Deductive

LOGIC

DEDUCTIVE
LOGIC

Second Edition

Hugues Leblanc
William A. Wisdom
Department of Philosophy
TEMPLE UNIVERSITY

Allyn and Bacon, Inc.
Boston, London, Sydney, Toronto

LIBRARY OF CONGRESS CATALOGING IN PUBLICATION DATA

Leblanc, Hugues, 1924–
    Deductive logic.

    Includes index.
    1. Logic. I. Wisdom, William A., joint author.
II. Title.
BC71.L38 1976   160   75-42443

ISBN 0-205-05496-X

To Gabrielle, Suzanne, Stephen, and Robert

CONTENTS

3. *METALOGIC*   *239*

PREFACE

We had various aims when preparing this second edition, among them: (i) to improve our account of such key notions as the notion of a compound in Chapter 1, the notion of truth (particularly, the truth of quantifications) in Chapter 2, etc.; (ii) to shorten some of the derivations in the first two chapters and some of the proofs in the third; and (iii) to eliminate errors (some purely typographical, some not) that had crept into the text and the exercises. The first aim was paramount; we hope that readers will find the passages concerned more effective than before.

Besides amending the text, we have also supplied answers to nearly half the exercises in Chapters 1 and 2. Collected at the end of the book, these answers should further illustrate such methods of the text as the truth-table method, Smullyan's tree method, and Gentzen's natural deduction method. They should also initiate the student to the art of proving *metatheorems,* i.e., the kind of *theorems about logic* to which we devote Chapter 3.

Our thanks go to Professor Alonzo Church (University of California at Los Angeles), Professor Kenton F. Machina (Illinois State University), Professor James E. Tomberlin (California State University, Northridge), Mr. William H. Ellis (Colby College), and various colleagues and students at Temple University, who spotted passages in the original edition which were either in error or unhappily written. Our thanks also go to teachers here and in Canada who used our text and informed us of their success with it in the classroom. Their comments vindicated our belief that consistency trees, derivation rules of the Gentzen sort, and the substitution interpretation of the quantifiers belong in an introduction to logic.

PREFACE TO THE
FIRST EDITION

Chapters 1 and 2 of this text are designed for use in a one-semester introduction to *deductive logic;* all three chapters are for use in a full-year course.

Chapter 1 is a detailed and systematic treatment of the logic of connectives, while Chapter 2 deals similarly with the logic of quantifiers. The first section of each chapter acquaints the reader with basic modes of statement composition and the logical matters that depend on statement composition. The next section develops a tree method of the Smullyan variety for testing the consistency of finite sets of statements, the logical truth of statements, the validity of arguments, and so on. And the third section supplies rules for deriving conclusions from premises. The method of "natural deduction" is employed; and, as we dispense throughout with the vexing distinction between "bound" and "free" variables, the rules for handling quantifiers will be found especially simple and convenient.

Since the tree and derivation methods serve much the same purpose—though in quite different ways—the instructor who has covered both of them in Chapter 1 may choose to omit one in Chapter 2. He should consult his own and the students' preferences on this matter—unless he intends to go on to Chapter 3, in which case Section 2.3 is required reading.

Certain features of our treatment are worth stressing. Throughout these first two chapters we deal with statements rather than statement forms, thus incessantly focusing our attention on the uses—some very ordinary, others not—to which logic can be put. And our account of matters like logical truth (i.e., truth on truth-functional or quantificational grounds), consistency, entailment, and so on, is entirely of the "truth-value" sort. Exploiting in Chapter 2 the "substitution" interpretation of the quantifiers, we characterize logical truth, for example, by changing just one word in the familiar definition of a tautology. The resulting semantics should accordingly be welcome as a simple and straightforward generalization of material from Chapter 1.

Chapter 3, which is largely the responsibility of the senior author, deals with the metatheory of truth-functional and quantificational logic. Professor Leblanc proves theorems of Post and Dubislav on modes of statement composition. He establishes that the derivation method of the previous two chapters is both sound and complete—the latter by a simplification of an argument of Henkin's. And he presents various results about trees, and about a new routine for making them. The truth-value semantics of the text is then matched against standard semantics, and some of the more important and arresting theorems in standard semantics are proven: one by Skolem, one due to Henkin and Beth, and so on. Finally, various sets of axioms for elementary logic are considered, and a familiar one is shown to permit the same derivations as does natural deduction.

Chapter 3 can be used in a variety of ways. Along with Chapters 1 and 2, it has served as the text in year-long introductory courses that go into metalogic. It has also been used (after quick review of the earlier chapters) in graduate courses, and in advanced undergraduate ones. (Incidentally, instructors covering only Chapters 1 and 2 in their classes have themselves found the third one helpful reading, and have recommended it to their better students.)

The book is entirely self-contained, and thus presupposes no special preparation. We use some set theory, of course, but all notions and notation employed are explained in Appendix I. Because our manual was written with logical considerations paramount, it should satisfy the interests of the general student, for whom this may be the only contact with deductive logic, and also meet the needs of students from philosophy, mathematics, formal linguistics, and related disciplines.

The exercises at the end of each section serve a number of purposes. Some will permit the student to review and test his mastery of the text, and may suggest areas where a second reading is in order. Others provide opportunities to develop technical skills in logic: skill at exposing the inconsistency of sets of statements, skill at deriving conclusions from premises, and so on. And yet others are of a more theoretical nature, pointing beyond the material of a section either to topics treated in later sections or to more advanced matters not covered in the text. Some of these theoretical exercises are relatively easy; the more difficult ones are starred.

We also wish to thank colleagues, students, and friends who helped us immeasurably in the preparation of this book. Professors Sidney Axinn, J. Robert Cassidy, Jack Nelson, and D. Paul Snyder of Temple University and Ms. Esen O. Traub of Rosemont College, all used an earlier version in their logic courses and provided us with many valuable suggestions. Professor Robert K. Meyer of Indiana University, Professor George Weaver of Bryn Mawr College, and Mr. Joseph Hetrick of Temple University read and most helpfully criticized all or part of the final version in manuscript form. And Mr. Barry Burd, Mr. Harold Goldberg, Mr. Maxim Maw, and Mr. Robert McArthur helped us with the proofreading.

And finally we wish to thank Temple University for its generous provision of clerical assistance throughout the writing of the book, and Haverford College for offering us the shelter of an office during the summers of 1968 and 1969.

Introduction

To satisfy the reader's quite natural curiosity about the kind of study he is approaching, we present here some of the key concepts examined and systematically developed in the text.

In large part, deductive logic concerns what can legitimately be inferred from what—i.e., whether a given *statement* would have to be true, or might still be false, if others offered as grounds for asserting it were true.[1] As logicians, we shall thus investigate how the *truth* or the *falsehood* of certain statements bears on that of others. And, since the truth or falsehood of a statement depends in turn on how it is put together, our attention will focus on the *composition* of statements.

Logic treats other things as well: whether a given statement could be false at all, or is necessarily true; whether, of two given statements, either one could be true and the other false; whether a number of statements could all be true together; and so on. These things too depend on how statements are put together, or are *compounded* from other statements.

We illustrate this central point. The truth or falsehood of the statement

Not all people over 30 are untrustworthy

depends in an obvious way on that of the statement 'All people over 30 are untrustworthy', from which it was as obviously composed.[2] If the latter is true, the former is false; if the latter is false, the former is true.

---

[1] Here we do not distinguish between statements and sentences. The reader who prefers to think of a statement not as a sentence, but as something conveyed by a sentence, is free to do so. The text readily adapts itself to that understanding of a statement. Note also that we limit ourselves to statements in the indicative mood, as distinct from the subjunctive, imperative, interrogative, etc.

[2] When *talking about* rather than *using* a statement, we always enclose it within single quotation marks, unless of course the statement is displayed on a separate line. We shall do likewise with individual words, phrases, and eventually symbols.

And, as we shall see in Chapter 2, whether the statement

> All people over 30 are untrustworthy

is true or is false depends in turn on the truth or falsehood of statements like 'If *Alan* is (a person) over 30, *he's* untrustworthy', and 'If *Barbara* is over 30, *she's* untrustworthy', and 'If *Charlie* is over 30, *he's* untrustworthy', and so on. These of course do not appear *verbatim* in 'All people over 30 are untrustworthy', the way 'All people over 30 are untrustworthy' does in 'Not all people over 30 are untrustworthy'. But, as we shall explain in Chapter 2, they still figure in the composition of 'All people over 30 are untrustworthy'—and hence in the composition of 'Not all people over 30 are untrustworthy'. Again, the statement

> If Alan is over 30, he's untrustworthy,

for example, would be false just in case the first constituent statement, 'Alan is over 30', were true while the second, 'Alan is untrustworthy', was false. And the statement

> Alan is untrustworthy

would be false if the constituent statement 'Alan is trustworthy' were true, and true if the latter were false.

Thus, to expose, in a logical fashion, the way a statement is composed *is* to expose, in terms of the truth or the falsehood of simpler statements, the circumstances under which it would be true or would be false.

Without such an understanding, it would be impossible to know whether any but the simplest statements (from which the others are composed) were true or were false. Furthermore, which of these simplest statements are true and which are false, and why, is *not* a logical issue. We rather want to know how their truth or falsehood—or that of any statements, for that matter—bears on the truth or falsehood of other statements composed from them.

Not only is this attention to a statement's composition—i.e., to the conditions for its truth and for its falsehood, in terms of the truth or falsehood of the statements built into it—usually necessary to determine whether the statement is true or is false, but sometimes it is *all* that is required. For example, 'All people over 30 are over 30' *must* be true, because all of the statements which might be involved in its composition—'If Alan is over 30, he's over 30', 'If Barbara is over 30, she's over 30', and so on—*must* be true. It is indeed impossible for the first occurrence of 'Alan is over 30' in 'If Alan is over 30, then Alan is over 30' to be true and the second false, for 'Barbara is over 30' to be both true and false, and so on. Statements which cannot be false and so have to be true, because of the way they are composed, could not properly be denied; they are called logical truths. And *logical truth* is one of the **logical properties** (in this case a property of some statements) which we shall investigate in the chapters to come.

Similarly, some statements are certifiably false by virtue of their manner of composition alone, such as 'Not all people over 30 are over 30'. Such statements could not properly be asserted, and are said to be *logically false*.

However, these properties of single statements, based on the way they are put together, represent only one kind of logical concern. Statements bear special **logical relations** to each other as well, on these same grounds (though the stories to be told about them may become more complicated). For example, 'Not all people over 30 are untrustworthy', while not logically true, would have to be true (or to be false) if 'Some people over 30 are trustworthy' were also true (or were false). For statements like 'Alan is over 30 and trustworthy', 'Barbara is over 30 and trustworthy', and so on,[3] are built into 'Some people over 30 are trustworthy' in such a way that this would be true or would be false under exactly the same circumstances as would 'Not all people over 30 are untrustworthy'. Statements bearing this relation to each other are said to be *equivalent*. So one cannot properly assert (deny) one statement and deny (assert) another which is equivalent to it.

Or we may address ourselves to a whole *set* of statements, to determine whether or not it is possible, as far as their composition is concerned, for all the statements in the set to be true together. If they could, the set of statements is said to be *consistent*. But a set of statements like

> You can believe Huntley if you can believe Brinkley, and vice versa
>
> If you can't believe either one of Huntley and Brinkley, you can't believe Cronkite
>
> You can believe Cronkite, but not Brinkley

is *inconsistent:* for given the ways their truth or falsehood is fixed by that of the simpler statements packed into them, these statements cannot all be true together. So one cannot properly assert together all the statements in an inconsistent set. Consistency and inconsistency are also logical properties—not of individual statements, but of sets of statements.

The validity and invalidity of arguments are the final (and most familiar) logical properties with which we shall be concerned. An **argument** is a complex of statements, the truth of some of which (the **premisses**) is, or might be, taken to justify asserting another (the **conclusion**). And an argument is said to be *valid* if, because of the ways the premisses and conclusion are composed, the premisses could not be true and the conclusion false—so that the latter would have to be true if the former

---

[3] And hence statements like 'Alan is over 30', 'Alan is trustworthy', 'Barbara is over 30', and so on.

were. Some arguments are obviously valid:

> Mary works hard
> She's a bright girl, and a charming one too
> She's sure to pass if she's bright and works hard
>
> ———————————————————————————
>
> Therefore, she'll pass or I'm a monkey's uncle.

Other arguments are not as obviously valid:

> Everybody loves a lover
> Tom doesn't love himself
>
> —————————————————
>
> Therefore, Tom doesn't love Sheila.

And of course some arguments are not valid at all, and are said to be *invalid:*

> Tigers are all mammals
> So are felines
>
> —————————————
>
> Therefore, tigers are felines.

(Note that an argument with false premisses and/or a false conclusion might nonetheless be valid; and an argument with true premisses and conclusion might nonetheless be invalid.)

Often, to be sure, the credibility of a conclusion is enhanced by premisses which do not guarantee its truth.[4] **Inductive logic** is the study of such arguments, and of the degrees of support that their premisses bestow on their conclusions. But in **deductive logic**—the subject of this book —the question is not how well the premisses of an argument support the conclusion, but whether or not they would *absolutely* preclude the falsehood, and hence ensure the truth, of the conclusion.

Reasoning in mathematics, science, philosophy, and everyday life often is deductive or has deductive phases. For example, to prove a theorem of number theory is to deduce it from the axioms of that theory or from other theorems that have already been proven. And quite often in science an hypothesis about some matter of fact is tested by finding out whether what would have to be true if the hypothesis were true is the case. Both the determination of these necessary consequences, and the decision

———————————

[4] For example:

> Most psychotics are irresponsible
> Charles is psychotic
>
> —————————————————————
>
> Therefore, Charles is irresponsible.

to reject the hypothesis whose "promise" is unfulfilled, are based on deductive reasoning.

The premisses of a valid argument are said to *entail* its conclusion. So entailment is the *logical relation* which a set of statements bears to a statement when it would be impossible, by virtue of their composition, for all the members of the set to be true and that statement false—or, to put it otherwise, when that statement would have to be true if all the members of the set were true.

These, then, are the logical properties preliminarily identified: logical truth and logical falsehood (of statements), consistency and inconsistency (of sets of statements), and validity and invalidity (of arguments). And these are the logical relations: equivalence (of one statement to another) and entailment (of a statement by a set of statements). They all hinge on the ways in which some statements are composed from others, i.e., on the ways in which the truth or the falsehood of some statements bears on that of others.

In Chapters 1 and 2 we shall develop techniques for representing these ways of composing statements—these "modes of statement composition"—on which logical properties and relations most often and importantly depend. And we shall develop methods of testing sets of statements for consistency, drawing conclusions from premisses that entail them, and so on. In Chapter 3 we shall prove the adequacy of the techniques and methods developed in the first two chapters, and examine some related topics. Together, these three chapters constitute a thorough introduction to deductive logic.

1

The Logic of Connectives

We are concerned with the *logical properties* that statements, sets of statements, and arguments might have. We are also concerned with the *logical relations* that statements, or sets of statements, might bear to other statements. These properties and relations depend in large part on the ways in which statements are compounded from other statements; and corresponding to some of these ways of compounding statements are particles called *statement connectives*. In this chapter we shall treat the five most common and logically important statement connectives.

1.1 Truth-Functional Composition

We call a **compound statement** any statement which contains, or could be treated as containing, one or more simpler statements as constituent parts. For example,

> Tom won't win the election

is a compound of the one statement

> Tom will win the election.

Similarly,

> Tom will win if we all work very hard for him

is a compound of the two statements

> Tom will win

and

> We all work very hard for Tom.

And three or more statements might be built into a compound:

> Tom will win unless he alienates either the party regulars or the big contributors, in which case he might as well give up

7

can be treated as a compound of the four statements

> Tom will win
> Tom alienates the party regulars
> Tom alienates the big contributors
> Tom might as well give up.

In general, any statement is compound if less than all of it is some one or more simpler statements; and these simpler statements are called its **components.** (These definitions must be considered somewhat provisional; the key terms 'statement', 'compound statement', and 'component' will be officially defined on pp. 20–22.)

Truth-Functionally Compound Statements

In this chapter we are not concerned with all compound statements, but only with truth-functional compounds. Call the truth or falsehood of a statement, as the case may be, its **truth-value.** A compound statement is said to be **truth-functionally compound** if *its* truth-value is entirely a function of the truth-values of its components—i.e., if its truth-value would be determined under any possible circumstance by the truth-values of its components, and by these truth-values alone. For example,

> Not every young man carries his draft card

would be false if the component 'Every young man carries his draft card' were true, and true if the component were false. Similarly,

> Most people are often happy, and Tom always is

would be true if, but only if, both 'Most people are often happy' and 'Tom is always happy' were true; if either component, or both, were false, the compound would be false. And again,

> Everything goes well if everyone helps; otherwise something goes wrong

is true just in case either (a) 'Everyone helps' and 'Everything goes well' are both true, or (b) 'Everyone helps' is false and 'Something goes wrong' is true; in any other case the compound is false. So its truth-value is determined under all possible circumstances by the truth-values of the components; the compound *is* truth-functional.

Of course, there are truth-functional compounds some of whose components are themselves truth-functional compounds: 'If the barometer falls and either the wind shifts or the temperature drops, then if I'm not mistaken we'll soon have rain and the pond will fill up'. And there are statements that are not truth-functionally compound at all; these latter we call **atomic statements.**[1] Among atomic statements are such non-compound statements as

The barometer falls	The wind shifts
The temperature drops	I'm mistaken
We'll soon have rain	The pond will fill up,

which occur as components of the previous illustration.

Also atomic are statements which, though compound, are not truth-functionally compound, such as

I wonder whether the Phillies will win the pennant next year

It's unlikely that Tom and Jack will both be here

I doubt that everyone will vote for Tom

I know that Paul is in the kitchen with Dinah

Tom lost a lot of support because he alienated the party regulars

Tom conceded defeat after he saw some of the early returns.

These are not truth-functional compounds—and hence count here as atomic statements—because their truth-values are not determined under *all* circumstances by those of their components. In the first example, whether or not the Phillies will win the pennant next year, I might or I might not wonder whether they will. So the truth-value of the compound does not depend in either case on that of its component. In the fourth example, the compound statement 'I know that Paul is in the kitchen with Dinah' is of course false if he is *not* in the kitchen with Dinah—i.e., if the statement 'Paul is in the kitchen with Dinah' is false. But the compound might be true or might be false if Paul *is* in the kitchen with Dinah. So the truth-value of the compound depends in one case, *but not in the other*, on the truth-value of its component.

Similarly, in either of the last two examples above, the compound would clearly be false if one or both of its components were false. But if both components were true, the compound might still be true or be false. (Even if he both lost a lot of support and alienated the party regulars, Tom might or might not have lost the support *because* he alienated the party regulars. And even if he both conceded defeat and saw some of the early returns, Tom might or might not have conceded defeat *after* seeing some of the early returns.) (See Exercise E1.1.1 on p. 42.)[2]

---

[1] In Chapter 2 we shall use the term 'atomic' in a more restricted sense, partly because some of the statements which must count as atomic (unanalyzable) in this chapter will be further analyzed in the next.

[2] In this and some later sections we indicate which exercises relate to the material just covered.

Truth-Functional Connectives

In general, statement connectives are particles—words or phrases—used to generate compound statements out of less complex statements. For example, 'and', 'because', 'if . . . then . . .', 'despite the fact that', 'after', and 'or' all can function as statement connectives. So can particles like 'not' and 'possibly', which are often used to generate compounds from single statements.

Connectives are called **truth-functional connectives** when the compound statements composed by means of them are truth-functional compounds. Few, if any, connectives in English are *always* truth-functional. However, a few *often* are; and others can sometimes be treated as having the logical force of these few, individually or in combination. We shall concentrate attention on the five most common and logically important truth-functional connectives, and on the five sorts of truth-functional compounds corresponding to them. (It will be proven in Chapter 3 that *all* truth-functional compounds can be represented by means of these five connectives alone—indeed, by means of as few as two of them.)

Negations. Negations are among the simplest and most obvious truth-functional compounds. We call one statement the negation of another when the former would be true if and only if the latter, its one component, were false. Often 'not' is used to express negations in English:

> Tom has not seen the evening paper
> Not all roses are red.

Often negations are expressed differently:

> Your dog ain't no better than mine
> The story of the Loch Ness monster is unbelievable
> I deny that I was in Transylvania when the poor lass died.

And of course one may negate compound as well as atomic statements:

> Tom isn't unhappy tonight
> Tom and Jack won't both win
> We won't see either Tom or Jack tonight.

We represent the negation of a statement A by prefixing a tilde '$\sim$' (read 'it is not the case that', or 'not' for short) to A:[3]

---

[3] The capital letter 'A' (and later 'B', 'C', and 'D') is not itself a statement or an abbreviation for a statement, but a device used, as here, to facilitate talk *about* any statement, whether compound or atomic. Except on pp. 21 and 23, where they serve a more general purpose, we thus use 'A', 'B', 'C', and 'D' to *refer* to any statement; and we use '$\sim A$', '$\sim B$', and so on to *refer* to the negation of any statement, and hence to any negation (or *denial,* as it is sometimes called).

In some other texts, the negation of a statement A is symbolized $-A$, or $\neg A$, or $\overline{A}$.

~Tom has seen the evening paper

~all roses are red

~your dog is better than mine

~the story of the Loch Ness monster is believable

~I was in Transylvania when the poor lass died

~~Tom is happy tonight

~(Tom will win and Jack will win)

~(we will see Tom tonight or we will see Jack tonight).

The whole point of '~' is given by this **truth-table** for the connective:

A	$\sim A$
T	**F**
F	**T**

Any negation $\sim A$ is false if its component A is true, and true if A is false.[4]

Conjunctions. When a compound of any two statements would be true if and only if *both* of these component statements were true, we call it the conjunction of the two statements. Often 'and' serves as the connective in English:

Roses are red and violets are blue

Roses and violets are flowers.

Often conjunctions are differently expressed. And, again, the statements conjoined may themselves be either compound or atomic:

Although he'll bring some grass if he comes, I doubt that he'll be here

Tom and Jack didn't show up, but we never missed them

I will not serve; no, again I insist that I will not serve.

We represent the conjunction of any two statements A and B by interposing the ampersand '&', and we call A and B the **conjuncts** of the conjunction A & B (read: A *and* B):[5]

---

[4] The reading of this and the other four truth-tables will be sharpened later.

[5] Again, we use 'A' and 'B' to *refer* to any two (not necessarily distinct) statements; and we use 'A & B' to *refer* to the conjunction of any two statements, and hence to *refer* to any conjunction. If we wanted to refer to any conjunction both conjuncts of which were the *same* statement, we would use 'A & A' (or 'B & B', and so on). In the future we shall omit these remarks, confident that the uses of 'A', 'B', etc.—either alone, or in contexts like '$\sim A$', 'A & B', and so on—are clear.

In some other texts, the conjunction of two statements A and B is symbolized $A \wedge B$, or $A.B$, or AB.

Roses are red & violets are blue

Roses are flowers & violets are flowers

He'll bring some grass if he comes & I doubt that he'll be here

(~Tom showed up & ~Jack showed up) & ~we missed them

~I will serve & ~I will serve.

The whole point of '&' is given by this truth-table for the connective:

A	B	$A \& B$
T	T	T
F	T	F
T	F	F
F	F	F

Any conjunction $A \& B$ is true if both of its conjuncts A and B are true; it is false if either one or both of its conjuncts are false.

Whether or not a statement in English *is* a conjunction, though, depends on the conditions under which it would be true and would be false. If these conditions are as above, use of '&' is appropriate. Consider, for example:

Tom and Mary are students

Tom and Mary are lovers.

The first certainly would, but the second probably would *not*, properly be represented as a conjunction:

Tom is a student & Mary is a student

Tom is a lover & Mary is a lover.

Or consider:

They got married and had a child

They had a child and got married.[6]

If, as Mary's mother would insist, the first is to be counted true and the second false, the 'and' is not our '&', but rather means 'and then', which is *not* a truth-functional connective. (A conjunction $A \& B$ is true if and only if $B \& A$ is true—the order makes no difference.)

In general, whether and how a statement in English is truth-functionally compound is a matter to be decided by a fluent speaker of the language, for whom the particular words used serve as clues only.

---

[6] We owe this illustration to P. F. Strawson, *Introduction to Logical Theory*, 1952, Methuen & Co., p. 80.

Disjunctions. When a compound of any two statements would be true if and only if *at least one* of these component statements were true, we call it the disjunction (some say "alternation") of the two statements. Usually 'or' serves as the connective in English:

> Someone's under the bed or I'm imagining things again
> Either there's dust on my lens or there are boulders on the moon
> He'll bring hamburgers or hot dogs with him
> Either some insects have eight legs, or this isn't an insect at all but a spider instead.

We represent the disjunction of two statements A and B by interposing the wedge 'V', and we call A and B the **disjuncts** of the disjunction $A \lor B$ (read: *A or B*):

> Someone's under the bed V I'm imagining things again
> There's dust on my lens V there are boulders on the moon
> He'll bring hamburgers with him V he'll bring hot dogs with him
> Some insects have eight legs V (~this is an insect & this is a spider).

The truth-table for 'V' is as follows:

A	B	$A \lor B$
T	T	T
F	T	T
T	F	T
F	F	F

The 'V' corresponds to what is often called the **inclusive** 'or', since a disjunction $A \lor B$ would be counted true if either one *or both* of its disjuncts A and B were true. A use of 'or' in English is *ex*clusive when the or-statement would be counted true only if *exactly* one of the components were true, and false if both (or neither) were true. Unless one is sure that an or-statement is meant to be exclusive, though, it is best to represent the connective by the inclusive 'V' so as not to unduly narrow the truth-conditions for the statement (i.e., so as not to be readier than is proper to consider someone a liar). The inclusive 'or' is of considerably more logical interest than its exclusive cousin. And the truth-functional force of the exclusive 'or' can be captured with our notation, whenever it is called for, simply by adding the appropriate "exclusion." So:

> Tom or Jack will drive (but not both)

becomes

> (Tom will drive V Jack will drive) & ~(Tom will drive & Jack will drive).

We cannot say, in the case of a true inclusive disjunction $A \lor B$ (as we could if the 'or' were exclusive), that if either A or B were true, the other would have to be false. What we *can* say is that if either disjunct were *false*, the other would have to be *true*. Indeed, asserting *A or B* is often tantamount to saying *If not A, then B* (as well as *If not B, then A*). Similarly, asserting *A or not B* is tantamount to saying *If not A, then not B* (as well as *If B, then A*). And asserting *not A or B* is tantamount to saying *If not not A, then B*—i.e., *If A, then B*. So statements like the following are often interchangeable:

(1)   Either you stop that or you'll get hurt

and

If you don't stop that, you'll get hurt;

(2)   He's perfectly trustworthy or else I'm not a good judge of character

and either

If he's not perfectly trustworthy, then I'm not a good judge of character

or

If I'm a good judge of character, then he's perfectly trustworthy;

(3)   Either that's not Tom, or he's grown a moustache

and

If that's Tom, he's grown a moustache.

A glance at the truth-table for '$\lor$' reveals why there is this particular relation between disjunctions and if-then statements. (Note in the disjunctions just given, by the way, that the 'or' is inclusive. We would count all three true if both disjuncts were true: he might stop, and still get hurt; he might be trustworthy even though I am not a good judge of character; and that might not be Tom, who might nonetheless have grown a moustache.) (See Exercise E1.1.2.)

Conditionals. When a compound of two statements A and B would be *false* if and only if A were true and B false, we call it the conditional of A and B (in that order). We represent it by interposing the horseshoe '$\supset$', and call A the **antecedent** and B the **consequent** of the conditional $A \supset B$ (read: *If A, then B*).[7] The truth-table for '$\supset$' is as follows:

---

[7] Some have called conditionals *implications* and have read '$\supset$' as 'implies'. Others, who use '(logical) implication' and '(logically) implies' where we would use 'entailment' and 'entails', have called them *material implications*. The reading of '$\supset$' as 'implies' has led to some confusions which can be avoided by reading it 'If . . . then'.

In some other texts, the conditional of two statements A and B is symbolized $A \to B$.

A	B	$A \supset B$
T	T	T
F	T	T
T	F	F
F	F	T

For us, then, a conditional $A \supset B$ is *false* if the antecedent A is true and the consequent B is false, hence if A and $\sim B$ are both true. And it is *true* if A is false or B is true, hence if $\sim A$ is true or B is. $A \supset B$ thus has the same logical force—is counted true and counted false under the same conditions—as the negation $\sim(A \& \sim B)$ of the conjunction $A \& \sim B$. And it has the same logical force as the disjunction $\sim A \vee B$ (as might have been anticipated, in view of the remarks on p. 14).

In ordinary language many statements of the kind *If A, then B* have just this force. Others have a causal force as well. 'If Peter keeps smoking that heavily, he'll contract cancer', for example, might well mean 'If Peter keeps smoking that heavily, he'll contract cancer, and he'll contract cancer *because* of his heavy smoking'. The corresponding conditionals $A \supset B$ do not have that force, and hence do not capture the full meaning of such statements. When presented with an if-then statement, the reader might check whether it would be true and would be false under the same conditions as the corresponding negation $\sim(A \& \sim B)$ or the corresponding disjunction $\sim A \vee B$. If the answer is Yes, rendition as $A \supset B$ is appropriate. Otherwise, it is not.

Our case for treating a number of if-then statements as truth-functional conditionals can be strengthened by reflection on the individual rows of the truth-table for '$\supset$'. Consider the first two. If a statement B is true, then it is true whether any statement A is true or is false, and we should want both *If A, then B* and *If not A, then B* to be true—which is what the first two rows ensure (with '$\supset$' read 'if . . . then . . .'). The third row is obvious, since any statement *If A, then B* is surely false if A is true but B is not. Indeed, one reason for asserting *If A, then B* is to rule out the possibility of B being false in case A is true (hence the similarity to $\sim(A \& \sim B)$). In the case of the fourth row, note that a statement *If A, then B* must have the same truth-conditions as its "contrapositive" *If not B, then not A:*

If today is Monday, then tomorrow is payday

means the same (in the sense of being true and being false under the same conditions) as

If tomorrow is not payday, then today is not Monday.

Now if both antecedent and consequent of the former are false (row 4), then both antecedent and consequent of the latter are true—in which case the latter is true (row 1). So the former must be true as well.

It may seem more natural to count a conditional true so long as its consequent is true, whether the antecedent be true or be false (rows 1 and 2), than to count a conditional true so long as its antecedent is false, whether the consequent be true or be false (rows 2 and 4). For of the two statements:

> If Hitler had invaded England, then he would have won the war

and

> If Hitler had invaded England, then he (still) would have lost the war,

we might—and historians do—want to consider one true and the other false, fully aware that the if-clause of each is false (in that Hitler did not invade England). This means at least that they are *not* properly rendered as truth-functional conditionals. But this might have been expected, as truth-functional conditionals are compounds of *indicative* statements, whereas these last are *subjunctive* conditionals. Indeed, one might not want to consider them compound statements at all, since one might not want to consider, e.g., 'Hitler would have won the war' an *independent statement* at all. For it could hardly have a truth-value; and the same applies to the subjunctive 'Hitler had invaded England' as well.

We give some examples of statements which probably could be rendered as truth-functional conditionals:

> If the Cohens come to dinner, then we won't serve both milk and meat
> They'll make it, provided that (so long as, etc.) they don't get lost
> This car is safe to drive if it has good brakes
> This car is safe to drive only if it has good brakes
> Ben Franklin could not read unless he had his glasses on
> He could not read without his glasses on.

These become (note what is antecedent and what consequent):

> The Cohens come to dinner ⊃ ~(we'll serve milk & we'll serve meat)
> ~they get lost ⊃ they'll make it
> This car has good brakes ⊃ it is safe to drive
> This car is safe to drive ⊃ it has good brakes
> ~Ben Franklin had his glasses on ⊃ ~he could read (or: Ben Franklin could read ⊃ he had his glasses on)
> ~he had his glasses on ⊃ ~he could read.

A statement A (or its truth) is sometimes said to be a *sufficient condition* for (the truth of) a statement B if $A \supset B$ is true; and a statement A

is said to be a *necessary condition* for a statement B if $\sim A \supset \sim B$, and hence $B \supset A$, is true. ($B \supset A$ is often called the **converse** of $A \supset B$.) According to the third example above, having good brakes is a sufficient condition for the car's being safe to drive; according to the fourth, it is a necessary condition.

Biconditionals. When a compound of two statements A and B would be true if A and B had the *same* truth-value, and false if their truth-values were different, we call it the biconditional of the two statements:

> 17 is even if and only if it's not odd
>
> Mary will get an A if she turns in a good paper; otherwise she won't
>
> Tom will come to the demonstration, unless of course the police lock him up
>
> Just one of them will be here—Tom or Jack.

We represent the biconditional of two statements A and B by interposing '$\equiv$' (read 'if and only if'):[8]

> 17 is even $\equiv$ $\sim$17 is odd
>
> Mary will get an A $\equiv$ she turns in a good paper
>
> Tom will come to the demonstration $\equiv$ $\sim$the police lock him up[9]
>
> Tom will be here $\equiv$ $\sim$Jack will be here (or: $\sim$Tom will be here $\equiv$ Jack will be here; or: $\sim$(Tom will be here $\equiv$ Jack will be here)).

The truth-table for '$\equiv$' is as follows:

A	B	$A \equiv B$
T	T	T
F	T	F
T	F	F
F	F	T

As may be clear from the name, the examples, and the truth-table, the biconditional $A \equiv B$ of two statements A and B has exactly the same

---

[8] Some have called biconditionals *equivalences,* and have read '$\equiv$' as 'is equivalent to'. Others have called them *material equivalences,* to distinguish them from logical equivalences.

In some other texts, the biconditional of two statements A and B is symbolized $A \leftrightarrow B$, or $A \sim B$.

[9] In many cases, A *unless B* means just A *if not B*—i.e., $\sim B \supset A$ (or, interestingly, $A \lor B$). 'Jimmy will die unless he is operated on' is a warning that if he is not operated on, he will die; it is not the doctor's promise as well that Jimmy will not die if he is operated on. In some cases, though, the converse $A \supset \sim B$ of $\sim B \supset A$, being obviously true on the occasion, sort of tags along, so that A *unless B* (e.g., 'Tom will come to the demonstration, unless of course the police lock him up') can properly be rendered as A *if and only if not B*—i.e., $A \equiv \sim B$. Likewise, 'Bob will drive us to the beach unless his car breaks down', for example, can surely be rendered as 'Bob will drive us to the beach $\equiv$ $\sim$Bob's car breaks down'.

logical force—would be true and would be false under exactly the same conditions—as the conjunction of the conditional $A \supset B$ with its converse $B \supset A$. (So when $A \equiv B$ is true, A is said to be a *necessary and sufficient condition* for B.)

In the following table we summarize the truth-conditions for these connectives.

TABLE I

A	B	$\sim A$	$A \supset B$	$A \ \& \ B$	$A \lor B$	$A \equiv B$
T	T	F	T	T	T	T
F	T	T	T	F	T	F
T	F		F	F	T	F
F	F		T	F	F	T

(See Exercise E1.1.2.)

Abbreviation, Punctuation, and Translation

Because we are not interested in whether or not plum pudding is tasty, but only in how 'Plum pudding is tasty' might figure in the composition of other statements, it will save us time and space, and cost us nothing of value, if we abbreviate the statement 'Plum pudding is tasty' (or any atomic statement) as, say, 'P'; 'The queen of France is bald' as, say, 'Q'; and so on. We shall use capital letters as abbreviations for atomic statements, avoiding in general the first few letters of the alphabet. We must remember that 'P', for example, is not a special symbol like the 'A' or 'B' which we have already used to *refer* to any statements, but actually *is* some particular atomic statement itself, or a shorthand way of writing one, which could always be written out, as before, in its fuller and more familiar form.

In any particular context, of course, we shall have to pick different letters to abbreviate different atomic statements. But, as the context changes, we can freely abbreviate new statements by letters used earlier for other statements. It will be helpful if we pick the initial letter of some key word in the statement being abbreviated, to remind us which statement the capital letter abbreviates. For instance, we shall abbreviate the atomic components of the next examples as follows:

> 'P': 'Percy will pass'
> 'Q': 'Quincy will pass'
> 'R': 'Reginald will pass'
> 'S': 'Percy studies hard'
> 'T': 'Percy is tired'.

When it makes no difference which statements are being abbreviated, we shall also use 'P', 'Q', 'R', and so on, and the reader can think of them as abbreviating any atomic statements he likes.

In ordinary language, there are a number of ways of indicating how the components of compound statements are to be grouped. Here, by contrast, we "officially" use only parentheses for this purpose. Sometimes no such punctuation is required in the representation of compound statements:

Reginald won't pass:	~R
Quincy won't fail:	~~Q
Quincy and Percy will both pass:	Q & P
Percy will pass only if he's not tired:	P ⊃ ~T
Percy will pass unless he's tired:	~T ⊃ P
Either Percy won't pass or Quincy will:	~P ∨ Q
Percy won't pass, but Quincy will:	~P & Q

Since the tilde '~' always governs as little as the punctuation will permit, the sixth example must be a disjunction whose left-hand disjunct is a negation, rather than the negation of a disjunction; and the last must be a conjunction whose left-hand conjunct is a negation, rather than the negation of a conjunction.

To represent the negation of any compound other than a negation, punctuation is required (compare these to the last two):

Neither Percy nor Quincy will pass:	~(P ∨ Q)
Percy and Quincy won't both pass:	~(P & Q)

And when two or more **binary connectives** ('⊃', '&', '∨', '≡') are used, punctuation must again group the components according to the sense of the compound translated:

Either Percy and Quincy will both pass, or Reginald will:
$$(P \& Q) \lor R$$
Percy will pass, and so will either Quincy or Reginald:
$$P \& (Q \lor R)$$
If Percy passes, then so will Quincy; and Percy will pass:
$$(P \supset Q) \& P$$
If Percy passes, then Quincy and Percy will both pass:
$$P \supset (Q \& P)$$
Percy will pass if Quincy does; otherwise neither of them will pass:
$$(Q \supset P) \& [\sim Q \supset (\sim P \& \sim Q)]$$
Either Quincy will pass if and only if Reginald doesn't, or Percy will pass if he studies hard and isn't tired:
$$(Q \equiv \sim R) \lor [(S \& \sim T) \supset P]$$

Although '(' and ')' will be our only "official" punctuation marks in Chapter 1, we use the brackets '[' and ']' as parentheses to facilitate reading when one set of parentheses encloses another.

As has already been suggested, the five connectives available permit representation of a wide variety of statements besides those containing 'not', 'and', 'or', etc. For one thing, all truth-functional compounds other than negations, conjunctions, disjunctions, etc., can be rendered in terms of just these compounds, a point to be fully established in Chapter 3. In addition, various statements which are not *overtly* truth-functional compounds can be *paraphrased* as such. We give examples of the latter, and supply translations.

Imagine only Percy and Quincy to be involved in some test-taking. Then we might have:

At least one of them will pass: $P \vee Q$
At most one of them will pass: $\sim(P \& Q)$, or $\sim P \vee \sim Q$
Exactly one of them will pass:
$(P \& \sim Q) \vee (\sim P \& Q)$, or $(P \vee Q) \& \sim(P \& Q)$, or $\sim(P \equiv Q)$

Now imagine all three of our characters involved:

They will all pass: $P \& (Q \& R)$, or $(P \& Q) \& R$
At least one of them will pass: $P \vee (Q \vee R)$, or $(P \vee Q) \vee R$[10]
At least two of them will pass: $(P \& Q) \vee [(P \& R) \vee (Q \& R)]$
At most one of them will pass:
$[P \supset (\sim Q \& \sim R)] \& ([Q \supset (\sim P \& \sim R)] \& [R \supset (\sim P \& \sim Q)])$
Exactly one of them will pass:
$[P \& (\sim Q \& \sim R)] \vee ([Q \& (\sim P \& \sim R)] \vee [R \& (\sim P \& \sim Q)])$

And so forth. (See Exercises E1.1.3–4.)

Statements and Components

We shall now present in a more succinct and "official" way material which has been rather freely exposited to this point.

We must first be more precise about what for us will count as a **statement.** There are, as we have already noted, compound statements in English which are not truth-functional compounds; and there are other truth-functional connectives besides the five we have presented. Here we count as **compound statements** only negations, conditionals, conjunctions, disjunctions, and biconditionals. But not every expression in which one of our five connectives appears (a tilde followed by one ex-

---

[10] Although it makes no difference in which order the components of this and the last example are grouped, they must of course be grouped in one way or the other.

pression, or a binary connective flanked by two) will count as a statement. So, to handle things more formally, any atomic statement (understood, for the purpose of Chapter 1, in any clear way the reader may please) will count as a statement. Second, an expression of the sort ~*A* will count as a statement if, but only if, *A* itself is a statement. And, third, an expression of one of the four sorts (*A* ⊃ *B*), (*A* & *B*), (*A* ∨ *B*), and (*A* ≡ *B*) will count as a statement if, but only if, both *A* and *B* are statements.[11]

When *A* is a statement, and hence ~*A* is one, we shall refer to *A* as the **immediate component** of ~*A*, and talk of the '~' shown as its **main connective.** Similarly, when both *A* and *B* are statements, we shall refer to *A* and *B* as the **immediate components** of (*A* ⊃ *B*), (*A* & *B*), (*A* ∨ *B*), and (*A* ≡ *B*)—for short, of *A* ⊃ *B*, *A* & *B*, *A* ∨ *B*, and *A* ≡ *B*—and talk of the '⊃', '&', '∨', and '≡' shown as their **main connectives.**

Besides the notion of an immediate component, the more general and important notion of a **component** of a statement must be rigorously defined. First, we take any statement to be a component of itself (this largely for technical reasons). Second, the immediate components of a compound statement count among its components. And, finally, any component of a component of a statement is a component of that statement. So the components of

$$(P \supset [Q \lor {\sim}(R \ \& \ S)])$$

are:

(1) (P ⊃ [Q ∨ ~(R & S)])
(2) P
(3) [Q ∨ ~(R & S)]
(4) Q
(5) ~(R & S)
(6) (R & S)
(7) R
(8) S.

(1) is a component of the original compound because it is that statement itself. (2) and (3) are components thereof because they are its immediate components. (4) and (5) are components of the original compound because they are immediate components, and hence components, of (3),

---

[11] Here we write '(*A* ⊃ *B*)' rather than '*A* ⊃ *B*', '(*A* & *B*)' rather than '*A* & *B*', and so on, to ensure that, when a compound is itself a component of another statement, it will be enclosed within the needed parentheses. But when the compound is not itself a component of another statement, the outermost parentheses are quite unnecessary and will regularly be omitted (as has been our practice in the preceding pages). Recall that we sometimes use the brackets '[' and ']' as parentheses, to facilitate the reading of longer statements. And note that on this occasion, as again in part **A** of Table II on p. 23, the two letters '*A*' and '*B*' are of course used to refer to *any* expression, and not just to statements.

which is a component of the original compound. (6) is a component of a component of the original statement, and hence is itself a component of that statement. And so on.

Any statement A will count as an **atomic component** of a statement B if (i) A is a component of B, and (ii) A is an atomic statement. So (2), (4), (7), and (8)—i.e., 'P', 'Q', 'R', and 'S'—are the atomic components of our example.

By means of the foregoing example, we can illustrate our account on p. 21 of what passes for a statement. (1), being of the sort $(A \supset B)$, will qualify as a statement if both (2) and (3), its immediate components, do. (2) does, since it is an atomic statement. (3), being of the sort $(A \lor B)$, will count as a statement if both (4) and (5) do. (4), an atomic statement, does. (5), being of the sort $\sim A$, will be a statement if (6) is. And (6), being of the sort $(A \& B)$, will make it if both (7) and (8) do—which of course they do. Hence (1) is a statement.[12] (See Exercise E1.1.5.)

Truth-Value Assignments

As suggested in the Introduction, we are not concerned here with how atomic statements get their truth-values, but only with the ways in which the truth-values of relatively less complex statements bear on those of more complex statements compounded from them. We proceed from the presumption that each non-compound statement has one or the other truth-value, we care not which.

For the sake of precision, we introduce the notion of a **truth-value assignment,** which is the result of giving one of the two truth-values **T** and **F** (but not both) to each one of a number of atomic statements.[13] Since the truth-value of a compound will ultimately depend on the truth-values of its atomic components, a truth-value assignment to certain atomic statements will determine a truth-value for any compound whose atomic components are among those atomic statements. To provide for this, we must sharpen our readings of the truth-tables for the five connectives. For example, the truth-table for '&' had been taken to say simply that a conjunction is true if and only if both of its conjuncts are true. We shall *now* understand it to say that a conjunction is *true on some assignment α of truth-values to its atomic components* if and only if both of its conjuncts are *true on* α. The readings of the truth-tables for the other four connec-

---

[12] Since all the statements we deal with come from ordinary discourse, they are all presumed to be finitely long, and hence to contain only finitely many connectives.

[13] Though a truth-value assignment is always an assignment of truth-values *to* certain atomic statements, we shall not invariably specify which atomic statements they are when this is clear from the context.

tives will be refined in the same way. We thus have no notion of truth *simpliciter:* all truth for us is *truth-on-a-truth-value-assignment.*

In Table II below we recapitulate the "official" definition of a statement and of a component of a statement. We also supply our new readings of the truth-tables for '~', '&', 'V', '⊃', and '≡'. Note that in **C** we speak of a statement as "true on an assignment of truth-values to its atomic components (and possibly to other atomic statements as well)." Since the parenthetical phrase is quite important, and will recur frequently throughout the work, we must pause to explain it. In considering the truth-value of, say, a conjunction *A & B* on an assignment α of truth-values to *its* atomic components, we will have to determine, among other things, the truth-value of *A* on the *same* assignment—which will often be to *more* atomic statements than are atomic components of *A*. (Of course those extra atomic statements will not affect the truth-value of *A*, but they could affect that of *B*.) So our account of things must not preclude the truth of

TABLE II

A. (1) An atomic statement is a **statement.**
    (2) If *A* is a statement, then so is ~*A*.
    (3) If *A* and *B* are (not necessarily distinct) statements, then (*A* ⊃ *B*), (*A* & *B*), (*A* V *B*), and (*A* ≡ *B*) are also statements.
    (4) Nothing else is a statement.

B. (1) Any statement is a **component** of itself.
    (2) *A* is a component of a statement ~*A*.
    (3) *A* and *B* are components of the statements (*A* ⊃ *B*), (*A* & *B*), (*A* V *B*), and (*A* ≡ *B*).
    (4) If a statement *A* is a component of a statement *B*, and *B* is a component of a statement *C*, then *A* is a component of *C*.
    (5) A statement *A* is an **atomic component** of a statement *B* if *A* is a component of *B*, and *A* is an atomic statement.

C. A statement is **true** on an assignment α of truth-values to its atomic components (and possibly to other atomic statements as well) if and only if
    (1) in case the statement is atomic, it is assigned **T** in α;
    (2) in case it is of the sort ~*A*, *A* is not true on α;
    (3) in case it is of the sort (*A* ⊃ *B*), either *A* is not true on α or *B* is true on α (or both);
    (4) in case it is of the sort (*A* & *B*), both *A* and *B* are true on α;
    (5) in case it is of the sort (*A* V *B*), at least one of *A* and *B* is true on α;
    (6) in case it is of the sort (*A* ≡ *B*), either both *A* and *B* are true on α, or neither one of *A* and *B* is true on α.

A statement is **false** on an assignment α of truth-values to its atomic components if and only if it is not true on α.

---

a statement on a truth-value assignment which reaches beyond the atomic components of that statement.

With the understanding that an *atomic* statement is true on a truth-value assignment α if and only if it is assigned **T** in α, we can be sure that any statement whose atomic components are all accorded a truth-value in some truth-value assignment will either be true or be false on that assignment. For a compound will be true on a truth-value assignment α if and only if its immediate components have certain truth-values (specified by the truth-table for that sort of compound) on α. Those immediate components, if compound, will be true on α if and only if *their* immediate components have certain truth-values (again specified by the truth-tables for compounds of those kinds) on α. And so on. And ultimately the atomic components of the original compound *will* have just one truth-value apiece on α.

Truth-Tables

Let us illustrate the point just made: that any assignment of truth-values to the atomic components of a statement determines a truth-value for that statement. Consider the conditional

$$\sim(P \& Q) \supset (R \lor \sim S).$$

Its truth-value is a function of the truth-value of the antecedent and that of the consequent. In turn, the truth-value of the antecedent '$\sim(P \& Q)$' is a function of the truth-value of the conjunction 'P & Q', which in turn is a function of the truth-values of the atomic components 'P' and 'Q'. The truth-value of the consequent 'R $\lor$ ~S' is a function of the truth-values of the disjuncts 'R' and '~S', and the truth-value of '~S' is a function of the truth-value of 'S'.

Let α, for example, be the result of assigning **F** to both 'P' and 'R', and **T** to both 'Q' and 'S'. Then 'P & Q' is false (since one conjunct is false) on α, and hence '~(P & Q)' is true on α; and '~S' is false on α, so 'R $\lor$ ~S' is also false (since both disjuncts are false) on α. Hence, because the antecedent of the original compound is true, and its consequent false, on α, the whole statement is false on α. This can be recorded thus:

P Q R S	P & Q	~(P & Q)	~S	R $\lor$ ~S	~(P & Q) $\supset$ (R $\lor$ ~S)
F T F T	F	T	F	F	F

As the reader can tell, we here work from the left end (the atomic components) to the right (the statement under consideration), determining the truth-values of the more complex components of the whole on the basis of the truth-values already obtained for (or assigned to) the less complex components. Note that the 'T' or 'F' accruing to a statement is written under its main connective if it is compound, and under the statement itself if it is atomic.

The process whereby '~(P & Q) ⊃ (R V ~S)' was shown to have the truth-value **F** on the truth-value assignment α can also be recorded in the following more compressed way. We number each 'T' or 'F' to show the order in which the truth-value is arrived at—the same order as above:

~	(P	&	Q)	⊃	(R	V	~	S)
T	**F**	**F**	**T**	**F**	**F**	**F**	**F**	**T**
3	1	2	1	6	1	5	4	1

'1' is used in connection with all four of 'P', 'Q', 'R', and 'S', since these statements are assigned a truth-value in α all at once.

This exercise should illustrate our dual concern with the *composition* of statements *from* atomic components, and with the *analysis* of compound statements *into* these elements. In ordinary and scientific discourse we encounter the finished products of composition. To determine their truth-values, we must break them down into their components, and these components into theirs, and so on, noting as we go just how the truth-values of more complex statements depend on those of less complex components (i.e., noting what connectives are appropriate where). Then we can work back from the truth-values (however arrived at) of the atomic components through the intermediate stages of logical complexity to the whole, following the course of composition already exposed.

As was stressed earlier, the logician's concern is a broad one precisely because it is not factual but, if you will, hypothetical. In the example just presented, only one of a number of possible truth-value combinations for the atomic components 'P', 'Q', 'R', and 'S' was considered—only one assignment of truth-values was made. There are of course others. And we are interested in such matters as: Is a given statement true on *all* truth-value assignments to its atomic components, or on just *some*, or on *none* at all? Is the statement true on *all* the truth-value assignments on which some other statements are true? And so on.

In order to answer questions like these, we must know how many truth-value assignments there are in any particular case, and how to arrive at them. For any n from 1 on, there are 2^n different ways of assigning one of the two truth-values **T** and **F** to each one of a statement's n atomic components $A_1, A_2, \ldots,$ and A_n. Note first that there are $2 \ (= 2^1)$ different ways of assigning a truth-value to just one atomic component, A_1. But, for each one of these 2 different ways of assigning a truth-value to A_1, there are 2 different ways of also assigning a truth-value to a second atomic component, A_2. So there are altogether $4 (= 2^1 \times 2 = 2^2)$ different ways of assigning a truth-value to both A_1 and A_2. Moreover, for each one of these 4 different ways of assigning a truth-value to A_1 and A_2, there are 2 different ways of also assigning a truth-value to a third atomic component, A_3. Hence, there are altogether $8 (= 2^2 \times 2 = 2^3)$ different ways of assigning a truth-value to all three of A_1, A_2, and A_3. Thus, by the same reasoning over and over, there are altogether 2^n different ways of assigning a truth-value to each one of a statement's n atomic components A_1, A_2, . . ., and A_n.

That is, if a statement has n distinct atomic components, there are 2^n different combinations of truth-values for these atomic components (or, to speak more dramatically, 2^n different ways the world might be which could have any bearing, in a truth-functional way, on the truth or falsehood of the statement).[14] A **truth-table** representing all of these possibilities can easily be produced by alternating 'T' and 'F' by ones (**T-F-T-F-** . . .) in a vertical column under the first atomic component, up to a total of 2^n entries; then by twos (**T-T-F-F-T-T-** . . .) for the second atomic component; by fours (**T-T-T-T-F-F-F-F-T-** . . .) for the third; by eights for the fourth—and, in general, by 2^{n-1}'s for the n-th atomic component of the statement under consideration.

Consider the earlier example. Because it has four distinct atomic components, there are $16 (= 2^4)$ different assignments of truth-values to those atomic components:

P Q R S	P & Q	~(P & Q)	~S	R V ~S	~(P & Q) ⊃ (R V ~S)
1. **T T T T**					
2. **F T T T**					
3. **T F T T**					
4. **F F T T**					
5. **T T F T**					
6. **F T F T**	F	T	F	F	F
7. **T F F T**					
8. **F F F T**					
9. **T T T F**					
10. **F T T F**					
11. **T F T F**					
12. **F F T F**					
13. **T T F F**					
14. **F T F F**					
15. **T F F F**					
16. **F F F F**					

---

[14] Although this holds *in general*, there may be exceptions to it. For example, if both 'My ball is blue all over' and 'My ball is red all over', or both 'Tom is five feet tall' and 'Tom is

The sixth truth-value assignment, or horizontal row, is the one for which we previously worked out the truth-value **F** for the entire statement. The student should complete this truth-table, either in the full style of p. 24, or in the more compressed style of p. 25. (Although it makes more sense to work horizontally, determining the truth-value of the whole statement on each truth-value assignment separately, it will go faster if one works vertically instead, determining first the truth-value for 'P & Q' on each assignment, then the truth-value for '~(P & Q)' on each assignment, and so on.)

Of course, in order to represent all of the conditions under which this or any statement might be true or be false, we must exhaust all of the possible assignments of truth-values to its atomic components. But since these represent all of the "ways things might be" which could have any bearing on the truth or falsehood of a truth-functionally compound statement, we shall find ourselves entitled to some rather strong claims about statements. In this case they are unimpressive: e.g., "This statement could either be true or be false, and I know under what circumstances it would be which." But the claims can sometimes be much stronger, as we shall proceed to show. (See Exercise E1.1.6.)

Truth-Table Tests for Logical Properties and Relations

A number of logical properties were defined in the Introduction in terms of the undefined concept of the *possible* truth or falsehood of statements. For example, an argument was said to be valid if its premises could not be true without its conclusion also being true. A set of statements was said to be consistent if all its members could be true together. And a statement was said to be logically true if it could not be false.

With the notion of a truth-value assignment on hand, we can now redefine these properties in a much sharper manner. And the truth-table method will enable us to determine whether or not statements are logically true on truth-functional grounds, sets of statements are consistent on truth-functional grounds, and so on. A similar treatment will be given the logical relations of entailment and equivalence.

On one clear sense of possibility, we may say that it is possible for a statement to be true if there are circumstances, or conditions, under which it would be true; and it is impossible for a statement to be true if there are no conditions under which it would be true. An assignment of truth-values to the atomic components of a statement *does* represent *one* con-

---

six feet tall', or both 'All men are mortal' and 'Some men are immortal' were among some n atomic statements, there would obviously be fewer than 2^n different truth-value combinations for those n statements ('My ball is blue all over' and 'My ball is red all over' can obviously not *both* get a 'T'). But our concern here is with *the most general case*, and not with occasional deviations from it.

dition that truth-functionally bears on the truth or the falsehood of that statement; and to run through all such truth-value assignments is to run through *all* the conditions (*all* the ways things might be) that truth-functionally affect the truth or the falsehood of the statement. We shall accordingly redefine validity, (in)consistency, logical truth, and so on, in terms of truth-value assignments. And note that because any statement or the members of any *finite* set of statements have only finitely many atomic components, truth-values can be assigned to those components in only finitely many different ways.[15] So the truth-value assignments to which we refer in the definitions below will always be finite in number, and hence within our power to write out as rows of 'T's and 'F's. That a statement is logically true, a set of statements inconsistent, and so on, will thus be—as announced—something that can be shown by the truth-table method, so long as the statement is logically true because of its truth-functional composition, the set inconsistent because of the truth-functional composition of its members, and so on.[16] (Of course a statement or set might have such a property by virtue of other structural features, or ways in which it or its members are composed. In this chapter, however, we limit ourselves to truth-functional modes of composition, and save further modes for Chapter 2.)

Truth-functional truth. A statement is **truth-functionally true**—logically true on truth-functional grounds—if it is true on every truth-value assignment to its atomic components. Such a statement would obviously have to be true no matter what, because it would be true under every condition bearing truth-functionally on its truth or its falsehood. A truth-functional truth is also called a **tautology.**[17] (In Chapter 2 we shall meet logical truths which are not truth-functionally true.)

In terms of truth-tables, a statement is truth-functionally true if its truth-table column (i.e., the one under its main connective) consists only of 'T's. For each entry corresponds to a different assignment of truth-values to its atomic components, and all possible assignments are represented. In the following examples, we display at the extreme right the statement being tested (ultimately, of course, it is only the column under *it* which will interest us). To the left of the statement we array *all* of its relatively less complex components, down to the atomic ones; and beneath

---

[15] All the sets of statements in this chapter will be understood to have finitely many members. Sets with infinitely many members will be discussed briefly in Section 2.1, and at length in Sections 3.2 and 3.6.

[16] The truth-table test is thus **mechanical:** after finitely many clerical operations, performed according to instructions fully specified in advance, it will always give a (correct) Yes or No answer to such questions as 'Is this statement truth-functionally true?', 'Is this set of statements truth-functionally consistent?', etc.

[17] Various truth-functional truths will be found in Exercises E1.1.7–9, E1.2.5, and E1.3.5, and in Section 1.3. Some have names (often of algebraic origin), which we append.

these atomic components we run all possible assignments of truth-values to them. The statements are so arrayed that the truth-value of any compound, on a given truth-value assignment, can be determined by reference to the truth-values (on that assignment) of statements on its left—and of course by reference to the truth-table for its main connective.

We show in this way that all three of 'P V ~P', '[(P ⊃ Q) ⊃ P] ≡ P', and '~(~P V Q) ⊃ [P V (Q & R)]' are truth-functionally true:

P	~P	P V ~P
T	F	T
F	T	T

P	Q	P ⊃ Q	(P ⊃ Q) ⊃ P	[(P ⊃ Q) ⊃ P] ≡ P
T	T	T	T	T
F	T	T	F	T
T	F	F	T	T
F	F	T	F	T

P Q R	~P	~P V Q	~(~P V Q)	Q & R	P V (Q & R)	~(~P V Q) ⊃ [P V (Q & R)]
T T T	F	T	F	T	T	T
F T T	T	T	F	T	T	T
T F T	F	F	T	F	T	T
F F T	T	T	F	F	F	T
T T F	F	T	F	F	T	T
F T F	T	T	F	F	F	T
T F F	F	F	T	F	T	T
F F F	T	T	F	F	F	T

We also give the more compressed version of this last truth-table, to illustrate the other way of exhibiting the material. Again we number the columns at the bottom to show the order in which they were produced— the same order as above:

~	(~ P V Q)	⊃	[P V (Q & R)]
F	F T T T	T	T T T T T
F	T F T T	T	F T T T T
T	F T F F	T	T T F F T
F	T F T F	T	F F F F T
F	F T T T	T	T T T F F
F	T F T T	T	F F T F F
T	F T F F	T	T T F F F
F	T F T F	T	F F F F F
4	2 1 3 1	7	1 6 1 5 1

We might have established the truth-functional truth of, say, '~(~P ∨ Q) ⊃ [P ∨ (Q & R)]' by a somewhat different line of thought. If there were any assignment α of truth-values to 'P', 'Q', and 'R' on which this conditional were false, then the antecedent '~(~P ∨ Q)' would have to be true and the consequent 'P ∨ (Q & R)' false on α. Now if '~(~P ∨ Q)' were true on α, '~P ∨ Q' would have to be false, '~P' false, and 'P' true on α. But if 'P ∨ (Q & R)' were false on α, 'P' would have to be false on α. So 'P' would have to be both true and false on α, which is impossible. Hence there can be no truth-value assignment on which '~(~P ∨ Q) ⊃ [P ∨ (Q & R)]' is false, so it must be true on every truth-value assignment to its atomic components—i.e., truth-functionally true. (This short-cut modification of the truth-table test—which amounts to a systematic hunt for a "disqualifying" truth-value assignment—could be used to establish truth-functional falsehood, equivalence, and inconsistency as well, and will be used on pp. 35–36 below in connection with truth-functional entailment. It will be the order of the day in Section 2.1, where truth-table tests are not generally available. And the tree technique to be developed in Sections 1.2 and 2.2 is reminiscent of it in some respects.) (See Exercises E1.1.7–9.)

Truth-functional falsehood and truth-functional indeterminacy. But of course not all statements are truth-functionally true (get 'T' in every row). Indeed, some get 'F' in every row of their truth-table column, or are false on every truth-value assignment (to their atomic components). Such statements are said to be **truth-functionally false,** or self-contradictory. Of course, the negation of any truth-functional truth is truth-functionally false (and vice versa). So are 'P & ~P', and '(P ∨ ~Q) & (Q & ~P)':

P	~P	P & ~P
T	F	F
F	T	F

P	Q	~Q	P ∨ ~Q	~P	Q & ~P	(P ∨ ~Q) & (Q & ~P)
T	T	F	T	F	F	F
F	T	F	F	T	T	F
T	F	T	T	F	F	F
F	F	T	T	T	F	F

A statement which is neither truth-functionally true nor truth-functionally false is **truth-functionally indeterminate,** or contingent: it shows at least one 'F' and at least one 'T' in its truth-table column (and hence the negation of a contingent statement must also be contingent). The statement '~(P & Q) ⊃ (R ∨ ~S)', used as an example on pp. 26–27 above, is truth-functionally indeterminate, as is '~(P & ~Q) ⊃ (Q ⊃ P)':

P Q	~Q	P & ~Q	~(P & ~Q)	Q ⊃ P	~(P & ~Q) ⊃ (Q ⊃ P)
T T	F	F	T	T	T
F T	F	F	T	F	F
T F	T	T	F	T	T
F F	T	F	T	T	T

Of course, most statements in ordinary discourse are truth-functionally indeterminate—as far as their *truth-functional* composition goes, they might be true and they might be false. But logic contributes importantly to an understanding of them (as well as of the more "dramatic" truth-functional truths and falsehoods) by exhibiting, in terms of the truth or the falsehood of the atomic statements of which they are composed, the circumstances under which they would be true and those under which they would be false.

Truth-functional equivalence. Two statements are **truth-functionally equivalent** if their truth-conditions are exactly the same—so that, on any truth-value assignment to the atomic components of both, either statement is true if the other one is. In terms of truth-tables, two statements are truth-functionally equivalent if their truth-table columns are the same. (Of course, the truth-table must be based on an exhaustion of truth-value combinations for the atomic components of *both* statements.) Or, what amounts to the same thing, two statements *A* and *B* are truth-functionally equivalent if their biconditional *A* ≡ *B* is truth-functionally true.[18] So the truth-table on p. 29 above shows that '(P ⊃ Q) ⊃ P' is truth-functionally equivalent to 'P'. 'P ⊃ Q' and its contrapositive '~Q ⊃ ~P' are also truth-functionally equivalent, as are 'P ∨ (P ≡ Q)' and 'Q ⊃ P':

P Q	~Q	~P	P ⊃ Q	~Q ⊃ ~P
T T	F	F	T	T
F T	F	T	T	T
T F	T	F	F	F
F F	T	T	T	T

---

[18] This may account for the unfortunate reading of '≡' as 'is equivalent to'. Note that, for us, a biconditional *A* ≡ *B* must be truth-functionally true, and not merely true, if *A* is to be truth-functionally equivalent to *B*. (In Chapter 2 we shall encounter equivalent statements that are not truth-functionally equivalent.)

P Q	P ≡ Q	P ∨ (P ≡ Q)	Q ⊃ P
T T	T	T	T
F T	F	F	F
T F	F	T	T
F F	T	T	T

But 'P ⊃ Q' and its converse 'Q ⊃ P' are not truth-functionally equivalent:

P Q	P ⊃ Q	Q ⊃ P
T T	T	T
F T	T	F
T F	F	T
F F	T	T

And we can provide from the truth-table two assignments of truth-values to their atomic components on which these statements would have different truth-values. (See Exercise E1.1.10.)

Truth-functional consistency and inconsistency. A finite but non-empty set $\{A_1, A_2, \ldots, A_n\}$ of statements is **truth-functionally consistent** if its members A_1, A_2, . . ., and A_n are all true on at least one assignment of truth-values to their atomic components.[19] And it is **truth-functionally inconsistent** if there is no such assignment, so that no matter which truth-value assignment is considered, at least one of the statements A_1, A_2, . . ., and A_n is false on the assignment.[20] Since our truth-value assignments represent all possible circumstances which could bear in a truth-functional way on the truth or the falsehood of A_1, A_2, . . ., and A_n, it would be (im)possible for those statements to be true together if $\{A_1, A_2, \ldots, A_n\}$ is truth-functionally (in)consistent. (A set of statements which is truth-functionally consistent may nonetheless be inconsistent on other grounds, such as those to be explored in Chapter 2.)

A truth-table for the consistency of a finite and non-empty set of statements consists in: (1) displaying all its members at the right, (2) array-

---

[19] At this point the reader unfamiliar with elementary set theory is advised to read Appendix I at the end of the book, where we explain all the notions and notation of set theory which he will encounter in the following pages.

Two things must be carefully noted here. (a) The consistency defined in the text is **semantic consistency**; a parallel notion, that of syntactic consistency, will be introduced in Chapter 3. (b) As pointed out in footnote 15, all sets of statements in this chapter are finite.

[20] Here is another clear case where a truth-value assignment might well reach beyond the atomic components of any one statement whose truth-value is determined by that assignment. We are asked, for example, to consider the truth-value of, say, A_1 on a truth-value assignment to atomic statements some of which will occur in A_1, but others of which may occur, say, in A_2 but not in A_1.

ing to the left all of the relatively less complex components of the members, down to their atomic components at the extreme left, (3) exhausting truth-value combinations, or assignments, to these atomic components, and then (4) calculating the truth-value of each member on each assignment, to see whether there is at least one row in which all the members get a 'T'. If there is, the set is truth-functionally consistent (*not* "truth-functionally consistent on that truth-value assignment," but just truth-functionally consistent); if there is *no* such truth-value assignment, the set is truth-functionally *in*consistent.

{P ⊃ ~Q, Q V ~R, P & R}[21] is such a truth-functionally inconsistent set. (All of the examples to follow will be done in the full rather than in the compressed style.)

P	Q	R	~Q	~R	P ⊃ ~Q	Q V ~R	P & R
T	T	T	F	F	F	T	T
F	T	T	F	F	T	T	F
T	F	T	T	F	T	F	T
F	F	T	T	F	T	F	F
T	T	F	F	T	F	T	F
F	T	F	F	T	T	T	F
T	F	F	T	T	T	T	F
F	F	F	T	T	T	T	F

But {P ⊃ ~Q, Q V ~R, P V R} is truth-functionally consistent:

P	Q	R	~Q	~R	P ⊃ ~Q	Q V ~R	P V R
T	T	T	F	F	F	T	T
F	T	T	F	F	T	T	T
T	F	T	T	F	T	F	T
F	F	T	T	F	T	F	T
T	T	F	F	T	F	T	T
F	T	F	F	T	T	T	F
T	F	F	T	T	T	T	T
F	F	F	T	T	T	T	F

If called upon to produce a truth-value assignment on which all the members of this last set were true (i.e., to defend our claim of truth-functional consistency), we could read off the table these two:

---

[21] As explained in Appendix I, we write

$$\{P \supset \text{~}Q, Q \lor \text{~}R, P \& R\}$$

where

$$\{\text{'}P \supset \text{~}Q\text{'}, \text{'}Q \lor \text{~}R\text{'}, \text{'}P \& R\text{'}\}$$

would be more proper. We shall follow this practice throughout.

$$
\begin{array}{lll}
\text{`P':} & \mathbf{F} \\
\text{`Q':} & \mathbf{T} \\
\text{`R':} & \mathbf{T}
\end{array}
\quad \text{and} \quad
\begin{array}{l}
\mathbf{T} \\
\mathbf{F} \\
\mathbf{F}
\end{array}
$$

(the first corresponding to the second row of the truth-table, and the other to the seventh).

Since the sets for which we have defined truth-functional inconsistency might have as few as one member, a word should be said about the truth-functional inconsistency of *unit sets*. The set $\{A\}$ which has some statement A as its only member is truth-functionally inconsistent if and only if A is truth-functionally false. For A is false on every truth-value assignment if and only if the members of $\{A\}$ are true on none.

If $\{A\}$ is truth-functionally consistent, we cannot say that A is truth-functionally true, but only that it is not truth-functionally false—and hence is *either* truth-functionally true *or* truth-functionally indeterminate. We can, however, say that a statement A is truth-functionally true if the set $\{{\sim}A\}$ which has the *negation* ${\sim}A$ of A as its only member is truth-functionally *inconsistent*. For ${\sim}A$ is false, and hence A is true, on every truth-value assignment if and only if the members of $\{{\sim}A\}$ are true on none. (As a result, two statements A and B are truth-functionally equivalent if and only if $\{{\sim}(A \equiv B)\}$ is truth-functionally inconsistent.) (See Exercise E1.1.11.)

Truth-functional entailment. A finite (*and possibly empty*) set $\{A_1, A_2, \ldots, A_n\}$ of statements **truth-functionally entails** a statement B if and only if there is no truth-value assignment on which $A_1, A_2, \ldots,$ and A_n are all true and B is false.[22] This can be put in a number of other ways. For example, $\{A_1, A_2, \ldots, A_n\}$ truth-functionally entails B (a) if and only if B is true on every truth-value assignment on which all of $A_1, A_2, \ldots,$ and A_n are true; or (b) if and only if $\{A_1, A_2, \ldots, A_n, {\sim}B\}$ is truth-functionally inconsistent; or (c) if and only if the conditional

$$
(A_1 \ \& \ A_2 \ \& \ \ldots \ \& \ A_n) \supset B
$$

(with the antecedent properly punctuated in one way or another) is truth-functionally true.[23] The reader should satisfy himself that a set of state-

---

[22] Two terminological remarks are in order. On the one hand, where we say that a set S of statements entails a statement A, other writers would say that S (logically) implies A (see footnote 7), or that A is a logical, or semantic, consequence of S, etc. And, on the other hand, some writers would say that S entails A only if stricter conditions than ours are met.

[23] So, a single statement A (or, more strictly, $\{A\}$) truth-functionally entails a statement B if and only if $A \supset B$ is truth-functionally true. This may account for the unfortunate reading of '$\supset$' as 'implies' (which, recall, is a frequent synonym of 'entails'). For us a conditional $A \supset B$ must be truth-functionally true, and not just true, if A is to truth-functionally entail B.

ments truth-functionally entails a statement on any one of these accounts if and only if it does on the other accounts as well. (Again, a set of statements which does not truth-functionally entail some statement may nonetheless entail it on other grounds, as we shall see in Chapter 2.)

Whether or not a set $\{A_1, A_2, \ldots, A_n\}$ of statements entails a statement B can be tested by arraying A_1, A_2, ..., A_n, and B to the right, and all their components to the left as before, producing a truth-table row for each truth-value assignment to the atomic components, and seeing whether or not each of A_1, A_2, ..., and A_n gets a 'T' and B gets an 'F' in any row. If there is *no* such row, then $\{A_1, A_2, \ldots, A_n\}$ truth-functionally entails B. If there *is* such a row, it does not, and a "disqualifying" truth-value assignment can be read at the left end of that row.

The following truth-table (in the full style) shows that the set $\{P \supset Q, \sim Q \vee R\}$ truth-functionally entails '$\sim R \supset \sim P$':

P	Q	R	~Q	~R	~P	P ⊃ Q	~Q ∨ R	~R ⊃ ~P
T	T	T	F	F	F	T	T	T
F	T	T	F	F	T	T	T	T
T	F	T	T	F	F	F	T	T
F	F	T	T	F	T	T	T	T
T	T	F	F	T	F	T	F	F
F	T	F	F	T	T	T	F	T
T	F	F	T	T	F	F	T	F
F	F	F	T	T	T	T	T	T

Each row (truth-value assignment) on which '$\sim R \supset \sim P$' is false is one on which at least one member of the set is false; hence there is none on which both members of the set are true and '$\sim R \supset \sim P$' false. (Notice that in *no* row of the truth-table for the corresponding set $\{P \supset Q, \sim Q \vee R, \sim(\sim R \supset \sim P)\}$ could all three members be true; this set is truth-functionally *in*consistent.)

We could have established this result by a short-cut method similar to that on p. 30. If $\{P \supset Q, \sim Q \vee R\}$ does *not* truth-functionally entail '$\sim R \supset \sim P$', then there must be a truth-value assignment α to 'P', 'Q', and 'R' on which both 'P $\supset$ Q' and '$\sim$Q $\vee$ R' are true and '$\sim R \supset \sim P$' is false. But if '$\sim R \supset \sim P$' is false on a truth-value assignment α, then '$\sim$R' is true and '$\sim$P' false—so 'R' is false and 'P' true—on α. Now 'Q' must be either true or false on α, but not both. On any assignment α on which 'Q' is true, '$\sim$Q' is false—and hence so is one member '$\sim$Q $\vee$ R' of $\{P \supset Q, \sim Q \vee R\}$ (since 'R' is also false on α). And on any assignment α on which 'Q' is false, so is the other member 'P $\supset$ Q' (since 'P' is true on α). So there is *no* truth-value assignment on which '$\sim R \supset \sim P$' is false while both 'P $\supset$ Q' and '$\sim$Q $\vee$ R' are true, and $\{P \supset Q, \sim Q \vee R\}$ therefore entails '~R ⊃ ~P'. (As we remarked before, reasoning of this kind will be quite important in Section 2.1, where truth-table tests are not generally available.)

The following truth-table, on the other hand, shows that {Q ∨ ~P, ~(~R & Q)} does *not* truth-functionally entail '~(~P ∨ ~R)':

P Q R	~P	~R	~R & Q	~P ∨ ~R	Q ∨ ~P	~(~R & Q)	~(~P ∨ ~R)
T T T	F	F	F	F	T	T	T
F T T	T	F	F	T	T	T	F
T F T	F	F	F	F	F	T	T
F F T	T	F	F	T	T	T	F
T T F	F	T	T	T	T	F	F
F T F	T	T	T	T	T	F	F
T F F	F	T	F	T	F	T	F
F F F	T	T	F	T	T	T	F

That all three statements under consideration are true on a truth-value assignment (the first) is irrelevant. What matters is that there is at least one truth-value assignment (indeed, there are three) on which 'Q ∨ ~P' and '~(~R & Q)' are both true and '~(~P ∨ ~R)' false (and hence '~~(~P ∨ ~R)' true); so the entailment fails, as these truth-value assignments bear out:

'P':	F		F		F
'Q':	T	and	F	and	F
'R':	T		T		F.

It was hinted on p. 34 that the empty set ∅ can be said to truth-functionally entail statements. *Which* statements it truth-functionally entails is an interesting question. Since a set {$A_1, A_2, \ldots, A_n$} of statements truth-functionally entails a statement B if and only if {$A_1, A_2, \ldots, A_n, {\sim}B$} is truth-functionally inconsistent, ∅ (i.e., {$A_1, A_2, \ldots, A_n$} where $n = 0$) truth-functionally entails B if and only if {${\sim}B$} is truth-functionally inconsistent. And, as we have already seen, {${\sim}B$} *is* truth-functionally inconsistent if and only if B is truth-functionally true. So the empty set ∅ truth-functionally entails all, and only, truth-functional truths.

Truth-functional validity and invalidity. Informally, an argument is valid if it would be impossible for all the premises to be true and the conclusion false. Therefore, in the present terms, an argument

$$A_1$$
$$A_2$$
.
$$A_n$$

———

$$\therefore B$$

is **truth-functionally valid** if $\{A_1,A_2,\ldots,A_n\}$ truth-functionally entails B; otherwise it is **truth-functionally invalid** (although, as we shall see in Chapter 2, it might still be valid on other than truth-functional grounds).[24] The argument

$$P \supset Q$$
$$\sim Q \vee R$$

———

$$\therefore \sim R \supset \sim P,$$

then, was just shown to be truth-functionally *valid;* and the argument

$$Q \vee \sim P$$
$$\sim(\sim R \;\&\; Q)$$

———

$$\therefore \sim(\sim P \vee \sim R)$$

was shown to be truth-functionally *in*valid (*not* "truth-functionally invalid on a certain truth-value assignment," but truth-functionally invalid). Whether or not an argument is truth-functionally valid can be ascertained by testing whether or not the premisses (as a set) truth-functionally entail the conclusion.

If we counted a single statement as (the conclusion of) an argument with no premisses—which we do not, but which would not be perfectly foolish—such an "argument" would be truth-functionally valid if and only if ∅ (the set consisting of all the "premisses") truth-functionally

———

[24] We have warned the reader that a statement which is logically true may fail to be truth-functionally true, that a set of statements which is inconsistent may be truth-functionally consistent, that an argument which is valid may be truth-functionally invalid, etc. But, of course, if a statement is truth-functionally true, it *is* logically true; if a set of statements is truth-functionally inconsistent, it *is* inconsistent; and if an argument is truth-functionally valid, it *is* valid. ('∴' is to be read 'therefore'.)

entailed its "conclusion," which it would if and only if that statement were truth-functionally true. This is just what we should want, incidentally. For to say that an argument is valid is to say that the conclusion would have to be true *so long as* the premises were true. Thus, to say that an "argument" with no premises is valid would be to say that the "conclusion" would have to be true *unconditionally*, which is just what we would expect about logical truths. (See Exercises E1.1.12–13.)

All the logical properties and relations presented above are naturally of interest in their own right. It is important, however, to see that they are not just so many disparate concepts, but rather are closely related to each other, so that whatever interest attaches to any attaches to the rest as well. At several points in the text, we showed that we could understand some of these concepts in terms of others—the truth-functional equivalence of two statements in terms of the truth-functional truth of their biconditional, the truth-functional truth of a statement in terms of its entailment by the empty set, and so on.

In the table on the facing page, we present our definitions of the logical properties and relations, as these are based on the truth-functional composition of statements. We parenthetically define them in terms of the truth-functional (in)consistency of sets of statements as well. On the one hand, we thus emphasize the interrelatedness of the concepts. And, on the other, we prepare the reader for Section 1.2, where we develop a new technique for testing the truth-functional (in)consistency of sets of statements, which technique can be applied—in accordance with these definitions—to test for other logical properties and relations as well. (See Exercises E1.1.14–16, 21.)

Truth-Functional Modes of (Statement) Composition[25]

Because interposing '&' between *two* statements is a way of truth-functionally compounding them, it is often called a **binary truth-functional mode of composition.** So is interposing 'V', '⊃', or '≡' between two statements. And prefacing *one* statement with '~' is known by analogy as a **singulary truth-functional mode of composition.**

There are other binary truth-functional modes of composition besides the four officially used here, and hence other binary truth-functional compounds besides conditionals, conjunctions, disjunctions, and biconditionals. We met one of those compounds on p. 13, and illustrations of two others on p. 19. The first was the **exclusive disjunction** of *A* and *B*—that compound of *A* and *B* which is true if and only if *exactly one*

---

[25] The remaining pages of this section, being of a more specialized nature, may be omitted on first reading.

TABLE III[26]

A. A finite (but non-empty) set S of statements is **truth-functionally consistent** if there is at least one assignment of truth-values to the atomic components of the members of S on which all the members of S are true; and it is **truth-functionally inconsistent** if it is not truth-functionally consistent.

B. (1) A statement A is **truth-functionally true** if A is true on every assignment of truth-values to its atomic components (so that $\{\sim A\}$ is truth-functionally inconsistent).

  (2) A statement A is **truth-functionally false** if A is true on no assignment of truth-values to its atomic components (so that $\{A\}$ is truth-functionally inconsistent).

  (3) A statement A is **truth-functionally indeterminate** if A is neither truth-functionally true nor truth-functionally false (so that both $\{\sim A\}$ and $\{A\}$ are truth-functionally consistent).

C. Two statements A and B are **truth-functionally equivalent** if there is no assignment of truth-values to the atomic components of A and of B on which A and B have different truth-values (so that $\{\sim(A \equiv B)\}$ is truth-functionally inconsistent).

D. A finite (and possibly empty) set S of statements **truth-functionally entails** a statement A if there is no assignment of truth-values (to the atomic components of the members of S and to those of A) on which all the members of S are true and A false (so that $S \cup \{\sim A\}$ is truth-functionally inconsistent).

E. An argument $A_1, A_2, \ldots, A_n/\,\therefore B$ is **truth-functionally valid** if $\{A_1, A_2, \ldots, A_n\}$ truth-functionally entails B (so that $\{A_1, A_2, \ldots, A_n, \sim B\}$ is truth-functionally inconsistent); otherwise, it is **truth-functionally invalid.**

---

of A and B is true. The second was that compound of A and B which is true if and only if neither one of A and B is true; in English it often runs

Neither A nor B,

in logic writings $A \downarrow B$, and it is called the **joint denial** of A and B. The third was that compound of A and B which is true if and only if *at least one* of A and B is false; in English it often runs

Either not A or not B (also: Not both A and B),

in logic writing $A|B$, and it is called the **alternative denial** of A and B.[27]

---

[26] It is common practice, when giving definitions, to write 'if' for the intended but cumbersome 'if and only if'. We follow suit here, and at various other points in the text.

[27] '|' is known in the literature as *Sheffer's stroke*.

Similarly, there are other singulary truth-functional modes of composition besides negation. And, since statements can be truth-functionally compounded three at a time, four at a time, and so on, there are also ternary truth-functional modes of composition, quaternary ones, and so on.

We shall survey these various truth-functional modes of composition in Section 3.1, and (as suggested on p. 20) establish that they are all reducible to modes we are already familiar with—in point of fact, to just negation, conjunction, and disjunction. That is, we shall show that to any truth-functional compound of n ($n \geq 1$) statements A_1, A_2, . . ., and A_n there corresponds a truth-functionally equivalent compound built out of the very same statements A_1, A_2, . . ., and A_n with the aid of just '~', '&', and 'V'.

Such "paraphrases" in terms of '~', '&', and 'V' are already available in some cases. As noted on p. 15, $A \supset B$ is truth-functionally equivalent to $\sim A \lor B$; and hence $A \equiv B$, which we explained as $(A \supset B) \mathbin{\&} (B \supset A)$, is truth-functionally equivalent to $(\sim A \lor B) \mathbin{\&} (\sim B \lor A)$. As for the exclusive disjunction of A and B, the joint denial $A \downarrow B$ of A and B, and the alternative denial $A \mid B$ of A and B, they are truth-functionally equivalent to $(A \lor B) \mathbin{\&} \sim(A \mathbin{\&} B)$, $\sim A \mathbin{\&} \sim B$, and $\sim A \lor \sim B$, respectively. What Section 3.1 guarantees is a paraphrase in terms of '~', '&', and 'V' of *each and every* truth-functional compound (not just conditionals, biconditionals, etc.), and a paraphrase that can be constructed by rote.

Because of this result, truth-functional compounds other than negations, conjunctions, and disjunctions are all dispensable. Indeed, since $A \lor B$ is truth-functionally equivalent to $\sim(\sim A \mathbin{\&} \sim B)$, and $A \mathbin{\&} B$ truth-functionally equivalent to $\sim(\sim A \lor \sim B)$, *either* disjunctions *or* conjunctions could also be dispensed with. Some accounts of truth-functional logic do just that, acknowledging as official compounds only negations and conjunctions, or only negations and disjunctions. However, conditionals, and to a lesser extent biconditionals, are so common in everyday discourse and play such a key role in logic that their absence would soon be felt. We accordingly prefer—in the more elementary Chapters 1 and 2—to include them, as well as *both* conjunctions and disjunctions, in our list of acknowledged compounds. Then, from the end of Section 3.1 on, we shall usually restrict ourselves to just two sorts of truth-functional compounds: negations and conditionals. For, like '~' and '&', or '~' and 'V', the two connectives '~' and '⊃' *also* permit paraphrase of every truth-functional compound,[28] and on a number of counts they prove a better choice of so-called **primitive connectives** than the other options open to us.

---

[28] Occurrences of '&' and 'V' in the paraphrases of Section 3.1 can indeed be turned in for occurrences of '⊃' and '~'. See the fourth and fifth definitions in the next paragraph.

Accounts of truth-functional logic in which only some of '~', '&', 'V', 'ⅅ', and '≡' figure as primitive usually reinstate the rest as so-called **defined connectives.** For example, those (like Whitehead and Russell's *Principia Mathematica*) that own only '~' and 'V' as primitive often reintroduce '&', 'ⅅ', and '≡' by means of the following definitions, which provide each one of $A \& B$, $A \supset B$, and $A \equiv B$ with a truth-functional equivalent compounded of A and B by means of just '~' and 'V':

$$(A \& B) =_{df} \sim(\sim A \lor \sim B)$$

$$(A \supset B) =_{df} (\sim A \lor B)$$

and

$$(A \equiv B) =_{df} \sim[\sim(\sim A \lor B) \lor \sim(\sim B \lor A)].$$

And those that own only '~' and 'ⅅ' as primitive often reintroduce '&', 'V', and '≡' by means of the following definitions, which provide each one of $A \& B$, $A \lor B$, and $A \equiv B$ with a truth-functional equivalent compounded of A and B by means of just '~' and 'ⅅ':

$$(A \& B) =_{df} \sim(A \supset \sim B)$$

$$(A \lor B) =_{df} (\sim A \supset B)$$

and

$$(A \equiv B) =_{df} \sim[(A \supset B) \supset \sim(B \supset A)].$$

Definitions like these play two different but related roles.

Consider, for example, the case where only '~' and 'ⅅ' serve as primitive. The definitions of '&', 'V', and '≡' which we just laid down make for greater compactness by allowing $\sim(A \supset \sim B)$ to be rewritten as $(A \& B)$, $(\sim A \supset B)$ as $(A \lor B)$, and $\sim[(A \supset B) \supset \sim(B \supset A)]$ as $(A \equiv B)$. And they provide paraphrases in terms of just '~' and 'ⅅ' of statements that also contain occurrences of any of '&', 'V', and '≡'. Indeed, systematic replacement of $(A \& B)$ by $\sim(A \supset \sim B)$, $(A \lor B)$ by $(\sim A \supset B)$, and $(A \equiv B)$ by $\sim[(A \supset B) \supset \sim(B \supset A)]$ in any such statement yields a paraphrase of it in terms of just '~' and 'ⅅ'. And the paraphrase is sure to be truth-functionally equivalent to the original, since—as we noted—the right-hand side of each definition (often known as the **definiens,** and sometimes the "definition") is truth-functionally equivalent to the left-hand side (often called the **definiendum**).

The last point is of special importance. Definiens and definiendum must be equivalent on truth-functional grounds if a (truth-functional) connective is to be properly defined. Similarly, in Chapter 2, definiens and definiendum will have to be equivalent on "quantificational" grounds if what will be called a *quantifier* is to be properly defined.

But other matters await us, to which we move on. (See Exercises E1.1.17–20.)

EXERCISES

E1.1.1. Which of the following statements could you construe as truth-functional compounds, and why?
- a. Hitler failed to invade England.
- b. Hitler lost the war because he failed to invade England.
- c. Tom and Jack are six feet tall.
- d. Tom and Jack are the same height.
- e. Bob has loved Mary ever since they were kids.
- f. He keeps calling her even though she won't talk to him.
- g. He calls her whenever he has a chance to.
- h. Neither Tweedledum nor Tweedledee makes any sense.
- i. They don't make any sense, but Alice does.
- j. The patient will die unless we operate immediately.
- k. It is just possible that there is life on Mars or Venus.
- l. Tom and Jack are probably lost by now.

E1.1.2. Give the truth-table for the exclusive 'or'.

E1.1.3. Using the abbreviations given, symbolize each of the statements below.

> 'P': 'Percy will pass'
>
> 'Q': 'Quincy will pass'
>
> 'R': 'Reginald will pass'
>
> 'S': 'Percy studies hard'
>
> 'T': 'Percy is tired'

- a. Percy studies hard unless he's tired, in which case he doesn't.
- b. Percy studies hard only if he's not tired.
- c. Percy will pass if, but only if, he either studies hard or isn't tired.
- d. Either Percy studies hard and will pass or he doesn't (and won't).
- e. If Percy will pass so long as he isn't tired, then he'll surely pass if he studies hard.
- f. Although he's tired, Percy will pass anyway.
- g. If Percy studies hard, then he'll pass provided that he isn't tired.
- h. Percy won't pass unless he studies hard.

i.   If either Quincy or Reginald will pass, then so will Percy unless he is tired.

j.   No more than one of them (Percy, Quincy, and Reginald, of course) will pass.

k.   Exactly two of them will pass.

l.   They won't all fail.

m. Reginald and Quincy will certainly pass; Percy, however, will fail if he doesn't study (and, for that matter, will fail even if he does).

n.   Percy won't pass, but at least one of the other two will.

o.   If neither Percy nor Quincy will pass, Reginald won't either.

E1.1.4. Supposing that Percy and Reginald will both pass, but not Quincy, and that Percy studies hard and is not tired, which of the statements in E1.1.3 are true, and which false?

E1.1.5. Assuming 'P', 'Q', and 'R' to be atomic statements, list all the components of each of the following statements (and identify the atomic ones):

a.   (P ⊃ Q) V (Q ⊃ P)

b.   ~~(P ⊃ ~Q) & (P V R)

c.   ~[~P ≡ ~(P & ~R)] ⊃ (~~R V P)

E1.1.6. Determine the truth-value of each of the following statements on the assignment of **T** to 'P' and 'Q', and **F** to 'R' and 'S':

a.   (P & R) V (Q & S)   f.   ~(P & ~S) V ~(~P & S)

b.   (P ⊃ Q) ⊃ (R ⊃ S)   g.   (~Q V S) ≡ [~(P V ~Q) V S]

c.   ~(R ⊃ Q)   h.   P & [R ⊃ (~Q V S)]

d.   ~(~R V ~S)   i.   (R & ~S) V (~P ≡ ~Q)

e.   (P & ~R) ⊃ ~~S   j.   ~S ⊃ ~[~(~P V R) ≡ (Q ⊃ S)]

E1.1.7. Give the truth-table for each of the following statements, and indicate which are truth-functionally true, which are truth-functionally false, and which are truth-functionally indeterminate:

a.   (P ⊃ ~P) V (~P ⊃ P)   f.   [P ⊃ (Q & ~R)] V (~P ≡ ~Q)

b.   (~P ⊃ P) & (P ⊃ ~P)   g.   ~(P ⊃ Q) & (~Q ⊃ ~P)

c.   (P V Q) ≡ [(P ⊃ Q) ⊃ Q]   h.   [(~P ⊃ Q) & (P ⊃ Q)] ≡ Q

d.   ~(~P ≡ Q) ⊃ (Q V ~R)   i.   (P & ~Q) V [Q ⊃ (R ≡ ~P)]

e.   ~(P ⊃ Q) ⊃ (~Q ⊃ ~P)   j.   (P ⊃ Q) ⊃ [~(Q V R) ⊃ ~(P & R)]

E1.1.8. Show by the short-cut method of p. 30 that each of the following conditionals is truth-functionally true:

a.   [P ⊃ (Q ⊃ R)] ⊃ [Q ⊃ (P ⊃ R)]

b.   [(P & Q) ⊃ R] ⊃ [P ⊃ (Q ⊃ R)]   (Exportation)

c.   [P ⊃ (Q ⊃ R)] ⊃ [(P & Q) ⊃ R]   (Importation)

d.   [(P ⊃ Q) & (Q ⊃ R)] ⊃ (P ⊃ R)   (Transitivity of '⊃')

e.   [(P ≡ Q) & (Q ≡ R)] ⊃ (P ≡ R)   (Transitivity of '≡')

f.   [(~P ⊃ Q) & (~P ⊃ ~Q)] ⊃ P   (Law of Indirect Proof)

E1.1.9. Show by the short-cut method of p. 30 that biconditionals of the following sorts are all truth-functionally true:

a. $\sim\sim A \equiv A$ (Law of Double Negation)

b. $\sim(A \,\&\, B) \equiv (\sim A \vee \sim B)$ (De Morgan's Law)

c. $\sim(A \vee B) \equiv (\sim A \,\&\, \sim B)$ (De Morgan's Law)

d. $(A \supset B) \equiv (\sim A \vee B)$

e. $\sim(A \supset B) \equiv (A \,\&\, \sim B)$

f. $(A \equiv B) \equiv [(A \,\&\, B) \vee (\sim A \,\&\, \sim B)]$

g. $\sim(A \equiv B) \equiv [(A \,\&\, \sim B) \vee (\sim A \,\&\, B)]$

E1.1.10. Match up the following into pairs of truth-functionally equivalent statements, and justify your answers with a truth-table for each pair:

a. $\sim P \supset Q$ f. $P \equiv \sim Q$

b. $\sim(P \,\&\, \sim Q)$ g. $\sim(P \vee \sim Q)$

c. $\sim(P \supset \sim Q)$ h. $(P \,\&\, \sim Q) \vee (\sim P \,\&\, Q)$

d. $\sim P \,\&\, Q$ i. $\sim(\sim P \,\&\, \sim Q)$

e. $\sim P \vee Q$ j. $P \,\&\, Q$

E1.1.11. Give the truth-table for each of the following sets of statements, indicate which are truth-functionally consistent and which are not, and justify this decision in each case:

a. $\{(P \supset \sim Q) \supset \sim Q, \sim(P \vee \sim Q)\}$ d. $\{\sim R, (P \vee \sim Q) \supset \sim(Q \,\&\, R), Q \supset \sim P\}$

b. $\{\sim[\sim(P \,\&\, Q) \equiv \sim Q], \sim(Q \supset P)\}$ e. $\{R \vee (P \,\&\, Q), P \supset (Q \,\&\, R), \sim R\}$

c. $\{\sim(P \vee R), P \vee (Q \supset R)\}$

E1.1.12. Determine by means of a truth-table whether or not the premises of each of the following arguments truth-functionally entail their conclusion (thus determining whether each argument is truth-functionally valid or invalid):

a. $P \supset Q$ b. $P \supset Q$
   $\overline{}$ $\overline{}$
   $\therefore \sim P \supset \sim Q$ $\therefore \sim Q \supset \sim P$

c. $P \vee Q$ d. $P \vee Q$
    $\sim P$ P
   $\overline{}$ $\overline{}$
   $\therefore Q$ $\therefore \sim Q$

e. $P \supset Q$ f. $P \supset (Q \supset R)$
    $Q \supset P$ $R \supset \sim P$
   $\overline{}$ $\overline{}$
   $\therefore P \vee Q$ $\therefore \sim P \vee \sim Q$

g. $P \supset Q$ h. $\sim(P \supset \sim Q)$
    $Q \supset \sim P$ $(Q \vee \sim R) \equiv P$
    P $P \,\&\, (R \supset Q)$
   $\overline{}$ $\overline{}$
   $\therefore R$ $\therefore \sim P \vee \sim Q$

i. $P \supset (Q \lor R)$
        $P \supset \sim Q$
       ———————
      ∴ $R \lor \sim P$

j. $(P \supset Q) \& (R \supset S)$
        $\sim Q \lor R$
       ———————
      ∴ $\sim P \lor S$

E1.1.13. When an argument in E1.1.12 was found truth-functionally valid, establish the result anew by the short-cut method of pp. 35–36.

E1.1.14.

(a) Show that all truth-functional truths are truth-functionally compound.

(b) Show that all truth-functional truths are truth-functionally equivalent to each other. And show that all truth-functional falsehoods are truth-functionally equivalent to each other.

(c) Might a truth-functionally valid argument all of whose premisses are true have a false conclusion? Why? Might a truth-functionally valid argument with a false premiss have a true conclusion? Why? Might a truth-functionally invalid argument all of whose premisses are true have a true conclusion? Why?

(d) If two statements A and B are truth-functionally equivalent, what do we know about the two arguments $A/ \therefore B$ and $B/ \therefore A$, and why?

E1.1.15. With S understood in each case to be a finite and non-empty set of statements, show that:

(a) S is truth-functionally inconsistent if and only if the conjunction of the members of S is truth-functionally false;[29]

(b) S is truth-functionally inconsistent if and only if some statement and its negation are both truth-functionally entailed by S;

(c) S is truth-functionally inconsistent if and only if every statement is truth-functionally entailed by S;

(d) S is truth-functionally inconsistent if and only if the negation $\sim A$ of any one member A of S is truth-functionally entailed by S *minus* A;

(e) S is truth-functionally inconsistent if and only if every finite superset of S is truth-functionally inconsistent;

(f) S is truth-functionally inconsistent if and only if at least one non-empty subset of S is truth-functionally inconsistent.

E1.1.16. With A understood to be a statement, show that:

(a) A is truth-functionally true if and only if A is truth-functionally entailed by every finite set of statements;

(b) A is truth-functionally entailed by a finite set S of statements if and only if A is truth-functionally entailed by every finite superset of S;

(c) A is truth-functionally entailed by a finite set S of statements if and only if A is truth-functionally entailed by at least one subset of S.

---

[29] A full and rigorous proof of (a) would require mathematical induction (presented in Chapter 3). It is possible, however, to suggest such a rigorous proof quite clearly and persuasively, and no more is expected of the student at this point. The same applies to E1.1.19 and later exercises.

E1.1.17.

    (a) Provide a truth-functional equivalent of ~*A* which is compounded
of *A* by means of just ' | ', and a truth-functional equivalent of each
of *A* & *B*, *A* ∨ *B*, and *A* ⊃ *B* which is compounded of *A* and *B* by
means of just ' | ' (thus showing that ' | ' permits definition of '~',
'&', '∨', and '⊃').

    (b) Do the same with '↓' in place of ' | '.

E1.1.18.

    (a) Define '∨' in terms of '⊃' alone.

    (b) Define '⊃' in terms of '&' and '≡', and then in terms of '∨' and '≡'.

E1.1.19.

    (a) Show that no truth-functional compound of *A* by means of just '⊃'
is truth-functionally equivalent to ~*A*, and that no truth-functional
compound of *A* and *B* by means of just '~' is truth-functionally
equivalent to *A* ⊃ *B* (thus showing that '⊃' does not permit definition of '~', nor '~' of '⊃').

    (b) Do the same with '&' in place of '⊃'.

    (c) Do the same with '∨' in place of '⊃'.

(These results will be important in Chapter 3.)

E1.1.20. Treating

        C unless *B*, in which case *A* (i.e., *A* if *B*, otherwise *C*)

as a ternary truth-functional compound of *A*, *B*, and *C*, complete the
following truth-table:

A	*B*	*C*	*C* unless *B*, in which case *A*
T	T	T	T
F	T	T	?
T	F	T	?
F	F	T	?
T	T	F	?
F	T	F	?
T	F	F	?
F	F	F	F

*E1.1.21. Consider this table for negation, where

    '2' is short for 'truth-functionally true',

    '1' is short for 'truth-functionally indeterminate', and

    '0' is short for 'truth-functionally false':

A	~*A*
2	0
1	1
0	2

Justify each entry under ~*A* above, and then supply the wanted entries in the following table:

A	B	A & B	A ∨ B	A ⊃ B	A ≡ B
2	2				
1	2				
0	2				
2	1				
1	1				
0	1				
2	0				
1	0				
0	0				

In most cases only one entry will be appropriate; but in some, more than one entry will be. When the latter is the case, offer an example for each one of the entries.[30]

1.2   Consistency Trees (1)

For all its merits, the truth-table method has a number of shortcomings. In the first place, it is often wasteful. For example, in the search for a row in which every member of a set of statements is true, one must often grind out and inspect a great many rows in which the members just cannot all be true. And the method quickly becomes intolerably long, as the number of rows doubles with each new atomic component. Second, the truth-table method, though it adjudicates on the (truth-functional) validity of arguments, does not reflect the ways in which we validly reason from premises to conclusions. In this respect it is "unnatural." And third, the truth-table method alone will not prove suitable in Chapter 2, where "quantificational" compounds as well as truth-functional ones are treated.

In this section and the next, we introduce two further methods for ascertaining whether statements, sets of statements, and arguments have certain logical properties. Both methods are tidier than the truth-table method; and both are serviceable in Chapter 2 as well as in Chapter 1. The method of this section, which stems from the truth-table method and stays close to it, is a systematic search for desired truth-value assignments.[1] The method of the next section is a formalization of natural patterns of valid reasoning from premises to conclusions. And in Sections 2.2 and 2.3, these methods will be extended to cover the logic of quantificational compounds.

---

[30] Starred exercises such as this are more difficult than the rest.

[1] The reader is therefore urged to review at this point the circumstances under which truth-functional compounds are true, and the results of E1.1.9.

Trees

A simple and telling technique has recently been devised for track-ing down the truth-value assignments on which all the members of a set of statements would be true. It can therefore be thought of as a test for truth-functional (in)consistency. And because truth-functional entail-ment, truth-functional truth, and so on, can be understood in terms of truth-functional inconsistency, the method serves to test for any logical property that depends on the truth-functional composition of statements. We present a version of the method due to Raymond M. Smullyan, and recently given currency by Richard C. Jeffrey.[2]

Consider the set {~P & ~~Q, P V ~R, Q ⊃ R}, which we display in this way:

1	~P & ~~Q
2	P V ~R
3	Q ⊃ R

Both conjuncts '~P' and '~~Q' of the first statement must be true on any truth-value assignment α on which all three members of the set (and the first in particular) are true—a fact which we record thus:

1	~P & ~~Q	
2	P V ~R	
3	Q ⊃ R	
	_____	from
4	~P	1
5	~~Q	1

If the first three statements are true on α, all five are true on α.

But if all five statements (and the fifth in particular) are true on α, then 'Q' must also be true on α—a fact which we record thus:

1	~P & ~~Q	
2	P V ~R	
3	Q ⊃ R	
	_____	from
4	~P	1
5	~~Q	1
6	Q	5

So, if the first three statements are true on α, all six are true on α.

_____

[2] The tree method is an adaptation by Smullyan of the "semantic tableaux" of Evert W. Beth, and of a method of Jaakko Hintikka for constructing "model sets." Beth's tableaux themselves stem from Gerhard Gentzen's tree method for proving so-called "Sequenzen" and,

And if the first three statements (and the second in particular) are true on α, then *at least one* of the disjuncts 'P' and '~R' of the second statement must be true on α:

1	~P & ~~Q	
2	P V ~R	
3	Q ⊃ R	
	―――――	from
4	~P	1
5	~~Q	1
6	Q	5
7	P ~R	2

If the first three statements are true on α, then *either* all seven statements from '~P & ~~Q' through 'P' on the left branch are true on α, *or* all seven statements from '~P & ~~Q' through '~R' on the right branch are true on α.

And if the first three statements (and the third in particular) are true on α, then *at least one* of the two statements '~Q' (the negation of the antecedent of the third statement) and 'R' (its consequent) must be true on α. For if a conditional is true on a truth-value assignment, then either its antecedent is false (and hence the negation of its antecedent true), or its consequent is true, on that assignment:

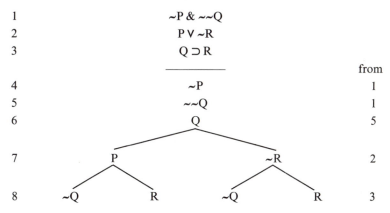

1	~P & ~~Q	
2	P V ~R	
3	Q ⊃ R	
	―――――	from
4	~P	1
5	~~Q	1
6	Q	5
7	P ~R	2
8	~Q R ~Q R	3

more generally, from the truth-table method. See Beth's *The Foundations of Mathematics,* 1959, North-Holland Publishing Company; Gentzen's "Untersuchungen über das logische Schliessen," *Mathematische Zeitschrift,* vol. 39, 1934–1935, pp. 176–210, 405–31; Hintikka's *Two Papers on Symbolic Logic, Acta Philosophica Fennica,* vol. 8, 1955; and Smullyan's *First-Order Logic,* 1968, Springer-Verlag New York Inc. The tree method made its first appearance in Richard C. Jeffrey's *Formal Logic: Its Scope and Limits,* 1967, McGraw-Hill Company.

Hence, if the first three statements—the members of the set under consideration—are all true on some truth-value assignment α, then *either* (1) all eight statements from '~P & ~~Q' through 'P' to '~Q' on the left-most branch are true on α; *or* (2) all eight statements from '~P & ~~Q' through 'P' to 'R' on the second branch are true on α; *or* (3) all eight statements from '~P & ~~Q' through '~R' to '~Q' on the third branch are true on α; *or* (4) all eight statements from '~P & ~~Q' through '~R' to 'R' on the right-most branch are true on α.

But there is no truth-value assignment on which all the statements on the first branch are true, for both 'P' and '~P' (as well as both 'Q' and '~Q') would have to be true on any such assignment, which is impossible. And both 'P' and '~P' would likewise have to be true on any truth-value assignment on which all the statements on the second branch were true. Similarly, there is no truth-value assignment on which all the statements on the third branch are true, for both 'Q' and '~Q' would have to be true on any such assignment. And there is, finally, no truth-value assignment on which all the statements on the fourth branch are true, for both 'R' and '~R' would have to be true on any such assignment. Hence, there is *no* truth-value assignment on which all three members of the original set are true, and the set is therefore truth-functionally inconsistent.

Notice that once 'P' had been entered on the left-hand branch at line 7 ('~P' already occurring on that branch at line 4), we could have ended the branch, knowing that *no* branch through 'P' could possibly correspond to a truth-value assignment. In the future we shall do just that, "closing" a branch with an 'x' as soon as a **contradiction** (some atomic statement and its negation) has appeared thereon, and indicating where the earlier half of the contradiction occurs on that branch. Such a

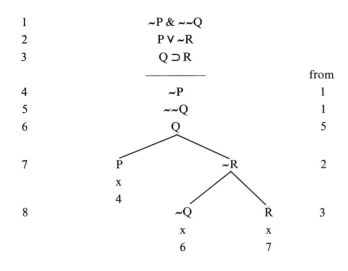

branch will be called a **closed branch;** one along which no contradiction
has appeared will be said to be an **open branch.**

Consider now the set {P ⊃ (Q & R), ~(P & ~Q) ⊃ ~R, P}, and the
"tree" obtained by application of the same principles as before. If all three
of these statements (and in particular the first) are true on some truth-
value assignment, then at least one of '~P' and 'Q & R' must be true on
that assignment:

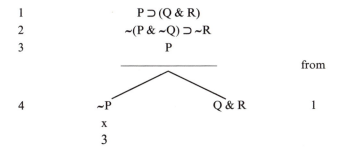

Since a contradiction has appeared along the left branch ('P' at line 3,
'~P' at line 4), we close the branch in the manner agreed upon.

But if all four statements on the open branch (and in particular
the fourth) are true on some truth-value assignment, then both 'Q' and
'R' must be true on that assignment:

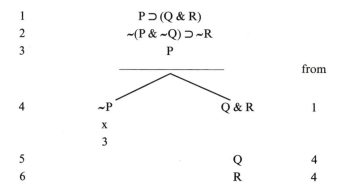

But if all three statements (and in particular the second) are true on
some truth-value assignment, then either the negation '~~(P & ~Q)' of
the antecedent '~(P & ~Q)' of the second statement, or the consequent
'~R', must be true on that assignment, and hence *either* all seven statements through '~~(P & ~Q)' *or* all seven statements through '~R' on the
following tree must be true on the assignment:

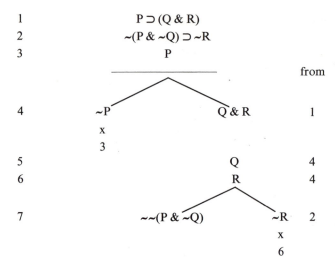

There is no truth-value assignment on which all the statements on the right-most branch are true, which is indicated in the usual way.

But if all seven statements on the remaining branch (and in particular the seventh) are true on some truth-value assignment, then 'P & ~Q', hence both 'P' and '~Q', and hence both 'Q' (line 5) and '~Q' are true on that assignment, which is impossible:

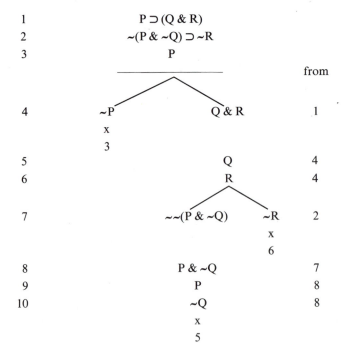

Hence, there is *no* truth-value assignment on which all three members of the original set are true, and the set is therefore truth-functionally inconsistent.

(This last tree differs from the first in a respect worth noting. Only one compound entered on the first tree required further treatment itself: '~~Q' at line 5. The second tree was more typical, in that several statements entered on it required further treatment themselves: 'Q & R' (line 4), '~~(P & ~Q)' (line 7), and 'P & ~Q' (line 8). When such lines occur, of course, they are handled in the same ways as are members of the set being tested.)

But now consider the set {P & (Q V ~R), Q ⊃ R}. By following *the same principles as before*, we arrive at the following tree for the set:[3]

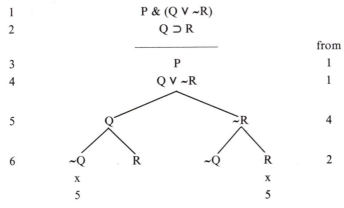

Again, we know that if the first two statements—the members of the set under consideration—are true on some truth-value assignment, then all the statements on the left-most branch are true on the assignment, or all those on the next branch are true on the assignment, and so on. We choose, however, to stress different features of the principles involved in making the tree than were stressed in the first two cases.

On the second branch, which runs from 'P & (Q V ~R)' through 'Q' to 'R' (the left-most branch which remains open), the atomic statements 'P', 'Q', and 'R' all occur unnegated. So consider the result α of assigning the truth-value **T** to all three. Since 'R' (line 6) is true on α, and a conditional is true on any truth-value assignment on which its consequent is true, 'Q ⊃ R' (line 2) from which 'R' came is true on α—quite regardless of whether the antecedent 'Q' is true or false on α. Since 'Q' (line 5) is true on α, and a disjunction is true on any truth-value assignment on which one of its disjuncts is true, 'Q V ~R' (line 4) from which 'Q' came is true on α—quite regardless of whether the right-hand disjunct '~R'

---

[3] Note that at line 6 '~Q' and 'R' are entered on every (open) branch through 'Q ⊃ R'.

is true or false on α. And since 'P' (line 3) is also true on α, and a conjunction is true on any truth-value assignment on which its two conjuncts are true, 'P & (Q ∨ ~R)' (line 1) from which 'P' and 'Q ∨ ~R' came
is true on α. So α *is* a truth-value assignment on which all the members
of the set are true, and hence the set is truth-functionally consistent.

On the third branch—the other open branch—the atomic statement
'P' occurs unnegated, and 'Q' and 'R' occur negated. So consider the
result α′ of assigning the truth-value **T** to 'P', and the truth-value **F** to
'Q' and 'R'. Since '~Q' (line 6) is true on α′, and a conditional is true
on any truth-value assignment on which the negation of its antecedent
is true, 'Q ⊃ R' (line 2) from which '~Q' came is true on α′. Since '~R'
(line 5) is true on α′, so is 'Q ∨ ~R' (line 4) from which '~R' came. And
since 'P' (line 3) is also true on α′, 'P & (Q ∨ ~R)' (line 1) from which 'P'
and 'Q ∨ ~R' came is also true on α′. So α′ is another (indeed, it is the
only other) truth-value assignment on which all the members of the set
are true.

Two related points were crucial in the preceding illustrations. On
the one hand, (a) if a compound statement is true on a truth-value
assignment α, then the statements obtained from it in accordance with
the appropriate principle—at least one of them where branching is involved, all of them where it is not—must also be true on α. And, on the
other hand, (b) if the one or two statements entered on some branch
in accordance with a principle are true on a truth-value assignment α,
then the compound from which they came must also be true on α.

The Rules

So far we have employed a few obvious principles in the construction
of trees. These principles could be schematized as follows:

The first, for example, could be read: when dealing with a conjunction,
write both conjuncts at the end of every open branch that goes through
the conjunction. The third could be read: when dealing with a conditional, put a fork at the end of every open branch that goes through
the conditional, writing the negation of the antecedent on the left branch
and the consequent on the right one.

Any statement not an atomic statement or a negated atomic statement
will be of just one of nine sorts: it will be a conditional, conjunction, disjunction, or biconditional; or it will be the negation of a negation, condi-

tional, conjunction, disjunction, or biconditional. So altogether we shall need nine rules for handling all truth-functional compounds other than negated atomic statements. (In the case of the negation $\sim A$ of an atomic statement A, one merely checks to see whether A itself appears on the same branch as $\sim A;$ that does not call for a special rule.)

The rules are as in the following table. (The point of the check marks will be explained on pp. 57–58.)

TABLE IV

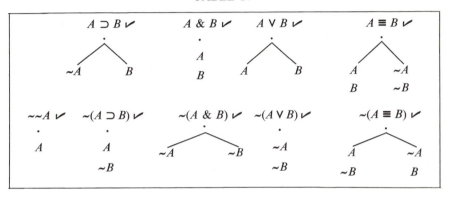

Reflection on the truth-tables for the various connectives should reveal the propriety of the new rules. The negation of a conditional is true (a conditional is false) if and only if both the antecedent and the negation of the consequent are true (the antecedent is true and the consequent false). The negation of a conjunction is true (a conjunction is false) if and only if the negation of at least one conjunct is true (at least one conjunct is false). The negation of a disjunction is true (a disjunction is false) if and only if the negations of both disjuncts are true (both disjuncts are false). The rules for biconditionals may need some explanation. The first, for example, could be read: when dealing with a biconditional, put a fork at the end of every open branch that goes through the biconditional, writing both halves of the biconditional on the left branch of the fork, and their negations on the right branch. The other rule could be read similarly. The truth-functional equivalence of a biconditional $A \equiv B$ to the disjunction $(A \& B) \lor (\sim A \& \sim B)$ of the two conjunctions $A \& B$ and $\sim A \& \sim B$, and of a negated biconditional $\sim(A \equiv B)$ to $(A \& \sim B) \lor (\sim A \& B)$ —which the reader should verify for himself—justifies these two rules.

The Tree Method

We are guided throughout by the manner of composition of each statement—how it is put together, and how statements put together in that way are true and are false. Indeed, the method proceeds precisely by *de*composing statements along the lines on which they were, or could be thought of as being, composed initially.

The gist of the method is this. We first assume that all the members of the set $\{A_1, A_2, \ldots, A_n\}$ to be tested are true on at least one assignment α of truth-values to their atomic components. Then, in accordance with the rules, we trace out the consequences of that assumption by entering on the branches of a tree various components of $A_1, A_2, \ldots$, and A_n, un-negated or negated according as the components have to be true or have to be false on α.[4] We also enter various components of the statements just entered on the tree, again unnegated or negated according as *these* components have to be true or have to be false on α. And so on. In this way connectives are systematically eliminated, and at some point or other the atomic components of $A_1, A_2, \ldots$, and A_n come to be entered on the tree, unnegated if they have to be true on α, negated if they have to be false on α. At *that* point, one of two cases obtains: *either* (1) a contradiction has turned up along every branch of the tree, the initial assumption proves untenable, and the set is truth-functionally *incon-sistent*; *or* (2) at least one branch of the tree remains open, the initial assumption is borne out, and the various truth-value assignments on which $A_1, A_2, \ldots$, and A_n are true can be picked off the open branches of the tree (by assigning **T** to every atomic statement on an open branch, **F** to every atomic statement whose negation is on *that* branch, and either **T** or **F** to any atomic component of $A_1, A_2, \ldots$, and A_n which does not occur on the branch).

The method will work only for non-empty sets of statements which have finitely many members. If a set had no members, there would be nothing for the method to work on. And if a set had infinitely many members, we could not even write them all down, much less decompose them. But we need not worry about these extreme situations, since truth-functional (in)consistency was defined in Section 1.1 only for finite and non-empty sets of statements. Thus, the method does satisfy our present needs.

Furthermore, all trees in this chapter will be finitely long, i.e., they will end after finitely many applications of the rules. Although this will not be true of all the trees of Chapter 2, one can count on it here. For, as we just saw, the method will be applied only to sets of statements with *finitely* many members, each of which contains *finitely* many connectives. So, with occurrences of binary connectives shed one by one, and tildes two at a time, finitely many applications of the rules are sure

---

[4] As the reader will gather from a glance at Table IV, the lines to be entered on a tree in accordance with the rule for any compound are all either components of the compound or negations thereof. For example, $\sim A$ is the *negation* of a component of $A \supset B$, while B itself is a component of $A \supset B$.

to leave one with just atomic statements or negations thereof, at which point there will be nothing more to do (except to "read" the resulting tree).

A tree is said to be **closed** if all of its branches are closed, and to be **open** if at least one of its branches is open. That a set of statements is truth-functionally *in*consistent if it has a closed tree (the first case on p. 56) is obvious. That the set is truth-functionally consistent if it has an open tree (the second case on p. 56), though following from remark (b) on p. 54, may merit further attention. So suppose a set $\{A_1, A_2, \ldots, A_n\}$ of statements has an open tree, and let α be the result of assigning **T** to every atomic statement that occurs unnegated on some open branch of the tree, **F** to every one that occurs negated on that branch, and either **T** or **F** to any atomic component of $A_1, A_2, \ldots$, and A_n that does not occur on the branch. Since (a) any atomic statement that occurs unnegated on the branch is true on α, (b) the negation of any one that occurs negated on that branch is likewise true on α, and (c) any compound on the branch other than a negated atomic statement is true on α if the one statement or the two statements on the branch that came from the compound are true on α, every statement on the branch is eventually sure to be true on α.[5] Hence, all of $A_1, A_2, \ldots$, and A_n must be true on α. So the set $\{A_1, A_2, \ldots, A_n\}$ itself is sure to be truth-functionally consistent.

A set of statements is therefore truth-functionally *in*consistent if and only if it has a closed tree, a fact on which we shall rely heavily throughout the rest of this section.

On Making Trees

We shall spell out the instructions for making and "reading" trees, give some strategy hints, and supply some sample trees to illustrate these remarks.

The two basic instructions have already been introduced, but we shall expand and comment on them here.

(1)   *When decomposing a compound, enter the statements into which it decomposes at the end of every open branch which goes through that compound,* noting to the right of those statements the line number of the compound from which they came, and check off the compound.[6] (a) Statements are entered *only* on branches which go through the compound being decomposed. Other branches which might be open at the time represent *alternatives* to the possibility under consideration, and

---

[5] A full and rigorous proof of the point will be given in Section 3.5. It calls for mathematical induction.

[6] A compound may occur more than once on a tree, in which case each one of its occurrences is decomposed separately.

they must not be confused with it. Otherwise, an undue contradiction might be generated. (b) A compound must be decomposed at the end of *every* open branch through it, to ensure that all of the alternative possibilities are represented on the tree. Failure to heed this might yield a tree erroneously suggesting truth-value assignments on which the members of the set tested are all true; and in the extreme case it might keep a due contradiction from appearing. (c) Since a compound need only be decomposed once, the check mark is a reminder that a compound has already been decomposed and is not to be treated again. (Decomposing a checked compound would merely add pointless lines to a tree.)

(2) *As soon as a contradiction has occurred along any one branch, that branch is to be closed with an* 'x' and indication of where the earlier half of the contradiction occurs on that branch. A branch, of course, is a single route through the tree, from a statement at the bottom up to the first member of the set tested. (a) Entering further statements on a branch along which a contradiction has occurred would clearly be wasteful. And in Chapter 2, failure to close such a branch immediately might make for an infinitely long tree when a finite one could be had. So it is good to get in the habit of closing branches as soon as possible. (b) Here we count as a contradiction only an *atomic* statement and its negation along a given branch. A branch could safely be closed upon the appearance on it of *any* statement and its negation (since every branch through it must eventually close). But to preserve the emphasis on truth-value assignments, which are always to atomic statements, we require that compounds be decomposed to their atomic components and negations thereof. (c) Since several rules have us enter a *pair* of statements on a single branch, it may happen that a contradiction will turn up in mid-application of a rule, *before* the second member of such a pair is entered. We require in such a case that the rule be fully applied, and both statements entered. The branch is then closed as usual with an indication of where the *earlier* half of the contradiction appears. The later half must therefore always be *either* the last statement on a closed branch *or* the one immediately preceding. (d) Sometimes a branch will close before every compound on that branch has been decomposed. This simply means that not all of the available information was needed to expose the impossibility of that alternative. In the extreme case, every branch may close before some one or more compound members of the set being tested are decomposed. Then the set *minus* all such members is also sure to be truth-functionally inconsistent.

Like the truth-table method from which it stems, the tree method of this chapter is a mechanical procedure: after a finite number of clerical operations have been performed, the method will always produce the right answer to the question "Is this set of statements truth-functionally consistent or not?" No imagination or foresight is required to apply the test. Ordinarily, however, a set of statements will have several differ-ent trees, depending on the order in which statements are decomposed (all of those trees open, or all of them closed, of course, as the set is truth-functionally consistent or inconsistent). So, although they are not needed in order to apply the method correctly, the following strategy hints will help to minimize the amount of effort expended, and to keep trees from becoming unnecessarily long and broad.

(1)   Always decompose first any statements on the tree which do *not* make for branches (conjunctions, and the negations of negations, conditionals, and disjunctions). (2) Then, when one has a choice between compounds which *do* make for branches, decompose any which will obviously generate a contradiction immediately or soon (so that one or both branches will close). (3) Then decompose unnegated or negated biconditionals, as these put *two* statements on each open branch and double the chances of its closing soon. (4) If none of these is appropriate, decompose any compound you please. This procedure will be followed in all of our examples.

EXAMPLE 1: {P V (Q & ~~R), R ⊃ ~Q, ~(P & ~Q)}.

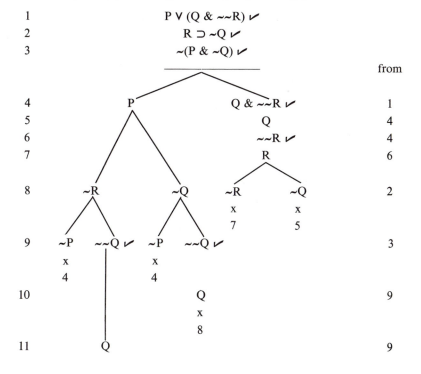

Here lines 4 through 7 serve to decompose line 1 completely. In the process, the trunk of the tree divides into two branches, which represent the only two ways in which line 1 can be true (on some truth-value assignment α): via the truth (on α) of 'P', and via the truth (on α) of both 'Q' and 'R'. Line 8 serves to decompose line 2; and in the course of its decomposition, each one of the original branches divides into two sub-branches. On the right, both of these close; and the ones on the left represent the only two ways in which line 1 *and* line 2 can be true together: via the truth of 'P' and the falsehood of 'R', and via the truth of 'P' and the falsehood of 'Q'. Lines 9 through 11 serve to decompose line 3 completely. In the process, each of the branches open at line 8 divides into two sub-branches. The first and third of these close immediately, and the fourth closes upon the decomposition of '~~Q' into 'Q'. But the second remains open even after the decomposition of '~~Q', and hence represents the one way in which lines 1 through 3 can all be true together: via the truth of 'P' and 'Q' and the falsehood of 'R'. So the set {P ∨ (Q & ~~R), R ⊃ ~Q, ~(P & ~Q)} is truth-functionally consistent.

Several of our earlier remarks on the making of trees are illustrated by this example. (i) It is not essential that line 1 be completely decomposed—i.e., that 'Q & ~~R' on line 4, and '~~R' on line 6, be decomposed—before line 2 or 3 is attacked. But decomposition of lines 2 and 3 calls for branches whereas that of lines 4 and 6 does not. (ii) Note that, and why, 'Q & ~~R' is decomposed only on the right branch. (iii) But note also that, and why, line 2 is decomposed at the ends of *two* branches rather than one. (iv) By the time line 9 is reached on the left of the tree, the compound statement '~Q' and its negation '~~Q' appear along the fourth sub-branch. But the branch is not closed then; rather, '~~Q' is decomposed into 'Q', and the branch is closed because of the contradiction 'Q' and '~Q'. And (v) note that, and why, all the results of decomposing line 2 occur on a single line (line 8), and all the results of decomposing line 3 occur on a single line (line 9), whereas each distinct occurrence of '~~Q' on line 9 is decomposed on a separate line. When the growth of a branch (such as the second sub-branch) is resumed, after such a delay, with a single column of one or more statements, a vertical bar will indicate the route clearly. This is unnecessary when delayed growth is resumed by branching, as at line 8 on the left.

Another tree will illustrate others of our remarks.

EXAMPLE 2: {Q, (~P & ~Q) ⊃ ~(~R & P), Q ⊃ ~(Q ∨ ~P)}.

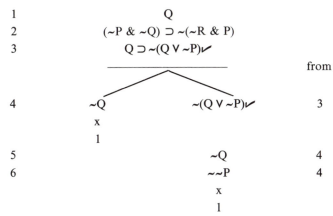

1   Q
2   (~P & ~Q) ⊃ ~(~R & P)
3   Q ⊃ ~(Q ∨ ~P)✔
                                                        from

4   ~Q   ~(Q ∨ ~P)✔   3
               x
               1

5   ~Q   4
6   ~~P   4
                                        x
                                        1

(i) All the branches on the tree must go through line 1, as it is a member
of the set tested; so line 1 can—and does—figure in contradictions. (ii)
The earlier half of the contradiction because of which the right-hand
branch is closed occurs on that branch at line 1 (as is indicated by the
notation), and the later half at line 5. Line 5, however, is not the last line
on the branch, since the decomposition of line 4 required the entry of
line 6 as well. (iii) Two compounds remain undecomposed on the tree:
'~~P' on line 6, because the branch closed before its decomposition was
called for; and line 2, because all branches closed before its decomposition was called for. So the set made up of just lines 1 and 3 is also truth-
functionally inconsistent. Of course, every branch would still have
closed had we decomposed line 2 before line 3, but we would obviously
have wasted a great deal of effort.

We have shown earlier that a truth-value assignment on which all
the members of a set of statements are true can be retrieved from any
open branch of a tree for that set, in this way: assign **T** to every atomic
statement that occurs unnegated on that branch, **F** to every atomic statement that occurs negated on the branch, and either **T** or **F** to any atomic
component (of members of the set) that does not occur on the branch.
As a matter of fact, *every* truth-value assignment on which all the
members of a set of statements are true can be retrieved from a tree for
that set, if some care is taken.
First, all of the truth-value assignments corresponding to branches
on which some atomic components do not occur must be gotten. (There
are two to be had from a branch from which one atomic component is

missing, four if two are missing, eight if three are missing, and so on.) And second, the tree must be completed. If we only wanted to ascertain whether or not {~(P & [(~P ≡ Q) & (~P ⊃ ~Q)])} was truth-functionally consistent, the following would suffice:

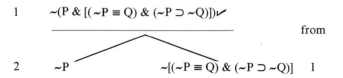

Since there are no statements on the left branch which are subject to decomposition, no contradiction *can* arise on that branch, whatever else were to happen on the right. Every (i.e., the one) member of this set is true on the assignment of **F** to 'P' and **T** to 'Q'. And it is true on the other truth-value assignment to be retrieved from the left branch: **F** to 'P' and **F** to 'Q'. But the whole tree is needed to track down *all* the truth-value assignments on which it is true:

EXAMPLE 3: {~(P & [(~P ≡ Q) & (~P ⊃ ~Q)])}.

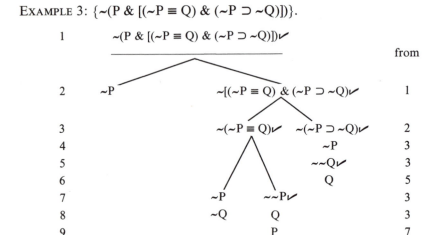

From the right-most branch we can retrieve the assignment of **F** to 'P' and **T** to 'Q', which we already had. From the branch to '~P' and '~Q' we can retrieve the assignment of **F** to 'P' and **F** to 'Q', which we also had. But from the branch to 'Q' and 'P' we retrieve the new assignment of **T** to 'P' and **T** to 'Q', bringing to three the total number of truth-value assignments on which line 1 is true.

Because one open branch may yield more than one truth-value assignment, and because several open branches may yield the same truth-value assignment, there is no simple correlation between the number of open branches on a tree and the number of truth-value assignments on which all the members of the set tested are true.

On Using Trees

Since all the logical properties and relations which depend on truth-functional composition can be—indeed have been—defined in terms of truth-functional (in)consistency (see Table III on p. 39), the tree method can be used in obvious ways to test for any of these.

Truth-functional entailment (validity). A set $\{A_1,A_2,\ldots,A_n\}$ of statements truth-functionally entails a statement B if and only if *every* branch of a tree for $\{A_1,A_2,\ldots,A_n,\sim B\}$ closes. However, if any branch remains open, we can obviously retrieve from it a truth-value assignment on which (the premisses) $A_1, A_2, \ldots$, and A_n would all be true and (the conclusion) B false.

EXAMPLE 4: Is the argument from the two premisses 'If the records all fell off the shelf, so did the philosophy book' and 'Either the philosophy book didn't fall off the shelf, or else somebody put it back' to the conclusion 'Unless (i.e., if it is not the case that) somebody put the philosophy book back, the records didn't all fall off the shelf' truth-functionally valid or not?

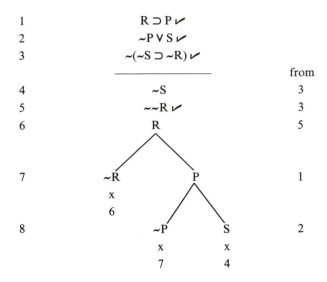

The third member of the set tested is the *negation* of the conclusion. As there is no assignment on which all three members are true, there is none on which the premises of the argument are true and the conclusion false, so the argument is truth-functionally valid.

EXAMPLE 5: Is the argument from 'The records didn't all fall off the shelf but not the philosophy book' and 'If the philosophy book fell off, then somebody put it back' to 'Either the philosophy book wasn't put back, or the records all fell off the shelf' truth-functionally valid or not?

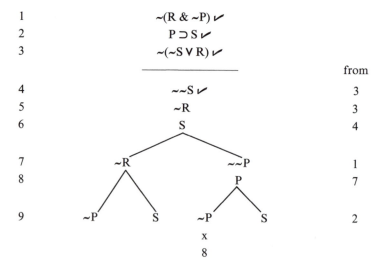

		from
1	~(R & ~P) ✔	
2	P ⊃ S ✔	
3	~(~S V R) ✔	
4	~~S ✔	3
5	~R	3
6	S	4
7	~R · · · ~~P	1
8	· · · P	7
9	~P · · S · · ~P · · S	2

As the tree does not close, the argument is not truth-functionally valid. Note that, although three branches stay open, they yield only two truth-value assignments on which the premises of the argument are true and the conclusion false: the assignment of **F** to both 'P' and 'R', and **T** to 'S'; and the assignment of **T** to both 'P' and 'S', and **F** to 'R'.[7]

Truth-functional falsehood and truth-functional truth. A statement *A* is truth-functionally false if and only if *every* branch of a tree for {*A*} closes. But from any branch which remains open, there can be retrieved a truth-value assignment on which *A* would be true.

EXAMPLE 6: Is the statement 'Neither the sandwiches nor the tomatoes are on the table unless the pickles are too, and the sandwiches but not the pickles are there' truth-functionally false?

---

[7] Example 1 on p. 59, by the way, could be taken to show that the set {P V (Q & ~~R), R ⊃ ~Q} does *not* entail 'P & ~Q', and to afford a truth-value assignment establishing this.

<pre>
1   [~P ⊃ ~(S ∨ T)] & (S & ~P) ✔
        _____   from

2   ~P ⊃ ~(S ∨ T) ✔   1
3   S & ~P ✔   1
4   S   3
5   ~P   3

6   ~~P ✔   ~(S ∨ T) ✔   2
7   P   6
              x
              5

8   ~S   6
9   ~T   6
                                         x
                                         4
</pre>

The statement is truth-functionally false, as there is no truth-value assignment on which it is true. (But Example 3 on p. 62 shows that '~(P & [(~P ≡ Q) & (~P ⊃ ~Q)])' is *not* truth-functionally false, by providing several truth-value assignments on which it would be true.)

By contrast, a statement *A* is truth-functionally true if and only if *every* branch of a tree for the set {~*A*}, which consists of the *negation* ~*A* of *A*, closes. But from any branch which remains open, there can be retrieved a truth-value assignment on which ~*A* would be true and hence *A* itself would be false.

EXAMPLE 7: Is the statement 'Sam is coming if Peter is, or Tom is coming if Sam is' truth-functionally true or not?

<pre>
1   ~[(P ⊃ S) ∨ (S ⊃ T)] ✔
        _____   from

2   ~(P ⊃ S) ✔   1
3   ~(S ⊃ T) ✔   1
4   P   2
5   ~S   2
6   S   3
7   ~T   3
                               x
                               5
</pre>

The statement is truth-functionally true, as there is no truth-value assignment on which its negation is true—and hence none on which the statement itself is false.

EXAMPLE 8: Is the statement 'If Sam is coming only if Peter is, then Sam is coming if Peter is' truth-functionally true or not?

1	~[(S ⊃ P) ⊃ (P ⊃ S)] ✔	
		from
2	S ⊃ P ✔	1
3	~(P ⊃ S) ✔	1
4	P	3
5	~S	3
6	~S P	2

The statement is *not* truth-functionally true, and indeed is false (since its negation is true) on the assignment of **T** to 'P' and **F** to 'S'.

Truth-functional equivalence. Two statements A and B are truth-functionally equivalent if and only if *every* branch of a tree for {~(A ≡ B)} closes. But from any branch which does not close, there can be retrieved a truth-value assignment on which A and B have different truth-values.

Note that the decomposition of the negation ~(A ≡ B) of A ≡ B yields the two alternatives under which A and B might have different truth-values: either A and ~B might both be true, or ~A and B might both be true. If neither alternative pans out, A and B *must* have the same truth-values.

EXAMPLE 9: Is 'Either Sam fell off the shelf, or he fell off it if and only if he wasn't holding on tightly' truth-functionally equivalent to 'Sam fell off the shelf if he wasn't holding on tightly'?

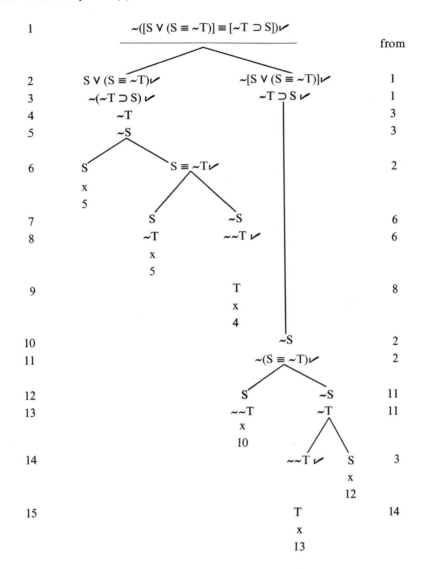

The two statements are truth-functionally equivalent.

The various uses to which the tree method has just been put can be tabulated as follows:

TABLE V

A. A set $\{A_1, A_2, \ldots, A_n\}$ of statements is **truth-functionally consistent** if and only if it has an open tree (a tree of which at least one branch is open); it is **truth-functionally inconsistent** if and only if it has a closed tree (a tree of which each branch is closed).

B. A set $\{A_1, A_2, \ldots, A_n\}$ of statements **truth-functionally entails** a statement B if and only if $\{A_1, A_2, \ldots, A_n, \sim B\}$ has a closed tree.

C. A statement A is **truth-functionally true** if and only if $\{\sim A\}$ has a closed tree; it is **truth-functionally false** if and only if $\{A\}$ has a closed tree.

D. Two statements A and B are **truth-functionally equivalent** if and only if $\{\sim (A \equiv B)\}$ has a closed tree.

All members of a set of statements are true on any result of assigning **T** to every atomic statement which occurs unnegated on an open branch of a tree for the set, **F** to every atomic statement which occurs negated on that branch, and either **T** or **F** to each atomic component which does not occur on the branch.

As mentioned earlier, the tree method will be extended in Chapter 2 to cover quantificational as well as truth-functional compounds.

EXERCISES

E1.2.1. Using the tree method, test each of the following sets of statements for truth-functional consistency. On the basis of the tree for each truth-functionally consistent set, provide one assignment of truth-values to the atomic components of its members on which each of the members would be true.

a. $\{P \supset \sim Q, \sim\sim(P \& Q)\}$

b. $\{\sim(\sim P \& Q), \sim P \lor Q\}$

c. $\{\sim(P \lor \sim Q), P \supset (\sim Q \& R)\}$

d. $\{P \equiv (Q \equiv P), \sim Q\}$

e. $\{\sim P \supset \sim Q, (P \& Q) \equiv Q\}$

f. $\{P \supset (Q \lor R), P \supset \sim R, \sim Q\}$

g. $\{Q, \sim(P \lor R), P \lor (Q \supset R)\}$

h. $\{R \lor (P \& Q), P \supset (Q \& R), \sim R\}$

i. $\{P \supset (Q \lor R), \sim P \& (\sim Q \& R), \sim R \supset \sim P\}$

j. $\{(P \lor \sim Q) \supset \sim(Q \& R), \sim R, Q \supset \sim P\}$

k. $\{(Q \& R) \supset P, \sim P \& R, Q\}$

l. $\{P \equiv (Q \lor R), P \equiv \sim Q, \sim(P \equiv R)\}$

m. $\{(P \equiv Q) \lor R, R \lor P, R \lor Q\}$

n. $\{P \equiv Q, R, \sim[(P \& R) \equiv (R \supset Q)]\}$

o. $\{\sim P \supset (Q \supset \sim R), \sim P \supset Q, R, \sim P\}$

p. $\{([(P \supset Q) \supset (\sim R \supset \sim S)] \supset R) \supset T, T \supset P, S, \sim P\}$

E1.2.2.   Using the tree method, test each of the following arguments for truth-functional validity. On the basis of the tree for each truth-functionally invalid argument, provide one assignment of truth-values to the atomic components of its premises and conclusion on which the premises would all be true and the conclusion false.

a.   If Jill passes Physics, then she'll graduate in June so long as she also passes Mathematics. Therefore, if Jill is sure to pass Mathematics if she passes Physics, then she'll graduate in June if she passes Physics. (P, G, M)

b.   If logic is pointless, so are both science and mathematics. So if either philosophy or science has a point, so does logic. (L: Logic has a point; S; M; P)

c.   If Alan is not appointed to the committee, Bob and Charlie will be. If either Alan or Bob is appointed, then Don will resign. So Don will resign, whether or not Charlie is appointed. (A, B, C, D)

d.   You can believe Huntley if you can believe Brinkley, and vice versa. If you can't believe either one of Huntley and Brinkley, you can't believe Cronkite. You can believe Cronkite. So you can believe Brinkley. (H, B, C)

e.   If the other side wants to negotiate but we think we can win on the battlefield, then we'll stall at the conference table. The war will drag on unless we stop stalling at the conference table. If the war drags on, then the other side obviously doesn't want to negotiate. So clearly the other side doesn't want to negotiate. (N, B, S, D)

f.   If you take Logic, then if you attend all the lectures and also do the homework, you will pass; however, if you neglect the homework, you'll fail. So if you take Logic and attend all the lectures, either you'll also do the homework and pass, or you won't and you'll fail. (T, A, H, P)

g.   If Peter's name has been removed from the membership list, then he received a bill for membership dues and failed to pay it or else he personally sent in his resignation from the club. Peter received a bill for membership dues and didn't send in his resignation from the club. Unless the treasurer's records are wrong, Peter paid his bill for membership dues. So if the treasurer's records aren't wrong, Peter's name hasn't been removed from the membership list. (N, B, P, R, T)

h.   If Debbie has a club left, she'll take this trick. If Steffie has a club left, she'll take the next trick. Debbie has a club left or Steffie does. If Debbie has a club left, Steffie won't take the next trick. And if Steffie has a club left, Debbie won't take this trick. So Debbie will take this trick if and only if Steffie doesn't take the next. (D, T, S, N)

i.   Either Mayor Trumble and Councilman Dimmit will both run for re-election, or the primary race will be wide open and the party will be taken over by young dissenters. Mayor Trumble will not run for re-election. So the party will be taken over by young dissenters. (T, D, O, P)

j.   If the grand jury convenes in September, the investigation will be resumed

and new evidence will be brought to light. If new evidence is brought to
light, labor boss Duffy will be deeply implicated. The local newspaper
will come out with sensational headlines if labor boss Duffy is implicated
at all. The mayor always has his way in town, and labor boss Duffy won't
be implicated in the least. So the grand jury will not convene in September.
(We leave to the reader the choice of abbreviations for the various atomic
components.)

k.   (P & Q) ⊃ R   l.   P ⊃ Q
       _____   _____
       ∴ ~(R & ~Q)   ∴ ~(P ⊃ ~Q)

m.   P ⊃ Q   n.   (P V Q) ≡ Q
       _____   _____
       ∴ (P V Q) ≡ P   ∴ P ⊃ Q

o.   (P ⊃ R) V (Q ⊃ R)   p.   P ⊃ (Q ⊃ ~P)
       _____   P ≡ ~Q
       ∴ (P & Q) ⊃ R   _____
                                                        ∴ ~P & Q

q.   P ⊃ (Q ⊃ R)   r.   P V ~Q
       P V (Q ⊃ R)   ~[(~P & Q) ≡ Q]
       Q   _____
       _____   ∴ Q ⊃ ~P
       ∴ R

s.   ~(P ⊃ ~Q)   t.   ~(~P V Q) ≡ (R & S)
       (Q V ~R) ≡ P   ~R ⊃ (T & U)
       P & (R ⊃ Q)   ~T ⊃ S
       _____   _____
       ∴ ~P V ~Q   ∴ ~P ⊃ T

E1.2.3. Using the tree method, determine which of the following statements are
truth-functionally true and which are not. From the tree for each one that is not,
provide one assignment of truth-values to its atomic components on which it would
be false.

   a.   P V (P ⊃ Q)

   b.   (P ⊃ Q) V (Q ⊃ R)

   c.   [(P ⊃ Q) ⊃ R] ⊃ [P ⊃ (Q ⊃ R)]

   d.   [P ⊃ (Q ⊃ R)] ⊃ [(P ⊃ Q) ⊃ R]

   e.   [(P ⊃ Q) ⊃ P] ≡ P

   f.   [(P ⊃ Q) ⊃ P] ≡ Q

   g.   [(P & Q) ⊃ R] ≡ [(P ⊃ R) V (Q ⊃ R)]

   h.   [(P V Q) ⊃ R] ≡ [(P ⊃ R) & (Q ⊃ R)]

   i.   [(P ⊃ Q) & ~P] ⊃ ~Q

   j.   P ⊃ [Q ≡ (~P ≡ ~Q)]

   k.   (P ⊃ Q) V (~P ⊃ R)

   l.   ~(P V ~Q) ≡ (Q & ~P)

E1.2.4.   Using the tree method, test the following pairs of statements for truth-functional equivalence:

   a.   'P ⊃ (Q ⊃ R)' and '(P ⊃ Q) ⊃ R'

   b.   '~(P & ~Q)' and 'Q V ~P'

   c.   'P' and '(P & Q) V (P & ~Q)'

   d.   '(P ≡ Q) ≡ R' and '(P ≡ Q) & (P ≡ R)'

E1.2.5.   Show by means of a tree in each case that the following biconditionals are truth-functionally true:

a. (P & Q) ≡ (Q & P)	(Commutativity of '&')
b. (P V Q) ≡ (Q V P)	(Commutativity of 'V')
c. (P ≡ Q) ≡ (Q ≡ P)	(Commutativity of '≡')
d. [P & (Q & R)] ≡ [(P & Q) & R]	(Associativity of '&')
e. [P V (Q V R)] ≡ [(P V Q) V R]	(Associativity of 'V')
f. [P ≡ (Q ≡ R)] ≡ [(P ≡ Q) ≡ R]	(Associativity of '≡')
g. [P & (Q V R)] ≡ [(P & Q) V (P & R)]	(Distributivity of '&' into 'V')
h. [P V (Q & R)] ≡ [(P V Q) & (P V R)]	(Distributivity of 'V' into '&')
i. [P ⊃ (Q & R)] ≡ [(P ⊃ Q) & (P ⊃ R)]	(Distributivity of '⊃' into '&')
j. [P ⊃ (Q V R)] ≡ [(P ⊃ Q) V (P ⊃ R)]	(Distributivity of '⊃' into 'V')
k. [P ⊃ (Q ⊃ R)] ≡ [(P ⊃ Q) ⊃ (P ⊃ R)]	(Distributivity of '⊃' into '⊃')
l. [P ⊃ (Q ≡ R)] ≡ [(P ⊃ Q) ≡ (P ⊃ R)]	(Distributivity of '⊃' into '≡')

E1.2.6.

   (a) Account (in more detail than does the text) for the conspicuous gap in the top row of Table IV on p. 55.

   (b) When picking a truth-value assignment off an open branch of a tree, we were told to assign *either one* of **T** and **F** to any atomic component that does not occur (unnegated or negated) on the branch. How can we be sure that the members of the set tested will all be true on the assignment, whether **T** was selected or **F** was?

   *(c) On p. 58 it is claimed that if some *compound* statement A and its negation ~A both occur on a branch of a tree, then on every branch through A and and ~A a contradiction (i.e., some *atomic* statement and its negation) is sure to occur. Show that this claim is true.

E1.2.7.

   (a) Show that any statement occurring on every open branch of a tree is truth-functionally entailed by the set tested.

   (b) How could we determine, from inspection of a tree for a set {A}, whether A is truth-functionally true?

E1.2.8.   Using the result in E1.2.7(a), answer the question following each one of these stories:

a.   If A passes the test, then B also does. Exactly one of B and C passes the test. Either both C and D pass the test or neither one of them does. At least one of D and E passes the test. E passes the test if and only if both A and D do.

Which of these five pass the test, and which don't?

b.   At least one of candidates X, Y, and Z will win the nomination for President. If pollster P is right in his prediction, then so are pollsters Q and R. If candidate Y wins the nomination, then pollster Q is wrong in his prediction. If candidate Z wins the nomination, then pollster R is wrong in his prediction. Pollster P is right in his prediction.

Which of these candidates win the nomination, and which don't?

c.   Harry will have a date from Barnard, one from Radcliffe, or one from Vassar. Harry will not have all three dates. If he has the date from Radcliffe, he'll have the one from Vassar too. If he doesn't have the date from Barnard or doesn't have the one from Radcliffe, he won't have the one from Vassar either.

Which dates will Harry have, and which will he not?

*E1.2.9.   Let the *conjunction associate* of an open *branch* of a tree be the conjunction of all the atomic statements and negations thereof that occur on the branch; and let the *disjunction associate* of an open *tree* be the disjunction of the conjunction associates of all the open branches of the tree. With these definitions on hand, show that if $\{A\}$ is truth-functionally consistent, then A is truth-functionally equivalent to the disjunction associate of any tree for $\{A\}$.

1.3   Derivations (1)

The tree method of the previous section affords a convenient shortcut to the truth-value assignments on which the members of a set of statements would all be true. But, like the truth-table method, it fails to embody a most important feature of reasoning: the "drawing" of a conclusion from premisses that entail it. For when inferring some statement from others, or when satisfying ourselves of the validity of some inference, we rarely search for a truth-value assignment to the atomic components of premisses and conclusion on which the former would all be true and the latter false. Rather we try (as in mathematics) to get from the premisses (or axioms), by a series of steps the soundness of which seems obvious, to other statements which would have to be true if those premisses were, to still other such statements, and finally to the conclusion (or theorem). Indeed, our ability to do this is closely tied to our sense of validity.

We shall develop here a technique which formalizes this kind of reasoning, and permits us to arrive at any conclusion truth-functionally entailed by a given set of premisses. The technique—commonly called **natural deduction**—can also be used, as we shall see, to establish truth-functional truth, falsehood, equivalence, and inconsistency.

Arguments and Derivations

Consider the argument from the Introduction:

> Mary works hard
> She's a bright girl, and a charming one too
> She's sure to pass if she's bright and works hard
> _____
> ∴. She'll pass or I'm a monkey's uncle.

In reasoning to the conclusion, or in certifying the validity of the argument, we might proceed by some such steps as these: On the *assumption* that all three premisses are true, Mary is both bright and charming; so she's bright. But (on that assumption) she also works hard; so she's bright and works hard. And (again on that assumption) if she's bright and works hard, she'll pass; so she'll pass. Therefore, if the premisses are all true, either she'll pass or I'm a monkey's uncle.

Here our logical intuitions guide us, in accordance with principles which certainly seem to be sound:

(a) If a conjunction follows from some assumptions, so does each conjunct;

(b) If two statements follow from some assumptions, so does their conjunction;

(c) If a conditional and its antecedent both follow from some assumptions, so does its consequent; and

(d) If a statement follows from some assumptions, so does its disjunction with any statement.

If these are sound principles, the line of thought above should satisfy us of the validity of the corresponding argument.

We reproduce this line of thought in a **derivation** of the conclusion from the premisses of the argument:

1	W	
2	B & C	
3	(B & W) ⊃ P	
4	B & C	line 2
5	B	from line 4, by (a)
6	W	line 1
7	B & W	from lines 5 and 6, by (b)
8	(B & W) ⊃ P	line 3
9	P	from lines 7 and 8, by (c)
10	P ∨ M	from line 9, by (d)

The vertical bar indicates the extent of the derivation (from line 1 through line 10). Above the horizontal bar are the three premises 'W', 'B & C', '(B & W) ⊃ P', serving here as the **assumptions** of the derivation; below are lines asserted on those assumptions.[1] To the right is the rationale for the assertion (on those assumptions) of every line past assumptions 1–3. Some lines are justified as being among the assumptions, others as following from some preceding line or lines in accordance with the principles enumerated earlier.

The Rules

We provide here a number of specific rules which entitle us to write lines in derivations when appropriate conditions have been satisfied. It is to one or another of these rules, rather than to our logical intuitions, that we shall appeal when justifying lines like 4–10 in the foregoing derivation.

Proof will be given in Chapter 3 that the rules permit construction of all the derivations we could (properly) want, without permitting construction of any we should not want. To put the matter more formally, let

$$\{A_1, A_2, \ldots, A_n\} \vdash B$$

be short for 'B is derivable from $\{A_1, A_2, \ldots, A_n\}$ in accordance with the rules of Section 1.3'. We shall establish in Chapter 3 that:

(1) If $\{A_1, A_2, \ldots, A_n\} \vdash B$, then $\{A_1, A_2, \ldots, A_n\}$ truth-functionally entails B (in view of which result the rules of this section will be said to be **sound**), and

---

[1] We talk of the *premises* of an argument, and the *assumptions* of a derivation. Of course, when deriving the conclusion of an argument from its premises, those premises *are* the assumptions of the derivation.

(2)   If $\{A_1,A_2,\ldots,A_n\}$ truth-functionally entails B, then $\{A_1,A_2,\ldots,A_n\}$
$\vdash B$ (in view of which result the rules of this section will be said
to be **complete**).

Incidentally, the form in which the rules are expressed and derivations
constructed is due largely to Frederic Brenton Fitch,[2] while the rules
themselves are adaptations of rules due to Stanislaw Jaśkowski and
Gerhard Gentzen.[3]

With the exception of the special rule Reiteration, each rule concerns a particular connective, and there are two rules for each one of
the five connectives. Because one permits the **introduction,** and one the
elimination, of a given connective, these are often called **intelim rules.**
The introduction rule for a given connective shows a way of *obtaining* a
compound with that as its main connective, and the elimination rule for
the connective shows what can be obtained *from* such a compound. By
exposing and clarifying the roles that the various sorts of compounds
can play in legitimate inferences, the pairs of intelim rules make for a
different and in some respects deeper understanding of the logical force
of '~', '⊃', '&', 'V', and '≡' than do truth-tables.

We shall first present and discuss the special rule Reiteration; we
shall then present and discuss the intelim rules one pair at a time.

THE REITERATION RULE ($=$ R):

1	A_1	
2	A_2	
.	.	
n	A_n	
.	.	
p	A_i	(R, i)

R is of very special importance. Each of the other rules governs the
introduction or elimination of a connective. R does not. Every other rule
presupposes that certain conditions have been fulfilled if some statement
is to be asserted on some assumptions in accordance with the rule. (For
example, some rules presuppose that certain other statements have been
derived first from the assumptions.) R does not. It simply says that any

---

[2] See *Symbolic Logic: An Introduction*, 1952, The Ronald Press, Chapter 2.
[3] See Jaśkowski's "On the rules of suppositions in formal logic," *Studia Logica*, 1934, no. 1.
The relevant paper by Gentzen is the one already mentioned in footnote 2 of Section 1.2.

member A_i of a set $\{A_1, A_2, \ldots, A_n\}$ of assumptions may be asserted on A_1, A_2, ..., and A_n, thereby permitting direct appeal to the assumptions.

Lines 4, 6, and 8 of our introductory derivation were justified by R, which fact we indicate in this manner:

1	W	
2	B & C	
3	(B & W) ⊃ P	
4	B & C	(R, 2)
5	B	
6	W	(R, 1)
7	B & W	
8	(B & W) ⊃ P	(R, 3)
9	P	
10	P ∨ M	

Any assumption which is used in a derivation must *be reiterated before being used; and* only *assumptions may be reiterated.*

THE INTELIM RULES FOR '⊃':

1	A_1			1	A_1	
2	A_2			2	A_2	
.	.			.	.	
n	A_n			n	A_n	
.	.			.	.	
p		B		p	$B \supset C$ (or B)	
.		.		.		
.		.		q	B (or $B \supset C$)	
q		C		.	.	
$q + 1$	$B \supset C$		$(\supset I, p-q)$	r	C	$(\supset E, p, q)$

The figures down the left side are call numbers for the lines in a derivation. And in parentheses next to the statement derived in accordance with each ⊃-rule we cite both that rule and the lines where the conditions for applying it are met.

⊃E says that if we have derived *both* a conditional *and* its antecedent from some assumptions, we may go on to assert its consequent on those assumptions (principle (c) on p. 73).

Line 9 of our introductory derivation thus follows by ⊃E, a fact we indicate in this way:

1	W	
2	B & C	
3	(B & W) ⊃ P	
4	B & C	(R, 2)
5	B	
6	W	(R, 1)
7	B & W	
8	(B & W) ⊃ P	(R, 3)
9	P	(⊃E, 7, 8)
10	P ∨ M	

Use of ⊃I involves a special feature of the technique developed here: a **subordinate derivation.** The rule says that we may assert a conditional on some assumptions if we can derive its consequent from those assumptions *and* the antecedent of the conditional. In effect, to show on some assumptions that if *B* then *C*, assume *B* as well and try to show that *C* follows. If this can be done, discard the provisional assumption *B* (and everything obtained on that assumption), and assert on the original assumptions alone that *if B then C*.

Consider the following argument, obviously valid:

> If Tom is arrested, he'll be indicted
> If he's indicted, he'll be tried
> If he's tried, he'll be convicted
> If he's convicted, he'll be jailed
>
> ---
>
> ∴ If Tom is arrested, he'll be jailed.

We may not know whether or not Tom will be arrested; and the premisses do not truth-functionally entail that he will be arrested or that he will be jailed. But if on the provisional assumption that he will be arrested it turns out that he would be jailed (as he obviously would), then we may confidently assert—on the strength of the original premisses alone—that *if* he is arrested, he'll be jailed. The line of thought is a natural way of establishing the validity of the argument. We reproduce it as a derivation of the conclusion from the premisses of the argument.

EXAMPLE 1:

1	A ⊃ I	
2	I ⊃ T	
3	T ⊃ C	
4	C ⊃ J	
5	A	
6	A	(R, 5)
7	A ⊃ I	(R, 1)
8	I	(⊃E, 6, 7)
9	I ⊃ T	(R, 2)
10	T	(⊃E, 8, 9)
11	T ⊃ C	(R, 3)
12	C	(⊃E, 10, 11)
13	C ⊃ J	(R, 4)
14	J	(⊃E, 12, 13)
15	A ⊃ J	(⊃I, 5–14)

As before, the vertical bars represent the extents of derivations, and their assumptions appear above the horizontal bars. It is important to note that at line 15 the provisional assumption 'A' (line 5) has been discarded or, to use the technical phrase, **discharged.** Line 15 (and anything that in some other derivation might follow that line) is asserted on the assumption of lines 1–4 alone, by virtue of the subordinate derivation running from line 5 through line 14. So we do not claim, when jotting down '(⊃I, 5–14)' next to 'A ⊃ J', that lines 5 and 14 entitle us to assert line 15 (indeed lines 5 and 14 may not be true on the assumptions on which we want to assert line 15). Rather, we assert line 15 because we are able to get *from* line 5 *to* line 14 (given lines 1 through 4), which fact we record by means of '(⊃I, 5–14)'.

By the way, attention to rule R reveals that only the assumptions of a given derivation may be reiterated into that derivation. Strictly speaking, then, rule ⊃I should appear this way:

$$
\begin{array}{c|l}
1 & A_1 \\
2 & A_2 \\
\cdot & \cdot \\
n & A_n \\
\cdot & \cdot \\
\end{array}
$$

p		A_1	
$p+1$		A_2	
$\cdot$		$\cdot$	
$p+n-1$		A_n	
$p+n$		B	
$\cdot$		$\cdot$	
q		C	
$q+1$	$B \supset C$		$(\supset I, p\text{--}q)$;

and the derivation of Example 1 should be written thus:

1	$A \supset I$	
2	$I \supset T$	
3	$T \supset C$	
4	$C \supset J$	
5	$A \supset I$	
6	$I \supset T$	
7	$T \supset C$	
8	$C \supset J$	
9	A	
10	A	(R, 9)
11	$A \supset I$	(R, 5)
12	I	$(\supset E, 10, 11)$
13	$I \supset T$	(R, 6)
14	T	$(\supset E, 12, 13)$
15	$T \supset C$	(R, 7)
16	C	$(\supset E, 14, 15)$
17	$C \supset J$	(R, 8)
18	J	$(\supset E, 16, 17)$
19	$A \supset J$	$(\supset I, 5\text{--}18)$

In practice, of course, we do not require that the assumptions common to a derivation and one subordinate to it reappear at the head of the latter derivation. But the reader is to imagine them there, and as a result is free to reiterate any of them into the subordinate derivation.

A similar remark will apply to all the rules which—like ⊃I—involve subordinate derivations: ~I, VE, and ≡I.

Consider another example, this one with subordinate derivations within subordinate derivations.

EXAMPLE 2: If Tom studies at all only when an exam is coming up, then he doesn't study at all unless he has to. Therefore, if Tom studies at all, then he has to study if an exam is coming up.

1	(S ⊃ E) ⊃ (S ⊃ H)	
2	S	
3	E	
4	S	
5	E	(R, 3)
6	S ⊃ E	(⊃I, 4–5)
7	(S ⊃ E) ⊃ (S ⊃ H)	(R, 1)
8	S ⊃ H	(⊃E, 6,7)
9	S	(R, 2)
10	H	(⊃E, 8, 9)
11	E ⊃ H	(⊃I, 3–10)
12	S ⊃ (E ⊃ H)	(⊃I, 2–11)

As will always be the case, our strategy here is dictated more by what we want to reach than by what is available at any stage (though of course both considerations are essential). So, after writing '(S ⊃ E) ⊃ (S ⊃ H)' above the horizontal line of what will be the derivation, and 'S ⊃ (E ⊃ H)' at the bottom (as what we are aiming at), we provisionally assume 'S', and write 'E ⊃ H' at the bottom of what will be a subordinate derivation. For if we can derive 'E ⊃ H' from 'S' and line 1, then by ⊃I we may assert 'S ⊃ (E ⊃ H)' on the strength of line 1 alone.[4] To arrive at 'E ⊃ H', we provisionally assume 'E', and write 'H' at the bottom of what will be another subordinate derivation. For if we can derive 'H' from 'E' and lines 1–2, then by ⊃I we may assert 'E ⊃ H' on the strength of lines 1–2 alone. Now for 'H'. Since 'H' is not one of lines 1–3, rule R will not deliver it; and, since it is atomic, no introduction rule will deliver

---

[4] Note that when asserting 'S ⊃ (E ⊃ H)' in line 12, we restore the parentheses which, strictly, belong around 'E ⊃ H' but are omitted as unnecessary in line 11. More generally, when asserting any compound ~B, B ⊃ C, B & C, B V C, and B ≡ C by an introduction rule, we enclose B and C within parentheses whenever B and C themselves are binary compounds. See p. 83, line 12, where we enclose 'P & Q' within parentheses when asserting its negation by ~I; p. 88, lines 9 and 15, where we enclose 'N & H' and 'N & M' within parentheses when asserting their disjunction by VI; and so on.

it either. So we must call at this point on an elimination rule. Only line 1 is compound—a conditional—so we think ⊃E. As it happens, if 'S ⊃ E' were derivable from lines 1–3, so would 'S ⊃ H' be by ⊃E (since '(S ⊃ E) ⊃ (S ⊃ H)' is obviously derivable from lines 1–3 by R); and if 'S ⊃ H' were derivable from lines 1–3, then so would 'H' be by ⊃E (since the antecedent 'S' of 'S ⊃ H' is obviously derivable from lines 1–3 by R). So all we need do is derive 'S ⊃ E' from lines 1–3, which we could do if we could derive 'E' from lines 1–3 and the provisional assumption 'S'. And this we can do by R, from line 3. So the derivation can be completed.

Note that 'S' at line 9 cannot be derived by R from line 4, an assumption which is unavailable for the purpose because it has been discharged by the time line 9 is reached.

The derivations 2–11, 3–10, and 4–5 are all subordinate derivations. A technical term which is to be used in Chapter 3 will permit a more precise characterization of them. Although the derivation 4–5 is subordinate to all of the other derivations, it is said to be an **immediate subordinate derivation** only of the derivation 3–10; this latter, though subordinate to the outer two, is an immediate subordinate derivation only of the derivation 2–11 (which itself is immediately subordinate only to the derivation 1–12).

(For exercises requiring just R and the intelim rules for '⊃', see E1.3.1, a–d.)

THE INTELIM RULES FOR '~':

~E says that if we can derive the double negation of some statement from some assumptions, we may go on to assert the statement itself on those assumptions (thus dropping two tildes at a time as we did in Section 1.2). The use of ~E will be amply illustrated below.

~I says that we may assert the negation ~B of any statement B on some assumptions if we can derive a contradiction (both C and ~C, for any statement C we please)[5] from those assumptions *and* B. In effect, to deny B on some assumptions, assume B and try to derive a contradiction. If this can be done, discard the provisional assumption B (and everything derived on that assumption), and assert *not* B on the original assumptions alone.

For example, suppose we knew that if the treaty had been honored, free elections would have been held, and that free elections were never held. We could show on these assumptions that the treaty was not honored, by showing the further assumption that it *was* honored to lead to an impossible situation: if that were true, along with the two original assumptions, then free elections both would and would not have been held. So the provisional assumption cannot be true, and its negation must be.

EXAMPLE 3:

1	T ⊃ E	
2	~E	
3	T	
4	T	(R, 3)
5	T ⊃ E	(R, 1)
6	E	(⊃E, 4, 5)
7	~E	(R, 2)
8	~T	(~I, 3–(6, 7))

EXAMPLE 4: Pat and Quincy will both come to the party only if Rachel comes too. Steve won't come if Pat and Quincy are going to be there. Rachel won't come unless Steve does. So Pat and Quincy won't both be at the party.

---

[5] Note that C is *not* required *here* to be atomic. We shall occasionally refer to C as the affirmative half, to ~C as the negative half, of the contradiction C and ~C. At one point in Chapter 3 it will prove convenient to break up the subordinate derivation of ~I into two subordinate derivations—one of C from B, and one of ~C from B.

1	(P & Q) ⊃ R	
2	(P & Q) ⊃ ~S	
3	R ⊃ S	
4	P & Q	
5	P & Q	(R, 4)
6	(P & Q) ⊃ R	(R, 1)
7	R	(⊃E, 5, 6)
8	R ⊃ S	(R, 3)
9	S	(⊃E, 7, 8)
10	(P & Q) ⊃ ~S	(R, 2)
11	~S	(⊃E, 5, 10)
12	~(P & Q)	(~I, 4–(9,11))

It will follow from material proved in Chapter 3 that a (finite and non-empty) set of statements is truth-functionally inconsistent if and only if some statement and its negation are both derivable from that set. Thus, use of ~I shows that some set $\{A_1, A_2, \ldots, A_n, B\}$ is truth-functionally inconsistent. But if there is no truth-value assignment on which A_1, $A_2, \ldots, A_n$, and B are all true, there is none on which $A_1, A_2, \ldots$, and A_n are all true and ~B is false; hence $\{A_1, A_2, \ldots, A_n\}$ truth-functionally entails ~B, and the inference in accordance with ~I is truth-functionally valid.

~I can often be used with ~E to permit the derivation of statements that are not negations but cannot be derived otherwise. In such a case, one can provisionally assume the *negation* ~A of the statement A one is after and try to reach a contradiction. The contradiction will entitle him to assert the *double*-negation ~~A of A by ~I, from which A itself can be reached in one more step by ~E. The reader may recognize in this maneuver what is often called **indirect** or **reductio (ad absurdum) proof:** to show that something is true, assume that it is not and derive a contradiction. However, ~I and ~E must both be used to get this effect.

EXAMPLE 5: If the kids didn't clean up the mess, then Mom was sure to be unhappy if she saw it. She certainly saw it if they didn't clean it up. But she was happy. So they must have cleaned it up.

1	$\sim C \supset (S \supset \sim H)$	
2	$\sim C \supset S$	
3	H	
4	$\quad \sim C$	
5	$\quad \sim C$	(R, 4)
6	$\quad \sim C \supset (S \supset \sim H)$	(R, 1)
7	$\quad S \supset \sim H$	($\supset$E, 5, 6)
8	$\quad \sim C \supset S$	(R, 2)
9	$\quad S$	($\supset$E, 5, 8)
10	$\quad \sim H$	($\supset$E, 7, 9)
11	$\quad H$	(R, 3)
12	$\sim\sim C$	($\sim$I, 4–(10,11))
13	C	($\sim$E, 12)

(For exercises requiring just R and the intelim rules for '$\supset$' and '$\sim$', see E1.3.1, e–h.)

THE INTELIM RULES FOR '&':

1	A_1		1	A_1			A_1	
2	A_2		2	A_2			A_2	
.	.		.	.			.	
n	A_n		n	A_n			A_n	
.	.		.	.			.	
p	B (or C)		p	$B \& C$			$B \& C$	
.	.		.	.			.	
q	C (or B)		q	B			C	(&E, p)[6]
.	.							
r	$B \& C$	(&I, p, q)						

&I says that if we have derived both conjuncts of a conjunction from some assumptions, we may go on to assert the conjunction itself on those assumptions (principle (b) on p. 73); and &E says that if we have de-

---

[6] Observe that there are two forms of &E, as there will be two forms of VI (see next page) and two forms of $\equiv$E (see p. 89). Proof will be sketched in Exercises E3.3.6–10 that in each case both forms are necessary if our rules are to be complete.

rived a conjunction from some assumptions, we may go on to assert either one of its conjuncts on those assumptions (principle (a) on p. 73).[7]

Line 5 of our introductory derivation thus follows by &E, and line 7 by &I:

1	W	
2	B & C	
3	(B & W) ⊃ P	
4	B & C	(R, 2)
5	B	(&E, 4)
6	W	(R, 1)
7	B & W	(&I, 5, 6)
8	(B & W) ⊃ P	(R, 3)
9	P	(⊃E, 7, 8)
10	P ∨ M	

(For exercises requiring just R and the intelim rules for '⊃', '~', and '&', see E1.3.1, i–l.)

THE INTELIM RULES FOR '∨':

---

[7] Note the similarity between &E and the rule of Section 1.2 for decomposing A & B.

VI says that if we have derived either of the disjuncts of a disjunction from some assumptions, we may go on to assert the disjunction on those assumptions (principle (d) on p. 73).

Line 10 of our introductory derivation thus follows by VI:

1	W	
2	B & C	
3	(B & W) ⊃ P	
4	B & C	(R, 2)
5	B	(&E, 4)
6	W	(R, 1)
7	B & W	(&I, 5, 6)
8	(B & W) ⊃ P	(R, 3)
9	P	(⊃E, 7, 8)
10	P ∨ M	(VI, 9)

VE says that if we can derive a disjunction from some assumptions, we may go on to assert on those assumptions anything derivable from the assumptions *and* each disjunct separately.[8] It is a more complicated rule, but it makes perfectly good sense. To illustrate matters, suppose we know that if Tom gets a vacation, he'll go either to the beach or to the mountains; that if he goes to the beach he'll spend a lot of money, and if he goes to the mountains he'll spend a lot of money too; and that he gets both a raise and a vacation. How might we assure ourselves of what is obvious enough: that he's going to spend a lot of money. We could first show that he does get a vacation, and thus that he'll go either to the beach or to the mountains. Then, without knowing which one of these he'll choose, but assured that he will choose one of them, we could first *assume* that he goes to the beach, and show that in that case he'll spend a lot of money; we could then *assume* that he goes to the mountains, and show that in that case too he'll spend a lot of money. In either case, therefore, he'll spend a lot of money. And since we can be sure that he'll go to the beach or the mountains on the strength of the original assumptions *alone,* we can assert that he'll spend a lot of money on the strength of those assumptions *alone.*

---

[8] VE does *not* say that if we can derive a disjunction from some assumptions, we may go on to assert either of its disjuncts on those assumptions. Such a rule would permit undesirable inferences.

EXAMPLE 6:

1	V ⊃ (B ∨ M)	
2	(B ⊃ S) & (M ⊃ S)	
3	R & V	
4	R & V	(R, 3)
5	V	(&E, 4)
6	V ⊃ (B ∨ M)	(R, 1)
7	B ∨ M	(⊃E, 5, 6)
8	B	
9	(B ⊃ S) & (M ⊃ S)	(R, 2)
10	B ⊃ S	(&E, 9)
11	B	(R, 8)
12	S	(⊃E, 10, 11)
13	M	
14	(B ⊃ S) & (M ⊃ S)	(R, 2)
15	M ⊃ S	(&E, 14)
16	M	(R, 13)
17	S	(⊃E, 15, 16)
18	S	(∨E, 7, 8–12, 13–17)

We can illustrate, in connection with this example, which lines in a derivation *may,* and which lines may *not,* be appealed to in any application of a rule—i.e., which call numbers may and which may not appear in the justifications down the right side.

(1) *Reiteration.* Within a given derivation, one may appeal in an application of R only to

(a) an *assumption* overtly heading that derivation (as line 4 was obtained by R from line 3, line 6 from line 1, line 11 from line 8, and line 16 from line 13); or to

(b) an *assumption* heading a derivation to which that one is subordinate (as lines 9 and 14 were each obtained by R from line 2). Such assumptions, remember, really belong at the head of every subordinate derivation.

One may *not* appeal, in an application of R, to any *other* assumption (line 8, for example, could *not* be used in the *second* subordinate derivation). Furthermore, had line 2 been reiterated into the principal derivation, and its conjuncts asserted there by &E, neither of these *derived* lines could have been appealed to within the subordinate derivations. This requirement could be relaxed, but it will not be. So one should wait until an assumption is needed before reiterating and "unpacking" it.

(2) *Intelim rules.* Within a given derivation one may appeal, when applying an intelim rule, *only* to

   (a) *derived* lines (so that line 5 may *not* be obtained by &E from line 3, nor line 10 or line 15 from line 2)

   (b) within *that* derivation (so that line 15 may *not* be obtained by &E from line 9; nor, in the next example, could line 6 or line 12 be obtained by &E from line 2).

EXAMPLE 7:   Nixon will be nominated, as will either Humphrey or Muskie. Therefore, either both Nixon and Humphrey will be nominated, or both Nixon and Muskie will.

1	N & (H ∨ M)	
2	N & (H ∨ M)	(R, 1)
3	H ∨ M	(&E, 2)
4	H	
5	N & (H ∨ M)	(R, 1)
6	N	(&E, 5)
7	H	(R, 4)
8	N & H	(&I, 6, 7)
9	(N & H) ∨ (N & M)	(VI, 8)
10	M	
11	N & (H ∨ M)	(R, 1)
12	N	(&E, 11)
13	M	(R, 10)
14	N & M	(&I, 12, 13)
15	(N & H) ∨ (N & M)	(VI, 14)
16	(N & H) ∨ (N & M)	(VE, 3, 4–9, 10–15)

Because line 16 is a disjunction, we might be tempted to reach it (from one of its disjuncts) by VI. But the assumptions truth-functionally entail neither one of 'N & H' and 'N & M', so we must resist the temptation. We might also be tempted to break off the first subordinate derivation at line 8, the second at line 14. But, as the subordinate derivations would no longer close on the *same* statement, VE could no longer be used to obtain line 16.

(For exercises requiring just R and the intelim rules for '⊃', '~', '&', and '∨', see E1.3.1, m–p.)

THE INTELIM RULES FOR '≡':

1	A_1			1	A_1			A_1	
2	A_2			2	A_2			A_2	
.	.			.	.			.	
n	A_n			n	A_n			A_n	
.	.			.	.			.	
p		B		p	$B \equiv C$ (or B)			$C \equiv B$ (or B)	
.		.		.	.			.	
q		C		q	B (or $B \equiv C$)			B (or $C \equiv B$)	
r		C		.	.			.	
.		.		r	C			C	($\equiv$E, p, q)
s		B							
$s+1$	$B \equiv C$		($\equiv$I, p–q, r–s)						

These rules treat $B \equiv C$ exactly as if it were truth-functionally equivalent to the conjunction of the two conditionals $B \supset C$ and $C \supset B$—which of course it is. For suppose in the first case that C is derivable from the set $\{A_1, A_2, \ldots, A_n, B\}$ and B is derivable from $\{A_1, A_2, \ldots, A_n, C\}$—for short, suppose that $\{A_1, A_2, \ldots, A_n, B\} \vdash C$ and $\{A_1, A_2, \ldots, A_n, C\} \vdash B$. Then $\{A_1, A_2, \ldots, A_n\} \vdash B \supset C$ and $\{A_1, A_2, \ldots, A_n\} \vdash C \supset B$ by $\supset$I, and hence $\{A_1, A_2, \ldots, A_n\} \vdash (B \supset C) \,\&\, (C \supset B)$ by &I. And in the second case suppose, for example, that $\{A_1, A_2, \ldots, A_n\} \vdash (B \supset C) \,\&\, (C \supset B)$. Then $\{A_1, A_2, \ldots, A_n\} \vdash B \supset C$ by &E, and hence if $\{A_1, A_2, \ldots, A_n\} \vdash B$ as well, then $\{A_1, A_2, \ldots, A_n\} \vdash C$ by $\supset$E. Indeed, the popular characterization of a biconditional as "a conditional which goes both ways" may be helpful in remembering how to obtain a biconditional, and what can be obtained from a biconditional.

EXAMPLE 8: Tom will pass if and only if he studies hard. So, if he studies hard if and only if he's interested in the subject, then he'll pass if and only if he is interested.

```
 1  | P ≡ S
    |-----
 2  |   | S ≡ I
    |   |-----
 3  |   |   | P
    |   |   |-----
 4  |   |   | P            (R, 3)
 5  |   |   | P ≡ S        (R, 1)
 6  |   |   | S            (≡E, 4, 5)
 7  |   |   | S ≡ I        (R, 2)
 8  |   |   | I            (≡E, 6, 7)
 9  |   |   | I
    |   |   |-----
10  |   |   | I            (R, 9)
11  |   |   | S ≡ I        (R, 2)
12  |   |   | S            (≡E, 10, 11)
13  |   |   | P ≡ S        (R, 1)
14  |   |   | P            (≡E, 12, 13)
15  |   | P ≡ I            (≡I, 3–8, 9–14)
16  | (S ≡ I) ⊃ (P ≡ I)    (⊃I, 2–15)
```

The reader should consider how the derivation through line 15 could be extended to produce a derivation of '$(S \equiv I) \equiv (P \equiv I)$' from '$P \equiv S$'.

Strategy Hints

Unlike the truth-table and tree methods, the derivation method as presented here is not mechanical—no clerical routine is supplied for turning out derivations corresponding to all, and only, truth-functionally valid arguments.[9] So, in order to minimize the amount of guesswork and luck required to produce a derivation, we recommend that the following guidelines be followed (whenever no easier way is obvious):

Stage 1—Work "from the bottom up" whenever possible. If, at any point in the construction of a derivation, the statement which you *want to reach* is compound, try to satisfy the conditions for asserting that sort of compound in accordance with the *introduction rule* for its *main connective*.

Associated with ⊃I, ~I, &I, and ≡I are sure-fire strategies for obtaining conditionals, negations, conjunctions, and biconditionals. (For example, if what you want to reach is a conditional $B \supset C$, draw a subordinate derivation bar all the way down from just below the last line

---

[9] Such a routine is available, but derivations constructed in keeping with it are so complicated that much of the value of "natural deduction" is lost in the process.

at the top of the derivation to just above the conditional, assume B, write C at the bottom of this subordinate derivation, and proceed—i.e., apply the guidelines to reach C. Or if what you want to reach is a conjunction B & C, write B half-way between the last line at the top of the derivation and the conjunction, write C immediately above the conjunction, and proceed—i.e., apply the guidelines to reach B, and then to reach C.) But the strategy similarly associated with VI is not so dependable.[10] For often a disjunction $B \vee C$ is truth-functionally entailed by assumptions that do not truth-functionally entail either of its disjuncts. When in doubt, settle the matter by means of a truth-table or a tree. If one disjunct is truth-functionally entailed by the assumptions on which $B \vee C$ is to be asserted (as in our introductory derivation), then write that disjunct immediately above $B \vee C$ and proceed—i.e., apply the guidelines to reach the disjunct. But if neither disjunct is truth-functionally entailed by—and hence neither is derivable from—the assumptions (as in Example 7 above and Example 14 below), or if the statement you want to reach is atomic (as in Examples 5 and 6 above), go on to Stage 2.

Stage 2—Check whether application of the appropriate *elimination rules* to available compounds would yield the line you are after (remembering that an assumption must be reiterated before an elimination rule is applied to it). The rule ⊃E may be applied to an available conditional $B \supset C$ to yield C (if B has also been derived); the rule VE may be applied to an available disjunction $B \vee C$ to yield any statement D which is derivable from the further provisional assumption of B, and of C, separately; the rule &E may be applied to an available conjunction B & C to yield either one of B and C; the rule ≡E may be applied to an available biconditional $B \equiv C$ to yield either B (if C has also been derived) or C (if B has also been derived); and the rule ~E may be applied to an available *double* negation ~~B to yield B.

  Hopefully, the derivation can be completed at this stage of the guidelines. But if there is *nothing* left to do—the conditions for reaching a line by the appropriate introduction rules cannot be produced, and the elimination rules appropriate to the available lines cannot be applied or will not help—then (but only then) turn to your last resort, **the indirect** or **negation route:**

Stage 3—Provisionally assume the negation of what you want to reach, derive a contradiction, assert by ~I the negation of your assumption— i.e., the *double* negation of what you are after—and apply ~E.

  Often, just the intelim rules for the connectives in the assumptions

---

[10] Namely, to reach a disjunction $B \vee C$, write one of the disjuncts immediately above $B \vee C$, and proceed.

and last line need be used in a derivation. But sometimes the indirect route is called for, even when no tilde occurs there. (This could be avoided by using different elimination rules for '⊃' and '≡', but the rules required would be far less "natural" than the indirect route.)[11] And it is often called for when the last line is a disjunction neither disjunct of which is truth-functionally entailed by the assumptions. Example 22 below illustrates both points.

~I is sometimes hard to use, because not only must you reach two statements instead of one, but—unlike all the others—this rule does not dictate what statements you must reach. So do not resort to it too readily. Especially, if a disjunction is available, it will sometimes be easier to reach what you want by VE rather than by ~I (see Example 15 below). But if you must use ~I—i.e., if you need a contradiction—check whether there is, either among or readily derivable from the undischarged assumptions—some negation ~C, the mate C of which can also be derived (see Examples 9–14). (The negation of an atomic statement or of a binary compound, to which of course no elimination rule applies, often serves as the negative half of a contradiction for ~I.) If no such negation is spotted, some thoughtful experimentation may be required.

But using ~I, however hard this may sometimes prove to be, has its advantages: if at any point in the construction of a derivation some statement and its negation are both available, then you will be able to reach *any* statement you may want (by ~I if it is a negation, by ~I and ~E if it is not). So remain alert to the availability of contradictions as you go along (see Examples 9, 11, and 12).

As the derivation grows, it will prove helpful to write as much as possible of the justification of a line just as soon as you decide how to reach it. This will prevent your forgetting, later on, the strategies adopted earlier. And it should keep you from making aimless assumptions. Since *all* provisional assumptions must eventually be discharged, one at a time, be quite certain, *as you are making it,* how each provisional assumption will be discharged, and to what avail. Four rules permit you to discharge assumptions (the four, of course, which involve subordinate derivations): ⊃I, ~I, VE, and ≡I.

The foregoing remarks on strategy will be illustrated shortly. But we pause to note how intimately the technique of natural deduction is related to the main theme of the book. The deriving of statements from sets of statements in accordance with R, ⊃I, ⊃E, and so on—like their truth-functional entailment by those sets—depends crucially on the composition of the statements involved. For example, a conjunction *B* & *C* is true on a truth-value assignment if and only if both its com-

---

[11] See on this matter H. Leblanc's "Proof routines for the propositional calculus," *Notre Dame Journal of Formal Logic,* vol. 4, 1963, pp. 81–104.

ponents *B* and *C* are true on the assignment. Accordingly, the intelim rules for '&' permit us to assert the *compound B & C* on some assumptions if we can derive both its *components B* and *C* from those assumptions, and to assert either one of *B* and *C* on some assumptions if we can derive *B & C* from those assumptions. And again, a conditional *B* ⊃ *C* is true on a truth-value assignment just in case, should its left-hand component *B* be true on the assignment, the right-hand one *C* is too. Accordingly, the intelim rules for '⊃' permit us to assert the *compound B* ⊃ *C* on some assumptions if we can derive its *component C* from those assumptions plus the *component B* of *B* ⊃ *C*, and to assert *C* on some assumptions if we can derive *B* ⊃ *C* and *B* from those assumptions. The reader is invited to see how like remarks hold in the other three cases.

Illustrations

Now for some sample derivations, which we run with the aid of '*A*', '*B*', and '*C*' to stress their exemplary character. Exactly the same moves would be made, whatever actual statements (be they atomic or compound) might appear in place of those three letters. The reader should try to reconstruct the strategies employed in each derivation. Notice particularly the uses of the indirect route when (but only when) absolutely necessary, and the ways in which **VE** is used (especially in Examples 15 and 16, where the recommendation in Stage 1 of the guidelines is rejected in favor of an **VE** strategy which seems simpler).

EXAMPLE 9:

1	~A		
2		A	
3			~B
4		A	(R, 2)
5			~A (R, 1)
6		~~B	(~I, 3–(4,5))
7		B	(~E, 6)
8	A ⊃ B		(⊃I, 2–7)

EXAMPLE 10:

1	~(A ⊃ B)	
2	B	
3	A	
4	B	(R, 2)
5	A ⊃ B	(⊃I, 3–4)
6	~(A ⊃ B)	(R, 1)
7	~B	(~I, 2–(5,6))

EXAMPLE 11:

1	~(A ⊃ B)	
2	~A	
3	A	
4	~B	
5	A	(R, 3)
6	~A	(R, 2)
7	~~B	(~I, 4–(5,6))
8	B	(~E, 7)
9	A ⊃ B	(⊃I, 3–8)
10	~(A ⊃ B)	(R, 1)
11	~~A	(~I, 2–(9,10))
12	A	(~E, 11)

EXAMPLE 12:

1	A ∨ B	
2	~A	
3	A ∨ B	(R, 1)
4	A	
5	~B	
6	A	(R, 4)
7	~A	(R, 2)
8	~~B	(~I, 5–(6,7))
9	B	(~E, 8)
10	B	
11	B	(R, 10)
12	B	(∨E, 3, 4–9, 10–11)

EXAMPLE 13:

1	~(A ∨ B)		~(A ∨ B)	
2	A		B	
3	A		B	(R, 2)
4	A ∨ B		A ∨ B	(VI, 3)
5	~(A ∨ B)		~(A ∨ B)	(R, 1)
6	~A		~B	(~I, 2–(4,5))

EXAMPLE 14:

1	~(A & B)	
2	~(~A ∨ ~B)	
3	~A	
4	~A	(R, 3)
5	~A ∨ ~B	(VI, 4)
6	~(~A ∨ ~B)	(R, 2)
7	~~A	(~I, 3–(5,6))
8	A	(~E, 7)
9	~B	
10	~B	(R, 9)
11	~A ∨ ~B	(VI, 10)
12	~(~A ∨ ~B)	(R, 2)
13	~~B	(~I, 9–(11,12))
14	B	(~E, 13)
15	A & B	(&I, 8, 14)
16	~(A & B)	(R, 1)
17	~~(~A ∨ ~B)	(~I, 2–(15,16))
18	~A ∨ ~B	(~E, 17)

EXAMPLE 15:

1	A ∨ B	
2	A ∨ B	(R, 1)
3	A	
4	~A & ~B	
5	~A & ~B	(R, 4)
6	~A	(&E, 5)
7	A	(R, 3)
8	~(~A & ~B)	(~I, 4–(6,7))
9	B	
10	~A & ~B	
11	~A & ~B	(R, 10)
12	~B	(&E, 11)
13	B	(R, 9)
14	~(~A & ~B)	(~I, 10–(12,13))
15	~(~A & ~B)	(VE, 2, 3–8, 9–14)

EXAMPLE 16:

1	A ∨ (B & C)	
2	A ∨ (B & C)	(R, 1)
3	A	
4	A	(R, 3)
5	A ∨ B	(VI, 4)
6	A ∨ C	(VI, 4)
7	(A ∨ B) & (A ∨ C)	(&I, 5, 6)
8	B & C	
9	B & C	(R, 8)
10	B	(&E, 9)
11	A ∨ B	(VI, 10)
12	C	(&E, 9)
13	A ∨ C	(VI, 12)
14	(A ∨ B) & (A ∨ C)	(&I, 11, 13)
15	(A ∨ B) & (A ∨ C)	(VE 2, 3–7, 8–14)

EXAMPLE 17:

1	$(A \lor B) \& (A \lor C)$	
2	$(A \lor B) \& (A \lor C)$	(R, 1)
3	$A \lor B$	(&E, 2)
4	$\quad A$	
5	$\quad A$	(R, 4)
6	$\quad A \lor (B \& C)$	(VI, 5)
7	$\quad B$	
8	$\quad (A \lor B) \& (A \lor C)$	(R, 1)
9	$\quad A \lor C$	(&E, 8)
10	$\quad\quad A$	
11	$\quad\quad A$	(R, 10)
12	$\quad\quad A \lor (B \& C)$	(VI, 11)
13	$\quad\quad C$	
14	$\quad\quad B$	(R, 7)
15	$\quad\quad C$	(R, 13)
16	$\quad\quad B \& C$	(&I, 14, 15)
17	$\quad\quad A \lor (B \& C)$	(VI, 16)
18	$\quad A \lor (B \& C)$	(VE, 9, 10–12, 13–17)
19	$A \lor (B \& C)$	(VE, 3, 4–6, 7–18)

EXAMPLE 18:

1	$\sim(\sim A \& B)$	
2	$\sim(\sim B \lor C)$	
3	$\quad \sim A$	
4	$\quad\quad B$	
5	$\quad\quad B$	(R, 4)
6	$\quad\quad \sim A$	(R, 3)
7	$\quad\quad \sim A \& B$	(&I, 5, 6)
8	$\quad\quad \sim(\sim A \& B)$	(R, 1)
9	$\quad \sim B$	($\sim$I, 4–(7,8))
10	$\quad \sim B \lor C$	(VI, 9)
11	$\quad \sim(\sim B \lor C)$	(R, 2)
12	$\sim\sim A$	($\sim$I, 3–(10,11))
13	A	($\sim$E, 12)

Theorems and Proofs

Recall that (1) a statement A is derivable from a (finite) set S of statements ($S \vdash A$, for short) if and only if S truth-functionally entails A, and (2) the empty set $\varnothing$ truth-functionally entails A if and only if A is truth-functionally true. (Proof of (2) was given on p. 36, and proof of (1) will be supplied in Chapter 3.) So, if (1) is true even when S is empty, then we should have it that $\varnothing \vdash A$ *if and only if A is truth-functionally true.* And indeed this is the case: all and only tautologies are derivable, in accordance with the rules of this section, from no assumptions at all.[12]

A derivation with no undischarged assumptions is sometimes called a **proof**, and a statement A is said to be **provable** or to be a **theorem** if there is a proof whose last line is A.

Proofs are no different from any other derivations, except that ⊃I, ~I (often followed by ~E), and ≡I will be relied on even more heavily than before, since they provide the assumptions (eventually discharged) from which to operate. In general, when constructing a proof, (a) write the line to be proved at the bottom (and nothing at the top), (b) draw a vertical bar all the way from the top, and (c) proceed as before, heeding the guidelines of pp. 90–92.

A few examples will illustrate how tautologies are proved. Again the reader should try to reconstruct the line of thought behind each proof.

EXAMPLE 19: To prove any statement of the sort $A \equiv {\sim}{\sim}A$.

1	A	
2	~A	
3	A	(R, 1)
4	~A	(R, 2)
5	~~A	(~I, 2–(3,4))
6	~~A	
7	~~A	(R, 6)
8	A	(~E, 7)
9	$A \equiv {\sim}{\sim}A$	(≡I, 1–5, 6–8)

---

[12] See also pp. 37–38. The undischarged assumptions of a derivation are the conditions on which the last line is asserted. If there are *no undischarged assumptions,* i.e., if all the assumptions of a derivation are provisional, and hence discharged by the time the last line is reached, then the last line can be asserted *un*conditionally.

EXAMPLE 20: To prove any statement of the sort $A \vee {\sim}A$.

1	${\sim}(A \vee {\sim}A)$	
2	A	
3	A	(R, 2)
4	$A \vee {\sim}A$	(VI, 3)
5	${\sim}(A \vee {\sim}A)$	(R, 1)
6	${\sim}A$	(${\sim}$I, 2–(4,5))
7	$A \vee {\sim}A$	(VI, 6)
8	${\sim}(A \vee {\sim}A)$	(R, 1)
9	${\sim}{\sim}(A \vee {\sim}A)$	(${\sim}$I, 1–(7,8))
10	$A \vee {\sim}A$	(${\sim}$E, 9)

$A \vee {\sim}A$ is sometimes known as the *Law of the Excluded Middle*.

EXAMPLE 21: $\vdash (A \supset B) \supset [({\sim}A \supset B) \supset B]$.

1	$A \supset B$	
2	${\sim}A \supset B$	
3	${\sim}B$	
4	A	
5	A	(R, 4)
6	$A \supset B$	(R, 1)
7	B	($\supset$E, 5, 6)
8	${\sim}B$	(R, 3)
9	${\sim}A$	(${\sim}$I, 4–(7,8))
10	${\sim}A \supset B$	(R, 2)
11	B	($\supset$E, 9, 10)
12	${\sim}B$	(R, 3)
13	${\sim}{\sim}B$	(${\sim}$I, 3–(11,12))
14	B	(${\sim}$E, 13)
15	$({\sim}A \supset B) \supset B$	($\supset$I, 2–14)
16	$(A \supset B) \supset [({\sim}A \supset B) \supset B]$	($\supset$I, 1–15)

EXAMPLE 22: ⊢ (A ⊃ B) ∨ (B ⊃ C).

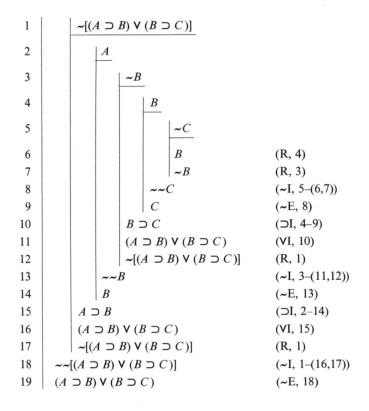

1	~[(A ⊃ B) ∨ (B ⊃ C)]	
2	A	
3	~B	
4	B	
5	~C	
6	B	(R, 4)
7	~B	(R, 3)
8	~~C	(~I, 5–(6,7))
9	C	(~E, 8)
10	B ⊃ C	(⊃I, 4–9)
11	(A ⊃ B) ∨ (B ⊃ C)	(VI, 10)
12	~[(A ⊃ B) ∨ (B ⊃ C)]	(R, 1)
13	~~B	(~I, 3–(11,12))
14	B	(~E, 13)
15	A ⊃ B	(⊃I, 2–14)
16	(A ⊃ B) ∨ (B ⊃ C)	(VI, 15)
17	~[(A ⊃ B) ∨ (B ⊃ C)]	(R, 1)
18	~~[(A ⊃ B) ∨ (B ⊃ C)]	(~I, 1–(16,17))
19	(A ⊃ B) ∨ (B ⊃ C)	(~E, 18)

Other Uses of Derivations

The derivation method has other uses besides establishing the truth-functional validity of (truth-functionally) valid arguments, and the truth-functional truth of tautologies.

Truth-functional falsehood. Since a statement A is truth-functionally false if and only if its negation ~A is truth-functionally true, a statement can be shown to be truth-functionally false by constructing a proof of its negation.

Truth-functional equivalence. Since two statements A and B are truth-functionally equivalent if and only if their biconditional $A \equiv B$ is truth-functionally true, two statements can be shown to be truth-functionally equivalent by constructing a proof of their biconditional (also of course, and with the saving of a line, by deriving each one of A and B from the other).

Truth-functional inconsistency. In order to show that not all of someone's claims are true (without necessarily identifying any culprit), we could and often do show that the *negation* of some one of those claims follows from the rest. The reader can assure himself that a set of statements is truth-functionally inconsistent if and only if the *negation* of any one member is truth-functionally entailed by—and hence is derivable from—the remaining members.[13] A set of statements can thus be shown to be truth-functionally inconsistent by deriving the negation of any one member from the rest.

The reader can also assure himself that a set of statements is truth-functionally inconsistent if and only if it truth-functionally entails a contradiction.[14] Another and simpler way of showing that a set of statements is truth-functionally inconsistent is thus to derive from it any contradiction one pleases. As a matter of fact, any derivation of, say, B and $\sim B$ from $\{A_1, A_2, \ldots, A_n\}$:

$$
\begin{array}{c|l}
1 & A_1 \\
2 & A_2 \\
\cdot & \cdot \\
n & A_n \\
\hline
\cdot & \cdot \\
p & B \\
\cdot & \cdot \\
q & \sim B
\end{array}
$$

can automatically be converted into a derivation of, say, $\sim A_i$ from $\{A_1, A_2, \ldots, A_{i-1}, A_{i+1}, \ldots, A_n\}$:

$$
\begin{array}{c|l}
1 & A_1 \\
2 & A_2 \\
\cdot & \cdot \\
i-1 & A_{i-1} \\
i & A_{i+1} \\
\cdot & \cdot \\
n-1 & A_n \\
\hline
\end{array}
$$

$$
\begin{array}{rl}
n & \quad A_i \\
\cdot & \quad \cdot \\
p & \quad B \\
\cdot & \quad \cdot \\
q & \quad \sim B \\
q+1 & \sim A_i \qquad (\sim I,\ n\text{--}(p,q))
\end{array}
$$

like lines $n + 1$ through q in the original derivation

---

[13] See Exercise E1.1.15(d) on this point.
[14] See Exercise E1.1.15(b) on this point.

Incidentally, the reader will have gathered from the guidelines of pp. 90–92, and some of our examples, that from a truth-functionally inconsistent set of statements *any* statement whatever is derivable. Indeed any derivation of, say, B and $\sim B$ from $\{A_1, A_2, \ldots, A_n\}$:

$$
\begin{array}{l|l}
1 & A_1 \\
2 & A_2 \\
\cdot & \cdot \\
n & A_n \\
\hline
\cdot & \cdot \\
p & B \\
\cdot & \cdot \\
q & \sim B
\end{array}
$$

can automatically be turned into a derivation of, say, C from $\{A_1, A_2, \ldots, A_n\}$:

$$
\begin{array}{l|l}
1 & A_1 \\
2 & A_2 \\
\cdot & \cdot \\
n & A_n \\
\hline
n+1 & \quad\; \sim C \\
\cdot & \quad\; \cdot \\
p & \quad\; B \\
\cdot & \quad\; \cdot \\
q & \quad\; \sim B \\
q+1 & \sim\sim C \qquad (\sim\!\text{I},\ n+1\text{–}(p,q)) \\
q+2 & C \qquad\quad (\sim\!\text{E},\ q+1)
\end{array}
$$

lines like $n+1$ through q in the original derivation

Any argument with truth-functionally inconsistent premisses is thus sure to be valid, but uninterestingly so, as the argument with the same premisses but the opposite conclusion would likewise be valid.

Like the tree method of Section 1.2, the present derivation method will be extended in Chapter 2 to cover quantificational as well as truth-functional matters.

EXERCISES

E1.3.1. Construct a derivation of the conclusion from the premisses of each of the following arguments:

a. P ⊃ (Q ⊃ R)   b. P ⊃ (P ⊃ Q)
    _____   _____
    ∴ Q ⊃ (P ⊃ R)   ∴ P ⊃ Q

c. (P ⊃ Q) ⊃ (P ⊃ R)   d. (P ⊃ Q) ⊃ (Q ⊃ R)
    Q   _____
    _____   ∴ Q ⊃ R
    ∴ P ⊃ R

e. P ⊃ (Q ⊃ ~P)   f. P ⊃ (Q ⊃ ~P)
    P ⊃ Q   _____
    _____   ∴ Q ⊃ ~P
    ∴ ~P

g. ~P ⊃ ~Q   h. ~~P
    _____   Q ⊃ ~P
    ∴ Q ⊃ P   _____
                                             ∴ ~(P ⊃ Q)

i. ~(P & ~Q)   j. P & ~Q
    _____   _____
    ∴ P ⊃ Q   ∴ ~(P ⊃ Q)

k. P ⊃ (R & S)   l. (P ⊃ ~Q) & (Q ⊃ ~R)
    Q ⊃ (~R & ~S)   S ⊃ Q
    _____   _____
    ∴ ~(P & Q)   ∴ S ⊃ (~P & ~R)

m. P V Q   n. P V Q
    P ⊃ R   Q ⊃ R
    Q ⊃ S   _____
    _____   ∴ ~P ⊃ R
    ∴ R V S

o. P ⊃ Q   p. P V Q
    ~(Q V R)   (P ⊃ R) & (~R ⊃ ~Q)
    _____   _____
    ∴ ~(P V R)   ∴ R

E1.3.2. Construct a derivation of the conclusion from the premisses of every truth-functionally valid argument in E1.2.2.

E1.3.3. Construct a derivation of the conclusion from the premisses of each of the following arguments:

   a. If Tom is sober, then he's rational but uninteresting. If he's polite but uninteresting, then Sylvia doesn't like him. Therefore, if Tom is sober and polite, Sylvia doesn't like him. (S, R, I, P, L)

b.   Len is old enough to vote if he's just 21. If he's under 21, he can't drink legally, and if he's over 21 he'll be drafted. So if Len is not old enough to vote, then either he can't drink legally or will be drafted. (Supply the missing but obvious premiss.) (V, T, U, L, O, D)

c.   If Bill heard Jane or Nancy, then he was eavesdropping. He was eavesdropping if and only if he was in the pay of the F. B. I. and the C. I. A. So if he wasn't in the pay of the F. B. I., he didn't hear Nancy. (J, N, E, F, C)

d.   If the number of hens stays about the same but people start buying more eggs, then omelettes will cost more. If omelettes will cost more if people buy more eggs, then the chicken farmers will make a fortune. The number of hens will stay about the same. So chicken farmers will make a fortune. (H, E, O, F)

e.   If Jim leaves on time, he'll reach Kansas City by 5:00 P.M. and be able to address the Jaycees. If Jim reaches Kansas City by 5:00 P.M., he'll have time for too many cocktails. If Jim is able to address the Jaycees, his name will get in the paper. If Jim has a late start, he'll have to drive at top speed. So Jim will have time for too many cocktails and his name will get in the paper, or else he'll have to drive at top speed. (Again supply the missing but obvious premiss.) (T, K, J, C, P, L, D)

f.   Rusty goes to church if and only if there's not something more interesting to do. And he only goes to church if the weather is warm and the sun is shining. In December either the sun doesn't shine or the weather isn't warm. Today isn't Christmas unless the month is December. So if today is Christmas, there's something more interesting to do than going to church. (G, I, W, S, D, C)

g.   If Jack is going to the party he'll invite Mary, but if he isn't he'll take Peggy to a show. If he invites Mary to the party, she'll go. If he's going to the party only if he invites Mary and he invites her only if she'll go, then either they'll both go or neither one of them will. If they both go to the party, Peggy will ge angry; and if neither of them goes, Mary will be angry. So one of the two girls will be angry. (G, I, T, M, P, A)

h.   If either one of his brothers plays with his toys, Steven will be angry; but if his sister plays with them he won't, but will be quite pleased instead. Either his sister plays with them, or his mother will take him out and buy him an ice cream cone. Surely he won't be taken out by both parents. So either his youngest brother doesn't play with his toys or his father won't take him out. ('O' for 'Steven's oldest brother plays with his toys', 'Y' for 'Steven's youngest brother plays with his toys', 'A' for 'Steven will be angry', 'S' for 'Steven's sister will play with his toys', 'P' for 'Steven will be quite pleased', 'M' for 'Steven's mother will take him out', 'I' for 'Steven's mother will buy him an ice cream cone', and 'F' for 'Steven's father will take him out'.)

i.   If Bob went to Canada to buy his new dog Rover, then it cost him a lot of money and so he's unlucky. If he didn't go to Canada to buy Rover, then he stayed in Peoria, and got inducted and sent to Vietnam. If he got sent to Vietnam, then he couldn't take Rover with him. If Rover didn't go with him, the poor thing is forlorn and unlucky. So either Bob or Rover or the Vietnamese are unlucky. (C, M, B, P, I, S, T, F, R, V)

j. Joe makes a lot of money only if he goes to graduate school. If Joe gets fed up, he'll join the circus. If Joe will go to graduate school if and only if he joins the circus, then either graduate schools or circuses have changed since my youth. Circuses haven't changed since I was young, nor have graduate schools. If Joe goes to graduate school, he'll surely get fed up. He won't join the circus unless he makes a lot of money. So if graduate schools have more buffoons than circuses do, then they have changed since my youth. (M, S, F, J, G, C, B)

k.   P   l.   (P ⊃ ~Q) & (Q ⊃ R)
      P ⊃ Q   (R V P) ≡ P
      (~Q ⊃ ~P) ⊃ ~P   ~S ⊃ Q

      ∴ R   ∴ S

m.   ~(P ⊃ Q)   n.   (P V Q) V (R & S)
      ~(Q ⊃ R)   (~P & S) & ~(~P & Q)

      ∴ S   ∴ ~P & R

o.   (~P & Q) & ~R   p.   P ≡ Q
      (S V T) ≡ (~R ≡ Q)   Q ≡ R

      ∴ T V S   ∴ [(P & Q) & R] V [(~P & ~Q) & ~R]

E1.3.4.   Construct a proof of every truth-functional truth in E1.2.3.

E1.3.5.   Construct a proof of each of the following truth-functional truths:

a.   [(P ⊃ Q) ⊃ P] ⊃ P   (Peirce's Law)

b.   (P V Q) ≡ [(P ⊃ Q) ⊃ Q]

c.   (P ⊃ Q) ≡ (~P V Q)

d.   P ≡ [Q ≡ (P ≡ Q)]

e.   [P V (Q ⊃ R)] ≡ [(P V Q) ⊃ (P V R)]   (Distributivity of 'V' into '⊃')

f.   [P V (Q ≡ R)] ≡ [(P V Q) ≡ (P V R)]   (Distributivity of 'V' into '≡')

E1.3.6.   Derive any contradiction you please from each truth-functionally inconsistent set of statements in E1.2.1.

E1.3.7.

(a) Show in connection with rule R that for any i from 1 through n $\{A_1, A_2, \ldots, A_n\}$ truth-functionally entails A_i.

(b) Show in connection with rule ⊃E that if $\{A_1, A_2, \ldots, A_n\}$ truth-functionally entails $B ⊃ C$ and B, then $\{A_1, A_2, \ldots, A_n\}$ truth-functionally entails C as well.

(c) Show in connection with rule $\supset I$ that if $\{A_1, A_2, \ldots, A_n, B\}$ truth-functionally entails C, then the subset $\{A_1, A_2, \ldots, A_n\}$ of $\{A_1, A_2, \ldots, A_n, B\}$ truth-functionally entails $B \supset C$.

(d) Obtain a similar result in connection with each one of $\sim E$, $\sim I$, $\&E$, $\&I$, VE, VI, $\equiv E$, and $\equiv I$.

E1.3.8.

(a) Need every assumption of a derivation be appealed to in the construction of a derivation?

(b) Show how any derivation of a statement A from a finite set S of statements can be converted into a derivation of A from any finite superset of S.

E1.3.9. Show that the following rule $\sim E^*$:

$$
\begin{array}{cll}
1 & A_1 & \\
2 & A_2 & \\
\cdot & \cdot & \\
n & A_n & \\
\cdot & \cdot & \\
p & \quad\quad \sim B & \\
\cdot & \quad\quad \cdot & \\
q & \quad\quad C \text{ (or } \sim C) & \\
\cdot & \quad\quad \cdot & \\
r & \quad\quad \sim C \text{ (or } C) & \\
r+1 & B & (\sim E^*,\ p\text{–}(q,r))
\end{array}
$$

can do duty for both $\sim E$ and $\sim I$. That is, with $\sim E^*$ as the *only* intelim rule for negation,

(a) show how to construct a derivation of B from $\{A_1, A_2, \ldots, A_n\}$ if you already know how to derive $\sim\sim B$ from $\{A_1, A_2, \ldots, A_n\}$, and

(b) show how to construct a derivation of $\sim B$ from $\{A_1, A_2, \ldots, A_n\}$ if you already know how to derive each one of C and $\sim C$ from $\{A_1, A_2, \ldots, A_n, B\}$.

E1.3.10. Suppose that $B \& C$ is defined as $\sim(B \supset \sim C)$, and that only R and the intelim rules for '$\sim$' and '$\supset$' are available. Show that:

(a) if *both* $\{A_1, A_2, \ldots, A_n\} \vdash B$ *and* $\{A_1, A_2, \ldots, A_n\} \vdash C$, then $\{A_1, A_2, \ldots, A_n\} \vdash \sim(B \supset \sim C) (= B \& C)$, and

(b) if $\{A_1, A_2, \ldots, A_n\} \vdash \sim(B \supset \sim C) (= B \& C)$, then both $\{A_1, A_2, \ldots, A_n\} \vdash B$ and $\{A_1, A_2, \ldots, A_n\} \vdash C$.

(That is, show how to construct a derivation of $\sim(B \supset \sim C)$ from $\{A_1, A_2, \ldots, A_n\}$ if you already know how to derive both B and C from $\{A_1, A_2, \ldots, A_n\}$; and show how to construct derivations of B and of C from $\{A_1, A_2, \ldots, A_n\}$ if you already know how to derive $\sim(B \supset \sim C)$ from $\{A_1, A_2, \ldots, A_n\}$.)

E1.3.11.   Suppose that $B \lor C$ is defined as $\sim B \supset C$, and that only R and the intelim rules for '$\sim$' and '$\supset$' are available. Show that:

(a) if either $\{A_1, A_2, \ldots, A_n\} \vdash B$ or $\{A_1, A_2, \ldots, A_n\} \vdash C$, then $\{A_1, A_2, \ldots, A_n\} \vdash \sim B \supset C \, (= B \lor C)$, and

(b) if $\{A_1, A_2, \ldots, A_n\} \vdash \sim B \supset C \; (= B \lor C)$, $\{A_1, A_2, \ldots, A_n, B\} \vdash D$, and $\{A_1, A_2, \ldots, A_n, C\} \vdash D$, then $\{A_1, A_2, \ldots, A_n\} \vdash D$.

(That is, show how to derive $\sim B \supset C$ from $\{A_1, A_2, \ldots, A_n\}$ if you already know how to derive either one of B and C from $\{A_1, A_2, \ldots, A_n\}$; and show how to derive D from $\{A_1, A_2, \ldots, A_n\}$ if you already know how to derive $\sim B \supset C$ from $\{A_1, A_2, \ldots, A_n\}$ and how to derive D from each one of the two supersets $\{A_1, A_2, \ldots, A_n, B\}$ and $\{A_1, A_2, \ldots, A_n, C\}$ of $\{A_1, A_2, \ldots, A_n\}$.)

2

The Logic of Quantifiers

There are other logically relevant ways of compounding statements besides those studied in Chapter 1. As we frequently remarked, truth-functional composition alone does not account for the logical truth of *all* logically true statements, the inconsistency of *all* inconsistent sets of statements, or the validity of *all* valid arguments. So in this chapter we shall treat other modes of composition. They correspond to particles like 'All' and 'Some', called *quantifiers;* and the statements they yield are accordingly called *quantificational compounds*.

In Section 2.1 we shall develop the basic notions and the notation appropriate to the logic of quantifiers. In Section 2.2 we shall extend the tree technique to test sets of statements for consistency generally— i.e., for consistency on quantificational as well as truth-functional grounds. And in Section 2.3 we shall extend the technique of natural deduction to permit the derivation of conclusions from premises that entail them generally—i.e., entail them either on truth-functional or on quantificational grounds.

2.1 Quantification

So far we have counted as atomic (non-compound) all those statements which could not be analyzed as *truth-functional* compounds—e.g., 'Peter is tall', 'All of Peter's friends are tall', 'Some insects have eight legs', etc. In Part One below we shall certify as atomic only *some* of them, and shall analyze the rest as quantificational compounds. In Part Two we shall specify the truth-conditions of the new compounds, and complete our account of the logical properties and relations first met in the Introduction.

Part One

Predicates, Individual Terms, and Atomic Statements

A great many statements are about one or more specific things. They are sometimes called **singular statements,** to distinguish them from **general statements** like 'All violets are blue' and 'Some teachers are infallible'. Only the former statements will turn out to be atomic on the definition to be given on p. 136.

Some singular statements can be understood as attributing a property to one specific thing:

>*Alan* frowns a lot
>
>*11* is even
>
>*Fatherhood* is quite a responsibility
>
>Heedless of any danger which might lurk ahead, *George* boldly struck off on another mission
>
>*The bingo game which was to have been held at the town hall next Saturday* has been postponed.

Other singular statements can be understood as attributing a relation to two or more things:

>*Alan* covets *Cynthia*
>
>It's better *to be red* than *(to be) dead*
>
>*Alan* is delighted with *fatherhood*
>
>*Alan* is delighted with himself (i.e., with *Alan*)
>
>*Cynthia* is sitting between *George* and *Alan*
>
>*Alan* invited *Cynthia* to *the bingo game which was to have been held at the town hall next Saturday*
>
>*Alan* loves *Cynthia* more than *George* (loves *Cynthia*)
>
>*Alan* loves *Cynthia* more than *(Alan* loves) *George.*

The italicized words—the words designating the specific things that are said to have certain properties or to stand in certain relations to other things—are called **individual terms,** or simply **terms.** A term either is a proper name ('Alan') or does the work of one ('the bingo game which was to have been held at the town hall next Saturday'). It is the sort of expression which functions as a grammatical subject or object in a sentence, identifying or singling out some particular thing about which a statement is made.

We use the word 'thing' here in the broadest possible sense. Things might thus be physical objects (Alan), properties (being red), relations (fatherhood), numbers (11), sets, events, and so on. Roughly, they are whatever things statements might be about; and, equally roughly, terms are the various expressions that would refer to those things.

Instead of expressions from the vernacular, however, we shall use the infinitely many symbols

$$a_1, \quad a_2, \quad a_3, \quad a_4, \ldots$$

as *our* terms, the first several of which will often be written

$$a, \quad b, \quad c, \quad d, \ldots .[1]$$

We invite the reader to follow suit, and turn in any expression he might use as a term for one or another of 'a_1', 'a_2', 'a_3', 'a_4', etc. (or, when the occasion permits, for one or another of 'a', 'b', 'c', 'd', etc.). These symbols will make for a compact and uniform rendition of singular statements, and reveal their articulation clearly.

Thus drafting 'a' to serve for 'Alan', 'b' to serve for 'the bingo game. . .', 'c' to serve for 'Cynthia', 'd' to serve for 'being dead', and so forth,[2] we could rewrite the examples above as

<u>a</u> frowns a lot

<u>e</u> is even

<u>f</u> is quite a responsibility

Heedless of any danger which might lurk ahead, <u>g</u> boldly struck off on another mission

<u>b</u> has been postponed

<u>a</u> covets <u>c</u>

<u>r</u> is better than <u>d</u>

<u>a</u> is delighted with <u>f</u>

<u>a</u> is delighted with <u>a</u>

<u>c</u> is sitting between <u>g</u> and <u>a</u>

<u>a</u> invited <u>c</u> to <u>b</u>

<u>a</u> loves c more than g loves <u>c</u>

<u>a</u> loves <u>c</u> more than <u>a</u> loves <u>g</u>.

In each case the underlined letters are to be thought of as *bona fide* terms, doing duty for terms in the vernacular which we identified on this occasion but might not on others.

---

[1] The terms 'a_{24}', 'a_{25}', and 'a_{26}' will *not* be written 'x', 'y', and 'z': these letters will soon be assigned a role of their own. Since there are $\aleph_0$ positive integers, we equip ourselves here with $\aleph_0$ terms (see Appendix I concerning $\aleph_0$).

[2] Though on this occasion 'a', for example, does duty for 'Alan', on another occasion it could do duty for an entirely different term, say, 'the oldest alligator in the Philadelphia Zoo'. 'a_1', 'a_2', 'a_3', and so on may indeed designate some things in one context and others in another context. We shall often remind the reader of this.

Incidentally, the order suggested when we introduced the terms

$$a_1, \quad a_2, \quad a_3, \quad a_4, \ldots,$$

will be known as their **alphabetic order,** and will prove of importance later on. 'a_1' is thus the *alphabetically first* (or earliest) of our terms, 'a_2' the *alphabetically second,* 'a_3' the *alphabetically third,* and so on.

Whatever is left once the terms have been removed from an atomic statement (i.e., whatever yields an atomic statement when fitted out with the right number of terms) is called a **predicate.** Predicates are the expressions used to talk *about* the things designated by terms—i.e., the expressions used to attribute properties and relations to things. Some predicates, like

> ... frowns a lot
>
> ... is even
>
> ... is quite a responsibility
>
> Heedless of any danger which might lurk ahead, ... boldly struck off on another mission
>
> ... has been postponed,

are called **one-place** or **monadic** predicates, as they show only one vacancy which could be filled by a term. Others are **many-place** or **polyadic** predicates—two-place (dyadic), three-place (triadic), four-place (tetradic), and so on—showing two, three, four, or more vacancies:

> ... covets ...
>
> ... is better than ...
>
> ... is delighted with ...
>
> ... is sitting between ... and ...
>
> ... invited ... to ...
>
> ... loves ... more than ... loves ... .[3]

---

[3] It would also do to understand by a predicate whatever is left once one or more individual terms are removed from an atomic statement. Thus, 'Alan covets Cynthia' can be thought of as consisting of the two-place predicate '... covets ...' flanked to left and right, respectively, by the terms 'Alan' and 'Cynthia'. It could also be thought of as consisting of the one-place predicate '... covets Cynthia' flanked on the left by the term 'Alan', or as consisting of the one-place predicate 'Alan covets ...' flanked on the right by the term 'Cynthia'.

Indeed, one might even (though we shall not) understand by a predicate whatever is left once *zero or more* individual terms are removed from a statement. Then 'Alan covets Cynthia' could be understood as the zero-place predicate 'Alan covets Cynthia' fitted out with the right number of terms, viz., none. The atomic statements of Chapter 1 would thus be drawn into the present account as zero-place predicates which we are not interested in analyzing. But we shall say no more of zero-place predicates, since in this chapter we are specifically interested in the analysis of atomic statements into predicates and terms, and in the compounding of general statements from statements whose atomic "components" are thus analyzed.

Monadic predicates are used to ascribe properties to single things; polyadic predicates are used to ascribe relations to (ordered) pairs, triples, quadruples, and so on, of things.[4]

In much of this section we still write out predicates; in the rest of the book, though, we shall use capital letters in their places. These capital letters served in Chapter 1 as abbreviations for atomic statements, but they are now free to assume another role. (Again we avoid where possible, but not fanatically, the four capital letters 'A', 'B', 'C', and 'D', and select the initial letter of some key word in the predicate to aid the memory. If we do not care which predicates are understood, we use 'F', 'G', and 'H'; the reader can think of these letters as abbreviating any of his favorite predicates.) When writing a statement in this kind of shorthand, we put the predicate letter first, and then string out the terms to the right in the proper order. So our examples could be represented thus:

Fa (Alan frowns a lot)	Ee (11 is even)
Rf	Hg
Pb	Cac (Alan covets Cynthia)
Brd	Daf
Daa	Scga
Iacb	Lacgc
Lacag.	

Statements which can be abbreviated in this way—as a predicate letter followed by one or more terms—are of course atomic in the sense of Chapter 1. And, as announced earlier, they are the *only* statements which henceforth will be considered atomic.

We still recognize truth-functional compounds of these atomic statements, just as in Chapter 1. So the statement

> Although Alan invited Cynthia to the bingo game, still if she's sitting between him and George then she doesn't love either one of them more than the other

would be represented as

$$\text{Iacb \& [Scag} \supset {\sim}\text{(Lcacg } \vee \text{ Lcgca)]}.$$

But statements like those identified as general on p. 110 above, though atomic in the sense of Chapter 1, will now be subjected to further analysis. (See Exercise E2.1.1.)

---

[4] Concerning ordered pairs, ordered triples, and so on, see Appendix I. A set-theoretic account of the role played by predicates will be found in Section 3.6.

Universal Quantification, and Term Variables

We begin with those general statements which can be construed as claims that *everything* is of a certain sort. They are called **universal statements.**

To say, for example,

Everything is lovely

is to say, in effect,

Whatever *thing* you may choose, *it* is lovely.

This will be rendered as

$(\forall x)(x$ is lovely$)$.

Here the second occurrence of '*x*' does duty for the neutral pronoun 'it' in 'it is lovely', while its antecedent 'thing' in 'Whatever thing you may choose' is represented by the first occurrence of '*x*'—the one in the **universal quantifier** '$(\forall x)$'. '$(\forall x)(x$ is lovely)' can be *read* as 'For all *x*, *x* is lovely'; but it is most readily seen to match 'Everything is lovely' if *understood* as shorthand for 'Whatever thing you may choose, it is lovely'.[5]

Again, to say

Nothing is going right

is to say, in effect,

Whatever *thing* you may consider, *it* is not going right.

This will accordingly be rendered as

$(\forall x){\sim}(x$ is going right$)$.

Again, to say

All violets are blue

is to say, in effect,

Everything which is a violet is blue,

that is,

Take any *thing* you will, if *it* is a violet, then *it* is blue.

_____

[5] In the literature, '(x)' is often used in place of '$(\forall x)$', and so are 'Λ_x' and 'Π_x'. '$\forall$' is of course the first letter of 'All' written upside down.

So this will be rendered

$$(\forall x)(x \text{ is a violet} \supset x \text{ is blue}).$$

Here the last two occurrences of 'x' do duty for the two occurrences of the neutral pronoun 'it' in 'if it is a violet, then it is blue', while their *common* antecedent 'thing' in 'Take any thing you will' is represented by the first occurrence of 'x'—the one in the universal quantifier '$(\forall x)$'. As before, though '$(\forall x)$' may be read 'For all x', it should be understood as akin to 'Take any thing you will', or some such universalizing prefix.

Incidentally, the parentheses which enclose 'x is lovely' in '$(\forall x)(x$ is lovely)', and 'x is going right' in '$(\forall x)\sim(x$ is going right)', are there only to facilitate the reading. If we abbreviated 'is lovely' as 'L', and 'is going right' as 'G', we would simply write '$(\forall x)Lx$' and '$(\forall x)\sim Gx$'. However, those surrounding 'x is a violet $\supset x$ is blue' in '$(\forall x)(x$ is a violet $\supset x$ is blue)' are indispensable, as would be those surrounding 'V$x \supset$ Bx' in '$(\forall x)($V$x \supset$ B$x)$'.

Consider now the claim

Everything attracts everything,

which clearly says

Whatever *thing* you may choose, *it* attracts everything,

or

$$(\forall x)(x \text{ attracts everything}).$$

This in turn becomes

$$(\forall x)(\text{whatever } \textit{thing} \text{ you may choose, } x \text{ attracts } \textit{it}),$$

which in the same spirit we render as

$$(\forall x)(\forall y)(x \text{ attracts } y).$$

There are *two* quantifiers here, and '$(\forall x)(\forall y)(x$ attracts $y)$' is thus shorthand for the admittedly awkward statement 'Whatever thing you may choose first, and whatever (not necessarily distinct) thing you may choose next, the former attracts the latter'. Fortunately, with fluency in the formal "language," the reader will soon skip this intermediate stage of translation from ordinary into "official" English, and pass directly from ordinary statements to their logical renditions. Problems of translation and punctuation will be discussed more fully later in the text.

Finally, consider the statement

Nobody owns everything,

which is to say

Take any *thing* you will, if *it* is a person then *it* does not own everything,

or

$(\forall x)[x$ is a person $\supset \sim(x$ owns everything$)]$.

This, in turn, says

$(\forall x)[x$ is a person $\supset \sim($take any *thing* you will, x owns *it*$)]$,

or, as we would have it,

$(\forall x)[x$ is a person $\supset \sim(\forall y)(x$ owns $y)]$.

The letters '*x*' and '*y*' in these symbolic renditions are called **term variables,** or **individual variables,** or simply **variables.** As term variables we shall use

$$x, \quad y, \quad z, \quad x', \quad y', \quad z', \quad x'', \ldots.$$

The order suggested here is called their **alphabetic order.**

We conclude our introduction to universal quantifications with a remark—to be expanded later—on the conditions they must meet to be true. The truth-value of a statement like '$(\forall x)(x$ fell off the shelf$)$' can obviously *not* depend on that of 'x fell off the shelf', for 'x fell off the shelf' is *not* a statement and hence has *no* truth-value. But it could depend—and will depend here—on the truth-values of various statements compositionally involved in '$(\forall x)(x$ fell off the shelf$)$'.

Ordinarily, to claim that everything is thus-and-so is to claim that the first thing you pick is thus-and-so, *and* the second one you pick is thus-and-so, *and* the third one you pick is thus-and-so, etc. In a similar way, we shall take

$(\forall x)(x$ fell off the shelf$)$

to be true just in case *all* the following statements (to be known as its *instances*)

a_1 fell off the shelf
a_2 fell off the shelf
a_3 fell off the shelf
etc.

are true. And we shall certify

I forgot everything on the morning of the exam,

i.e.,

$(\forall x)(I$ forgot x on the morning of the exam$)$,

true just in case *all* of the statements

> I forgot a_1 on the morning of the exam
> I forgot a_2 on the morning of the exam
> I forgot a_3 on the morning of the exam
> etc.

are true.

The same terms occur of course in both batches of instances:

a_1 fell off the shelf	I forgot a_1 on the morning of the exam
a_2 fell off the shelf	I forgot a_2 on the morning of the exam
a_3 fell off the shelf	I forgot a_3 on the morning of the exam

and so on. But there is nothing anomalous in this. Like the pronoun 'everything', which obviously covers one batch of things in 'Everything fell off the shelf' and quite another in 'I forgot everything on the morning of the exam', the terms 'a_1', 'a_2', 'a_3', and so on can be used to designate some things on one occasion and others on another. The set of those things one is talking about on any particular occasion will be called the **universe of discourse,** or **domain;** and one's individual terms will designate members of this set.

Existential and Mixed Quantification

General statements which can be construed as claims that *something* is of a certain sort are called **existential statements.** For example, to say

> Something fell off the shelf

is to say, in effect,

> There is something which fell off the shelf,

or

> There is a *thing* such that *it* fell off the shelf.

This will be rendered as

> $(\exists x)(x$ fell off the shelf$)$.

As before, the second occurrence of the term variable 'x' does duty for the neutral pronoun 'it' in 'it fell off the shelf', while its antecedent 'thing' in 'There is a thing such that' is represented by the first occurrence of the *same* variable—the one in the **existential quantifier** '$(\exists x)$'. And while '$(\exists x)$' can be read simply as 'For some x', it should be understood as 'There is an x such that', or—better yet—as 'There exists *at least one* x such that'.[6]

---

[6] In the literature, '(Ex)' is often used in place of '$(\exists x)$', and so are 'V_x' and 'Σ_x'. '$\exists$' is of course the first letter of 'Exists' reversed.

Note in this connection that both 'Something fell off the shelf' and 'Some things fell off the shelf' would be translated '$(\exists x)(x$ fell off the shelf$)$', even though the first statement might be to the effect that just one thing did, and the second to the effect that more than one did. In either case, at least one thing fell off the shelf; and it is this common bit of information which the translation conveys.

Again, to say

Something does not fit in

is to say, in effect,

There exists at least one *thing* such that *it* does not fit in.

This will accordingly be rendered as

$(\exists x){\sim}(x$ fits in$)$.

Again, to say

Some teachers are infallible

is to say, in effect,

There is at least one *thing* such that *it* is a teacher and *it* is infallible.

So this will be rendered

$(\exists x)(x$ is a teacher & x is infallible$)$.

Here the last two occurrences of 'x' do duty for the two occurrences of the neutral pronoun 'it' in 'it is a teacher and it is infallible', while their common antecedent 'thing' in 'There is at least one thing such that' is represented by the first occurrence of 'x'—the one in the existential quantifier '$(\exists x)$'.

Again, to say

Something reminds me of something

is to say

There is at least one *thing* such that *it* reminds me of something,

or

$(\exists x)(x$ reminds me of something$)$.

This in turn becomes

$(\exists x)($there is at least one *thing* such that x reminds me of *it*$)$,

or, as we would have it,

$(\exists x)(\exists y)(x$ reminds me of $y)$.

And, again, to say

> Somebody lost something

is to say

> There is some person who lost something,

or, more "officially,"

> There is at least one *thing* such that *it* is a person and *it* lost something.

In our notation this becomes

> $(\exists x)\,(x$ is a person $\&\ x$ lost something),

hence

> $(\exists x)\,(x$ is a person $\&$ there is at least one *thing* such that x lost *it*),

and hence

> $(\exists x)[x$ is a person $\&\ (\exists y)\,(x$ lost $y)]$.

The conditions which existential statements must meet to be true are obvious. Ordinarily, to claim that something is thus-and-so is to claim that *either* the first thing you pick is thus-and-so, *or* the second thing you pick is thus-and-so, *or* the third thing you pick is thus-and-so, etc. In a similar manner, we shall certify the statement

> Something escapes me,

i.e.,

> $(\exists x)\,(x$ escapes me),

true just in case *at least one* of the following statements (to be known as its *instances*)

> a_1 escapes me
> a_2 escapes me
> a_3 escapes me
> etc.

is true. And we shall take

> Some teachers are dull,

i.e.,

> $(\exists x)\,(x$ is a teacher $\&\ x$ is dull)

to be true just in case *one or more* of the statements

> a_1 is a teacher & a_1 is dull
> a_2 is a teacher & a_2 is dull
> a_3 is a teacher & a_3 is dull
> etc.

are true.

When more than one quantifier occurs in a statement, as was the case in several of the examples above, we speak of **multiple quantification.** When at least one is universal and another existential, we speak of **mixed multiple quantification.** A case in point is the statement

> Everything has a cause,

that is

> Take any *thing* you will, something caused *it*.

This becomes

> $(\forall x)$ (something caused x),

that is

> $(\forall x)$ (there is a *thing* such that *it* caused x),

which we run

> $(\forall x)(\exists y)(y$ caused $x)$.

A second is the related, but different, statement

> Something caused everything,

that is

> There is a *thing* such that *it* caused everything.

This becomes

> $(\exists y)(y$ caused everything),

or

> $(\exists y)$ (take any *thing* you will, y caused *it*),

which we render

> $(\exists y)(\forall x)(y$ caused $x)$.[7]

---

[7] We used 'y' first, and then 'x', to expose more clearly the difference between this and the former statement. Had we used 'x' first, 'Something caused everything' would have been rendered '$(\exists x)(\forall y)(x$ caused $y)$', which differs only notationally from '$(\exists y)(\forall x)(y$ caused $x)$'.

Yet another is the statement

Somebody loves everybody.

As a first step toward its rendition we get

$(\exists x)(x$ is a person & x loves everybody$)$.

This in turn says

$(\exists x)[x$ is a person & (take any *thing* you will, if *it* is a person then x loves *it*)],

which we run

$(\exists x)[x$ is a person & $(\forall y)(y$ is a person $\supset x$ loves $y)]$.

Special problems of translation arise with mixed multiple quantification, and these will be treated below.

Note in closing that there are truth-functional compounds of quantifications, just as there are truth-functional compounds of atomic and of truth-functionally compound statements. So, for example,

If something is going wrong, then not everybody is working hard

would be rendered as the *conditional* statement

$(\exists x)(x$ is going wrong$) \supset {\sim}(\forall x)(x$ is a person $\supset x$ is working hard$)$.

Many other examples will come our way as we proceed.

Translation

To suggest the wide scope of quantificational logic, we next exhibit and comment on a number of statements which can be translated into our symbolism. In the final, more difficult, cases we indicate how the translating was done. (In Sections 2.2 and 2.3 we shall use translations without pausing—as the reader should pause—to justify them.)

Universal statements. Statements which can be construed as claims that *everything* is thus-and-so are rendered on the pattern

$(\forall x)(x$ is thus-and-so$)$

(or '$(\forall y)(y$ is thus-and-so$)$', or '$(\forall z)(z$ is thus-and-so$)$', etc., since which term variable is chosen does not matter in this case). As we have seen, the part 'x is thus-and-so' may itself be either atomic or compound. (In the examples to follow, we indicate what the predicate letters abbreviate only when called for.)

Everything is lovely	– $(\forall x)Lx$
Everything is self-identical	– $(\forall x)Ixx$ (where 'Ixy' would be read 'x is identical with y')
Peter hates everything	– $(\forall x)Hpx$
Nothing is going right	– $(\forall x)\sim Gx$
Peter knows nothing about New York City (or: Peter doesn't know anything about New York City)	– $(\forall x)\sim Kpxn$ (where '$Kxyz$' would be read 'x knows y about z')
Everything is either material or spiritual	– $(\forall x)(Mx \lor Sx)$
Everything is a delusion caused by God	– $(\forall x)(Dx \,\&\, Cgx)$
Nothing is both round and square	– $(\forall x)\sim(Rx \,\&\, Sx)$
All and only material objects are subject to physical laws (or: A thing is subject to physical laws if and only if it is material)	– $(\forall x)(Px \equiv Mx)$
Peter saw everything but the cobras	– $(\forall x)(Spx \equiv \sim Cx)$

In several of these examples, the 'everything' would surely not be meant in the broadest sense possible, but would encompass just those things appropriate in the context (the things which make up the universe of discourse, or domain, on that occasion). For example, 'Peter saw everything but the cobras' would not commit a speaker to Peter's having seen the Eleusinian Mysteries and the square root of 2, but only—perhaps —everything at the zoo. In cases like these, some authors would require that the restriction be built into the translation itself:

> Take what you will, *if* it was at the zoo,
>   *then* Peter saw it if and only if it wasn't a cobra,

i.e.,

$$(\forall x)[Zx \supset (Spx \equiv \sim Cx)].$$

The same remarks would apply to earlier examples as well, such as

> Everything fell off the shelf,

which these authors would render as

> Take what you will, *if* it was on the shelf, *then* it fell off,

i.e.,

$$(\forall x)(Sx \supset Fx).$$

We do not require this, and usually take the statements at face value. But a statement explicitly saying that all things *of a certain sort* (such-

and-such) are of some other sort (so-and-so) as well *is* rendered on the pattern

$$(\forall x)\,(x \text{ is such-and-such} \supset x \text{ is so-and-so}).$$

To the *left* of '⊃' (i.e., in the "antecedent" 'x is such-and-such') is identified the sort of things about all of which the claim is made, and to the *right* (in the "consequent" 'x is so-and-so') what is said about all things of that sort. Of course the parts 'x is such-and-such' and 'x is so-and-so' may themselves be either atomic or compound.

All pacifists are Quakers	
Pacifists are (all) Quakers	
A pacifist is a Quaker	
To be a pacifist is to be a Quaker	
Every (any, each) pacifist is a Quaker	$- (\forall x)\,(Px \supset Qx)$
If anyone's (someone's) a pacifist, he's a Quaker	
Anyone who's a pacifist is a Quaker	
Only (None but) Quakers are pacifists	
Only pacifists are Quakers	$- (\forall x)\,(Qx \supset Px)$
Peter gets everything (anything) he wants	$- (\forall x)\,(Wpx \supset Gpx)$
God loves everybody	$- (\forall x)\,(Px \supset Lgx)\,(Px\text{: } x \text{ is a person})$
Peter's friends all love God	$- (\forall x)\,(Fxp \supset Lxg)$
No adults are trustworthy	$- (\forall x)\,(Ax \supset {\sim}Tx)$
No babies are unattractive	$- (\forall x)\,(Bx \supset {\sim}{\sim}Ax)$
Nothing which Peter saw was new	$- (\forall x)\,(Spx \supset {\sim}Nx)$
No capitalists like Marx	$- (\forall x)\,(Cx \supset {\sim}Lxm)$
Mama doesn't like anybody	$- (\forall x)\,(Px \supset {\sim}Lmx)$
No triangles are both equilateral and scalene	$- (\forall x)\,[Tx \supset {\sim}(Ex \,\&\, Sx)]$
Old doctors are all conservative	$- (\forall x)\,[(Dx \,\&\, Ox) \supset Cx]$
Doctors and lawyers are all conservative	$- (\forall x)\,[(Dx \lor Lx) \supset Cx]$
People are interesting if they're witty	$- (\forall x)\,[Px \supset (Wx \supset Ix)]$
People are interesting if and only if they're witty	$- (\forall x)\,[Px \supset (Ix \equiv Wx)]$
No intelligent men are lonely if they're young and healthy	$- (\forall x)\,[(Mx \,\&\, Ix) \supset ([Yx \,\&\, Hx] \supset {\sim}Lx)]$

Incidentally, when the universal force of a statement is signaled by a word like 'always' or 'everywhere', the statement may be construed as a claim about all times or places:

God is everywhere	$- (\forall x)(Px \supset Agx)$ (Px: x is a place; Axy: x is at (place) y)
Jack isn't getting anywhere	$- (\forall x)(Px \supset {\sim}Gjx)$ (Gxy: x is getting to y)
Everywhere that Mary went, her lamb [Lambert] was sure to go	$- (\forall x)[(Px \,\&\, Wmx) \supset Wlx]$
Charles is always happy	$- (\forall x)(Tx \supset Hcx)$ (Tx: x is a time; Hxy: x is happy at (time) y)
Alice drools whenever she eats	$- (\forall x)[(Tx \,\&\, Eax) \supset Dax]$ (Exy: x eats at y; Dxy: x drools at y)
Charles is never happy unless Barbara is	$- (\forall x)[(Tx \,\&\, {\sim}Hbx) \supset {\sim}Hcx]$.

Existential statements. Statements which can be construed as claims that *something* (at least one thing) is thus-and-so are rendered on the pattern

$$(\exists x)\,(x \text{ is thus-and-so})$$

(or '$(\exists y)(y$ is thus-and-so)', etc.). Again, the part 'x is thus-and-so' may itself be either atomic or compound. In particular, a claim to the effect that something *of a certain sort* (such-and-such) is of some other sort (so-and-so) as well is rendered

$$(\exists x)\,(x \text{ is such-and-such} \,\&\, x \text{ is so-and-so}),$$

where again the parts 'x is such-and-such' and 'x is so-and-so' may be either atomic or compound.

Something is a centaur There are centaurs There is a centaur Centaurs exist	$- (\exists x)Cx$
Peter doesn't understand something (or: There is something Peter doesn't understand)	$- (\exists x){\sim}Upx$
Some teachers are foolish (or: There are foolish teachers)	$- (\exists x)(Tx \,\&\, Fx)$
Some teachers aren't foolish	$- (\exists x)(Tx \,\&\, {\sim}Fx)$
Some teachers who are young are foolish	$- (\exists x)[(Tx \,\&\, Yx) \,\&\, Fx]$

Some of Mary's friends don't understand her	$- (\exists x)\,(\mathrm{F}xm\ \&\ {\sim}\mathrm{U}xm)$
Some of Mary's male friends don't understand themselves	$- (\exists x)\,[(\mathrm{F}xm\ \&\ \mathrm{M}x)\ \&\ {\sim}\mathrm{U}xx]$
Some tigers are mean if they're hungry	$- (\exists x)\,[\mathrm{T}x\ \&\ (\mathrm{H}x \supset \mathrm{M}x)]$
There are old tigers that are mean if and only if they're hungry	$- (\exists x)\,[(\mathrm{T}x\ \&\ \mathrm{O}x)\ \&\ (\mathrm{M}x \equiv \mathrm{H}x)]$
Some young people are neither rich nor unhappy	$- (\exists x)\,[(\mathrm{P}x\ \&\ \mathrm{Y}x)\ \&\ {\sim}(\mathrm{R}x \lor {\sim}\mathrm{H}x)]$
There are people who have never met Spiro, but who love and admire him anyway	$- (\exists x)\,[(\mathrm{P}x\ \&\ {\sim}\mathrm{M}xs)\ \&\ (\mathrm{L}xs\ \&\ \mathrm{A}xs)]$
Ulysses feared something he saw	$- (\exists x)\,(\mathrm{S}ux\ \&\ \mathrm{F}ux).$
Tom is sometimes confused	$- (\exists x)\,(\mathrm{T}x\ \&\ \mathrm{C}tx)$ ($\mathrm{T}x$: x is a time; $\mathrm{C}xy$: x is confused at y)
Jack sometimes snores when he's asleep	$- (\exists x)\,[(\mathrm{T}x\ \&\ \mathrm{A}jx)\ \&\ \mathrm{S}jx]$
Bob is lost somewhere in Antarctica	$- (\exists x)\,[(\mathrm{P}x\ \&\ \mathrm{I}xa)\ \&\ \mathrm{L}bx]$ ($\mathrm{P}x$: x is a place; $\mathrm{I}xy$: x is in y; $\mathrm{L}xy$: x is lost at y)

Multiple quantification. As already remarked, what is said of every x or of some x, namely

$$x \text{ is thus-and-so,}$$

may itself be compound. It may be truth-functionally compound, as in the cases above. It may be quantificationally compound, or involve quantifications:

Everything attracts everything	$- (\forall x)\,(\forall y)\mathrm{A}xy$
Something attracts something	$- (\exists x)\,(\exists y)\mathrm{A}xy$
Something attracts everything	$- (\exists x)\,(\forall y)\mathrm{A}xy$
Everything attracts something (or other)	$- (\forall x)\,(\exists y)\mathrm{A}xy$
Something is attracted by everything	$- (\exists x)\,(\forall y)\mathrm{A}yx$
Everything is attracted by something (or other)	$- (\forall x)\,(\exists y)\mathrm{A}yx$
If one thing weighs less than another, then that other doesn't weigh less than the first	$- (\forall x)\,(\forall y)\,(\mathrm{W}xy \supset {\sim}\mathrm{W}yx)$
If a thing weighs less than another and that other weighs less than a third, then the first weighs less than the third	$- (\forall x)\,(\forall y)\,(\forall z)\,[(\mathrm{W}xy\ \&\ \mathrm{W}yz) \supset \mathrm{W}xz].$

In these last examples, the quantifiers have all been initially placed, and translation was a rather straightforward matter. In more complicated cases, however, it may be best to proceed by stages, capturing first the overall import of the statement in a coarse rendition, and then refining that by translating its parts coarsely, and then theirs, and so on, working inward until the whole statement is cast in logical notation. Consider, for example, the Pauline doctrine (Titus 1:12)

> The Cretians are alway liars.

Translating coarsely, we first get

> $(\forall x)$ (x is a Cretian $\supset x$ is alway a liar).

The part

> x is alway a liar

in turn is rendered

> $(\forall y)$ (y is a time $\supset x$ is a liar at y).

Abbreviating the predicates, then, the whole becomes

> $(\forall x) [Cx \supset (\forall y) (Ty \supset Lxy)]$.

Or consider the statement

> Somebody can beat everyone on A's team.

As a first step, we render this as

> $(\exists x)$ (x is a person & x can beat everyone on A's team).

The part

> x can beat everyone on A's team,

construed as about every person on A's team, becomes

> $(\forall y) [(y$ is a person & y is on A's team) $\supset x$ can beat $y]$.

Reassembling, and abbreviating, we get

> $(\exists x) (Px \& (\forall y) [(Py \& Ay) \supset Bxy])$.

Likewise, we would first render

> There is somebody on A's team whom everybody on C's team can beat

as

> $(\exists x) [(x$ is a person & x is on A's team) & everybody on C's team can beat $x]$.

In turn,

> everybody on C's team can beat x

becomes

$(\forall y) [(y$ is a person $\& y$ is on C's team$) \supset y$ can beat $x]$.

In abbreviated form, then, our final translation runs

$(\exists x) [(Px \& Ax) \& (\forall y) ([Py \& Cy] \supset Byx)]$.

More deceptive, perhaps, is a statement like

If something's (anything's) a large mastiff, then it should be avoided if all dogs are vicious.

Despite the 'something', this is clearly a claim about *all* large mastiffs:

$(\forall x) (x$ is a large mastiff $\supset$ if all dogs are vicious then x should be avoided$)$.

The clause

x is a large mastiff

easily goes into

$Mx \& Lx$;

while

if all dogs are vicious *then* x is to be avoided

becomes

$(\forall y) (Dy \supset Vy) \supset Ax$.

Putting everything in its proper place, we get

$(\forall x) [(Mx \& Lx) \supset ((\forall y) (Dy \supset Vy) \supset Ax)]$.

(Because of our later account of statementhood, we must use a term variable other than 'x' when translating the clause 'all dogs are vicious' in this context.)

In the next two examples, we expedite things somewhat by putting the ordinary English into "official" prose which goes more readily into symbols. The statement

There's always a war somewhere

surely means

For every time there is some place where some war is going on.

Using '$Gxyz$' for 'x is going on at (time) y and (place) z', we can skip the intermediate stages of translation and go directly to the symbolization:

$(\forall x) (Tx \supset (\exists y) [Py \& (\exists z) (Wz \& Gzxy)])$.

And again, to say

> There's never a war everywhere

is surely to say

> For every time there is some place where no war is going on,

or, in symbols,

$$(\forall x)(Tx \supset (\exists y)[Py \ \& \sim(\exists z)(Wz \ \& \ Gzxy)]).$$

Translation of the familiar

> Everybody loves a lover

turns out to be quite elaborate. Conceived as a claim about all people, saying that each one loves every person who is a lover, this would first be rendered

$$(\forall x)(Px \supset x \text{ loves every person who is a lover}).$$

The clause

> x loves every person who is a lover

would in turn be construed as saying of each person who is a lover that x loves him:

$$(\forall y)[(Py \ \& \ y \text{ is a lover}) \supset Lxy].$$

Finally,

> y is a lover

obviously means

> y loves somebody,

which would be rendered

$$(\exists z)(Pz \ \& \ Lyz).$$

Putting all the pieces back together, we get

$$(\forall x)[Px \supset (\forall y)([Py \ \& \ (\exists z)(Pz \ \& \ Lyz)] \supset Lxy)].$$

Our last example of a mixed quantification will prove to be considerably more difficult:

> Somebody gives all his gifts to a single person.

Instead of attacking this directly, we begin with some simpler statements that lead up to it.

(1)   Consider first

> Alan gives all his gifts to Bob,

i.e.,

> If Alan gives anything to anybody, he gives it to Bob.

This could be rendered

> $(\forall x)$ (Alan gives x to somebody $\supset$ Alan gives x to Bob),

or, in symbols,

> $(\forall x)[(\exists y)(Py \,\&\, Gaxy) \supset Gaxb]$.

(2)   Consider then

> Alan gives all his gifts to a single person.

This says simply that there is a person like Bob in (1). Without further ado, we can render it as

> $(\exists z)(Pz \,\&\, (\forall x)[(\exists y)(Py \,\&\, Gaxy) \supset Gaxz])$.[8]

(3)   Consider, at last, the original statement

> Somebody gives all his gifts to a single person.

This, in turn, says simply that there is some person like Alan in (2). So it can straightway be translated

> $(\exists x')[Px' \,\&\, (\exists z)(Pz \,\&\, (\forall x)[(\exists y)(Py \,\&\, Gx'xy) \supset Gx'xz])]$.

Truth-functional compounds of quantifications. We shall often be interested in the logical features of statements which, while obviously involving quantifiers, are not themselves quantifications but truth-functional compounds thereof (we called attention to one such statement on p. 121). Furthermore, some statements which *can* be translated as quantifications are tantamount to—and hence can be faithfully rendered as—truth-functional compounds of quantifications.

To illustrate this latter point, we (correctly) translate as truth-functional compounds of quantifications some statements which have already been (equally correctly) translated as quantifications:

Peter doesn't know anything about New York City	$- \sim(\exists x)Kpxn$
Charles is never happy unless Barbara is	$- \sim(\exists x)[(Tx \,\&\, \sim Hbx) \,\&\, Hcx]$
There's never a war everywhere	$- \sim(\exists x)(Tx \,\&\, (\forall y)[Py \supset (\exists z)(Wz \,\&\, Gzxy)])$

---

[8] Our translation merely says that there is at least one person like Bob in (1). The original went farther, adding that there is at most one such person. But obviously one cannot give all of one's gifts to more than one person, so we ignore the addition (concerning which, see Exercise E3.1.5).

There is something Peter doesn't
understand (i.e., he doesn't
understand everything) $- \sim(\forall x)\mathrm{U}px$

Some teachers aren't foolish
(i.e., not all teachers are
foolish) $- \sim(\forall x)(\mathrm{T}x \supset \mathrm{F}x)$

Doctors and lawyers are all
conservative $- (\forall x)(\mathrm{D}x \supset \mathrm{C}x)\ \&\ (\forall x)(\mathrm{L}x \supset \mathrm{C}x)$

If something's a large mastiff,
then it should be avoided if
all dogs are vicious $- (\forall x)(\mathrm{D}x \supset \mathrm{V}x) \supset$
$(\forall x)[(\mathrm{M}x\ \&\ \mathrm{L}x) \supset \mathrm{A}x].$

On p. 132 we shall give another striking example of a pair of statements
—one a quantification and the other a truth-functional compound—
which have the same force.

Sometimes the English gives a clue to the fact that a statement should
be rendered not as a quantification but as a truth-functional compound
of quantifications:

Some things are red *and* some
flat $- (\exists x)\mathrm{R}x\ \&\ (\exists x)\mathrm{F}x$

Some things are red *and* some
aren't $- (\exists x)\mathrm{R}x\ \&\ (\exists x)\sim\mathrm{R}x$

If all the Trustees are nominated, *then* some of them will
be re-elected $- (\forall x)(\mathrm{T}x \supset \mathrm{N}x) \supset (\exists x)(\mathrm{T}x\ \&\ \mathrm{R}x)$

All crocodiles are dangerous
if any are $- (\exists x)(\mathrm{C}x\ \&\ \mathrm{D}x) \supset (\forall x)(\mathrm{C}x \supset \mathrm{D}x)$

None of Peter's friends believe
him, *or else* some of them are
gullible $- (\forall x)(\mathrm{F}xp \supset \sim\mathrm{B}xp)\ \vee$
$(\exists x)(\mathrm{F}xp\ \&\ \mathrm{G}x).$

But these clues may be misleading. The statement

If something is rare, then it's valuable

is *not* a conditional with an existential antecedent, but a universal statement:

$(\forall x)(\mathrm{R}x \supset \mathrm{V}x).$

Or these clues may be absent altogether. The statement

There are females at Harvard and Yale

is *not* to be rendered as

$(\exists x)[\mathrm{F}x\ \&\ (\mathrm{H}x\ \&\ \mathrm{Y}x)],$

but rather as

$$(\exists x)\,(Fx\ \&\ Hx)\ \&\ (\exists x)\,(Fx\ \&\ Yx)$$

(with 'Fx' for 'x is a female', 'Hx' for 'x is at Harvard', and 'Yx' for 'x is at Yale').

One must therefore attend closely to the meaning of a statement whose translation will involve quantifiers, and make it either a quantification or a truth-functional compound as that meaning dictates.

Some general remarks on translation. There can be no hard and fast rules for translation into symbols. To translate a statement from ordinary English is to produce a symbolic rendition which has the same or very nearly the same force—i.e., the same truth-conditions—as the original. So to translate a statement from the vernacular is to produce one in logical notation which would be true and would be false under the same or very nearly the same conditions as would the original. The truth-conditions of statements in English are familiar to fluent speakers of the language (since being familiar with them is a large part of what fluency is). The truth-conditions of quantifications have already been introduced on pp. 116–17 and 119–20, and will be discussed later.

As already noted, a routine reliance on the grammatical form of statements may sometimes lead to error. We cannot treat all the potentially dangerous cases, but we can cover enough of them to put the reader on his guard. For example, while

Scouts are helpful

and

A Scout is helpful

would ordinarily mean

$$(\forall x)\,(Sx \supset Hx)$$

(with 'Hx' abbreviating 'x is helpful'), the apparently similar statements

Scouts are helping me

and

A Scout is helping me

would ordinarily mean

$$(\exists x)\,(Sx\ \&\ Hx)$$

(with 'Hx' here abbreviating 'x is helping me').

Again, while the two statements

Peter likes everybody he meets

and

Peter likes anybody he meets

would both be translated

$$(\forall x)\,[(Px\ \&\ Mpx) \supset Lpx],$$

the similar statements

Peter doesn't like everybody he meets

and

Peter doesn't like anybody he meets

would become, respectively,

$$\sim(\forall x)\,[(Px\ \&\ Mpx) \supset Lpx],$$

and

$$\sim(\exists x)\,[(Px\ \&\ Mpx)\ \&\ Lpx].$$

Thus, 'any' in some contexts has the force of 'every', and in others the force of 'some'. This is also apparent from a pair of statements like

If there are any abominable snowmen, I'll eat my hat

and

If there are any abominable snowmen, I'll find them.

The first could properly be translated

$$(\exists x)Sx \supset Eih,$$

but the second would have to be translated

$$(\forall x)\,(Sx \supset Fix).$$

(The first could also be rendered as '$(\forall x)(Sx \supset Eih)$', but *not* as '$(\forall x)Sx \supset Eih$'—'If everything is an abominable snowman, I'll eat my hat'.)

And there may be a temptation to use '&' where '$\supset$' would be appropriate, and *vice versa*. A statement like

All new things are exciting

or

Everything which is new is exciting

or

Anything (A thing) is exciting if it is new

is to be rendered as

$$(\forall x)(Nx \supset Ex),$$

and *not* as (the stronger)

$$(\forall x)(Nx \ \& \ Ex).$$

There are a number of cases where '&' is appropriate—as when translating statements like 'Everything is new and exciting', or 'Everything is a delusion caused by God': '$(\forall x)(Dx \ \& \ Cgx)$'. But it is *not* appropriate for the even more common statements to the effect that

Everything which is such-and-such is so-and-so.

On the other hand, a statement like

Some expensive things are ugly

or

Some things which are expensive are also ugly

or

Some things are both expensive and ugly,

is to be rendered as

$$(\exists x)(Ex \ \& \ Ux),$$

and *not* as (the weaker)

$$(\exists x)(Ex \supset Ux).$$

There are (rare) occasions on which '$\supset$' is appropriate. 'There is something which will hurt Mary's feelings *if* she hears about it' is to be symbolized '$(\exists x)(Hmx \supset Fxm)$'—where '$Hxy$' abbreviates '$x$ hears about y', and 'Fxy' abbreviates 'x will hurt y's feelings'. But it is *not* appropriate for the immensely more common statements to the effect that

Something which is such-and-such is so-and-so.

Punctuation. One must be scrupulously careful about the use of parentheses to mark off the "scope" of logical operators generally, and of quantifiers in particular. In Chapter 1 we noted the difference between, say,

~Da ∨ Ga   – Either Archie's not really dead, or he's come back as a ghost

and

~(Da ∨ Ga)   – Archie's neither dead nor a ghost.

Like the tilde '~', quantifiers govern as little as the punctuation allows. So

$(\forall x)Bx \supset Hb$ – If *everything* gets broken at the party, then Bobby will get hell

is a conditional statement with a universal antecedent, whereas

$(\forall x)(Bx \supset Hb)$ – If *anything* gets broken at the party, then Bobby will get hell

is a universal quantification with the quantifier '$(\forall x)$' governing a "conditional." Furthermore, while

$(\forall x)(Bx \supset Rx)$ – If anything gets broken, it will have to be replaced

is a statement, the expression

$(\forall x)Bx \supset Rx$ – If everything gets broken, x will have to be replaced

is *not*.

In general, then, make sure that the parentheses in translations are so placed that what you have produced is a statement, and a statement that says what you want to say. (See Exercises E2.1.2–3.)

Instances, Statements, and Subformulas

We next introduce or formally define a number of notions that will be used frequently in the rest of the text and for this reason must be clearly understood. The reader will notice our use of the capital letter 'X' to refer to any term variable (be it 'x', or 'y', or 'z', etc.), and of the capital letter 'T' to refer to any term (be it 'a_1', or 'a_2', or 'a_3', etc.).[9] In the next few pages we use 'A' and 'B' to refer indiscriminately to *any* expression; however, after specifying what we understand by a statement, we shall use them to refer only to statements, and to expressions (such as 'x fell off the shelf', 'x is a teacher & x is dull', and '$(\forall x)(y$ caused $x)$') which show term variables at places where statements would show terms.[10]

By an **instance** of an expression of the sort $(\forall X)A$ or of the sort $(\exists X)A$ we shall understand any result $A(T/X)$ of substituting some term T for

---

[9] On some occasions we shall also use 'Y' to refer to any term variable, and 'T'' to refer to any term.

[10] Expressions of that sort, which obviously become statements when prefaced with suitable quantifiers, are called **quasi-statements,** or **open statements.** On some occasions we shall also use 'C' and 'D' to refer to statements and "quasi-statements".

every occurrence of the term variable X in A.[11] Roughly, then, an instance $A(T/X)$ of a universal statement $(\forall X)A$ says of the particular thing named by the term T what $(\forall X)A$ says of everything; and an instance $A(T/X)$ of an existential statement $(\exists X)A$ says of that particular thing what $(\exists X)A$ says of something.

As already noted, the instances of

$$(\forall x)(x \text{ fell off the shelf})$$

are the *infinitely many* results of successively substituting 'a$_1$', 'a$_2$', 'a$_3$', etc. for the term variable 'x' in 'x fell off the shelf':[12]

a$_1$ fell off the shelf —i.e., $(x$ fell off the shelf$)(a_1/x)$,
a$_2$ fell off the shelf —i.e., $(x$ fell off the shelf$)(a_2/x)$,
a$_3$ fell off the shelf —i.e., $(x$ fell off the shelf$)(a_3/x)$,

etc.;

and those of

$$(\exists x)(x \text{ is a teacher } \& \ x \text{ is dull})$$

are

a$_1$ is a teacher & a$_1$ is dull
a$_2$ is a teacher & a$_2$ is dull
a$_3$ is a teacher & a$_3$ is dull

etc.

The instances of

$$(\exists y)(\forall x)(y \text{ caused } x)$$

are

$(\forall x)(a_1 \text{ caused } x)$
$(\forall x)(a_2 \text{ caused } x)$
$(\forall x)(a_3 \text{ caused } x)$

etc.;

---

[11] '$A(T/X)$' may be read 'A with T in place of X'. When X does not occur in A, $A(T/X)$ is of course the same as A, this for any term T. We shall refer to the result of putting T for X in a negation $\sim A$ by means of '$(\sim A)(T/X)$', to the result of putting T for X in a conditional $A \supset B$ by means of '$(A \supset B)(T/X)$', and so on. $(\sim A)(T/X)$ is easily seen to be the same as $\sim A(T/X)$, the negation of the result of putting T for X in A; $(A \supset B)(T/X)$ is easily seen to be the same as $A(T/X) \supset B(T/X)$, the conditional with $A(T/X)$ as antecedent and $B(T/X)$ as consequent; and so on.

[12] There are infinitely many terms; so, whenever X occurs in A, $(\forall X)A$ and $(\exists X)A$ both have infinitely many instances. When we put T for X in A, we say that we *instantiate* $(\forall X)A$ or $(\exists X)A$ *by means of T*.

and those of

$$(\forall x)[x \text{ is a person} \supset (\exists y)(y \text{ is a person \& } x \text{ loves } y)]$$

are

a₁ is a person $\supset$ ($\exists y$)(y is a person & a₁ loves y)
a₂ is a person $\supset$ ($\exists y$)(y is a person & a₂ loves y)
a₃ is a person $\supset$ ($\exists y$)(y is a person & a₃ loves y)
etc.

And so on.

Since '$(\forall x)(a_1 \text{ caused } x)$', '$(\forall x)(a_2 \text{ caused } x)$', '$(\forall x)(a_3 \text{ caused } x)$', and so on, are themselves quantifications, they each have their own instances. '$(\forall x)(a_1 \text{ caused } x)$' and '$(\forall x)(a_2 \text{ caused } x)$', for example, have the following instances:

a₁ caused a₁   a₂ caused a₁
a₁ caused a₂   a₂ caused a₂
a₁ caused a₃   a₂ caused a₃
etc.   etc.

But these of course do *not* count as instances of the original statement '$(\exists y)(\forall x)(y \text{ caused } x)$'.[13]

As suggested on p. 116 and p. 119, the truth-value of a quantification depends upon the truth-values of its instances. The notion we just defined will thus prove crucial when we review the conditions under which statements are true or are false. And we use it when specifying what counts as a **statement.**

First, we certify as a statement—indeed, as an **atomic statement**—any expression of the sort

$$P(T_1, T_2, \dots, T_m),$$

where P is an abbreviation for an m-place predicate ($m \geq 1$), and T_1, T_2, ..., and T_m are m (not necessarily distinct) terms. (In practice we have omitted, and shall keep omitting, the parentheses and commas shown here, thus writing 'Fa₁' for 'F(a₁)', 'Ga₂a₅' for 'G(a₂,a₅)', and so on.) Next, we certify as a statement any expression of the sort $\sim A$, where A is a statement, or of the four sorts $(A \supset B)$, $(A \& B)$, $(A \lor B)$, and $(A \equiv B)$, where A and B are statements. And, finally, we certify as a statement any expression of either of the sorts $(\forall X)A$ and $(\exists X)A$, where for some term T the instance $A(T/X)$ of $(\forall X)A$ or $(\exists X)A$ is a statement. (We shall call our earlier connectives and the two quantifier letters '$\forall$' and '$\exists$' **logical opera-**

---

[13] They will be included, though, among what we later call the *subformulas* of '$(\exists y)(\forall x)$ (y caused x)'.

tors. Thus, the **main logical operator** of a universal quantification $(\forall X)A$ is the '$\forall$' shown, and that of an existential quantification $(\exists X)A$ is the '$\exists$' shown.)

It is readily verified that if $A(T/X)$ counts as a statement for any one term T, it does so for every term T. Hence, in effect, $(\forall X)A$ and $(\exists X)A$ count as statements if all their instances do[14] (just as a truth-functional compound counts as a statement if its immediate components do).

Proof that under the definition above

$$(\exists x)[x \text{ is a person } \& (\forall y)(y \text{ is a person } \supset x \text{ loves } y)], \tag{1}$$

for example, is a statement, could run as follows. (1) is a statement if any one of its instances, say,

$$a_1 \text{ is a person } \& (\forall y)(y \text{ is a person } \supset a_1 \text{ loves } y)$$

is a statement, which it is if

$$a_1 \text{ is a person}$$

and

$$(\forall y)(y \text{ is a person } \supset a_1 \text{ loves } y)$$

are statements. The former is an atomic statement, and hence a statement. As for the latter, it is a statement if any one of its instances, say,

$$a_2 \text{ is a person } \supset a_1 \text{ loves } a_2$$

is a statement, which it is if both

$$a_2 \text{ is a person}$$

and

$$a_1 \text{ loves } a_2$$

are statements. But, like 'a_1 is a person', 'a_2 is a person' and 'a_1 loves a_2' are atomic statements, and hence statements. So (1) is a statement.

Three points are to be noted before we leave the subject of statements.

(1) Even when X does not occur in A, $(\forall X)A$ and $(\exists X)A$ still count as statements if, for any term T, $A(T/X)$—i.e., A—is a statement. $(\forall X)A$ and $(\exists X)A$ are then known as **vacuous quantifications,** and unlike other quantifications each has *just one* instance: A. Cases in point are '$(\forall x)Fa$' and '$(\exists y)(\forall x)(Fx \& Gx)$'. The former has '$Fa$' as its one instance, the latter '$(\forall x)(Fx \& Gx)$'.

---

[14] The converse also holds true, the instances of $(\forall X)A$ and $(\exists X)A$ counting as statements if $(\forall X)A$ and $(\exists X)A$ do.

(2) When $(\forall X)$ or $(\exists X)$ already occurs in A, then neither $(\forall X)A$ nor $(\exists X)A$ counts as a statement, since $A(T/X)$ is not a statement for any term T. Take '$Fx \equiv (\forall x)Gx$'. None of '$Fa_1 \equiv (\forall a_1)Ga_1$', '$Fa_2 \equiv (\forall a_2)Ga_2$', etc., counts as a statement; so neither does '$(\forall x)[Fx \equiv (\forall x)Gx]$'.[15] (3) In Chapter 3 we shall have occasion to speak of the **length** of a statement. $P_1, P_2, \ldots,$ and P_j being the various predicates that occur in a statement A, the length of A is simply the number of times $P_1, P_2, \ldots,$ and P_j occur in A *plus* the number of times '$\sim$', '$\supset$', '&', '$\lor$', '$\equiv$', '$\forall$', and '$\exists$' do. For example, the length of 'a_1 is lovely' and of 'a_1 caused a_2' is 1; the length of '$(\forall x) \sim (x$ is going right)' is 3; and the length of '$(\forall x)[x$ is a person $\supset (\forall y)(y$ is a person $\supset x$ loves $y)]$' is 7. Note in the last case that the predicate 'is a person' occurs twice, the predicate 'loves' once, the connective '$\supset$' twice, and the quantifier letter '$\forall$' twice.

Finally, we introduce the notion of a **subformula**. The instances of a quantification play pretty much the same roles as the immediate components of a truth-functional compound do: not only does the truth-value of a quantification depend upon those of its instances, but—as we shall soon see—the quantification itself can be thought of as compounded from some of its instances. We could, of course, number the instances of a quantification among its components; however, as they do not actually appear in the quantification, this might prove misleading. So we rather talk of them as subformulas of the quantification, and for the sake of uniformity *rename all the statements which previously counted as components of a statement A subformulas of A as well*. Thus, any statement will count as a subformula of itself. Also, A will count as a subformula of a negation $\sim A$; A and B will count as subformulas of a conditional $A \supset B$, a conjunction $A \& B$, a disjunction $A \lor B$, and a biconditional $A \equiv B$; and— for any term T whatever—$A(T/X)$ will count as a subformula of a universal quantification $(\forall X)A$ and an existential quantification $(\exists X)A$. Finally, A will count as a subformula of B if A is a subformula of some subformula of B. (Note that under this account of things an instance $A(T/X)$ of $(\forall X)A$ and $(\exists X)A$ is an "immediate" subformula of $(\forall X)A$ and $(\exists X)A$, just as A is an "immediate" subformula of $\sim A$.)[16] And, of course,

---

[15] Note, by the way, that although '$(\forall x)[Fx \equiv (\forall x)Gx]$' does not count as a statement. '$(\forall x)Fx \equiv (\forall x)Gx$' does: the two occurrences of $(\forall x)$ here do not overlap. And all of '$(\forall y)[Fy \equiv (\forall x)Gx]$', '$(\forall z)[Fz \equiv (\forall x)Gx]$', etc., where the quantifiers overlap but contain different variables, also count as statements.

By not allowing two occurrences of the same quantifier to overlap, we eschew the irksome distinction—which plagues many other texts—between *bound* and *free* variables.

[16] Note also that the subformulas of $\sim A$ are $\sim A$ plus the subformulas of A; those of $A \supset B$, for example, are $A \supset B$, plus the subformulas of A, plus the subformulas of B; and those of $(\forall X)A$, for example, are $(\forall X)A$ plus the subformulas of each and every instance of $(\forall X)A$.

a statement will count as an **atomic subformula** of another if it is a subformula of that other and is atomic. This last notion will prove particularly important later, when truth-values are assigned to the atomic subformulas of statements, and matters like logical truth, consistency, entailment, and so on, are defined in terms of truth-value assignments to those atomic subformulas.

For illustration's sake, consider the statement

$$(\forall x)[Fx \supset \sim(\exists y)(Gyx \ \& \ Ha_1)]. \tag{2}$$

(2) is—for technical reasons—a subformula of itself, and its immediate subformulas (instances) are

$$Fa_1 \supset \sim(\exists y)(Gya_1 \ \& \ Ha_1)$$
$$Fa_2 \supset \sim(\exists y)(Gya_2 \ \& \ Ha_1)$$
$$Fa_3 \supset \sim(\exists y)(Gya_3 \ \& \ Ha_1)$$
etc.

These are all conditional statements, and their immediate subformulas (antecedents and consequents)

Fa_1	$\sim(\exists y)(Gya_1 \ \& \ Ha_1)$
Fa_2	$\sim(\exists y)(Gya_2 \ \& \ Ha_1)$
Fa_3	$\sim(\exists y)(Gya_3 \ \& \ Ha_1)$
etc.	etc.,

being subformulas of subformulas of (2), are themselves subformulas of (2)—and 'Fa_1', 'Fa_2', 'Fa_3', and so on, are atomic subformulas of (2). The immediate subformulas

$$(\exists y)(Gya_1 \ \& \ Ha_1)$$
$$(\exists y)(Gya_2 \ \& \ Ha_1)$$
$$(\exists y)(Gya_3 \ \& \ Ha_1)$$
etc.,

of the negations '$\sim(\exists y)(Gya_1 \ \& \ Ha_1)$', '$\sim(\exists y)(Gya_2 \ \& \ Ha_1)$', '$\sim(\exists y)(Gya_3 \ \& \ Ha_1)$', and so on, are themselves subformulas of (2), as are their immediate subformulas (instances)

$Ga_1a_1 \ \& \ Ha_1$	$Ga_1a_2 \ \& \ Ha_1$	$Ga_1a_3 \ \& \ Ha_1$	·	·	·
$Ga_2a_1 \ \& \ Ha_1$	$Ga_2a_2 \ \& \ Ha_1$	$Ga_2a_3 \ \& \ Ha_1$	·	·	·
$Ga_3a_1 \ \& \ Ha_1$	$Ga_3a_2 \ \& \ Ha_1$	$Ga_3a_3 \ \& \ Ha_1$	·	·	·
·	·	·	·	·	·
·	·	·	·	·	·
·	·	·	·	·	·

And the immediate subformulas (conjuncts) of these are subformulas—indeed, the remaining atomic subformulas—of (2). These, then, are all the atomic subformulas of (2):

Ha_1	Fa_1	Ga_1a_1	Ga_1a_2	Ga_1a_3	$\cdot$ $\cdot$ $\cdot$
	Fa_2	Ga_2a_1	Ga_2a_2	Ga_2a_3	$\cdot$ $\cdot$ $\cdot$
	Fa_3	Ga_3a_1	Ga_3a_2	Ga_3a_3	$\cdot$ $\cdot$ $\cdot$
	$\vdots$	$\vdots$	$\vdots$	$\vdots$	$\vdots$ $\vdots$ $\vdots$

Note that, and why, 'Ha_2', 'Ha_3', and so on, do not turn up among the atomic subformulas of (2).[17]

Fortunately, there is an easier way to track down the atomic subformulas of a statement A. Consider each expression in A consisting only of a predicate and its terms or term variables (like 'Fx', 'Gyx', and 'Ha_1' in (2)). If that expression shows no variable (as 'Ha_1' shows none), then it is an atomic subformula of A. If it does show variables (as 'Fx' and 'Gyx' do), then any result of putting terms for its term variables (the same term for each occurrence of a given variable) is also an atomic subformula of A.[18]

We spoke in the Introduction of statements which—whether or not they appear *verbatim* in a statement—partake in its composition. These, of course, are the subformulas of the statement. And, as we suggested then and will soon document, to track them down is to track down the ways in which the statement may be true or may be false. (See Exercises E2.1.5-7, 9.)

Quantification as a Mode of Statement Composition

Given what we called in Chapter 1 the immediate component A of a negation $\sim A$, we can manufacture $\sim A$ by prefacing A with a tilde. For this reason, negation is said to be a *mode of statement composition,* and the statements it delivers are considered compound ones. Similarly, given nearly any instance $A(T/X)$ of a universal quantification $(\forall X)A$ or an existential one $(\exists X)A$, we can manufacture $(\forall X)A$ or $(\exists X)A$. Two operations are required: (i) substituting X for every occurrence of T in $A(T/X)$, and (ii) prefacing the result with whichever one of $(\forall X)$ and $(\exists X)$ is desired. So we may likewise think of "universalization" and "existentializa-

---

[17] It follows from our definition of a statement, and that of a subformula, that the subformulas of a statement are statements themselves. So 'Fx' and 'Gyx' are *not* subformulas of (2).

[18] If the expression shows both terms and term variables, then terms should be put only for the *variables*. Thus, the atomic subformulas of '$(\forall x)\sim Fa_1x$' are just 'Fa_1a_1', 'Fa_1a_2', 'Fa_1a_3', and so on.

tion" as modes of statement composition, and treat the statements they deliver as compound statements.[19]

To illustrate matters, take a universal quantification which contains no term at all, say,

$$(\forall x)\,(x \text{ is a violet} \supset x \text{ is blue}).$$

We can assemble it from any one of its instances

$(a_1 \text{ is a violet} \supset a_1 \text{ is blue})$

$(a_2 \text{ is a violet} \supset a_2 \text{ is blue})$

$(a_3 \text{ is a violet} \supset a_3 \text{ is blue})$

etc.,

by putting 'x' for 'a_1' in the first instance, for 'a_2' in the second, for 'a_3' in the third, and so on, and prefacing the result '$(x$ is a violet $\supset x$ is blue)' with '$(\forall x)$'.

Or take an existential quantification which contains no term either, say,

$$(\exists x)\,(x \text{ is a teacher \& } x \text{ is infallible}).$$

We can assemble it from any one of '$(a_1$ is a teacher & a_1 is infallible)', '$(a_2$ is a teacher & a_2 is infallible)', '$(a_3$ is a teacher & a_3 is infallible)', and so on, by substituting 'x' for the term there, and prefacing the result '$(x$ is a teacher & x is infallible)' with '$(\exists x)$'.

The same holds true of any quantification which contains no term at all: the quantification can be assembled—and hence compounded—from any one of its instances, and is thus a compound of a sort.

Now take a quantification which contains one term, say,

$$(\forall x)\,(x \text{ is on the Board} \supset x \text{ voted for } a_1). \tag{3}$$

The quantification cannot be compounded from the instance

$(a_1 \text{ is on the Board} \supset a_1 \text{ voted for } a_1),$

which rather yields

$$(\forall x)\,(x \text{ is on the Board} \supset x \text{ voted for } x).$$

But it can be compounded from all the other instances of (3). Substitute 'x' for every occurrence of 'a_2' in

$(a_2 \text{ is on the Board} \supset a_2 \text{ voted for } a_1),$

preface the result with '$(\forall x)$', and you get (3).

---

[19] Universalization and existentialization are in effect the inverse of "instantiation". Instantiation decomposes a quantification into its various instances; universalization and existentialization compound the quantification from what we shall later call its *generating instances*.

Or take a quantification which contains two terms, say,

$(\forall x)[(x$ is on the Board & x dislikes $a_1) \supset x$ voted for $a_2]$.   (4)

The quantification cannot be compounded from the instance

$[(a_1$ is on the Board & a_1 dislikes $a_1) \supset a_1$ voted for $a_2]$,

which rather yields

$(\forall x)[(x$ is on the Board & x dislikes $x) \supset x$ voted for $a_2]$;

nor can it be compounded from the instance

$[(a_2$ is on the Board & a_2 dislikes $a_1) \supset a_2$ voted for $a_2]$,

which rather yields

$(\forall x)[(x$ is on the Board & x dislikes $a_1) \supset x$ voted for $x]$.

But it can be compounded from all the other instances of (4). Substitute 'x' for every occurrence of 'a_3' in

$[(a_3$ is on the Board & a_3 dislikes $a_1) \supset a_3$ voted for $a_2]$,

preface the result with '$(\forall x)$', and you get (4). And so on.

To formalize matters, call an instance $A(T/X)$ of a quantification $(\forall X)A$ or $(\exists X)A$ a **generating instance** if the quantification is vacuous or the "instantiating" term T is foreign to it.[20] It is clear from examples (3) and (4) above that a quantification which contains terms can be compounded from every one of its generating instances, and hence from all but finitely many of its instances (all but one in the case of (3), all but two in the case of (4), and more generally all but n instances when the quantification contains n different terms). Since quantifications which contain no terms have generating instances only, we may conclude more generally that *any* quantification can be compounded from all its generating instances, and hence from all but finitely many of its instances.

The point is a useful one. It allows us to think of all statements that are not atomic as compounds of one sort or another: *truth-functional* ones in the case of $\sim A$, $A \supset B$, A & B, $A \lor B$, and $A \equiv B$, *quantificational* ones in the case of $(\forall X)A$ and $(\exists X)A$.[21]

---

[20] A term is of course said to be **foreign to a statement** if it does not occur in the statement. We shall analogously say that a term is **foreign to a set of statements** if it is foreign to every member of the set; and that a term is **foreign to a branch of a tree** if it is foreign to every statement on that branch of the tree.

[21] A compound was said in Chapter 1 to be truth-functional if its truth-value depends entirely upon those of its *components*. Since the truth-value of a quantification depends upon those of its instances, and instances are *not* components of the quantification, universal and existential quantifications are *not* truth-functional compounds. The demarcation line between

One last notion remains to be defined. By a **term variant** of a statement A we shall understand any result $A(T'/T)$ of substituting some term T' for every occurrence of T in A. So 'a$_2$ caused a$_3$' is a term variant of 'a$_1$ caused a$_3$', which itself is a term variant of 'a$_1$ caused a$_2$'. The first statement results from substituting 'a$_2$' for 'a$_1$' in the second, which itself results from substituting 'a$_3$' for 'a$_2$' in the third. ('a$_2$ caused a$_3$', however, is *not* a term variant of 'a$_1$ caused a$_2$'.)

In particular, then, a term variant of an instance $A(T/X)$ of a quanti-

TABLE VI

A. (1) The **terms** are 'a$_1$', 'a$_2$', 'a$_3$', *ad infinitum.*

(2) The **term variables** are 'x', 'y', 'z', 'x''', 'y''', 'z''', *ad infinitum.*

The order suggested here is the **alphabetic order** of the terms and of the term variables.

B. An **instance** of an expression of the sort $(\forall X)A$ or the sort $(\exists X)A$ is the result $A(T/X)$ of substituting some term T for every occurrence of the term variable X in A. When $(\forall X)A$ or $(\exists X)A$ is vacuous or T is foreign to $(\forall X)A$ or $(\exists X)A$, the instance is said to be a **generating** or **conservative instance.**

C. An **atomic statement** is an expression of the sort $P(T_1,T_2,\ldots,T_m)$, where P is an abbreviation for an m-place predicate ($m \geq 1$), and T_1, T_2, $\ldots$, and T_m are m (not necessarily distinct) terms.

D. (1) An atomic statement is a **statement.**

(2) If A is a statement, then so is $\sim A$.

(3) If A and B are (not necessarily distinct) statements, then $(A \supset B)$, $(A \,\&\, B)$, $(A \lor B)$, and $(A \equiv B)$ are also statements.

(4) If—for some term T—the instance $A(T/X)$ of $(\forall X)A$ and $(\exists X)A$ is a statement, then $(\forall X)A$ and $(\exists X)A$ are also statements.

(5) Nothing else is a statement.

E. (1) Any statement is a **subformula** of itself.

(2) A is a subformula of the statement $\sim A$.

(3) A and B are subformulas of the statements $(A \supset B)$, $(A \,\&\, B)$, $(A \lor B)$, and $(A \equiv B)$.

(4) For any term T the instance $A(T/X)$ of the statements $(\forall X)A$ and $(\exists X)A$ is a subformula of $(\forall X)A$ and $(\exists X)A$.

(5) If a statement A is a subformula of a statement B, and B is a subformula of a statement C, then A is a subformula of C.

(6) A statement A is an **atomic subformula** of a statement B if A is a subformula of B, and A is an atomic statement.

F. A **term variant** of a statement A is the result $A(T'/T)$ of substituting some term T' for every occurrence of a term T in A.

---

truth-functional and quantificational compounds becomes less sharp if one thinks of a universal quantification as the conjunction, and an existential quantification as the disjunction, of its infinitely many instances. But infinite conjunctions and disjunctions fall beyond the scope of this text (see footnote 12 of Section 1.1).

fication $(\forall X)A$ or $(\exists X)A$ is any result $(A(T/X))(T'/T)$ of substituting T' for every occurrence of T in $A(T/X)$. It is easily verified that, when T and T' differ, $(A(T/X))(T'/T)$ is an instance of $(\forall X)A$ or $(\exists X)A$ if and only if $A(T/X)$ is a generating instance of $(\forall X)A$ or $(\exists X)A$. For this reason, the generating instances of a quantification are also known as its **conservative instances.** The point will prove of importance in Section 2.3.

We summarize in Table VI on p. 143 the main notions defined so far.[22] (See Exercises E2.1.4,8.)

Part Two

Truth

As in Chapter 1, we shall primarily be interested in how the truth-values of compound statements depend upon those of the simpler statements—and ultimately of the atomic statements—involved in their composition. Of course, our notion of a compound statement has been broadened to include quantifications as well as truth-functional compounds; and the simpler statements which figure—either truth-functionally or quantificationally—in the composition of a statement are what we call its *subformulas.* So the truth-values of compound statements will now depend upon those of their subformulas—and ultimately of their atomic subformulas.

Again we presume that atomic statements—i.e., statements of the sort $P(T_1, T_2, \ldots, T_m)$—are either true or false (but not both). Which truth-value any one has, and why it is assigned that truth-value, matters not. What *does* matter is that all the atomic subformulas of a *compound statement* thus come with truth-values. And again various possibilities arise here: the subformulas in question might all come with the truth-value **T**, or they might all come with the truth-value **F**, or some might come with the truth-value **T** and the rest with the truth-value **F**. Using the same phrase as before, we shall talk of these possibilities as **truth-value assignments**—more fully, as truth-value assignments to the atomic subformulas of the compound; and on each one of them the statement will have a uniquely determined truth-value. For a compound statement will be rated true on a truth-value assignment just in case its immediate subformulas (immediate components if the compound is truth-functional, instances if it is a quantification) have certain truth-values on the assignment; and an atomic statement ("the end of the line" for us) will be

---

[22] In part **D** of the table we again let '*A*' and '*B*' refer to any expression.

declared true on the assignment just in case it is assigned **T** in the assignment.

We shall first specify under which conditions a statement, be it atomic or compound, is certified true on a truth-value assignment to its atomic subformulas, and comment at length on the truth-conditions for universal and existential quantifications. We shall then return to such matters as logical truth, consistency, and entailment, informally encountered in the Introduction, and formally treated for the first time on pp. 28–38. Some brief remarks on infinite sets of statements and quantificational modes of composition in general will bring the section to a close.

Truth, our initial concern, we define as follows:

TABLE VII

A. A statement is **true** on an assignment α of truth-values to its atomic subformulas (and possibly to other atomic statements as well) if and only if:

(1) in case the statement is atomic, it is assigned **T** in α;

(2) in case it is of the sort $\sim\!A$, A is not true on α;

(3) in case it is of the sort $(A \supset B)$, either A is not true on α or B is true on α (or both);

(4) in case it is of the sort $(A \,\&\, B)$, both A and B are true on α;

(5) in case it is of the sort $(A \lor B)$, at least one of A and B is true on α;

(6) in case it is of the sort $(A \equiv B)$, either both A and B are true on α, or neither one of A and B is true on α;

(7) in case it is of the sort $(\forall X)A$, $A(T/X)$ is true on α for every term T (i.e., every instance of $(\forall X)A$ is true on α);

(8) in case it is of the sort $(\exists X)A$, $A(T/X)$ is true on α for at least one term T (i.e., at least one instance of $(\exists X)A$ is true on α).

B. A statement is **false** on an assignment α of truth-values to its atomic subformulas if and only if it is not true on α.

For the sake of illustration, consider the following statement from p. 121:

$(\exists x)\,(x \text{ is going wrong}) \supset \sim\!(\forall x)\,(x \text{ is a person} \supset x \text{ is working hard}),$

and let α be the result of assigning **T** to 'a_1 is going wrong', **T** to 'a_2 is a person', **F** to 'a_2 works hard', and either one of **T** and **F** to the remaining atomic subformulas of the statement. Then, by virtue of clauses (1) and (8) above, '$(\exists x)\,(x$ is going wrong)' is true on α. On the other hand, by virtue of clauses (1) and (3), 'a_2 is a person $\supset a_2$ works hard' is not true on α; hence, by virtue of clause (7), '$(\forall x)\,(x$ is a person $\supset x$ works hard)' is not true either on α; and hence, by virtue of clause (2), '$\sim\!(\forall x)\,(x$ is a person $\supset x$ is working hard)' is true on α. So, by virtue of clause (3) again, '$(\exists x)\,(x$ is going wrong) $\supset \sim\!(\forall x)\,(x$ is a person $\supset x$ is working hard)' is true on α. The statement would also prove true on the result of assigning

F to each one of 'a_1 is going wrong', 'a_2 is going wrong', 'a_3 is going wrong', ..., and either **T** or **F** to the rest of its atomic subformulas. It would prove false on the result of assigning **T** to any one of 'a_1 is going wrong', 'a_2 is going wrong', 'a_3 is going wrong', ..., **F** to each one of 'a_1 as a person', 'a_2 is a person', 'a_3 is a person', ..., and either **T** or **F** to 'a_1 is working hard', 'a_2 is working hard', 'a_3 is working hard', ... And so on.

As suggested on pp. 116 and 119, clause (7) in Table VII mirrors the common understanding of

> Everything is thus-and-so

as

> The first thing you pick is thus-and-so, *and* the second you pick is thus-and-so, *and* the third you pick is thus-and-so, and so on;

while clause (8) reflects the corresponding interpretation of

> Something is thus-and-so

as

> The first thing you pick is thus-and-so, *or* the second you pick is thus-and-so, *or* the third you pick is thus-and-so, etc.

But our account of quantified statements has some problems, due either to its deviation in certain respects from the ordinary account, or to its apparent inability to represent the concept of truth under certain conditions. We shall discuss four of these problems here. Treatment of a fifth, which arises in connection with infinite sets of statements, is postponed until the end of the section, since infinite sets play no role in this chapter. Some of these problems are more difficult than others; none is insurmountable. (Incidentally, the account which we discuss in Chapter 3 as "standard semantics" is not affected by all five of these difficulties; but it is vastly more complicated than our own in many respects. The reader is invited to compare the two accounts.)

(1) The first issue which deserves attention here has already been introduced on pp. 116–17. On some particular occasion we might explicate our claim that

> *Everything* fell off the shelf

as

> *The vase* fell off the shelf,
> *The goldfish bowl* fell off the shelf,
> *The dictionary* fell off the shelf,

and so on, thus instantiating our quantification by means of 'the vase', 'the goldfish bowl', 'the dictionary', and so on. But asked on another occasion what we meant by

> I forgot *everything* on the morning of the exam,

we might reply

> I forgot *the perfect passive participle of 'amo'* on the morning of the exam,
>
> I forgot *the Latin word for 'locomotive'* on the morning of the exam,
>
> I forgot *my name* on the morning of the exam,

and so on, instantiating our quantification this time by means of quite different terms. By contrast, we would *officially* construe the two claims as follows:

a_1 fell off the shelf	I forgot a_1 on the morning of the exam
a_2 fell off the shelf	I forgot a_2 on the morning of the exam
a_3 fell off the shelf	I forgot a_3 on the morning of the exam
etc.	etc.,

using the *same* terms in each case.

The discrepancy arises from the fact that we commonly use 'everything' to refer to some things in one context and to others in another, while we here use the single run of individual terms 'a_1', 'a_2', 'a_3', and so on. But this causes no difficulty, since our terms need not designate the same things on all occasions.[23] So at one time they might designate things on the shelf, and at another the things to be remembered at examination time. All that logic will require of terms, be they ours or the layman's, is that they designate one thing apiece. What that thing is does not matter in the least.

(2) A similar discrepancy between the everyday account and ours stems from the fact that a claim about *everything* is often about only finitely many things. The layman's recital of the instances of, say,

> Everything fell off the shelf

would eventually come to an end, whereas ours would not, just growing and growing. This difference is unavoidable. Our terms are to serve as many occasions as possible: those where a mere handful would do, and those where a host of them—perhaps as many as there are positive integers—are called for. So we enlist $\aleph_0$ terms, enough to designate all five things on the shelf (vase, bowl, dictionary, telephone, ashtray), or all twenty things I learned in Latin 1 this year, or even all of the $\aleph_0$ integers 1, 2, 3, etc. As a result, all of our quantifications come to have infinitely many instances.

But there is no great difficulty here: although our terms must each

---

[23] The same, of course, holds true of terms in the vernacular: 'The President of the United States' referred to one person in 1946, another in 1956, and still another in 1966.

designate something, they need not designate *different* things.[24] So 'a$_1$', 'a$_2$', 'a$_3$', and 'a$_4$' might respectively name the vase, the goldfish bowl, the dictionary, and the telephone, and the remaining terms 'a$_5$', 'a$_6$', 'a$_7$', etc. might all name the ashtray, so that

> a$_5$ fell off the shelf,
> a$_6$ fell off the shelf,
> a$_7$ fell off the shelf,
> etc.

are all just so many notationally different ways of saying 'The ashtray fell off the shelf'.

(3) We have remarked several times that each of our terms 'a$_1$', 'a$_2$', 'a$_3$', etc. is required to designate something. This means that they cannot do duty for expressions like 'Beethoven's Twelfth Symphony' or 'squaring the circle'. This requirement is built into our account of truth. For on any truth-value assignment on which

> a$_1$ is thus-and-so

(and possibly no other instance of '$(\exists x)\,(x$ is thus-and-so)') is true, the *existential* quantification

> There *exists* an x such that x is thus-and-so

would be certified true, which it could hardly be if 'a$_1$' did not designate anything. Similarly, on any truth-value assignment on which

> a$_2$ is thus-and-so

(and possibly no other instance of '$(\exists x)\,(x$ is thus-and-so)') is true, the quantification

> There *exists* an x such that x is thus-and-so

would count true, which again it could hardly be if 'a$_2$' designated nothing. And so on.[25]

For example, we surely want to count the singular statement

> Squaring the circle is impossible

---

[24] The same, of course, holds true of terms in the vernacular: 'Shakespeare' and 'the Bard of Avon' refer to the same person, 'the Morning Star' and 'the Evening Star' to the same star.

[25] By presupposing that each of our terms designates something, we presuppose that at least one thing exists. So the *domains* we discuss in (4) below, and will treat more fully in Section 3.6, must be non-empty sets.

true, and the existential one

There exists an x such that x is impossible

false. But if any one of our terms were to do duty for 'squaring the circle', then the latter statement would have to be true since the former is. One might be tempted to avoid this problem by allowing some terms not to designate anything, and then counting an existential quantification $(\exists X)A$ true just in case $A(T/X)$ is true for some *designating* term T. This has been worked out, but the resulting *presupposition-free logic* is too complicated and unorthodox for presentation here.[26]

(4) The fourth issue is best discussed in terms of *universes of discourse* or, as the more recent logical literature calls them, *domains,* which we mentioned briefly on p. 117. On any occasion one's domain consists of the various things he would have in mind when claiming that *everything* is thus-and-so: it constitutes, so to speak, the subject matter on that occasion. For example, when remarking that everything fell off the shelf, one clearly has in mind the things that were on the shelf: *they* would make up his domain on this particular occasion. And when reporting that he forgot everything on the morning of the exam, he would be talking about the things he was expected to know at that time: *they* would make up his domain on that occasion.

We construe

Everything is thus-and-so

as

a_1 is thus-and-so, and a_2 is thus-and-so, and a_3 is thus-and-so, etc.

The account is appropriate in a great many cases—those obviously where each member of the domain is named by a term. It is not, to be sure, suitable in the remaining cases, a point we illustrate in (i) below. However, so far as defining consistency, logical truth, etc. goes, we may confine ourselves (as it turns out) to the cases our account suits, a point we discuss in (ii).

---

[26] Presupposition-free logic (known for short as *free logic*) grew out of two papers published simultaneously: Hintikka's "Existential presuppositions and existential commitments," *The Journal of Philosophy,* vol. 56, 1959, pp. 125–37, and Leblanc and (Theodore) Hailperin's "Nondesignating singular terms," *The Philosophical Review,* vol. 68, 1959, pp. 129–36. Both made use of the identity sign '='. In a later paper, Karel Lambert devised a free logic which does without '=' and which Leblanc and Meyer have recently shown to be both sound and complete. See Lambert's "Existential import revisited," *Notre Dame Journal of Formal Logic,* vol. 4, 1963, pp. 288–92, and Leblanc and Meyer's "On prefacing $(\forall X)A \supset A(Y/X)$ with $(\forall Y)$: A free quantificational theory without identity," *Zeitschrift für Mathematische Logik und Grundlagen der Mathematik,* vol. 16, 1970, pp. 447–62.

As suggested earlier, there is an alternative account of the truth of quantifications, known as the *standard* account and presented in Section 3.6. It fits *all* cases. We nonetheless prefer our interpretation: besides yielding suitable definitions of our logical properties and relations, it is far simpler to expound and to master.[27]

(i) When the domain is *finite or denumerably infinite,* i.e., when it has finitely many or $\aleph_0$ members, all of them *might* have names from our denumerably infinite list 'a_1', 'a_2', 'a_3', etc.; but they might *not.* Suppose, for example, that our domain consisted of the positive integers, and that our terms named only the odd ones—or for that matter that they all named the number 1. Then

$$(\forall x)\ (x \text{ is odd}),$$

which would be certified false if every integer were named, would turn out true—since each of 'a_1 is odd', 'a_2 is odd', 'a_3 is odd', etc. would be true.

When the domain is *non-denumerably infinite,* i.e., when it has more than $\aleph_0$ members, only *some* of its members can be handed names from the list 'a_1', 'a_2', 'a_3', etc., and under no circumstances would

a_1 is thus-and-so, and a_2 is thus-and-so, and a_3 is thus-and-so, etc.

do as a paraphrase of

$$(\forall x)\ (x \text{ is thus-and-so}).$$

One example of a non-denumerably infinite domain is the set consisting of all the real numbers (all the rational numbers and all the irrational ones); another is the set of all the points on some line segment; still another is the set consisting of all the subsets of any infinite set. And much larger domains turn up in the more advanced chapters of mathematics.

So the presumption that each and every thing one might ever have in mind is sure to figure among a_1, a_2, a_3, etc. is not appropriate in every case. We nonetheless abide by the truth-conditions for $(\forall X)A$ and $(\exists X)A$ laid down on p. 145, this because of one fundamental theorem due to Thoralf Skolem, and another due to Leon Henkin and Evert W. Beth.

(ii) Skolem's Theorem, proved in Section 3.6, assures us that, when

---

[27] The interpretation, known as **the substitution interpretation of the quantifiers,** is to be found in works of Russell and the early Wittgenstein, and has been more recently championed by Ruth Barcan Marcus and others. At the hands of Belnap (Nuel D., Jr.,), Beth, Dunn (J. Michael), Hintikka, Leblanc, Meyer (Robert K.), Schütte (Kurt), and others, it has developed into the new semantics for logic, sometimes called **truth-value semantics,** which we present in this section.

doing elementary logic, we may ignore all non-denumerably infinite domains: exactly the same statements prove logically true, the same sets of statements (in)consistent, and so on, whether we acknowledge non-denumerably infinite domains or systematically overlook them. Domains with more than $\aleph_0$ members do matter elsewhere, and attention to them would call for the standard account of truth (the one supplied in Section 3.6); but here they may be safely discounted. (Skolem's Theorem even assures us that, when doing elementary logic, we may discount all finite domains as well. We shall not press that point here, however.)

The Henkin-Beth Theorem, also proved in Section 3.6, goes one step further. It assures us that we may ignore domains any members of which have not been christened 'a_1' or 'a_2' or 'a_3' etc.: exactly the same statements prove logically true, the same *finite* sets of statements (in)consistent, and so on, whether we acknowledge such domains or not. (Infinite sets of statements are another matter, as we shall soon see; but these come in for detailed treatment only in Chapter 3.)

Thus because of Skolem's result we may confine ourselves here to finite and denumerably infinite sets; and because of the Henkin-Beth one we may further confine ourselves to those whose members go by the names 'a_1', 'a_2', 'a_3', and so on. For the purposes at hand, though admittedly not for some others, our interpretation of quantified statements is therefore adequate.

Truth-Tables for the Quantifiers

In Chapter 1 we met several kinds of truth-tables. There were truth-tables for '$\sim$', '$\supset$', '&', '$\vee$', and '$\equiv$', summarizing the conditions under which truth-functional compounds are true and are false. On pp. 24–25 we recorded, as a single row of a truth-table, our calculation of the truth-value of a compound on a given truth-value assignment. And then there were the full-blown truth-tables displayed on pp. 29, 30, etc., by means of which we tested statements for truth-functional truth, sets of statements for truth-functional consistency, and so on.

Our account of the truth of quantifications in terms of truth-value assignments to atomic subformulas permits—indeed, encourages—us to think of the quantifiers as having truth-tables just as the truth-functional connectives do, and to imagine truth-table tests for the logical properties and relations to be studied below.

But immediately an important difference becomes clear. In Chapter 1 truth-tables were all finitely long. But because most quantifications (all but the vacuous ones) have infinitely many subformulas, their truth-tables will be infinitely long in both directions: infinitely many columns, one for each subformula, and infinitely many rows, because the two truth-values can be allocated to these infinitely many subformulas in infinitely many ways.[28]

Still, truth-tables for the quantifiers can be suggestive; and, as we shall soon see, portions of truth-table rows can serve various purposes.

First, we give truth-tables for the two quantifiers, analogous to those for the five connectives (but only analogous, since those were complete, while these are necessarily incomplete).

TABLE VIII

$A(a_1/X)$	$A(a_2/X)$	$A(a_3/X)$	$A(a_4/X)$	·	·	·	$(\forall X)A$
T	T	T	T	·	·	·	T
F	T	T	T	·	·	·	F
T	F	T	T	·	·	·	F
F	F	T	T	·	·	·	F
T	T	F	T	·	·	·	F
·	·	·	·	·	·	·	·
·	·	·	·	·	·	·	·
·	·	·	·	·	·	·	·

$A(a_1/X)$	$A(a_2/X)$	$A(a_3/X)$	$A(a_4/X)$	·	·	·	$(\exists X)A$
F	F	F	F	·	·	·	F
T	F	F	F	·	·	·	T
F	T	F	F	·	·	·	T
T	T	F	F	·	·	·	T
F	F	T	F	·	·	·	T
·	·	·	·	·	·	·	·
·	·	·	·	·	·	·	·
·	·	·	·	·	·	·	·

In the columns under the instances, we so alternate the 'T's and 'F's as to show the only row in which a universal quantification $(\forall X)A$ gets a 'T', and the only row in which an existential quantification $(\exists X)A$ gets an 'F'. Of course, Table VIII merely summarizes in graphic form the truth-conditions for quantifications already given: a universal (existential) quantification is true on a given assignment of truth-values to its atomic

---

[28] To be more precise, in $2^{\aleph_0}$ different ways. Proof of the fact can be retrieved from primers of set theory.

subformulas if and only if every (at least one) instance of the quantification is true on that assignment.

Although we cannot display every row, or even all of any one row, of a truth-table for a quantificational compound, we can sometimes give or suggest enough of one row to do for such a statement what we did on pp. 24–25 for a truth-functional compound: calculate its truth-value on a given assignment of truth-values to its atomic subformulas.

Consider the statement '$(\exists x)(Fx \,\&\, Gx)$', and let α be the result of assigning **T** to both 'Fa$_2$' and 'Ga$_2$', and either **T** or **F** to each of the remaining atomic subformulas 'Fa$_1$', 'Fa$_3$', 'Fa$_4$', ..., 'Ga$_1$', 'Ga$_3$', 'Ga$_4$', ... The following finite portion of a truth-table row shows that '$(\exists x)(Fx \,\&\, Gx)$' is true on α:

Fa$_2$	Ga$_2$	Fa$_2$ & Ga$_2$	$(\exists x)(Fx \,\&\, Gx)$
T	T	T	T

We used dots in the previous tables to suggest statements and truth-values which mattered to us but were not displayed. We omit the dots here since the truth-values of the infinitely many other subformulas of '$(\exists x)(Fx \,\&\, Gx)$' are irrelevant.

Consider now the statement '$(\exists x)Fx \supset (\forall x)Fx$', and let α be the result of assigning **T** to 'Fa$_4$', **F** to 'Fa$_{12}$', and **T** or **F** to each of the remaining atomic subformulas. The following finite portion of a truth-table row shows that '$(\exists x)Fx \supset (\forall x)Fx$' is false on α:

Fa$_4$	Fa$_{12}$	$(\exists x)Fx$	$(\forall x)Fx$	$(\exists x)Fx \supset (\forall x)Fx$
T	F	T	F	F

'$(\exists x)Fx$' is of course true on α because its instance 'Fa$_4$' is, and '$(\forall x)Fx$' is false on α because not every one of its instances is true on α ('Fa$_{12}$' being false on α).

But consider the statement '$(\forall x)(Fx \supset Gx)$', and let α be the result of assigning **F** to every one of 'Fa$_1$', 'Fa$_2$', 'Fa$_3$', ..., and either **T** or **F** to each of 'Ga$_1$', 'Ga$_2$,' 'Ga$_3$', ... Although '$(\forall x)(Fx \supset Gx)$' is true on α, a finite portion of a truth-table row can only suggest this rather than show it:

Fa$_1$	Fa$_2$	Fa$_3$	...	Fa$_1 \supset$ Ga$_1$	Fa$_2 \supset$ Ga$_2$	Fa$_3 \supset$ Ga$_3$	...	$(\forall x)(Fx \supset Gx)$
F	F	F	...	T	T	T	...	T

(Here the dots '...' suggest the truth-value **F** for the rest of 'Fa$_4$', 'Fa$_5$', ..., and **T** for the remaining instances of '$(\forall x)(Fx \supset Gx)$'. *Every* instance of '$(\forall x)(Fx \supset Gx)$' will be true on any truth-value assignment in which 'Fa_1', 'Fa_2', 'Fa_3', ... are all assigned **F**, and hence '$(\forall x)(Fx \supset Gx)$' will also be true on any such assignment.

This sort of display will sometimes prove helpful in summarizing reasoning about logical properties and relations at the quantificational level. (See Exercise E2.1.10.)

Logical Properties and Relations

In the Introduction, we defined logical truth, consistency, entailment, and so on, in terms of the possible truth or falsehood of statements. For example, we took a statement to be logically true if it could not be false; we took a set of statements to be consistent if its members could all be true together; and so on.

These definitions were sharpened a first time in Chapter 1. On one clear sense of possibility, we noted, it is possible for a statement to be true (false) if there are *conditions* under which it would be true (false). Having shown that for each and every truth-value assignment to its *atomic components* a *truth-functional compound* has a unique truth-value, we used those assignments as the conditions under which the compound might be true or might be false. We were thus led to declare a statement logically true on truth-functional grounds—for short, *truth-functionally true*—if the statement was true on all truth-value assignments to its atomic components; we likewise declared a set of statements consistent on truth-functional grounds—for short, *truth-functionally consistent*—if there was a truth-value assignment to the atomic components of the members of the set on which all these members were true; and so on.

Now that we acknowledge quantificational as well as truth-functional compounds, a second (and final) sharpening of our early definitions is called for. And since for each and every truth-value assignment to its *atomic subformulas* the truth-value of any such compound is uniquely determined, we shall think of those assignments as the conditions under which the compound might be true or might be false. We shall accordingly take a statement to be logically true on quantificational as well as truth-functional grounds—for short, *logically true*—if the statement is true on all truth-value assignments to its atomic subformulas; we shall likewise take a set of statements to be consistent on quantificational as well as truth-functional grounds—for short, *consistent*—if there is a truth-value assignment to the atomic subformulas of its members on which all these members are true; and so on.

Our final account of logical truth, consistency, entailment, and so on, thus arises in a simple, straightforward, and natural manner from the provisional one in Chapter 1. Indeed, reading 'subformulas' for 'components'

—and lifting the qualification 'truth-functionally'—everywhere in Table III on p. 39 does the trick.

Two remarks are in order as we tabulate the resulting definitions,

(1) A statement which on the narrower grounds of Chapter 1 happened to be logically true, will be logically true on the broader ones of this chapter. And a set of statements which on truth-functional grounds alone was inconsistent or entailed some statement, will still be inconsistent or still entail that statement here.

However, a statement which was *not* truth-functionally true may well prove logically true under the new standards. For example, 'Horses are horses', an atomic statement so far as Chapter 1 is concerned, is not truth-functionally true. But its rendition here, '$(\forall x)(Hx \supset Hx)$', is logically true: on any truth-value assignment to the atomic subformulas 'Ha', 'Hb', 'Hc', etc., '$(\forall x)(Hx \supset Hx)$' is of course sure to be true. Likewise, an argument which was *not* truth-functionally valid may prove valid on the new definition. For example, 'Horses are animals'—to be symbolized, say, 'A' in Chapter 1—does not truth-functionally entail 'Tails of horses are tails of animals'—say, 'T'. But, in the notation of this

TABLE IX

A.	A finite (but non-empty) set S of statements is **consistent** if there is at least one assignment of truth-values to the atomic subformulas of the members of S on which all the members of S are true; and it is **inconsistent** if it is not consistent.[29]
B. (1)	A statement A is **logically true** if A is true on every assignment of truth-values to its atomic subformulas (so that $\{\sim A\}$ is inconsistent).
(2)	A statement A is **logically false** if A is true on no assignment of truth-values to its atomic subformulas (so that $\{A\}$ is inconsistent).
(3)	A statement A is **logically indeterminate** if A is neither logically true nor logically false (so that both $\{\sim A\}$ and $\{A\}$ are consistent).
C.	Two statements A and B are **equivalent** if there is no assignment of truth-values to the atomic subformulas of A and of B on which A and B have different truth-values (so that $\{\sim(A \equiv B)\}$ is inconsistent).
D.	A finite (and possibly empty) set S of statements **entails** a statement A if there is no assignment of truth-values (to the atomic subformulas of the members of S and to those of A) on which all the members of S are true and A false (so that $S \cup \{\sim A\}$ is inconsistent).
E.	An argument $A_1, A_2, \ldots, A_n / \therefore B$ is **valid** if $\{A_1, A_2, \ldots, A_n\}$ entails B (so that $\{A_1, A_2, \ldots, A_n, \sim B\}$ is inconsistent); otherwise, it is **invalid.**

[29] As mentioned earlier, we again define consistency (and entailment) only for finite sets of statements. We shall consider infinite sets of statements briefly toward the end of this section, and in Chapter 3. Remember that the consistency here defined is **semantic consistency.** The related concept of *syntactic consistency* will be defined and discussed in Chapter 3.

chapter, '$(\forall x)(Hx \supset Ax)$' does entail '$(\forall x)[(\exists y)(Hy \;\&\; Txy) \supset (\exists y)(Ay \;\&\; Txy)]$': there is no truth-value assignment to the atomic subformulas of the premiss and the conclusion on which the former is true and the latter false. Similarly, a truth-functionally consistent set of statements may prove inconsistent here. And so on.

(2) In more advanced texts, further kinds of components are acknowledged besides the truth-functional compounds of Chapter 1 and the quantificational ones of this chapter. There one meets statements which—though not logically true on the grounds considered here—are nonetheless held logically true; sets of statements which—though consistent by the present standards—are nonetheless held inconsistent; and so on. But we have the viewpoint of this book, and hence identify logical truth with what is known elsewhere as truth-functional or quantificational truth, consistency with what is known elsewhere as truth-functional or quantificational consistency, and so on.

As announced, the definitions in Table IX are obtained by changing just one word in the corresponding definitions from Chapter 1. But this apparently slight change has dramatic and far-reaching consequences, all stemming from the fact that statements have only finitely many (truth-functional) components, but may have—and often do have—infinitely many subformulas.

Using truth-tables, we could mechanically test statements and sets of them for logical truth, consistency, entailment, etc., as understood in Chapter 1. But on our broadened definitions, these properties and relations are now beyond the reach of truth-tables. For to tabulate and then inspect infinitely many different truth-value assignments, each to infinitely many atomic subformulas, is obviously out of the question.

Furthermore, not only do *truth-tables* fail us at this juncture, but—as Alonzo Church showed in 1936—there can be *no* mechanical way of ascertaining, in each and every case, whether or not a statement is logically true, a set of statements consistent, an argument valid, etc. The result is of major importance, for in the light of it we must abandon all hope of settling such issues by rote.

But there are other than mechanical ways of coping with these problems. For example, we can resort to the approach sketched on pp. 30 and 35–36 of Chapter 1. Each of the logical properties and relations depends on there *being*, or *not being*, a truth-value assignment of a certain sort. A statement A is logically true if, but only if, there is *no* assignment on which A is false; a set S of statements is consistent if, but only if, there *is* an assignment on which all its members are true; and so on. And in all cases, the composition of statements and of their subformulas determines whether there *is*, or there *is not,* such an assignment. Thus, knowing the truth-conditions for any sort of statement (and hence for any of its subformulas as well), we can conduct a carefully reasoned search for the critical assignment.

Such a search will end in one of three ways. (1) We may hit upon a suitable assignment: so *A* is not logically true, *S* is consistent, or whatever. Here tables like those on p. 153 can be quite serviceable for documenting our findings. For, once in our hands, the assignment can be displayed or suggested in a partial truth-table row, and the truth-values of relevant subformulas of *A* or of the members of *S* calculated on that assignment. (2) We may, on the contrary, hit upon reasons why there *cannot* be an assignment of the requisite sort: so *A* is logically true, *S* is inconsistent, or whatever. We could then substantiate the point by spelling out the reasons why such an assignment is not forthcoming.[30] Or (3) we may give up in despair before hitting upon anything which would be to the point.

We use this approach below in a number of relatively simple cases. In difficult ones, however, systematic techniques like the tree or the derivation method are more serviceable. The expanded tree technique of Section 2.2 is as nearly effective a procedure as can be found in this area, where (as we just noted) a fully effective procedure is impossible. And the expanded derivation technique of Section 2.3 accomplishes much the same task in a somewhat different way.

In Table IX we parenthetically defined several of our logical properties and relations in terms of (in)consistency, which as a result came first. This made for a more unified account of things, and it prepares the reader for the various uses of the tree method in Section 2.2. But in the discussion which follows we begin with logical truth, falsehood, and indeterminacy; then treat equivalence; and so on.

Logical truth, falsehood, and indeterminacy. In view of the definitions in Table IX, a statement is **logically true** if it is false on no truth-value assignment to its atomic subformulas, **logically false** if true on none, and **logically indeterminate** if false on one but true on another.

Consider, then, a statement like

All men are wicked, and none is,

which we would render

$$(\forall x)(Mx \supset Wx) \& (\forall x)(Mx \supset \sim Wx).$$

This is obviously not logically true. For '$(\forall x)(Mx \supset Wx) \& (\forall x)(Mx \supset \sim Wx)$' would be false on any truth-value assignment on which either conjunct was false. And the left-hand conjunct, being a universal quantification, would be false on any assignment on which some *one* of its

---

[30] In a few very simple cases, these reasons can be suggested by a finite portion of a truth-table, in sample rows of which truth-values are assigned to and calculated for sample subformulas. But this device is regularly so cumbersome and unilluminating—having far more dots than substance—that we do not use it.

instances 'Ma$_1$ ⊃ Wa$_1$', 'Ma$_2$ ⊃ Wa$_2$', ... was false. Such an assignment is of course easy to come by, as shown by this finite portion of a truth-table row:

Ma$_1$	Wa$_1$	Ma$_1$ ⊃ Wa$_1$	(∀x)(Mx ⊃ Wx)	(∀x)(Mx ⊃ Wx) & (∀x)(Mx ⊃ ~Wx)
T	F	F	F	F

'(∀x)(Mx ⊃ Wx) & (∀x)(Mx ⊃ ~Wx)' is false on the result of assigning **T** to 'Ma$_1$', **F** to 'Wa$_1$', and either one of **T** or **F** to each of its remaining atomic subformulas. Hence, it is not logically true.

One might perhaps wonder if '(∀x)(Mx ⊃ Wx) & (∀x)(Mx ⊃ ~Wx)' is logically *false*—true on *no* truth-value assignment. But an assignment is easily found on which all the instances of the conjuncts—and hence the conjuncts themselves—prove true. Indeed, 'Ma$_1$ ⊃ Wa$_1$', 'Ma$_2$ ⊃ Wa$_2$',..., *and* 'Ma$_1$ ⊃ ~Wa$_1$', 'Ma$_2$ ⊃ ~Wa$_2$', ... are all true on the result of assigning **F** to their antecedents 'Ma$_1$', 'Ma$_2$', ..., and either one of **T** or **F** to 'Wa$_1$', 'Wa$_2$', ... We cannot *display* all the relevant subformulas and truth-values in a truth-table row. But we can *suggest* them clearly enough to establish that '(∀x)(Mx ⊃ Wx) & (∀x)(Mx ⊃ ~Wx)' is not logically false:[31]

Ma$_1$	Ma$_2$	...	Ma$_1$ ⊃ Wa$_1$	Ma$_2$ ⊃ Wa$_2$	...	(∀x)(Mx ⊃ Wx)
F	F	...	T	T	...	T

Ma$_1$ ⊃ ~Wa$_1$	Ma$_2$ ⊃ ~Wa$_2$	...	(∀x)(Mx ⊃ ~Wx)	(∀x)(Mx ⊃ Wx) & (∀x)(Mx ⊃ ~Wx)
T	T	... T		T

Since '(∀x)(Mx ⊃ Wx) & (∀x)(Mx ⊃ ~Wx)' has been shown by the two partial truth-table rows above to be true on one truth-value assignment and false on another, it is logically indeterminate.

Consider, next, the statement

If some lions are male, then some are not,

or, in symbols,

$$(∃x)(Lx \,\&\, Mx) ⊃ (∃x)(Lx \,\&\, {\sim}Mx).$$

---

[31] Our feeling that 'All men are wicked, and none is' is logically false stems from our knowledge that there are men. Indeed, '[(∀x)(Mx ⊃ Wx) & (∀x)(Mx ⊃ ~Wx)] & (∃x)Mx' *is* logically false. But, while it may be *indubitable* that there are men, it is not *necessary*—logically true—that there should be any. And hence, though 'All men are wicked, and none is' is surely false, it is not *logically* false.

This is obviously not logically false; and a truth-value assignment show-ing this—on which the conditional would be true—is readily produced. For '$(\exists x)(Lx \,\&\, Mx) \supset (\exists x)(Lx \,\&\, {\sim} Mx)$' would be true on any assign-ment on which its consequent '$(\exists x)(Lx \,\&\, {\sim} Mx)$' was true; and the latter would be true on any assignment on which any *one* of its instances 'La$_1$ & ~Ma$_1$', 'La$_2$ & ~Ma$_2$', . . . was true. A suitable assignment is captured in the following bit of a truth-table row:

La$_1$ Ma$_1$	~Ma$_1$	La$_1$ & ~Ma$_1$	$(\exists x)(Lx \,\&\, {\sim} Mx)$	$(\exists x)(Lx \,\&\, Mx) \supset (\exists x)(Lx \,\&\, {\sim} Mx)$
T **F**	**T**	**T**	**T**	**T**

One might suppose, though, that '$(\exists x)(Lx \,\&\, Mx) \supset (\exists x)(Lx \,\&\, {\sim} Mx)$' is logically true—true on every truth-value assignment. But an assign-ment α on which its antecedent '$(\exists x)(Lx \,\&\, Mx)$' proves true and its con-sequent '$(\exists x)(Lx \,\&\, {\sim} Mx)$' false can be found with little effort. As long as some one instance—say 'La$_1$ & Ma$_1$'—of '$(\exists x)(Lx \,\&\, Mx)$' is true on α, the conditional will prove false on α if every instance of '$(\exists x)(Lx \,\&\, {\sim} Mx)$' is false on α. Assign **T** to both 'La$_1$' and 'Ma$_1$', and **F** to 'La$_2$', 'La$_3$', . . ., and we have α made.[32] Thus, although the following truth-table row does not display all of the relevant subformulas and truth-values, it clearly suggests enough of them to guarantee that '$(\exists x)(Lx \,\&\, Mx) \supset (\exists x)(Lx \,\&\, {\sim} Mx)$' is not logically true:

Ma$_1$ La$_1$ La$_2$ La$_3$ . . .	La$_1$ & Ma$_1$	$(\exists x)(Lx \,\&\, Mx)$	~Ma$_1$	La$_1$ & ~Ma$_1$	La$_2$ & ~Ma$_2$
T **T** **F** **F** . . .	**T**	**T**	**F**	**F**	**F**

La$_3$ & ~Ma$_3$ . . .	$(\exists x)(Lx \,\&\, {\sim} Mx)$	$(\exists x)(Lx \,\&\, Mx) \supset (\exists x)(Lx \,\&\, {\sim} Mx)$
F . . .	**F**	**F**

As '$(\exists x)(Lx \,\&\, Mx) \supset (\exists x)(Lx \,\&\, {\sim} Mx)$' has been shown by the two partial truth-table rows above to be true on one truth-value assignment and false on another, it is logically indeterminate.

The previous examples, being logically indeterminate, were neither logically true nor logically false. But consider the statement

$$[(\forall x)(Fx \supset Gx) \,\&\, (\forall x)Fx] \supset (\forall x)Gx.$$

---

[32] Like any truth-value assignment on which '$(\exists x)(Lx \,\&\, Mx) \supset (\exists x)(Lx \,\&\, {\sim}'Mx)$' is false, this one requires both that there are lions, and that all of them are male. Our temptation to consider 'If some lions are male, then some are not' logically true is easily accounted for. It would indeed be odd to say 'Some lions are male' if we knew they *all* were; so, on being told only that *some* are male, we might conclude that some (perhaps) are not. But neither 'Some lions are male' nor '$(\exists x)(Lx \,\&\, Mx)$' *logically* requires that there be lions that are not male.

If this conditional were not logically true, there would be a truth-value assignment on which it was false. Any such assignment is one on which the antecedent '$(\forall x)(Fx \supset Gx) \& (\forall x)Fx$' would be true; hence one on which both conjuncts '$(\forall x)(Fx \supset Gx)$' and '$(\forall x)Fx$' would be true; hence one on which all their instances 'Fa$_1 \supset$ Ga$_1$' and 'Fa$_1$', 'Fa$_2 \supset$ Ga$_2$' and 'Fa$_2$', ... would be true. But every instance 'Ga$_1$', 'Ga$_2$', ... of '$(\forall x)Gx$'— and hence '$(\forall x)Gx$' itself—would be true on that assignment. So there can be *no* truth-value assignment on which the antecedent '$(\forall x)(Fx \supset Gx) \& (\forall x)Fx$' would be true and the consequent '$(\forall x)Gx$' false. Thus, there can be no truth-value assignment on which the conditional is false. So '$[(\forall x)(Fx \supset Gx) \& (\forall x)Fx] \supset (\forall x)Gx$' is logically true (and its negation '$\sim([(\forall x)(Fx \supset Gx) \& (\forall x)Fx] \supset (\forall x)Gx)$' logically false, of course).

Consider now the existential quantification

$$(\exists x)[(\exists y)Fy \supset Fx].$$

On any truth-value assignment on which '$(\exists x)[(\exists y)Fy \supset Fx]$' would be false, *every one* of its instances '$(\exists y)Fy \supset$ Fa$_1$', '$(\exists y)Fy \supset$ Fa$_2$', ... would likewise be false. But on any truth-value assignment on which '$(\exists y)Fy \supset$ Fa$_1$', '$(\exists y)Fy \supset$ Fa$_2$', ... would all be false, their common antecedent '$(\exists y)Fy$' would be true, and every one of 'Fa$_1$', 'Fa$_2$', ... (their respective consequents) false—which is obviously impossible. So there can be *no* truth-value assignment on which '$(\exists x)[(\exists y)Fy \supset Fx]$' is false, and the quantification is therefore logically true (and, again, its negation '$\sim(\exists x)[(\exists y)Fy \supset Fx]$' logically false). (See Exercises E2.1.14–16. Various logical truths—many of them biconditionals—will be found in Exercises E2.2.5 and E2.3.4, and in Section 2.3.)[33]

Equivalence. Two statements are **equivalent** if there is no truth-value assignment to their atomic subformulas on which one is true and the other false. Consider, for example, any universal quantification

$$(\forall X)A$$

and the corresponding negation

$$\sim(\exists X)\sim A.$$

(Here we shall be reasoning "wholesale" about all such pairs of statements, rather than about two specific statements.) $(\forall X)A$ is true on any truth-value assignment α if and only if $A(T/X)$ is true—and hence

---

[33] The remaining pages of Section 2.1 can be omitted on first reading. They first treat equivalence, entailment, validity, and (in)consistency in the manner in which logical truth and falsehood have just been treated; they then deal briefly with two rather specialized topics: the (in)consistency of infinite sets of statements, and quantificational modes of statement composition.

$\sim A(T/X)$ is false—on α for every term T. But $\sim A(T/X)$ is false on α for every term T if and only if $(\exists X)\sim A$ is false—and hence $\sim(\exists X)\sim A$ is true—on α. So there can be *no* truth-value assignment on which either of $(\forall X)A$ and $\sim(\exists X)\sim A$ is true and the other false; they are therefore equivalent.

And again, consider any existential quantification

$$(\exists X)A$$

and the corresponding negation

$$\sim(\forall X)\sim A.$$

$(\exists X)A$ is true on any truth-value assignment α if and only if $A(T/X)$ is true—and hence $\sim A(T/X)$ is false—on α for at least one term T. But $\sim A(T/X)$ is false on α for at least one term T if and only if $(\forall X)\sim A$ is false—and hence $\sim(\forall X)\sim A$ is true—on α. So there can be *no* truth-value assignment on which either of $(\exists X)A$ and $\sim(\forall X)\sim A$ is true and the other false; they are therefore equivalent.

But consider the two statements

$$(\exists x)(Fx \,\&\, Gx)$$

and

$$(\exists x)Fx \,\&\, (\exists x)Gx.$$

These will fail to be equivalent if there is a truth-value assignment on which, say, '$(\exists x)Fx \,\&\, (\exists x)Gx$' is true and '$(\exists x)(Fx \,\&\, Gx)$' false. Such an assignment is not hard to come by; indeed, any one in which 'Fa_1' and 'Ga_2' are assigned **T,** and all of 'Ga_1', 'Fa_2', 'Fa_3', . . . are assigned **F** will do, as this partial truth-table row shows:

Ga_1	Ga_2	Fa_1	Fa_2	Fa_3	Fa_4	$\cdots$	$(\exists x)Fx$	$(\exists x)Gx$	$Fa_1 \,\&\, Ga_1$
F	**T**	**T**	**F**	**F**	**F**	$\cdots$	**T**	**T**	**F**

$Fa_2 \,\&\, Ga_2$		$Fa_3 \,\&\, Ga_3$	$\cdots$	$(\exists x)(Fx \,\&\, Gx)$	$(\exists x)Fx \,\&\, (\exists x)Gx$
F		**F**	$\cdots$	**F**	**T**

So '$(\exists x)(Fx \,\&\, Gx)$' and '$(\exists x)Fx \,\&\, (\exists x)Gx$' are not equivalent. (The reader can satisfy himself, by the way, that there is *no* truth-value assignment on which '$(\exists x)(Fx \,\&\, Gx)$' is true and '$(\exists x)Fx \,\&\, (\exists x)Gx$' false.) (See Exercise E2.1.12.)

Entailment and validity. A set $\{A_1, A_2, \ldots, A_n\}$ **entails** a statement B—or an argument

$$A_1$$
$$A_2$$
$$\cdot$$
$$\underline{A_n}$$
$$\therefore B$$

is **valid**—if and only if there is no assignment of truth-values to the atomic subformulas of A_1, A_2, ..., A_n, and of B on which A_1, A_2, ..., and A_n are all true and B false.

Consider, for example, the argument

$$(\forall x)(Fx \supset Gx)$$
$$\underline{(\exists x)Fx}$$
$$\therefore (\exists x)(Fx \,\&\, Gx).$$

Is this valid or not? Any "disqualifying" truth-value assignment α must be one on which both '$(\forall x)(Fx \supset Gx)$' and '$(\exists x)Fx$' are true. But some instance 'Fa_i' $(i \geq 1)$ of '$(\exists x)Fx$' must be true on α if '$(\exists x)Fx$' is; and the instance '$Fa_i \supset Ga_i$' of '$(\forall x)(Fx \supset Gx)$' is sure to be true on α if '$(\forall x)(Fx \supset Gx)$' is. So '$Ga_i$'—hence '$Fa_i \,\&\, Ga_i$', and hence '$(\exists x)(Fx \,\&\, Gx)$'—must be true on α. Thus there is *no* truth-value assignment on which both members of $\{(\forall x)(Fx \supset Gx), (\exists x)Fx\}$ are true and '$(\exists x)(Fx \,\&\, Gx)$' false, the set entails '$(\exists x)(Fx \,\&\, Gx)$', and the corresponding argument is valid.

But does $\{(\forall x)(Fx \supset Gx)\}$ alone entail '$(\exists x)(Fx \,\&\, Gx)$'? It does *not* if there is a truth-value assignment on which '$(\forall x)(Fx \supset Gx)$'—and hence each of its instances '$Fa_1 \supset Ga_1$', '$Fa_2 \supset Ga_2$', ...—is true, while '$(\exists x)(Fx \,\&\, Gx)$'—and hence each of its instances '$Fa_1 \,\&\, Ga_1$', '$Fa_2 \,\&\, Ga_2$', ...—is false. Such an assignment is easy to come by; indeed, any one in which all of 'Fa_1', 'Fa_2', ... are assigned **F** will do, as this partial truth-table row shows:

Fa_1 Fa_2 ...	$Fa_1 \supset Ga_1$ $Fa_2 \supset Ga_2$ ...	$Fa_1 \,\&\, Ga_1$ $Fa_2 \,\&\, Ga_2$ ...	
F **F** ...	**T** **T** ...	**F** **F** ...	

$(\forall x)(Fx \supset Gx)$	$(\exists x)(Fx \,\&\, Gx)$
T	**F**

So there is an assignment on which '$(\forall x)(Fx \supset Gx)$' is true and '$(\exists x)(Fx \,\&\, Gx)$' false, $\{(\forall x)(Fx \supset Gx)\}$ does not entail '$(\exists x)(Fx \,\&\, Gx)$', the corresponding argument is invalid, and '$(\exists x)Fx$' did make a crucial difference between this and the previous case.[34]

Now for a somewhat more complicated pair of cases. First, does (the set consisting just of)

$$(\exists x)(\forall y)Cxy$$

entail

$$(\forall y)(\exists x)Cxy?$$

A disqualifying assignment α would have to be one on   which '$(\exists x)(\forall y)Cxy$' is true, hence one on which *at least one* of its instances

$(\forall y)Ca_1y$
$(\forall y)Ca_2y$
$(\forall y)Ca_3y$

.

.

.

is true, and hence one on which *all* the statements in *at least one* of the following rows are true:

$Ca_1a_1, Ca_1a_2, Ca_1a_3, \ldots$
$Ca_2a_1, Ca_2a_2, Ca_2a_3, \ldots$
$Ca_3a_1, Ca_3a_2, Ca_3a_3, \ldots$

.   .   .   . . .

.   .   .   . . .

.   .   .   . . .

But notice that if *all* the statements in any *one* of these rows are true on α, then *all* of the following statements must be true on α:

$$(\exists x)Cxa_1, (\exists x)Cxa_2, (\exists x)Cxa_3, \ldots.$$

---

[34] In Aristotelian logic—an historically important, but comparatively limited, antecedent of our own—a universal statement of the sort 'All men are mortal' was taken to entail the corresponding existential statement 'Some men are mortal'. On our account it does not, and this largely because of the way we translate such universal statements—as tantamount to 'If anything is a man, it is mortal'. '$(\forall x)(Fx \supset Gx)$' entails neither '$(\exists x)(Fx \& Gx)$' nor '$(\exists x)Fx$', and hence has no "existential import." As a matter of fact, '$\sim(\exists x)Fx$' (i.e., 'There aren't any men') *does* entail '$(\forall x)(Fx \supset Gx)$' (i.e., 'They're all mortal'), as well of course as '$(\forall x)(Fx \supset \sim Gx)$' (i.e., 'None of them is mortal').

Two facts justify our rendition of universal statements, as against Aristotle's. (1) Many universal statements in ordinary usage—indistinguishable in form from those with existential import—have no such import (e.g., 'All trespassers will be prosecuted' and 'Cars without brakes aren't safe to drive', which we might well want to count true, even if there are no trespassers or brakeless cars). And (2) we have a way of rendering universal statements whose existential import happens to matter: we use the model '$(\forall x)(Fx \supset Gx) \& (\exists x)Fx$', which *does* entail '$(\exists x)(Fx \& Gx)$'.

And if they are all true on α, then so is '$(\forall y)(\exists x)Cxy$', which is therefore entailed by $\{(\exists x)(\forall y)Cxy\}$. So the argument from '$(\exists x)(\forall y)Cxy$' to '$(\forall y)(\exists x)Cxy$' is valid.

But is the argument from

$$(\forall y)(\exists x)Cxy$$

to

$$(\exists x)(\forall y)Cxy$$

also valid? A disqualifying truth-value assignment α to their atomic subformulas 'Ca_1a_1', 'Ca_1a_2', 'Ca_1a_3', . . ., 'Ca_2a_1', 'Ca_2a_2', 'Ca_2a_3', . . ., 'Ca_3a_1', 'Ca_3a_2', 'Ca_3a_3', . . . must be one on which the premiss '$(\forall y)(\exists x)Cxy$'—and hence each of its instances '$(\exists x)Cxa_1$', '$(\exists x)Cxa_2$', . . . —is true, while the conclusion '$(\exists x)(\forall y)Cxy$'—and hence each of its instances '$(\forall y)Ca_1y$', '$(\forall y)Ca_2y$', . . .—is false. There are infinitely many different truth-value assignments which would do the job. For example, let α simply be the result of assigning T to every one of 'Ca_1a_1', 'Ca_2a_2', 'Ca_3a_3', . . ., and F to the remaining atomic subformulas of '$(\forall y)(\exists x)Cxy$' and '$(\exists x)(\forall y)Cxy$'. Every instance of '$(\forall y)(\exists x)Cxy$'—and hence '$(\forall y)(\exists x)Cxy$' itself—is true on α: '$(\exists x)Cxa_1$' because 'Ca_1a_1' is, '$(\exists x)Cxa_2$' because 'Ca_2a_2' is, and so on. And every instance of '$(\exists x)(\forall y)Cxy$'—and hence '$(\exists x)(\forall y)Cxy$' itself—is false on α: '$(\forall y)Ca_1y$' because 'Ca_1a_2' is, '$(\forall y)Ca_2y$' because 'Ca_2a_1' is, '$(\forall y)Ca_3y$' because 'Ca_3a_1' is, and so on. Thus, there is a truth-value assignment on which '$(\forall y)(\exists x)Cxy$' is true and '$(\exists x)(\forall y)Cxy$' false, the argument

$$(\forall y)(\exists x)Cxy$$

$$\therefore (\exists x)(\forall y)Cxy$$

is invalid, and $\{(\forall y)(\exists x)Cxy\}$ does not entail '$(\exists x)(\forall y)Cxy$'. (The truth-value assignment used to show this is not clearly suggested by any relatively short truth-table row, so we forego the usual tabulation.)

Consistency and inconsistency. A set $\{A_1, A_2, . . ., A_n\}$ of statements is **consistent** if there *is* a truth-value assignment on which A_1, A_2, . . ., and A_n are all true, and **inconsistent** if there is *not*. To find such an assignment, or to show why there can be none, we would proceed in the manner amply illustrated above.

Indeed, we have already achieved a number of consistency results, in other guises. While showing on p. 158 above that '$(\forall x)(Mx \supset Wx) \mathbin{\&} (\forall x)(Mx \supset \sim Wx)$' is not logically false, we established along the way that $\{(\forall x)(Mx \supset Wx), (\forall x)(Mx \supset \sim Wx)\}$ is a consistent set. In showing on p. 161 that '$(\exists x)(Fx \mathbin{\&} Gx)$' and '$(\exists x)Fx \mathbin{\&} (\exists x)Gx$' are not equivalent, we established (or by one more entry could have established) that $\{\sim(\exists x)(Fx \& Gx), (\exists x)Fx \& (\exists x)Gx\}$ is a consistent set. And in showing on pp. 162–63 that the argument '$(\forall x)(Fx \supset Gx), (\exists x)Fx/$ $\therefore(\exists x)(Fx \& Gx)$' is valid, but '$(\forall x)(Fx \supset Gx)/\therefore(\exists x)(Fx \& Gx)$' invalid, we established in effect that $\{(\forall x)(Fx \supset Gx), (\exists x)Fx, \sim(\exists x)(Fx \& Gx)\}$ is inconsistent, while $\{(\forall x)(Fx \supset Gx), \sim(\exists x)(Fx \& Gx)\}$ is consistent.

We shall not further illustrate this approach to (in)consistency. At best it is somewhat unsystematic, whereas the tree technique of Section 2.2 will be a much more rigorous way of achieving essentially the same results. Before presenting this technique, though, we pause briefly to treat two somewhat special topics. (See Exercises E2.1.11, 13.)

Infinite Sets of Statements

Many texts talk of (in)consistency in connection with infinite as well as finite sets of statements. We could easily have done so in Section 1.1, by declaring an infinite set S of statements truth-functionally consistent (inconsistent) if there is (there is no) truth-value assignment to the atomic components of the members of S on which all these members are true. In the present context, though, difficulties would arise if we similarly extended our account of (in)consistency. The Henkin–Beth Theorem guarantees that, whether or not all the members of a finite or denumerably infinite domain go by the names 'a_1', 'a_2', 'a_3', etc., exactly the same *finite* sets of statements prove to be (in)consistent. *Infinite* sets, however, are something else.

Consider, for example, the set

$$\{Fa_1, Fa_2, Fa_3, \ldots, \sim(\forall x)Fx\},$$

which is to consist of all the instances of '$(\forall x)Fx$', and also '$\sim(\forall x)Fx$'. On the one truth-value assignment on which all of 'Fa_1', 'Fa_2', 'Fa_3', and so on, are true, '$(\forall x)Fx$' is true, and hence '$\sim(\forall x)Fx$' is false. And on the remaining truth-value assignments, one or more of 'Fa_1', 'Fa_2', 'Fa_3', and so on, are false. Accordingly there is no truth-value assignment on which all the members of the set are true. So on a straightforward extension of **A** and **D** in Table III, the set would be declared inconsistent, and $\{Fa_1, Fa_2, Fa_3, \ldots\}$ would be said to entail '$(\forall x)Fx$'.

The result is a welcome one when all the members of the domain answer the names 'a_1', 'a_2', 'a_3', etc.; but when they do not, it is obviously improper. Suppose, as on a previous occasion, that the domain consisted of the positive integers, and that 'a_1', 'a_2', 'a_3', etc., were respectively understood to designate 2, 4, 6, etc. Then the infinitely many truths 'a_1 is an even integer', 'a_2 is an even integer', 'a_3 is an even integer', etc., would come to entail the falsehood '$(\forall x)(x$ is an even integer)'.

Sets of statements to which infinitely many terms are foreign are said to be **infinitely extendible.** The problem above arises with certain sets which, like $\{Fa_1, Fa_2, Fa_3, \ldots, \sim(\forall x)Fx\}$, are *not* infinitely extendible —i.e., to which no term is foreign, or just one is, or just two are, etc. There are various ways of coping with them, and properly accounting for their (in)consistency. However, we postpone our treatment of the matter until Section 3.6, where we shall attend to the Henkin–Beth Theorem, its scope, and its limits. (See Exercise E2.1.17.)

Quantificational Modes of (Statement) Composition

Universalization and existentialization are sometimes called **elementary quantificational modes of composition.** Just as there are truthfunctional modes of statement composition which we did not study because they are both rare in ordinary discouse and reducible to those we did study, there are other elementary quantificational modes—six others, to be exact. One, for example, delivers compounds which are true if and only if all their instances are true or none is; another delivers compounds which are true if and only if some, but not all, of their instances are true; and so on. We shall review these extra modes of composition in Section 3.1, and establish that—given negation, conjunction, and disjunction— they are all reducible to universalization.

Because of this result, elementary quantificational compounds other than universal and existential quantifications are all dispensable. Indeed, since $(\exists X)A$ is equivalent to $\sim(\forall X)\sim A$, and $(\forall X)A$ is equivalent to $\sim(\exists X)\sim A$, *either* existential quantifications *or* universal ones could also be dispensed with. For the time being, we include both kinds of quantifications in our list of acknowledged compounds; but in much of Chapter 3 we shall retain only universal ones. There we shall construe compounds of the sort $(\exists X)A$ as shorthand for compounds of the sort $\sim(\forall X)\sim A$, by adding

$$(\exists X)A =_{df} \sim(\forall X)\sim A$$

to the definitions displayed on p. 41. The number of **primitive logical operators** will thereby be reduced to three: the two connectives '$\sim$' and '$\supset$' (which permit definition of all other truth-functional connectives) and the one quantifier symbol '$\forall$' (which, given the connectives mentioned above, permits definition of all other elementary quantifier symbols).

Examples of non-elementary quantificational compounds are 'Less than five things are thus-and-so', 'More than twenty things are thusand-so', 'As many things as not are thus-and-so', etc. They too play a role in reasoning, but their analysis lies beyond the scope of this text.

EXERCISES

E2.1.1.   In the statements below, indicate the words or phrases which could count as *terms,* and what *sort of thing* (physical object, property, relation, set, event, etc.) each would designate. (Recall that what is left when the terms are removed from an atomic statement is its predicate—one-place if one has been removed, two-place if two, and so on.)

   a.   I buried Paul.

   b.   Mourning becomes Electra.

   c.   'Inquiry' is sometimes spelled with 'E'.

   d.   Charles Darwin discovered that species of finches.

   e.   Three plus seven equals six plus four.

   f.   Multiplication is easier than division, but harder than tying shoes.

   g.   Paul Revere announced the redcoats' arrival.

   h.   Sodomy is illegal in Pennsylvania, but not in Illinois.

   i.   Cheetahs are in danger of becoming extinct.

   j.   I bought my way into the jet set.

   k.   January 1 will come and go, and I'll still have the smoking habit.

   l.   What really happened that night may never be known.

   m.   To err is human, to be forgiven is divine.

   n.   The senior class is much brighter than the junior class, and Pete is the brightest boy in it.

   o.   Paternity is far more often at issue than maternity.

   p.   The blue of Jane's eyes is deeper than the Mediterranean Sea.

   q.   'Either it's raining or it isn't' is a tautology.

   r.   The falsehood of what he said was perfectly obvious to us.

   s.   After seeing the vision, Alexander devised his plan for conquest.

   t.   The heavy responsibility of being President eventually took its toll from Johnson.

E2.1.2.   Using the abbreviations suggested, symbolize each of the following statements:

   1.   Doctors are professionals.   (Dx, Px)

   2.   Doctors are in the audience.   (Dx, Ax)

   3.   Only doctors are in the audience.   (Dx, Ax)

   4.   A doctor is devoted to the relief of suffering.   (Dx, Rx)

   5.   A doctor is devoted to my wife.   (Dx, Wx: x is devoted to my wife)

   6.   Doctors are not all rich.   (Dx, Rx)

   7.   No doctors are rich.   (Dx, Rx)

   8.   Doctors who are poor are honest.   (Dx, Px, Hx)

   9.   Doctors who are poor are non-existent.   (Dx, Px)

10. Doctors and lawyers who are rich are admired only if they're also honest. (Dx, Lx, Rx, Ax, Hx)

11. All young people are attractive except those who giggle.   (Yx, Px, Ax, Gx)

12. Some of the people on the committee were neither willing nor able to do the job.   (Px, Cx, Wx, Ax)

13. Not all of the books on the shelf are worth reading.   (Bx, Sx, Wx)

14. Not one of the books on the shelf is worth reading.   (Bx, Sx, Wx)

15. Someone can get into the club if he's rich or knows the right people, unless he's black.   (Px, Cx, Rx, Kx, Bx)

16. There are fine universities in Connecticut and Kansas.   (Fx, Ux, Cx, Kx)

17. Someone can sneak into the ballpark only if George isn't on duty.   (Px: x is a person; Sx: x can sneak into the ballpark; Dx: x is on duty; g: George)[35]

18. Something is missing unless Tom counted incorrectly.   (Mx: x is missing; Cx: x counted correctly; t: Tom)

19. If something is worth doing, then cynics are wrong.   (Dx: x is worth doing; Cx; Wx)

20. If something is worth doing, then it's worth doing well.   (Dx; Wx: x is worth doing well)

21. If all tax-evaders are caught, then my uncle Joe will be.   (Tx: x is a tax-evader; Cx: x is caught; j: my uncle Joe)

22. If any tax-evaders are caught, then my uncle Joe will be.   (Tx; Cx; j)

23. If someone makes a joke and no one laughs, then he feels pretty silly.   (Px: x is a person; Jx: x makes a joke; Lx: x laughs; Sx: x feels pretty silly)

24. If someone tries hard, then he'll succeed unless some people who try hard have bad luck.   (Px; Tx: x tries hard; Sx: x will succeed; Bx: x has bad luck)

25. If a novel is badly written or obscene (or both), then unless people have changed it will sell.   (Nx; Bx; Ox; Px; Cx; Sx)

26. There are men who are unhappy unless everything is going well.   (Mx; Hx; Wx: x is going well)

27. All draft dodgers who have gone to Canada will be free from prosecution if any one of them is.   (Dx: x is a draft dodger; Cx: x has gone to Canada; Fx: x will be free from prosecution)

28. Students work hard if they are well-motivated and challenged; otherwise they don't.   (Sx; Hx: x works hard; Mx: x is well-motivated; Cx)

29. There is someone who will get a spanking if he keeps misbehaving.   (Px: x is a person; Sx: x will get a spanking; Mx: x keeps misbehaving)

30. Either all my friends are lucky, or else none breaks the law.   (Fx: x is a friend of mine; Lx: x is lucky; Bx: x breaks the law)

---

[35] Hence, with 'Dx' for 'x is on duty' and 'g' for 'George', 'Dg' would be 'George is on duty'.

31. Bob likes anyone who pays attention to him. (Lxy: x likes y; Axy: x pays attention to y; Px: x is a person; b: Bob)[36]

32. If Tom doesn't like anyone, then he surely doesn't like everyone.   (Px; Lxy: x likes y; t: Tom)

33. There's no time like the present.   (Tx: x is a time; Lxy: x is like y; p: the present moment)

34. Tom is taller than anyone he knows.   (Px; Txy: x is taller than y; Kxy: x knows y; t: Tom)

35. Tom has confidence in himself only if someone else does too.   (Px; Cxy: x has confidence in y; Ixy: x is identical with y; t: Tom)

36. Everybody doesn't like something, but nobody doesn't like Sara Lee. (Px; Lxy; s: Sara Lee)

37. Everybody likes, and is liked by, somebody; but nobody likes, or is liked by, everybody.   (Px; Lxy)

38. Nobody gives anything away which is given him by one of his children. (Px; Gxyz: x gives y to z; Cxy: x is a child of y)

39. Only philosophers and logicians understand everything.   (Px: x is a philosopher; Lx: x is a logician; Uxy: x understands y)

40. Only philosophers and logicians understand anything.   (Px; Lx; Uxy)

41. Whenever a lecher sees a girl, he gets excited.   (Tx: x is a time; Lx: x is a lecher; Sxyz: x sees y at (time) z; Gx: x is a girl; Exy: x gets excited at (time) y)

42. Whither thou goest, I will go.   (Px: x is a place; Gxy: x goes to (place) y; u: thou; i: I)

43. No one on A's team can beat everyone on C's team.   (Px: x is a person; Ax: x is on A's team; Bxy: x can beat y; Cx: x is on C's team)

44. No one on A's team can beat anyone on C's team.   (Px; Ax; Bxy; Cx)

45. Anyone on A's team who can beat someone on C's team can beat everyone on D's team.   (Px; Ax; Bxy; Cx; Dx)

46. Peter once had some wits, but Mack never had any.   (Tx: x was a time; Wx: x is a wit; Hxyz: x had y at (time) z; p; m)

47. A thing is part of another thing if and only if whatever overlaps the first also overlaps the second.   (Pxy: x is part of y; Oxy: x overlaps y)

48. If a thing overlaps all the parts of another thing, then the second is part of the first.   (Pxy; Oxy)

49. A thing overlaps another thing if and only if the two things have a part in common.   (Pxy; Oxy)

50. You (i.e., any person) can fool some of the people all of the time, and all of the people some of the time, but you cannot fool all of the people all of the time.   (Px: x is a person; Tx: x is a time; Fxyz: x can fool y at (time) z)

---

[36] With 'Axy' for 'x pays attention to y' and 'b' for 'Bob', 'Ax·b' would be 'x pays attention to Bob'. Similarly, with 'Lxy' for 'x likes y', 'Lbx' would be 'Bob likes x'.

E2.1.3.   Treating

'P*x*'   as short for '*x* is a person',

'H*xy*'   as short for '*x* has *y*',

'G*xyz*'   as short for '*x* gives *y* to *z*' (or, as the
                  occasion warrants, '*x* gave *y* to *z*'),

'a'   as short for 'Alan', and

'b'   as short for 'Barbara',

put the following statements into smooth, straightforward, natural English:

a. $(\exists x)(Hbx \& Gaxb)$

b. $(\forall x)(Hbx \supset Gbxa)$

c. $(\forall x)[Gaxb \supset (\exists y)(Py \& Gbxy)]$

d. $(\forall x)[(Px \& (\exists y)Gxya) \supset (\exists y)Gxyb]$

e. $(\exists x)[Px \& (\exists y)(Gxyb \& \sim Gxya)]$

f. $(\forall x)[Px \supset (\exists y)Hxy]$

g. $\sim(\exists x)[Px \& (\forall y)Hxy]$

h. $(\forall x)[Px \supset (\exists y)Gxyx]$

i. $(\exists x)(\forall y)[Py \supset \sim(\exists z)(Pz \& Gyxz)]$

j. $(\exists x)(Px \& (\forall y)[Py \supset \sim(\exists z)(Gxzy \vee Gyzx)])$

k. $(\exists x)[Px \& (\forall z)(\exists y)(Pz \supset Gxyz)]$

l. $(\exists x)[Px \& (\exists y)(\forall z)(Pz \supset Gxyz)]$

m. $(\forall x)(Px \supset (\forall y)(\forall z)[(Py \& Hyz) \supset Hxz])$

n. $(\forall x)(Px \supset (\forall y)[(\exists z)(Pz \& Gxyz) \supset \sim Hxy])$

o. $(\forall x)(Px \supset (\forall y)[(\exists z)(Pz \& Gzyx) \supset Hxy])$

p. $(\forall x)(Px \supset (\forall y)[\sim Hxy \supset \sim(\exists z)(Pz \& Gxyz)])$

q. $\sim(\exists x)(Px \& (\forall y)[Hxy \supset (\exists z)(Pz \& Gxyz)])$

r. $\sim(\exists x)(Px \& (\forall y)[Hxy \supset (\exists z)(Pz \& Gzyx)])$

s. $(\exists x)[Px \& (\exists y)(Py \& (\forall z)[(\exists x')(Px' \& Gxzx') \supset Gxzy])]$

t. $\sim(\exists x)[Px \& (\exists y)(Py \& (\forall z)[(\exists x')(Px' \& Gx'zx) \supset Gyzx])]$

E2.1.4.   Note the manner in which the instances of quantifications were exhibited on pp. 135–36: the first three instances, followed by 'etc.' Exhibit in the same manner the instances of each of the following quantifications, indicating in each case whether the instance is or is not conservative.

a. $(\exists x)Fa_3 x$ b. $(\exists x)[Fx \& (\forall y)(\forall z)(\sim Fy \supset \sim Gxz)]$

c. $(\exists x)(Fa_2 a_1 \& Ga_1)$ d. $(\forall x)([Fx \& Gx] \supset [(\forall y)(Gy \supset Hy) \supset Hx])$

e. $(\forall y)[(\exists x)\sim Fxy \vee Ga_1 a_3]$ f. $(\forall x)(\forall y)(Fya_1 \supset \sim Fa_2 x)$

E2.1.5.   Note the manner in which the subformulas of a statement were exhibited on pp. 139–40. Exhibit in the same manner the subformulas of the six statements in

E2.1.4, and those of the following eight:

g. $\sim\sim Fa_1 \mathbin{\&} \sim(Fa_1 \equiv Ga_1)$

h. $(\exists x)(Fx \mathbin{\&} \sim Ga_1) \supset (Ga_1 \supset (\forall x)Hx)$

i. $\sim(\forall x)\sim(Fx \supset Gx)$

j. $\sim(\forall x)[(\sim Fx \mathbin{\&} Gx) \supset (Hx \vee \sim Fa_2)]$

k. $(\exists x)Gx \supset \sim(\forall x)(Px \supset Wx)$

l. $Scag \supset [Iacb \mathbin{\&} \sim(Lcacg \vee Lcgca)]$

m. $(\forall x)(Mx \supset Wx) \mathbin{\&} (\forall x)(Mx \supset \sim Wx)$

n. $(\exists x)(Lx \mathbin{\&} Mx) \supset (\exists x)(Lx \mathbin{\&} \sim Mx)$

E2.1.6.

(a) Show that when $A(T/X)$ qualifies as a statement for any one term T, then it qualifies as one for every term T.[37]

(b) Show that (i) if $A \supset B(T/X)$ is a statement for some term T, then $A \supset (\forall X)B$ is a statement; and (ii) if $A(T/X) \supset B$ is a statement for some term T, then $(\exists X)A \supset B$ is a statement.

(c) Vacuous quantifications could be ruled out by inserting one restriction in the definition of a quantificational statement (Part **D** of Table VI, p. 143). What should the restriction be?

(d) With $A(X/T)$ understood to be the result of putting X for T in A, show that clause (4') below could replace clause (4) in the definition of a statement:

(4') If A is a statement and X is a term variable foreign to A, then $(\forall X)A(X/T)$ and $(\exists X)A(X/T)$ are also statements.

Under which circumstances would $(\forall X)A(X/T)$ and $(\exists X)A(X/T)$ then prove to be vacuous quantifications?

E2.1.7.

(a) With A understood to be a statement, and its length to be as on p. 138, show that:

(i) in case A is atomic, then A is of length 1;

(ii) in case A is of the sort $\sim B$, then A is of length $l + 1$, where l is the length of B;

(iii) in case A is of one of the four sorts $(B \supset C)$, $(B \mathbin{\&} C)$, $(B \vee C)$, and $(B \equiv C)$, then A is of length $l + l' + 1$, where l is the length of B and l' is that of C;

(iv) in case A is of one of the two sorts $(\forall X)B$ and $(\exists X)B$, then A is of length $l + 1$, where l is the length of any instance $B(T/X)$ of A.

(b) Calculate the length of each of statements a–n in E2.1.4–5.

E2.1.8.

(a) Supply the one statement which is an instance of all three of the existential quantifications

$$(\exists x)Fxx$$

$$(\exists x)Fa_1 x$$

$$(\exists x)Fxa_1.$$

Of which of these statements is the instance supplied a generating one?

---

[37] A full and rigorous proof of (a) would require mathematical induction. It is possible, however, to suggest such a rigorous proof quite clearly and persuasively, and no more is expected of the student at this point.

(b) With $A(X/T)$ understood as in E2.1.6(d), show that if $A(T/X)$ is a generating instance of $(\forall X)A$, then $(\forall X)[(A(T/X))(X/T)]$—the result of putting X for T in $A(T/X)$ and prefacing that with $(\forall X)$—is $(\forall X)A$ itself.

(c) With T and T' presumed to be distinct terms, show that the term variant $(A(T/X))(T'/T)$ of $A(T/X)$ counts as an instance of $(\forall X)A$ if and only if T is foreign to $(\forall X)A$—and, hence, if and only if $A(T/X)$ is a conservative instance of $(\forall X)A$. Show why the result fails when T' and T are the same.

(d) Show that, if $A(T/X)$ is a conservative instance of $(\forall X)A$, then any instance $A(T'/X)$ of $(\forall X)A$ is the term-variant $(A(T/X))(T'/T)$ of $A(T/X)$.

E2.1.9.

(a) Under precisely which circumstances are the atomic subformulas of a statement finite in number, and under which are they infinite?

(b) Let S be a finite (but non-empty) set of statements, let S^* consist of all the atomic subformulas of the members of S, and let S^{**} consist of all the statements whose atomic subformulas belong to S^*. Show that S^* may be finite, but S^{**} is sure to be infinite. (Sets like S^* and S^{**} will play a key role in Section 3.4.)

*(c) Show that truth-values can be assigned to $\aleph_0$ atomic statements in $2^{\aleph_0}$ different ways.

E2.1.10.

(a) Let α be the result of assigning **T** to every one of 'Fa$_1$', 'Fa$_2$', 'Fa$_3$', etc., and **F** to every one of 'Ga$_1$', 'Ga$_2$', 'Ga$_3$', etc., and every one of 'Ha$_1$', 'Ha$_2$', 'Ha$_3$', etc.; and let α' be the result of assigning **T** to 'Fa$_1$', 'Ga$_1$', and 'Ha$_1$', and **F** to every one of 'Fa$_2$', 'Fa$_3$', etc., 'Ga$_2$', 'Ga$_3$', etc., and 'Ha$_2$', 'Ha$_3$', etc. Calculate the truth-value of each of the statements g–j in E2.1.5 on α, and then on α'.

(b) For each of the following statements, find a truth-value assignment to its atomic subformulas on which it would be false, and display that assignment and the truth-values of relevant subformulas in a truth-table row as on pp. 153–54. (In each case, only finitely many atomic subformulas need be attended to.)

   i. $Fa \supset (\forall x)Fx$

   ii. $(\exists x)Fx \supset Fa$

   iii. $[(\forall x)Fx \supset (\forall x)Gx] \supset (\forall x)(Fx \supset Gx)$

   iv. $[(\forall x)Fx \equiv (\forall x)Gx] \supset (\forall x)(Fx \equiv Gx)$

   v. $[(\forall x)Fx \supset Ga] \supset (\forall x)(Fx \supset Ga)$

   vi. $(\exists x)(Fx \supset Ga) \supset [(\exists x)Fx \supset Ga]$

E2.1.11. Using the method of the text (pp. 157–60), determine whether each of the following statements is logically true, logically false, or logically indeterminate. (Note that when a conditional $A \supset B$ is *logically true*, the set $\{A, \sim B\}$ is *inconsistent* and $\{A\}$ *entails* B. And, when a biconditional $A \equiv B$ is *logically true*, A and B are *equivalent*.)

   a. $\sim(\exists x)Fx \supset (\forall x)(Fx \supset Gx)$

   b. $\sim(\exists x)Fx \supset (\forall x)(Fx \supset \sim Gx)$

c. $(\exists x)(Fx \ \& \ Gx) \supset [(\exists x)Fx \ \& \ (\exists x)Gx]$

d. $[(\exists x)Fx \ \& \ (\forall x)Gx] \supset (\exists x)(Fx \ \& \ Gx)$

e. $(\forall x)(Fx \lor Gx) \supset [(\forall x)Fx \lor (\forall x)Gx]$

f. $(\forall x)(Fx \lor Gx) \supset [(\forall x)Fx \lor (\exists x)Gx]$

g. $(\exists x)(Fx \supset Gx) \supset (\exists x)(Fx \ \& \ Gx)$

h. $(\forall x)(Fx \supset Gx) \equiv {\sim}(\exists x)(Fx \ \& \ {\sim}Gx)$

i. $[(\forall x)(Fx \supset Gx) \ \& \ (\forall x)(Gx \supset Hx)] \supset (\forall x)(Fx \supset Hx)$

j. $[(\exists x)(Fx \ \& \ Gx) \ \& \ (\forall x)(Gx \supset Hx)] \supset (\exists x)(Fx \ \& \ Hx)$

k. $(\forall x)[Fx \supset (\forall y)Fy]$

l. $(\forall x)[Fx \supset (\exists y)Fy]$

m. $(\exists x)Fxx \equiv (\exists x)(\exists y)Fxy$

n. $(\forall x)Fxx \equiv (\forall x)(\forall y)Fxy$

E2.1.12.
   (a)   Show that if $(\forall X)A$ is vacuous, then all three of $(\forall X)A$, $(\exists X)A$, and A are equivalent.

   (b)   Show that if our supply of terms were finite, then in view of clauses (7) and (8) in the definition of truth, a universal quantification would be equivalent to the conjunction, and an existential quantification equivalent to the disjunction, of its instances.

E2.1.13.   In Table IX logical truth, equivalence, and entailment were defined in terms of consistency. Show that all the logical properties and relations in question can likewise be defined in terms of (i) logical truth or falsehood, (ii) equivalence, and (iii) entailment.

E2.1.14.
   *(a)   Show that the term variants of a logical truth are all logically true, and those of a logical falsehood all logically false.

   (b)   Construct a logically indeterminate statement with a logically true term variant, and construct one with a logically false term variant.

E2.1.15.
   (a)   Show that if $(\forall X)A$ is logically true, so is $(\exists X)A$; and, if $(\exists X)A$ is logically false, so is $(\forall X)A$.

   (b)   Show that:
      (i)   If $(\forall X)A$ is logically true, so is every instance of $(\forall X)A$;
      (ii)   If every instance of $(\forall X)A$ is logically true, so is $(\forall X)A$;
      * (iii)   If any one *conservative* instance of $(\forall X)A$ is logically true, so is $(\forall X)A$;
      (iv)   If $(\exists X)A$ is logically false, so is every instance of $(\exists X)A$;
      (v)   If every instance of $(\exists X)A$ is logically false, so is $(\exists X)A$;
      (vi)   If any one *conservative* instance of $(\exists X)A$ is logically false, so is $(\exists X)A$.

   (c)   In connection with (iii) and (vi), construct a non-conservative instance of $(\forall X)A$ which is logically true, though $(\forall X)A$ itself is not; and construct a non-conservative instance of $(\exists X)A$ which is logically false, though $(\exists X)A$ itself is not.

E2.1.16. With '2' short for 'logically true', '1' for 'logically indeterminate', and '0' for 'logically false', and $A(T/X)$ presumed to be an arbitrary *conservative* instance of $(\forall X)A$, supply the wanted entries in the following table:

$A(T/X)$	$(\forall X)A$	$(\exists X)A$
2		
1		
0		

When more than one entry is appropriate, offer an example for each.

E2.1.17. Show that the members of each one of the following three sets cannot all be true on any truth-value assignment to their atomic subformulas:

a. $\{\sim Fa_1, \sim Fa_2, \sim Fa_3, \ldots, (\exists x)Fx\}$

b. $\{Fa_1, Fa_2, Fa_3, \ldots, Ga_1, Ga_2, Ga_3, \ldots, (\forall x)Fx \supset \sim(\forall x)\ Gx\}$

c. $\{Fa_2, Fa_3, Fa_4, \ldots, Ga_2, Ga_3, Ga_4, \ldots, \sim(\forall x)Fx, \sim Fa_1 \supset (Ga_1 \ \& \ (\exists x)\sim Gx)\}$.

2.2   Consistency Trees (2)

As the reader will recall, a set of statements which on truth-functional grounds alone is consistent may nonetheless be inconsistent on quantificational ones. And hence a statement which on truth-functional grounds alone fails to be entailed by a set of statements, or fails to be logically true, may nonetheless be entailed by the set, or be logically true, on quantificational grounds. The techniques of Chapter 1 must therefore be extended to cover quantificational matters; and, since the truth-table method cannot be so extended, a technique like the tree method of Section 1.2, or the derivation method of Section 1.3, is indispensable at this point.

In Section 2.3 we shall extend the derivation method to quantificational matters. In this section we extend the tree method, and—borrowing again from Smullyan and Jeffrey—devise a full-fledged technique for ascertaining whether or not, given a set S of statements, there is a truth-value assignment to the atomic subformulas of the members of S on which all these members are true. We shall then have a comprehensive test for (in)consistency, entailment, logical truth, and the like.[1]

The method of Section 1.2 worked as follows. We first assumed a set $\{A_1, A_2, \ldots, A_n\}$ of statements to be truth-functionally consistent. We then traced out the consequences of that assumption, entering on the branches

---

[1] When talking in this section of the (in)consistency of a set of statements, we automatically presume that the set is finite and non-empty; and, when talking of the entailment of a statement by a set of statements, we automatically presume that the set is finite.

of a tree components of A_1, A_2, . . ., and A_n (unnegated or negated), components of these components (again unnegated or negated), and so on, down to the atomic components of A_1, A_2, . . ., and A_n (also unnegated or negated). The rules we used to decompose A_1, A_2, . . ., and A_n were such that, if $\{A_1,A_2,. . .,A_n\}$ was truth-functionally consistent, then *either* the set consisting of all the entries on the left-most branch of the tree was truth-functionally consistent, *or* the set consisting of all those on the next branch was, . . ., *or* the set consisting of all those on the right-most branch was. So, if a contradiction turned up along *every* branch (and the sets consisting of the entries on the various branches of the tree were *all* truth-functionally *in*consistent), then $\{A_1,A_2,. . .,A_n\}$ *was* truth-functionally *in*consistent. Furthermore, if any branch of the tree remained open to the end, we could be sure that $\{A_1,A_2,. . .,A_n\}$ was truth-functionally consistent—indeed, we could retrieve from that branch a truth-value assignment to the atomic components of A_1, A_2, . . ., and A_n on which all of A_1, A_2, . . ., and A_n were sure to be true.

The present method will work in much the same way, but with *subformulas* substituting for components. On the assumption that a set $\{A_1,A_2,. . .,A_n\}$ of statements is consistent, we shall enter on the branches of a tree subformulas of A_1, A_2, . . ., and A_n (unnegated or negated), subformulas of these subformulas (unnegated or negated), and so on, down to various atomic subformulas of A_1, A_2, . . ., and A_n (unnegated or negated). Of course, this will require some extra rules for decomposing quantifications and their negations. But the rules will be such that, if $\{A_1,A_2,. . .,A_n\}$ is consistent, then *either* the set consisting of all the entries on the left-most branch of the tree is consistent as well, *or* the set consisting of all the entries on the next branch is, . . ., *or* the set consisting of all the entries on the right-most branch is. So, if a contradiction turns up along *every* branch, then $\{A_1,A_2,. . .,A_n\}$ can confidently be declared inconsistent.

Detailed proof of this result will be given in Section 3.5; and proof can be found in Smullyan and in Jeffrey that if $\{A_1,A_2,. . .,A_n\}$ is inconsistent, then $\{A_1,A_2,. . .,A_n\}$ has a closed tree.[2] The reader may thus rest assured that $\{A_1A_2,. . .,A_n\}$ is inconsistent if and only if it has a closed tree. What an open tree would tell us about $\{A_1,A_2,. . .,A_n\}$ will be discussed at length below.[3]

---

[2] See Chapter V of Smullyan's *First-Order Logic*, and Chapter 8 of Jeffrey's *Formal Logic: Its Scope and Limits*.

[3] Though similar to the method of Section 1.2, the present one differs from it in many respects. For one thing, an unnegated universal quantification $(\forall X)A$, or a negated existential one $\sim(\exists X)A$, may have to be decomposed more than once if a due contradiction is to appear on some branch of a tree. So $(\forall X)A$ and $\sim(\exists X)A$ will not be checked off. Also, besides claiming—when $\{A_1,A_2,. . .,A_n\}$ was consistent—that the entries on any open branch of a tree for $\{A_1,A_2,. . .,A_n\}$ had to be true on some truth-value assignment on which A_1, A_2, . . ., and A_n

The New Rules

The rules of Table IV on p. 55 will serve, as before, to decompose truth-functional compounds. Four new rules will be used to decompose quantificational compounds and their negations. Each application of the latter will yield a subformula—either unnegated or negated—of a quantificational compound or of the negation of one, and will thereby cut down by one the number of occurrences of '∀' and '∃'.

Decomposing a universal quantification (and hence eliminating one universal quantifier) presents no problem. For suppose a universal quantification $(\forall X)A$ turns up on a branch of a tree, and the set consisting of all the statements entered so far on that branch is consistent. Then the same set *plus any instance of* $(\forall X)A$ *we please,* say $A(T/X)$, will be consistent as well, and we should have license to add $A(T/X)$ to the branch. Indeed, as $A(T/X)$ is true on any truth-value assignment on which $(\forall X)A$ is, $A(T/X)$ will be true on *all* the truth-value assignments on which the original entries were true. The move will be called **instantiating $(\forall X)A$ by means of the term T,** and the rule that condones it can be schematized thus:

$$
\boxed{
\begin{array}{c}
(\forall X)A \\
\cdot \\
A(T/X)
\end{array}
}
$$

The quantificational compound $(\forall X)A$ is not checked off after application of the rule. This for a simple, but compelling, reason: by checking off $(\forall X)A$, we might keep a due contradiction from turning up along some branch through $(\forall X)A$, and thereby mistake an inconsistent set of statements for a consistent one. We shall illustrate the point shortly. Note, by the way that, as $(\forall X)A$ is not checked off, it remains available for further instantiations.

The fact that a universal quantification is not checked off opens up an entirely new possibility. In Chapter 1, we could always count on producing a *finite* tree, even when the set tested was consistent: after finitely many applications of the rules, there remained nothing more to do. But things are different here. However many instances of a universal quantification have been entered on an *open* branch, another can still be added

---

were true, we could—and did—claim that if $A_1, A_2, \ldots$, and A_n were true on any truth-value assignment α, then the entries on some open branch or other had to be true on α. As the example in footnote 6 shows, we cannot make this extra claim here.

in accordance with the rules. Indeed, if every line that could be entered on an open branch of a tree did appear there, the tree might be *infinite,* i.e., infinitely many statements might turn up on one or more of its open branches. Some consistent sets (say, $\{(\forall x)Fx\}$) have only infinite trees. Fortunately, every inconsistent one has a closed, and hence finite, tree. (An inconsistent set may also have an infinite tree, but not one on which every possible line has been entered; we shall illustrate this below.)

Decomposing the *negation* of an *existential* quantification (and thereby eliminating one existential quantifier) is done in a similar manner.[4] Suppose a negated existential quantification $\sim(\exists X)A$ turns up on a branch of a tree, and the set consisting of all the statements entered so far on that branch is consistent. Then the same set *plus the negation $\sim A(T/X)$ of any instance $A(T/X)$ of $(\exists X)A$* will be consistent as well, and we should have license to add $\sim A(T/X)$ to the branch. Indeed, as $\sim A(T/X)$ is true on any truth-value assignment on which $\sim(\exists X)A$ is, $\sim A(T/X)$ will be true on *all* the truth-value assignments on which the original entries were true.

Of course, $\sim A(T/X)$ is *not* a subformula of $\sim(\exists X)A$, as $A(T/X)$ was one of $(\forall X)A$. It is, however, the negation of one (recall that $A(T/X)$ is a subformula of $(\exists X)A$, and that $(\exists X)A$ is a subformula of $\sim(\exists X)A$). So what we enter under $\sim(\exists X)A$ is a negated subformula of $\sim(\exists X)A$. The situation is not novel. Of the two statements $\sim A$ and B which we entered under $A \supset B$ in Section 1.2, one was the negation of a component—rather than a component—of $A \supset B$; and both statements which we entered under $\sim(A \lor B)$ were negated components of the compound.

Nor, of course, is $\sim A(T/X)$ an instance of $\sim(\exists X)A$: negations of quantifications are not quantifications, and hence have no instances. Note, however, that $\sim A(T/X)$ *is* an instance of the equivalent quantification $(\forall X)\sim A$ (which equivalence accounts, as already noted, for the similarities between our first two rules). So, to simplify the terminology, we shall consider $\sim A(T/X)$ a **quasi-instance** of $\sim(\exists X)A$. We shall refer both to instances and to quasi-instances as **"instances"** (in rhetorical quotes); and by **"instantiating"** (again in quotes) we shall mean either instantiating or quasi-instantiating, as is appropriate. The move from $\sim(\exists X)A$ to $\sim A(T/X)$ will thus be called **"instantiating" $\sim(\exists X)A$ by means of the term T,** and the rule that condones it can be schematized as follows:

$$\sim(\exists X)A$$
$$\cdot$$
$$\sim A(T/X)$$

---

[4] This because $\sim(\exists X)A$ is equivalent to $(\forall X)\sim A$.

Again, $\sim(\exists X)A$ is *not* checked off, $\sim(\exists X)A$ thus remaining available for further "instantiation."

To summarize things before we go on: the first of our new rules allows us to enter an instance $A(T/X)$ of $(\forall X)A$ on any branch through $(\forall X)A$, the second to enter a quasi-instance $\sim A(T/X)$ of $\sim(\exists X)A$ on any branch through $\sim(\exists X)A$, using in either case any term T we please. (Some choices of T will of course generate due contradictions sooner than others, but this is not the issue here.)[5]

The rules for decomposing (unnegated) existential quantifications and negated universal ones also resemble each other, but differ from the first two rules in important ways.

Suppose an existential quantification $(\exists X)A$ turns up on a branch of a tree, and the set consisting of all the statements entered so far on that branch is consistent. Then the same set *plus* any instance $A(T/X)$ of $(\exists X)A$ is sure to be consistent as well, *so long as T is foreign to the branch.* $A(T/X)$ need *not* be true on *every* truth-value assignment on which $(\exists X)A$ is true,[6] nor as a result on all the assignments on which the various entries on the branch are true. But it is sure to be true on *at least one* of them. So the set consisting of the original entries on the branch *plus* $A(T/X)$ is certain to be consistent, and we should have license to add $A(T/X)$ to the branch.[7]

The italicized restriction on T is crucial. Take the consistent set $\{\sim Fa, (\exists x)Fx\}$. Each one of the further sets $\{\sim Fa, (\exists x)Fx, Fb\}$, $\{\sim Fa, (\exists x)Fx, Fc\}$, etc., is consistent as well. But $\{\sim Fa, (\exists x)Fx, Fa\}$ is not. So entering 'Fa' under '$(\exists x)Fx$' would make for a contradiction and a closed tree. No mishap of this sort will occur, though, if any one of 'Fb', 'Fc', etc., is entered under '$(\exists x)Fx$'. All these show in place of 'x' in 'Fx' a term foreign to $\{\sim Fa, (\exists x)Fx\}$.

---

[5] When X does not occur in A, $A(T/X)$ is the same as A ($\sim A(T/X)$ the same as $\sim A$) for every term T. So by the first rule, A may be entered on any open branch through a vacuous quantification $(\forall X)A$; and by the second, $\sim A$ may be entered on any open branch through the negation $\sim(\exists X)A$ of a vacuous quantification $(\exists X)A$.

[6] For example, let α be the result of assigning **T** to every atomic subformula of '$(\exists x)Fx$' other than 'Fa', and **F** to that one. Then '$(\exists x)Fx$' is true on α, but of course 'Fa' is not. So, to illustrate the point made in footnote 3, the entries of this one-branch tree for the set $\{(\exists x)Fx\}$

$$(\exists x)Fx \checkmark$$

$$Fa$$

are not true on α.

[7] Note also that if $A(T/X)$ is true on any truth-value assignment α, then $(\exists X)A$—the entry from which $A(T/X)$ would come—is sure to be true on α. This point will prove important on p. 185.

Since $A(T/X)$ will frequently be entered on several branches, we require here that T *be foreign to each and every branch on which $A(T/X)$ is to be entered.* On p. 188, though, we shall relax the restriction some.

The move from $(\exists X)A$ to $A(T/X)$ will be called **instantiating $(\exists X)A$ by means of the term T,** and the rule that condones it can be schematized thus:

$$\boxed{\begin{array}{l} (\exists X)A\checkmark \\[4pt] \quad \bullet \\[4pt] A(T/X) \end{array}}$$

Note that $(\exists X)A$—unlike $(\forall X)A$ and $\sim(\exists X)A$—*is* checked off. Exactly the same sets of statements as before would be found inconsistent if $(\exists X)A$ were also left unchecked; but among the consistent ones, only those whose members show no quantifiers would have finite trees. With just one shot at $(\exists X)A$ allowed, it is imperative, by the way, that we enter $A(T/X)$ on *every* open branch through $(\exists X)A$; otherwise, a due contradiction might fail to turn up along some branch through $(\exists X)A$.

Decomposing the *negation* of a *universal* quantification is done in a similar manner.[8] Suppose a negated universal quantification $\sim(\forall X)A$ turns up on a branch of a tree, and the set consisting of all the statements entered so far on the branch is consistent. Then the same set *plus* the negation $\sim A(T/X)$ of any instance $A(T/X)$ of $(\forall X)A$ will be consistent as well, *so long as T is foreign to the branch.* Again, $\sim A(T/X)$ need not be true on every truth-value assignment on which $\sim(\forall X)A$ is true, nor as a result on all the assignments on which the various entries on the branch are true. But it is sure to be true on at least one of them, and we should have license to add $\sim A(T/X)$ to the branch.[9]

The restriction on T is crucial; and, as $\sim A(T/X)$ will frequently be entered on several branches, we require here that T *be foreign to each and every branch on which $\sim A(T/X)$ is to be entered.*

Again, $\sim A(T/X)$ is not a subformula of $\sim(\forall X)A$. It is, however, the negation of one, and what we enter under $\sim(\forall X)A$ here is a negated subformula of $\sim(\forall X)A$. Nor is $\sim A(T/X)$ an instance of $\sim(\forall X)A$. It is, however, an instance of the equivalent $(\exists X)\sim A$, and hence an "instance" of $\sim(\forall X)A$. The move from $\sim(\forall X)A$ to $\sim A(T/X)$ will thus be called "in-

---

[8] This because $\sim(\forall X)A$ is equivalent to $(\exists X)\sim A$.

[9] Note also that if $\sim A(T/X)$ is true on any truth-value assignment α, then $\sim(\forall X)A$—the entry from which $\sim A(T/X)$ would come—is sure to be true on α. This point will prove important on p. 185.

stantiating" $\sim(\forall X)A$ **by means of the term** T, and the rule that condones
it can be schematized as follows:

$$
\boxed{
\begin{array}{c}
\sim(\forall X)A\, \checkmark \\[2pt]
\cdot \\[2pt]
\sim A(T/X)
\end{array}
}
$$

Again, we check off $\sim(\forall X)A$, and therefore require $\sim A(T/X)$ to be entered
on every open branch through $\sim(\forall X)A$.[10]

For ease of reference, we collect our four new rules in a single table:[11]

TABLE X

$(\forall X)A$	$\sim(\exists X)A$	$(\exists X)A\ \checkmark$	$\sim(\forall X)A\ \checkmark$
$\cdot$	$\cdot$	$\cdot$	$\cdot$
$A(T/X)$	$\sim A(T/X)$	$A(T/X)$	$\sim A(T/X)$

Restriction: In the third and fourth cases, T must be a term foreign to every
branch on which $A(T/X)$ and $\sim A(T/X)$ are to be entered.

Examples and Strategies

We shall now present some sample trees, and—in connection with
the first of these—two strategy hints. The reader should review the instructions laid down in Section 1.2, the strategy hints of p. 59, and Table
V of p. 55 on the various uses to which the tree method can be put, as
all these remain pertinent (with the appropriate changes in terminology
made). With infinitely many shots at universal quantifications and negated
existential quantifications allowed, we expressly require that a branch be
closed immediately upon the appearance of an atomic statement and its
negation. Otherwise, the branch might just keep getting longer and
longer and longer, never permitting (as did the branches of trees in Section 1.2) a check for contradictions.

---

[10] When $(\exists X)A$ is a vacuous quantification, our third rule permits us to enter A under
$(\exists X)A$. For (1) there is sure to be a term T which is foreign to all the branches through $(\exists X)A$,
and (2) for that term T as well as any other, $A(T/X)$ is the same as A. By the same token, our
fourth rule permits us to enter $\sim A$ under the negation $\sim(\forall X)A$ of any vacuous quantification
$(\forall X)A$.

[11] Our rules are adaptations of those on p. 54 of Smullyan's *First-Order Logic*. All the tree
rules of this section and of Section 1.2 are gathered in Appendix II.

EXAMPLE 1: {Something was left unsaid, Nothing was left unsaid}—an obviously inconsistent set of statements.

(a)   1 $(\exists x)Lx$ ✔
           2                    $(\forall x)\sim Lx$
                   ─────────────────   from
           3   La   1
           4              $\sim$La   2
                          x
                          3

The rationale behind the tree is as follows. Suppose that something was left unsaid (line 1); suppose also that nothing was left unsaid (line 2); and refer to what—according to line 1—was left unsaid by means of 'a', a term foreign to lines 1–2. Then a was left unsaid (line 3). But, as according to line 2 nothing was left unsaid, a was not left unsaid (line 4), a flat contradiction. Note, incidentally, that a like contradiction would arise whatever term be used to instantiate '$(\exists x)Lx$' (and '$(\forall x)\sim Lx$').

The following tree would also expose the inconsistency of the set $\{(\exists x)Lx, (\forall x)\sim Lx\}$:

(b)   1 $(\exists x)Lx$ ✔
           2                    $(\forall x)\sim Lx$
                   ─────────────────   from
           3              $\sim$La   2
           4   Lb   1
           5              $\sim$Lb   2
                          x
                          4

But effort is wasted here: since 'a' has already been used to instantiate line 2, another term must be used to instantiate line 1, and hence an extra line has to be entered on the tree to yield the due contradiction.

(b) prompts our first strategy hint: *In view of the restriction imposed on T in the last two rules of Table X, existential quantifications and negated universal quantifications should be "instantiated" before universal quantifications and negated existential quantifications.* Otherwise, as we just saw, terms by means of which certain statements might have been "instantiated" will no longer be available for that purpose, and the tree will have longer branches than necessary.

By contrast, the following infinite tree, where all the instances of '$(\forall x)\sim Lx$' other than '$\sim$La' are presumed to be successively entered as lines 4, 5, 6, and so on, does *not* expose the inconsistency of $\{(\exists x)Lx,$ $(\forall x)\sim Lx\}$:

(c)   1 $(\exists x)Lx$ ✔

         2                          $(\forall x)\sim Lx$

                                    —————————   from

         3   La   1

         4                             $\sim$Lb   2

         5                             $\sim$Lc   2

         6                             $\sim$Ld   2

         .   .   .

         .   .   .

         .   .   .

As '$(\exists x)Lx$', which was instantiated at line 3 by means of 'a', can be instantiated only once, failure to use 'a' when the time came to instantiate '$(\forall x)\sim Lx$' prevented any contradiction from arising.

(c) prompts our second strategy hint: *Before they are "instantiated" by means of a fresh term, universal quantifications and negated existential quantifications should be "instantiated" on a given branch by means of every term already occurring along that branch.* Otherwise, as we just saw, a tree that could have closed might not.

EXAMPLE 2: {God created everything or else nothing is worth living for, Something that God didn't create is worth living for}—again an obviously inconsistent set of statements.

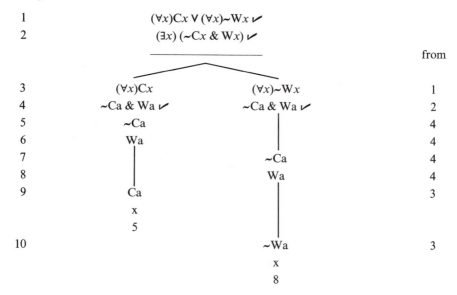

1                          $(\forall x)Cx \lor (\forall x)\sim Wx$ ✔

2                          $(\exists x) (\sim Cx \ \& \ Wx)$ ✔

                    ——————————————————   from

3            $(\forall x)Cx$ $(\forall x)\sim Wx$ 1

4           $\sim$Ca & Wa ✔ $\sim$Ca & Wa ✔   2

5             $\sim$Ca   4

6   Wa   4

7 $\sim$Ca   4

8   Wa   4

9   Ca   3
              x
              5

10 $\sim$Wa   3
                                               x
                                               8

Here line 1 is first decomposed in accordance with the rule for disjunctions; on each of the resulting branches line 2 is instantiated as line 4, and line 4 decomposed in accordance with the rule for conjunctions; and then on each branch line 3 is instantiated by means of 'a' to produce a contradiction. A contradiction would likewise arise if 'b', or 'c', or 'd', etc., were used instead of 'a' to instantiate line 2. The tree illustrates an earlier remark of ours: if the instance '~Ca & Wa' of the existential quantification '(∃x)(~Cx & Wx)' were entered only on the left branch of the tree, the right one would never close, as the only lines that could possibly be entered on it would be instances of '(∀x)~Wx'.

EXAMPLE 3: Does {All Greeks are men, All men are fallible, Aristotle is a Greek} entail 'Not all Greeks are infallible'?

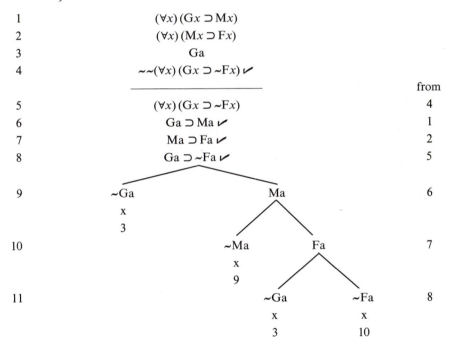

1	(∀x)(Gx ⊃ Mx)	
2	(∀x)(Mx ⊃ Fx)	
3	Ga	
4	~~(∀x)(Gx ⊃ ~Fx) ✔	
		from
5	(∀x)(Gx ⊃ ~Fx)	4
6	Ga ⊃ Ma ✔	1
7	Ma ⊃ Fa ✔	2
8	Ga ⊃ ~Fa ✔	5
9	~Ga / Ma	6
10	~Ma / Fa	7
11	~Ga / ~Fa	8

Since the set made up of lines 1–4 is inconsistent, lines 1–3 do entail '~(∀x)(Gx ⊃ ~Fx)'.

Here line 4 was first decomposed in accordance with the rule for double negations, and all three of lines 1, 2, and 5 were then instantiated by means of 'a'. The remaining moves were all truth-functional ones.

EXAMPLE 4: Is 'There is something that was left unsaid if anything was' logically true or not?

		from
1	$\sim(\exists x)(\forall y)(Ly \supset Lx)$	
2	$\sim(\forall y)(Ly \supset La)$ ✔	1
3	$\sim(Lb \supset La)$ ✔	2
4	Lb	3
5	$\sim La$	3
6	$\sim(\forall y)(Ly \supset Lb)$ ✔	1
7	$\sim(Lc \supset Lb)$ ✔	6
8	Lc	7
9	$\sim Lb$	7
	x	
	4	

Since the set made up of line 1 is inconsistent, '$(\exists x)(\forall y)(Ly \supset Lx)$' is logically true.

The tree illustrates two earlier remarks of ours. (1) Line 1 had to be decomposed twice before a contradiction could be arrived at. (Note also that when line 2 was quasi-instantiated, a term other than 'a' had to be used; when line 6 was, a term other than 'a' and 'b'.) (2) Had we checked off line 1 after quasi-instantiating it as line 2, we could not have decomposed it twice, the (one branch of the) tree would have ended at line 5 without closing, and we would have declared the set made up of line 1 consistent, when in fact it is not.

All the sets we have tested so far were inconsistent; and, as promised on p. 175, each one proved to have a closed tree. Now for some consistent sets.

EXAMPLE 5: {Mary forgot something or misunderstood something, Mary remembered something, Mary understood something}.

			from
1	$(\exists x)Fx \vee (\exists x)Mx$ ✔		
2	$(\exists x)\sim Fx$ ✔		
3	$(\exists x)\sim Mx$ ✔		
4	$(\exists x)Fx$ ✔	$(\exists x)Mx$ ✔	1
5	$\sim Fa$	$\sim Fa$	2
6	$\sim Mb$	$\sim Mb$	3
7	Fc		4
8		Mc	4

The left branch of the tree is still open, and yet—lines 1–4 being all checked off—no further line can be added to it. Can we then pick off the branch a truth-value assignment on which all of lines 1–3 are sure to be true? Yes. Assigning **T** to 'Fc' (the one atomic statement that occurs unnegated on the branch), **F** to 'Fa' and 'Mb' (the two atomic statements that occur negated on the branch), and either one of **T** and **F** to the remaining atomic subformulas of lines 1–3 will do the trick. Indeed, 'Fc' being true on the assignment, '($\exists x$)Fx' will be true on it, and hence so will line 1; 'Fa' being false on the assignment, '~Fa' will be true on it, and hence so will line 2; and, 'Mb' being false on the assignment, '~Mb' will be true on it, and hence so will line 3. As the right branch of the tree is also open, and no further line can be added to it, assigning **T** to 'Mc', **F** to 'Fa' and 'Mb', and either one of **T** and **F** to the remaining atomic subformulas of lines 1–3 will likewise do the trick.[12]

More generally, take *any* finite tree with an open branch that is **completed,** i.e., with an open branch to which no further line can be added. The set tested by such a tree is sure to be consistent, and a truth-value assignment on which all its members are true can be picked off any open and completed branch: **T** to every atomic statement that occurs unnegated on the branch, and **F** to all the other atomic subformulas. (Note that every atomic statement occurring negated on that branch is thereby assigned **F**. Exactly which truth-value is assigned to the remaining atomic subformulas matters not.)

Proof of the fact is essentially as on p. 57. (a) Any atomic statement that occurs unnegated on the branch is true on α. (b) The negation of any one that occurs negated on the branch is likewise true on α. And (c) any compound on the branch (other than a negated atomic statement) is true on α if the statements on the branch which came from the compound are true on α. (Note in connection with (c) that there can be no (unnegated) universal quantifications or negated existential quantifications on the branch, since it is presumed to be both open and completed. There can of course be (unnegated) existential or negated universal quantifications on the branch, but—as pointed out in footnotes 7 and 9— these are sure to be true on α if the statements on the branch which came from them are true on α.) Hence, every statement on the branch is true on α. Hence, all the members of the set tested, being on the branch, are true on α.[13]

---

[12] Were it not for the restriction placed on T in the rule for existential quantifications, at line 7 of the foregoing tree '($\exists x$)Fx' could have been instantiated as 'Fa', which would have contradicted line 5; and at line 8 '($\exists x$)Mx' could have been instantiated as 'Mb', which would have contradicted line 6. With both branches thus closing, we would have declared inconsistent a set which is consistent.

[13] See Section 3.5, where a rigorous proof of the result is given. In general, nothing of interest can be learned from finite branches that are still open but not completed.

EXAMPLE 6: {Something just fell off the shelf or there is something wrong with my ears. Nothing just fell off the shelf}.

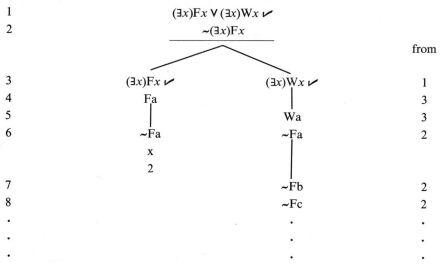

1                                    $(\exists x)Fx \lor (\exists x)Wx$ ✔

2 $\sim(\exists x)Fx$ from

3	$(\exists x)Fx$ ✔	$(\exists x)Wx$ ✔	1
4	Fa		3
5		Wa	3
6	~Fa	~Fa	2
	x		
	2		
7		~Fb	2
8		~Fc	2

(All the quasi-instances of '$\sim(\exists x)Fx$' are presumed to be successively entered on the right branch of the tree as lines 6, 7, 8, 9, etc.)

Lines 1–2 are clearly true on the result α of assigning **T** to the one atomic statement ('Wa') that occurs unnegated on the right branch of the tree, and **F** to the remaining atomic subformulas of lines 1–2. For, with 'Wa' true on α, so is '$(\exists x)Wx$', and hence so is line 1; and, with 'Fa', 'Fb', 'Fc', and so on, all false on α, then '$(\exists x)Fx$' is false on α, and hence line 2 is true on α.

More generally, take *any* infinite tree with a finite branch that is both open and completed, *or* with an infinite branch that meets the following four conditions: (a) no contradiction occurs on the branch, (b) any compound on the branch other than a negated atomic statement, a universal quantification, or a negated existential quantification is decomposed, (c) every instance of any universal quantification on the branch is on the branch, and (d) every quasi-instance of any negated existential quantification on the branch is on the branch. The set tested by the tree is then sure to be consistent, and a truth-value assignment on which all its members are true can be retrieved from the tree. In the first case select any finite branch which is open and completed, and in the second any infinite one which meets conditions (a)–(d). Assigning **T** to every atomic statement occurring unnegated on the branch, and **F** to all the other subformulas, will again do the trick. Proof of the fact is essentially as on p. 185.[14]

---

[14] See Exercises E3.5.7–8 on this matter. In general, nothing of interest can be learned from infinite branches (like that of the third tree under Example 1) which do not meet conditions (a)–(d).

But these are matters which we cannot pursue any further, infinite trees being only a marginal concern of ours.

The Routine

As noted before, every inconsistent set of statements has a closed tree. But, as also noted, *not* every tree for an inconsistent set closes. So it would be good to know—when testing a set of statements for (in)consistency—that the tree we are constructing *will* be one of those which close *if* the set happens to be inconsistent. Fortunately, a routine for making trees is available which guarantees just this (the two strategy hints we gave earlier being part of it).[15] The reader who heeds it can be sure that any step he takes is towards a contradiction *if* one is due, and hence that the tree he is making will sooner or later close *if* the set tested is inconsistent. The tree could often stand pruning; but a closed tree it will be, and one that exposes the inconsistency of the set (CASE 1).

If, however, the set tested is consistent, following the routine to make a tree will lead to one of three situations:

(a)   We may *eventually* be told to proceed no further, and that the set is consistent. *Either*

    (i)   some one or more open branches may just have been completed; and from *any one* of them a truth-value assignment on which the members of the set are all true can be retrieved. (The tree will be **stunted** if there remain branches to which further lines—finitely many or indefinitely many—could still be added.) (CASE 2) *Or*

    (ii)   no open branch has been completed; but, in view of the lines already on the tree, entering new lines would be pointless. Here a truth-value assignment guaranteeing the consistency of the set can be retrieved from *at least one* (though not necessarily from every) open branch of the stunted tree (CASE 3).

(b)   On the other hand, we may *never* be told to stop, but will rather be instructed to add line after line to the tree, endlessly but to no avail. In that event, although the set tested is consistent, the routine will never apprise us of the fact (CASE 4).

Preferable, of course, would be a routine which would apprise us of the consistency of *every* consistent set. However, in view of Church's result reported on p. 156, no such routine can be devised.

---

[15] Our routine was inspired by (but differs considerably from) that on p. 114 of Jeffrey's *Formal Logic*.

The ground rules of the routine, with some of which the reader is already familiar, are as follows:

A. A branch must be closed as soon as an atomic statement and its negation have appeared along the branch.

B. Any statement not an (unnegated) universal quantification or negated existential one must be checked off when decomposed by application of a rule, and the statements into which it decomposes must be entered on each open branch through the statement.

C. When decomposing an (unnegated) existential quantification or negated universal one, "instantiate" it on each open branch through the statement by means of *the alphabetically earliest term foreign to that branch* (or, if preferred, by means of the alphabetically earliest term foreign to every branch on which it is to be "instantiated")

D. When decomposing an (unnegated) universal quantification or negated existential one, "instantiate" it on each open branch through the statement by means of *all (and only) the terms that have occurred so far along that branch*, omitting such "instances" of the statement as are already on the branch.[16] If no term has yet occurred along a given branch, use 'a_1' ($=$ 'a').

Incidentally, when terms occur in members of the set tested, we presuppose that 'a_1' ($=$ 'a') is among them. In Example 7 below, we accordingly refer to Bob by means of 'a' (rather than, say, 'b'). This will simplify the description on pp. 190–91 of the truth-value assignment for CASE 3.

Three incidental remarks about making trees via the routine are appropriate. First, when the routine does not say which of two or more statements on a tree to decompose first, the reader may select any one he wishes. We regularly work from the uppermost statement down, and from left to right when there are two or more statements to attend to on a given line. Instructions to proceed in this way could have been incorpor-

---

[16] The parenthesized '*and only*' is crucial. A number of trees whose open branches would otherwise all grow endlessly are stunted because of it.

THE ROUTINE

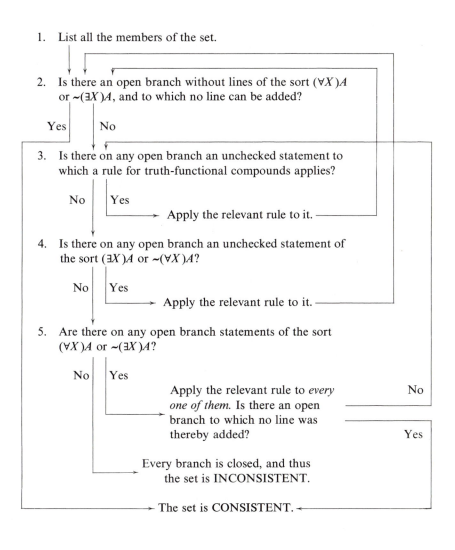

1.   List all the members of the set.

2.   Is there an open branch without lines of the sort $(\forall X)A$
     or $\sim(\exists X)A$, and to which no line can be added?

     Yes   No

3.   Is there on any open branch an unchecked statement to
     which a rule for truth-functional compounds applies?

             No   Yes

                   ⟶   Apply the relevant rule to it. ⟶

4.   Is there on any open branch an unchecked statement of
     the sort $(\exists X)A$ or $\sim(\forall X)A$?

            No   Yes

                  ⟶   Apply the relevant rule to it. ⟶

5.   Are there on any open branch statements of the sort
     $(\forall X)A$ or $\sim(\exists X)A$?

           No   Yes

                            Apply the relevant rule to *every*   No
                            one of them. Is there an open
                            branch to which no line was
                            thereby added?   Yes

                      Every branch is closed, and thus
                         the set is INCONSISTENT.

                    ⟶ The set is CONSISTENT. ←

ated in the guidelines or the routine itself, to make its use more mechanical; but this would complicate things quite unnecessarily.

Second, the reader will notice that when the work assigned in Stage 3 or Stage 4 is done, he is sent back to Stage 2, and properly so: an open branch of the tree might *now* be completed. However, upon completing the work assigned in Stage 5, he is sent back to Stage 3 rather than to Stage 2, and again properly so: there is sure to be an (unnegated) universal or negated existential quantification on every open branch, so the answer to the question at Stage 2 would have to be No.

Third, at Stages 3 and 4 the reader is asked to decompose *one* statement and return to Stage 2. But at Stage 5 he must "instantiate" all the (unnegated) universal quantifications and negated existential ones on the branch. Why the instructions were so phrased will be illustrated under Example 8.

Now for CASES 1–4 from p. 187.

If a time comes when the one question posed at Stages 2, 3, and 4, and the first question posed at Stage 5, is answered No, then every branch of the tree will be closed, for reasons which study of the routine will reveal (CASE 1). If a time comes when the question posed at Stage 2 is answered Yes, then the reader will have, for his efforts, an open branch which is completed (i.e., one to which no further line can be added), and the construction of the tree will stop, whether or not more lines could have been added to other branches. Of course, there will be no (unnegated) universal or negated existential quantifications on that branch (CASE 2). If a time comes when both of the questions posed at Stage 5 are answered Yes, then the construction of the tree will again stop. Though there are (unnegated) universal or negated existential quantifications on every open branch, "instantiating" them is demonstrably pointless (CASE 3). However, if every time the reader reaches Stage 5, he answers the first question Yes and the second No, then he is caught in an endless cycle of "instantiations," and the tree will just keep growing (CASE 4).

(The first tree under Example 1, and those under Examples 2–4, were all constructed by following the routine, and were closed trees. Had we followed the routine in Example 5, the set $\{(\exists x)Fx \vee (\exists x)Mx, (\exists x)\sim Fx, (\exists x)\sim Mx\}$ would have been declared consistent the minute we completed the left-hand branch with 'Fc', and 'Mc' would not have been entered on the tree (CASE 2). And had we followed the routine in Example 6, the tree would have been stunted after we entered '~Fa' on it. Indeed, in view of ground rule **D,** (1) no other quasi-instance of '~(∃x)Fx' could be entered on the branch, since 'a' was the only term to have occurred on it so far, and (2) '~Fa' itself could not be entered again (CASE 3).)

As noted on p. 187, a truth-value assignment on which all the members of the set S being tested are true can be retrieved from the tree in CASE 2 and CASE 3. In the instructions below, understand S^* to consist of the atomic subformulas of the members of S:

CASE 2. Pick any open and completed branch, and assign (i) **T** to every member of S^* which occurs unnegated on that branch, and (ii) **F** to the remaining members of S^*.

CASE 3. Pick any open branch to which no new line has been added since you last entered Stage 5, and—with **the a_1-rewrite (= a-rewrite) of a member A of S^*** held to be the result of putting 'a_1' (= 'a') for every term in A which is foreign to *that* branch—assign (i) **T** to every member of S^* which occurs unnegated, or whose a_1-rewrite occurs unnegated, on the branch, and (ii) **F** to the remaining members of S^*.[17]

The assignment for CASE 2 is familiar from p. 185. On pp. 195–96 we shall illustrate the assignment for CASE 3, and in Section 3.5 we shall prove that every member of S is true thereon.

Further Examples

We append as samples seven extra trees, all constructed by following the routine. The first three are closed, the next three are stunted, and the seventh is a portion of a tree which would keep growing endlessly (CASE 4). We do some pruning on the trees by enclosing unnecessary lines within square brackets.

---

[17] Note that each member of S^* is thereby assigned the same truth-value as its a_1-rewrite. The point will prove important in Section 3.5. In Example 11 on p. 195, the various statements of which 'Fa' is the a-rewrite are, of course, 'Fb', 'Fc', 'Fd', etc. And in Example 12 on p. 196, those of which 'Dba' is the a-rewrite are 'Dbc', 'Dbd', 'Dbe', etc. (but *not* 'Dbb', since 'b' already occurs on the left-hand branch of the tree).

EXAMPLE 7: Is the argument from the four premisses 'Only grown-ups and children accompanied by their parents were admitted', 'All grown-ups who stayed till the end liked the show', 'Bob was admitted', and 'Bob didn't like the show', to the conclusion 'Some grown-ups didn't stay till the end or Bob was (a child) accompanied by his parents', valid or not?

1	$(\forall x)[Ax \supset (Gx \lor Cx)]$	
2	$(\forall x)[(Gx \& Sx) \supset Lx]$	
3	Aa	
4	$\sim La$	
5	$\sim[(\exists x)(Gx \& \sim Sx) \lor Ca]\checkmark$	

from

6	$\sim(\exists x)(Gx \& \sim Sx)$	5
7	$\sim Ca$	5
8	$Aa \supset (Ga \lor Ca)\checkmark$	1
9	$(Ga \& Sa) \supset La\checkmark$	2
10	$\sim(Ga \& \sim Sa)\checkmark$	6

11	8
12	11
13	10
14	13
15	9
16	15

The argument is valid.

EXAMPLE 8: Is the argument from 'There is something which is the cause of everything' to 'Everything has a cause' valid or not?

		from
1	$(\exists x)(\forall y)Cxy$✔	
2	$\sim(\forall y)(\exists x)Cxy$✔	
3	$(\forall y)Cay$	1
4	$\sim(\exists x)Cxb$	2
5	[Caa]	3
6	Cab	3
7	$\sim$Cab	4
	x	
	6	

The argument is valid.[18] (Note that line 5 is unnecessary.)

To illustrate, as promised, a remark on p. 190, suppose the first question posed at Stage 5 had read: "*Is* there on any open branch *a* statement, etc. . . .," and the instructions in case of a Yes answer had read: "Apply the rule to *it*." Then, after entering 'Caa' and 'Cab' as lines 5 and 6 respectively, we would have returned to Stage 3, and passed through Stage 4 to Stage 5 again. Faced once more with line 3, to which the rule for (un-negated) universal quantifications applies, we might have chosen to apply the rule to that statement again (instead of treating line 4). But, since 'Caa' and 'Cab' have already been entered on the tree, and since the only terms to have occurred so far are 'a' and 'b', no new line would thereby have been added to the tree. So we would have answered Yes to the second question of Stage 5, thus mistakenly declaring the set consistent.

With the first question at Stage 5 and the attendant instructions phrased as they are, we must decompose line 4 as well as line 3 before answering the second question. And application of the rule for negated existential quantifications to that line yields '$\sim$Cab', which closes the tree.

---

[18] This result was established by a different method on pp. 163–64.

EXAMPLE 9: Is the argument from 'Horses are animals' to 'Tails of horses are tails of animals' valid or not?

		from
1	$(\forall x)(Hx \supset Ax)$	
2	$\sim(\forall x)[(\exists y)(Hy \mathbin{\&} Txy) \supset (\exists y)(Ay \mathbin{\&} Txy)]\checkmark$	

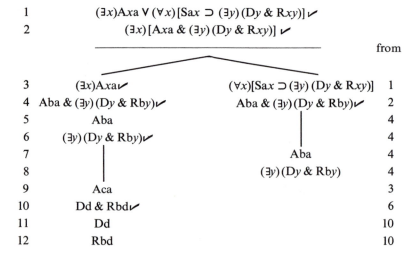

3	$\sim[(\exists y)(Hy \mathbin{\&} Tay) \supset (\exists y)(Ay \mathbin{\&} Tay)]\checkmark$	2
4	$(\exists y)(Hy \mathbin{\&} Tay)\checkmark$	3
5	$\sim(\exists y)(Ay \mathbin{\&} Tay)$	3
6	$Hb \mathbin{\&} Tab\checkmark$	4
7	Hb	6
8	Tab	6
9	$[Ha \supset Aa]$	1
10	$Hb \supset Ab\checkmark$	1
11	$[\sim(Aa \mathbin{\&} Taa)]$	5
12	$\sim(Ab \mathbin{\&} Tab)\checkmark$	5
13	$\sim Hb$ Ab	10
	x 7	
14	$\sim Ab$ $\sim Tab$	12
	x x	
	13 8	

The argument is valid. (Note that lines 9 and 11 are unnecessary.)

EXAMPLE 10: Is the set made up of 'Unless the accused has an alibi, anything he says will raise fresh doubts' and 'Indeed, some of his alibis will themselves raise fresh doubts anyway' consistent or not? (We use 'A' as short for 'is an alibi of'.)

		from
1	$(\exists x)Axa \lor (\forall x)[Sax \supset (\exists y)(Dy \mathbin{\&} Rxy)]\checkmark$	
2	$(\exists x)[Axa \mathbin{\&} (\exists y)(Dy \mathbin{\&} Rxy)]\checkmark$	

3	$(\exists x)Axa\checkmark$	$(\forall x)[Sax \supset (\exists y)(Dy \mathbin{\&} Rxy)]$	1
4	$Aba \mathbin{\&} (\exists y)(Dy \mathbin{\&} Rby)\checkmark$	$Aba \mathbin{\&} (\exists y)(Dy \mathbin{\&} Rby)\checkmark$	2
5	Aba		4
6	$(\exists y)(Dy \mathbin{\&} Rby)\checkmark$		4
7		Aba	4
8		$(\exists y)(Dy \mathbin{\&} Rby)$	4
9	Aca		3
10	$Dd \mathbin{\&} Rbd\checkmark$		6
11	Dd		10
12	Rbd		10

At this point the routine instructs us to stop and declare the set made up of lines 1–2 consistent: even though further work could be done on the right-hand branch, the left-hand one is open and completed (CASE 2). (Note incidentally that if the routine had not provided for stunting on an occasion like this, the tree would have grown forever.) As expected, a truth-value assignment on which lines 1–2 would both be true can be read off the completed branch: **T** to each of 'Aba', 'Aca', 'Dd', and 'Rbd', and **F** to the remaining atomic subformulas of lines 1–2.

EXAMPLE 11: Is the argument from the two premisses 'All Greeks are men' and 'All men are fallible' to the conclusion 'Not all Greeks are infallible' valid or not?

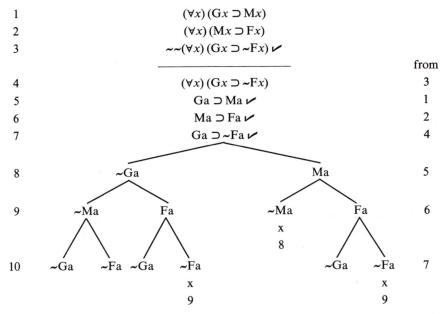

1	$(\forall x)(Gx \supset Mx)$	
2	$(\forall x)(Mx \supset Fx)$	
3	$\sim\sim(\forall x)(Gx \supset \sim Fx)$ ✔	from
4	$(\forall x)(Gx \supset \sim Fx)$	3
5	$Ga \supset Ma$ ✔	1
6	$Ma \supset Fa$ ✔	2
7	$Ga \supset \sim Fa$ ✔	4

(branching tree structure:
line 8: ~Ga   Ma — from 5
line 9: ~Ma   Fa   ~Ma(x 8)   Fa — from 6
line 10: ~Ga   ~Fa   ~Ga   ~Fa(x 9)   ~Ga   ~Fa(x 9) — from 7)

At this point the routine instructs us to stop and declare the set made up of lines 1–3 consistent: applying the rule for (unnegated) universal quantifications would add no new line to *any* of the four open branches. Indeed, in view of ground rule **D,** (1) no other instances of lines 1, 2, and 4 can be entered on those branches, since 'a' is the only term that has occurred so far, and (2) lines 5, 6, and 7 cannot be entered again (CASE 3). As promised on pp. 190–91, a truth-value assignment on which lines 1–3 would all be true can be retrieved from, say, the third branch: **T** to 'Fa', and hence also to 'Fb', 'Fc', 'Fd', etc., of which 'Fa' is the a-rewrite; and **F** to the remaining atomic subformulas of lines 1–3.

The proposed argument is therefore invalid, and the extra premiss 'Ga'—which insures that there are Greeks—made the difference in Example 3 on p. 183.

EXAMPLE 12: Is the set made of 'Nothing is fun or everything has dire consequences' and 'Adultery has dire consequences' consistent or not? (We use 'D' as short for 'is a dire consequence of'.)

		from
1	$(\forall x)\sim Fx \lor (\forall x)(\exists y)Dyx$ ✔	
2	$(\exists x)Dxa$ ✔	

3	$(\forall x)\sim Fx$	$(\forall x)(\exists y)Dyx$	1
4	Dba	Dba	2
5	$\sim Fa$		3
6	$\sim Fb$		3
7		$(\exists y)Dya$ ✔	3
8		$(\exists y)Dyb$ ✔	3
9		Dca	7
10		Ddb	8
11		$(\exists y)Dyc$	3
12		$(\exists y)Dyd$	3

At this point the routine instructs us to stop and declare the set made up of lines 1–2 consistent. The first time we went through Stage 5 (and instantiated both '$(\forall x)\sim Fx$' and '$(\forall x)(\exists y)Dyx$'), two lines were entered on each branch, and the ones on the right-hand branch had to be instantiated in turn as lines 9 and 10. But the second time around, though two new lines were again entered on the right-hand branch, none was entered on the left-hand one (CASE 3). Here a truth-value assignment on which lines 1–2 would both be true can be retrieved from the left-hand branch (though not from the right-hand one): T to 'Dba', and hence also to 'Dbc', 'Dbd', 'Dbe', etc., of which 'Dba' is the a-rewrite; and F to the remaining atomic subformulas of lines 1–2.

EXAMPLE 13: Is the argument from 'Everything has a cause' to 'There is something which is the cause of everything' (the converse, so to speak, of the argument in Example 8) valid or not?

		from
1	$(\forall y)(\exists x)Cxy$	
2	$\sim(\exists x)(\forall y)Cxy$	
	—————	
3	$(\exists x)Cxa$✓	1
4	$\sim(\forall y)Cay$ ✓	2
5	Cba	3
6	$\sim Cac$	4
7	$(\exists x)Cxb$ ✓	1
8	$(\exists x)Cxc$ ✓	1
9	$\sim(\forall y)Cby$ ✓	2
10	$\sim(\forall y)Ccy$ ✓	2
11	Cdb	7
12	Cec	8
13	$\sim Cbf$	9
14	$\sim Ccg$	10

The routine instructs us next to "instantiate" lines 1 and 2 by means of 'd', 'e', 'f', and 'g'; then to "instantiate" the resulting lines by means of a fresh term for each; and so on (CASE 4). But we break off at this point as we see ourselves caught in an endless cycle of "instantiations": we will forever be returned from Stage 5 to Stage 3, no matter how long we proceed, and hence will never be told to stop. Seeing this, we conclude that the tree will never close (and hence that the set is consistent, and the corresponding argument invalid).[19] Of course, we have not rigorously established the consistency of the set tested, as we do in CASES 2 and 3. There can be no generally effective way of showing that we are caught in CASE 4. Sometimes, as here, it is relatively easy to see this; sometimes, however, it can be extremely difficult.

EXERCISES

E2.2.1.   Using the tree method, test each of the following sets of statements for consistency. On the basis of the tree for each consistent set, provide where possible a truth-value assignment on which all its members would be true. (a–l do not require use of the routine on p. 189; m–p do).

_____

[19] The invalidity of this argument was established by a different method on p. 164. There we were also able to supply a truth-value assignment—not so readily afforded by this tree—which discredited the argument.

a. $\{(\forall x)Fx, (\forall x)(Fx \supset Gx), \sim Ga\}$

b. $\{(\forall x)(Fx \supset Gx), \sim(\exists x)(Fx \& Gx), (\exists x)Fx\}$

c. $\{(\forall x)Fx \supset (\exists x)(Fx \& Gx), (\exists x)(Fx \& \sim Gx)\}$

d. $\{(\forall x)(Fx \supset Gx) \supset (\exists x)(Gx \& Hx), (\exists x)\sim Gx, Fa \& \sim(Gb \lor \sim Hb)\}$

e. $\{\sim(\forall x)[Fx \supset (\forall y)(Gy \supset Hx)], (\exists x)Fx \& (\exists x)\sim(Fx \lor Gx), \sim(\forall x)(Fc \supset Hx)\}$

f. $\{(\exists x)Gx \supset (\forall x)(Fx \supset Gx), (\exists x)Hx \supset (\forall x)(Gx \supset Hx),$
     $\sim[(\exists x)(Gx \& Hx) \supset (\forall x)(Fx \supset Hx)]\}$

g. $\{(\forall x)(Fx \supset Gx) \supset [(\forall x)Gx \supset (\sim(\exists x)Hx \supset \sim(\forall x)Fx)], Fa, \sim Hb\}$

h. $\{(\forall x)(Fx \supset Gx), (\forall x)(Hx \supset Ix), \sim[(\forall x)(Gx \supset Hx) \supset (\forall x)(Fx \supset Ix)]\}$

i. $\{(\exists x)Fxa \supset (\forall x)Gxx, Faa, (\forall x)\sim(\exists y)Gxy\}$

j. $\{(\exists x)(Fax \equiv \sim Gx), (\exists x)(Gx \equiv \sim(\forall y)Hy), \sim((\exists x)Fxa \supset (\forall y)Hy)\}$

k. $\{(\forall x)[Fx \supset (\forall y)(Gy \supset Hxy)], \sim(\forall x)[Fx \supset (\forall y)(\sim Fy \supset Hxy)],$
     $(\forall x)(Fx \lor Gx)\}$

l. $\{(\forall x)(\forall y)(\forall z)[(Fxy \& Fyz) \supset Fxz], \sim(\exists x)Fxx, \sim(\forall x)(\forall y)(Fxy \supset \sim Fyx)\}$

m. $\{(\forall x)(Fx \supset Gx), \sim(\exists x)(Fx \& Gx)\}$

n. $\{(\forall x)[\sim Fx \supset (Gx \lor Hx)] \supset (\forall x)(\exists y)\sim Ixy\}$

o. $\{\sim(\forall x)Fx \supset \sim(\exists x)(Gx \lor (\forall y)Hyx), \sim(\forall x)Gx\}$

p. $\{(\forall x)(Fax \equiv Gx), (\exists x)((\exists y)Fxy \equiv (\exists y)Gy)\}$

E2.2.2.   Using the tree method, test each of the following arguments for validity. On the basis of the tree for each invalid argument, provide where possible a truth-value assignment on which the premises would all be true and the conclusion false. Only i, j, s, and t require use of the routine on p. 189.

a. $(\forall x)(Fx \lor Gx)$
    ───────────────
    $\therefore (\exists x)Fx \lor (\forall x)Gx$

b. $(\forall x)Fx \supset (\forall x)Gx$
    ───────────────
    $\therefore (\exists x)(Fx \supset Gx)$

c. $(\forall x)Fx \supset (\forall x)Gx$
    ───────────────
    $\therefore (\forall x)(Fx \supset Gx)$

d. $(\exists x)(\exists y)(Fxy \lor Fyx)$
    ───────────────
    $\therefore (\exists x)(\exists y)Fxy$

e. $(\forall x)(Fx \equiv \sim Gx)$
    $\sim(\exists x)Fx$
    ───────────────
    $\therefore (\forall x)Gx$

f. $(\forall x)(\forall y)(\sim Fxy \lor Gxy)$
    $\sim(\exists x)(\exists y)Gxy$
    ───────────────
    $\therefore (\forall x)(\forall y)\sim Fxy$

g. $(\forall x)(\forall y)Fxy \supset (\exists x)(Fxx \& Gx)$ h. $(\forall x)(Dx \supset Mx)$

$(\exists x)Fxx$ $(\forall x)[(\exists y)(My \& Wxy) \supset Gx]$

$(\exists x)(Gx \& Hx)$ $(\exists x)(Ox \& (\exists y)[(Ny \& Dy) \& Wxy])$

$\therefore (\exists x)Gx \supset (\forall x)(Gx \supset Hx)$ $\therefore (\exists x)(Ox \& Gx)$

i. $(\forall x)[Fx \supset (Gx \lor Hx)]$ j. $(\forall x)(\forall y)(\sim Fxy \lor Gxy)$

$(\exists x)(Fx \& \sim Gx)$ $\sim(\exists x)(\exists y)Gxy$

$\therefore \sim(\exists x)(Fx \& \sim Hx)$ $\therefore (\exists x)(\exists y)Fxy$

k. Either all columnists are prejudiced or no reporters are honest. Thus, if some reporters are columnists, then some columnists are either prejudiced or dishonest. (Use 'Cx' for 'x is a columnist', 'Px' for 'x is prejudiced', 'Rx' for 'x is a reporter', and 'Hx' for 'x is honest'.)

l. There is a Greek shipper who is richer than Croesus. Croesus is neither Greek nor a shipper, but Aristotle is both. So anyone who is richer than Aristotle is richer than Croesus. (Use 'Gx' for 'x is Greek', 'Sx' for 'x is a shipper', 'Rxy' for 'x is richer than y', 'Px' for 'x is a person', 'c' for 'Croesus', and 'a' for 'Aristotle'.)

m. All the students who do well on the final examination will pass Biology. Joann is a student, and she occasionally attends lab. Therefore, if all the students who occasionally attend lab do well on the final examination, then Joann will pass Biology. (Sx, Dx, Px, Ax, j)

n. If all the members of the platform committee were pledged to the front-runner, then no candidate who favored a stronger platform was invited to testify. Some candidates who favored a stronger platform were invited to testify. So some members of the platform committee weren't pledged to the frontrunner. (Mx, Px, Cx, Fx, Ix)

o. If a thing weighs less than another, then that other does not weigh less than the first. So nothing weighs less than itself. (Wxy)

p. If no women love Archie, then there's a rotten mother. Some women don't love Archie. So whoever is Archie's mother is rotten. (Wx, Lxy, Mxy, Rx, a)

q. Doctors and lawyers are professionals. Some doctors overcharge. Some lawyers are crooks. So some crooks are professionals and some professionals overcharge. (Dx, Lx, Px, Ox, Cx)

r. Fathers are parents (i.e., anyone's father is his parent). Artists are dreamers. So the fathers of artists are parents of artists, and fathers of dreamers. (Fxy, Pxy, Ax, Dx)

s. Lions and tigers are felines. Felines and wolves are carnivores. Carnivores are vicious predators. So some tigers are vicious. (Lx, Tx, Fx, Wx, Cx, Vx, Px)

t. No politicians are honest. Therefore, if Dick is a Republican, then if all Republicans are honest, Dick is a politician. (Px, Hx, Rx, d)

E2.2.3. Using the tree method and the routine on p. 189, determine which of the following statements are logically true and which are not. From the tree for each statement that is not, provide where possible one truth-value assignment to its atomic subformulas on which it would be false.

a. $(\forall x)(Fx \supset {\sim}Gx) \supset (\exists x)(Fx \ \& \ {\sim}Gx)$

b. $[(\exists x)Fx \supset (\exists x)Gx] \supset (\exists x)(Fx \supset Gx)$

c. $(\exists x)(Fx \supset Gx) \supset [(\exists x)Fx \supset (\exists x)Gx]$

d. $(\forall x)(Fx \supset Gx) \supset [(\forall x)Fx \supset (\forall x)Gx]$

e. $[(\forall x)Fx \supset (\forall x)Gx] \supset (\forall x)(Fx \supset Gx)$

f. $(\forall x)(Fx \equiv Gx) \supset [(\forall x)Fx \equiv (\forall x)Gx]$

g. $[(\forall x)Fx \equiv (\forall x)Gx] \supset (\forall x)(Fx \equiv Gx)$

h. $(\exists x)[(\exists y)Fy \supset Fx]$

i. $(\forall x)(\forall y)Fxy \supset (\exists x)Fxx$

j. $(\forall x)Fxx \supset {\sim}(\exists x)(\exists y)Fxy$

k. $(\forall x)(Fax \equiv Gx) \supset (\exists x)[(\exists y)Fxy \equiv (\exists y)Gy]$

l. $[(\forall x)(\forall y)(\forall z)[(Fxy \ \& \ Fyz) \supset Fxz] \ \& \ (\forall x){\sim}Fxx] \supset (\forall x)(\forall y)(Fxy \supset {\sim}Fyx)$

E2.2.4. Using the tree method and the routine on p. 189, test the following pairs of statements for equivalence:

a. '$(\exists x)(Fx \ \& \ Gx)$' and '$(\exists x)Fx \ \& \ (\exists x)Gx$'

b. '$(\forall x)Fx \lor (\forall x)Gx$' and '$(\forall x)(Fx \lor Gx)$'

c. '$(\exists x)(Fx \supset Gx)$' and '$(\forall x)Fx \supset (\exists x)Gx$'

d. '$(\forall x)(Fx \supset {\sim}Gx)$' and '${\sim}(\exists x)(Fx \ \& \ Gx)$'

E2.2.5. Show by means of a tree in each case that the following biconditionals are logically true:

a. $(\forall x)(Fx \ \& \ Gx) \equiv [(\forall x)Fx \ \& \ (\forall x)Gx]$ (Distributivity of '$\forall$' into '&')

b. $(\exists x)(Fx \lor Gx) \equiv [(\exists x)Fx \lor (\exists x)Gx]$ (Distributivity of '$\exists$' into '$\lor$')

c. $(\forall x)(Fx \ \& \ Ga) \equiv [(\forall x)Fx \ \& \ Ga]$ (Confinement of '$\forall$')

d. $(\forall x)(Fa \ \& \ Gx) \equiv [Fa \ \& \ (\forall x)Gx]$ (''   )

e. $(\forall x)(Fx \lor Ga) \equiv [(\forall x)Fx \lor Ga]$ (''   )

f. $(\forall x)(Fa \lor Gx) \equiv [Fa \lor (\forall x)Gx]$ (''   )

g. $(\forall x)(Fx \supset Ga) \equiv [(\exists x)Fx \supset Ga]$ (''   )

h. $(\forall x)(Fa \supset Gx) \equiv [Fa \supset (\forall x)Gx]$ (''   )

i. $(\exists x)(Fx \ \& \ Ga) \equiv [(\exists x)Fx \ \& \ Ga]$ (Confinement of '$\exists$')

j. $(\exists x)(Fa \ \& \ Gx) \equiv [Fa \ \& \ (\exists x)Gx]$ (''   )

k. $(\exists x)(Fx \lor Ga) \equiv [(\exists x)Fx \lor Ga]$ (''   )

l. $(\exists x)(Fa \lor Gx) \equiv [Fa \lor (\exists x)Gx]$ (''   )

m. $(\exists x)(Fx \supset Ga) \equiv [(\forall x)Fx \supset Ga]$ (''   )

n. $(\exists x)(Fa \supset Gx) \equiv [Fa \supset (\exists x)Gx]$ (Confinement of '∃')

o. $(\forall x)(\forall y)Fxy \equiv (\forall y)(\forall x)Fxy$ (Permutativity of '∀')

p. $(\exists x)(\exists y)Fxy \equiv (\exists y)(\exists x)Fxy$ (Permutativity of '∃')

E2.2.6.   Show that:

  (a) '$(\exists x)Fx$' and '$(\forall y)(\exists x)[(Fy \supset Fy) \supset Fx]$' are equivalent, and yet

  (b) $\{(\exists x)Fx\}$ has only finite trees, whereas $\{(\forall y)(\exists x)[(Fy \supset Fy) \supset Fx]\}$ has only infinite ones.

E2.2.7.   In Section 1.2, we could be sure that any statement occurring on every open branch of a tree was entailed by the set tested (see Exercise E1.2.7). Show that this is still true in this section when all the quantifiers are universal and initially placed, but not necessarily in other cases.

E2.2.8.   Show that:

  (a) If the answer to the first question at Stage 5 of the routine on p. 189 is No, then every branch of the tree being constructed is closed;

  (b) If the answer there is Yes, then there is an unnegated universal or negated existential quantification on every open branch.

E2.2.9.   With S understood to be a finite and non-empty set of statements, show by reference to the tree rules that:

  (a) If none of the three connectives '~', '⊃', and '≡' occurs in any member of S, then *every* branch of every tree for S is sure to be open; and

  (b) If the connective '~' does not occur in any member of S, then *at least one* branch of every tree for S is sure to be open.

2.3   Derivations (2)

The tree method of the preceding section, though broad enough to adjudicate on all elementary logical matters, still fails to capture an important aspect of reasoning: the "drawing" of a conclusion from premises that entail it. To make up for this, we supplement the derivation method of Section 1.3, and—borrowing again from Gentzen and Fitch—provide intelim rules for the two quantifiers. There will be four of these, as expected. Two introduction rules, respectively called ∀I and ∃I, show how to *obtain* a quantification, whether universal or existential. And two elimination rules, respectively called ∀E and ∃E, show what can be obtained *from* a quantification. Added to the rules of Section 1.3, they will permit us to derive from any finite set of statements (the null set ∅ included) *all,* and of course *only,* the statements that are entailed by the set.[1] Proof of the fact will be given in Sections 3.3–3.4, where we show that R and the intelim rules for our various operators are both *complete* and *sound.* ∀I and ∃E, incidentially, are special cases of more general rules, called ∀I* and ∃E*, which we present towards the end of the section and use in the next chapter. We also present a substitute for ∃E (and ∃E*) which does without a subordinate derivation.

Like the intelim rules for '∼', '⊃', '&', '∨', and '≡', those for '∀' and '∃' lead to a deeper understanding of the operators involved. The "infinite" truth-tables of Section 2.1, and the rules of Section 2.2 for decomposing quantifications, shed light on the logical force of '∀' and '∃'. But the quantifiers are perhaps best understood when met with—and successfully coped with—in the course of a derivation.

The Rules ∀E *and* ∃I

∀E and ∃I are very straightforward rules. Because every one of its instances is true on any truth-value assignment on which a universal quantification $(\forall X)B$ is true, a finite set of statements that entails $(\forall X)B$ is sure to entail $B(T/X)$ for any term T. So ∀E permits us—whenever we can derive $(\forall X)B$ from some assumptions A_1, A_2, . . ., and A_n—to assert *any* instance of $(\forall X)B$ we please on those same assumptions. (Roughly, whatever has been shown to be true of everything may be asserted of any particular thing.) Similarly, because an existential quantification $(\exists X)B$ is true on any truth-value assignment on which at least one of its instances is true, a finite set of statements that entails $B(T/X)$ for some term T or other, is sure to entail $(\exists X)B$. So ∃I permits us—whenever we can derive *some* instance or other of $(\exists X)B$ from some assumptions A_1, A_2, . . ., and A_n—to assert $(\exists X)B$ on those same assumptions. (Roughly, whatever has been shown to be true of a particular thing may be asserted of something or other.)[2]

---

[1] Again we limit ourselves to finite sets, postponing study of the derivability of statements from infinite sets of statements until Section 3.2.

[2] When X does not occur in B and hence $B(T/X)$ is the same as B for any term T, ∀E allows us of course to pass from the vacuous universal quantification $(\forall X)B$ to B, and ∃I to pass from B to the vacuous existential quantification $(\exists X)B$. Note the similarity between ∀E and the rule of Section 2.2 for instantiating universal quantifications. Because of that similarity, we occasionally refer to applications of ∀E as **instantiations.**

Graphically:

$$
\begin{array}{ll}
1 & A_1 \\
2 & A_2 \\
\cdot & \cdot \\
n & \underline{A_n} \\
\cdot & \cdot \\
p & (\forall X)B \\
\cdot & \cdot \\
q & B(T/X) \quad (\forall E, p)
\end{array}
\qquad\qquad
\begin{array}{ll}
1 & A_1 \\
2 & A_2 \\
\cdot & \cdot \\
n & \underline{A_n} \\
\cdot & \cdot \\
p & B(T/X) \\
\cdot & \cdot \\
q & (\exists X)B \quad (\exists I, p)
\end{array}
$$

The following derivation makes use of both rules.

EXAMPLE 1: Everything is outrageous. So something is.

$$
\begin{array}{lll}
1 & (\forall x)Ox & \\
2 & (\forall x)Ox & (R, 1) \\
3 & Oa & (\forall E, 2) \\
4 & (\exists x)Ox & (\exists I, 3)
\end{array}
$$

In line 3 we could of course pick any instance of '$(\forall x)Ox$' we please.

The instantiating term T may or may not occur in the universal quantification $(\forall X)B$ from which $B(T/X)$ is obtained by $\forall$E, or in the existential quantification $(\exists X)B$ which is obtained from $B(T/X)$ by $\exists$I. So all of the following are proper derivations (let 'C' be the two-place predicate 'will take care of' in all five cases):

$$
\begin{array}{lll}
1 & (\forall x)Cax & \\
2 & (\forall x)Cax & \\
3 & Cab &
\end{array}
\qquad
\begin{array}{lll}
(\forall x)Cax & \\
(\forall x)Cax & (R, 1) \\
Caa & (\forall E, 2)
\end{array}
$$

$$
\begin{array}{lll}
1 & Caa & \\
2 & Caa & \\
3 & (\exists x)Cxx &
\end{array}
\qquad
\begin{array}{ll}
Caa \\
Caa \\
(\exists x)Cax
\end{array}
\qquad
\begin{array}{ll}
Caa \\
Caa & (R, 1) \\
(\exists x)Cxa & (\exists I, 2)
\end{array}
$$

If Archie will take care of everything, then not only will he take care of Barbara, but he will take care of himself as well. And if Archie will take care of himself, then not only will something take care of itself, but Archie will take care of something, and something will take care of Archie.

(For exercises requiring $\forall$E and $\exists$I, see E2.3.1, a–d.)

The Rule ∀I

Were all the instances of a universal quantification $(\forall X)B$ derivable from a set of assumptions, we should have license to assert $(\forall X)B$ on those assumptions. Of course, the instances are infinite in number, and we cannot actually construct infinitely many derivations. We can rest assured, however, that *every* instance is derivable from the set if *one* that meets certain restrictions is.

Consider a derivation of an instance $B(T/X)$ of a universal quantification $(\forall X)B$ from a set $\{A_1, A_2, \ldots, A_n\}$ of assumptions. Suppose that the instantiating term T is foreign to each and every one of $A_1, A_2, \ldots,$ and A_n (Condition One), and that T is also foreign to $(\forall X)B$, in which case of course $B(T/X)$ counts as a *conservative* instance of $(\forall X)B$ (Condition Two). And substitute for T some term T' other than T in every line of the derivation of $B(T/X)$ from $\{A_1, A_2, \ldots, A_n\}$. What results is sure to constitute a derivation of $(B(T/X))(T'/T)$—the result of putting T' for T in $B(T/X)$—from $\{A_1(T'/T), A_2(T'/T), \ldots, A_n(T'/T)\}$, the result of putting T' for T in each one of $A_1, A_2, \ldots,$ and A_n. But since, in virtue of Condition One, T does not occur in any one of $A_1, A_2, \ldots,$ and A_n, then $A_1(T'/T), A_2(T'/T), \ldots,$ and $A_n(T'/T)$ are the same as $A_1, A_2, \ldots,$ and A_n, respectively; and since, in virtue of Condition Two, T does not occur in $(\forall X)B$, then $(B(T/X))(T'/T)$ is the same as $B(T'/X)$—the instance of $(\forall X)B$ which results from putting T' for the term variable X in B.[3] Hence, the result of putting T' for T in every line of the derivation of $B(T/X)$ from $\{A_1, A_2, \ldots, A_n\}$ is sure to constitute a derivation of the instance $B(T'/X)$ of $(\forall X)B$ from $\{A_1, A_2, \ldots, A_n\}$.

So, if from a set $\{A_1, A_2, \ldots, A_n\}$ of assumptions one can derive an instance $B(T/X)$ of a universal quantification $(\forall X)B$, *and* if the term T is foreign both to $\{A_1, A_2, \ldots, A_n\}$ and to $(\forall X)B$, then every instance of that universal quantification is sure to be derivable from $\{A_1, A_2, \ldots, A_n\}$, and $(\forall X)B$ may be asserted on those assumptions.[4]

---

[3] To illustrate the last point (already made in another context), let $(\forall X)B$ be '$(\forall x)\sim$(Peter enjoys x)'; and let T *first* be 'Al', which does *not* occur in $(\forall X)B$, so that $B(T/X)$ is the *conservative* instance '$\sim$(Peter enjoys Al)' of '$(\forall x)\sim$(Peter enjoys x)'. With T' successively taken to be 'Al', 'Barbara', 'Charlene', etc., $(B(T/X))(T'/T)$ will be '$\sim$(Peter enjoys Al)', '$\sim$(Peter enjoys Barbara)', '$\sim$(Peter enjoys Charlene)', etc., all of them instances of '$(\forall x)\sim$(Peter enjoys x)'. But *now* let T be 'Peter', which *does* occur in $(\forall X)B$, so that $B(T/X)$ is the non-conservative instance '$\sim$(Peter enjoys Peter)' of '$(\forall x)\sim$(Peter enjoys x)'. With T' as before, $(B(T/X))(T'/T)$ will be '$\sim$(Al enjoys Al)', '$\sim$(Barbara enjoys Barbara)', '$\sim$(Charlene enjoys Charlene)', etc., none of which is an instance of '$(\forall x)\sim$(Peter enjoys x)'.

[4] Proof will be given in Section 3.3 that if $B(T/X)$ is entailed by $\{A_1, A_2, \ldots, A_n\}$, and if T is foreign to $\{A_1, A_2, \ldots, A_n\}$ and to $(\forall X)B$, then $(\forall X)B$ is entailed by—and hence should be derivable from—$\{A_1, A_2, \ldots, A_n\}$. The justification of ∀I above should suffice for the moment, however. When X does not occur in B, ∀I allows us to infer $(\forall X)B$ from B without further ado, this for reasons like the ones presented in footnote 10 on p. 180.

Graphically:

$$
\begin{array}{r|l}
1 & A_1 \\
2 & A_2 \\
\cdot & \cdot \\
n & A_n \\
\\
\cdot & \cdot \\
p & B(T/X) \\
\cdot & \cdot \\
q & (\forall X)B \qquad (\forall I, p)
\end{array}
$$

Restriction: T must be foreign to each and every one of $A_1, A_2, \ldots$, and A_n, and to $(\forall X)B$.

The following two derivations make use of $\forall I$ (as well as $\forall E$, and some truth-functional rules):

EXAMPLE 2: Al's students are human beings. Human beings make mistakes. Al is a lousy teacher. Therefore, Al's students make mistakes, and Al is a lousy teacher (anyway).

1	$(\forall x)(Sxa \supset Hx)$	
2	$(\forall x)(Hx \supset Mx)$	
3	Ta	
4	Sba	
5	Sba	(R, 4)
6	$(\forall x)(Sxa \supset Hx)$	(R, 1)
7	Sba $\supset$ Hb	($\forall$E, 6)
8	Hb	($\supset$E, 5, 7)
9	$(\forall x)(Hx \supset Mx)$	(R, 2)
10	Hb $\supset$ Mb	($\forall$E, 9)
11	Mb	($\supset$E, 8, 10)
12	Sba $\supset$ Mb	($\supset$I, 4–11)
13	$(\forall x)(Sxa \supset Mx)$	($\forall$I, 12)[5]
14	Ta	(R, 3)
15	$(\forall x)(Sxa \supset Mx)$ & Ta	(&I, 13, 14)

---

[5] The parentheses which—strictly—belong around 'Sba $\supset$ Mb' in line 12 are omitted as unnecessary. However, when passing from line 12 to line 13 by $\forall$I, we enclose 'Sxa $\supset$ Mx'

The last line is a conjunction, so in view of &I we try to derive each conjunct from lines 1–3. The right-hand conjunct 'Ta' is derivable from lines 1–3 by R, so we address ourselves to the left-hand one. ∀I says that we may assert '(∀x)(Sxa ⊃ Mx)' on lines 1–3 if we can derive from those lines any result of putting for 'x' in 'Sxa ⊃ Mx' a term foreign to lines 1–3 and to '(∀x)(Sxa ⊃ Mx)'. Since 'a' occurs in lines 1–3 and in '(∀x)(Sxa ⊃ Mx)', we pick 'b', and try to derive 'Sba ⊃ Mb' from lines 1–3. But 'Sba ⊃ Mb' is a conditional. So, in view of ⊃I, we assume the antecedent 'Sba' and try to derive the consequent 'Mb' from the *four* lines 1–4. Reiterating lines 1 and 2, instantiating them by means of 'b', and reiterating line 4, gives us all we need to reach 'Mb' by two applications of ⊃E. Note both that the results of substituting 'a', 'c', 'd', etc., for 'b' in lines 1–12 would count, respectively, as derivations of 'Saa ⊃ Ma', 'Sca ⊃ Mc', 'Sda ⊃ Md', and so forth, from lines 1–3; and that 'Saa ⊃ Ma', 'Sba ⊃ Mb', 'Sca ⊃ Mc', 'Sda ⊃ Md', etc., are *all* the instances of '(∀x)(Sxa ⊃ Mx)'. So we should certainly have license to derive '(∀x)(Sxa ⊃ Mx)' from lines 1–3.

EXAMPLE 3: All textbooks are dull. So if everything is a textbook, everything is dull.

1	(∀x)(Tx ⊃ Dx)	
2	(∀x)Tx	
3	(∀x)Tx	(R, 2)
4	Ta	(∀E, 3)
5	(∀x)(Tx ⊃ Dx)	(R, 1)
6	Ta ⊃ Da	(∀E, 5)
7	Da	(⊃E, 4, 6)
8	(∀x)Dx	(∀I, 7)
9	(∀x)Tx ⊃ (∀x)Dx	(⊃I, 2–8)

Since the last line is a conditional (it is *not* a universal quantification), we assume the antecedent '(∀x)Tx', and try to derive the consequent '(∀x)Dx' from lines 1 and 2. ∀I says that we may assert '(∀x)Dx' on lines 1–2 if we can derive from those lines any result of putting for 'x' in 'Dx' a term foreign to lines 1–2 and to '(∀x)Dx'. Since no term occurs there, we pick 'a' and try to derive 'Da' from lines 1–2. Two reiterations, two instantiations (by means of 'a', of course), and one application of ⊃E yield 'Da', and the derivation can be completed. Again note that the results of substituting 'b', 'c', 'd', etc., for 'a' in lines 1–7 would count, respectively, as derivations of 'Db', 'Dc', 'Dd', and so forth, from lines 1–2; and that 'Da',

---

within parentheses. More generally, when passing from $B(T/X)$ to $(∀X)B$ by ∀I or to $(∃X)B$ by ∃I, we enclose B within parentheses whenever B is a *binary* compound. See p. 209, line 12, where we put parentheses around 'Gx & Hx' when passing from 'Ga & Ha' to '(∃x)(Gx & Hx)' by ∃I.

'Db', 'Dc', 'Dd', etc., are all the instances of '$(\forall x)Dx$'. So we should certainly have license to derive '$(\forall x)Dx$' from lines 1–2.

(For exercises requiring $\exists$I and the intelim rules for '$\forall$', see E2.3.1, e–h.)

The Rule $\exists$E

Consider a derivation of an existential quantification $(\exists X)B$ from a set $\{A_1,A_2,\ldots,A_n\}$ of assumptions; a further derivation of some statement C from the same assumptions *plus* some instance $B(T/X)$ of $(\exists X)B$; and a truth-value assignment α (to the atomic subformulas of A_1, A_2, ..., A_n, and $(\exists X)B$) on which all of A_1, A_2, ..., and A_n are true. Since $(\exists X)B$ is derivable from—and hence entailed by—$\{A_1,A_2,\ldots,A_n\}$, at least one instance of $(\exists X)B$ is sure to be true on α. So, if for *every* term T' other than T we could also derive C from $\{A_1,A_2,\ldots,A_n\}$ *plus* $B(T'/X)$, we should have license to assert C on just the assumptions A_1, A_2, ..., and A_n. Whichever instance of $(\exists X)B$ is true on α—and at least one is, though we may not know which—C would indeed be known to be derivable from $\{A_1,A_2,\ldots,A_n\}$ plus *that* instance.

Again, we cannot construct infinitely many derivations. We can rest assured, however, that for any term T' other than T the statement C would be derivable from $\{A_1,A_2,\ldots,A_n\}$ plus $B(T'/X)$—as well as from $\{A_1,A_2,\ldots,A_n\}$ plus $B(T/X)$—if T satisfies certain restrictions. The result of substituting T' for T in every line of the original derivation of C from $\{A_1,A_2,\ldots,A_n\}$ plus $B(T/X)$ is sure to constitute a derivation of $C(T'/T)$ from $\{A_1(T'/T), A_2(T'/T),\ldots,A_n(T'/T)\}$ plus $(B(T/X))(T'/T)$. Hence, if (1) T is foreign to each and every one of A_1,A_2, ..., and A_n (so that, for any i from 1 through n, $A_i(T'/T)$ is the same as A_i), (2) T is foreign to $(\exists X)B$ (so that $(B(T/X))(T'/T)$ is the same as $B(T'/X)$), and (3) T is foreign to C (so that $C(T'/T)$ is the same as C), the resulting derivation will be one of C from $\{A_1,A_2,\ldots,A_n\}$ plus $B(T'/X)$.

Note incidentally that if T meets condition (2), $B(T/X)$ will be a *conservative* instance of $(\exists X)B$, as it was of $(\forall X)B$ in rule $\forall$I.

The line of thought behind $\exists$E is a very natural one. Imagine, for example, that 'Something sells better than the Bible nowadays' is derivable from some assumptions A_1, A_2, ..., and A_n; and suppose that A_1, A_2, ..., and A_n are all true. Then one or more instances of 'Something sells better than the Bible nowadays' are sure to be true, since the quantification itself is sure to be true. If—just for the sake of the argument, as the expression goes—we assume that '*Portnoy's Complaint* sells better than the Bible nowadays' is one of them, and given that extra assumption we can reach a statement C that makes no mention of *Portnoy's Complaint*, then we may assert C on the original assumptions A_1, A_2, ..., and

A_n alone, so long as they make no mention of *Portnoy's Complaint* either.[6]
For under those circumstances, we *could* have reached C, given any instance of 'Something sells better than the Bible nowadays' that is true
(or, if only one instance of the quantification is true, given that instance).[7]
    Graphically:

$$
\begin{array}{ll}
1 & A_1 \\
2 & A_2 \\
. & . \\
n & A_n \\
. & . \\
p & (\exists X)B \\
. & . \\
q & \quad B(T/X) \\
. & \quad . \\
r & \quad C \\
r+1 & C \qquad (\exists E,\ p,\ q\text{--}r)
\end{array}
$$

Restriction: T must be foreign to each and every one of A_1, A_2, . . ., and
A_n, to $(\exists X)B$, and to C.

Like $\supset$I, $\sim$I, $\lor$E, and $\equiv$I, $\exists$E involves a subordinate derivation, whose provisional assumption $B(T/X)$ is said to be *discharged* by the time C is en-
tered in the same column as $(\exists X)B$.[8]

---

    [6] Note that '*Portnoy's Complaint* sells better than the Bible nowadays' *is* a conservative
instance of 'Something sells better than the Bible nowadays'.
    [7] Proof will be sketched in Exercise E3.3.1 that if (a) $(\exists X)B$ is entailed by $\{A_1,A_2,. . .,A_n\}$,
(b) C is entailed by $\{A_1,A_2,. . .,A_n,\ B(T/X)\}$, and (c) T is foreign to $\{A_1,A_2,. . .,A_n\}$, to $(\exists X)B$,
and to C, then C is entailed by—and hence should be derivable from—$\{A_1,A_2,. . .,A_n\}$. Do *not*
conclude that if $(\exists X)A$ is entailed by $\{A_1,A_2,. . .,A_n\}$, then at least one instance of $(\exists X)B$ is
sure to be entailed by $\{A_1,A_2,. . .,A_n\}$. '$(\exists x)Fx$', for example, which entails itself, does not entail any one of 'Fa', 'Fb', 'Fc', etc. On any particular truth-value assignment on which '$(\exists x)Fx$'
is true, at least one of the statements 'Fa', 'Fb', 'Fc', etc., is true; but no *one* of them is sure to be
true on *every* truth-value assignment on which '$(\exists x)Fx$' is true.
    When X does not occur in B, $\exists$E allows us to infer C from $\{A_1,A_2,. . .,A_n\}$ if $(\exists X)B$ is
derivable from $\{A_1,A_2,. . .,A_n\}$ and if C is derivable from $\{A_1,A_2,. . .,A_n,B\}$, this again for reasons like the ones presented in footnote 10 on p. 180.
    [8] All the derivation rules of this section and of Section 1.3 are gathered in Appendix II.

The following three derivations make use of ∃E.[9]

EXAMPLE 4: Some Greeks are famous. All famous people are happy. So some Greeks are happy.

1	$(\exists x)(Gx \mathbin{\&} Fx)$	
2	$(\forall x)(Fx \supset Hx)$	
3	$(\exists x)(Gx \mathbin{\&} Fx)$	(R, 1)
4	Ga & Fa	
5	Ga & Fa	(R, 4)
6	Ga	(&E, 5)
7	Fa	(&E, 5)
8	$(\forall x)(Fx \supset Hx)$	(R, 2)
9	Fa ⊃ Ha	(∀E, 8)
10	Ha	(⊃E, 7, 9)
11	Ga & Ha	(&I, 6, 10)
12	$(\exists x)(Gx \mathbin{\&} Hx)$	(∃I, 11)
13	$(\exists x)(Gx \mathbin{\&} Hx)$	(∃E, 3, 4–12)

The following strategy is used here: we reiterate line 1, assume an instance of it (since no term occurs in lines 1, 2, and 13, 'Ga & Fa' will do), and try to derive the corresponding instance 'Ga & Ha' of line 12 from lines 1, 2, *and* 4. This is easily done, once line 2 is reiterated and instantiated by means of 'a'. We next conclude to '$(\exists x)(Gx \mathbin{\&} Hx)$' by ∃I, and—as ∃E allows—reassert that very conclusion on the strength of lines 1–2 alone. Incidentally, there was no hope of deriving 'Ga & Ha' from lines 1–2 alone: though entailing '$(\exists x)(Gx \mathbin{\&} Hx)$', they do not entail any of its instances.

Note that the results of substituting 'b', 'c', 'd', etc., for 'a' in lines 1–2 and 4–12 would count, respectively, as derivations of '$(\exists x)(Gx \mathbin{\&} Hx)$' from lines 1–2 *plus* 'Gb & Fb', from lines 1–2 *plus* 'Gc & Fc', from lines 1–2 *plus* 'Gd & Fd', and so forth; and 'Ga & Fa', 'Gb & Fb', 'Gc & Fc', 'Gd & Fd', etc., are all the instances of '$(\exists x)(Gx \mathbin{\&} Fx)$'. We should therefore have license to assert '$(\exists x)(Gx \mathbin{\&} Hx)$' on the strength of just lines 1–2. Informally, although we do not know whether it is Aristotle or (our own) Spiro or Zorba, etc., who in view of line 1 is a famous Greek, it follows from lines 1–2 that *somebody* is; and, *whoever* it is, it would follow that *he* is a happy Greek, and hence that at least one Greek is happy. So we conclude to '$(\exists x)(Gx \mathbin{\&} Hx)$' given just lines 1–2.

---

[9] On many occasions the existential quantification $(\exists X)B$ coincides with one of the A's. Line 3 in Example 4 coincides with the first assumption, line 3 in Example 5 coincides with the second assumption, and so on.

EXAMPLE 5: If anything got broken during the party, Bobby will get hell.
So if something got broken during the party, Bobby will get hell.

1	$(\forall x)(\text{B}x \supset \text{Hb})$	
2	$(\exists x)\text{B}x$	
3	$(\exists x)\text{B}x$	(R, 2)
4	Ba	
5	Ba	(R, 4)
6	$(\forall x)(\text{B}x \supset \text{Hb})$	(R, 1)
7	Ba $\supset$ Hb	($\forall$E, 6)
8	Hb	($\supset$E, 5, 7)
9	Hb	($\exists$E, 3, 4–8)
10	$(\exists x)\text{B}x \supset \text{Hb}$	($\supset$I, 2–9)

To reach the last line, which is a conditional (*not* an existential quantification), we assume the antecedent '$(\exists x)\text{B}x$' and try to reach the consequent 'Hb'. The following strategy is used here: we reiterate line 2,
assume an instance of it (since 'a' does not occur in lines 1, 2, and 9, we
pick 'Ba'),[10] and try to derive 'Hb' from lines 1, 2, *and* 4. This is easily
done once line 1 is reiterated, and instantiated by means of 'a'. Note
again what the results of substituting 'b', 'c', 'd', etc., for 'a' in lines 1–2
and 4–8 would be like, and why this entitles us to declare 'Hb' derivable
from just lines 1–2. Informally, although we do not know whether it is a
cheap glass or a rare piece of china or a windowpane, etc., that in view of
assumption 2 got broken during the party, it follows from lines 1–2 that
something did; and, *whatever* it was, it would follow that Bobby is to get
hell because *it* got broken.

EXAMPLE 6: There is something that is the cause of everything. Therefore
everything has a cause.

1	$(\exists x)(\forall y)\text{C}xy$	
2	$(\exists x)(\forall y)\text{C}xy$	(R, 1)
3	$(\forall y)\text{Cb}y$	
4	$(\forall y)\text{Cb}y$	(R, 3)
5	Cba	($\forall$E, 4)
6	$(\exists x)\text{Cx}a$	($\exists$I, 5)
7	$(\exists x)\text{Cx}a$	($\exists$E, 2, 3–6)
8	$(\forall y)(\exists x)\text{C}xy$	($\forall$I, 7)

---

[10] Note that line 1 does belong at the head of the subordinate derivation 2–9. So the term
by means of which '$(\exists x)\text{B}x$' is instantiated should be foreign to that line as well as to line 2.

To obtain '$(\forall y)(\exists x)Cxy$' by $\forall$I, we need only derive one instance of it, say, '$(\exists x)Cxa$' ('a' is foreign to lines 1 and 8), from line 1. But, since line 1 does not entail any instance of '$(\exists x)Cxa$', we must reach '$(\exists x)Cxa$' by $\exists$E rather than $\exists$I. So we provisionally assume an instance of '$(\exists x)(\forall y)Cxy$' (since 'a' occurs in '$(\exists x)Cxa$', we pick '$(\forall y)Cby$'), and try to derive '$(\exists x)Cxa$' from '$(\forall y)Cby$', which is easily done once '$(\forall y)Cby$' is reiterated and instantiated by means of 'a'. Informally, we assume that, say, God ($=$ b) is the cause of everything, and show on this extra assumption that something is the cause of, say, the pimple on my nose ($=$ a). Because we could have shown this *whatever* is the cause of everything, and because in view of line 1 *something* is the cause of everything, we conclude on the strength of just line 1 that the pimple on my nose has a cause. But because we could have shown in exactly the same manner that *any* thing has a cause, we may go on to assert on the strength of just line 1 that everything has a cause. The derivation uses all four of our new rules, and hence deserves close attention.

(For exercises requiring the intelim rules for '$\forall$' and '$\exists$', see E2.3.1, i–l.)

A Word on Restrictions

The reader who has little patience with restrictions should nonetheless heed those placed on T in $\forall$I and $\exists$E. Otherwise, he might arrive at conclusions that are *not* entailed by his premisses.

(1)   As regards $\forall$I, if T were free to occur in any one of $A_1, A_2, \ldots$, and A_n, then 'Everything will take care of itself' could be derived as follows from 'Archie will take care of himself':

1	Caa		
2	Caa	(R, 1)	
3	$(\forall x)Cxx$	($\forall$I, 2)	(erroneous!)

(2)   As regards $\forall$I again, if T were free to occur in $(\forall X)B$, then 'Archie will take care of everything' could be derived as follows from 'Everything will take care of itself':

1	$(\forall x)Cxx$		
2	$(\forall x)Cxx$	(R, 1)	
3	Caa	($\forall$E, 2)	
4	$(\forall x)Cax$	($\forall$I, 3)	(erroneous!)

(3)   As regards $\exists$E, if T were free to occur in any one of $A_1, A_2, \ldots$, and A_n, then 'Nothing is self-explanatory' could be derived as follows from 'Some things are self-explanatory' and 'The instructor doesn't explain a thing':

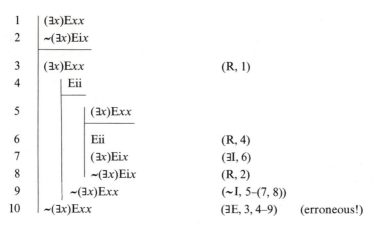

1	$(\exists x)Exx$	
2	$\sim(\exists x)Eix$	
3	$(\exists x)Exx$	(R, 1)
4	Eii	
5	$(\exists x)Exx$	
6	Eii	(R, 4)
7	$(\exists x)Eix$	($\exists$I, 6)
8	$\sim(\exists x)Eix$	(R, 2)
9	$\sim(\exists x)Exx$	($\sim$I, 5–(7, 8))
10	$\sim(\exists x)Exx$	($\exists$E, 3, 4–9) (erroneous!)

(4)   As regards $\exists$E again, if T were free to occur in $(\exists X)B$, then 'Something is self-caused' could be derived as follows from 'Everything has a cause':

1	$(\forall x)(\exists y)Cyx$	
2	$(\forall x)(\exists y)Cyx$	(R, 1)
3	$(\exists y)Cya$	($\forall$E, 2)
4	Caa	
5	Caa	(R, 4)
6	$(\exists x)Cxx$	($\exists$I, 5)
7	$(\exists x)Cxx$	($\exists$E, 3, 4–6) (erroneous!)

(5)   As regards $\exists$E again, if T were free to occur in C, then 'I irritate Peter' could be derived as follows from 'Something irritates Peter':

1	$(\exists x)Ixp$	
2	$(\exists x)Ixp$	(R, 1)
3	Iip	
4	Iip	(R, 3)
5	Iip	($\exists$E, 2, 3–4) (erroneous!)

Note incidentally that if $(\forall X)B$ is to be obtained by $\forall$I in the course of a *subordinate* derivation, T must be foreign not only to the assumptions of that derivation, but also to those of any derivation to which it is subordinate: such assumptions really belong at the head of the derivation. A similar remark is in order when a line is to be obtained by $\exists$E in a *subordinate* derivation.[11]

---

[11] See Example 5 and footnote 10 for an illustration.

Uses of Derivations

Our derivation method as expanded in this section can still be put to any of the uses discussed in Section 1.3. The reader is therefore urged to review pp. 98–102, making all the changes necessitated by the subsequent extension of the method to quantificational matters.

An argument is of course shown to be *valid* by constructing a derivation of its conclusion from its premisses; and a statement is shown to be *logically true* by constructing a proof of that statement, i.e., by constructing a derivation of the statement from no assumptions at all. Furthermore, a statement is shown to be *logically false* by constructing a proof of its negation; two statements are shown to be *equivalent* by constructing a proof of their biconditional; and a finite set of statements is shown to be *inconsistent* by constructing a derivation of some contradiction from the set.

In the examples later, we shall use the method to establish the validity of a number of arguments, and the logical truth of a few statements, without making an issue of the difference. For whether a derivation does or does not have any undischarged assumptions is of no significance so far as its construction, or the application of the rules, is concerned.

Strategy Hints

Again, we could give mechanical instructions for producing a derivation *whenever* one can be had.[12] But following them is such a tedious business that much of the point of natural deduction would be lost in the process. So we rather supplement the guidelines of Section 1.3, to make the construction of derivations at the quantificational level as straightforward as possible.

Because those earlier guidelines remain fully appropriate, the reader is urged to review pp. 90–92, substituting 'main logical operator(s)' for 'main connective(s)' throughout. The guidelines will thus include reference to ∀I and ∃I, when the statement one is after is a universal or existential quantification, and to ∀E and ∃E, when a universal or existential quantification is available. Presuming such review to have been done, we go on to comment on derivations that involve quantifications.

Stage 1—Introduction Rules. Associated with ∀I is a sure-fire strategy for obtaining universal quantifications (as &I afforded a sure-fire route to

---

[12] The reader will recall that following the routine on p. 189 will yield a closed tree for $\{A_1, A_2, \ldots, A_n, \sim B\}$ *whenever* $\{A_1, A_2, \ldots, A_n\}$ entails B. Mechanical instructions could be given for converting the tree into a derivation of B from $\{A_1, A_2, \ldots, A_n\}$ done in accordance with our rules.

conjunctions). You can count on being able to derive *any* instance, and hence the *right sort* of instance, of a universal quantification $(\forall X)B$ from any assumptions entailing $(\forall X)B$. So pick any term T that is foreign to those assumptions and to $(\forall X)B$, write $B(T/X)$ immediately above $(\forall X)B$, and proceed—i.e., apply the guidelines to reach $B(T/X)$, after which you may assert $(\forall X)B$ by $\forall$I (as in Examples 2 and 3 above).

However, the strategy similarly associated with $\exists$I is not so dependable.[13] For often an existential quantification $(\exists X)B$ is entailed by assumptions that do not entail *any* of its instances. When you are in doubt, a tree test may help. If some instance is entailed by the assumptions on which $(\exists X)B$ is to be asserted (as in Example 1 above), then write the instance immediately above $(\exists X)B$ and proceed—i.e., apply the guidelines to reach that instance.

Stage 2—Elimination Rules. But if no instance of $(\exists X)B$ is entailed by— and hence none is derivable from—those assumptions (as in Examples 4 and 6), then go on to Stage 2 of the guidelines, and consider applying to the statements available the elimination rules for their main logical operators (connectives or quantifiers).

When all the quantifiers in the assumptions and last line are initially placed, and are universal in the assumptions, the following simple procedure will often—though *not* always—do the trick. Choose as a target any instance of the last line (if it has one quantifier; an instance of an instance if it has two; an instance of an instance of an instance if it has three; and so on). Make sure that the terms selected to match different term variables in the last line are different, and that those selected to match universally quantified variables occur neither in the assumptions nor in the last line itself. That line will readily follow from the target one by $\forall$I and/or $\exists$I. The only other quantificational moves may be applications of $\forall$E to eliminate quantifiers in the assumptions and put terms for variables (in the positions dictated by their positions in the target). In some cases (such as Examples 1 and 15), no other moves will be needed. In most of the others (such as Example 7), the remaining moves will all be truth-functional. (But see Example 17 for a case in which this procedure will not work, even though it satisfies the conditions mentioned at the beginning of this paragraph: no instance of the last line is logically true.)

On the other hand, if there is an existential quantification $(\exists X)B$, as well as universal ones, among the assumptions, it will regularly be best to (a) reiterate $(\exists X)B$, (b) begin the subordinate derivation that $\exists$E calls for (i.e., assume $B(T/X)$ for some term T foreign to $(\exists X)B$, to the line you want to reach by $\exists$E, and to the assumptions on which it is

---

[13] Namely, to reach an existential quantification $(\exists X)B$, write one of its instances immediately above $(\exists X)B$, and proceed.

to be asserted), (c) write the line you are after at the bottom of the subordinate derivation, and (d) proceed to reach that line. You can often expect universal quantifications among the assumptions to be eventually reiterated, and instantiated by means of T. But do not reiterate and instantiate them before there is a point to doing so (see Examples 4 and 5 above).

Stage 3—The Indirect Route. Often just the intelim rules for the logical operators in the assumptions and last line need be used in a derivation. But sometimes the indirect route is called for, even when no tilde occurs there.[14] And it is often called for when the last line is an existential quantification no instance of which is entailed by the assumptions. (Examples 11 and 13 illustrate the latter point; Example 17 illustrates both.)

Again, if resort to ~I is indicated, check whether there is, either among or readily derivable from the undischarged assumptions, some negation ~C, the mate C of which can also be derived. The negation of a quantification, to which of course no elimination rule applies, often serves as the negative half of a contradiction for ~I. The point is illustrated by Examples 10, 11, 13, 17, and 21 below. Example 10, in particular, shows how—given the negation ~$(\exists X)A$ of an existential quantification $(\exists X)A$—one may obtain the negation ~$A(T/X)$ of *any* instance $A(T/X)$ of $(\exists X)A$, and then go on to obtain $(\forall X)$~A. And Example 11 shows how—given the negation ~$(\forall X)A$ of a universal quantification $(\forall X)A$—one may obtain $(\exists X)$~A, this even though no instance ~$A(T/X)$ of $(\exists X)$~A is entailed by ~$(\forall X)A$. Lines 2–9 of this example also show how to get from the negated quantification ~$(\exists X)$~A to $(\forall X)A$ along the lines laid down in Example 10.

Special problems arise when (a) one is after a contradiction for ~I, (b) an existential quantification $(\exists X)A$ is among the assumptions needed to reach that contradiction, but (c) no negation that might serve as the negative half is readily available (as in Example 14 below). In such cases one can often reach a contradiction *within* a subordinate derivation headed by an instance $B(T/X)$ of $(\exists X)B$, but neither half of the contradiction can be asserted by $\exists$E because it shows the very term T. Since under those circumstances *any* statement can be reached within the subordinate derivation headed by $B(T/X)$ (see p. 92), the trick is to reach some statement that (1) *can* be asserted by $\exists$E, and (2) will lead to a contradiction. The negation ~C of any assumption C not yet discharged will do, since that assumption can then be reiterated and the desired contradiction C and ~C completed.

---

[14] This could be avoided by using different elimination rules for '⊃' and '≡', and adding a rule for introducing the universal quantifier into certain disjunctions. See H. Leblanc's "Two separation theorems for natural deduction," *Notre Dame Journal of Formal Logic*, vol. 7, pp. 159–80. However, the new rules would be far less natural to use than the indirect route.

One must be *very* careful about the selection of terms when applying the intelim rules for '∀' and '∃'. $B(T/X)$ must in each case be an *instance* of the quantification $(\forall X)B$ or $(\exists X)B$ involved. In the cases of ∀I and ∃E, $B(T/X)$ must—as we saw—be a *conservative* instance of the quantification, and T must be foreign to other statements as well. When preparing to apply ∀I or ∃E, therefore, one should choose a term T for $B(T/X)$ which is entirely foreign to the derivation, rather than wonder whether a particular term will do (see Examples 2, 5, and 6 above). In applications of ∀E and ∃I, on the other hand, where there are no such restrictions, one should pick T in such a way as to make the best use of available statements: instantiate $(\forall X)B$ by means of terms already occurring in the derivation (if there are any),[15] and when trying to reach $(\exists X)B$, aim at an instance $B(T/X)$ of $(\exists X)B$ such that T already occurs in the derivation. Of course, *which* term T to pick for applications of ∀E and ∃I will be dictated by what is available and what one is after (as in Example 2 lines 1 and 2 were obviously to be instantiated by means of 'b' rather than 'a', and in Example 5 line 1 was obviously to be instantiated by means of 'a' rather than 'b').

These guidelines and suggestions should prove satisfactory for derivations involving statements with one quantifier apiece. However, things can become more difficult when multiple quantification is involved, as in Examples 15–21 below. In such cases, a certain amount of ingenuity and a great deal of care may be called for. But the examples and comments which follow should suggest how one can proceed, always trying to match what one has and what one is after, and observing scrupulously the restrictions imposed by ∀I and ∃E on the choice of instantiating terms.

Illustrations

The first eight of the examples to follow are run as paradigm derivations. Exactly the same moves would be made whatever A, B, C, and D might be, and whatever the term T might be, so long as the specified restrictions on T are met. So, for instance, Example 8 establishes the equivalence of the conjunction of *any two* universal quantifications $(\forall X)A$ and $(\forall X)B$ to $(\forall X)(A \ \& \ B)$; Example 10 shows how to get from the negation $\sim(\exists X)A$ of *any* existential quantification $(\exists X)A$ to the corresponding universal quantification $(\forall X)\sim A$; and Example 12 shows how to get from a statement like 'There aren't any unicorns (heffalumps,

---

[15] Occasionally it will prove appropriate to instantiate $(\forall X)B$ by means of a term already occurring in $(\forall X)B$. See Example 20 or 21 below, where a statement opening with two universal quantifiers is first instantiated by means of a certain term, and the result then instantiated by means of that term again (so that the *same* term is substituted for two *different* variables).

honest men, etc.)' to one like 'All (or none) of them are green (tall, happy, etc.)'.

Examples 15–21 involve multiple quantification and, except 17, polyadic predicates as well. The key to each lies in the selection of the right instantiating terms. As this can sometimes be difficult, the reader is urged to study the examples closely, and to reconstruct the line of thought which yielded each.

In Examples 19–21 we simplify the translations and derivations by limiting our attention to people (more formally, by taking our domain to consist only of people). We can thus treat 'Everybody loves a lover', for example, as 'Everything loves anything which loves something'. Otherwise, we would have to render this as

$$(\forall x)\,[Px \supset (\forall y)\,([Py \,\&\, (\exists z)\,(Pz \,\&\, Lyz)] \supset Lxy)],$$

where the predicate 'P' reads 'is a person' (see p. 128), and add the premisses 'Tom is a person' and 'Mary is a person', which is unnecessarily complicated.

To compress matters in the rest of this section, we extend a previous convention, and write

$$\{A_1, A_2, \ldots, A_n\} \vdash B$$

when B is derivable from $\{A_1, A_2, \ldots, A_n\}$ in accordance with R and the intelim rules of Section 1.3 and of this section.

EXAMPLE 7: $\{(\forall X)\,[(A \lor B) \supset C], (\forall X)\,(C \supset D)\} \vdash (\forall X)\,(A \supset D)$.

Let T be foreign to $(\forall X)[(A \lor B) \supset C]$, $(\forall X)(C \supset D)$, and (hence) $(\forall X)(A \supset D)$.

1	$(\forall X)\,[(A \lor B) \supset C]$	
2	$(\forall X)\,(C \supset D)$	
3	$A(T/X)$	
4	$(\forall X)\,[(A \lor B) \supset C]$	(R, 1)
5	$(\forall X)\,(C \supset D)$	(R, 2)
6	$[A(T/X) \lor B(T/X)] \supset C(T/X)$	(∀E, 4)
7	$C(T/X) \supset D(T/X)$	(∀E, 5)
8	$A(T/X)$	(R, 3)
9	$A(T/X) \lor B(T/X)$	(∨I, 8)
10	$C(T/X)$	(⊃E, 6, 9)
11	$D(T/X)$	(⊃E, 7, 10)
12	$A(T/X) \supset D(T/X)$	(⊃I, 3–11)
13	$(\forall X)\,(A \supset D)$	(∀I, 12)

Note that line 6 is the same as $[(A \lor B) \supset C](T/X)$, line 7 the same as $(C \supset D)(T/X)$, and line 12 the same as $(A \supset D)(T/X)$. The hypothesis on T is needed of course to swing line 13.

EXAMPLE 8: $\vdash (\forall X)(A \,\&\, B) \equiv [(\forall X)A \,\&\, (\forall X)B]$.

Let T be foreign to $(\forall X)(A \,\&\, B)$, and hence to $(\forall X)A$ and $(\forall X)B$ as well.

1	$(\forall X)(A \,\&\, B)$	
2	$(\forall X)(A \,\&\, B)$	(R, 1)
3	$A(T/X) \,\&\, B(T/X)$	($\forall$E, 2)
4	$A(T/X)$	(&E, 3)
5	$(\forall X)A$	($\forall$I, 4)
6	$B(T/X)$	(&E, 3)
7	$(\forall X)B$	($\forall$I, 6)
8	$(\forall X)A \,\&\, (\forall X)B$	(&I, 5, 7)
9	$(\forall X)A \,\&\, (\forall X)B$	
10	$(\forall X)A \,\&\, (\forall X)B$	(R, 9)
11	$(\forall X)A$	(&E, 10)
12	$A(T/X)$	($\forall$E, 11)
13	$(\forall X)B$	(&E, 10)
14	$B(T/X)$	($\forall$E, 13)
15	$A(T/X) \,\&\, B(T/X)$	(&I, 12, 14)
16	$(\forall X)(A \,\&\, B)$	($\forall$I, 15)
17	$(\forall X)(A \,\&\, B) \equiv [(\forall X)A \,\&\, (\forall X)B]$	($\equiv$I, 1–8, 9–16)

Note that lines 3 and 15 are the same as $(A \,\&\, B)(T/X)$. The hypothesis on T is needed of course to swing lines 5, 7, and 16.

EXAMPLE 9: $\{(\exists X)(A \lor B)\} \vdash (\exists X)A \lor (\exists X)B$.
   Let T be foreign to $(\exists X)(A \lor B)$.

1	$(\exists X)(A \lor B)$	
2	$(\exists X)(A \lor B)$	(R, 1)
3	$A(T/X) \lor B(T/X)$	
4	$A(T/X) \lor B(T/X)$	(R, 3)
5	$A(T/X)$	
6	$A(T/X)$	(R, 5)
7	$(\exists X)A$	($\exists$I, 6)
8	$(\exists X)A \lor (\exists X)B$	(VI, 7)
9	$B(T/X)$	
10	$B(T/X)$	(R, 9)
11	$(\exists X)B$	($\exists$I, 10)
12	$(\exists X)A \lor (\exists X)B$	(VI, 11)
13	$(\exists X)A \lor (\exists X)B$	(VE, 4, 5–8, 9–12)
14	$(\exists X)A \lor (\exists X)B$	($\exists$E, 2, 3–13)

Note that line 3 is the same as $(A \lor B)(T/X)$. The reader is invited to derive line 1 from line 14. One application of $\equiv$I will then give him a proof of $(\exists X)(A \lor B) \equiv [(\exists X)A \lor (\exists X)B]$.

EXAMPLE 10: $\{\sim(\exists X)A\} \vdash (\forall X)\sim A$.
   Let T be foreign to $(\forall X)\sim A$.

1	$\sim(\exists X)A$	
2	$A(T/X)$	
3	$A(T/X)$	(R, 2)
4	$(\exists X)A$	($\exists$I, 3)
5	$\sim(\exists X)A$	(R, 1)
6	$\sim A(T/X)$	($\sim$I, 2–(4, 5))
7	$(\forall X)\sim A$	($\forall$I, 6)

Note that line 6 is the same as $(\sim A)(T/X)$.

EXAMPLE 11: $\{\sim(\forall X)A\} \vdash (\exists X)\sim A$.

Let T be foreign to $\sim(\forall X)A$.

1.	$\sim(\forall X)A$	
2	$\sim(\exists X)\sim A$	
3	$\sim A(T/X)$	
4	$\sim A(T/X)$	(R, 3)
5	$(\exists X)\sim A$	($\exists$I, 4)
6	$\sim(\exists X)\sim A$	(R, 2)
7	$\sim\sim A(T/X)$	($\sim$I, 3–(5, 6))
8	$A(T/X)$	($\sim$E, 7)
9	$(\forall X)A$	($\forall$I, 8)
10	$\sim(\forall X)A$	(R, 1)
11	$\sim\sim(\exists X)\sim A$	($\sim$I, 2–(9,10))
12	$(\exists X)\sim A$	($\sim$E, 11)

Note that line 4 is the same as $(\sim A)(T/X)$, and line 7 the same as $\sim(\sim A(T/X))$.

The reader is invited to elaborate the above examples into proofs of the two biconditionals $(\forall X)A \equiv \sim(\exists X)\sim A$ and $(\exists X)A \equiv \sim(\forall X)\sim A$.

EXAMPLE 12: $\{\sim(\exists X)A\} \vdash (\forall X)(A \supset B)$.

Let T be foreign to $(\forall X)(A \supset B)$.

1	$\sim(\exists X)A$	
2	$A(T/X)$	
3	$\sim B(T/X)$	
4	$A(T/X)$	(R, 2)
5	$(\exists X)A$	($\exists$I, 4)
6	$\sim(\exists X)A$	(R, 1)
7	$\sim\sim B(T/X)$	($\sim$I, 3–(5, 6))
8	$B(T/X)$	($\sim$E, 7)
9	$A(T/X) \supset B(T/X)$	($\supset$I, 2–8)
10	$(\forall X)(A \supset B)$	($\forall$I, 9)

Note that line 7 is the same as $\sim(\sim B(T/X))$, and line 9 the same as $(A \supset B)(T/X)$.

EXAMPLE 13: $\{\sim(\forall X)(A \supset \sim B)\} \vdash (\exists X)(A \,\&\, B)$.
    Let T be foreign to $(\forall X)(A \supset \sim B)$.

1	$\sim(\forall X)(A \supset \sim B)$	
2	$\sim(\exists X)(A \,\&\, B)$	
3	$A(T/X)$	
4	$B(T/X)$	
5	$A(T/X)$	(R, 3)
6	$B(T/X)$	(R, 4)
7	$A(T/X) \,\&\, B(T/X)$	(&I, 5, 6)
8	$(\exists X)(A \,\&\, B)$	($\exists$I, 7)
9	$\sim(\exists X)(A \,\&\, B)$	(R, 2)
10	$\sim B(T/X)$	($\sim$I, 4–(8, 9))
11	$A(T/X) \supset \sim B(T/X)$	($\supset$I, 3–10)
12	$(\forall X)(A \supset \sim B)$	($\forall$I, 11)
13	$\sim(\forall X)(A \supset \sim B)$	(R, 1)
14	$\sim\sim(\exists X)(A \,\&\, B)$	($\sim$I, 2–(12, 13))
15	$(\exists X)(A \,\&\, B)$	($\sim$E, 14)

Note that line 7 is the same as $(A \,\&\, B)(T/X)$, and line 11 the same as $(A \supset \sim B)(T/X)$.

In traditional logic, the statements which we render on the patterns $(\forall X)(A \supset B)$, $(\forall X)(A \supset \sim B)$, $(\exists X)(A \,\&\, B)$, and $(\exists X)(A \,\&\, \sim B)$ were known, respectively, as A-statements, E-statements, I-statements, and O-statements. In view of Example 13, an I-statement is derivable from the negation of an E-statement; and in view of the next, the negation of an I-statement is derivable from an E-statement.

EXAMPLE 14: $\{(\forall X)(A \supset \sim B\} \vdash \sim(\exists X)(A \& B)$.

Let T be foreign to $(\exists X)(A \& B)$.

1	$(\forall X)(A \supset \sim B)$	
2	$(\exists X)(A \& B)$	
3	$(\exists X)(A \& B)$	(R, 2)
4	$A(T/X) \& B(T/X)$	
5	$(\exists X)(A \& B)$	
6	$A(T/X) \& B(T/X)$	(R, 4)
7	$A(T/X)$	(&E, 6)
8	$(\forall X)(A \supset \sim B)$	(R, 1)
9	$A(T/X) \supset \sim B(T/X)$	($\forall$E, 8)
10	$\sim B(T/X)$	($\supset$E, 7, 9)
11	$B(T/X)$	(&E, 6)
12	$\sim(\exists X)(A \& B)$	($\sim$I, 5–(10, 11))
13	$\sim(\exists X)(A \& B)$	($\exists$E, 3, 4–12)
14	$\sim(\exists X)(A \& B)$	($\sim$I, 2–(3, 13))

Note that line 4 is the same as $(A \& B)(T/X)$, and line 9 the same as $(A \supset \sim B)(T/X)$.

Because line 5 plays no part in the derivation of $\sim B(T/X)$ and $B(T/X)$, it could have been $(\forall X)(A \supset \sim B)$, lines 12 and 13 could have been $\sim(\forall X)(A \supset \sim B)$, and line 14 could have been $(\forall X)(A \supset \sim B)$, yielding an equally satisfactory contradiction for $\sim$I.

EXAMPLE 15: Everything is equally dependent on the will of God. So there's something on which God's will is as dependent as anything is. (We use 'D' as short for '... is as dependent on ... as ... is'.)

1	$(\forall x)(\forall y)Dxgy$	
2	$(\forall x)(\forall y)Dxgy$	(R, 1)
3	$(\forall y)Dggy$	($\forall$E, 2)
4	$Dgga$	($\forall$E, 3)
5	$(\forall x)Dggx$	($\forall$I, 4)
6	$(\exists y)(\forall x)Dgyx$	($\exists$I, 5)

EXAMPLE 16:   There is a cause. So something has a cause.

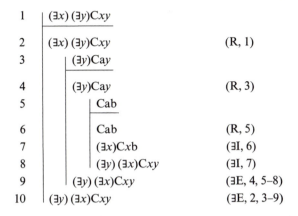

1	(∃x)(∃y)Cxy	
2	(∃x)(∃y)Cxy	(R, 1)
3	(∃y)Cay	
4	(∃y)Cay	(R, 3)
5	Cab	
6	Cab	(R, 5)
7	(∃x)Cxb	(∃I, 6)
8	(∃y)(∃x)Cxy	(∃I, 7)
9	(∃y)(∃x)Cxy	(∃E, 4, 5–8)
10	(∃y)(∃x)Cxy	(∃E, 2, 3–9)

EXAMPLE 17:   There's something that makes sense if anything does.

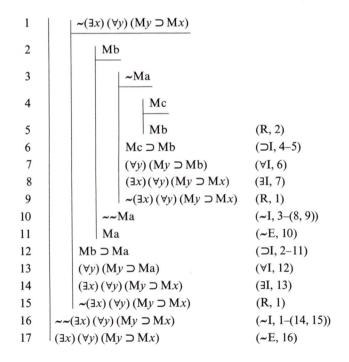

1	~(∃x)(∀y)(My ⊃ Mx)	
2	Mb	
3	~Ma	
4	Mc	
5	Mb	(R, 2)
6	Mc ⊃ Mb	(⊃I, 4–5)
7	(∀y)(My ⊃ Mb)	(∀I, 6)
8	(∃x)(∀y)(My ⊃ Mx)	(∃I, 7)
9	~(∃x)(∀y)(My ⊃ Mx)	(R, 1)
10	~~Ma	(~I, 3–(8, 9))
11	Ma	(~E, 10)
12	Mb ⊃ Ma	(⊃I, 2–11)
13	(∀y)(My ⊃ Ma)	(∀I, 12)
14	(∃x)(∀y)(My ⊃ Mx)	(∃I, 13)
15	~(∃x)(∀y)(My ⊃ Mx)	(R, 1)
16	~~(∃x)(∀y)(My ⊃ Mx)	(~I, 1–(14, 15))
17	(∃x)(∀y)(My ⊃ Mx)	(~E, 16)

EXAMPLE 18:   Horses are animals. So horses' tails are tails of animals.

1	$(\forall x)\,(Hx \supset Ax)$	
2	$(\exists y)\,(Hy \,\&\, Tay)$	
3	$(\exists y)\,(Hy \,\&\, Tay)$	(R, 2)
4	$Hb \,\&\, Tab$	
5	$Hb \,\&\, Tab$	(R, 4)
6	Hb	(&E, 5)
7	$(\forall x)\,(Hx \supset Ax)$	(R, 1)
8	$Hb \supset Ab$	($\forall$E, 7)
9	Ab	($\supset$E, 6, 8)
10	Tab	(&E, 5)
11	$Ab \,\&\, Tab$	(&I, 9, 10)
12	$(\exists y)\,(Ay \,\&\, Tay)$	($\exists$I, 11)
13	$(\exists y)\,(Ay \,\&\, Tay)$	($\exists$E, 3, 4–12)
14	$(\exists y)\,(Hy \,\&\, Tay) \supset (\exists y)\,(Ay \,\&\, Tay)$	($\supset$I, 2–13)
15	$(\forall x)\,[(\exists y)\,(Hy \,\&\, Txy) \supset (\exists y)\,(Ay \,\&\, Txy)]$	($\forall$I, 14)

EXAMPLE 19: You can't be loved, or love someone, unless you love your-self too. Charlene loves Bob. So somebody loves Charlene.

1	$(\forall x)\,[(\exists y)\,(Lyx \lor Lxy) \supset Lxx]$	
2	Lcb	
3	$(\forall x)\,[(\exists y)\,(Lyx \lor Lxy) \supset Lxx]$	(R, 1)
4	$(\exists y)\,(Lyc \lor Lcy) \supset Lcc$	($\forall$E, 3)
5	Lcb	(R, 2)
6	$Lbc \lor Lcb$	(VI, 5)
7	$(\exists y)\,(Lyc \lor Lcy)$	($\exists$I, 6)
8	Lcc	($\supset$E, 4, 7)
9	$(\exists x)Lxc$	($\exists$I, 8)

EXAMPLE 20: Everybody loves a lover. Tom doesn't love himself. So Tom doesn't love Sheila.

1	$(\forall x)(\forall y)[(\exists z)Lyz \supset Lxy]$	
2	~Ltt	
3	Lts	
4	$(\forall x)(\forall y)[(\exists z)Lyz \supset Lxy]$	(R, 1)
5	$(\forall y)[(\exists z)Lyz \supset Lty]$	($\forall$E, 4)
6	$(\exists z)Ltz \supset Ltt$	($\forall$E, 5)
7	Lts	(R, 3)
8	$(\exists z)Ltz$	($\exists$I, 7)
9	Ltt	($\supset$E, 6, 8)
10	~Ltt	(R, 2)
11	~Lts	(~I, 3–(9,10))

EXAMPLE 21: People are prejudiced against anyone who is liked by someone they dislike. But nobody's prejudiced against himself. So people don't like anyone who dislikes them.

1	$(\forall x)(\forall y)[(\exists z)(Lzy \;\&\; {\sim}Lxz) \supset Pxy]$	
2	${\sim}(\exists x)Pxx$	
3	~Lba	
4	Lab	
5	$(\forall x)(\forall y)[(\exists z)(Lzy \;\&\; {\sim}Lxz) \supset Pxy]$	(R, 1)
6	$(\forall y)[(\exists z)(Lzy \;\&\; {\sim}Lbz) \supset Pby]$	($\forall$E, 5)
7	$(\exists z)(Lzb \;\&\; {\sim}Lbz) \supset Pbb$	($\forall$E, 6)
8	Lab	(R, 4)
9	~Lba	(R, 3)
10	Lab & ~Lba	(&I, 8, 9)
11	$(\exists z)(Lzb \;\&\; {\sim}Lbz)$	($\exists$I, 10)
12	Pbb	($\supset$E, 7, 11)
13	$(\exists x)Pxx$	($\exists$I, 12)
14	${\sim}(\exists x)Pxx$	(R, 2)
15	~Lab	(~I, 4–(13, 14))
16	~Lba $\supset$ ~Lab	($\supset$I, 3–15)
17	$(\forall y)({\sim}Lya \supset {\sim}Lay)$	($\forall$I, 16)
18	$(\forall x)(\forall y)({\sim}Lyx \supset {\sim}Lxy)$	($\forall$I, 17)

We next comment on some features of Examples 15–21.

All the quantifiers in the assumptions and last line of Example 15 are initially placed, and universal in the assumptions. So, as suggested on p. 214 above, we aim for a suitable instance 'Dgga' of the last line '$(\exists y)(\forall x)Dgyx$' ('a' being foreign to line 1), reiterate line 1, and apply ∀E to get rid of quantifiers and put terms in the right positions.

No instance of the last line '$(\exists y)(\exists x)Cxy$' of Example 16 is entailed by the assumption '$(\exists x)(\exists y)Cxy$'. Resorting to ∃E, we instantiate line 1 (reiterated as line 2) by means of 'a', and instantiate the result (reiterated as line 4) by means of 'b'. Then we reintroduce by ∃I the two existential quantifiers in the reverse order, and apply ∃E twice.

Example 17 relies heavily on the indirect route. No instance of the last line is logically true, so none is derivable from the null set from which the last line is to be derived. The indirect route is unavoidable. Since the assumption '$\sim(\exists x)(\forall y)(My \supset Mx)$' is the only negation in sight, we try to reach '$(\exists x)(\forall y)(My \supset Mx)$' as the affirmative half of the contradiction. (This is of course the same as the last line; but with line 1 available, it can now be reached directly.) At this point no instance is easier to obtain than any other, so we try to reach '$(\forall y)(My \supset Ma)$'. As this in turn is a universal quantification, we pick a term foreign to lines 1 and 13, and try to reach the instance 'Mb ⊃ Ma' of '$(\forall y)(My \supset Ma)$' by assuming 'Mb' and aiming for 'Ma'. 'Ma' being atomic, and no elimination rules being applicable to lines 1–2, the indirect route is again unavoidable. On the extra assumption '$\sim$Ma', the same contradiction we set out to reach as lines 14–15 is readily forthcoming once line 6 has been obtained. Note how that line was reached.

Example 18 is rather straightforward. It should be obvious that, although line 12 could be asserted on the strength of any instance, including 'Aa & Taa', the one to aim for is 'Ab & Tab' (and 'b' is the term by means of which to instantiate line 7).

Example 19 illustrates the fact (already mentioned on p. 203) that we may assert an existential quantification $(\exists X)B$ by ∃I if we can reach *any* instance $B(T/X)$ of $(\exists X)B$, *including* one in which T already occurs. One might be tempted to aim for 'Lbc'; but this is not entailed by, and hence is not derivable from, lines 1–2. Seeing 'Lxx' in line 1, though, we might suspect (correctly so, as it turns out) that both 'Lbb' and 'Lcc' are derivable from lines 1–2; and we aim for 'Lcc' since it *is* an instance from which we may pass on to line 9. (The "somebody" who loves Charlene is Charlene herself.) The rest is easy.

An analogous point is illustrated by Examples 20 and 21: *any* instance $B(T/X)$ follows from a universal quantification $(\forall X)B$, *including* one in which T already occurs (as in Example 20 line 6 follows from line 5, and in Example 21 line 7 follows from line 6, by ∀E). Example 20 is straightforward enough at the outset; we are to assume 'Lts' and reach 'Ltt' and '$\sim$Ltt' as our contradiction. But how to reach 'Ltt'? Instantiation of line 1 (reiterated as line 4) first by means of 't', and then by means of 't' again, will yield a conditional whose consequent is what we want; and fortunately, as it turns out, the antecedent is easily obtained from line 3 (reiterated for the purpose as line 7). So 'Ltt' is easily had after all.

Example 21 is straightforward up to the assumption of 'Lab' at line 4, and the decision to aim for '($\exists x$)Pxx' and '$\sim$($\exists x$)Pxx' as our contradiction (since we are to expect the negation of a quantification to turn up as the negative half of a contradiction for $\sim$I). We can reach '($\exists x$)Pxx' if we can reach either 'Paa' or 'Pbb', but it may be by no means clear which one to aim for. Considering lines 3 and 4, we see that 'Lab & $\sim$Lba' would "match" the 'Lzy & $\sim Lxz$' of line 1 if 'b' were put for both 'x' and 'y', and 'a' were put for 'z'. And we see that instantiating line 1 (reiterated as line 5) first by means of 'b' for 'x', and then by means of 'b' again for 'y', would yield a conditional with 'Pbb' in the consequent. It turns out that the antecedent '($\exists z$) (Lzb & $\sim Lbz$)' is easy to reach, and the derivation is completed.

The Rules $\forall$I* and $\exists$E*[16]

Reconsider Example 2 on p. 205, and suppose that two of the four references to Al were dropped, so that the argument ran:

> Students are human beings. Human beings make mistakes. Al is a lousy teacher. Therefore, students make mistakes, and Al is a lousy teacher.

The derivation could be adapted to read:

1	($\forall x$) ($Sx \supset Hx$)	
2	($\forall x$) ($Hx \supset Mx$)	
3	Ta	
4	$\quad$ Sb	
5	$\quad$ Sb	(R, 4)
6	$\quad$ ($\forall x$) ($Sx \supset Hx$)	(R, 1)
7	$\quad$ $Sb \supset Hb$	($\forall$E, 6)
8	$\quad$ Hb	($\supset$E, 5, 7)
9	$\quad$ ($\forall x$) ($Hx \supset Mx$)	(R, 2)
10	$\quad$ $Hb \supset Mb$	($\forall$E, 9)
11	$\quad$ Mb	($\supset$E, 8, 10)
12	$Sb \supset Mb$	($\supset$I, 4–11)
13	($\forall x$) ($Sx \supset Mx$)	($\forall$I, 12)
14	Ta	(R, 3)
15	($\forall x$) ($Sx \supset Mx$) & Ta	(&I, 13, 14)

---

[16] The reader who does not intend to go on to Chapter 3 may omit the rest of this section.

As in the original derivation, use of the term 'b' in lines 4–12 is of course proper: 'b' is foreign to the assumptions 1–3, and to line 13 itself (which is obtained from line 12 by ∀I). And also proper would be use of the later terms 'c', 'd', 'e', etc., since they too are foreign to lines 1–3 and 13. But how about 'a' *this* time around? Although 'a' occurs in line 3, it is foreign to lines 1–2 and 13, and *only* lines 1–2 are needed to obtain line 12. So should we not have license here to assume 'Sa' in line 4, and derive 'Ma' in line 11, 'Sa ⊃ Ma' in line 12, and '(∀x)(Sx ⊃ Mx)' in line 13?

∀I prohibits this sort of thing, but ∀I*—the broader introduction rule for '∀' that we mentioned on p. 202—allows it, at the cost of an extra subordinate derivation. The rule reads:

$$
\begin{array}{lll}
1 & A_1 & \\
2 & A_2 & \\
\cdot & \cdot & \\
n & A_n & \\
& & \\
\cdot & \cdot & \\
p & & A_1' \\
p+1 & & A_2' \\
\cdot & & \cdot \\
p+j-1 & & A_j' \\
& & \\
\cdot & & \cdot \\
q & & B(T/X) \\
q+1 & (\forall X)B & (\forall \text{I*}, p\text{–}q)
\end{array}
$$

Restrictions: (a) A_1', A_2', ..., and A_j' ($j \geq 0$) must all belong to $\{A_1, A_2, ..., A_n\}$. (b) T must be foreign to A_1', A_2', ..., A_j', and to $(\forall X)B$.

With T presumed to be foreign to $(\forall X)B$, ∀I* thus permits assertion of $(\forall X)B$ on the assumptions A_1, A_2, ..., and A_n if $B(T/X)$ is derivable from some subset of $\{A_1, A_2, ..., A_n\}$ to which T is foreign; and ∀I is simply the subcase of ∀I* where the subset of $\{A_1, A_2, ..., A_n\}$ happens to be $\{A_1, A_2, ..., A_n\}$ itself (and one does not bother moving into a fresh column and writing A_1, A_2, ..., and A_n all over again).

The following derivation of '$(\forall x)(Sx \supset Mx)$ & Ta' from the set $\{(\forall x)(Sx \supset Hx), (\forall x)(Hx \supset Mx), Ta\}$ makes use of $\forall I^*$ (and 'a'):

EXAMPLE 22:

1	$(\forall x)(Sx \supset Hx)$	
2	$(\forall x)(Hx \supset Mx)$	
3	Ta	
4	$(\forall x)(Sx \supset Hx)$	
5	$(\forall x)(Hx \supset Mx)$	
6	Sa	
7	Sa	(R, 6)
8	$(\forall x)(Sx \supset Hx)$	(R, 4)—*not* R, 1!
9	Sa $\supset$ Ha	($\forall$E, 8)
10	Ha	($\supset$E, 7, 9)
11	$(\forall x)(Hx \supset Mx)$	(R, 5)—*not* R, 2!
12	Ha $\supset$ Ma	($\forall$E, 11)
13	Ma	($\supset$E, 10, 12)
14	Sa $\supset$ Ma	($\supset$I, 6–13)
15	$(\forall x)(Sx \supset Mx)$	($\forall$I*, 4–14)
16	Ta	(R, 3)
17	$(\forall x)(Sx \supset Mx)$ & Ta	(&I, 15, 16)

Formatwise, $\exists E^*$ departs little from $\exists E$. With T presumed to be foreign both to $(\exists X)B$ and to C, it permits assertion of C on the assumptions $A_1, A_2, \ldots,$ and A_n if $(\exists X)B$ is derivable from $\{A_1, A_2, \ldots, A_n\}$, and C is derivable—given the extra assumption $B(T/X)$—from some subset of $\{A_1, A_2, \ldots, A_n\}$ to which T is foreign. $\exists E$ is thus the subcase of $\exists E^*$ where the subset of $\{A_1, A_2, \ldots, A_n\}$ is $\{A_1, A_2, \ldots, A_n\}$ itself, and one does not trouble writing $A_1, A_2, \ldots,$ and A_n all over again.

$$\begin{array}{ll} 1 & A_1 \\ 2 & A_2 \\ \cdot & \cdot \\ n & A_n \\ \cdot & \cdot \\ p & (\exists X)B \\ \cdot & \cdot \\ q & A'_1 \\ q+1 & A'_2 \\ \cdot & \cdot \\ q+j-1 & A'_j \\ q+j & B(T/X) \\ \cdot & \cdot \\ r & C \\ r+1 & C \qquad (\exists E^*, p, q\text{-}r) \end{array}$$

Restrictions: (a) A'_1, A'_2, . . ., and A'_j ($j \geq 0$) must all belong to $\{A_1, A_2, . . ., A_n\}$.
(b) T must be foreign to A'_1, A'_2, . . ., A'_j, $(\exists X)B$, and C.

For illustration's sake, consider the following modification of Example 4 on p. 209:

EXAMPLE 23: Aristotle is a Greek. Some Greeks are famous. All famous people are happy. So some Greeks are happy.

$$\begin{array}{lll} 1 & Ga \\ 2 & (\exists x)(Gx \,\&\, Fx) \\ 3 & (\forall x)(Fx \supset Hx) \\ \\ 4 & (\exists x)(Gx \,\&\, Fx) & (R, 2) \\ 5 & \quad (\forall x)(Fx \supset Hx) \\ 6 & \quad Ga \,\&\, Fa \\ \\ 7 & \quad Ga \,\&\, Fa & (R, 6) \\ 8 & \quad Ga & (\&E, 7) \\ 9 & \quad Fa & (\&E, 7) \\ 10 & \quad (\forall x)(Fx \supset Hx) & (R, 5)\text{—}not\ R, 3! \\ 11 & \quad Fa \supset Ha & (\forall E, 10) \\ 12 & \quad Ha & (\supset E, 9, 11) \\ 13 & \quad Ga \,\&\, Ha & (\&I, 8, 12) \\ 14 & \quad (\exists x)(Gx \,\&\, Hx) & (\exists I, 13) \\ 15 & (\exists x)(Gx \,\&\, Hx) & (\exists E^*, 4, 5\text{-}14) \end{array}$$

Here the occurrence of 'a' among the assumptions from which the last line '$(\exists x)(Gx \ \& \ Hx)$' is to be derived does not prevent our using 'a' at line 6, since line 1 is nowhere used in the subordinate derivation of '$(\exists x)(Gx \ \& \ Hx)$', and 'a' is foreign to line 5 (i.e., to line 3), which *is* used.

$\forall$I* and $\exists$E* make for slightly longer and more complicated-looking derivations than $\forall$I and $\exists$E did. Otherwise, they have the edge over $\forall$I and $\exists$E. As indicated before, they place less stringent restrictions on the term T. And they permit more straightforward proof of the following result:

(a) If $S \vdash B$, then $S \cup S' \vdash B$,

where S and S' are two finite sets of statements.

This result, according to which a statement that is derivable from a finite set of statements is derivable as well from any finite superset of the set, is wanted on two counts.[17] First, the following counterpart of it:

(b) If S entails B, then $S \cup S'$ entails B,

where S and S' are as before, holds true, and matters like derivability, provability, etc., should exactly match matters like entailment, logical truth, and so forth.[18] (In case proof of (b) is desired, suppose S entails B. Then there is no truth-value assignment to the atomic subformulas of the members of $S \cup \{\sim B\}$ on which all the members of $S \cup \{\sim B\}$ are true. But if so, there clearly is no truth-value assignment to the atomic subformulas of the members of $S \cup S' \cup \{\sim B\}$ on which all the members of $S \cup S' \cup \{\sim B\}$ are true. Hence, $S \cup S'$ entails B.) And second, we shall repeatedly use (a) in Chapter 3, when showing that our derivation rules are both sound and complete.

For proof of (a), suppose—as in Chapter 3—that we make $\forall$I* our official introduction rule for '$\forall$', and $\exists$E* our official elimination rule for '$\exists$'; and suppose there is a derivation of B from the original set $\{A_1, A_2, \ldots, A_n\}$ ($= S$) of assumptions. Then the result:

---

[17] Any finite superset of S is of course of the sort $S \cup S'$, where S' is finite.

[18] Derivability, provability, and the like will soon be called *syntactic* matters; entailment, logical truth, and the like will be called *semantic* matters.

$$
\begin{array}{c|c}
1 & A_1 \\
2 & A_2 \\
\cdot & \cdot \\
n & A_n \\
n+1 & A_{n+1} \\
n+2 & A_{n+2} \\
\cdot & \cdot \\
n+k & A_{n+k} \\
\hline
\cdot & \cdot \\
\cdot & \cdot \\
\cdot & \cdot \\
p & B
\end{array}
$$

of entering any k additional assumptions A_{n+1}, A_{n+2}, ..., and A_{n+k} between A_n and the first horizontal bar of the original derivation is sure to count as a derivation of B from the enlarged set $\{A_1, A_2, ..., A_n\}$ $\cup$ $\{A_{n+1}, A_{n+2}, ..., A_{n+k}\}$ $(= S \cup S')$ of assumptions. Inspection of rule R, the intelim rules of Section 1.3 for '$\sim$', '$\supset$', '&', '$\lor$', and '$\equiv$', and the four rules $\forall$I*, $\forall$E, $\exists$I, and $\exists$E* will quickly bear this out. As a matter of fact, one need only note, as regards $\forall$I* and $\exists$E*, that the j assumptions A_1', A_2', ..., and A_j' to which the term T of $\forall$I* and $\exists$E* must be foreign, all belong to the superset $\{A_1, A_2, ..., A_n\}$ $\cup$ $\{A_{n+1}, A_{n+2}, ..., A_{n+k}\}$ of $\{A_1, A_2, ..., A_n\}$ if they all belong to $\{A_1, A_2, ..., A_n\}$ itself.

(a) also holds true when $\forall$I serves as introduction rule for '$\forall$', and $\exists$E as elimination rule for '$\exists$'. Some editing may prove necessary, though, before the additional assumptions A_{n+1}, A_{n+2}, ..., and A_{n+k} are entered beneath A_n: a term which was foreign to each and every one of A_1, A_2, ..., and A_n might turn up in one of A_{n+1}, A_{n+2}, ..., and A_{n+k}, and hence might have to be replaced throughout by a totally new term.

*The Rule $\exists$E***

Interestingly enough, there is an elimination rule for '$\exists$'—we call it $\exists$E**—which like $\forall$I, $\forall$E, and $\exists$I does without a subordinate derivation:

$$
\begin{array}{r|l}
1 & A_1 \\
2 & A_2 \\
\cdot & \cdot \\
n & A_n \\
\cdot & \cdot \\
p & (\exists X)B \\
\cdot & \cdot \\
q & B(T/X) \qquad (\exists E^{**}, p)
\end{array}
$$

Restriction: The term T must be foreign to $A_1, A_2, \ldots$, and A_n, to $(\exists X)B$, and to any line obtained by an earlier application of $\exists E^{**}$.

When $\exists E^{**}$ does duty as elimination rule for '$\exists$', a further restriction must be placed upon the term T in rule $\forall I$: *T is to be foreign to any line obtained by application of* $\exists E^{**}$. Otherwise, we could derive any universal quantification from the corresponding existential quantification thus (with T understood to be foreign to $(\forall X)A$, and hence also to $(\exists X)A$):

$$
\begin{array}{r|ll}
1 & (\exists X)A & \\
2 & (\exists X)A & (R, 1) \\
3 & A(T/X) & (\exists E^{**}, 2) \\
4 & (\forall X)A & (\forall I, 3) \qquad \text{(erroneous!)}
\end{array}
$$

We again derive '$(\forall y)(\exists x)Cxy$' from '$(\exists x)(\forall y)Cxy$', using $\exists E^{**}$ instead of $\exists E$:

EXAMPLE 24:

$$
\begin{array}{r|ll}
1 & (\exists x)(\forall y)Cxy & \\
2 & (\exists x)(\forall y)Cxy & (R, 1) \\
3 & (\forall y)Cay & (\exists E^{**}, 2) \\
4 & Cab & (\forall E, 3) \\
5 & (\exists x)Cxb & (\exists I, 4) \\
6 & (\forall y)(\exists x)Cxy & (\forall I, 5)
\end{array}
$$

Thus, derivations using $\exists E^{**}$ will be shorter than the corresponding derivations using $\exists E$. But one warning is in order. With $\exists E$ (or $\exists E^*$) serving as elimination rule for '$\exists$', any statement derivable from a set of statements is sure to be entailed by that set. But this is not necessarily so when

∃E** serves in that capacity, as the following derivation of 'Alcohol un-does me' from 'Something undoes me' reveals:

1	$(\exists x)Ux$	
2	$(\exists x)Ux$	(R, 1)
3	Ua	(∃E**, 2)

So this further proviso must be met when using ∃E**: *The last line of a derivation should contain no occurrence of any term introduced by* ∃E** *in the course of the derivation.*[19]

EXERCISES

E2.3.1. Construct a derivation of the conclusion from the premises of each of the following arguments:

a. $(\forall x)(Fx \supset Gx)$
     Fa
    ————————
     $\therefore Ha \supset Ga$

b. $(\forall x)(Fx \supset Gx)$
     $(\forall x)\sim Gx$
    ————————
     $\therefore \sim Fa \lor \sim Ha$

c. $(\forall x)(Fx \supset \sim Gx)$
     $(\forall x)(Fx \& Hx)$
    ————————
     $\therefore (\exists x)\sim Gx$

d. $(\forall x)[(\exists y)Fxy \supset Gbx]$
     $(\forall x)(\forall y)Fyx$
    ————————
     $\therefore (\exists x)Gxx$

e. $(\exists x)Fx \supset (\forall x)Gx$
    ————————
     $\therefore (\forall x)(\sim Gx \supset \sim Fx)$

f. $(\exists x)Fxb \supset (\forall x)Gx$
     $(\forall x)Fax$
    ————————
     $\therefore (\forall x)(Hxc \supset Gx)$

g. $\sim(\forall x)\sim Fx$
    ————————
     $\therefore (\exists x)Fx$

h. $(\forall x)(\forall y)[(\exists z)Fyz \supset Fxy]$
     Fab
    ————————
     $\therefore (\forall x)(\forall y)Fyx$

i. $(\exists x)Fx \& (\forall x)Gx$
    ————————
     $\therefore (\exists x)(Fx \& Gx)$

j. $(\exists x)Fx$
     $(\exists x)Gx$
    ————————
     $\therefore (\exists x)[(\exists y)Fy \& Gx]$

k. $(\exists x)(Fx \& Gx)$
    ————————
     $\therefore \sim(\forall x)(Fx \supset \sim Gx)$

l. $(\forall x)(Fx \supset Gx)$
     $(\forall x)[(\exists y)(Gy \& Ixy) \supset Hx]$
     $(\exists x)[Jx \& (\exists y)(Fy \& Ixy)]$
    ————————
     $\therefore (\exists x)(Jx \& Hx)$

---

[19] W. V. Quine in his *Methods of Logic*, revised edition, 1959, Henry Holt and Company, Inc., uses an elimination rule for 'ヨ' of the same sort as ∃E**. So did I. M. Copi in the first two editions of his *Symbolic Logic,* The Macmillan Company; the 1967 edition, however, uses an analogue of our ∃E. In these two texts and others, the introduction rules for '∀' and 'ヨ' are respectively called UG and EG ('G' for 'Generalization'), and the elimination ones are respectively called UI and EI ('I' for 'Instantiation').

E2.3.2. Construct a derivation of the conclusion from the premises of each of the following arguments:

a. All tigers are felines. All mammals are vertebrates. So, if all felines are mammals, then all tigers are vertebrates. (Tx, Fx, Mx, Vx)

b. No beauty queens are unattractive. There aren't any attractive gangsters. So beauty queens are never gangsters. (Qx, Ax, Gx)

c. All beautiful things are desirable. Nothing desirable has scales. Mermaids have scales. So beautiful mermaids always lure sailors to their doom. (Bx, Dx, Sx, Mx, Lx)

d. Philosophers are stuffy woolgatherers. Metaphysicians are not stuffy if they are logicians. Some philosophers are careful thinkers if and only if they are logicians. Only metaphysicians are either stuffy or unintelligible. So not all philosophers are logicians. (Px, Sx, Wx, Mx, Lx, Cx, Ix)

e. Only grownups, and children accompanied by their parents, saw the show. All the grownups who remained till the end liked the show. Peter saw the show, but he didn't like it. So some grownups didn't remain till the end, or else Peter was accompanied by his parents. (Gx, Cx, Ax, Sx, Rx, Lx, p)

f. If any undergraduate enrolls in the course, and all the graduate students who enroll are doctoral candidates, he (the undergraduate) will have rough competition. If some graduate students who enroll in the course are doctoral candidates, then no graduate student enrolls unless he's a doctoral candidate. So, if any undergraduate enrolls in the course, and some graduate students who are doctoral candidates enroll too, then he'll have rough competition. (Ux, Ex, Gx, Cx, Hx)

g. If any men are lovers, they all are. If a woman is still young or beautiful, then if all men are lovers she's a social success. So, if a beautiful woman is intelligent but no longer young, then if some lovers are men she's a social success if she's a good cook. (Mx, Lx, Wx, Yx, Bx, Sx, Ix, Cx)

h. There is a dirty book which has been read by every person who has read any books. Everybody has read at least one book. Members of the D. A. R. are grand people. So there's a dirty book which every D. A. R. member has read. (Dx, Bx, Px, Rxy, Mx, Gx)

i. People like anything liked by anyone they like. Not everybody dislikes everybody. People like those who like them. So somebody likes himself. (Px, Lxy)

j. Every line of the President's message is addressed to posterity. People who address something they wrote to posterity take themselves too seriously. A friend of mine wrote a line of the President's message. So a friend of mine takes himself too seriously. (Lx, Ax, Px, Wxy, Sxy, Fxy, i)

k. Any psychiatrist who heeds the advice of a doctor is sick. Psychiatrists are doctors. So any psychiatrist who heeds his own advice is sick. (Px, Hxy, Dx, Sx)

l. Everybody wants whatever anybody has. All God's children are nasty people, but He nonetheless gives them whatever they want. A person has whatever is given to him. You and I (at least) are lovely people, and so is

God. I have shoes. You have shoes. So all God's children have shoes. (Px, Wxy, Hxy, Cxy, Nx, Gxyz, Lx, Sx, g, i, u)

m.   Ga $\supset$ ($\forall x$)Fx

    ($\exists x$)Fx $\supset$ Ga

    ―――――――

    $\therefore$ ($\forall x$) (Ga $\equiv$ Fx)

n.   ($\exists x$) ($\exists y$)Fxy $\vee$ ($\forall x$) ($\forall y$)Gyx

    ―――――――――――――

    $\therefore$ ($\exists x$) ($\exists y$) (Fxy $\vee$ Gxy)

o.   ($\forall x$) ($\sim$Fx $\supset$ Gx)

    ($\forall x$) [($\sim$Gx $\vee$ Fx) $\equiv$ $\sim$Gx]

    ($\exists x$) (Hx $\equiv$ Fx)

    ――――――――――――

    $\therefore$ $\sim$($\forall x$) (Hx $\equiv$ Gx)

p.   ($\forall x$) (Fx $\equiv$ Gx)

    ($\forall x$) (Hx $\equiv$ Ix)

    ($\exists x$) [Ix & ($\forall y$) (Fy $\supset$ Jy)]

    ――――――――――――

    $\therefore$ ($\exists x$) [Hx & ($\forall y$) (Jy $\vee$ $\sim$Gy)]

q.   ($\forall x$) (Fxa $\supset$ Fxb)

    ――――――――――――――――――

    $\therefore$ ($\forall x$) [($\exists y$) (Gxy & Fya) $\supset$ ($\exists y$) (Gxy & Fyb)]

r.   ($\forall x$) ($\forall y$) [(Fx & Gy) $\supset$ Hxy]

    ($\exists x$) ($\exists y$) [(Fx & $\sim$Fy) & $\sim$Hxy]

    ――――――――――――――

    $\therefore$ ($\exists x$) ($\sim$Fx & $\sim$Gx)

s.   ($\forall x$) ($\exists y$) (Fx $\supset$ Gy)

    ―――――――――

    $\therefore$ ($\exists y$) ($\forall x$) (Fx $\supset$ Gy)

t.   ($\forall x$) ($\exists y$) (Fy $\supset$ Gx)

    ―――――――――

    $\therefore$ ($\exists y$) ($\forall x$) (Fy $\supset$ Gx)

E2.3.3. Construct a proof of every logical truth in E2.2.3.

E2.3.4. Construct a proof of each of the following logical truths:

a.   ($\forall x$) ($\exists y$) (Fy $\supset$ Fx)

b.   ($\exists x$)Fx $\vee$ ($\forall x$) (Fx $\supset$ Gx)

c.   ($\forall x$) (Fx $\vee$ Ga) $\equiv$ [($\forall x$)Fx $\vee$ Ga]

d.   ($\forall x$) (Fx $\supset$ Ga) $\equiv$ [($\exists x$)Fx $\supset$ Ga]

e.   ($\exists x$) (Fx $\supset$ Ga) $\equiv$ [($\forall x$)Fx $\supset$ Ga]

f.   ($\exists x$) (Fx $\supset$ Gx) $\equiv$ [($\forall x$)Fx $\supset$ ($\exists x$)Gx]

E2.3.5. Derive any contradiction you please from each inconsistent set of statements in E2.2.1.

E2.3.6. Suppose that ($\exists X$)B is defined as $\sim$($\forall X$)$\sim$B, and that the intelim rules for '$\exists$' are not available. Show that:

  (a) if $\{A_1, A_2, \ldots, A_n\}$ $\vdash$ B(T/X) for some T, then $\{A_1, A_2, \ldots, A_n\}$ $\vdash$ $\sim$($\forall X$)$\sim$B
    (= ($\exists X$)B), and

(b) if $\{A_1,A_2,\ldots,A_n\} \vdash \sim(\forall X)\sim B \,(= (\exists X)B)$ and $\{A_1,A_2,\ldots,A_n, B(T/X)\} \vdash C$, then $\{A_1,A_2,\ldots,A_n\} \vdash C$, so long as T is foreign to $\{A_1,A_2,\ldots,A_n\}$ and to both $\sim(\forall X)\sim B$ and C.

(That is, show how to construct a derivation of $\sim(\forall X)\sim B$ from $\{A_1,A_2,\ldots,A_n\}$ if you already know how to derive $B(T/X)$ from $\{A_1,A_2,\ldots,A_n\}$ for some term T; and show how to construct a derivation of C from $\{A_1,A_2,\ldots,A_n\}$ if you already know how to derive $\sim(\forall X)\sim B$ from $\{A_1,A_2,\ldots,A_n\}$ and know how to derive C from the superset $\{A_1,A_2,\ldots,A_n, B(T/X)\}$, where T is a term foreign to $\{A_1,A_2,\ldots,A_n\}$ and to both $\sim(\forall X)\sim B$ and C.)

E2.3.7.

(a) Show that if $S \vdash \sim(\forall X)A$ and $S \cup \{\sim A(T/X)\} \vdash B$, then $S \vdash B$, so long as T is foreign to S and to both $\sim(\forall X)A$ and B.

(b) Show that if $S \vdash \sim(\exists X)A$, then $S \vdash \sim A(T/X)$ for any term T.

E2.3.8.   Do E2.3.1–4 over, using $\exists E^{**}$ in place of $\exists E$.

3

Metalogic

In Chapters 1 and 2 we introduced the reader to various ways of turning out compound statements whose truth-values depend on just the truth-values of their components or just those of their subformulas. We also defined various logical properties and relations which statements —either individually or as a set—might have, or bear to other statements, *because* of their manner of composition: properties like logical truth, consistency, and so on; and relations like equivalence, entailment, and so on. We then developed techniques—the truth-table technique of Section 1.1, and the tree technique of Sections 1.2 and 2.2—for testing the (in)consistency of finite sets of statements. Lastly, we developed in Sections 1.3 and 2.3 a technique for deriving statements from the finite sets of statements that entail them.

In this chapter we shall first establish various results about modes of statement composition in general, both truth-functional modes of composition and quantificational ones (Section 3.1). After a section devoted to auxiliary matters like mathematical induction, derivability from infinite sets of statements, and so on (Section 3.2), we shall prove that the technique of Chapters 1 and 2 for deriving statements from finite sets of statements is both sound and complete (Sections 3.3–3.4). We shall next establish that any set of statements declared INCONSISTENT by the routine of p. 189 is indeed inconsistent, and any one declared CONSISTENT is sure to be consistent (Section 3.5). Returning to the notions of consistency, entailment, and logical truth, we shall then compare and contrast our "truth-value" account of these with the one normally given in the literature (Section 3.6). Lastly, we shall present an alternative technique for deriving statements from sets of statements, and show that it permits the same derivations as does the technique of Sections 1.3 and 2.3 (Section 3.7).

As the foregoing summary indicates, we shall mostly be concerned

239

with establishing results *about* matters from Chapters 1 and 2, and comparing our account of these matters with other accounts in the literature. This sort of thing is often referred to as **metalogic,** 'meta' (the Greek word for 'after') doing duty here and in related contexts for 'about'. And, because they are theorems *about* logical matters, the results we shall obtain are often called **metatheorems.** As often as not, though, the shorter appellation 'theorem' is used instead, and we shall follow suit, thus talking of the Soundness Theorem for the principal metatheorem of Section 3.3, the Completeness Theorem for the principal metatheorem of Section 3.4, and so on.

Besides 'metalogic', which serves as the title of this chapter, two other technical terms will prove useful hereafter: 'syntax' and 'semantics'. Inasmuch as (1) the truth-value of an atomic statement depends in part upon the *meaning* of the predicate and that of each term occurring in the statement, and (2) the conditions under which compound statements are certified true or false depend upon the *meanings* of the seven operators '∼', '⊃', '&', 'V', '≡', '∀', and '∃', truth and falsehood are commonly called **semantic** notions. And so are consistency, entailment, logical truth, and so on, in whose definitions *truth* plays a role. On the other hand, statementhood, derivability, provability, and the like, have to do with *form* rather than meaning or truth. For example, a statement counts as a compound statement if it is of one of seven specified forms: $\sim A$, $A \supset B$, etc., and this quite regardless of its meaning. A statement may be asserted by &I on some given assumptions if it is of the form $A \& B$, and both A and B are derivable from those assumptions, again whatever the meaning of the statement or the meanings of the assumptions. And so on. Notions like statementhood, derivability, and provability are accordingly called **syntactic** notions.

Though of different kinds, the syntactic notion of derivability and the semantic one of entailment are nonetheless expected to match; and proof is given that they do as regards finite sets of statements. Indeed, according to the Soundness Theorem of Section 3.3, a statement A is entailed by a finite set S of statements if it is derivable from S; and, according to the Completeness Theorem of Section 3.4, A is derivable from S if it is entailed by S. Since a statement is logically true if and only if entailed by the null set of statements, and provable if and only if derivable from that set, the syntactic notion of provability and the semantic one of logical truth also match.

We included consistency in our list of semantic notions, and rightly so, since a finite set of statements was said in Section 2.1 to be consistent if there is a truth-value assignment on which all its members are *true*. The notion has a syntactic counterpart, a set being called *syntactically consistent* if no contradiction is derivable from it. Syntactic consistency played no official role in Chapters 1 and 2, but will play a major one in Sections 3.2–3.6.

'Semantics' will be the more heavily used of the two terms we just introduced. It appears in the title of 3.6, a section where—as already announced—we compare the standard or "model-theoretic" account of consistency, entailment, and logical truth with our own, and prove as we go along a number of theorems that link *standard* and *truth-value* semantics. In the early days of modern logic, matters of syntax were paramount; recently, however, it is matters of semantics that have attracted the most attention, and in its modest way our text reflects this trend.

One major result about elementary logic had to be left unproved. This is Church's 1936 theorem according to which there can be no mechanical way of determining—in each and every case—whether or not a statement is logically true, a finite set of statements entails another statement, a finite and non-empty set of statements is consistent, and so on. The mathematical preliminaries called for were too numerous to include here.[1]

3.1   Modes of Statement Composition

Truth-Functional Modes of (Statement) Composition

The reader will recall from Section 1.1 that, for any n from 1 on, there are in general 2^n different ways of assigning a truth-value to each one of n atomic statements, and by the same token to each one of any n statements, atomic or compound. Relying upon this result, we shall now establish that, for any n from 1 on, there are 2^{2^n} different ways of truth-functionally compounding n statements at a time—i.e., 2^{2^n} different ways of compounding n statements, say, $A_1, A_2, \ldots,$ and A_n, into a further statement whose truth-value depends just on the truth-values of $A_1, A_2, \ldots,$ and A_n.

For proof consider Table XI on the next page.

The first blank under compound B can be filled either with a 'T' or with an 'F', and hence in 2 different ways. But, for each one of these 2 different ways of filling the first blank under compound B, there are likewise 2 different ways of filling the second one. Hence, there are 2×2 different ways of filling the first two blanks under compound B. Moreover,

---

[1] Church's Theorem is in a paper entitled "A note on the Entscheidungsproblem," *The Journal of Symbolic Logic,* vol. 1, 1936, pp. 40–41, 101–2. It follows (via a result of J. Barkley Rosser's on recursive enumerability) from a theorem of Kurt Gödel's in "Ueber formal unentscheidbare Sätze der *Principia Mathematica* und verwandter Systeme I," *Monatshefte für Mathematik und Physik,* vol. 38, 1931, pp. 173–98. There are numerous expositions of Gödel's and Church's Theorems. Excellent ones will be found in Stephen C. Kleene's *Mathematical Logic,* 1967, John Wiley & Sons, Inc., and Joel W. Robbin's *Mathematical Logic, A First Course,* 1969, W. A. Benjamin, Inc.

TABLE XI

Truth-value assignments	Components					Compound
	A_1	A_2	A_3	$\cdots$	A_n	B
Assignment 1	T	T	T	$\cdots$	T	
Assignment 2	F	T	T	$\cdots$	T	
Assignment 3	T	F	T	$\cdots$	T	
Assignment 4	F	F	T	$\cdots$	T	
Assignment 5	T	T	F	$\cdots$	T	
.	.	.	.	$\cdots$	.	
.	.	.	.	$\cdots$	.	
.	.	.	.	$\cdots$	.	
Assignment 2^n	F	F	F	$\cdots$	F	

for each one of these 2×2 different ways of filling the first two blanks under compound B, there are 2 different ways of filling the third one. Hence, there are $2 \times 2 \times 2$ different ways of filling the first three blanks under compound B. Thus, by the same reasoning over and over, there are $\underbrace{2 \times 2 \times \ldots \times 2}_{2^n \text{ times}}$ different ways of filling the 2^n blanks under compound

B. But $\underbrace{2 \times 2 \times \ldots \times 2}_{2^n \text{ times}}$ equals 2^{2^n}. Hence, there are 2^{2^n} different ways of

filling the 2^n blanks under compound B—i.e., of compounding $A_1, A_2, \ldots,$ and A_n into a further statement whose truth-value depends just on the truth-values of $A_1, A_2, \ldots,$ and A_n. Hence, for any n from 1 on, there are 2^{2^n} different ways of truth-functionally compounding n statements at a time. Or, as the matter is often put:

> (*3.1.1*)   For any n from 1 on, there are 2^{2^n} n-ary truth-functional modes of composition.

('(3.1.1)' identifies the result as being the first in Section 3.1.)

For example, suppose n to be 1. Then there are 4 ($= 2^{2^1}$) different ways of filling the 2 ($= 2^1$) blanks under B in Table XI:

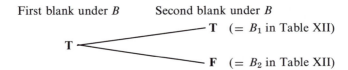

First blank under B Second blank under B

T   ($= B_1$ in Table XII)

T

F   ($= B_2$ in Table XII)

T $(= B_3$ in Table XII)

F

F $(= B_4$ in Table XII)

The resulting *singular* truth-functional modes of composition can be tabulated as follows:

TABLE XII

A $(= A_1)$	B_1	B_2	B_3	B_4
T	T	T	F	F
F	T	F	T	F

The third mode of composition in Table XII is familiar enough: it is negation, B_3 having the same truth-values as $\sim A$. The second is sometimes known as *identity*, B_2 having the same truth-values as A (the reader may wish to read B_2 as "It is the case that A"[1]). The first delivers a truth-functional compound of A which is true no matter which truth-value is assigned to A, and hence has the same truth-values as, say, $A \vee \sim A$; and the fourth delivers a truth-functional compound of A which is false no matter which truth-value is assigned to A, and hence has the same truth-values as, say, $A \,\&\sim A$.

Suppose next that n in (3.1.1) equals 2. Then there are 16 $(= 2^{2^2})$ different ways of filling the 4 $(= 2^2)$ blanks under B in Table XI:

1st blank under B 2d blank under B 3d blank under B 4th blank under B

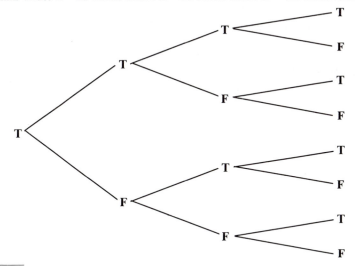

---

[1]Or, more simply, as A. Note that we use the phrase 'truth-functional compound' more broadly here than in Chapter 1, in that each statement now counts as a truth-functional compound of itself. This broader understanding of the phrase would have been distracting in Chapter 1, but is quite welcome, as every statement already counted as a *component* of itself.

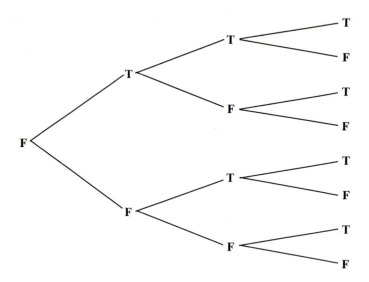

The resulting *binary* truth-functional modes of composition can be tabulated as follows:

TABLE XIII

A_1	A_2	B_1	B_2	B_3	B_4	B_5	B_6	B_7	B_8
T	T	T	T	T	T	T	T	T	T
F	T	T	T	T	T	F	F	F	F
T	F	T	T	F	F	T	T	F	F
F	F	T	F	T	F	T	F	T	F

A_1	A_2	B_9	B_{10}	B_{11}	B_{12}	B_{13}	B_{14}	B_{15}	B_{16}
T	T	F	F	F	F	F	F	F	F
F	T	T	T	T	T	F	F	F	F
T	F	T	T	F	F	T	T	F	F
F	F	T	F	T	F	T	F	T	F

Seven of these modes of composition are familiar. B_2 is $A_1 \lor A_2$; B_3 is $A_1 \supset A_2$; B_7 is $A_1 \equiv A_2$; B_8 is $A_1 \& A_2$; B_9 is the alternative denial

$A_1 \mid A_2$ of A_1 and A_2; B_{10} is the exclusive disjunction of A_1 and A_2; and B_{15} is the joint denial $A_1 \downarrow A_2$ of A_1 and A_2.

At least one of the 256 ($2^{2^3} = 2^8$) ternary truth-functional modes of composition is sometimes met in everyday discourse, the one that delivers

$$A_1 \text{ unless } A_2, \text{ in which case } A_3$$

or—equivalently—

$$A_3 \text{ if } A_2, \text{ otherwise } A_1.$$

It has the following truth-table:

A_1	A_2	A_3	A_1 unless A_2, in which case A_3
T	T	T	T
F	T	T	T
T	F	T	T
F	F	T	F
T	T	F	F
F	T	F	F
T	F	F	T
F	F	F	F

However, truth-functional modes of composition other than singulary and binary ones can—to all intents and purposes—be discounted, and so can most singulary and binary ones, as we shall establish shortly.

Note by the way that, where α is any truth-value assignment to n ($n \geq 1$) statements $A_1, A_2, \ldots,$ and A_n, there corresponds to α a conjunction C which is true just on α. The conjunction, to be known as **the conjunction associate of α**, is

$$\pm A_1 \mathbin{\&} \pm A_2 \mathbin{\&} \ldots \mathbin{\&} \pm A_n,^2$$

where—for each i from 1 through n—$\pm A_i$ is A_i itself if A_i is assigned the truth-value **T** in α, otherwise $\pm A_i$ is $\sim A_i$. To illustrate matters, we tabulate the eight different ways in which A_1, A_2, and A_3 can be assigned a truth-value each, and the conjunction associates of the resulting eight truth-value assignments to A_1, A_2, and A_3:

---

[2] In this and a few similar cases, we omit easily restored parentheses.

TABLE XIV

Truth-value assignments to A_1 A_2 A_3			Conjunction associates
T	T	T	A_1 & A_2 & A_3
F	T	T	$\sim A_1$ & A_2 & A_3
T	F	T	A_1 & $\sim A_2$ & A_3
F	F	T	$\sim A_1$ & $\sim A_2$ & A_3
T	T	F	A_1 & A_2 & $\sim A_3$
F	T	F	$\sim A_1$ & A_2 & $\sim A_3$
T	F	F	A_1 & $\sim A_2$ & $\sim A_3$
F	F	F	$\sim A_1$ & $\sim A_2$ & $\sim A_3$

Clearly, the first conjunction in the right-most column ($= A_1$ & A_2 & A_3) is true if and only if A_1, A_2, and A_3 are all assigned the truth-value **T**—and hence is true just on the first of our eight truth-value assignments. The second conjunction ($= \sim A_1$ & A_2 & A_3) is true if and only if A_1 is assigned the truth-value **F** and both A_2 and A_3 are assigned the truth-value **T**—and hence is true just on the second of our eight truth-value assignments. And so on.

We next proceed to show that, for any n from 1 on, any n statements A_1, A_2, . . ., and A_n, and any truth-functional compound B of A_1, A_2, . . ., and A_n, there corresponds to B a truth-functionally equivalent compound built out of A_1, A_2, . . ., and A_n by means of just '$\sim$', '&', and 'V'. Since the result is due to Emil L. Post, the compound in question is sometimes known as **the Post paraphrase of B.**[3]

Consider first the case where B is not true on any of the 2^n truth-value assignments to A_1, A_2, . . ., and A_n. Since

$$A_1 \text{ \& } \sim A_1 \text{ \& } A_2 \text{ \& } A_3 \text{ \& } \ldots \text{ \& } A_n \qquad (1)$$

is not true either on any of these assignments, (1) is truth-functionally equivalent to B. But (1) is a compound of A_1, A_2, . . ., and A_n by means of just '$\sim$' and '&', and hence by means of just '$\sim$', '&', and 'V'. Hence, (1) will do in this case as the Post paraphase of B.

Consider next the case where B is true on at least one of the 2^n truth-value assignments to A_1, A_2, . . ., and A_n; let α_1, α_2, . . ., and α_j ($1 \leq j \leq 2^n$) be all the truth-value assignments to A_1, A_2, . . ., and A_n on which B is

---

[3] See Post's "Introduction to a general theory of elementary propositions," *The American Journal of Mathematics,* vol. 43, 1921, pp. 163–85.

true; and, for each i from 1 through j, let C_i be the conjunction associate of α_i. We first show that the disjunction

$$C_1 \vee C_2 \vee \ldots \vee C_j \qquad (2)$$

of the conjunction associates $C_1, C_2, \ldots$, and C_j of $\alpha_1, \alpha_2, \ldots$, and α_j is true on each one of $\alpha_1, \alpha_2, \ldots$, and α_j; we go on to show that (2) is false on any other truth-value assignment to $A_1, A_2, \ldots$, and A_n; and we conclude that (2) will do in this case as the Post paraphrase of B.

Part One.   Since C_1 is true on α_1, (2) (of which C_1 is a disjunct) is sure to be true on α_1. Similarly, since C_2 is true on α_2, (2) (of which C_2 is also a disjunct) is also sure to be true on α_2. And so on. Hence, (2) is sure to be true on each one of $\alpha_1, \alpha_2, \ldots$, and α_j.

Part Two.   Since C_1 is true just on α_1, C_1 is false on any truth-value assignment to $A_1, A_2, \ldots$, and A_n other than α_1, and hence is false on any truth-value assignment to $A_1, A_2, \ldots$, and A_n other than $\alpha_1, \alpha_2, \ldots$, and α_j. Similarly, since C_2 is true just on α_2, C_2 is false on any truth-value assignment to $A_1, A_2, \ldots$, and A_n other than $\alpha_1, \alpha_2, \ldots$, and α_j. And so on. Hence, $C_1, C_2, \ldots$, and C_j are all false on any truth-value assignment to $A_1, A_2, \ldots$, and A_n other than $\alpha_1, \alpha_2, \ldots$, and α_j. Hence, their disjunction (2) is likewise false on any truth-value assignment to $A_1, A_2, \ldots$, and A_n other than $\alpha_1, \alpha_2, \ldots$, and α_j.

Part Three.   Since (2) is true on all and only those truth-value assignments to $A_1, A_2, \ldots$, and A_n on which B is true, (2) is truth-functionally equivalent to B. But (2) is a compound of $A_1, A_2, \ldots$, and A_n by means of just '~', '&', and 'V'. Hence, (2) will do in this case as the Post paraphrase of B.[4]

So, whether or not B is true on any truth-value assignment to $A_1, A_2, \ldots$, and A_n, there is a truth-functional equivalent of B built out of $A_1, A_2, \ldots$, and A_n by means of just '~', '&', and 'V'. Hence, as the matter is often put:

> (*3.1.2*)   All truth-functional modes of composition are reducible to just negation, conjunction, and disjunction.

The result can be sharpened in two different ways, as the reader may recall from Section 1.1. Since $\sim(\sim A \mathbin{\&} \sim B)$ is equivalent to $A \vee B$, any occurrence of the connective 'V' in the Post paraphrase of a truth-

---

[4] The Post paraphrase of B is not always the shortest one available by means of just '~', '&', and 'V'. The Post paraphrase of $A_1 \supset A_2$, for example, is $(A_1 \mathbin{\&} A_2) \vee (\sim A_1 \mathbin{\&} A_2) \vee (\sim A_1 \mathbin{\&} \sim A_2)$, which is of course longer than the familiar $\sim A_1 \vee A_2$; and that of $A_1 \vee A_2$ is $(A_1 \mathbin{\&} A_2) \vee (\sim A_1 \mathbin{\&} A_2) \vee (A_1 \mathbin{\&} \sim A_2)$. However, compactness is not the issue here.

functional compound can be turned in for three occurrences of '~' and one of '&'. Hence:

>(3.1.3) All truth-functional modes of composition are reducible to just negation and conjunction.

Similarly, since ~(~A ∨ ~B) is equivalent to A & B, any occurrence of the connective '&' in the Post paraphrase of a truth-functional compound can be turned in for three occurrences of '~' and one of '∨'. Hence:

>(3.1.4) All truth-functional modes of composition are reducible to just negation and disjunction.

Other reductions are of course feasible. Since ~(A ⊃ ~B) is equivalent to A & B, and ~A ⊃ B equivalent to A ∨ B, any occurrence of the connective '&' in the Post paraphrase of a truth-functional compound can be turned in for two occurrences of '~' and one of '⊃', and any occurrence of '∨' turned in for one occurrence each of '~' and '⊃'. Hence:

>(3.1.5) All truth-functional modes of composition are reducible to just negation and conditional.

Since A | A is equivalent to ~A, (A | B) | (A | B) equivalent to A & B, and (A | A) | (B | B) equivalent to A ∨ B, any occurrence of '~' in the Post paraphrase of a truth-functional compound can be turned in for one occurrence of ' | ', and any occurrence of either one of '&' and '∨' turned in for three occurrences of ' | '. Hence:

>(3.1.6) All truth-functional modes of composition are reducible to just alternative denial.

Similarly, since A ↓ A is equivalent to ~A, (A ↓ A) ↓ (B ↓ B) equivalent to A & B, and (A ↓ B) ↓ (A ↓ B) equivalent to A ∨ B, any occurrence of '~' in the Post paraphrase of a truth-functional compound can be turned in for one occurrence of '↓', and any occurrence of either one of '&' and '∨' turned in for three occurrences of '↓'. Hence:

>(3.1.7) All truth-functional modes of composition are reducible to just joint denial.

Post's Theorem and its five corollaries (3.1.3)–(3.1.7) can of course be reformulated as **definability theorems:** (1) '~', '&' and '∨' *together* permit definition of all the other (truth-functional) connectives; (2) so do '~' and '&' *together*, '~' and '∨' *together*, and '~' and '⊃' *together*; and (3) so does ' | ' *by itself*, and '↓' *by itself*. The Post paraphrase of any truth-functional compound not a negation, a conjunction, or a disjunction qualifies indeed as a definition of the compound by means of just '~', '&', and '∨'. Hence (1), of which (2)–(3) are mere corollaries.

Note in connection with (1)–(2) that any statement compounded of an atomic statement A by means of just '&', or just '∨', or just '⊃' is sure to be true on the result α of assigning **T** to A.[5] But $\sim A$ is not true on α. Hence, no statement compounded of A by means of just '&', or just '∨', or just '⊃', is equivalent to $\sim A$. Hence, none of '&', '∨', and '⊃' *alone* permits definition of every (truth-functional) connective.

Similarly, no statement compounded of A by means of just '$\sim$' is logically true.[6] But $\sim(A \ \& \ \sim A)$, $A \lor \sim A$, and $A \supset A$ are all three logically true. Hence, no statement compounded of A by means of just '$\sim$' is equivalent to any one of $\sim(A \ \& \ \sim A)$, $A \lor \sim A$, and $A \supset A$. Hence, '$\sim$' *alone* does not permit definition of '&', '∨', and '⊃'. Hence, '$\sim$' *alone* does not permit definition of every (truth-functional) connective.

Quantificational Modes of (Statement) Composition

We remarked in Section 2.1 that $(\forall X)A$ and $(\exists X)A$ can be thought of as quantificational compounds of their conservative instances. Indeed, as prefacing a statement A with '$\sim$' yields its negation $\sim A$, so prefacing with $(\forall X)$ the result A of putting X for T in a conservative instance of $(\forall X)A$ delivers that universal quantification, and prefacing with $(\exists X)$ the result A of putting X for T in a conservative instance of $(\exists X)A$ delivers that existential quantification. Hence, like negation, universalization and existentialization are here considered modes of (statement) composition. To distinguish them from the modes of composition treated in Chapter 1, we have called them *quantificational* modes of composition.

We have only tentative inventories of the various sorts of quantified statements—and, hence, of the various quantificational modes of composition—that are commonly in use. Included in all of them, of course, are statements of the sorts

> Everything is F,
> Something is F,
> Nothing is F,

and so on; also statements of the sorts

> Most things are F,
> Few things are F,
> As many things as not are F,

---

[5] The point is taken up in Exercise E3.2.2.
[6] The point is taken up in Exercise E3.2.4.

and so on; also statements of the sorts

> At least n things are F,
> At most n things are F,
> Exactly n things are F,
> Roughly n things are F,

this for any positive integer n; and so on. Included in inventories made by mathematicians are also statements of the sorts

> Finitely many things are F,
> Infinitely many things are F,
> Denumerably many things are F,
> Non-denumerably many things are F,

and so on.

Exactly eight of the above sorts of quantified statements—and hence exactly eight quantificational modes of composition, to be known here as **elementary quantificational modes of composition**—can be accommodated within elementary logic.[7] They are occasionally tabulated as follows, where $A(T/X)$ is an arbitrary instance of $(\forall X)A$, and α is an arbitrary truth-value assignment to $A(a_1/X)$, $A(a_2/X)$, $A(a_3/X)$, and so on:[8]

TABLE XV

	$A(T/X)$	$(Q_1X)A$	$(Q_2X)A$	$(Q_3X)A$	$(Q_4X)A$
	for every T	T	T	T	T
true on α	for some T's only	T	T	F	F
	for no T at all	T	F	T	F

	$A(T/X)$	$(Q_5X)A$	$(Q_6X)A$	$(Q_7X)A$	$(Q_8X)A$
	for every T	F	F	F	F
true on α	for some T's only	T	T	F	F
	for no T at all	T	F	T	F

---

[7] When the identity predicate '=' is on hand, the quantificational compounds 'For at least n x, Fx', 'For at most n x, Fx', and 'For exactly n x, Fx' can be accommodated in elementary logic for any positive integer n. The rest of the compounds above, however, still cannot. A statement of the kind $T_1 = T_2$ is of course certified true if the terms T_1 and T_2 designate the same thing; otherwise, it is certified false. See Exercise E3.1.5 on this matter.

[8] We take $(Q_iX)A$ to be a statement if—for some term T—$A(T/X)$ is a statement. With $A(T/X)$ presumed here to be an instance of $(\forall X)A$ for any term T whatever, and hence to be a statement, $(Q_iX)A$ is sure to be a statement.

$(Q_1X)A$ is thus the quantificational compound which is true on α no matter what. $(Q_2X)A$, more familiar as $(\exists X)A$, is the quantificational compound which is true on α if and only if $A(T/X)$ is true on α for every T or for some T's only, hence if and only if $A(T/X)$ is true on α for at least one T. $(Q_3X)A$ is the quantificational compound which is true on α if and only if $A(T/X)$ is true on α for every T or for no T at all; it may be read

For every X or for no X at all, A.

$(Q_4X)A$, more familiar as $(\forall X)A$, is the quantificational compound which is true on α if and only if $A(T/X)$ is true on α for every T. $(Q_5X)A$ is the quantificational compound which is true on α if and only if $A(T/X)$ is true on α for some T's only or for no T at all; it may be read

Not for every X, A.

$(Q_6X)A$ is the quantificational compound which is true on α if and only if $A(T/X)$ is true on α for some T's only; it may be read

For some X, but not every X, A.

$(Q_7X)A$ is the quantificational compound which is true on α if and only if $A(T/X)$ is true on α for no T at all; it may be read

For no X, A.

And $(Q_8X)A$ is the quantificational compound which is false on α no matter what.

We go on to show that, for any i from 1 through 8, there corresponds to $(Q_iX)A$ an equivalent compound built out of the two *universal quantifications* $(\forall X)A$ and $(\forall X)\sim A$ by means of just '$\sim$', '&', and 'V'. Since the result is due to Walter Dubislav, the compound in question will be called here **the Dubislav paraphrase of $(Q_iX)A$.**[9]

Note first that, where $A(T/X)$ and α are as in Table XV,

(i) $A(T/X)$ is true on α for every T—the first possibility listed in the table under $A(T/X)$—if and only if $(\forall X)A$ is true on α,

(ii) $A(T/X)$ is true on α for some T's only—the second possibility listed in the table under $A(T/X)$—if and only if $\sim(\forall X)\sim A$ & $\sim(\forall X)A$ is true on α, and

(iii) $A(T/X)$ is true on α for no T at all—the third possibility listed in the table under $A(T/X)$— if and only if $(\forall X)\sim A$ is true on α.

---

[9] See Dubislav's "Elementarer Nachweis der Widerspruchslosigkeit des Logik-Kalküls," *Journal für die reine und angewandte Mathematik*, vol. 161, 1929, pp. 107–12. The converse of Dubislav's result also holds true: every truth-functional compound of $(\forall X)A$ and $(\forall X)\sim A$ is indeed equivalent to one of $(Q_1X)A$–$(Q_8X)A$. See Exercise E3.1.7 on this matter.

Now refer to $(\forall X)A$, $\sim(\forall X)\sim A$ & $\sim(\forall X)A$, and $(\forall X)\sim A$ as C_1, C_2, and C_3, respectively. It is clear that:

$C_1 \vee C_2 \vee C_3 (= D_1)$ is true on α if and only if $(Q_1 X)A$ is true on α,

$C_1 \vee C_2 (= D_2)$ is true on α if and only if $(Q_2 X)A$ is true on α,

$C_1 \vee C_3 (= D_3)$ is true on α if and only if $(Q_3 X)A$ is true on α,

$C_1 (= D_4)$ is true on α if and only if $(Q_4 X)A$ is true on α,

$C_2 \vee C_3 (= D_5)$ is true on α if and only if $(Q_5 X)A$ is true on α,

$C_2 (= D_6)$ is true on α if and only if $(Q_6 X)A$ is true on α,

$C_3 (= D_7)$ is true on α if and only if $(Q_7 X)A$ is true on α, and

C_1 & $\sim C_1 (= D_8)$ is true on α if and only if $(Q_8 X)A$ is true on α.

Hence, for each i from 1 through 8, D_i is equivalent to $(Q_i X)A$. But D_i is a compound of the two universal quantifications $(\forall X)A$ and $(\forall X)\sim A$ by means of just '$\sim$', '&', and '$\vee$'. Hence, for each i from 1 through 8, D_i will do as the Dubislav paraphrase of $(Q_i X)A$.

Hence, as the matter is sometimes put:

(3.1.8) All elementary quantificational modes of composition are reducible to just negation, conjunction, disjunction, and universal quantification.

Hence, in view of results obtained a few pages back:

(3.1.9) All truth-functional and elementary quantificational modes of composition are reducible to just negation, conditional, and universal quantification;

and

(3.1.10) All truth-functional and elementary quantificational modes of composition are reducible to just alternative denial and universal quantification, or just joint denial and universal quantification.

Other reductions are also feasible. Since $\sim(\exists X)\sim A$ is equivalent to $(\forall X)A$, any occurrence of '$\forall$' in the Dubislav paraphrase of $(Q_i X)A$ can be turned in for two occurrences of '$\sim$' and one of '$\exists$'. Since $(Q_3 X)A$ & $A(T/X)$, for any term T, is equivalent to $(\forall X)A$, any occurrence of '$\forall$' in the Dubislav paraphrase of $(Q_i X)A$ can be turned in for one occurrence each of '&' and 'Q_3'.[10] And so on.

The Dubislav paraphrase of an elementary quantificational compound other than $(\forall X)A$ qualifies as a definition of the compound by means of just '$\sim$', '&', '$\vee$', and '$\forall$'. So the foregoing results can be reformulated as definability theorems: (1) '$\sim$', '&', '$\vee$', and '$\forall$' *together* permit

---

[10] That 'Q_3' and '&' together permit definition of '$\forall$' was first noted in H. Leblanc and R. H. Thomason's "All or none: a novel choice of primitives for elementary logic," *The Journal of Symbolic Logic,* vol. 32, 1967, pp. 345–51. See Exercise E3.1.4.

definition of all the other (truth-functional) connectives and elementary quantifiers; (2) so do '~', '&', 'V', and '∃'; (3) so do '~', '⊃', and '∀'; and so on.

The quantificational modes of composition in Table XV are **singulary** ones. There are of course binary ones of the same sort, ternary ones, and so on. To illustrate matters briefly, we have translated 'Whatever is F is also G' as '$(\forall x)(Fx \supset Gx)$', thus treating it as a quantificational compound of, say, 'Fa ⊃ Ga'; we have translated 'Something which is F is G' as '$(\exists x)(Fx \mathbin{\&} Gx)$', thus treating it as a quantificational compound of, say, 'Fa & Ga'; and so on. However, since 'Fa ⊃ Ga' and 'Fa & Ga' are themselves compounds of 'Fa' and 'Ga', we could have gone one step further, and treated 'Whatever is F is also G' and 'Something which is F is G' as quantificational compounds of 'Fa' and 'Ga'. Under this other approach, our two statements—respectively translated, say, as '$(Q^2_1 x)(Fx, Gx)$' and '$(Q^2_2 x)(Fx, Gx)$'—would count as **binary** quantificational compounds of 'Fa' and 'Ga'.[11] And the quantificational modes of composition which deliver these compounds would count as **binary** ones.

There are, for each n from 1 on, $2^{(2^{2^n})-1}$ n-ary quantificational modes of composition of this sort: 8 singulary ones (those in Table XV), 32,768 binary ones, and so on. And all of them are reducible to just negation, conjunction, disjunction, and universal quantification.[12]

'~', '⊃', and '∀' as Primitive Operators

In Chapters 1 and 2 we restricted ourselves to just *five* connectives: '~', '⊃', '&', 'V', and '≡', and just *two* elementary quantifiers: the universal quantifier and the existential one. No theoretical loss was thereby incurred, since in view of (3.1.2) and (3.1.8) every truth-functional compound and every elementary quantificational compound has an (equivalent) paraphrase using just '~', '&', 'V', and '∀'.

In much of this chapter we shall further restrict ourselves to just *two* connectives: '~' and '⊃', and just *one* elementary quantifier: the universal quantifier.[13] So we shall usually acknowledge only *three* sorts of compound statements: negations, conditionals, and universal quantifications. In view of (3.1.9) we lose nothing thereby; and proofs in which each and every recognized sort of compound statement must be considered separately will be much simplified.

---

[11] The superscript '2' in the quantifiers '$(Q^2_1 x)$' and '$(Q^2_2 x)$' signals that they are "binary."

[12] The two results (concerning which see E3.1.10–11) are due to Ludwig Borkowski in "On proper quantifiers I," *Studia Logica*, vol. 8, 1958, pp. 65–130.

[13] In Section 3.5, and in exercises that specifically relate to Chapters 1 and 2, all seven of '~', '⊃', '&', 'V', '≡', '∀', and '∃' will again serve as primitive operators. The exercises in question are clearly distinguished from the rest.

We nonetheless reserve our right to use '&', '∨', '≡', and '∃' by adopting the following four definitions, already met in Sections 1.1 and 2.1:

D&. $(A \& B) =_{df} \sim(A \supset \sim B)$

D∨. $(A \lor B) =_{df} (\sim A \supset B)$

D≡. $(A \equiv B) =_{df} \sim[(A \supset B) \supset \sim(B \supset A)]$[14]

D∃. $(\exists X)A =_{df} \sim(\forall X)\sim A.$

As already explained, these officially construe $(A \& B)$ as shorthand for $\sim(A \supset \sim B)$, $(A \lor B)$ as shorthand for $(\sim A \supset B)$, $(A \equiv B)$ as shorthand for $\sim[(A \supset B) \supset \sim(B \supset A)]$, and $(\exists X)A$ as shorthand for $\sim(\forall X)\sim A$.

Because of the reduction in primitive operators which we just effected, a statement A will now be said to be derivable from a finite set S of statements (again $S \vdash A$, for short) if and only if A is derivable from S in accordance with just rules R, ~I, ~E, ⊃I, ⊃E, ∀I*, and ∀E. The remaining intelim rules of Sections 1.3 and 2.3 can still be had, however, as **derived rules of inference,** which we proceed to show. In virtue of (3.1.12), for example, $A \& B$—which is now shorthand for $\sim(A \supset \sim B)$—is sure to be derivable from S in accordance with just rules R, ~I, ~E, ⊃I, ⊃E, ∀I*, and ∀E if both A and B are derivable from S in accordance with them; and the proof of (3.1.12) shows how, given derivations of both A and B from S in accordance with R, ~I, ~E, ⊃I, ⊃E, ∀I*, and ∀E, one may derive the paraphrase $\sim(A \supset \sim B)$ of $A \& B$ from S in accordance with those seven rules. So all the inferences that could be performed with the help of &I can be performed here; and (3.1.13)–(3.1.19) show that this is true for all the other rules we give up.

When proving (3.1.12), and many of (3.1.13)–(3.1.19), we avail ourselves of the following fact (proved on pp. 231–32):

(3.1.11)   If $S \vdash A$, then $S \cup S' \vdash A$ for any finite set S' of statements.

(3.1.12)   If $S \vdash A$ and $S \vdash B$, then $S \vdash A \& B$. ($= \&$I)

PROOF: Suppose first that $S \vdash A$. Then $S \cup \{A \supset \sim B\} \vdash A$ by (3.1.11). But $S \cup \{A \supset \sim B\} \vdash A \supset \sim B$ by R. Hence $S \cup \{A \supset \sim B\} \vdash \sim B$ by ⊃E. Suppose also that $S \vdash B$. Then $S \cup \{A \supset \sim B\} \vdash B$ by (3.1.11). Hence $S \vdash \sim(A \supset \sim B)$ by ~I. Hence (3.1.12) by D&.

(3.1.13)   If $S \vdash A \& B$, then $S \vdash A$ and $S \vdash B$. ($= \&$E)

PROOF: (i) $S \cup \{\sim A, A, B\} \vdash A$ and $S \cup \{\sim A, A, B\} \vdash \sim A$ by R. Hence $S \cup \{\sim A, A\} \vdash \sim B$ by ~I, and hence $S \cup \{\sim A\} \vdash A \supset \sim B$ by ⊃I. But if $S \vdash \sim(A \supset \sim B)$, then $S \cup \{\sim A\} \vdash \sim(A \supset \sim B)$ by (3.1.11).

---

[14] By virtue of D≡ and D&, $(A \equiv B)$ is also short for the more familiar $[(A \supset B) \& (B \supset A)]$, a fact on which we shall frequently rely.

Hence, if $S \vdash \sim(A \supset \sim B)$, then $S \vdash \sim\sim A$ by $\sim$I, and hence $S \vdash A$ by $\sim$E. (ii) $S \cup \{\sim B, A\} \vdash \sim B$ by R, and hence $S \cup \{\sim B\} \vdash A \supset \sim B$ by $\supset$I. But if $S \vdash \sim(A \supset \sim B)$, then $S \cup \{\sim B\} \vdash \sim(A \supset \sim B)$ by (3.1.11). Hence, if $S \vdash \sim(A \supset \sim B)$, then $S \vdash \sim\sim B$ by $\sim$I and hence $S \vdash B$ by $\sim$E. Hence (3.1.13) by D&.

(3.1.14)   If $S \vdash A$ or $S \vdash B$, then $S \vdash A \lor B$. (= VI)

PROOF: (i) Suppose $S \vdash A$. Then $S \cup \{\sim A, \sim B\} \vdash A$ by (3.1.11). But $S \cup \{\sim A, \sim B\} \vdash \sim A$ by R. Hence $S \cup \{\sim A\} \vdash \sim\sim B$ by I, hence $S \cup \{\sim A\} \vdash B$ by $\sim$E, and hence $S \vdash \sim A \supset B$ by $\supset$I. (ii) Suppose $S \vdash B$. Then $S \cup \{\sim A\} \vdash B$ by (3.1.11), and hence $S \vdash \sim A \supset B$ by $\supset$I. Hence (3.1.14) by DV.

(3.1.15)   If $S \vdash A \lor B$, $S \cup \{A\} \vdash C$, and $S \cup \{B\} \vdash C$, then $S \vdash C$. (= VE)

PROOF: Suppose first that $S \vdash \sim A \supset B$. Then $S \cup \{\sim C, \sim A\} \vdash \sim A \supset B$ by (3.1.11). But $S \cup \{\sim C, \sim A\} \vdash \sim A$ by R. Hence $S \cup \{\sim C, \sim A\} \vdash B$ by $\supset$E. Suppose next that $S \cup \{B\} \vdash C$. Then $S \cup \{\sim C, \sim A, B\} \vdash C$ by (3.1.11), hence $S \cup \{\sim C, \sim A\} \vdash B \supset C$ by $\supset$I, and hence $S \cup \{\sim C, \sim A\} \vdash C$ by $\supset$E. But $S \cup \{\sim C, \sim A\} \vdash \sim C$ by R. Hence $S \cup \{\sim C\} \vdash \sim\sim A$ by $\sim$I, and hence $S \cup \{\sim C\} \vdash A$ by $\sim$E. Suppose finally that $S \cup \{A\} \vdash C$. Then $S \cup \{\sim C, A\} \vdash C$ by (3.1.11). But $S \cup \{\sim C, A\} \vdash \sim C$ by R. Hence $S \cup \{\sim C\} \vdash \sim A$ by $\sim$I, hence $S \vdash \sim\sim C$ by $\sim$I again, and hence $S \vdash C$ by $\sim$E. Hence (3.1.15) by DV.

(3.1.16)   If $S \cup \{A\} \vdash B$ and $S \cup \{B\} \vdash A$, then $S \vdash A \equiv B$. (= ≡I)

PROOF: If $S \cup \{A\} \vdash B$ and $S \cup \{B\} \vdash A$, then $S \vdash A \supset B$ and $S \vdash B \supset A$ by $\supset$I, and hence $S \vdash (A \supset B) \& (B \supset A)$ by (3.1.12). Hence (3.1.16) by D≡ and D&.

(3.1.17)   If (i) either $S \vdash A \equiv B$ or $S \vdash B \equiv A$, and (ii) $S \vdash A$, then $S \vdash B$. (= ≡E)

PROOF: Suppose $S \vdash A \equiv B$ or $S \vdash B \equiv A$. Then $S \vdash A \supset B$ by (3.1.13), D≡, and D&. Hence, if $S \vdash A$, then $S \vdash B$ by $\supset$E. Hence (3.1.17).

(3.1.18)   If $S \vdash A(T/X)$ for some term T, then $S \vdash (\exists X)A$. (= ∃I)

PROOF: Suppose $S \vdash A(T/X)$ for some term T. Then $S \cup \{(\forall X)\sim A\} \vdash A(T/X)$ by (3.1.11). But $S \cup \{(\forall X)\sim A\} \vdash (\forall X)\sim A$ by R, and hence $S \cup \{(\forall X)\sim A\} \vdash \sim A(T/X)$ by $\forall$E. Hence $S \vdash \sim(\forall X)\sim A$ by $\sim$I. Hence (3.1.18) by D∃.

(3.1.19)   If $S \cup S' \vdash (\exists X)A$ and $S \cup \{A(T/X)\} \vdash B$, then $S \cup S' \vdash B$, so long at T is foreign to S, $(\exists X)A$, and B. (= ∃E*)

PROOF: Suppose first that $S \cup \{A(T/X)\} \vdash B$, where T is foreign to S, $(\exists X)A$, and B. Then $S \cup \{\sim B, A(T/X)\} \vdash B$ by (3.1.11). But $S \cup \{\sim B, A(T/X)\} \vdash \sim B$ by R. Hence $S \cup \{\sim B\} \vdash \sim A(T/X)$ by $\sim$I, and hence $S \cup S' \cup \{\sim B\} \vdash (\forall X)\sim A$ by $\forall$I* and the hypothesis on T. Suppose also that $S \cup S' \vdash \sim(\forall X)\sim A$. Then $S \cup S' \cup \{\sim B\} \vdash \sim(\forall X)\sim A$ by (3.1.11), hence $S \cup S' \vdash \sim\sim B$ by $\sim$I, and hence $S \cup S' \vdash B$ by $\sim$E.

EXERCISES

E3.1.1. Find the Post paraphrase of all the truth-functional compounds in Table XII on p. 243 and Table XIII on p. 244.

E3.1.2. Supply definitions—as compact as you can make them—of '$\supset$' and '$\equiv$' by means of each one of ' $|$ ' and '$\downarrow$'.

E3.1.3. With D_1–D_8 defined as on p. 252, show that for each i from 1 through 8, D_i is equivalent to $(Q_iX)A$.

E3.1.4. Show that, for any term T, each one of $(Q_3X)A$ & $A(T/X)$ and $\sim(Q_6X)A$ & $A(T/X)$ is equivalent to $(\forall X)A$. (Thus, 'Q_3' and '&' permit definition of '$\forall$', and so do 'Q_6', '$\sim$', and '&'.)

E3.1.5. With the identity predicate '$=$' on hand,
    (a) supply a paraphrase of 'For at most one x, Fx' and 'For exactly one x, Fx', and
    (b) supply more generally a paraphrase of

$$\text{For at least } n \ X, A$$
$$\text{For at most } n \ X, A$$
$$\text{For exactly } n \ X, A$$

    for any positive integer n.

E3.1.6. Show that if (i) the disjunction $A_1 \lor A_2 \lor \ldots \lor A_n$ of n given statements A_1, A_2, ..., and A_n is logically true or (ii) their conjunction A_1 & A_2 & ... & A_n is logically false, then there are just 2^{2^n-1} different ways of truth-functionally compounding A_1, A_2, ..., and A_n.

E3.1.7. Using the result in E3.1.6, show that there are just 8 different ways of truth-functionally compounding two statements $(\forall X)A$ and $(\forall X)\sim A$, or two statements $(\exists X)A$ and $(\exists X)\sim A$.

E3.1.8. α being a truth-value assignment to $A(a_1/X)$, $A(a_2/X)$, $A(a_3/X)$, ..., $B(a_1/X)$, $B(a_2/X)$, $B(a_3/X)$, ..., let $(|X)(A,B)$—known as *the universalized alternative denial of A and B*—be true on α if and only if for every term T at least one of $A(T/X)$ and $B(T/X)$ is false on α. Show that alternative denial and universal quantification are reducible to universalized alternative denial.

E3.1.9. α being as in E3.1.8, let $(\downarrow X)(A,B)$—known as the *universalized joint denial of A and B*—be true on α if and only if neither one of $A(T/X)$ and $B(T/X)$ is true on α for any term T. Show that joint denial and universal quantification are reducible to universalized joint denial.

E3.1.10. Show that the disjunction of the four existential quantifications $(\exists X)(A$ & $B)$, $(\exists X)(\sim A$ & $B)$, $(\exists X)(A$ & $\sim B)$, and $(\exists X)(\sim A$ & $\sim B)$ is logically true, and hence in view of E3.1.6 that there are just 32,768 different ways of truth-functionally compounding the four existential quantifications in question. (These correspond of course to Borkowski's 32,768 binary quantificational modes of composition.)

E3.1.11.

(1) $A_1, A_2, \ldots$, and A_n being n ($n \geq 1$) statements,

(2) $\alpha_1, \alpha_2, \ldots$, and α_{2^n} being the 2^n different ways in which $A_1, A_2, \ldots$, and A_n can be assigned a truth-value each, and

(3)   for each i from 1 through 2^n, C_i being the conjunction associate of α_i, show that the disjunction of the 2^n existential quantifications $(\exists X)C_1(X/T)$, $(\exists X)C_2(X/T), \ldots$, and $(\exists X)C_{2^n}(X/T)$ is logically true, and hence in view of E3.1.6 that there are just $2^{(2^{2^n})-1}$ different ways of truth-functionally compounding the 2^n existential quantifications in question.

3.2   Auxiliary Material

Mathematical Induction

At many points in Sections 3.3–3.7 we shall use a method of proof which comes from arithmetic: **mathematical induction.** There are two forms of this method. One works as follows. In order to show that something is true of every natural number, i.e., that every natural number has a certain property P, show first that

$$0 \text{ (zero) has property } P, \tag{1}$$

and show next, of an arbitrary natural number n larger than 0, that

$$\text{If } n{-}1 \text{ has property } P, \text{ then } n \text{ also has property } P.^1 \tag{2}$$

It readily follows from (1) and (2) that each one of 0, 1, 2, and so on has property P, and hence that every natural number has property P. For, in virtue of (1), 0 has property P; hence, in virtue of (2), so does 1; hence, in virtue of (2) again, so does 2; and so on.

The part of the proof which is devoted to establishing (1) is known as **the basis of the induction,** and the part devoted to establishing (2) is known as **the inductive step of the induction.** A common way of establishing (2) is to assume the antecedent

$$n{-}1 \text{ has property } P \tag{3}$$

of (2) as a provisional assumption, and derive from it (and other relevant data) the consequent

$$n \text{ has property } P \tag{4}$$

---

[1] Or, equivalently, show of an arbitrary natural number n ($n \geq 0$) that if n has property P, then $n{+}1$ also has property P.

of (2). Then (3) is usually referred to as **the hypothesis of the induction.**

When the point to be proved concerns the natural numbers from 1 on (i.e., the positive integers) or—more generally—the natural numbers from a certain natural number k ($k \geq 1$) on, rather than all the natural numbers, both the basis and the inductive step of the induction must be adjusted. The basis is now to the effect that k has property P, and the inductive step is to the effect that an arbitrary natural number n larger than k is sure to have property P if $n-1$ does.

As an illustration let us establish that, for any n from 0 on, a set S with n members has 2^n subsets.[2]

BASIS: To show that when S has 0 members, S has 2^0 ($=$ 1) subsets. This is obvious, inasmuch as S—being the empty set—can have no subset other than itself.

INDUCTIVE STEP: Assuming that any set with $n - 1$ members has 2^{n-1} subsets (this is of course the hypothesis of the induction), to show that a set S with n members has 2^n subsets, where n is an arbitrary natural number larger than 0.[3] Let s be an arbitrary member of S, and let S' be S *minus s* (and hence have $n - 1$ members). The subsets of S clearly fall into two groups: those that do not have s as a member, and those that do. The former are the various subsets of S'; the latter are exactly the same subsets *plus s*. Hence, S has twice the number of subsets that S' has. But, by the hypothesis of the induction, S' has 2^{n-1} subsets. Hence, S has $2 \times 2^{n-1}$ ($= 2^n$) subsets.

The proof would be said to be *by induction on n*, the number of members of S.[4]

We shall use this kind of mathematical induction at one point in Section 3.4. Having constructed an infinite array S_0, S_1, S_2, and so on, of sets of statements, we shall first establish that S_0 is what we call *syntactically consistent;* we shall then establish that if S_{n-1} is syntactically consistent, where $n > 0$, then so is S_n; and we shall conclude therefrom that each one of the sets S_0, S_1, S_2, and so on, is syntactically consistent.[5] The proof would be said to be by induction on n, the rank (if you will) of S_n.

---

[2] I.e., for any n from 0 on, n is such that, if S has n members, then S has 2^n subsets.

[3] Since 'n' already occurs in the statement to be proved ('If a set S has n members, then S has 2^n subsets'), some writers would use 'n'' or some fresh letter (say, 'm') in place of 'n' in the inductive step. We don't bother.

[4] Taking cues from this proof, the reader may wish to prove afresh, and more formally than we have in Section 1.1, that n ($n \geq 1$) atomic statements can be assigned a truth-value each in 2^n different ways.

[5] I.e., for any n from 0 on, n is such that S_n is syntactically consistent.

Strong Mathematical Induction

There are some occasions in arithmetic, and a great many in logic, when a second kind of mathematical induction, called **strong mathematical induction** or **course-of-values induction,** is needed. The basis of the induction is as before:

$$0 \text{ has property } P. \tag{5}$$

But the inductive step, which previously was to the effect that

> If $n-1$ has property P, then n has property P,

will now be to the effect that

> If *each and every natural number smaller than n* has property P,
> then n has property P, $\tag{6}$

and the antecedent

> *Each and every natural number smaller than n* has property P $\tag{7}$

of (6) will now serve as the hypothesis of the induction. It is clear that under these circumstances every natural number is sure again to have property P. For, in virtue of (5), 0 has property P. But, if so, each and every natural number smaller than 1 has property P. Hence, in virtue of (6), 1 has property P. But, if so, 0 and 1 both have property P, and hence each and every natural number smaller than 2 has property P. Hence, in virtue of (6) again, 2 has property P. And so on. (Again, when the point to be proved concerns the natural numbers from some k ($k \geq 1$) on, the appropriate adjustments must be made.)

Strong mathematical induction is used in many textbooks to establish that, for any n from 2 on, n is a prime or a product of two or more primes. The basis presents no difficulty: 2 is indeed a prime, and hence is a prime or a product of two or more primes. Consider then an integer n larger than 2, assume that each and every integer from 2 through $n-1$ is a prime or a product of two or more primes (this is the hypothesis of the induction), and suppose first that n is a prime. Then, of course, n is a prime or a product of two or more primes. Suppose next that n is not a prime. Then n is sure to be divisible by an integer larger than 1 and smaller than n, and hence n is sure to be the product of two integers larger than 1 and smaller than n: one of them—call it p—being a divisor of n, the other—call it q—being the quotient of n divided by p. But, if both p and q are larger than 1 and smaller than n, then by the hypothesis of the induction both p and q are primes or products of two or more primes.[6] Hence n, the

---

[6] Note that under the circumstances neither one of p and q can equal $n - 1$. Hence, merely assuming that $n-1$ is a prime or a product of two or more primes would not do the trick here, and *strong* mathematical induction is called for.

product of p and q, is a product of two or more primes, and thus is a prime or a product of two or more primes. So whether or not a prime, n is a prime or a product of two or more primes.

A simple, but useful, application of strong mathematical induction to logical matters is as follows. Let S be a finite (but non-empty) set of statements; let α be a truth-value assignment to *just* the atomic subformulas of the members of S; let α' be a truth-value assignment to the atomic subformulas of the members of S *and other atomic statements as well;* and suppose that the atomic subformulas of the members of S are assigned the same truth-values in α' as in α. It is readily shown of any subformula A of any member of S—and hence, in particular, of any member A of S—that A *is true on* α *if and only if* A *is true on* α'. The proof is by strong mathematical induction on what we called in Section 2.1 the *length l of A.*[7]

BASIS: $l = 1$. Then A is an atomic subformula of a member of S, and hence is assigned the same truth-value in α' as in α. Hence, A is true on α if and only if A is true on α'.

INDUCTIVE STEP: $l > 1$. Then A is of one of the three sorts $\sim B$, $B \supset C$, and $(\forall X)B$. Suppose that, so long as it is of a length less than l, any subformula of any member of S is true on α if and only if true on α' (= hypothesis of the induction).

CASE 1: A is of the sort $\sim B$. B—being a subformula of A—is a subformula of a member of S, and is of a length less than l. So, by the hypothesis of the induction, B is true on α if and only if B is true on α'. Hence B is not true on α if and only if B is not true on α'. Hence, $\sim B \ (= A)$ is true on α if and only if $\sim B$ is true on α'.

CASE 2: A is of the sort $B \supset C$. Each one of B and C—being a subformula of A—is a subformula of a member of S, and each one is of a length less than l. So, by the hypothesis of the induction, B is true on α if and only if B is true on α', and C is true on α if and only if C is true on α'. Hence, B is not true on α or C is true on α if and only if B is not true on α' or C is true on α'. Hence, $B \supset C \ (= A)$ is true on α if and only if $B \supset C$ is true on α'.

CASE 3: A is of the sort $(\forall X)B$. Suppose $(\forall X)B$ is true on α. Then $B(a_1/X)$, $B(a_2/X)$, $B(a_3/X)$, etc., are all true on α. But each one of $B(a_1/X)$, $B(a_2/X)$, $B(a_3/X)$, etc.—being a subformula of A—is a subformula of a member of S, and each one is of a length less than l. Hence,

---

[7] For a slightly different proof that any member of S is true on α if and only if true on α', see Exercise E3.2.1.

by the hypothesis of the induction, $B(a_1/X)$, $B(a_2/X)$, $B(a_3/X)$, etc., are all true on α'. Hence, $(\forall X)B$ is true on α'. Hence, if $(\forall X)B$ is true on α, then $(\forall X)B$ is true on α'. But, by exactly the same reasoning, $(\forall X)B$ is true on α if $(\forall X)B$ is true on α'. Hence, $(\forall X)B$ $(= A)$ is true on α if and only if $(\forall X)B$ is true on α'.

The reader will have noticed that when $\sim B$ $(= A)$ is of length l, B *is* of length $l - 1$; and when $(\forall X)B$ $(= A)$ is of length l, each one of $B(a_1/X)$, $B(a_2/X)$, $B(a_3/X)$, etc., *is* of length $l-1$. However, when $B \supset C$ $(= A)$ is of length l, *neither one* of B and C is of length $l-1$. Hence, assuming the result to be proved just for subformulas of length $l-1$ would not do the trick. We must assume it for subformulas of any length from 1 through $l-1$, and use *strong* mathematical induction.

It follows from our result that:

(1) If the members of a finite but non-empty set S of statements are true on some truth-value assignment α to *just* the atomic subformulas of the members of S, then they are sure to be true on a number of truth-value assignments *to other atomic statements as well*, namely: all the assignments in which the atomic subformulas of the members of S have the same truth-values as in α; and

(2) If the members of S are true on some truth-value assignment α' to the atomic subformulas of the members of S *and to other atomic statements as well*, then they are sure to be true on one truth-value assignment to *just* the atomic subformulas of the members of S, namely: the one which assigns to these subformulas the same truth-values as in α'.

Hence:

> (*3.2.1*)   Let S be a finite but non-empty set of statements. Then the members of S are true on some truth-value assignment to *just* the atomic subformulas of the members of S if and only if they are true on some truth-value assignment to these atomic subformulas *and to other atomic statements as well.*

We shall call upon (3.2.1) on p. 269.

Now for a more sophisticated use of strong mathematical induction. The result it yields, when generalized as in (3.2.2) below, will play a key role in our forthcoming proof that $\forall I^*$ is sound.[8]

(1) Let A be a statement; let T_1 and T_2 be two distinct terms either one of which may, but need not, occur in A; let Σ_T be a finite set of terms consisting of all the terms distinct from T_1 and T_2 that occur in A (and

---

[8] See p. 277. On a first study of this section the reader may skip from here to p. 265.

possibly other terms distinct from T_1 and T_2 as well);[9] and let Σ'_T consist of all the remaining terms. *Example:* Supposing A to be '$\sim Fa_1a_2 \supset (\forall x)(Fxa_1 \supset Ga_3x)$', T_1 to be 'a_1', and T_2 to be 'a_2', then Σ_T could consist, for example, of 'a_3' (which does occur in A) and 'a_4' (which does not), in which case Σ'_T would consist of 'a_5', 'a_6', 'a_7', and so on.

(2) Supposing the number of terms in Σ_T to be p ($p \geq 0$), let **the image f(T) of a term T** be as in the following table, where the terms in Σ_T and those in Σ'_T are understood to be listed in alphabetic order:[10]

$$f(T_1) \quad = T_2,$$
$$f(T_2) \quad = T_2,$$

images of the terms in Σ_T
$$f(T_3) \quad = T_3,$$
$$f(T_4) \quad = T_4,$$
$$\cdot \qquad \cdot$$
$$\cdot \qquad \cdot$$
$$\cdot \qquad \cdot$$
$$f(T_{p+2}) = T_{p+2},$$

images of the terms in Σ'_T
$$f(T_{p+3}) = T_1,$$
$$f(T_{p+4}) = T_{p+3},$$
$$f(T_{p+5}) = T_{p+4},$$
$$\cdot \qquad \cdot$$
$$\cdot \qquad \cdot$$
$$\cdot \qquad \cdot$$

Example continued: Let T_1, T_2, Σ_T, and Σ'_T be as in (1). Then the images of 'a_1'–'a_5' will respectively be 'a_2', 'a_2', 'a_3', 'a_4', and 'a_1', and for each i from 6 on the image of 'a_i' will be 'a_{i-1}'.

(3) Where B is a subformula of A (or is like a subformula of A except for containing term variables at places where the subformula would contain terms), let **the image f(B) of B** be the result of simultaneously replacing all the terms that occur in B by their respective images. Should B contain no other terms than those in A, its image f(B) will thus be the result of putting T_2 for T_1 in B. Hence, in particular, the image f(A) of A will be the term variant $A(T_2/T_1)$ of A. On the other hand, when B contains

---

[9] It is with an eye to (3.2.2) that we put in the parenthetical 'and possibly other terms distinct from T_1 and T_2 as well'. Σ_T will then consist of the various terms distinct from T_1 and T_2 which occur in members of a finite set S of statements. Were it not for that eventual generalization of our result, Σ_T could be taken to contain just the terms distinct from T_1 and T_2 which occur in A.

[10] So that—when $p > 0$—T_3 is the alphabetically first member of Σ_T, T_4 is the alphabetically second, and so on; and T_{p+3} is the alphabetically first member of Σ'_T, T_{p+4} the alphabetically second member, and so on.

other terms as well, f(B) will be the result of putting T_2 for T_1 in B, leaving every term from Σ_T unchanged, putting T_1 for T_{p+3}, and for each i from 4 on putting T_{p+i-1} for T_{p+i}.

Example continued: Supposing A, T_1, T_2, Σ_T, and Σ'_T to be as in (1), then each statement (subformula of A) on the left has as its image the statement to its right:

$$\sim\!Fa_1a_2 \quad - \quad \sim\!Fa_2a_2$$
$$(\forall x)\,(Fxa_1 \supset Ga_3x) \quad - \quad (\forall x)\,(Fxa_2 \supset Ga_3x)$$
$$Fa_1a_1 \supset Ga_3a_1 \quad - \quad Fa_2a_2 \supset Ga_3a_2$$
$$Fa_2a_1 \supset Ga_3a_2 \quad - \quad Fa_2a_2 \supset Ga_3a_2$$
$$Fa_3a_1 \supset Ga_3a_3 \quad - \quad Fa_3a_2 \supset Ga_3a_3$$
$$Fa_4a_1 \supset Ga_3a_4 \quad - \quad Fa_4a_2 \supset Ga_3a_4$$
$$Fa_5a_1 \supset Ga_3a_5 \quad - \quad Fa_1a_2 \supset Ga_3a_1$$
$$Fa_6a_1 \supset Ga_3a_6 \quad - \quad Fa_5a_2 \supset Ga_3a_5$$

(The last six statements on the left are instances of '$(\forall x)\,(Fxa_1 \supset Ga_3x)$'; those to their right are instances of the image '$(\forall x)\,(Fxa_2 \supset Ga_3x)$' of '$(\forall x)\,(Fxa_1 \supset Ga_3x)$'. In general, the instances of a subformula of A of the sort $(\forall X)C$ have as their images the instances of the image f$((\forall X)C)$ of $(\forall X)C$. See CASE 3 on pp. 264–65.)

(4) Where α is an arbitrary truth-value assignment to the atomic subformulas of A, to those of f(A), and possibly to other atomic statements as well, let f(α) be the result of assigning to every atomic subformula of A the truth-value assigned in α to the image of that subformula, and to any other atomic statement which is assigned a truth-value in α an arbitrary truth-value.

Example continued: Supposing A, T_1, T_2, Σ_T, and Σ'_T to be as in (1), the atomic subformula 'Fa_1a_2' of A would be assigned in f(α) whatever truth-value is assigned in α to its image 'Fa_2a_2'; the atomic subformula 'Ga_3a_6' of A would be assigned in f(α) whatever truth-value is assigned in α to its image 'Ga_3a_5'; and so on.

We establish by strong mathematical induction on the length l of an arbitrary subformula B of A that B *is true on* f(α) *if and only if* f(B) *is true on* α, and hence that A itself—which counts as one of its subformulas—is true on f(α) if and only if f(A) ($= A(T_2/T_1)$) is true on α.

BASIS: $l = 1$. Then B is an atomic subformula of A. But, by the very construction of f(α), B is assigned the same truth-value in f(α) as f(B) is in α. Hence, B is true on f(α) if and only if f(B) is true on α.

INDUCTIVE STEP: $l > 1$. Then B is of one of the sorts $\sim\!C$, $C \supset D$, and $(\forall X)C$. Suppose any subformula of A of a length less than l to be true on f(α) if and only if its image is true on α (= hypothesis of the induction).

CASE 1: B is of the sort $\sim C$. C—being a subformula of B—is a subformula of A and is of a length less than l. So, by the hypothesis of the induction, C is true on f(α) if and only if f(C) is true on α. Hence, C is not true on f(α) if and only if f(C) is not true on α. Hence, $\sim C$ is true on f(α) if and only if $\sim$f(C) is true on α. But $\sim$f(C) is the same as f($\sim C$). Hence, $\sim C$ (= B) is true on f(α) if and only if f($\sim C$) (= f(B)) is true on α.

CASE 2: B is of the sort $C \supset D$. Each one of C and D—being a subformula of B—is a subformula of A, and each one is of a length less than l. So, by the hypothesis of the induction, C is true on f(α) if and only if f(C) is true on α, and D is true on f(α) if and only if f(D) is true on α. Hence, C is not true on f(α) or D is true on f(α) if and only if f(C) is not true on α or f(D) is true on α. Hence, $C \supset D$ is true on f(α) if and only if f(C) $\supset$ f(D) is true on α. But f(C) $\supset$ f(D) is the same as f($C \supset D$). Hence, $C \supset D$ (= B) is true on f(α) if and only if f($C \supset D$) (= f(B)) is true on α.

CASE 3: B is of the sort $(\forall X)C$. PART ONE: Since T_1 is the image of T_{p+3}, (f(C))(T_1/X) is the same as f($C(T_{p+3}/X)$);[11] since T_2 is the image of T_1, (f(C))(T_2/X) is the same as f($C(T_1/X)$); since for each i from 3 through $p + 2$, T_i is its own image, (f(C)) (T_i/X) is the same as f($C(T_i/X)$); and, since for each i from $p+3$ on T_i is the image of T_{i+1}, (f(C)) (T_i/X) is the same as f($C(T_{i+1}/X)$). So, (i) each instance of $(\forall X)$f(C) (= f($(\forall X)C$)) is the image of some instance of $(\forall X)C$. On the other hand, f($C(T_1/X)$) and f($C(T_2/X)$) are the same as (f(C))(T_2/X); for each i from 3 through $p+2$, f($C(T_i/X)$) is the same as (f(C))(T_i/X); f($C(T_{p+3}/X)$) is the same as (f(C))(T_1/X); and, for each i from $p+4$ on, f($C(T_i/X)$) is the same as (f(C))(T_{i-1}/X). So, (ii) the image of each instance of $(\forall X)C$ is an instance of $(\forall X)$f(C) (= f($(\forall X)C$)). PART TWO: Suppose first that $(\forall X)C$ is true on f(α), and hence that each instance $C(T/X)$ of $(\forall X)C$ is true on f(α). Since $C(T/X)$—being a subformula of B—is a subformula of A and is of a length less than l, by the hypothesis of the induction the image of each instance of $(\forall X)C$ is true on α, hence by (i) each instance of $(\forall X)$f(C) is true on α, and hence f($(\forall X)C$) itself is true on α. Suppose next that $(\forall X)C$ is not true on f(α), and hence that at least one instance $C(T/X)$ of $(\forall X)C$ is not true on f(α). Since $C(T/X)$ is a subformula of A and is of a length less than l, by the hypothesis of the induction the image of at least

---

[11] Note that (f(C)) (T_1/X) is the result of replacing X by T_1 in the result f(C) of simultaneously replacing all the terms that occur in C by their respective images, whereas f($C(T_{p+3}/X)$) is the result of simultaneously replacing all the terms that occur in C by their respective images and X by the image of T_{p+3}. With T_1 appointed as the image of T_{p+3}, (f(C)) (T_1/X) and f($C(T_{p+3}/X)$) are sure to be the same.

one instance of $(\forall X)C$ is not true on α, hence by (ii) at least one instance of $(\forall X)f(C)$ is not true on α, and hence $f((\forall X)C)$ itself is not true on α. Hence, $(\forall X)C (= B)$ is true on $f(\alpha)$ if and only if $f((\forall X)C) (= f(B))$ is true on α.[12]

The result we have just obtained readily generalizes to any member of a finite (but non-empty) set S of statements. Indeed, let T_1 and T_2 again be two distinct terms; let Σ_T consist of all the terms distinct from T_1 and T_2 which occur in members of S; let Σ_T' consist of all the remaining terms; let the image of a term T be defined as in (2) above; let the image of a subformula B of a member A of S be defined as in (3) above; let α be a truth-value assignment to the atomic subformulas of both the members of S and their term variants (hence, in particular, to the atomic subformulas of the results of putting T_2 for T_1 in the members of S); and let α' be the result of assigning to every atomic subformula of a member of S the truth-value assigned in α to the image of that subformula, and to any other atomic statement that is assigned a truth-value in α an arbitrary truth-value. Then, by the foregoing result, each and every member A of S is true on α' if and only if the image of A is true on α. But, as we noted in (3) above, the image of A is the result $A(T_2/T_1)$ of putting T_2 for T_1 in A. Hence, each and every member A of S is true on α' if and only if $A(T_2/T_1)$ is true on α. Hence:

> (3.2.2)   Let S be a finite (but non-empty) set of statements; let T_1 and T_2 be distinct terms; and let α be a truth-value assignment to the atomic subformulas of both the members of S and their term variants. Then there exists a truth-value assignment α' (to the same atomic statements as are assigned a truth-value in α) such that the term variant $A(T_2/T_1)$ of any member A of S is true on α if and only if A is true on α'.

In the rest of this chapter we shall save the appellation 'mathematical induction' for strong mathematical induction, and on the one occasion when we use the other kind, we shall refer to it as **weak mathematical induction.**

Mathematical induction is the one prerequisite for Section 3.3. There are three others for Section 3.4.

Derivability From Infinite Sets of Statements

So far, when talking about the derivability of a statement from a set of statements, we have always understood the set to be finite. But later in this section, and in Sections 3.4–3.7, we shall want to speak of the deriv-

---

[12] We owe much of the above proof to R. K. Meyer of Indiana University.

ability of statements from sets that are or may be infinite. We can do this if we adopt the following definition, which reflects the finitist stance of contemporary logic:

Where A is a statement and S is an infinite *set of statements, take A to be derivable from S in accordance with* R, ~I, ~E, ⊃I, ⊃E, ∀I*, *and* ∀E *if (and only if) A is derivable in accordance with these rules from some* finite *subset or other of S.*

For example, since a statement of the sort ~B ⊃ ~A is derivable from the set {A ⊃ B} in accordance with R, ~I, ⊃I, and ⊃E, ~B ⊃ ~A will be held derivable in accordance with these rules from any infinite set of statements that has {A ⊃ B} as a subset (i.e., that has A ⊃ B as a member). Since a statement of the sort (∀X)B is derivable from the set {(∀X)(A ⊃ B), (∀X)A} in accordance with R, ⊃E, ∀I*, and ∀E, (∀X)B will be held derivable in accordance with these rules from any infinite set of statements that has {(∀X)(A ⊃ B), (∀X)A} as a subset (i.e., that has both (∀X)(A ⊃ B) and (∀X)A as members). And so on.

It has also been understood so far that a set of statements said to entail some statement must be finite. Like the syntactic notion of derivability, the semantic notion of entailment can be generalized to the infinite case. But this task is postponed until Section 3.6, where the matter can be treated more naturally.

Various results concerning the derivability of statements from sets of statements hold whatever the size of the sets, hence in particular whether the sets be finite or infinite. We demonstrate some eleven of them which will come in handy later in this section and in Sections 3.4–3.6. Most of them are generalizations of rules from Sections 1.3 and 2.3. (3.2.5), for example, is a generalization of rule R, (3.2.6) of rule ~I, and (3.2.13) of rule ∀E. To abridge matters, we again write 'S ⊢ A' for 'A is derivable from S' (with S now either finite or infinite).

(3.2.3) If S ⊢ A, then S' ⊢ A for any superset S' of S (i.e., for any set S' of statements of which S is a subset).

PROOF: Let S' be an arbitrary superset of S.
CASE 1: Both S and S' are finite. Let S'' consist of all the members of S' that do not belong to S, and suppose S ⊢ A. Then S ∪ S'' ⊢ A by (3.1.11). But S' is the same as S ∪ S''. Hence S' ⊢ A.
CASE 2: S is finite, but S' is infinite. Suppose S ⊢ A. Since S is a finite subset of S', by definition S' ⊢ A.
CASE 3: Both S and S' are infinite. Suppose S ⊢ A. Then by definition there is a finite subset of S, say S'', such that S'' ⊢ A. But S'', being a subset of S, is also one of S'. Hence S' ⊢ A by Case 2.

(*3.2.4*) $S \vdash A$ if and only if there is a finite subset S' of S such that $S' \vdash A$.

PROOF: (i) Suppose $S \vdash A$, with S finite. Since S is one of its own subsets, there is a finite subset S' of S, S itself, such that $S' \vdash A$. Suppose $S \vdash A$, with S infinite. Then by definition there is a finite subset S' of S such that $S' \vdash A$. (ii) Suppose there is a finite subset S' of S such that $S' \vdash A$. Then $S \vdash A$ by (3.2.3).

(*3.2.5*)   If A belongs to S, then $S \vdash A$.

PROOF: $\{A\} \vdash A$ by R. But, if A belongs to S, then $\{A\}$ is a subset of S. Hence (3.2.5) by (3.2.3).

(*3.2.6*)   If $S \cup \{A\} \vdash B$ and $S \cup \{A\} \vdash \sim B$, then $S \vdash \sim A$.

PROOF: Suppose $S \cup \{A\} \vdash B$ and $S \cup \{A\} \vdash \sim B$. Then by (3.2.4) there is a finite subset of $S \cup \{A\}$, say S', from which B is derivable, and a finite subset of $S \cup \{A\}$, say S'', from which $\sim B$ is derivable. Now let $(S' \cup S'')_{-A}$ consist of all the members of S', *plus* all the members of S'', *minus* A. Since each one of S' and S'' is a subset of $(S' \cup S'')_{-A} \cup \{A\}$, then $(S' \cup S'')_{-A} \cup \{A\} \vdash B$ and $(S' \cup S'')_{-A} \cup \{A\} \vdash \sim B$ by (3.2.3), and hence $(S' \cup S'')_{-A} \vdash \sim A$ by $\sim$I.[13] But, since each one of S' and S'' is a subset of $S \cup \{A\}$, and A does not belong to $(S' \cup S'')_{-A}$, $(S' \cup S'')_{-A}$ is a subset of S. Hence, there is a finite subset of S from which $\sim A$ is derivable. Hence $S \vdash \sim A$ by (3.2.4).

(*3.2.7*)   If $S \vdash \sim\sim A$, then $S \vdash A$.

PROOF: Suppose $S \vdash \sim\sim A$. Then by (3.2.4) there is a finite subset S' of S such that $S' \vdash \sim\sim A$, and hence by $\sim$E such that $S' \vdash A$. Hence $S \vdash A$ by (3.2.4).

(*3.2.8*)   If $S \cup \{A\} \vdash B$, then $S \vdash A \supset B$.

PROOF: Suppose $S \cup \{A\} \vdash B$. Then by (3.2.4) there is a finite subset S' of $S \cup \{A\}$ such that $S' \vdash B$. Now let S'_{-A} consist of all the members of S' *minus* A. Then $S'_{-A} \cup \{A\} \vdash B$ by (3.2.3), and hence $S'_{-A} \vdash A \supset B$ by $\supset$I. Hence $S \vdash A \supset B$ by (3.2.4).

(*3.2.9*)   If $S \vdash A \supset B$ and $S \vdash A$, then $S \vdash B$.

PROOF: Suppose $S \vdash A \supset B$ and $S \vdash A$. Then by (3.2.4) there is a finite subset of S, say S', from which $A \supset B$ is derivable, and a finite

---

[13] If S'' is empty, and A belongs to S', then $(S' \cup S'')_{-A} \cup \{A\}$ is of course the same as S', and $(S' \cup S'')_{-A} \cup \{A\} \vdash B \,(= S' \vdash B)$ without appeal to (3.2.3). The same applies to $(S' \cup S'')_{-A} \cup \{A\} \vdash \sim B$.

subset of S, say S'', from which A is derivable. But, if $S' \vdash A \supset B$ and $S'' \vdash A$, then $S' \cup S'' \vdash A \supset B$ and $S' \cup S'' \vdash A$ by (3.2.3), and hence $S' \cup S'' \vdash B$ by $\supset$ E. Hence, there is a finite subset of S from which B is derivable. Hence $S \vdash B$ by (3.2.4).

(3.2.10)   If $S \vdash {\sim}A$ or $S \vdash B$, then $S \vdash A \supset B$.

PROOF: (i) Suppose $S \vdash {\sim}A$. Then $S \cup \{A,{\sim}B\} \vdash {\sim}A$ by (3.2.3). But $S \cup \{A,{\sim}B\} \vdash A$ by (3.2.5). Hence $S \cup \{A\} \vdash {\sim}{\sim}B$ by (3.2.6), hence $S \cup \{A\} \vdash B$ by (3.2.7), and hence $S \vdash A \supset B$ by (3.2.8). (ii) Suppose $S \vdash B$. Then $S \cup \{A\} \vdash B$ by (3.2.3), and hence $S \vdash A \supset B$ by (3.2.8).

(3.2.11) $S \vdash A \supset A$.

PROOF: $S \cup \{A\} \vdash A$ by (3.2.5), and hence $S \vdash A \supset A$ by (3.2.8).

(3.2.12)   If $S \vdash A(T/X)$, then $S \vdash (\forall X)A$, so long as T is foreign to S and to $(\forall X)A$.

PROOF like that of (3.2.7).

(3.2.13)   If $S \vdash (\forall X)A$, then $S \vdash A(T/X)$ for any term T.

PROOF like that of (3.2.7).

Syntactic Consistency and Inconsistency

To repeat a point from p. 240, the notions of consistency and inconsistency that we introduced in Sections 1.1 and 2.1 (and for which we supplied a test in Sections 1.2 and 2.2) are semantic ones. As they have syntactic counterparts, and these counterparts are to play a major role in Sections 3.4 and 3.6, some sharpening in terminology and another pair of definitions are in order.

A finite but non-empty set S of statements will hereafter be called **semantically consistent** (rather than just consistent, as was our practice) if there is a truth-value assignment to the atomic subformulas of the members of S on which every member of S is true. And the set will be called **semantically inconsistent** (rather than just inconsistent) if it is not semantically consistent—i.e., if there is *no* such assignment. On the other hand, a set S of statements will be called **syntactically consistent** if there is *no* statement A such that both $S \vdash A$ and $S \vdash {\sim}A$. And the set will be called **syntactically inconsistent** if it is not syntactically consistent—i.e., if there *is* a statement A such that both $S \vdash A$ and $S \vdash {\sim}A$.

Since our original concept of derivability has been extended to suit infinite as well as finite sets of statements, S is free in the last two definitions to be infinite as well as finite. S is also free in those two definitions to be empty. We shall wait until Section 3.6 before extending the concept of semantic consistency (and inconsistency) to the case where S is infinite. It pays, however, to extend it right away to the case where S is empty, and *declare $\varnothing$ semantically consistent* by special dispensation. The move is a rather natural one inasmuch as $\varnothing$ will be shown in Section 3.3 to be syntactically consistent.

Our proof later of the Soundness Theorem (If $S \vdash A$, then S entails A) will have as a corollary that if a finite set of statements is semantically consistent, the set is syntactically consistent as well. And our proof of the Completeness Theorem (If S entails A, then $S \vdash A$) will follow from a lemma of Leon Henkin's to the effect that if a finite and non-empty set of statements is syntactically consistent, the set is semantically consistent as well. As regards finite and non-empty sets of statements, then, the new concept of syntactic consistency exactly parallels the familiar one of semantic consistency.

We record a corollary of (3.2.1) which will prove handy later on, and then verify with the reader six results on syntactic inconsistency. S is of course free in these six results to be of any size whatever.

> (*3.2.14*) Let S be a finite and non-empty set of statements. Then S is semantically consistent (inconsistent) if and only if there is a (no) truth-value assignment to the atomic subformulas of the members of S—and possibly to other atomic statements as well—on which every member of S is true.[14]

> (*3.2.15*) If S is syntactically inconsistent, then $S \vdash A$ for any statement A.

PROOF: Let S be syntactically inconsistent, and A be an arbitrary statement. By definition there is a statement B such that both $S \vdash B$ and $S \vdash \sim B$, and hence by (3.2.3) such that both $S \cup \{\sim A\} \vdash B$ and $S \cup \{\sim A\} \vdash \sim B$. Hence $S \vdash \sim\sim A$ by (3.2.6). Hence $S \vdash A$ by (3.2.7).

> (*3.2.16*) If S is syntactically inconsistent, then so is any superset of S (i.e., any set of statements of which S is a subset).

PROOF: Let S and A be as in the proof of (3.2.15), and let S' be an arbitrary superset of S. Then $S \vdash \sim(A \supset A)$ by (3.2.15), and hence $S' \vdash \sim(A \supset A)$ by (3.2.3). But $S' \vdash A \supset A$ by (3.2.11). Hence, by definition, S' is syntactically inconsistent.

---

[14] Had we taken a finite set S of statements (said set possibly empty) to be semantically consistent if there is a truth-value assignment to the atomic subformulas of the members of S—*and possibly to other atomic statements as well*—on which all the members of S are true, then $\varnothing$ would automatically prove to be semantically consistent (every member of $\varnothing$ is indeed true on the result of assigning any truth-value whatsoever to any atomic statements whatsoever), and (3.2.14) could be dispensed with. But lugging around the clause 'and possibly to other atomic statements' seemed too high a price.

(*3.2.17*)   If S is syntactically inconsistent, then at least one finite subset of S is syntactically inconsistent.

PROOF: Let S and A be as in the proof of (3.2.15). Then $S \vdash$ $\sim(A \supset A)$ by (3.2.15), and hence by (3.2.4) there is a finite subset of S, say S', such that $S' \vdash \sim(A \supset A)$. But by (3.2.11) $S' \vdash A \supset A$. Hence, by definition, there is a finite subset of S that is syntactically inconsistent.

(*3.2.18*)   (a) S is syntactically inconsistent if and only if at least one finite subset of S is syntactically inconsistent.
(b) S is syntactically consistent if and only if every finite subset of S is syntactically consistent.

PROOF by (3.2.16)–(3.2.17).

(*3.2.19*)   If $S \cup \{A\}$ is syntactically inconsistent, then $S \vdash \sim A$.

PROOF: Suppose $S \cup \{A\}$ is syntactically inconsistent. Then by (3.2.15) $S \cup \{A\} \vdash B$ and $S \cup \{A\} \vdash \sim B$ for any statement B. Hence $S \vdash \sim A$ by (3.2.6).

(*3.2.20*)   If $S \cup \{\sim A\}$ is syntactically inconsistent, then $S \vdash A$.

PROOF: If $S \cup \{\sim A\}$ is syntactically inconsistent, then $S \vdash \sim\sim A$ by (3.2.19) and hence $S \vdash A$ by (3.2.7).

Alphabetic Ordering of Statements

At a critical point in Section 3.4 we shall presume that the members of a certain set S^{**} of statements come in a definite order, called **the alphabetic order of the members of S^{**},** and hence that some specific member of the set is indeed the alphabetically first member of the set, some specific member its alphabetically second member, and so on. There are many different ways of ordering the members of a given set S of statements. We adopt the following, which stems from R. M. Smullyan.[15]

We first assign a number, to be known as its **code number,** to each one of our primitive operators, punctuation signs, term variables, and terms. We also assign a code number to each one of the abbreviations (capital letters with zero or more primes) that serve as predicates in

---

[15] See *Theory of Formal Systems,* Princeton University Press, 1961, pp. 11–12; also Jeffrey's *Formal Logic: Its Scope and Limits,* pp. 202–6.

members of the given set S. We then take *the code number of a member A of S* to be the number whose decimal expression is the decimal expression for the code number of the left-most symbol or abbreviation in A, followed by the decimal expression for the code number of the next symbol or abbreviation in A, and so on.[16] We next say that a given member A of S *alphabetically precedes* another member B of S if the code number of A is smaller than the code number of B. Finally, we take a member A of S to be *the alphabetically first (or earliest) member of S* if A alphabetically precedes all other members (i.e., has the smallest code number of all); to be *the alphabetically second member of S* if it alphabetically precedes all other members but the first (i.e., has the second smallest code number of all); and so on.

Before glancing at the table of code numbers on p. 272, the reader should recall that our term variables and our terms have already been arranged in a definite order, the former coming in the alphabetic order

$$x, \quad y, \quad z, \quad x', \quad y', \quad z', \quad x'', \quad y'', \quad z'', \dots ,$$

the latter in the alphabetic order

$$a_1, \quad a_2, \quad a_3, \dots .$$

That order determines their respective code numbers. As for the abbreviations which—for any set S and any m from 1 on—serve in members of S as m-place predicates, they too can be arranged in some alphabetic order of their own, so long as there are only finitely many of them (as will be the case with set S^{**} in Section 3.4) or only $\aleph_0$ of them. To illustrate the latter case, if for some m or other

$$F, \quad G, \quad H, \quad F', \quad G', \quad H', \quad F'', \quad G'', \quad H'', \dots ,$$

were all the abbreviations that serve in members of a given set S as m-place predicates, then the order in which we just displayed them would do as their alphabetic order. The one agreed upon determines their respective code numbers.

An example will show how code numbering and alphabetic ordering work. Consider the set

$$\{(\forall x)(\sim F(x) \supset (\forall y)H(y, x)), \ \sim(\forall x)\sim I(a_3, x), \ (H(a_2, a_4) \supset \sim G(a_1))\}.$$

Take 'F' here to be the alphabetically first 1-place predicate, 'G' to be the second; and take 'H' to be the alphabetically first 2-place predicate,

---

[16] We illustrate this below. It will be obvious that no two members of S could have the same code number. Some positive integers (1, for example) will not be the code numbers of any members of any given set S, but that makes no difference for the purpose of alphabetic ordering. On this occasion, we presume the members of S to display all official parentheses and commas.

TABLE OF CODE NUMBERS

Code numbers for the three primitive operators:

$\sim$ 12
$\supset$ 122
$\forall$ 1222

Code numbers for the three punctuation signs:

(13
)   133
,   1333

Code numbers for the term variables:

the alphabetically first term variable $(= x)$ 14
the alphabetically second term variable $(= y)$ 144
the alphabetically third term variable $(= z)$ 1444
etc. . .

Code numbers for the terms:

the alphabetically first term $(= a_1)$ 15
the alphabetically second term $(= a_2)$ 155
the alphabetically third term $(= a_3)$ 1555
etc . . .

Code numbers for the m-place ($m \geq 1$) predicates in members of S:

the alphabetically first m-place predicate $\underbrace{11\ldots1}_{m \text{ times}}6$

the alphabetically second m-place predicate $\underbrace{11\ldots1}_{m \text{ times}}66$

the alphabetically third m-place predicate $\underbrace{11\ldots1}_{m \text{ times}}666$

etc. . . .[17]

'I' to be the second. Then, as the reader can verify for himself, the code number of

$$(\forall x)(\sim F(x) \supset (\forall y)H(y,x))$$

is

131222141331312161314133122131222144133116131441333314133133.

The code number of

$$\sim(\forall x)\sim I(a_3, x)$$

_____

[17] For each m and each n from 1 on, the code number of the alphabetically n–th one among the m-place predicates that occur in members of S thus has as its decimal expression a sequence of m ones followed by n sixes.

is

12131222141331211661315551333314133.

And the code number of

$$(H(a_2, a_4) \supset \sim G(a_1))$$

is

13116131551333155551331221216613151331313.

Inspection will reveal that the code number of '$\sim(\forall x)\sim I(a_3, x)$' is smallest, and hence that this statement is the alphabetically first member of the given set. '$(H(a_2, a_4) \supset \sim G(a_1))$' is the alphabetically second member of the set, because its code number is smaller than that of '$(\forall x)(\sim F(x) \supset (\forall y)H(y, x))$', which is therefore the alphabetically third member of the set.

In view of the foregoing, any set S of statements is sure to have at most $\aleph_0$ members (hence to be finite or denumerably infinite). For each member can be assigned a positive integer of its own as code number, and there are $\aleph_0$ positive integers. And S is sure to have at most $2^{\aleph_0}$ sub-sets. If it has n members, then (as we saw on p. 258) it will have 2^n subsets; and if it has $\aleph_0$ members, then it will have $2^{\aleph_0}$ subsets.

EXERCISES

E3.2.1.   With S, α, and α' understood to be as on p. 260, and A understood to be any statement whose atomic subformulas are all assigned a truth-value in α, show by mathematical induction on the length of A that A is true on α if and only if true on α', and hence again that any member of S is true on α if and only if true on α'. (Note: The proof can be run like that on pp. 260–61, but details will differ.)

E3.2.2.   With A understood to belong to a set S of statements if and only if A is an atomic statement or A is of one of the three sorts $B \supset C$, $B \& C$, and $B \lor C$, where B and C both belong to S, show by mathematical induction on the length of A that A is sure to be true on the result of assigning **T** to all the atomic subformulas of the members of S. (As pointed out on p. 249, it follows from this result that none of '$\supset$', '$\&$', and '$\lor$' permits definition of '$\sim$'.)

E3.2.3.   Generalizing upon the result in E3.2.2, show that none of the modes of composition corresponding to B_1–B_8 in Table XIII, p. 244, permits definition of '$\sim$'.

E3.2.4.   With A understood to belong to a set S of statements if and only if A is an atomic statement or A is of the sort $\sim B$, where B belongs to S, show that A is sure to be truth-functionally indeterminate. (Hint: α being the result of assigning **T** to all the atomic subformulas of the members of S, and α' the result of assigning **F** to all of them, show by mathematical induction on the length of A that A is true on α if and only if A is not true on α'. As pointed out on p. 249, it follows from this result that '$\sim$' does not permit definition of any one of '$\supset$', '$\&$', and '$\lor$'.)

E3.2.5. Generalizing upon the results in E3.2.2 and E3.2.4, show that: (a) When just '~', '⊃', and '∀' serve as primitive operators, every logical truth is sure to contain at least one occurrence of '⊃', and (b) When just '~', '&', '∨', '∀', and '∃' serve as primitive operators, every logical truth is sure to contain at least one occurrence of '~' and at least one of '&' or '∨'.

E3.2.6. Supposing A, T_1, T_2, Σ_T, Σ'_T, f(T), f(B), and f(α) to be as on pp. 261-62, construct a truth-value assignment α to the atomic subformulas of A and to those of f(A) on which f(A) is true; construct one on which f(A) is false; and show that in each case A is true on f(α) if and only if f(A) is true on α.

E3.2.7 With S understood to be a finite set of statements, and $S(T'/T)$ to consist of the results of putting T' for T in the members of S, show by means of (3.2.2) that if S entails A, then $S(T'/T)$ entails $A(T'/T)$.

E3.2.8. With S and S' free to be infinite as well as finite, all seven of '~', '⊃', '&', '∨', '≡', '∀', and '∃' understood to serve as primitive operators, and all fifteen of the rules of Sections 1.3 and 2.3 to serve as derivation rules, show that:

    (a) $S \vdash A \& B$ if and only if $S \vdash A$ and $S \vdash B$;

    (b)   If $S \vdash A$ or $S \vdash B$, then $S \vdash A \lor B$;

    (c)   If $S \vdash A \lor B$, $S \cup \{A\} \vdash C$, and $S \cup \{B\} \vdash C$, then $S \vdash C$;

    (d)   If $S \vdash \sim(A \lor B)$, then $S \vdash \sim A$ and $S \vdash \sim B$;

    (e)   If $S \cup \{A\} \vdash B$ and $S \cup \{B\} \vdash A$, then $S \vdash A \equiv B$;

    (f)   If (i) either $S \vdash A \equiv B$ or $S \vdash B \equiv A$, and (ii) $S \vdash A$, then $S \vdash B$;

    (g)   If $S \vdash \sim(A \equiv B)$, then $S \vdash \sim(A \& B)$ and $S \vdash \sim(\sim A \& \sim B)$;

    (h)   If $S \vdash A(T/X)$ for some term T, then $S \vdash (\exists X)A$;

    (i)   If $S \cup S' \vdash (\exists X)A$ and $S \cup \{A(T/X)\} \vdash B$, then $S \cup S' \vdash B$, so long as T is foreign to S, $(\exists X)A$, and B;

    (j)   If $S \vdash (\forall X)\sim A$, then $S \vdash \sim(\exists X)A$.

(These results will be used in a later exercise.)

E3.2.9. Using the result proved on pp. 260-61, show that if $\{A\}$ entails B, then either $\{A\}$ is semantically inconsistent, or B is logically true, or A and B have at least one atomic subformula in common.

E3.2.10. Using the result in E3.2.9, show that if a finite set S of statements entails A, then either S is semantically inconsistent, or A is logically true, or at least one member of S has an atomic subformula in common with A.

E3.2.11. Using the result in E3.2.10, show that if a finite set S of statements entails A and '~' is foreign to S, then either A is logically true or at least one member of S has an atomic subformula in common with A.

E3.2.12. Using the result proved on pp. 260-61, show that if a disjunction $A \lor B$ is logically true but neither of A and B is, then A and B have at least one atomic subformula in common.

3.3   The Soundness Theorem

Making good a repeated promise, we proceed to show that if a state-ment A is derivable from a finite set S of statements in accordance with R and the intelim rules of Sections 1.3 and 2.3 for '~', '⊃', and '∀', then A is sure to be entailed by S; and hence that if A is provable in accordance with these rules, then A is sure to be logically true. The argument em-ployed readily generalizes to the case where all seven of '~', '⊃', '&', '∨', '≡', '∀', and '∃' serve as primitive operators, and A is derivable from S in accordance with all fifteen of the rules of Sections 1.3 and 2.3.[1]

To simplify at one point the wording of the argument, we assume that the subordinate derivation in ~I:

$$
\begin{array}{|l}
B \\[4pt]
\hline
\\[-6pt]
\cdot \\
C \quad (\text{or} \sim C) \\
\cdot \\
\sim C \quad (\text{or } C)
\end{array}
$$

is split into two derivations, one headed by B and ending with C, the other headed by B and ending with $\sim C$.[2] We also assume that derivations are recorded in full, so that all the assumptions which belong at the head of a subordinate derivation appear there. And recall that ∀I* (rather than ∀I) serves in this chapter as introduction rule for '∀'. The change in rule is inconsequential: since ∀I is just a special case of ∀I*, any derivation done with the help of ∀I can obviously be done with the help of ∀I*.

Entailment Lemmas

Preparatory to proving our main result, we establish a number of entailment lemmas, one for each of our seven rules. Throughout, the reader should bear in mind that a finite set S of statements entails a statement A if and only if $S \cup \{\sim A\}$ is semantically inconsistent, hence by (3.2.14) if and only if there is no truth-value assignment to the atomic subformulas of the members of $S \cup \{\sim A\}$—and possibly to other atomic statements as well—on which all the members of $S \cup \{\sim A\}$ are true. Hence, S entails A if and only if A is true on any truth-value assignment to the atomic subformulas of the members of $S \cup \{\sim A\}$—and possibly to other atomic statements as well—on which all the members of S are true. Note also that the atomic subformulas of the members of a set $S \cup \{A\}$

---

[1] See Exercise E3.3.2 on this matter.
[2] For a derivation that uses this format of ~I, see p. 278.

are those of the members of S *plus* those of A; that the atomic subformulas of $\sim A$ are those of A; that the atomic subformulas of $A \supset B$ are
those of A *plus* those of B; and that the atomic subformulas of $(\forall X)A$ are
those of $A(a_1/X)$, *plus* those of $A(a_2/X)$, *plus* those of $A(a_3/X)$, and so on.

(3.3.1)   If A belongs to S, then S entails A.

PROOF: Suppose A belongs to S. Then there can be no truth-value
assignment to the atomic subformulas of the members of $S \cup \{\sim A\}$
on which all the members of $S \cup \{\sim A\}$ are true; for if there were,
both A (which by hypothesis belongs to S) and $\sim A$ (which belongs to
$S \cup \{\sim A\}$) would be true on the assignment, which is impossible.
Hence, $S \cup \{\sim A\}$ is semantically inconsistent. Hence, S entails A.

(3.3.2)   If $S \cup \{A\}$ entails both B and $\sim B$, then S entails $\sim A$.

PROOF: Suppose $S \cup \{A\}$ entails both B and $\sim B$, and let α be an
arbitrary truth-value assignment to the atomic subformulas of the
members of S, to those of A, and to those of B, on which all the
members of S are true. A cannot be true on α; for if it were, both B
and $\sim B$ would be true on α. Hence, $\sim A$ is sure to be true on α. Hence,
$\sim A$ is sure to be true on any truth-value assignment to the atomic
subformulas of the members of S, to those of A, and to those of B,
on which all the members of S are true. Hence, S entails $\sim A$.

(3.3.3)   If S entails $\sim\sim A$, then S entails A.

PROOF: Suppose S entails $\sim\sim A$, and let α be an arbitrary truth-
value assignment to the atomic subformulas of the members of S and
to those of A, on which all the members of S are true. Then $\sim\sim A$
is sure to be true on α, hence $\sim A$ is sure not to be true on α, and
hence A is sure to be true on α. Hence, S entails A.

(3.3.4)   If $S \cup \{A\}$ entails B, then S entails $A \supset B$.

PROOF: Suppose $S \cup \{A\}$ entails B, and let α be an arbitrary truth-
value assignment to the atomic subformulas of the members of S, to
those of A, and to those of B, on which all the members of S are true.
If A is also true on α (and, hence, all the members of $S \cup \{A\}$ are
true on α), then B is sure to be true on α, and hence so is $A \supset B$. If,
on the other hand, A is not true on α, then again $A \supset B$ is true on α.
In either case, therefore, $A \supset B$ is true on α. Hence, S entails $A \supset B$.

(3.3.5)   If S entails both $A \supset B$ and A, then S entails B.

PROOF: Suppose S entails both $A \supset B$ and A, and let α be as in the
proof of (3.3.4). Then $A \supset B$ and A are sure to be true on α, and
hence so is B. Hence, S entails B.

(3.3.6) If S entails $A(T/X)$, then $S \cup S'$ entails $(\forall X)A$, so long as T is foreign to S and to $(\forall X)A$.

PROOF: We first consider the special case where S' is empty (and, hence, $S \cup S'$ is just S). We then pass on to the general case.

CASE 1: Suppose S entails $A(T/X)$, where T is foreign to S and to $(\forall X)A$, and let α be a truth-value assignment to the atomic subformulas of both the members of $S \cup \{(\forall X)A\}$ and their term variants, on which all the members of S are true. We shall establish that, for any term T', $A(T'/X)$ is true on α, hence that $(\forall X)A$ is true on α, and hence that S entails $(\forall X)A$.

CASE 1.1: T' is the same as T. Then $A(T'/X)$ is the same as $A(T/X)$. But, since S entails $A(T/X)$, $A(T/X)$ is sure to be true on α. Hence, $A(T'/X)$ is sure to be true on α.

CASE 1.2: T' is distinct from T. *Suppose the result $(A(T/X))(T'/T)$ of putting T' for T in $A(T/X)$ is not true on α.* In view of (3.2.2) there exists a truth-value assignment α' (to the same atomic statements as are assigned a truth-value in α) such that: (a) if the result $B(T'/T)$ of putting T' for T in a member B of S is true on α, then B itself is true on α', and (b) if $(A(T/X))(T'/T)$ is not true on α, then $A(T/X)$ itself is not true on α'.[3] But, with T presumed to be foreign to S, $B(T'/T)$ is the same as B, and hence is true on α. Hence, there exists a truth-value assignment (to the same atomic statements as are assigned a truth-value in α) on which all the members of S are true, but $A(T/X)$ is not. Hence, S does not entail $A(T/X)$. But S was presumed from the very start to entail $A(T/X)$. Hence, our original supposition proves untenable, and $(A(T/X))(T'/T)$ is sure to be true on α. But, with T presumed to be foreign to $(\forall X)A$ (and, hence, to A), $(A(T/X))(T'/T)$ is the same as $A(T'/X)$. Hence, $A(T'/X)$ is sure to be true on α.

CASE 2: Suppose S entails $A(T/X)$, where T is foreign to S and to $(\forall X)A$, and let α be an arbitrary truth-value assignment to the atomic subformulas of the members of $S \cup S'$ and to those of $(\forall X)A$, on which all the members of $S \cup S'$ are true. Since S entails $A(T/X)$, S entails $(\forall X)A$ by Case 1 and the hypothesis on the term T. But, since every member of $S \cup S'$ is true on α, so is every member of S. Hence, $(\forall X)A$ is true on α. Thus, $S \cup S'$ entails $(\forall X)A$, so long as T is foreign to S and to $(\forall X)A$.

---

[3] Indeed, think of $S \cup \{A(T/X)\}$ as the set S of (3.2.2), and of T and T' as the terms T_1 and T_2 of (3.2.2). Then (a) for any member B of $S \cup \{A(T/X)\}$ other than $A(T/X)$, B is true on α' if and only if $B(T'/T)$ is true on α, and (b) member $A(T/X)$ of $S \cup \{A(T/X)\}$ is true on α' if and only if $(A(T/X))(T'/T)$ is true on α.

(*3.3.7*)   If S entails $(\forall X)A$, then S entails $A(T/X)$ for any term T.

PROOF: Suppose S entails $(\forall X)A$, and let α be an arbitrary truth-value assignment to the atomic subformulas of the members of S and to those of $(\forall X)A$, on which all the members of S are true. Then $(\forall X)A$ is sure to be true on α, and hence so is $A(T/X)$ for any term T. Hence, S entails $A(T/X)$ for any term T.

One last preliminary before we embark upon the proof of our theorem: **the degree of complexity of a derivation.** A derivation that contains no subordinate derivation will be declared of degree of complexity zero; one that contains one or more subordinate derivations will be declared of degree of complexity $d+1$, d being the sum of the degrees of complexity of its *immediate* subordinate derivations. To illustrate matters, consider the following derivation (recorded in full form) of '$(\forall x)\sim Fx$' from $\{(\forall x)(Fx \supset Gx), (\forall x)\sim Gx\}$:

1	$(\forall x)(Fx \supset Gx)$	
2	$(\forall x)\sim Gx$	
3	$(\forall x)(Fx \supset Gx)$	
4	$(\forall x)\sim Gx$	
5	$(\forall x)(Fx \supset Gx)$	
6	$(\forall x)\sim Gx$	
7	Fa_1	
8	$(\forall x)(Fx \supset Gx)$	(R, 5)
9	$Fa_1 \supset Ga_1$	($\forall$E, 8)
10	Fa_1	(R, 7)
11	Ga_1	($\supset$E, 9, 10)
12	$(\forall x)(Fx \supset Gx)$	
13	$(\forall x)\sim Gx$	
14	Fa_1	
15	$(\forall x)\sim Gx$	(R, 13)
16	$\sim Ga_1$	($\forall$E, 15)
17	$\sim Fa_1$	($\sim$I, 5–11, 12–16)
18	$(\forall x)\sim Fx$	($\forall$I*, 3–17)

The derivation running from line 5 through line 11 is of degree of complexity 0, and so is the one running from line 12 through line 16. Hence, the derivation running from line 3 through line 17, which has as its only immediate subordinate derivations the derivations respectively running from line 5 through line 11 and from line 12 through line 16, is of degree of complexity $(0+0)+1$ $(= 1)$. Hence, the derivation of '$(\forall x)\sim Fx$' from $\{(\forall x)(Fx \supset Gx), (\forall x)\sim Gx\}$, which has as its only immediate subordinate derivation the derivation running from line 3 through line 17, is of degree of complexity $1 + 1$ $(= 2)$.

Proof of the Soundness Theorem

The last line—call it B—of any derivation done in accordance with the rules R, $\sim$I, $\sim$E, $\supset$I, $\supset$E, $\forall$I*, and $\forall$E, is entailed by the assumptions A_1, A_2, . . ., and A_n $(n \geq 0)$ of the derivation (and, hence, any statement derivable in accordance with these rules from a finite set of statements is entailed by the set).

This is proved by mathematical induction on the degree of complexity d of the derivation. We first show that the result holds when $d = 0$ (basis of the induction on d); then, assuming that it holds of any derivation of a degree of complexity less than d, we show that the result holds when $d > 0$ (inductive step of the induction on d); and we conclude therefrom that the result holds of any d, i.e., whatever the degree of complexity of the derivation of B from $\{A_1, A_2, . . ., A_n\}$. Within the basis of the induction on d, we conduct another induction (this time on a certain number i) which we indent, and whose basis and inductive step we respectively identify as Basis' and Inductive Step'. And, within the inductive step of the induction on d, we conduct yet another induction (this time on a certain number k) which we also indent, and whose basis and inductive step we respectively identify as Basis'' and Inductive Step''.

BASIS: $d = 0$. Then the derivation of B from $\{A_1, A_2, . . ., A_n\}$ is sure to be of the sort

$$
\begin{array}{r|l}
1 & A_1 \\
2 & A_2 \\
\cdot & \cdot \\
n & A_n \\
\hline
n+1 & A_{n+1} \\
n+2 & A_{n+2} \\
\cdot & \cdot \\
n+p & A_{n+p} \qquad (= B),
\end{array}
$$

where, for each i from 1 to p, A_{n+i} is obtained by one of the four among our seven rules that do not involve subordinate derivations, namely: R, $\sim$E, $\supset$E, and $\forall$E. We establish by mathematical induction on i that, for each i from 1 through p, $\{A_1,A_2,\ldots,A_n\}$ entails A_{n+i}; and hence that $\{A_1,A_2,\ldots,A_n\}$ entails the last line B $(= A_{n+p})$ of the derivation.

BASIS': $i = 1$. Then A_{n+i} is obtained by rule R, hence A_{n+i} belongs to $\{A_1,A_2,\ldots,A_n\}$, and hence by (3.3.1) $\{A_1,A_2,\ldots,A_n\}$ entails A_{n+i}.

INDUCTIVE STEP': $i > 1$. Suppose $\{A_1,A_2,\ldots,A_n\}$ entails A_{n+1}, $A_{n+2}, \ldots$, and A_{n+i-1} (hypothesis of the induction on i), and suppose that A_{n+i} is obtained by rule R. Then, by the same reasoning as before, $\{A_1,A_2,\ldots,A_n\}$ entails A_{n+i}. Or suppose that A_{n+i} is obtained from *one* of the lines A_{n+1}, $A_{n+2}, \ldots$, and A_{n+i-1} by one of the two rules $\sim$E and $\forall$E. Since, by the hypothesis of the induction on i, $\{A_1,A_2,\ldots,A_n\}$ entails the line in question, by (3.3.3) or (3.3.7) $\{A_1,A_2,\ldots,A_n\}$ entails A_{n+i}. Or suppose that A_{n+i} is obtained from *two* of the lines A_{n+1}, $A_{n+2}, \ldots$, and A_{n+i-1} by $\supset$E. Since, by the hypothesis of the induction on i, $\{A_1,A_2,\ldots,A_n\}$ entails the two lines in question, by (3.3.5) $\{A_1,A_2,\ldots,A_n\}$ entails A_{n+i}.

INDUCTIVE STEP: $d > 0$. Then at least one of the lines directly under the assumptions A_1, A_2, $\ldots$, and A_n of the derivation is obtained by one of the three among our seven rules that involve subordinate derivations. Let B_1, B_2, $\ldots$, and B_t be all the lines in the derivation that are directly under the assumptions A_1, A_2, $\ldots$, and A_n; and suppose that the theorem to be proved holds of derivations of a degree of complexity less than d (hypothesis of the induction on d). We establish by mathematical induction on k that for each k from 1 through t, $\{A_1,A_2,\ldots,A_n\}$ entails B_k, and hence that $\{A_1,A_2,\ldots,A_n\}$ entails the last line B $(= B_t)$ of the derivation.

BASIS": $k = 1$. Then B_k *is* obtained by one of the four rules R, $\sim$I, $\supset$I, and $\forall$I*.

CASE 1: B_k is obtained by rule R. Proof as in BASIS' above.
CASE 2: B_k is obtained by rule $\sim$I, and hence B_k is of the sort $\sim$C. Then the derivation of B from $\{A_1,A_2,\ldots,A_n\}$ is sure to be of the sort

$$
\begin{array}{r|l}
1 & A_1 \\
2 & A_2 \\
\cdot & \cdot \\
n & A_n \\
\hline
\end{array}
$$

$n + 1$	A_1
$n + 2$	A_2
$\cdot$	$\cdot$
$2n$	A_n
$2n + 1$	C
$\cdot$	$\cdot$
p	D
$p + 1$	A_1
$p + 2$	A_2
$\cdot$	$\cdot$
$p + n$	A_n
$p + n + 1$	C
$\cdot$	$\cdot$
q	$\sim D$
$q + 1$	$\sim C$ $(= B_k)$
$\cdot$	$\cdot$
r	$B.$

But the derivations running from line $n + 1$ through line p and from line $p + 1$ through line q are immediate subordinate derivations of the derivation of B from $\{A_1, A_2, \ldots, A_n\}$. Hence, by definition, each one is of a degree of complexity less than d. Hence, by the hypothesis of the induction on d, $\{A_1, A_2, \ldots, A_n, C\}$ entails both D and $\sim D$. Hence, by (3.3.2), $\{A_1, A_2, \ldots, A_n\}$ entails $\sim C$ $(= B_k)$.

CASE 3: B_k is obtained by $\supset$I. The proof, which is like that of CASE 2 except for using (3.3.4) in place of (3.3.2), is left to the reader.

CASE 4: B_k is obtained by rule $\forall$I*, and hence B_k is of the sort $(\forall X)C$. Then the derivation of B from $\{A_1, A_2, \ldots, A_n\}$ is sure to be of the sort

$$
\begin{array}{l|l}
1 & A_1 \\
2 & A_2 \\
\cdot & \cdot \\
n & A_n \\
\end{array}
$$

$$
\begin{array}{l|l}
n+1 & A'_1 \\
n+2 & A'_2 \\
\cdot & \cdot \\
n+j & A'_j \\
\\
\cdot & \cdot \\
p & C(T/X) \\
p+1 & (\forall X)C \quad (= B_k) \\
\cdot & \cdot \\
q & B, \\
\end{array}
$$

where $A'_1, A'_2, \ldots$, and $A'_j(j \geq 1)$ all belong to $\{A_1, A_2, \ldots, A_n\}$, and T is foreign to $A'_1, A'_2, \ldots$, and A'_j, and $(\forall X)C$. But the subordinate derivation running from line $n+1$ through line p is an immediate subordinate derivation of the derivation of B from $\{A_1, A_2, \ldots, A_n\}$, and hence is of a degree of complexity less than d. Hence, by the hypothesis of the induction on d, $\{A'_1, A'_2, \ldots, A'_j\}$ entails $C(T/X)$. Hence, by (3.3.6) and the hypothesis on T, $\{A_1, A_2, \ldots, A_n\}$ entails $(\forall X)C$ $(= B_k)$.

INDUCTIVE STEP''': $k > 1$. Suppose $\{A_1, A_2, \ldots, A_n\}$ entails B_1, $B_2, \ldots$, and B_{k-1} (hypothesis of the induction on k).

CASE 1: B_k is obtained by one of the four rules R, $\sim$E, $\supset$E, and $\forall$E. Then, by the same reasoning as in Inductive Step' (but using the hypothesis of the induction on k instead of the hypothesis of the induction on i), $\{A_1, A_2, \ldots, A_n\}$ entails B_k.
CASE 2: B_k is obtained by one of the three rules $\sim$I, $\supset$I, and $\forall$I*. Then, by essentially the same reasoning as in Basis'', $\{A_1, A_2, \ldots, A_n\}$ entails B_k.

Hence (as announced on p. 279) the **Soundness Theorem:**

> (3.3.8) Let S be a finite set of statements. If a statement A is derivable from S in accordance with rules R, $\sim$I, $\sim$E, $\supset$I, $\supset$E, $\forall$I*, and $\forall$E, then A is entailed by S.

Incidentally, our first five entailment lemmas on p. 276 do hold with 'truth-functionally entails' in place of 'entails'; so the foregoing argument *minus* all references to the intelim rules for '$\forall$' guarantees that the last line of any derivation done in accordance with just rules R, ~I, ~E, ⊃I, and ⊃E is truth-functionally entailed by the assumptions of the derivation. Hence:

> (3.3.9) Let S be a finite set of statements. If A is derivable from S in accordance with rules R, ~I, ~E, ⊃I, and ⊃E, then A is truth-functionally entailed by S.

Corollaries

Our Soundness Theorem has two interesting corollaries.

First, suppose that a statement A is provable in accordance with rules R, ~I, ~E, ⊃I, ⊃E, ∀I*, and ∀E, and hence is derivable from the set ∅ in accordance with these rules. Then, in view of (3.3.8), A is entailed by ∅. Hence, $\{\sim A\}$ is semantically inconsistent. Hence, A is logically true.

> (3.3.10) If A is provable in accordance with rules R, ~I, ~E, ⊃I, ⊃E, ∀I*, and ∀E, then A is logically true.

Hence, by the same reasoning, but appealing to (3.3.9) rather than (3.3.8):

> (3.3.11) If A is provable in accordance with rules R, ~I, ~E, ⊃I, and ⊃E, then A is truth-functionally true (i.e., A is a tautology).

Next, suppose that a finite but non-empty set S of statements is syntactically inconsistent. Then there is a statement A such that $S \vdash A$ and $S \vdash \sim A$, and hence in view of (3.3.8) such that S entails both A and $\sim A$. But, if so, then S is semantically inconsistent. For suppose there were a truth-value assignment to the atomic subformulas of the members of S on which all these members are true. Then by (3.2.1) there would be one to the atomic subformulas of the members of S and to those of A and of $\sim A$ on which all the members of S are true. But, as S entails both A and $\sim A$, these two statements would have to be true on that assignment, which is impossible. Hence:

> (3.3.12) Let S be a finite but non-empty set of statements. If S is semantically consistent, then S is syntactically consistent.

Finally, suppose ∅ were syntactically inconsistent. Then there would be a statement A such that $\vdash A$ and $\vdash \sim A$, and hence in view of (3.3.10) such that both A and $\sim A$ are logically true, which is impossible. Hence:

> (3.3.13) ∅ is syntactically consistent.

Hence, as announced on p. 269 of Section 3.2:

> (3.3.14) Let S be a finite set of statements. If S is semantically consistent, then S is syntactically consistent.

EXERCISES

E3.3.1.
   (a) Show in connection with ∃I that if $\{A_1, A_2, \ldots, A_n\}$ entails $B(T/X)$ for some
       term T, then $\{A_1, A_2, \ldots, A_n\}$ entails $(\exists X)B$.
   (b) Show in connection with ∃E that if (i) $\{A_1, A_2, \ldots, A_n\}$ entails $(\exists X)B$, (ii)
       $\{A_1, A_2, \ldots, A_n, B(T/X)\}$ entails C, and (iii) T is foreign to $\{A_1, A_2, \ldots, A_n\}$ and
       to both $(\exists X)B$ and C, then $\{A_1, A_2, \ldots, A_n\}$ entails C. (Note: Proof of (b)
       can be retrieved from the proof of (3.1.19), using (3.3.1) in place of R,
       (3.3.2) in place of ~I, and so on.)

E3.3.2.   Using the results in E1.3.7(d) and E3.3.1, show that (3.3.8) generalizes to
the case where A is derivable from S in accordance with R and the intelim rules of
Sections 1.3 and 2.3 for all seven of '~', '⊃', '&', 'V', '≡', '∀', and '∃'.

E3.3.3.   With S understood to be an infinite set of statements, show that:
   (a) If there is a truth-value assignment to the atomic subformulas of the mem-
       bers of S on which all the members of S are true, then S is syntactically
       consistent;
   (b) If every finite subset of S is semantically consistent, then S is syntactically
       consistent.

E3.3.4.   Using the result in E3.3.3(b), show that $\{Fa_1, Fa_2, \ldots, Fa_n, \ldots, \sim(\forall x)Fx\}$,
and each one of the sets in E2.1.17, is syntactically consistent.

E3.3.5.   Show that:
   (a) Any statement of any one of the six sorts A1–A6 on p. 328 is logically true,
       and
   (b) If any conservative instance of $(\forall X)A$ is logically true, then $(\forall X)A$ is log-
       ically true as well.

E3.3.6.   With a conjunction understood in this exercise and the next to be true on a
truth-value assignment α if and only if its left-hand conjunct is true on α, show that:
   (a) If $\{A_1, A_2, \ldots, A_n\}$ entails each one of B and C, then $\{A_1, A_2, \ldots, A_n\}$ still
       entails B & C;
   (b) If $\{A_1, A_2, \ldots, A_n\}$ entails B & C, then $\{A_1, A_2, \ldots, A_n\}$ still entails B; but
   (c) $\{P \& Q\}$ no longer entails 'Q'.

E3.3.7.   When a conjunction B & C is derivable from a set $\{A_1, A_2, \ldots, A_n\}$ of assumptions, one form of &E permits assertion of B on these assumptions, the other
permits assertion of C. With A a statement and S a finite set of statements, show
that:
   (a) If A can be derived from S without using the second form of &E, then A
       is sure to be entailed by S under the reinterpretation of '&' in E3.3.6.
and hence that:
   (b) 'Q' cannot be derived from $\{P \& Q\}$.

E3.3.8.   Using a similar line of reasoning, show that 'P' cannot be derived from
$\{P \& Q\}$ without using the first form of &E. (This time around, provisionally take
B & C to be true on a truth-value assignment α if and only if C is true on α.)

E3.3.9.   One form of VI permits assertion of a disjunction B V C on some assumptions A_1, A_2, ..., and A_n when B is derivable from $\{A_1,A_2,...,A_n\}$; the other form of VI permits assertion of $B \lor C$ when C is derivable from $\{A_1,A_2,...,A_n\}$. Show that:

(a) 'P $\lor$ Q' cannot be derived from $\{P\}$ without using the first form of VI, and

(b) 'P $\lor$ Q' cannot be derived from $\{Q\}$ without using the second form of VI.

(Note: When proving (a), take $B \lor C$ to be true on a truth-value assignment α if and only if C is true on α; when proving (b), take $B \lor C$ to be true on a truth-value assignment α if and only if B is true on α.)

E3.3.10   One form of $\equiv$E permits assertion of C on some assumptions A_1, A_2, ..., and A_n when $B \equiv C$ and B are both derivable from $\{A_1,A_2,...,A_n\}$; the other form of $\equiv$E permits assertion of C when $C \equiv B$ and B are both derivable from $\{A_1,A_2,...,A_n\}$. Show that:

(a) 'Q' cannot be derived from $\{P, P \equiv Q\}$ without using the first form of $\equiv$E, and

(b) 'Q' cannot be derived from $\{P, Q \equiv P\}$ without using the second form of $\equiv$E.

(Note: When proving (a), take $B \equiv C$ to be true on a truth-value assignment α if and only if C is false on α or B is true on α; when proving (b), take $B \equiv C$ to be true on a truth-value assignment α if and only if B is false on α or C is true on α.)

*E3.3.11.   Let S be a finite set of statements.

(a) Supposing that each member of $S \cup \{A\}$ is an atomic statement, show that S entails A if and only if A belongs to S.

(b) Supposing that each member of $S \cup \{A\}$ is an atomic statement or a conjunction of two or more atomic statements, show that S entails A if and only if each atomic component of A occurs in some member or other of S.

(c) Supposing that each member of $S \cup \{A\}$ is an atomic statement or a disjunction of two or more atomic statements, show that S entails A if and only if each atomic component of some one member of S occurs in A.

3.4   The Completeness Theorem

Making good a second promise, we go on to show that any statement entailed by a finite set of statements is sure to be derivable from the set in accordance with rules R, $\sim$I, $\sim$E, $\supset$I, $\supset$E, $\forall$I*, and $\forall$E; and hence that any logical truth is provable in accordance with these rules.

The theorem follows in a mere seven lines from the result of Henkin's reported earlier: *If a finite (but non-empty) set S of statements is syntactically consistent, then S is semantically consistent as well,* or—to put it the other way round—if a finite (but non-empty) set S of statements is semantically inconsistent, then S is syntactically inconsistent as well. For suppose a finite (but this time possibly empty) set S' of statements does entail a statement A. Then by definition the set $S' \cup \{\sim A\}$ (which is not empty even when S' is) is semantically inconsistent, hence by Henkin's result $S' \cup \{\sim A\}$ is syntactically inconsistent as well, and hence by (3.2.20) $S' \vdash A$. Hence, any statement entailed by a finite set of statements is derivable from the set in accordance with rules R, ~I, ~E, ⊃I, ⊃E, ∀I*, and ∀E.

To prove Henkin's result, *we assume the above set S to be syntactically consistent*, construct another set S_∞ (this one infinite), supply a truth-value assignment α on which all the members of S_∞ are demonstrably true, and—S being a subset of S_∞—conclude that all the members of S are true on α. Since a semantically consistent set of statements is one whose members are all true on some common truth-value assignment, we shall have it that, if S is syntactically consistent, then S is semantically consistent as well.

The Two Sets S* and S**

Before we embark upon the construction of S_∞, we must introduce two auxiliary sets which will play a considerable part in the whole undertaking: $S*$ and $S**$.

A statement A will belong to $S*$ if and only if A is an atomic subformula of a member of S; and a statement A will belong to $S**$ if and only if every atomic subformula of A belongs to $S*$. $S*$ will thus consist of the atomic subformulas of the members of S; and $S**$ will consist of the various statements whose atomic subformulas all belong to $S*$, i.e., of the various statements (among them the members of S) which can be truth-functionally or quantificationally compounded from the members of $S*$. As regards size, $S*$ will be infinite just in case at least one member of S has a non-vacuous quantification among its subformulas. $S**$, on the other hand, is sure to be infinite. Suppose, for example, that S—and, hence, $S*$—had just one member: 'Fa$_1$'. Since 'Fa$_1$' is the one atomic subformula of '~Fa$_1$', '~~Fa$_1$', '~~~Fa$_1$', and so on, these infinitely many negations (plus infinitely many other truth-functional compounds of 'Fa$_1$') would all belong to $S**$.[1]

The following will be recalled later:

(a) S is a subset of $S**$;
(b) Every atomic statement in $S**$ belongs to $S*$;
(c) If A belongs to $S**$ and all the atomic subformulas of B are among those of A, then B also belongs to $S**$; and
(d) Every subformula of every statement in $S**$ belongs to $S**$.

(a)–(b) are obvious. As for (c), if A belongs to $S**$, then all the atomic subformulas of A belong to $S*$. Hence, if all the atomic subformulas of B are among those of A, then all the atomic subformulas of B belong to $S*$,

---

[1] Since $S**$ is sure to be infinite, and like any other set of statements has *at most* $\aleph_0$ members, $S**$ has *exactly* $\aleph_0$ members.

and hence B belongs to S^{**}. And as for (d), suppose B is a subformula of a member A of S^{**}. Since all the atomic subformulas of B are sure to be among those of A, B is sure in virtue of (c) to belong to S^{**}.

As explained in Section 3.2, the members of S^{**} can be arranged in some definite order, known as their *alphabetic order*. Accordingly, we shall feel free in the next few pages to talk of a given member of S^{**} as being the alphabetically n–th (say, the alphabetically first, or tenth, or one-millionth) member of S^{**}. Since the terms 'a_1', 'a_2', 'a_3', and so on, already come in alphabetic order, we shall also feel free to talk of a given term as being the alphabetically earliest one to be foreign to a given statement or to a given set of statements.

The Set S_∞

We construct S_∞ by so adding statements to the set S that we can prove (e)–(j) below and, via these, (k)–(m) on p. 290.[2]

First, take S_0 to be S itself. Next, A_n being for each n from 1 on the alphabetically n th member of S^{**}, define S_n as follows:

(i)   if $S_{n-1} \cup \{A_n\}$ is syntactically inconsistent, take S_n to be $S_{n-1} \cup \{\sim A_n\}$,

(ii) if $S_{n-1} \cup \{A_n\}$ is syntactically consistent, and A_n is *not* of the sort $\sim(\forall X)B$, take S_n to be $S_{n-1} \cup \{A_n\}$, and

(iii) if $S_{n-1} \cup \{A_n\}$ is syntactically consistent, and A_n is the negation $\sim(\forall X)B$ of a universal quantification $(\forall X)B$, take S_n to be $S_{n-1} \cup \{\sim(\forall X)B, \sim B(T/X)\}$, where T is the alphabetically earliest term that is foreign to S_{n-1} and A_n.[3]

Finally, take S_∞ to be the union of S_0, S_1, S_2, and so on (i.e., let S_∞ consist of all the members of S_0 $(= S)$, *plus* whichever statement or statements were added to S_0 to obtain S_1, *plus* whichever statement or statements were added to S_1 to obtain S_2, and so on). Note, incidentally, that—however large n may be—there is sure to be in case (iii) at least one term that is foreign to S_{n-1} and $\sim(\forall X)B$, since only finitely many terms occur in any one statement and S_{n-1} has only finitely many members.[4]

S_∞ has a number of crucial features:

(e) S is a subset of S_∞;

(f) S_∞ is a subset of S^{**};

---

[2] Exercise E3.4.3 sheds further light on this matter.

[3] If X does not occur in B, then of course $\sim B(T/X)$ is the same as $\sim B$.

[4] The same would hold true if S were infinite, but infinitely many terms were nonetheless foreign to S. Sets of statements to which infinitely many terms are foreign were called *infinitely extendible*. They will play a major role in Section 3.6.

(g) S_∞ is syntactically consistent (if, as assumed here, S is syntactically consistent);

(h)   For every statement A in S^{**}, either A or $\sim A$ belongs to S_∞;

(i)   For every statement in S^{**} of the sort $\sim(\forall X)B$, if $\sim(\forall X)B$ belongs to S_∞, then there is at least one term T such that $\sim B(T/X)$ also belongs to S_∞; and

(j)   For every statement A in S^{**}, if $S_\infty \vdash A$, then A belongs to S_∞.

Incidentally, since S^{**} has infinitely many members, so does S_∞ in view of (h). Hence our use of results from pp. 266–70 in what follows.[5]

(e) is obvious. And so is (f). For in view of (a) on p. 286, S ($= S_0$) is a subset of S^{**}; and in view of (c) on the same page $\sim A_n$ belongs to S^{**} if A_n does, and $\sim B(T/X)$ belongs to S^{**} if $\sim(\forall X)B$ does.

To prove (g) we first establish that, for each n from 0 on, S_n is syntactically consistent. The proof, as announced in Section 3.2, is by *weak* mathematical induction on n.

BASIS: $n = 0$. Then S_n is S, and by assumption is syntactically consistent.

INDUCTIVE STEP: $n > 0$. Let A_n be the alphabetically n-th member of S^{**}.

CASE 1: $S_{n-1} \cup \{A_n\}$ is syntactically inconsistent, in which case S_n is $S_{n-1} \cup \{\sim A_n\}$. Suppose S_n is syntactically inconsistent. Then

$$S_{n-1} \vdash A_n \tag{1}$$

by (3.2.20). But, since in this case $S_{n-1} \cup \{A_n\}$ is syntactically inconsistent,

$$S_{n-1} \vdash \sim A_n \tag{2}$$

by (3.2.19). Hence, in view of (1) and (2), S_{n-1} is syntactically inconsistent. Hence, if S_n is syntactically inconsistent, then so is S_{n-1}. Hence, if S_{n-1} is syntactically consistent, then so is S_n.

CASE 2: $S_{n-1} \cup \{A_n\}$ is syntactically consistent, but A_n is not of the sort $\sim(\forall X)B$, in which case S_n is $S_{n-1} \cup \{A_n\}$. Then S_n is syntactically consistent, and hence is syntactically consistent if S_{n-1} is.

CASE 3: $S_{n-1} \cup \{A_n\}$ is syntactically consistent and A_n is the negation $\sim(\forall X)B$ of a universal quantification $(\forall X)B$, in which case S_n is $S_{n-1} \cup \{\sim(\forall X)B, \sim B(T/X)\}$, where T is a term foreign to S_{n-1} and $\sim(\forall X)B$. Suppose S_n is syntactically inconsistent. Then $S_{n-1} \cup \{\sim(\forall X)B\}$ $\vdash B(T/X)$ by (3.2.20), and—T being foreign to S_{n-1} and $(\forall X)B$—

$$S_{n-1} \cup \{\sim(\forall X)B\} \vdash (\forall X)B \tag{3}$$

---

[5] In view of one of these results, $S_\infty \vdash A$ if A belongs to S_∞; so, in view of (j), derivability from S_∞ and membership in S_∞ match each other exactly.

by $\forall I^*$. But

$$S_{n-1} \cup \{\sim(\forall X)B\} \vdash \sim(\forall X)B \tag{4}$$

by R. Hence, in view of (3) and (4), $S_{n-1} \cup \{\sim(\forall X)B\}$ is syntactically inconsistent. But $S_{n-1} \cup \{\sim(\forall X)B\}$ is $S_{n-1} \cup \{A_n\}$, which in this case is presumed to be syntactically consistent. Hence, our supposition that S_n is syntactically inconsistent proves untenable. Hence, S_n is syntactically consistent, and hence is syntactically consistent if S_{n-1} is.

This established, suppose S_∞ were syntactically inconsistent. Then in view of (3.2.18) some finite subset of S_∞, call it S'_∞, would also be syntactically inconsistent. But every member of the set S'_∞ which does not belong to S_0 belongs to S_1, or—if it does not belong to S_1—to S_2, or—if it does not belong to S_2—to S_3, and so on. Hence, since S'_∞ is finite, there is sure to be an n such that every member of S'_∞ belongs to S_n (and, of course, to S_{n+1}, S_{n+2}, S_{n+3}, and so on). Hence, in view of (3.2.18), S_n (plus, of course, S_{n+1}, S_{n+2}, S_{n+3}, and so on) would also be syntactically inconsistent, when—as we just saw—none of S_0, S_1, S_2, and so on, is syntactically inconsistent. Hence S_∞ is sure to be syntactically consistent.

That (h) holds true is obvious from the construction of S_∞. A, being a member of S^{**}, is sure to be—for some n or other—the alphabetically n-th member of S^{**}, and hence either A or $\sim A$ belongs to S_n. But S_n is a subset of S_∞. Hence, either A or $\sim A$ belongs to S_∞.

That (i) holds true follows from the construction of S_∞ and from (g). $\sim(\forall X)B$, being a member of S^{**}, is sure to be—for some n or other—the alphabetically n-th member of S^{**}. Now suppose that $\sim(\forall X)B$ belongs to S_∞ and hence in view of (3.2.5) is derivable from S_∞. Then $S_{n-1} \cup \{\sim(\forall X)B\}$ is sure to be syntactically consistent. For, if $S_{n-1} \cup \{\sim(\forall X)B\}$ were syntactically inconsistent, then in view of (3.2.20) $(\forall X)B$ would be derivable from S_{n-1} and hence in view of (3.2.3) from S_∞, and S_∞ would be syntactically inconsistent, as against (g). But, if $S_{n-1} \cup \{\sim(\forall X)B\}$ is syntactically consistent, then S_n is $S_{n-1} \cup \{\sim(\forall X)B, \sim B(T/X)\}$ for some term T. Hence, if $\sim(\forall X)B$ belongs to S_∞, then there is at least one term T such that $\sim B(T/X)$ belongs to S_n and hence to S_∞.[6]

Finally, that (j) holds true follows from (g) and (h). Suppose indeed that, for some statement A in S^{**}, A were derivable from S_∞ and yet did not belong to S_∞. Then in view of (h) $\sim A$ would belong to S_∞, hence, in view of (3.2.5) $\sim A$ would also be derivable from S_∞, and hence S_∞ would be syntactically inconsistent, as against (g). Hence, if $S_\infty \vdash A$, then A belongs to S_∞.

Because of (e)–(j) S_∞ has three further features which bring us to the very heart of the matter, namely: *For every statement A in S^{**},*

---

[6] Note that if X does not occur in B, $\sim B(T/X)$ belongs to S_∞ (if $\sim(\forall X)B$ does) for every term T, this because $\sim B(T/X)$ is the same as $\sim B$.

(k)   If A is a negation $\sim B$, then A belongs to S_∞ if and only if B does not belong to S_∞;

(l)   If A is a conditional $B \supset C$, then A belongs to S_∞ if and only if B does not belong to S_∞ or C belongs to S_∞; and

(m)   If A is a universal quantification $(\forall X)B$, then A belongs to S_∞ if and only if $B(T/X)$ belongs to S_∞ for every term T.

Proof of (k) is as follows. Suppose that both $\sim B$ and B belong to S_∞. Then in view of (3.2.5) both $\sim B$ and B are derivable from S_∞, and hence S_∞ is syntactically inconsistent, as against (g). Hence, if $\sim B$ belongs to S_∞, then B does not. Conversely, by hypothesis $\sim B \, (= A)$ belongs to S^{**}, hence by (d) on p. 286 B also belongs to S^{**}, hence by (h) either B or $\sim B$ belongs to S_∞, and hence B belongs to S_∞ if $\sim B$ does not. Hence, $\sim B$ belongs to S_∞ if and only if B does not belong to S_∞.

For proof of (l), suppose first that both $B \supset C$ and B belong to S_∞. Then in view of (3.2.5) both $B \supset C$ and B are derivable from S_∞, hence in view of (3.2.9) C is derivable from S_∞, and hence by (j) C belongs to S_∞. Hence, if $B \supset C$ belongs to S_∞, then either B does not belong to S_∞ or else C does. Next, suppose that B does not belong to S_∞. By hypothesis $B \supset C (= A)$ belongs to S^{**}, hence by (d) on p. 286 B also belongs to S^{**}, and hence by (k) $\sim B$ belongs to S_∞. So, in view of (3.2.5) $\sim B$ is derivable from S_∞, hence in view of (3.2.10) $B \supset C$ is derivable from S_∞, and hence by (j) $B \supset C$ belongs to S_∞. Finally, suppose that C belongs to S_∞. Then in view of (3.2.5) C is derivable from S_∞, hence in view of (3.2.10) again $B \supset C$ is derivable from S_∞, and hence by (j) $B \supset C$ belongs to S_∞. So, $B \supset C$ belongs to S_∞ if and only if B does not belong to S_∞ or C belongs to S_∞.

And, for proof of (m), suppose first that $(\forall X)B$ belongs to S_∞. Then in view of (3.2.5) $(\forall X)B$ is derivable from S_∞, hence in view of (3.2.13) $B(T/X)$ is derivable from S_∞ for every term T, and hence by (j) $B(T/X)$ belongs to S_∞ for every term T. Suppose next that $(\forall X)B$ does not belong to S_∞. Then by (h) $\sim(\forall X)B$ belongs to S_∞ (and hence, by (f), to S^{**}). Hence, by (i) there is at least one term T such that $\sim B(T/X)$ belongs to S_∞ (and hence, by (f), to S^{**}). Hence, by (k) there is at least one term T such that $B(T/X)$ does not belong to S_∞. So $(\forall X)B$ belongs to S_∞ if and only if $B(T/X)$ belongs to S_∞ for every term T.

The Truth-Value Assignment α

Let α be the result of assigning **T** to every member of S^* that belongs to S_∞, and **F** to the remaining members of S^*. Given (k)–(m) it is readily shown by mathematical induction on the length l of an arbitrary member A of S^{**} that A is true on α if and only if A belongs to S_∞. Hence, every member of S^{**} that belongs to S_∞ is true on α. Hence, in view of (f) every member of S_∞ is true on α.

The induction is as follows.

BASIS: $l = 1$. Then A is atomic, and hence in view of (b) on p. 286 belongs to S^*. But, by the very construction of α, A is assigned **T** in α if and only if A belongs to S_∞. Hence, A is true on α if and only if A belongs to S_∞.

INDUCTIVE STEP: $l > 1$. Then A is of one of the three sorts $\sim B$, $B \supset C$, and $(\forall X)B$. Assume any member of S^{**} of a length less than l to be true on α if and only if it belongs to S_∞.

CASE 1: A is of the sort $\sim B$. In view of (d) on p. 286 B belongs to S^{**}. Hence, by the hypothesis of the induction, B is true on α if and only if B belongs to S_∞. Hence, B is not true on α if and only if B does not belong to S_∞. Hence, $\sim B$ is true on α if and only if B does not belong to S_∞. Hence, in view of (k), $\sim B$ is true on α if and only if $\sim B$ belongs to S_∞.

CASE 2: A is of the sort $B \supset C$. In view of (d) both B and C belong to S^{**}. Hence, by the hypothesis of the induction, B is true on α if and only if B belongs to S_∞, and C is true on α if and only if C belongs to S_∞. Hence, B is not true on α or C is true on α if and only if B does not belong to S_∞ or C belongs to S_∞. Hence, $B \supset C$ is true on α if and only if B does not belong to S_∞ or C belongs to S_∞. Hence, in view of (l), $B \supset C$ is true on α if and only if $B \supset C$ belongs to S_∞.

CASE 3: A is of the sort $(\forall X)B$. Suppose that $(\forall X)B$ is true on α. Then each one of $B(a_1/X)$, $B(a_2/X)$, $B(a_3/X)$, and so on, is true on α. But in view of (d) each one of $B(a_1/X)$, $B(a_2/X)$, $B(a_3/X)$, and so on, belongs to S^{**}. Hence, by the hypothesis of the induction, each one of $B(a_1/X)$, $B(a_2/X)$, $B(a_3/X)$, and so on, belongs to S_∞. Hence, in view of (m), $(\forall X)B$ belongs to S_∞. Hence, if $(\forall X)B$ is true on α, then $(\forall X)B$ belongs to S_∞. But, by the same reasoning, if $(\forall X)B$ is not true on α, then $(\forall X)B$ does not belong to S_∞. Hence, $(\forall X)B$ is true on α if and only $(\forall X)B$ belongs to S_∞.

Now for the final (and expected) moves in the whole undertaking. Since every member of S_∞ is true on α, and since in view of (e) S is a subset of S_∞, every member of S is true on α. Hence, there is a truth-value assignment to the members of S^* on which every member of S is true. But the members of S^* are the atomic subformulas of the members of S. So, there is a truth-value assignment to the atomic subformulas of the members of S on which every member of S is true.[7] Hence, S is seman-

---

[7] In view of footnote 4, the result would still hold true if S were infinite, but infinitely extendible, a point we shall recall in Section 3.6. Then all of (a)–(m) would still go through, and hence so would the induction we just conducted.

tically consistent. Hence, if S is syntactically consistent (the assumption under which our whole proof has proceeded), then S is semantically consistent as well. Hence, Henkin's Lemma:

> *(3.4.1)*   Let S be a finite and non-empty set of statements. If S is syntactically consistent, then S is semantically consistent.

Hence (by the reasoning on pp. 285–86), the **Completeness Theorem:**

> *(3.4.2)*   Let S be a finite set of statements. If a statement A is entailed by S, then A is derivable from S in accordance with rules R, $\sim$I, $\sim$E, $\supset$I, $\supset$E, $\forall$I*, and $\forall$E.

The argument[8] readily generalizes to the case where all seven of '$\sim$', '$\supset$', '&', '$\lor$', '$\equiv$', '$\forall$', and '$\exists$' serve as primitive operators. Then A, if entailed by S, is sure to be derivable from S in accordance with all fifteen of the rules of Sections 1.3 and 2.3.[9]

If (i) S^* is taken to consist of the atomic components—in the sense of Section 1.1—of the various members of S, (ii) S^{**} is taken to consist of the various statements whose atomic components all belong to S^*, (iii) S_0 is again taken to be S, (iv) S_n is taken to be $S_{n-1} \cup \{\sim A_n\}$ if there is a statement B such that both B and $\sim B$ are derivable from $S_{n-1} \cup \{A_n\}$ in accordance with rules R, $\sim$I, $\sim$E, $\supset$I, and $\supset$E, otherwise to be $S_{n-1} \cup \{A_n\}$, (v) S_∞ is again taken to be the union of S_0, S_1, S_2, and so on, and (vi) α is again taken to be the result of assigning **T** to every member of S^* that belongs to S_∞, and **F** to every one that does not, it is possible to show—using just R, $\sim$I, $\sim$E, $\supset$I, and $\supset$E—that every member of S is true on α. So, by the same reasoning as on pp. 285–86:

> *(3.4.3)*   Let S be a finite set of statements. If A is truth-functionally entailed by S, then A is derivable from S in accordance with rules R, $\sim$I, $\sim$E, $\supset$I, and $\supset$E.

Corollaries

First, suppose that A is logically true. Then $\{\sim A\}$ is semantically inconsistent, and hence $\varnothing$ entails A. Hence, in view of (3.4.2):

> *(3.4.4)*   If A is logically true, then A is provable in accordance with rules R, $\sim$I, $\sim$E, $\supset$I, $\supset$E, $\forall$I*, and $\forall$E.[10]

---

[8] An adaptation of Henkin's own in "The completeness of the first-order functional calculus." *The Journal of Symbolic Logic,* vol. 14, 1949, pp. 159–66.

[9] See Exercise E3.4.5 on this matter.

[10] Kurt Gödel was the first to show that means of proof to the same effect as R, $\sim$I, $\sim$E, $\supset$I, $\supset$E, $\forall$I*, and $\forall$E permit proof of every logical truth: see "Die Vollständigkeit der Axiome des logischen Funktionenkalküls," *Monatshefte für Mathematik und Physik,* vol. 37, 1930, pp. 349–60.

Hence, appealing to (3.4.3) rather than (3.4.2):

> (*3.4.5*)   If A is truth-functionally true (i.e., if A is a tautology), then A is provable in accordance with rules R, $\sim$ I, $\sim$ E, $\supset$ I, and $\supset$ E.

Second, $\varnothing$ was declared semantically consistent by definition. Hence, (3.4.1) generalizes to any finite set of statements:

> (*3.4.6*)   Let S be a finite set of statements. If S is syntactically consistent, then S is semantically consistent.

Hence, in view of (3.3.14), the result we announced on p. 269:

> (*3.4.7*)   Let S be a finite set of statements. Then S is semantically consistent if and only if S is syntactically consistent.

EXERCISES

E3.4.1.   Show that if a given member A of S^{**} does not belong to S_∞, then $S_\infty \cup \{A\}$ is syntactically inconsistent (and hence that as many members of S^{**} belong to S_∞ as syntactic consistency permits).

E3.4.2.
  (a)   With S, S^*, S^{**}, and A_n understood to be as in the text, take S_0 to be S, take S_n to be $S_{n-1} \cup \{A_n\}$ if $S_{n-1} \vdash A_n$, otherwise to be S_{n-1}, and take S_∞ to be the union of S_0, S_1, S_2, etc. This done, show that (e), (f), (g), and (j) on pp. 287–88 still hold true.
  (b)   With S, S^*, S^{**}, and A_n again understood to be as in the text, take S_0 to be S, take S_n to be $S_{n-1} \cup \{A_n\}$ if $S_{n-1} \cup \{A_n\}$ is syntactically consistent, otherwise to be $S_{n-1} \cup \{\sim A_n\}$, and take S_∞ to be as before. This done, show that (e), (f), (g), (h), and (j) on pp. 287–88 still hold true.

E3.4.3.   Supposing '&', 'V', '$\equiv$', and '$\exists$' to serve as primitive (rather than defined) operators, show that S_∞ as defined on p. 287 has the following four extra features: *For every statement A in S^{**},*
  (n)   If A is a conjunction $B \ \& \ C$, then A belongs to S_∞ if and only if both B and C belong to S_∞,
  (o)   If A is a disjunction $B \ V \ C$, then A belongs to S_∞ if and only if at least one of B and C belongs to S_∞,
  (p)   If A is a biconditional $B \equiv C$, then A belongs to S_∞ if and only if both B and C belong to S_∞ or neither one does, and
  (q)   If A is an existential quantification $(\exists X)B$, then A belongs to S_∞ if and only if there is at least one term T such that $B(T/X)$ belongs to S_∞.

(Hint: Use results (a)–(j) in E3.2.8.)

E3.4.4.   With all seven of '$\sim$', '$\supset$', '&', 'V', '$\equiv$', '$\forall$', and '$\exists$' understood to serve as primitive operators, show on the basis of E3.4.3 that if a statement A is entailed by a finite set S of statements, then A is sure to be derivable from S in accordance with R and the intelim rules of Sections 1.3 and 2.3.

E3.4.5. Reversing the procedure in the text, obtain (3.4.2) as a corollary of (3.4.4). (Hint: Use the definitions on p. 155, (3.1.11), and the two rules R and ⊃E.)

E3.4.6. Supposing a set S to be non-empty and infinitely extendible, show that S is syntactically consistent if and only if there is a truth-value assignment to the atomic subformulas of the members of S on which these members are true.

E3.4.7. Using E3.2.10, show that if $S \vdash A$, then either S is syntactically inconsistent, or $\vdash A$, or at least one member of S has an atomic subformula in common with A.

*E3.4.8.

    (a) Supposing S and A to be as in E3.3.11(a), and S to entail A, show that just R is necessary to derive A from S.

    (b) Supposing S and A to be as in E3.3.11(b), and S to entail A, show that just R, &I, and &E are necessary to derive A from S.

    (c) Supposing S and A to be as in E3.3.11(c), and S to entail A, show that just R, VI, and VE are necessary to derive A from S.

3.5 Trees: Some Metalogical Results

Returning to the topic of trees, we first show that any set of statements declared INCONSISTENT at Stage 5 of the routine on p. 189 is certain to be semantically inconsistent. We then go on to show that any set of statements declared CONSISTENT either at Stage 2 or at Stage 5 of the routine is certain to be semantically consistent. To keep in closer touch with Sections 1.2 and 2.2, we assume throughout this section that all seven of the operators '~', '⊃', '&', 'V', '≡', '∀', and '∃' are primitive.

Closed Trees

Proof that if a tree closes, the set being tested is semantically inconsistent, calls for one lemma, (3.5.1). The thirteen clauses there match the rules for decomposing compounds (see Appendix II). For example, clause (a) matches the rule for decomposing a conjunction $A \& B$; it guarantees that if $A \& B$ turns up on a branch of a tree, and the set consisting of all the entries so far on that branch is semantically consistent, then the set consisting of those entries *plus* both A and B is semantically consistent as well. Clause (b) matches the rule for decomposing a disjunction $A \vee B$; it guarantees that if $A \vee B$ turns up on a branch of a tree, and the set consisting of all the entries so far on that branch is semantically consistent, then *either* the set consisting of those entries *plus* A *or* the one consising of those entries *plus* B is semantically consistent as well. And so on. We leave to the reader proof of the first nine clauses, which match the truth-functional rules.

> *(3.5.1)*
> (a)   If $S \cup \{A \& B\}$ is semantically consistent, so is $S \cup \{A \& B, A, B\}$;
> (b)   If $S \cup \{A \vee B\}$ is semantically consistent, so is one of $S \cup \{A \vee B, A\}$ and $S \cup \{A \vee B, B\}$;
> (c)   If $S \cup \{A \supset B\}$ is semantically consistent, so is one of $S \cup \{A \supset B, \sim A\}$ and $S \cup \{A \supset B, B\}$;
> (d)   If $S \cup \{A \equiv B\}$ is semantically consistent, so is one of $S \cup \{A \equiv B, A, B\}$ and $S \cup \{A \equiv B, \sim A, \sim B\}$;
> (e)   If $S \cup \{\sim\sim A\}$ is semantically consistent, so is $S \cup \{\sim\sim A, A\}$;
> (f)   If $S \cup \{\sim(A \& B)\}$ is semantically consistent, so is one of $S \cup \{\sim(A \& B), \sim A\}$ and $S \cup \{\sim(A \& B), \sim B\}$;
> (g)   If $S \cup \{\sim(A \vee B)\}$ is semantically consistent, so is $S \cup \{\sim(A \vee B), \sim A, \sim B\}$;
> (h)   If $S \cup \{\sim(A \supset B)\}$ is semantically consistent, so is $S \cup \{\sim(A \supset B), A, \sim B\}$;
> (i)   If $S \cup \{\sim(A \equiv B)\}$ is semantically consistent, so is one of $S \cup \{\sim(A \equiv B), A, \sim B\}$ and $S \cup \{\sim(A \equiv B), \sim A, B\}$;
> (j)   If $S \cup \{(\forall X)A\}$ is semantically consistent, so is $S \cup \{(\forall X)A, A(T/X)\}$ for any term T;
> (k)   If $S \cup \{\sim(\exists X)A\}$ is semantically consistent, so is $S \cup \{\sim(\exists X)A, \sim A(T/X)\}$ for any term T;
> (l)   If $S \cup \{(\exists X)A\}$ is semantically consistent, so is $S \cup \{(\exists X)A, A(T/X)\}$ for any term T foreign to S and to $(\exists X)A$;
> (m)   If $S \cup \{\sim(\forall X)A\}$ is semantically consistent, so is $S \cup \{\sim(\forall X)A, \sim A(T/X)\}$ for any term T foreign to S and to $\sim(\forall X)A$.

PROOF: (j) On any truth-value assignment on which $(\forall X)A$ is true, $A(T/X)$ is true as well for any term T. Hence (j). (k) On any truth-value assignment on which $\sim(\exists X)A$ is true, $(\forall X)\sim A$ is true as well. Hence (k) by (j). (l) With T understood to be foreign to S and to $(\exists X)A$, suppose $S \cup \{(\exists X)A, A(T/X)\}$ is semantically inconsistent. Then $S \cup \{(\exists X)A, A(T/X)\} \vdash \sim(\exists X)A$ by (3.2.15). But $S \cup \{(\exists X)A\} \vdash (\exists X)A$ by R. Hence $S \cup \{(\exists X)A\} \vdash \sim(\exists X)A$ by $\exists$E* and the hypothesis on T. But, as just noted, $S \cup \{(\exists X)A\} \vdash (\exists X)A$ by R. Hence $S \cup \{(\exists X)A\}$ is syntactically inconsistent, and hence by (3.3.12) semantically inconsistent as well. Hence, if $S \cup \{(\exists X)A, A(T/X)\}$ is semantically inconsistent, so is $S \cup \{(\exists X)A\}$. Hence (l). (m) On any truth-value assignment on which $\sim(\forall X)A$ is true, $(\exists X)\sim A$ is true as well. Hence (m) by (l).

Now suppose that every branch of a tree for some set S of statements closes, and let S_1 consist of all the entries on the left-most branch of the tree, S_2 consist of all the entries on the next branch, . . ., and S_n ($n \geq 1$) consist of all the entries on the right-most branch. If S is semantically consistent, then by virtue of (3.5.1) at least one of S_1, S_2, . . ., and S_n is sure to be semantically consistent as well. But, as a contradiction (i.e., an atomic statement and its negation) appears on every branch of the tree, a contradiction *does* belong to each one of S_1, S_2, . . ., and S_n. Hence, none of these sets can be semantically consistent, and S itself must be semantically inconsistent.

Should an illustration be needed, take the tree on p. 182. If

$$\{(\forall x)Cx \text{ V } (\forall x)\sim Wx, (\exists x)(\sim Cx \text{ \& } Wx)\},$$

the set S being tested, is semantically consistent, then by clause (b) in (3.5.1) so is one of the two sets

$$\{(\forall x)Cx \text{ V } (\forall x)\sim Wx, (\exists x)(\sim Cx \text{ \& } Wx), (\forall x)Cx\}$$

and

$$\{(\forall x)Cx \text{ V } (\forall x)\sim Wx, (\exists x)(\sim Cx \text{ \& } Wx), (\forall x)\sim Wx\}.$$

But, if the set $\{(\forall x)Cx \text{ V } (\forall x)\sim Wx, (\exists x)(\sim Cx \text{ \& } Wx), (\forall x)Cx\}$ is semantically consistent, then by clause (l) so is

$$\{(\forall x)Cx \text{ V } (\forall x)\sim Wx, (\exists x)(\sim Cx \text{ \& } Wx), (\forall x)Cx, \sim Ca \text{ \& } Wa\},$$

hence by clause (a) so is

$$\{(\forall x)Cx \text{ V } (\forall x)\sim Wx, (\exists x)(\sim Cx \text{ \& } Wx), (\forall x)Cx, \sim Ca \text{ \& } Wa, \sim Ca, Wa\},$$

and hence by clause (j) so is

$$\{(\forall x)Cx \text{ V } (\forall x)\sim Wx, (\exists x)(\sim Cx \text{ \& } Wx), (\forall x)Cx, \sim Ca \text{ \& } Wa, \sim Ca, Wa, Ca\} (= S_1).$$

And, if the set $\{(\forall x)Cx \text{ V } (\forall x)\sim Wx, (\exists x)(\sim Cx \text{ \& } Wx), (\forall x)\sim Wx\}$ is semantically consistent, then by the very same clauses in (3.5.1) so is

$$\{(\forall x)Cx \text{ V } (\forall x)\sim Wx, (\exists x)(\sim Cx \text{ \& } Wx), (\forall x)\sim Wx, \sim Ca \text{ \& } Wa, \sim Ca, Wa, \sim Wa\}$$
$$(= S_2).$$

But neither one of S_1 and S_2 can be semantically consistent. So S is sure to be semantically inconsistent.

Hence:

> (3.5.2)   If a finite and non-empty set of statements has a closed tree, then the set is semantically inconsistent.

Hence, in particular:

> (3.5.3)   If a finite and non-empty set of statements is declared INCONSISTENT at Stage 5 of the routine on p. 189, then the set is semantically inconsistent.

As remarked on p. 175, the converse of (3.5.2) also holds true: if a finite and non-empty set of statements is semantically inconsistent, then the set is sure to have a closed tree. Proof can further be given that if a finite and non-empty set of statements has a closed tree, then the tree constructed by the routine of p. 189 is sure to close. Practice in constructing trees by the routine should reveal, informally, why this is so: no opportunity for generating a contradiction is overlooked.

Hintikka Sets

When testing a set S of statements for (in)consistency via the tree routine of p. 189, the reader is sometimes notified that S is semantically *consistent* (CASES 2 and 3 on p. 190). In CASE 2, he will have answered Yes to the question posed at Stage 2 of the routine, as there is on the tree an *open and completed branch*.[1] In CASE 3, he will have answered Yes to both questions posed at Stage 5, as there is on the tree an *open branch* to which no addition was made since last entering Stage 5. (A branch of this sort will hereafter be called *characteristic of* CASE 3.) In each of the two CASES, we told the reader how to retrieve from that open branch a truth-value assignment on which—as we shall now establish—all the members of S are true.

One auxiliary notion is needed: that of a Hintikka set of statements.[2] S being a non-empty set of statements, and Σ_T consisting of all the terms (if any) which occur in the various members of S, call S a **Hintikka set** when S meets the following fourteen conditions:

(a)   If the negation $\sim A$ of an atomic statement A belongs to S, then A does *not* belong to S;

(b)   If the negation $\sim\sim A$ of a negation $\sim A$ belongs to S, then A also belongs to S;

(c)   If a conjunction $A \& B$ belongs to S, then both A and B also belong to S;

(d)   If the negation $\sim(A \& B)$ of a conjunction $A \& B$ belongs to S, then at least one of $\sim A$ and $\sim B$ also belongs to S;

(e)   If a disjunction $A \lor B$ belongs to S, then at least one of A and B also belongs to S;

---

[1] Recall that a completed branch is one to which no addition can be made. Hence, an open and completed branch has no line of the sort $(\forall X)A$ or $\sim(\exists X)A$.

[2] For the related notion of a *full Hintikka set*, see E3.5.4 below. Sets like those which we call Hintikka or full Hintikka sets were first studied by Hintikka under the name of *model sets;* see his *Two Papers on Symbolic Logic* in this connection.

(f)   If the negation $\sim(A \vee B)$ of a disjunction $A \vee B$ belongs to S, then both $\sim A$ and $\sim B$ also belong to S;

(g)   If a conditional $A \supset B$ belongs to S, then at least one of $\sim A$ and B also belongs to S;

(h)   If the negation $\sim(A \supset B)$ of a conditional $A \supset B$ belongs to S, then both A and $\sim B$ also belong to S;

(i)   If a biconditional $A \equiv B$ belongs to S, then either both A and B also belong to S or both $\sim A$ and $\sim B$ also belong to S;

(j)   If the negation $\sim(A \equiv B)$ of a biconditional $A \equiv B$ belongs to S, then either both A and $\sim B$ also belong to S or both $\sim A$ and B also belong to S;

(k)   If a universal quantification $(\forall X)A$ belongs to S, then *for each term T in* $\Sigma_T A(T/X)$ also belongs to S;

(l)   If the negation $\sim(\forall X)A$ of a universal quantification $(\forall X)A$ belongs to S, then there is at least one term T such that $\sim A(T/X)$ belongs to S;

(m)   If an existential quantification $(\exists X)A$ belongs to S, then there is at least one term T such that $A(T/X)$ also belongs to S; and

(n)   If the negation $\sim(\exists X)A$ of an existential quantification $(\exists X)A$ belongs to S, then *for each term T in* $\Sigma_T \sim A(T/X)$ also belongs to S.

It is easily verified that the set consisting of all the lines on an open and completed branch is a Hintikka set. Take, for example, the second tree on p. 194. The set consisting of the ten lines on the left-hand branch is a Hintikka set (to which belongs no unnegated universal or negated existential quantification): one disjunct of line 1 belongs to the set, one instance of each one of lines 2, 3, and 6 belongs to the set, and both conjuncts of each one of lines 4 and 10 belong to the set.

Similarly, the set consisting of all the lines on a branch characteristic of CASE 3 is a Hintikka set. This time unnegated universal or negated existential quantifications will belong to the set, but these quantifications are sure to be "instantiated" in the set by means of all the terms there. Take, for example, the tree on p. 196. The set

$$\{(\forall x)\sim Fx \vee (\forall x)\,(\exists y)Dyx, (\exists x)Dxa, (\forall x)\sim Fx, Dba, \sim Fa, \sim Fb\}$$

consisting of all the lines on the left-hand branch is a Hintikka set: the one unnegated universal quantification belonging to the set is instantiated in the set by means of all the terms there. By contrast, the set consisting of the various lines on the right-hand branch is not a Hintikka set: lines 11–12 are not instantiated in the set.

The First Consistency Theorem

Attending first to CASE 2, we establish that if a Hintikka set of statements has no unnegated universal or negated existential quantifications among its members, then every member of the set is sure to be true on any truth-value assignment meeting condition (iii) below.

> (*3.5.4*)   Let S be a non-empty set of statements, S^* consist of all the atomic subformulas of the members of S, and α be a truth-value assignment to the members of S^*. If:
>
>   (i) S is a Hintikka set,
>   (ii) no member of S is of the sort $(\forall X)B$ or the sort $\sim(\exists X)B$, and
>   (iii) every member of S^* which belongs to S is assigned $\mathbf{T}$ in α, and every one whose negation belongs to S is assigned $\mathbf{F}$ in α,
>
> then every member of S is true on α.

PROOF by mathematical induction on the length l of an arbitrary member A of S.

BASIS: $l = 1$. Then A—being atomic—belongs to S^*, hence in view of (iii) is assigned $\mathbf{T}$ in α, and hence is true on α.

INDUCTIVE STEP: $l > 1$. Then in view of (ii) A is of one of the twelve sorts $\sim B$, where B is atomic, $\sim\sim B$, $B \supset C$, $\sim(B \supset C)$, $B \,\&\, C$, $\sim(B \,\&\, C)$, $B \lor C$, $\sim(B \lor C)$, $B \equiv C$, $\sim(B \equiv C)$, $\sim(\forall X)B$, and $(\exists X)B$. Suppose any member of S of a length less than l to be true on α.

CASE 1: A is of the sort $\sim B$, where B is atomic. Then B belongs to S^*, and in view of (iii) is assigned $\mathbf{F}$ in α. Hence, $\sim B\,(= A)$ is true on α.
CASE 2: A is of the sort $\sim\sim B$. Then in view of (i) B belongs to S. But B is of a length less than l. Hence, by the hypothesis of the induction, B is true on α, and hence so is $\sim\sim B\,(= A)$.
CASE 3: A is of the sort $B \supset C$. Then in view of (i) $\sim B$ belongs to S or C does. But each one of $\sim B$ and C is of a length less than l. Hence, by the hypothesis of the induction, $\sim B$ is true on α or C is, and hence $B \supset C\,(= A)$ is true on α.
CASE 4. A is of the sort $\sim(B \supset C)$. Then in view of (i) both B and $\sim C$ belong to S. But each one of B and $\sim C$ is of a length less than l. Hence, by the hypothesis of the induction, both B and $\sim C$ are true on α, and hence so is $\sim(B \supset C)\,(= A)$.
CASES 5–10: A is of one of the six sorts $B \,\&\, C$, $\sim(B \,\&\, C)$, $B \lor C$, $\sim(B \lor C)$, $B \equiv C$, and $\sim(B \equiv C)$. Proofs left to the reader.

CASE 11: A is of the sort $(\exists X)B$. Then in view of (i) there is a term T such that $B(T/X)$ belongs to S. But $B(T/X)$ is of a length less than l. Hence, by the hypothesis of the induction, $B(T/X)$ is true on α, and hence so is $(\exists X)B (= A)$.

CASE 12: A is of the sort $\sim(\forall X)B$. Proof like that of CASE 11.

Now suppose that, as you enter or re-enter Stage 2 of the routine, there is an open and completed branch; and consider the truth-value assignment recommended on p. 190 for CASE 2: **T** to every atomic statement which occurs unnegated on that branch, and **F** to the remaining atomic subformulas of the members of the set tested. Since the set consisting of all the lines on the branch meets conditions (i)–(ii) in (3.5.4), and the foregoing truth-value assignment meets condition (iii) in (3.5.4), every line on the branch—and hence every member of the set tested—is sure to be true on the assignment. Hence, our first consistency theorem:

> (3.5.5) If a finite and non-empty set of statements is declared CONSISTENT at Stage 2 of the routine on p. 189, then every member of the set is true on the truth-value assignment of p. 190 for CASE 2, and hence the set is semantically consistent.

The Second Consistency Theorem

CASE 3 demands more sophisticated treatment. Suppose that an unnegated universal quantification $(\forall X)B$ belongs to a Hintikka set S of statements. Were each one of 'a_1', 'a_2', 'a_3', etc., to occur in some member or other of S, then all the instances of $(\forall X)B$ would belong to S. But if S consists of just the statements on a branch characteristic of CASE 3, then some terms (indeed infinitely many) will be foreign to these statements, some instances of $(\forall X)B$ (indeed infinitely many) will *not* belong to S, and any truth-value assignment for CASE 3 must ensure that the missing instances of $(\forall X)B$ behave like those which *do* belong to S.

Proof that the assignment recommended on p. 191 does the trick has three main parts.

Part One. (1) Let A be a statement; let S^* consist of all the atomic subformulas of A and possibly other atomic statements as well; let Σ_T consist of 'a_1', all the terms occurring in A, and possibly other terms as well; let Σ_T' consist of all the remaining terms; let **the a_1-rewrite of a member B of S^*** be the result of putting 'a_1' for each term in B which belongs to Σ_T'; and let α be a truth-value assignment to the members of S^* in which every member of S^* is assigned the same truth-value as its a_1-rewrite.[3]

---

[3] Clearly, the a_1-rewrite of each member B of S^* belongs to S^*. For if B appears in A, then B is its own a_1-rewrite, and hence belongs to S^*. And if B does *not* appear in A, then some

(2) If T belongs to Σ_T, let **the image f(T) of T** be T itself; if T is the alphabetically earliest member of Σ'_T, let the image f(T) of T be 'a$_1$'; and, for each i from 2 on, if T is the alphabetically i-th member of Σ'_T, let the image f(T) of T be the alphabetically $(i - 1)$th member of Σ'_T. And, where B is a subformula of A (or is like a subformula of A except for containing term variables at places where the subformula would contain terms), let **the image f(B) of B** be the result of simultaneously replacing all the terms in B by their respective images.

We proceed to show by mathematical induction on the length l of an arbitrary subformula B of A that *if the atomic subformulas of* f(B) *all belong to* S^* (and, hence, are all assigned truth-values in α), *then B is true on α if and only if* f(B) *is true on α.*

BASIS: $l = 1$, in which case B belongs to S^* and f(B) is atomic. Suppose that the atomic subformulas of f(B) all belong to S^*—i.e., suppose that f(B) belongs to S^*. By the very construction of α, each one of B and f(B) is assigned the same truth-value in α as its a$_1$-rewrite. But, as the reader may verify on his own, B and f(B) have the same a$_1$-rewrite. So B and f(B) must have the same truth-value on α. Hence, if the atomic subformulas of f(B) all belong to S^*, then B is true on α if and only if f(B) is true on α.

INDUCTIVE STEP: $l > 1$, in which case B is of one of the seven sorts $\sim C$, $C \supset D$, $C \,\&\, D$, $C \lor D$, $C \equiv D$, $(\forall X)C$, and $(\exists X)C$. Suppose that if a subformula of A is of a length less than l and the atomic subformulas of its image all belong to S^*, then the subformula is true on α if and only if its image is true on α (= hypothesis of the induction). Suppose also that the atomic subformulas of f(B) all belong to S^*.

> CASE 1: B is of the sort $\sim C$. C is a subformula of A, and is of a length less than l. Furthermore, the atomic subformulas of f(C), being those of f($\sim C$), all belong to S^*. Hence, by the hypothesis of the induction, C is true on α if and only if f(C) is true on α. Hence, $\sim C$ is true on α if and only if $\sim$f(C) (= f($\sim C$)) is true on α.
>
> CASES 2–5: B is of one of the four sorts $C \supset D$, $C \,\&\, D$, $C \lor D$, and $C \equiv D$. Proofs similar to that of CASE 1.
>
> CASE 6: B is of the sort $(\forall X)C$. PART ONE: (i) If T belongs to Σ_T, then (f(C))(T/X) is the same as f($C(T/X)$); and, for each i from 1 on, if T is the alphabetically i-th term in Σ'_T, and T' the alphabetically $(i + 1)$th one, then (f(C))(T/X) is the same as f($C(T'/X)$). So, each instance of $(\forall X)$f(C) (= f(($\forall X$)C)) is the image of some instance of $(\forall X)C$. (ii) If T belongs to Σ_T, then f($C(T/X)$) is the same as (f(C))

---

expression like B, except for containing term variables at places where B contains terms, *does* appear in A; hence, every result of putting terms for the variables in that expression belongs to S^*; hence, in particular, the result of putting 'a$_1$' for those variables belongs to S^*.

(T/X); if T is the alphabetically earliest member of Σ'_T, then $f(C(T/X))$ is the same as $(f(C))(a_1/X)$; and, for each i from 2 on, if T is the alphabetically i-th term in Σ'_T, and T' is the alphabetically $(i-1)$th one, then $f(C(T/X))$ is the same as $(f(C))(T'/X)$. So, the image of each instance of $(\forall X)C$ is an instance of $(\forall X)f(C)$ $(= f((\forall X)C))$. And (iii) the atomic subformulas of the image of each instance of $(\forall X)C$—being those of some instance of $(\forall X)f(C)$—all figure among the atomic subformulas of $(\forall X)f(C)$, and hence all belong to S^*. PART TWO: Suppose first that $(\forall X)C$ is true on α, and hence that every instance $C(T/X)$ of $(\forall X)C$ is true on α. Since $C(T/X)$ is a subformula of A and is of a length less than l, by the hypothesis of the induction and (iii) the image of each instance of $(\forall X)C$ is true on α; hence by (i) each instance of $(\forall X)f(C)$ is true on α; and hence $f((\forall X)C)$ is true on α. Suppose next that $(\forall X)C$ is not true on α, and hence that at least one instance of $(\forall X)C$ is not true on α. Then by the hypothesis of the induction and (iii) the image of at least one instance of $(\forall X)C$ is not true on α, hence by (ii) at least one instance of $(\forall X)f(C)$ is not true on α, and hence $f((\forall X)C)$ is not true on α. Hence, $(\forall X)C$ $(= B)$ is true on α if and only if $f((\forall X)C)$ $(= f(B))$ is true on α.

CASE 7: B is of the sort $(\exists X)C$. Proof similar to that of CASE 6.

Part Two. The italicized result on p. 301 has a crucial corollary. Suppose indeed that A is a universal quantification $(\forall X)B$, and that the subformula $B(T/X)$ of $(\forall X)B$ is true on α for every term T in Σ_T. Then in particular $B(a_1/X)$ is true on α. Now let T_1 be the alphabetically earliest member of Σ'_T. Since no term from Σ'_T occurs in B, $f(B(T_1/X))$ is the same as $B(a_1/X)$ and hence is true on α. But all the atomic subformulas of $B(a_1/X)$ figure among those of $(\forall X)B$, and hence they all belong to S^*. So, by the result on p. 301, $B(T_1/X)$ is likewise true on α. Next, let T_2 be the alphabetically second member of Σ'_T. Since no term from Σ'_T occurs in B, $f(B(T_2/X))$ is the same as $B(T_1/X)$ and hence is true on α. But all the atomic subformulas of $B(T_1/X)$ figure among those of $(\forall X)B$, and hence they all belong to S^*. So, by the result on p. 301, $B(T_2/X)$ is likewise true on α. And so on. Hence, $B(T/X)$ is true on α for every term in Σ'_T as well as every term in Σ_T.[4] Hence, $(\forall X)B$ is true on α. So, *if A is of the sort $(\forall X)B$ and $B(T/X)$ is true on α for every term T in Σ_T, then A is true on α;* and, by a like reasoning, *if A is of the sort $\sim(\exists X)B$ and $\sim B(T/X)$ is true on α for every term T in Σ_T, then A is true on α.*[5]

---

[4] In the language of p. 300, $B(T_i/X)$ behaves like $B(T_{i-1}/X)$ for each i from 2 on. And since $B(T_1/X)$ behaves like $B(a_1/X)$, each one of $B(T_1/X)$, $B(T_2/X)$, $B(T_3/X)$, etc., behaves like $B(a_1/X)$. So if $B(T/X)$ is true on α for every term T in Σ'_T, and hence $B(a_1/X)$ is true on α, then $B(T/X)$ is sure to be true on α for *every* term T.

[5] The foregoing proof owes some to George Weaver.

This corollary readily generalizes to the case where A is a member of a set of statements:

(3.5.6)   Let S be a non-empty set of statements; let S^* consist of all the atomic subformulas of the members of S; let Σ_T consist of all the terms occurring in the various members of S; let Σ'_T consist of all the remaining terms; let the a_1-rewrite of a member C of S^* be the result of putting 'a_1' for each term in C which belongs to Σ'_T; let α be a truth-value assignment to the members of S^*; and let A be a member of S of one of the two sorts $(\forall X)B$ and $\sim(\exists X)B$. If

(i)   'a_1' belongs to Σ_T and
(ii)   each member of S^* is assigned in α the same truth-value as its a_1-rewrite,

then in the case that A is of the sort $(\forall X)B$, A is true on α so long as $B(T/X)$ is true on α for every term T in Σ_T, and in the case that A is of the sort $\sim(\exists X)B$, A is true on α so long as $\sim B(T/X)$ is true on α for every term T in Σ_T.

Part Three. With (3.5.6) on hand, proof of the following generalization of (3.5.4) is trivial.

(3.5.7)   Let S, S^*, Σ_T, Σ'_T, the a_1-rewrite of a member of S^*, and α be as in (3.5.6). If

(i) S is a Hintikka set,
(ii)   'a_1' occurs in at least one member of S,
(iii)   every member of S^* which belongs to S is assigned **T** in α, and every member of S^* whose negation belongs to S is assigned **F** in α, and
(iv)   every member of S^* is assigned in α the same truth-value as its a_1-rewrite,

then every member of S is true on α.[6]

PROOF like that of (3.5.4), but with the following extra cases in the Inductive Step.

CASE 13: A is of the sort $(\forall X)B$. Since $(\forall X)B$ belongs to S, in view of (i) $B(T/X)$ belongs to S for every term T in Σ_T. But $B(T/X)$ is of a length less than l. Hence, by the hypothesis of the induction, $B(T/X)$ is true on α for every term T in Σ_T. Hence, in view of (3.5.6), (ii), and (iv), $(\forall X)B$ $(= A)$ is true on α.

CASE 14: A is of the sort $\sim(\exists X)B$. Proof like that of CASE 13.

---

[6] So long as Σ_T is not empty, any one of its members can of course play the role assigned in (3.5.7) to 'a_1'. Hence, so long as at least one number of a Hintikka set S shows a term, there is sure to be a truth-value assignment on which all the members of S are true.

Now suppose that, as you complete the work in Stage 5 of the routine, there is an open branch to which no addition was made; and consider the truth-value assignment recommended on pp. 190–91 for CASE 3: **T** to every atomic statement which occurs unnegated, or whose a_1-rewrite occurs unnegated, on the branch, and **F** to the remaining atomic subformulas. Since the set consisting of all the lines on the branch meets conditions (i)–(ii) in (3.5.7),[7] and the foregoing truth-value assignment meets conditions (iii)–(iv) in (3.5.7), every line on the branch—and, hence, every member of the set tested—is sure to be true on the assignment. Hence, our second consistency theorem:

> *(3.5.8)*   If a finite and non-empty set of statements is declared CONSIST-
> ENT at Stage 5 of the routine on p. 189, then every member of the set is true
> on the truth-value assignment of pp. 190–91 for CASE 3, and hence the set
> is semantically consistent.

EXERCISES

E3.5.1.   Prove clauses (a)–(i) in (3.5.1).

E3.5.2.   Show that none of the sets in E2.1.17 and E3.3.4 is a Hintikka set.

E3.5.3.   With A, S^*, Σ_T, Σ'_T, the a_1-rewrite of a member of S^*, and α understood to be as on p. 300, show in more detail than does footnote 3 on p. 300 that the a_1-rewrite of each member of S^* belongs to S^*, and hence is sure to be assigned a truth-value in α. With $f(B)$ defined as on p. 301, go on to show that, in case B is atomic, B and $f(B)$ have the same a_1-rewrite.

E3.5.4.   A non-empty set S of statements is said to be a **full Hintikka set** when S meets conditions (a)–(j) on pp. 297–98, conditions (l)–(m), and the following strength-ened versions of conditions (k) and (n):

>   (k′) If $(\forall X)A$ belongs to S, then so does $A(T/X)$ for every term T,
>   (n′) If $\sim(\exists X)A$ belongs to S, then so does $\sim A(T/X)$ for every term T.

Given this definition, and with S^* understood to consist of all the atomic sub-formulas of the members of S, show that if S is a full Hintikka set, then every member of S is sure to be true on the result of assigning **T** to every member of S^* which belongs to S, and **F** to the remaining members of S^*.

E3.5.5.   Show that if a tree has an infinite branch which meets conditions (a)–(d) on p. 186, then the set consisting of all the statements on that branch is a full Hintikka set and hence is semantically consistent.

E3.5.6.   With all seven of '$\sim$', '$\supset$', '&', '$\vee$', '$\equiv$', '$\forall$', and '$\exists$' understood to serve as primitive operators, and S and S_∞ to be as on p. 285 and p. 287, show that if S is syntactically consistent, then S_∞ is a full Hintikka set.

---

[7] Because of the conventions on p. 188, 'a_1' is sure to occur along each branch of any tree constructed via the routine on p. 189.

E3.5.7.   With all seven of '~', '⊃', '&', '∨', '≡', '∀', and '∃' understood to serve as primitive operators, show that:

(a) If S is a Hintikka set *at least one of whose members contains a term,* then there is a truth-value assignment on which all the members of S are true;

(b) If S is a subset of some Hintikka set *of the sort described in* (a), then there is a truth-value assignment on which all the members of S are true; and

(c) If there is a truth-value assignment on which all the members of S are true, then S is a subset of some Hintikka set. (Hint: Use the result in E3.5.6 to prove (c).)

E3.5.8.   Using the results in E3.5.7, show that a statement A is logically true if and only if $\sim A$ does not belong to any Hintikka set *of the sort described in E3.5.7(a).*

E3.5.9.   Show by means of counterexamples that the results in E3.5.7(a), E3.5.7(b), and E3.5.8 would fail if the italicized restrictions were lifted.

3.6   Standard Semantics

Domains, Interpretations, and the Like[1]

Domains and interpretations are the first items of business in standard semantics. *Domains* are *non-empty* sets, be it of things (like the molecules in a glassful of water), or of people (like the United States senators), or of numbers (like the real numbers between 0 and 1).[2] *Interpretations*—to be more precise, *D-interpretations*—are results of assigning to each one of the terms 'a_1', 'a_2', 'a_3', and so on, a member of some domain D, and to each one of a number of predicates a set of members of D when the predicate is 1-place, a set of pairs of members of D when the predicate is 2-place, a set of triples of members of D when the predicate is 3-place, and so on. The predicates concerned will usually be those that occur in a given statement A or in members of a given set S of statements.

Domains—or universes of discourse, as we also called them—are familiar from Section 2.1. Interpretations are not. Recall, however, that since 'a_1', 'a_2', 'a_3', and so on, were drafted in Section 2.1 to serve as names, there should correspond to any term T a certain thing, the one which goes by the name T. Note also that to any 1-place predicate there

---

[1] The reader should review the latter portion of Appendix I before embarking upon this section.

[2] On the requirement that domains be non-empty, see footnote 26 of Section 2.1.

corresponds a certain set of things, to any 2-place predicate a certain set of pairs of things, to any 3-place predicate a certain set of triples of things, and so on: the things, or pairs of things, or triples of things, and so on, to which the predicate applies. For example, there corresponds to the 1-place predicate 'weighs more than a ton' a certain set of things: those, like the Liberty Bell, which weigh more than a ton. There corresponds to the 2-place predicate 'is the father of' a certain set of pairs of things (people): those like $<$Adam, Cain$>$ which consist of a father and some offspring of his (in that order). There corresponds to the 3-place predicate 'is the sum of ... and' a certain set of triples of things (numbers): those like $<12, 5, 7>$ which consist of a number and some two numbers that add up to it. And so on. Viewed from this angle, a D-interpretation is just an invitation—given a certain domain D—to think of each one of the terms 'a_1', 'a_2', 'a_3', and so on as standing for a specific member of D, and of each one of a certain number of predicates as applying to the members of a specific subset of D when the predicate is 1-place, to those of a specific subset of $D \times D$ when the predicate is 2-place, to those of a specific subset of $D \times D \times D$ when the predicate is 3-place, and, in general, to those of a specific subset of D^m when the predicate is m-place.

Several things should be noted in connection with D-interpretations.

(1)   Though every term must be assigned a member of the domain D, not every member of D need be assigned to a term. Indeed, when D has more than $\aleph_0$ members, at most $\aleph_0$ of those members can be assigned to 'a_1', 'a_2', 'a_3', and so on. However, D-interpretations in which every member of the domain is assigned to a term are of special interest, as will soon appear. We shall call them *Henkin D-interpretations*.

(2)   The same member of D may be assigned to more than one term (though of course only one member of D can be assigned to any one term). Indeed, when D has only finitely many members, infinitely many terms are sure to be assigned the same member of D.

(3)   Though every one of the 1-place predicates at hand (if any) must be assigned a subset of D, not every subset of D need be assigned to one of those predicates. Indeed, when D has more subsets than there are 1-place predicates available, some of these subsets cannot be assigned to any 1-place predicate. The like holds true of 2-place predicates, 3-place predicates, and so on.

(4)   The same subset of D may be assigned to more than one 1-place predicate (though of course only one subset of D can be assigned to any 1-place predicate). Indeed, when D has fewer subsets than there are 1-place predicates available, at least one subset of D is sure to be assigned to more than one 1-place predicate. The like holds true of 2-place predicates, 3-place predicates, and so on.

(5)   Since the null set $\varnothing$ does count as a subset of D, $D \times D$, $D \times D \times D$, and so on, $\varnothing$ may be assigned to any predicate.[3] A predicate which is assigned $\varnothing$ is to be thought of as not applying to any thing, or to any pair of things, or to any triple of things, and so on.

(6)   As should be clear by now, but cannot be too emphatically stressed, for any domain D the terms 'a$_1$', 'a$_2$', 'a$_3$', and so on, and the various members of a given set Σ_P of predicates, are susceptible of more than one D-interpretation. Even when the domain has just one member, say Molly Bloom, and there is only one predicate in Σ_P, say the one-place 'F', the terms 'a$_1$', 'a$_2$', 'a$_3$', and so on, and the predicate 'F' are susceptible of two different interpretations: the one that assigns Molly Bloom to every term and the null set $\varnothing$ to 'F', and the one that assigns Molly Bloom to every term and the whole domain D to 'F'.

The next item of business in standard semantics is to specify the conditions under which A is to be *true on* I_D, where A is a statement, Σ_P is a set of predicates to which belongs every predicate occurring in A, D is a domain, and I_D is a D–interpretation of the terms 'a$_1$', 'a$_2$', 'a$_3$', etc., and of the predicates in Σ_P. The matter is readily handled in three cases. (1) Let A be of the sort $P(T_1,T_2,\ldots,T_m)$; for each i from 1 through m, let $I_D(T_i)$ be the member of D assigned in I_D to the term T_i; and let $I_D(P)$ be the subset of D^m assigned in I_D to predicate P. Then A is certified true on I_D if $<I_D(T_1),I_D(T_2),\ldots,I_D(T_m)>$ belongs to $I_D(P)$, i.e., if the m-tuple made up of $I_D(T_1)$, $I_D(T_2)$, $\ldots$, and $I_D(T_m)$ in that order is one of the m-tuples in $I_D(P)$. (2) Let A be of the sort $\sim B$. Then A is certified true on I_D if B is not true on I_D. (3) Let A be of the sort $B \supset C$. Then A is certified true on I_D if B is not true on I_D or C is true on I_D.

What, however, when A is of the sort $(\forall X)B$? Then B is not a statement, except in the trivial case where X does not occur in B. But the result $B(T/X)$ of replacing X everywhere in B by an arbitrary term T foreign to $(\forall X)B$ *is* a statement, and therein lies the answer. Of course, certifying $(\forall X)B$ true on I_D if $B(T/X)$ is true on I_D would not do: T stands for just one member of D, the one assigned to T in I_D. And certifying $(\forall X)B$ true on I_D if $B(T/X)$ is true on I_D for every term T would have familiar limitations: such members of D as are not assigned in I_D to any one of 'a$_1$', 'a$_2$', 'a$_3$', etc. would again be left out of account. Rather, we shall construe $(\forall X)B$ as true on I_D if $B(T/X)$ is true on I_D *and* on all the D-interpretations which are like I_D except for assigning to T another member of D than I_D does—more compactly, if $B(T/X)$ is true on all the D-interpretations (to be known as *the T-variants of* I_D) which are like I_D except for *possibly* assigning to T another member of D than I_D does. On this

---

[3] And would normally be assigned to such a 1-place predicate as 'is an odd integer divisible by 2', to such a 2-place predicate as 'is the childless father of', and so on.

account, A—when of the sort $(\forall X)B$—will be true on I_D if *in effect* $B(T/X)$ is true on I_D whichever member of D is assigned to T in I_D.[4]

This matter once disposed of, a set S of statements (said set *possibly infinite*) is declared semantically consistent if—for some domain D—there is a D-interpretation of the terms 'a_1', 'a_2', 'a_3', etc., and of the predicates that occur in members of S and possibly other predicates as well, on which every member of S is true; otherwise, S is taken to be semantically inconsistent. A set S of statements (said set *possibly infinite*) is said to entail a statement A if $S \cup \{\sim A\}$ is semantically inconsistent. And a statement A is declared logically true if $\{\sim A\}$ is semantically inconsistent.

We now provide formal definitions and illustrations of the concepts just discussed. Throughout, Σ_T is presumed to be $\{\,'a_1','a_2',\ldots,'a_n',\ldots\}$.[5]

(1)   By a **domain** we shall understand any *non-empty* set.

(2)   Let D be a domain, and Σ_P consist of one or more predicates. By a **D-interpretation of (the members of) $\Sigma_T \cup \Sigma_P$** we shall understand any result I_D of assigning a member of D—referred to as $I_D(T)$—to each term T in Σ_T, and for each m from 1 on a subset of D^m—referred to as $I_D(P)$—to each m-place predicate P in Σ_P.

EXAMPLE: Let D consist of Tom, Dick, and Harry, and Σ_P consist of the 1-place predicate 'F' (say, 'is a member of the Board') and the 2-place predicate 'G' (say, 'voted for'). Then

$$I_D \begin{cases} I_D('a_1') &= \text{Tom} \\ I_D('a_2') &= \text{Dick} \\ I_D(T) &= \text{Harry, for every term } T \text{ from '}a_3\text{' on} \\ I_D('F') &= D\,(= \{\text{Tom,Dick,Harry}\}) \\ I_D('G') &= \{<\text{Tom,Harry}>,<\text{Dick,Harry}>,<\text{Harry,Dick}>\} \end{cases}$$

qualifies as a D-interpretation of $\Sigma_T \cup \Sigma_P$.

(3)   Let D and Σ_P be as in (2); let I_D and I'_D be (not necessarily distinct) D-interpretations of $\Sigma_T \cup \Sigma_P$; and let T be a term. Then I'_D will count as a **T-variant of I_D** if: (i) for every term T' other than T, $I'_D(T') = I_D(T')$, and (ii) for every predicate P in Σ_P, $I'_D(P) = I_D(P)$.

EXAMPLE CONTINUED: Let D, Σ_P, and I_D be as before, and let T be 'a_1'. Then I_D has three T-variants: itself and the following two D-interpretations of $\Sigma_T \cup \Sigma_P$:

---

[4] We shall establish that when I_D is a Henkin D-interpretation (i.e., a D-interpretation in which each and every member of D is assigned to one of 'a_1', 'a_2', 'a_3', etc.), $B(T/X)$ is true on every T-variant of I_D if and only if $B(T/X)$ is true on I_D for every term T, and hence that $(\forall X)B$ is true on I_D if and only if $B(T/X)$ is true on I_D for every term T. However, not every D-interpretation is a Henkin one. Hence the broader account of things in the text.

[5] Note the switch from Sections 3.2 and 3.5, where 'Σ_T' played a different role.

$$I'_D \begin{cases} I'_D(\text{'}a_1\text{'}) = \text{Dick} \\ I'_D(\text{'}a_2\text{'}) = \text{Dick} \\ I'_D(T) = \text{Harry, for every term } T \text{ from 'a}_3\text{' on} \\ I'_D(\text{'F'}) = D \\ I'_D(\text{'G'}) = \{<\text{Tom,Harry}>,<\text{Dick,Harry}>,<\text{Harry,Dick}>\} \end{cases}$$

$$I''_D \begin{cases} I''_D(\text{'}a_1\text{'}) = \text{Harry} \\ I''_D(\text{'}a_2\text{'}) = \text{Dick} \\ I''_D(T) = \text{Harry, for every term } T \text{ from 'a}_3\text{' on} \\ I''_D(\text{'F'}) = D \\ I''_D(\text{'G'}) = \{<\text{Tom,Harry}>,<\text{Dick,Harry}>,<\text{Harry,Dick}>\} \end{cases}$$

(4)   Let A be a statement, Σ_P consist of all the predicates that occur in A (and possibly other predicates as well), T be any term that is foreign to A, D be a domain, and I_D be a D-interpretation of $\Sigma_T \cup \Sigma_P$. Then A is said to be **true on I_D** if (and only if):

   (a)   in case A is of the sort $P(T_1,T_2,....,T_m)$ for some m from 1 on, $<I_D(T_1),I_D(T_2),...,I_D(T_m)>$ belongs to $I_D(P)$;
   (b)   in case A is of the sort $\sim B$, B is not true on I_D;
   (c)   in case A is of the sort $B \supset C$, B is not true on I_D or C is true on I_D; and
   (d)   in case A is of the sort $(\forall X)B$, $B(T/X)$ is true on every T-variant of I_D.[6]

EXAMPLE CONTINUED: Let A be '$\sim(\forall x)(Fx \supset Gxa_3)$'—say, 'Not every Board member voted for Harry'; let T be 'a_1' (it could be any term except 'a_3'); and let Σ_P, D, I_D, I'_D, and I''_D be as before. In view of (b), A is true on I_D if and only if '$(\forall x)(Fx \supset Gxa_3)$' is not true on I_D; in view of (d), '$(\forall x)(Fx \supset Gxa_3)$' is true on I_D if and only if '$Fa_1 \supset Ga_1a_3$' is true on all three of I_D, I'_D, and I''_D; in view of (c), '$Fa_1 \supset Ga_1a_3$' is true on I''_D if and only if 'Fa_1' is not true on I''_D or 'Ga_1a_3' is true on I''_D; and, in view of (a), 'Fa_1' is true on I''_D if and only if $I''_D(\text{'}a_1\text{'})$ belongs to $I''_D(\text{'F'})$, and 'Ga_1a_3' is true on I''_D if and only if $<I''_D(\text{'}a_1\text{'}),I''_D(\text{'}a_3\text{'})>$ belongs to $I''_D(\text{'G'})$. But $I''_D(\text{'}a_1\text{'})$ ($=$ Harry) belongs to $I''_D(\text{'F'})$ ($=$ {Tom,Dick,Harry}), and $<I''_D(\text{'}a_1\text{'}),I''_D(\text{'}a_3\text{'})>$ ($=$ $<$Harry,Harry$>$) does not belong to $I''_D(\text{'G'})$ ($=$ {$<$Tom,Harry$>$,$<$Dick,Harry$>$,$<$Harry,Dick$>$}). Hence, 'Fa_1' is true on I''_D, and 'Ga_1a_3' is not. Hence, '$Fa_1 \supset Ga_1a_3$' is not true on I''_D.[7]

---

[6] When all seven of '$\sim$', '$\supset$', '&', '$\vee$', '$\equiv$', '$\forall$', and '$\exists$' serve as primitive operators, four extra clauses are required: (e) in case A is of the sort B & C, both B and C are true on I_D, (f) in case A is of the sort $B \vee C$, at least one of B and C is true on I_D, (g) in case A is of the sort $B \equiv C$, both B and C are true on I_D or neither one is, and (h) in case A is of the sort $(\exists X)B$, $B(T/X)$ is true on at least one T-variant of I_D.

[7] We attended to I''_D, rather than I_D and I'_D, precisely *because* '$Fa_1 \supset Ga_1a_3$', while true on I_D and I'_D, is *not* true on I''_D. (On all three D-interpretations, Board members Tom and Dick *did* vote for Harry, but Board member Harry did *not*.)

Hence, '$(\forall x)(Fx \supset Gxa_3)$' is not true on I_D. Hence, A is true on I_D.

(5) Let S be a set of statements and Σ_P consist of all the predicates that occur in members of S (and possibly other predicates as well).[8] Then S is said to be **semantically consistent in the standard sense** if there is a domain D and a D-interpretation I_D of $\Sigma_T \cup \Sigma_P$ such that every member of S is true on I_D; and S is said to be **semantically inconsistent in the standard sense** if S is not semantically consistent in the standard sense.

EXAMPLE CONTINUED: Let S be $\{Fa_3, \sim Ga_3a_3, \sim(\forall x)(Fx \supset Gxa_3)\}$, and Σ_P be as before. It is easily verified that 'Fa_3' and '$\sim Ga_3a_3$' are both true on the D-interpretation I_D of p. 308. Hence, there is a domain D—namely: $\{Tom, Dick, Harry\}$—and a D-interpretation of $\Sigma_T \cup \Sigma_P$—namely: I_D—on which all the members of S are true. Hence, S is semantically consistent in the standard sense.

(6) Let S be a set of statements and A be a statement. Then S is said to **entail A in the standard sense** if $S \cup \{\sim A\}$ is semantically inconsistent in the standard sense.

EXAMPLE CONTINUED: Let S be $\{Fa_1, (\forall x)(Fx \supset Gxa_3)\}$; let A be 'Ga_1a_3'; let Σ_P be any set of predicates to which both 'F' and 'G' belong; let D be an arbitrary domain; and let I_D be an arbitrary D-interpretation of $\Sigma_T \cup \Sigma_P$. If '$(\forall x)(Fx \supset Gxa_3)$' is true on I_D, then '$Fa_1 \supset Ga_1a_3$' is true on every 'a_1'-variant of I_D, and hence on I_D (I_D counts indeed as an 'a_1'-variant of itself). Hence, if 'Fa_1' as well is true on I_D, then 'Ga_1a_3' is sure to be true on I_D, and hence '$\sim Ga_1a_3$' sure not to be true on I_D. Hence, $\{Fa_1, (\forall x)(Fx \supset Gxa_3), \sim Ga_1a_3\}$ $(= S \cup \{\sim A\})$ is semantically inconsistent in the standard sense. Hence, S entails A in the standard sense.

(7) A statement A is said to be **logically true in the standard sense** if $\{\sim A\}$ is semantically inconsistent in the standard sense.

EXAMPLE CONCLUDED: Let A be '$Fa_1 \supset [(\forall x)(Fx \supset Gxa_3) \supset Ga_1a_3]$'. It is easily verified that $\{\sim(Fa_1 \supset [(\forall x)(Fx \supset Gxa_3) \supset Ga_1a_3])\}$ is semantically inconsistent in the standard sense. Hence, A is logically true in the standard sense.

A few extra definitions are in order.

When D is a domain and I_D is—for some set Σ_P of predicates—a D-interpretation of $\Sigma_T \cup \Sigma_P$, the pair $<D, I_D>$ is often called *a model*, and

---

[8] We could require Σ_P to consist of *just* the predicates that occur in members of S, but to keep in closer touch with the literature we allow it to contain other predicates as well. Under the present understanding of Σ_P, $\varnothing$ automatically proves to be semantically consistent in the standard sense, a result we don't bother to record separately. Indeed, let D be $\{1\}$, and I_D be the result of assigning the integer 1 to every term, and $\{1\}$ (or $\varnothing$) to the 1-place predicate 'F'. Then every member of $\varnothing$ is clearly true on I_D.

more particularly *a model with D as a domain*. Adapting the latter phrase
to our own purposes, we shall say of a set S of statements and a non-
empty set D that **S has a model with D as a domain** if—Σ_P consisting of all
the predicates that occur in members of S and possibly other predicates
as well—there is a D-interpretation I_D of $\Sigma_T \cup \Sigma_P$ such that every member of S is true on I_D. Furthermore, we shall say of a set S of statements
that *S has a model with a finite (denumerably infinite, non-denumerably
infinite) domain* if there is a finite (denumerably infinite, non-denumerably
infinite) set D such that S has a model with D as a domain. It can be
shown that if a set S of statements is semantically consistent in the standard sense, then S has a model with a denumerably infinite—and, hence,
with a finite or a denumerably infinite—domain. This is Skolem's
Theorem, which we discussed briefly on p. 149, and prove a few pages
hence.

Finally, for Henkin D-interpretations and, by extension, Henkin
models. Where D is a domain and—for some set Σ_P of predicates—I_D is a
D-interpretation of $\Sigma_T \cup \Sigma_P$, we shall count I_D as a **Henkin D-interpretation
of $\Sigma_T \cup \Sigma_P$** if for every member d of D there is a term T such that $I_D(T) = d$.
And, where S is a set of statements, we shall say that **S has a Henkin
model** if—Σ_P consisting of all the predicates that occur in members
of S and possibly other predicates as well—there is a domain D and a
Henkin D-interpretation I_D of $\Sigma_T \cup \Sigma_P$ such that every member of S is
true on I_D. Sharpening Skolem's result, we shall establish that if a *finite*
set S of statements is semantically consistent in the standard sense, then S
has a Henkin model. This is the Henkin-Beth Theorem, on which we also
commented in Section 2.1.[9]

Infinitely extendible sets of statements, which have put in an appearance in sundry footnotes and exercises, are due for a major role in what
follows. As the reader will recall, a set of statements is said to be *infinitely
extendible* if infinitely many terms (to be precise, $\aleph_0$ terms) are foreign to
the set. The set

$$\{Fa_2, Fa_4, \ldots, Fa_{2n}, \ldots, \sim(\forall x)Fx\}$$

is infinitely extendible; for even though infinitely many terms do occur in
members of the set, namely: 'a_2', 'a_4', 'a_6', and so on, equally many do
not, namely: 'a_1', 'a_3', 'a_5', and so on. But the set

$$\{Fa_1, Fa_2, \ldots, Fa_n, \ldots, \sim(\forall x)Fx\},$$

about which a good deal will be heard, is not infinitely extendible.[10]

---

[9] Not every set of statements that has a model with a finite or a denumerably infinite domain has a Henkin model (though, of course, every one that has a Henkin model has a model
with a finite or a denumerably infinite domain). The set $\{Fa_1, Fa_2, \ldots, Fa_n, \ldots, \sim(\forall x)Fx\}$, which
we mention in the next paragraph, has a model with a finite domain, but has no Henkin model.
Hence, the Henkin-Beth Theorem is a genuine sharpening of Skolem's.

[10] Note, by the way, that every finite set of statements is infinitely extendible.

So much, however, for preliminaries. We now go on to show that rules R, ~I, ~E, ⊃I, ⊃E, ∀I*, and ∀E are both sound and complete under the standard account of entailment; establish a number of key results in standard semantics (among them the Skolem and Henkin-Beth Theorems); and study the relationship between Henkin models and truth-value assignments. The extent to which standard and truth-value semantics match will become obvious as we proceed. Ways of accounting in truth-value semantics for the semantic consistency of *infinite* sets of statements and the entailment of statements by *infinite* sets of statements will be sketched in the closing pages of the section.

Soundness Revisited

Proof that, where A is a statement and S a *finite* set of statements, A is sure to be entailed by S in the standard sense if A is derivable from S in accordance with rules R, ~I, ~E, ⊃I, ⊃E, ∀I*, and ∀E, is as in Section 3.3, but with (3.6.1)–(3.6.5) and (3.6.8)–(3.6.9) below substituting for (3.3.1)–(3.3.7). (3.6.9) calls for (3.6.6), an important lemma which we shall have further occasion to use. (3.6.8) calls for the more trivial (3.6.7).

(3.6.1)   If A belongs to S, then S entails A in the standard sense.

PROOF: Let Σ_P consist of all the predicates occurring in members of S; and suppose A belongs to S. Then, whatever domain D may be, there can be no D-interpretation I_D of $\Sigma_T \cup \Sigma_P$ on which all the members of $S \cup \{\sim A\}$ are true; for if there were, both A and $\sim A$ would be true on I_D, which is impossible. Hence, $S \cup \{\sim A\}$ is semantically inconsistent in the standard sense. Hence, S entails A in the standard sense.

(3.6.2)   If $S \cup \{A\}$ entails both B and $\sim B$ in the standard sense, then S entails $\sim A$ in the standard sense.

PROOF: Let Σ_P consist of all the predicates occurring in members of S, all those in A, and all those in B; and suppose $S \cup \{A\}$ entails both B and $\sim B$ in the standard sense (in which case both $S \cup \{A,\sim B\}$ and $S \cup \{A,\sim\sim B\}$ are semantically inconsistent in the standard sense). Then, whatever domain D may be, there can be no D-interpretation I_D of $\Sigma_T \cup \Sigma_P$ on which all the members of $S \cup \{A\}$ are true; for if there were, either all the members of $S \cup \{A,\sim B\}$ or all those of $S \cup \{A,\sim\sim B\}$ would be true on I_D, which is impossible in this case. But, if there can be no D-interpretation of $\Sigma_T \cup \Sigma_P$ on which all the members of $S \cup \{A\}$ are true, there can be none on which all those of $S \cup \{\sim\sim A\}$ are true. Hence, $S \cup \{\sim\sim A\}$ is semantically inconsistent in the standard sense. Hence, S entails $\sim A$ in the standard sense.

(3.6.3)   If S entails $\sim\sim A$ in the standard sense, then S entails A in the standard sense.

(3.6.4)   If $S \cup \{A\}$ entails B in the standard sense, then S entails $A \supset B$ in the standard sense.

(3.6.5)   If S entails both $A \supset B$ and A in the standard sense, then S entails B in the standard sense.

Proofs of (3.6.3)–(3.6.5) are left to the reader.

(3.6.6)   Let A be a statement, T and T' be terms, Σ_P consist of all the predicates that occur in A (and possibly other predicates as well), D be a domain, and B be a subformula of A. Then $B(T'/T)$ is true on a D-interpretation I_D of $\Sigma_T \cup \Sigma_P$ if and only if B is true on the T-variant I'_D of I_D such that $I'_D(T) = I_D(T')$.[11]

PROOF: Let I_D be an arbitrary D-interpretation of $\Sigma_T \cup \Sigma_P$, and I'_D be the T-variant of I_D such that $I'_D(T) = I_D(T')$. Proof that $B(T'/T)$ is true on I_D if and only if B is true on I'_D, is by mathematical induction on the length l of B.

BASIS: $l = 1$. Then B is of the sort $P(T_1,T_2,...,T_m)$ for some m from 1 on, and hence $B(T'/T)$ is of the sort $P(T'_1,T'_2,...,T'_m)$, where—for each i from 1 through m—T'_i is T_i itself if T_i is distinct from T, otherwise T'_i is T'. But, by the definition of a T-variant of a D-interpretation in general and the construction of I'_D in particular, (i) $I'_D(T_i) = I_D(T'_i)$ for each i from 1 through m and (ii) $I'_D(P) = I_D(P)$. Hence, $<I'_D(T_1),I'_D(T_2),...,I'_D(T_m)>$ belongs to $I'_D(P)$ if and only if $<I_D(T'_1), I_D(T'_2),...,I_D(T'_m)>$ belongs to $I_D(P)$. Hence, $B(T'/T)$ is true on I_D if and only if B is true on I'_D.

INDUCTIVE STEP: $l > 1$. Suppose (3.6.6) holds true of any subformula of A of a length less than l.

CASE 1: B is of the sort $\sim C$, and hence $B(T'/T)$ is of the sort $\sim C(T'/T)$. Since C is a subformula of A and is of a length less than l, by the hypothesis of the induction $C(T'/T)$ is true on I_D if and only if C is true on I'_D. Hence, $\sim C(T'/T)$ is true on I_D if and only if $\sim C$ is true on I'_D.

CASE 2: B is of the sort $C \supset D$, and hence $B(T'/T)$ is of the sort $C(T'/T) \supset D(T'/T)$. The proof is left to the reader.

CASE 3: B is of the sort $(\forall X)C$, and hence $B(T'/T)$ is of the sort $((\forall X)C)(T'/T)$. We establish in (i) that if $(\forall X)C(T'/T)(=((\forall X)C)(T'/T))$ is not true on I_D, then $(\forall X)C$ is not on I'_D, and in (ii) that if

---

[11] Hence, in particular, $A(T'/T)$ is true on I_D if and only if A is true on I'_D. Note the similarity between (3.6.6) and (3.2.2).

$(\forall X)C$ is not true on I_D', then $(\forall X)C(T'/T)$ is not true on I_D. (i)
Suppose that $(\forall X)C(T'/T)$ is not true on I_D and let T'' be an arbitrary term foreign to both $(\forall X)C$ and $(\forall X)C(T'/T)$. Then there is a
T''-variant of I_D, say I_D'', on which $(C(T'/T))(T''/X)$ is not true.
But, with T'' foreign to $(\forall X)C(T'/T)$ and hence to $C(T'/T)$,
$(C(T''/X))(T'/T)$ is the same as $(C(T'/T))(T''/X)$. Hence,
$(C(T''/X))(T'/T)$ is not true on I_D''. But $C(T''/X)$ is a subformula of
A and is of a length less than l. Hence, by the hypothesis of the induction $C(T''/X)$ is not true on the T-variant I_{D}'' of I_D'' such that
$I_{D}''(T) = I_D''(T')$. But I_{D}'' is a T''-variant of I_D'. Indeed, since I_{D}'' is a
T-variant of I_D'', and I_D'' is a T''-variant of I_D, then I_{D}'' and I_D can differ
only in what they respectively assign to T and T''. But I_D', being a
T-variant of I_D, can differ from I_D only in what it assigns to T. So I_{D}''
and I_D' can differ only in what they respectively assign to T and T''.
But $I_{D}''(T) = I_D'(T)$.[12] So I_{D}'' and I_D' can differ only in what they respectively assign to T''. So—as claimed earlier—I_{D}'' is a T''-variant
of I_D'. So there is a T''-variant of I_D' on which $C(T''/X)$ is not true.
So $(\forall X)C$ is not true on I_D'.[13] (ii) Suppose that $(\forall X)C$ is not true on
I_D', and let T'' be as in (i). Then there is a T''-variant of I_D', say I_D'',
on which $C(T''/X)$—a subformula of A of a length less than l—is
not true. Now let I_D''' be the T''-variant of I_D such that $I_D'''(T'') =
I_D''(T'')$. Then I_D''' is the T-variant of I_D''' such that $I_D''(T) = I_D'''(T')$.
Indeed, since I_D'' is a T''-variant of I_D', and I_D' is a T-variant of I_D, then
I_D'' and I_D can differ only in what they respectively assign to T'' and T.
But I_D''', being a T''-variant of I_D, can differ from I_D only in what it
assigns to T''. So I_D'' and I_D''' can differ only in what they respectively
assign to T'' and T. But $I_D''(T'') = I_D'''(T'')$. So I_D'' and I_D''' can differ
only in what they respectively assign to T. But $I_D''(T) = I_D'''(T')$.[14]
So—as claimed earlier—I_D'' is the T-variant of I_D''' such that $I_D''(T) =
I_D'''(T')$. So by the hypothesis of the induction $(C(T''/X))(T'/T)$ is
not true on I_D'''. But, with T'' foreign to $(\forall X)C(T'/T)$ and hence to
$C(T'/T)$, $(C(T'/T))(T''/X)$ is the same as $(C(T''/X))(T'/T)$.
Hence, $(C(T'/T))(T''/X)$ is not true on I_D'''. So there is a T''-variant
of I_D on which $(C(T'/T))(T''/X)$ is not true. So $(\forall X)C(T'/T)$ is
not true on I_D.

(3.6.7) Let A be a statement, T be a term foreign to A, Σ_p consist of all the
predicates that occur in A (and possibly others as well), D be a domain, I_D

---

[12] Note for proof that: (a) since I_D'' is a T''-variant of I_D and hence can differ from I_D
only in what it assigns to T'', $I_D''(T') = I_D(T')$, and hence $I_D''(T') = I_D'(T)$; and (b) $I_D''(T) =
I_D''(T')$.

[13] Recall that, as T'' is foreign to $(\forall X)C$, $(\forall X)C$ is true on I_D' only if $C(T''/X)$ is true
on every T''-variant of I_D'.

[14] Note for proof that: (a) since I_D'' is a T''-variant of I_D' and hence can differ from I_D'
only in what it assigns to T'', $I_D''(T) = I_D'(T)$, and hence $I_D''(T) = I_D(T')$, and (b) since I_D''' is a
T''-variant of I_D and hence can differ from I_D only in what it assigns to T'', $I_D'''(T') = I_D(T')$.

be a D-interpretation of $\Sigma_T \cup \Sigma_P$, and I'_D be any T-variant of I_D. Then A is true on I_D if and only if A is true on I'_D.

PROOF by mathematical induction of the length of A. Limiting ourselves to the one arduous case, let A be of the sort $(\forall X)B$, and let T''' be foreign to A and distinct from T.[15] (i) Suppose A is true on I_D and hence $B(T'''/X)$ is true on every T'''-variant of I_D. Then by the hypothesis of the induction $B(T'''/X)$ is true on every T-variant of every T'''-variant of I_D. But every T'''-variant of I'_D is a T-variant of some T'''-variant of I_D. So $B(T'''/X)$ is true on every T'''-variant of I'_D and hence A is true on I'_D. (ii) Suppose A is not true on I_D and hence $B(T'''/X)$ is not true on some T'''-variant of I_D. Then by the hypothesis of the induction $B(T'''/X)$ is not true on any T-variant of some T'''-variant of I'_D. But every T'''-variant of I_D has some T'''-variant of I'_D among its T-variants. So $B(T'''/X)$ is not true on some T'''-variant of I'_D and hence A is not true on I'_D.

(3.6.8) If S entails $A(T/X)$ in the standard sense, then $S \cup S'$ entails $(\forall X)A$ in the standard sense, so long as T is foreign to S and to $(\forall X)A$.

PROOF: With T presumed to be foreign to S and to $(\forall X)A$, suppose S entails $A(T/X)$ in the standard sense; let Σ_P consist of all the predicates occurring in members of $S \cup S'$ and all those in $(\forall X)A$; let D be a domain; and let I_D be a D-interpretation of $\Sigma_T \cup \Sigma_P$ on which all the members of $S \cup S'$ (and hence all the members of S) are true. Since T is presumed to be foreign to S, every member B of S is sure by (3.6.7) to be true on any T-variant of any D-interpretation of $\Sigma_T \cup \Sigma_P$ on which B is true. Hence, all the members of S are true on every T-variant of I_D. But S entails $A(T/X)$ in the standard sense. Hence, $A(T/X)$ is true on every T-variant of I_D. But T is foreign to $(\forall X)A$. Hence, $(\forall X)A$ is true on I_D. Hence, $(\forall X)A$ is true on any— and thus on every—D-interpretation of $\Sigma_T \cup \Sigma_P$ on which all the members of $S \cup S'$ are true. Hence, $S \cup S'$ entails $(\forall X)A$ in the standard sense.

(3.6.9) If S entails $(\forall X)A$ in the standard sense, then S entails $A(T/X)$ in the standard sense for any term T.

PROOF: Suppose S entails $(\forall X)A$ in the standard sense; let T be an arbitrary term; let T' be an arbitrary term foreign to $(\forall X)A$; let Σ_P consist of all the predicates occurring in members of S and all those in $(\forall X)A$; let D be a domain; let I_D be a D-interpretation of $\Sigma_T \cup \Sigma_P$ on which all the members of S are true; and let I'_D be the T'-variant of I_D such that $I'_D(T') = I_D(T)$. Then $(\forall X)A$ is true on I_D, hence $A(T'/X)$ is true on I'_D, and hence by (3.6.6)[16] $(A(T'/X))(T/T')$ is true on I_D. But, with T' presumed to be foreign to $(\forall X)A$, $A(T/X)$ is

---

[15] As the reader will discover, the restriction on T is needed in the Basis of the induction.
[16] With 'T' and 'T'' interchanged throughout.

the same as $(A(T'/X))(T/T')$. Hence, $A(T/X)$ is true on I_D. Hence, S entails $A(T/X)$ in the standard sense for any term T.

Hence (by the same reasoning as on pp. 279–82):

> (*3.6.10*)   Let S be a finite set of statements. If A is derivable from S in accordance with rules R, $\sim$I, $\sim$E, $\supset$I, $\supset$E, $\forall$I*, and $\forall$E, then A is entailed by S in the standard sense.

Rules R, $\sim$I, $\sim$E, $\supset$I, $\supset$E, $\forall$I*, and $\forall$E, then, are sound under the standard (as well as under the truth-value) account of entailment.

Completeness Revisited

Proof of the converse of (3.6.10) calls for the following corollary of (3.6.6), which incidentally will serve later on to link truth-value and standard semantics.

> (*3.6.11*)   Let $(\forall X)A$ be a statement, Σ_P consist of all the predicates that occur in $(\forall X)A$ (and possibly other predicates as well), D be a domain, and I_D be a Henkin D-interpretation of $\Sigma_T \cup \Sigma_P$. Then $(\forall X)A$ is true on I_D if and only if $A(T/X)$ is true on I_D for every term T.

PROOF: Suppose first that $(\forall X)A$ is true on I_D. Then, by the same reasoning as in the proof of (3.6.9), $A(T/X)$ is sure to be true on I_D for every term T. Suppose next that $A(T/X)$ is true on I_D for every term T, and let T' be an arbitrary term foreign to $(\forall X)A$. Then $(A(T'/X))(T/T')$ is the same as $A(T/X)$, and hence is true on I_D for every term T. Now let I_D' be an arbitrary T'-variant of I_D, and let d be the member of D that is assigned in I_D' to T'. With I_D presumed to be a Henkin D-interpretation of $\Sigma_T \cup \Sigma_P$, there is sure to be a term, say T'', to which d is assigned in I_D. Hence, $I_D'(T') = I_D(T'')$. Hence, I_D' is the T'-variant of I_D such that $I_D'(T') = I_D(T'')$. But, since $(A(T'/X))(T/T')$ is true on I_D for every term T, $(A(T'/X))$ (T''/T') is true on I_D. Hence, by (3.6.6), $A(T'/X)$ is true on I_D'. Hence, if $A(T/X)$ is true on I_D for every term T, then $A(T'/X)$ is true on any—and hence on every—T'-variant of I_D, and hence $(\forall X)A$ is true on I_D. Hence (3.6.11).

With (3.6.11) at hand, proof is readily had that if an infinitely extendible but non-empty set S of statements (hence, in particular, if a finite but non-empty set S of statements) is syntactically consistent, then S is semantically consistent in the standard sense. (The completeness of our rules will follow from this result.) Let S^*, S^{**}, and S_∞ be defined exactly as on p. 286 and p. 287. With S presumed to be infinitely extendible, there is sure to be for any n whatever at least one term that is foreign to S_{n-1} and $\sim(\forall X)B$. Hence, with S also presumed to be syntactically consistent, S_∞ is sure to have features (k)–(m) on p. 290.[17]

---

[17] See footnote 4 to Section 3.4.

Now let D be Σ_T, i.e., $\{\text{'}a_1\text{'},\text{'}a_2\text{'},\ldots,\text{'}a_n\text{'},\ldots\}$;[18] and let I_D be the result of assigning:

(i)   to each term T the term T itself,

(ii) to each 1-place predicate P that occurs in members of S_∞ the subset of D $(= \Sigma_T)$ consisting of every term T such that $P(T)$ belongs to S_∞,

(iii) to each 2-place predicate P that occurs in members of S_∞ the subset of $D \times D$ $(= \Sigma_T \times \Sigma_T)$ consisting of every pair $<T_1,T_2>$ of terms such that $P(T_1,T_2)$ belongs to S_∞,

(iv) to each 3-place predicate P that occurs in members of S_∞ the subset of $D \times D \times D$ $(= \Sigma_T \times \Sigma_T \times \Sigma_T)$ consisting of every triple $<T_1,T_2,T_3>$ of terms such that $P(T_1,T_2,T_3)$ belongs to S_∞, and so on.

It is easily shown by mathematical induction on the length l of an arbitrary member A of S^{**} that A is true on I_D if and only if A belongs to S_∞. Hence, every member of S_∞ is sure to be true on I_D, and hence so is every member of S. Hence, there is a domain D and a D-interpretation I_D of the terms 'a_1', 'a_2', 'a_3', and so on, and of the predicates that occur in members of S_∞ (and hence in members of S), such that every member of S is true on I_D. Hence, S is semantically consistent in the standard sense.

The induction is as follows:

BASIS: $l = 1$. Then A is of the sort $P(T_1,T_2,\ldots,T_m)$ for some m from 1 on. But, by the very construction of I_D, $<I_D(T_1),I_D(T_2),\ldots,I_D(T_m)>$ belongs to $I_D(P)$ if and only if $P(T_1,T_2,\ldots,T_m)$ belongs to S_∞. Hence, A is true on I_D if and only if A belongs to S_∞.

INDUCTIVE STEP: $l > 1$.
CASES 1–2: A is of the sort $\sim B$, and A is of the sort $B \supset C$. The proofs, which are essentially like those of CASES 1–2 on p. 291, are left to the reader.
CASE 3: A is of the sort $(\forall X)B$. Since for every member T of D $(= \Sigma_T)$ there is a term T' (namely, T itself) such that $I_D(T') = T$, I_D is a Henkin D-interpretation of the terms 'a_1', 'a_2', 'a_3', and so on, and of the predicates that occur in members of S_∞. Hence, by (3.6.11), $(\forall X)B$ is true on I_D if and only if $B(a_1/X)$, $B(a_2/X)$, $B(a_3/X)$, and so on, are true on I_D. But by (d) on p. 286 $B(a_1/X)$, $B(a_2/X)$, $B(a_3/X)$, and so on, belong to S^{**} (and, of course, each one of them is of a length less than l). Hence, by the hypothesis of the induction, $B(a_1/X)$, $B(a_2/X)$, $B(a_3/X)$, and so on, are true on I_D if and only if they belong to S_∞. Hence, $(\forall X)B$ is true on I_D

---

[18] Using Σ_T (or part thereof) as a domain is a ploy that goes back to Henkin. We shall frequently resort to it.

if and only if $B(a_1/X)$, $B(a_2/X)$, $B(a_3/X)$, and so on, belong to S_∞. Hence, by (m) on p. 290, $(\forall X)B$ is true on I_D if and only if $(\forall X)B$ belongs to S_∞.

Since $\varnothing$ is semantically consistent in the standard sense, the foregoing result generalizes to:

> (3.6.12) Let S be an *infinitely extendible* set of statements. If S is syntactically consistent, then S is semantically consistent in the standard sense.

But, as remarked earlier, any finite set of statements is infinitely extendible. Hence:

> (3.6.13) Let S be a *finite* set of statements. If S is syntactically consistent, then S is semantically consistent in the standard sense.

Hence, by exactly the same steps as on pp. 285–86:

> (3.6.14) Let S be a *finite* set of statements. If A is entailed by S in the standard sense, then A is derivable from S in accordance with rules R, $\sim$I, $\sim$E, $\supset$I, $\supset$E, $\forall$I*, and $\forall$E.

Rules R, $\sim$I, $\sim$E, $\supset$I, $\supset$E, $\forall$I*, and $\forall$E, then, are complete under the standard (as well as the truth-value) account of entailment.

Note by the way that the converse of (3.6.13) follows from (3.6.10) by essentially the same reasoning as on p. 283:

> (3.6.15) Let S be a *finite* set of statements. If S is semantically consistent in the standard sense, then S is syntactically consistent.

Hence, in view of (3.4.7):

> (3.6.16) Let S in (a)–(b) be a *finite* set of statements.
>
> (a) S is semantically consistent in the truth-value sense if and only if S is semantically consistent in the standard sense.[19]
>
> (b) S entails A in the truth-value sense if and only if S entails A in the standard sense.
>
> (c) A is logically true in the truth-value sense if and only if A is logically true in the standard sense.

Our account in Section 2.1 of the semantic consistency of *finite* sets of statements, of the entailment of individual statements by *finite* sets of statements, and of the logical truth of individual statements, thus exactly matches the standard one.[20] We shall arrive again at this conclusion on pp. 323–24, but by a more intuitive route.

---

[19] For a forerunner of this result, see Beth's *The Foundations of Mathematics*, Section 89.
[20] We presume the truth-value account of semantic consistency to be as in Section 3.2, where $\varnothing$ was declared semantically consistent by special dispensation.

Further Results

Sets of statements that are not infinitely extendible are also sure to be semantically consistent in the standard sense if they are syntactically consistent. Proof of the fact calls for an auxiliary notion (reminiscent of one in Section 3.2) and three lemmas. Let **the double image f'(T) of a term T** be 'a_2' when T is 'a_1', 'a_4' when T is 'a_2', 'a_6' when T is 'a_3', and so on; let **the double image f'(A) of a statement A** be the result of simultaneously replacing all the terms that occur in A by their respective double images: and let **the double image f'(S) of a set S of statements** be the set consisting of the double images of the various members of S. The reader may wish to verify that:

(*3.6.17*)

    (a) The double image of any set of statements is infinitely extendible.

    (b) The double image of any syntactically consistent set of statements is syntactically consistent.

    (c) Let A be a statement, $f'(A)$ be the double image of A, Σ_P consist of all the predicates that occur in A (and possibly other predicates as well), D be Σ_T, I_D be a D-interpretation of $\Sigma_T \cup \Sigma_P$, and $f'(I_D)$ be like I_D except for assigning to each term T in Σ_T the member of D assigned in I_D to the double image $f'(T)$ of T. Then A is true on $f'(I_D)$ if and only if $f'(A)$ is true on I_D.[21]

Consider now a set S of statements which is syntactically consistent, but is *not* infinitely extendible. Then in view of clauses (a)–(b) in (3.6.17) its double image $f'(S)$ is sure to be syntactically consistent *and* infinitely extendible. Next, let S^* consist of the atomic subformulas of the various members of $f'(S)$: let S^{**} consist as before of the various statements whose atomic subformulas all belong to S^*; let S_∞ be defined as on p. 287, but with S_0 taken to be $f'(S)$ rather than S: let D be Σ_T; let I_D be as on p. 317; and let $f'(I_D)$ be as in clause (c) of (3.6.17). As shown before, every member of $f'(S)$ is sure to be true on I_D. Hence, in view of clause (c) in (3.6.17), every member of S is sure to be true on $f'(I_D)$. Hence, there is a domain D and a D-interpretation (of the members of Σ_T and of the predicates that occur in members of S) on which every member of S is true. Hence, S is semantically consistent in the standard sense. Hence:

(*3.6.18*)   Let S be a set of statements that is not infinitely extendible. If S is syntactically consistent, then S is semantically consistent in the standard sense.

---

[21] Proof of (a) is immediate. Proof of (c) is by mathematical induction on the length of an arbitrary subformula of A, and presents no difficulty. Proof of (b) is somewhat more difficult; see E3.6.10.

Hence:

> (*3.6.19*) If a set S of statements is syntactically consistent, then S (whether
> or not infinitely extendible) is semantically consistent in the standard sense.

These last two results go beyond those of Section 3.4. The members
of any syntactically consistent set of statements that is infinitely extendible are sure to be true on at least one truth-value assignment to their
atomic subformulas.[22] But the members of $\{Fa_1, Fa_2, \ldots, Fa_n, \ldots, {\sim}(\forall x)Fx\}$,
and of many other syntactically consistent sets that are *not* infinitely extendible, cannot be true on any truth-value assignment.[23] We shall return
to this matter a few pages hence.

In view of (3.6.15), the converse of (3.6.19) holds true:

> (*3.6.20*) If a set S of statements is semantically consistent in the standard
> sense, then S is syntactically consistent.

PROOF: Suppose first that S is finite. Then (3.6.20) by (3.6.15).
Suppose next that S is infinite and syntactically inconsistent. Then
by (3.2.18) some finite subset of S is syntactically inconsistent, hence
by (3.6.15) some finite subset of S is semantically inconsistent in the
standard sense, and hence S itself is semantically inconsistent in the
standard sense.

(3.6.19) and (3.6.20) have corollaries worth recording. The first two
are known in the literature as **Compactness Theorems;**[24] the third is a
generalization of (3.6.10) and (3.6.14). *Note that in all three S may be infinite as well as finite.*

> (*3.6.21*) A set S of statements is semantically consistent in the standard
> sense if and only if every finite subset of S is semantically consistent in the
> standard sense.

PROOF: In view of (3.6.19)–(3.6.20) S is semantically consistent in
the standard sense if and only if S is syntactically consistent, hence
in view of (3.2.18) if and only if every finite subset of S is syntactically
consistent, and hence in view of (3.6.19)–(3.6.20) if and only if every
finite subset of S is semantically consistent in the standard sense.

> (*3.6.22*) S entails A in the standard sense if and only if at least one finite
> subset of S entails A in the standard sense.

PROOF by (3.6.21).

---

[22] See footnote 7 to Section 3.4.
[23] Proof that $\{Fa_1, Fa_2, \ldots, Fa_n, \ldots, {\sim}(\forall x)Fx\}$ is semantically consistent in the standard
sense, and hence is syntactically consistent, is given on p. 322. See also E3.3.4.
[24] Note the analogy between (3.2.18) and (3.6.21).

(*3.6.23*)   *A* is derivable from *S* in accordance with rules R, $\sim$I, $\sim$E, $\supset$I, $\supset$E, $\forall$I*, and $\forall$E if and only if *A* is entailed by *S* in the standard sense.

PROOF: In view of (3.2.4) $S \vdash A$ if and only if there is a finite subset S' of S such that $S' \vdash A$, hence in view of (3.6.10) and (3.6.14) if and only if there is a finite subset S' of S such that A is entailed by S' in the standard sense, and hence in view of (3.6.22) if and only if A is entailed by S in the standard sense.

The Skolem and the Henkin-Beth Theorems

The results recorded above as (3.6.18) and (3.6.12) can be significantly sharpened.

The reader will have noticed that the domain used on pp. 317–18 to prove (3.6.12) and on p. 319 to prove (3.6.18)—namely, Σ_T—is of size $\aleph_0$. Hence any syntactically consistent set of statements has a model with a denumerably infinite domain. But by (3.6.20) any set of statements that is semantically consistent in the standard sense is syntactically consistent. Hence the following result, first obtained by Thoralf Skolem and known as **the Skolem Theorem:**[25]

(*3.6.24*)   If a set *S* of statements is semantically consistent in the standard sense, then *S* has a model with a denumerably infinite domain.

Hence, of course:

(*3.6.25*)   If a set *S* of statements is semantically consistent in the standard sense, then *S* has a model with a finite or a denumerably infinite domain.

The Skolem Theorem thus guarantees that, as regards semantic consistency, entailment, logical truth, and the like, models with finite domains or with non-denumerably infinite domains can simply be ignored. Roughly, we can always pretend in connection with these matters that there are exactly $\aleph_0$ things at hand—or, in view of the weaker (3.6.25), that there are just finitely many or just $\aleph_0$ things at hand. We made that very claim in Section 2.1, p. 149.

The reader will also have noticed that the *D*-interpretation used on pp. 317–18 to prove (3.6.12) is a Henkin one. Hence, any syntactically consistent set of statements that is infinitely extendible has a Henkin model. Hence by (3.6.20):

---

[25] Skolem published his theorem, a generalization of an earlier result of L. Löwenheim, in a paper of 1920 entitled "Logisch-kombinatorische Untersuchungen über die Erfüllbarkeit oder Beweisbarkeit mathematischer Sätze nebst einem Theoreme über dichte Mengen." See *Skrifter utgit av Videnskapsselskapet i Kristiania, I. Matematisk-naturvidenskabelig Klasse 1919*, no. 3, 1920, pp. 1–36.

(*3.6.26*)   Let S be an infinitely extendible set of statements. If S is semantically consistent in the standard sense, then S has a Henkin model.

Hence the following result, which we have called **the Henkin-Beth Theorem** because it stems from the work of these two:[26]

(*3.6.27*)   If a *finite* set S of statements is semantically consistent in the standard sense, then S has a Henkin model.

With sets of statements presumed as in Chapters 1 and 2 to be *finite*, (3.6.27) thus guarantees that, as regards semantic consistency, entailment, logical truth, and the like, models not of the Henkin sort can simply be ignored. Roughly, we can always pretend in connection with these matters that all the things there are go by the names 'a_1', 'a_2', 'a_3', and so on. We made that very claim in Section 2.1, pp. 149–50.

By contrast, the D-interpretation which we employed on p. 319 to prove (3.6.18) was not a Henkin one: only 'a_2', 'a_4', 'a_6', and so on, among the members of D, were assigned in that D-interpretation to the various terms 'a_1', 'a_2', 'a_3', and so on. And indeed some sets of statements that are semantically consistent in the standard sense *but are not* infinitely extendible, do not boast a Henkin model. The ubiquitous $\{Fa_1, Fa_2, \ldots, Fa_n, \ldots, \sim(\forall x)Fx\}$ is a case in point. The set is semantically consistent in the standard sense (and hence, as noted on p. 320, syntactically consistent). For let D be $\{1, 2, \ldots, n, \ldots\}$; let I_D be the result of assigning the integer 1 to each one of 'a_1', 'a_2', 'a_3', and so on, and $\{1\}$ to 'F'; let T be 'a_1'; and let I_D' be the T-variant of I_D that assigns to T the integer 2. Then 'Fa_1', 'Fa_2', 'Fa_3', and so on, are all true on I_D (this because 1 belongs to $\{1\}$). On the other hand, 'Fa_1' is not true on I_D' (this because 2 does not belong to $\{1\}$), hence '$(\forall x)Fx$' is not true on I_D, and hence '$\sim(\forall x)Fx$' is true on I_D. Hence, all the members of $\{Fa_1, Fa_2, \ldots, Fa_n, \ldots, \sim(\forall x)Fx\}$ are true on I_D. But the set cannot have any Henkin model, since '$(\forall x)Fx$' is true on a Henkin model if and only if all of 'Fa_1', 'Fa_2', 'Fa_3', and so on, are true on the model.

Henkin Models and Truth-Value Assignments

That $\{Fa_1, Fa_2, \ldots, Fa_n, \ldots, \sim(\forall x)Fx\}$, though semantically consistent in the standard sense, has no Henkin model, is to be expected: Henkin models and truth-value assignments match one-to-one. Indeed, to every Henkin model there corresponds a truth-value assignment, and to every truth-value assignment there corresponds a Henkin model, such that a

---

[26] See Henkin's paper, "The completeness of the first-order functional calculus," and Beth's *The Foundations of Mathematics*, Section 89.

statement is true on the model if and only if it is true on the truth-value assignment. Proof of the fact makes use of (3.6.11).

(3.6.28) Let A be a statement, and Σ_P consist of all the predicates that occur in A.

(a) Let D be a domain, I_D be a Henkin D-interpretation of $\Sigma_T \cup \Sigma_P$, and α be the truth-value assignment to the atomic subformulas of A in which every atomic subformula of A that is true on I_D is assigned the truth-value **T**, and the remaining ones the truth-value **F**. Then, for every subformula B of A, B is true on I_D if and only if B is true on α.

(b) Let α be a truth-value assignment to the atomic subformulas of A; let D be Σ_T; and let I_D be the D-interpretation of $\Sigma_T \cup \Sigma_P$ such that: (i) for each term T in Σ_T, $I_D(T) = T$, and (ii) for each m from 1 on and each m-place predicate P in Σ_P, $<T_1, T_2, \ldots, T_m>$ belongs to $I_D(P)$ if and only if $P(T_1, T_2, \ldots, T_m)$ is assigned **T** in α. Then, for every subformula B of A, B is true on α if and only if B is true on I_D.

PROOF by mathematical induction on the length of an arbitrary subformula B of A. The only case that is not immediate is the one under the Inductive Step where B is of the sort $(\forall X)C$. But the D-interpretation I_D in (b) is a Henkin one (this because every member of D is assigned to itself and hence to a term), and the one in (a) is explicitly required to be a Henkin one. Hence, by (3.6.11), $(\forall X)C$ is true on I_D if and only if $C(T/X)$ is true on I_D for every term T. But by the hypothesis of the induction $C(T/X)$ is true on I_D if and only if $C(T/X)$ is true on α. Hence, $(\forall X)C$ is true on I_D if and only if $C(T/X)$ is true on α for every term T. But $(\forall X)C$ is true on α if and only if $C(T/X)$ is true on α for every term T. Hence, $(\forall X)C$ is true on I_D if and only if $(\forall X)C$ is true on α.

Hence:

(3.6.29)   A non-empty set S of statements has a Henkin model if and only if there is a truth-value assignment to the atomic subformulas of S on which every member of S is true.

Since any set of statements that has a Henkin model is semantically consistent in the standard sense, and $\varnothing$ is semantically consistent both in the standard and the truth-value sense, we may conclude from the Henkin-Beth Theorem and (3.6.29) that:

(a) Where S is a *finite* set of statements, S is semantically consistent in the standard sense if and only if S is semantically consistent in the truth-value sense;

(b) Where S is again a *finite* set of statements and A is a statement, A is entailed by S in the standard sense if and only if A is entailed by S in the truth-value sense; and

(c) Where A is a statement, A is logically true in the standard sense if and only if A is logically true in the truth-value sense.

As regards finite sets of statements, and of course individual statements, the truth-value semantics of Section 2.1 thus exactly coincides—to note it again—with standard semantics.

Addenda to Section 2.1

There are many different ways of attending in truth-value semantics to the semantic consistency of *infinite* sets of statements and the entailment of statements by *infinite* sets of statements.

One way, the simplest of all, is to certify an *infinite* set S of statements *semantically consistent in the truth-value sense* if every finite subset of S is semantically consistent in the truth-value sense; certify S *semantically inconsistent in the truth-value sense* if S is not semantically consistent in the truth-value sense; and, where A is a statement, take S *to entail A in the truth-value sense* if $S \cup \{\sim A\}$ is semantically inconsistent in the truth-value sense.

With the truth-value counterpart of (3.6.21) thus turned—as regards infinite sets of statements—into a definition, it immediately follows that:

(d) A set S of statements (said set either finite or infinite) is semantically consistent in the standard sense if and only if S is semantically consistent in the truth-value sense, and

(e) A set S of statements (said set either finite or infinite) entails a statement A in the standard sense if and only if S entails A in the truth-value sense.

And of course it follows from (3.6.22)–(3.6.23) that, where S is a set of statements of any size whatever and A is a statement:

(f) S entails A in the truth-value sense if and only if at least one finite subset of S entails A in the truth-value sense, and

(g) A is derivable from S in accordance with rules R, $\sim$I, $\sim$E, $\supset$I, $\supset$E, $\forall$I*, and $\forall$E if and only if A is entailed by S in the truth-value sense.

Another, but slightly more complicated way of handling things, is as follows:

(i) Where S is an infinite set of statements that is infinitely extendible, certify S semantically consistent in the truth-value sense if there is a truth-value assignment to the atomic subformulas of the members of S on which all the members of S are true, and

(ii)   Where S is an infinite set of statements that is not infinitely extendible, certify S semantically consistent in the truth-value sense if what we called above the double image $f'(S)$ of S semantically consistent in the truth-value sense.

This done, an infinite set S of statements may again be said to be semantically inconsistent in the truth-value sense if it is not semantically consistent in the truth-value sense, and to entail a statement A in the truth-value sense if $S \cup \{\sim A\}$ is semantically inconsistent in the truth-value sense. Proof that under this substitute account of things (d)–(g) still hold true is left to the reader.[27]

EXERCISES

E3.6.1.   Show that if a domain D has n members, then for each m from 1 on D^m has n^m members and hence 2^{n^m} subsets. (It follows from this result that in a D-interpretation a subset of D^m can be assigned to an m-place predicate in 2^{n^m} different ways.)

E3.6.2.   For each set in E2.2.1 which is semantically consistent, supply—for some domain D—a D-interpretation (of 'a_1', 'a_2', 'a_3', etc., and of the predicates occurring in members of the set) on which all the members of the set are true.

E3.6.3.   For each argument in E2.2.2 which is not valid, supply—for some domain D—a D-interpretation (of 'a_1', 'a_2', 'a_3', etc., and of the predicates occurring in the argument) on which the premises are all true and the conclusion is not.

E3.6.4.   For each statement in E2.2.3 which is not logically true, supply—for some domain D—a D-interpretation (of 'a_1', 'a_2', 'a_3', etc., and of the predicates occurring in the statement) on which the statement is not true.

E3.6.5.   Show that:

(a)   Any statement of any one of the six sorts A1–A6 on p. 328 is logically true in the standard sense;

(b)   If any conservative instance of $(\forall X)A$ is logically true in the standard sense, so is $(\forall X)A$;

(c)   Neither one of '$(\forall x)[Fa \supset (Gb \supset Fx)]$' and '$(\forall y)[(\forall x)Fxa \supset Fby]$' on p. 329 is logically true in the standard sense.

E3.6.6.   Prove (3.6.3)–(3.6.5) in the text; and do E3.3.1 over, with 'entails in the standard sense' substituting for 'entails.'

E3.6.7.

(a)   Complete the proof of (3.6.7).

(b)   With A, T, Σ_P, and D understood to be as in (3.6.7), and I_D to be a D-inter-

---

[27] The account, first published in H. Leblanc's "A simplified account of validity and implication for quantificational logic," *The Journal of Symbolic Logic*, vol. 33, 1968, pp. 231–35, stems in part from Hintikka.

pretation of $\Sigma_T \cup \Sigma_P$, show that A is true on all the T-variants of I_D or else A is true on none of them.

E3.6.8. With $(\forall X)A$, Σ_P, and D understood to be as in (3.6.11), I_D to be a D-interpretation of $\Sigma_T \cup \Sigma_P$, and Σ_T' to be a proper subset of Σ_T, show that if each member of D is assigned in I_D to a member of Σ_T', then $(\forall X)A$ is true on I_D if and only if $A(T/X)$ is true on I_D for every member T of Σ_T'.

* *E3.6.9.* Prove part (c) of (3.6.17).

**E3.6.10.* Prove part (b) of (3.6.17). (A relatively easy proof of (b) is sketched in E3.7.13, where derivability and hence syntactic consistency are accounted for axiomatically.)

E3.6.11. With A_1 understood to be '$(\exists x)Fx$', A_2 to be '$(\exists x)(\exists y)[(Fx \,\&\, Fy) \,\&\, (Gx \equiv {\sim}Gy)]$', A_3 to be '$(\exists x)(\exists y)(\exists z)([(Fx \,\&\, Fy) \,\&\, Fz] \,\&\, ([(Gx \equiv {\sim}Gy) \,\&\, (Hx \equiv {\sim}Hz)] \,\&\, (Iy \equiv {\sim}Iz)))$', B to be '$(\forall x)Fx$', and Σ_P to consist of the four predicates 'F', 'G', 'H', and 'I', show that for any domain D:

(a) If D has at least i members ($i = 1$, 2, or 3), there is a D-interpretation of $\Sigma_T \cup \Sigma_P$ on which A_i is true;

(b) If D has fewer than i members, there is no D-interpretation of $\Sigma_T \cup \Sigma_P$ on which A_i is true;

(c) If D has at least $i + 1$ members, there is a D-interpretation of $\Sigma_T \cup \Sigma_P$ on which $A_i \supset B$ is not true; and

(d) If D has fewer than $i + 1$ members, $A_i \supset B$ is true on every D-interpretation of $\Sigma_T \cup \Sigma_P$.

E3.6.12. Show that the set

$$\{(\forall x){\sim}Fxx, (\forall x)(\exists y)Fxy, (\forall x)(\forall y)(\forall z)[(Fxy \,\&\, Fyz) \supset Fxz]\}$$

has at least one model with a denumerably infinite domain, but has none with a finite domain.

E3.6.13. With A understood to be a statement, Σ_P to consist of all the predicates that occur in A (and possibly other predicates as well), and D and D' to be domains of the same size, show that there is a D-interpretation of $\Sigma_T \cup \Sigma_P$ on which A is true if and only if there is a D'-interpretation of $\Sigma_T \cup \Sigma_P$ on which A is true.

E3.6.14. Generalizing upon the result in E3.6.13, show that if a set S of statements has a model with a given set D as a domain, then S has a model with any set of the same size as D as a domain.

**E3.6.15.* Using (3.6.24) and the result in E3.6.14, show that if a set S of statements has a model with non-denumerably infinite domain D, then S has a model with any denumerably infinite subset of D as a domain.

**E3.6.16.* Show that if a set S of statements has a model with a given set D as a domain, then S has a model with any set larger in size than D as a domain.

* *E3.6.17.* With S understood to be a Hintikka set of statements (see pp. 297–98) or a full Hintikka one (see E3.5.4), and Σ_T' understood to consist of all the terms that occur in members of S, show that if Σ_T' is not empty, then S has a model with Σ_T' as a domain. (Hint: Use Σ_T' as a domain, and assign to each term that belongs to Σ_T' that very term, to each one that does not belong to Σ_T' the alphabetically earliest member of Σ_T'.)

E3.6.18.

    (a) Using the result in E3.6.17, show that if the routine on p. 189 declares a set S of statements CONSISTENT, then S is sure to have a model with a finite domain (and hence to be semantically consistent in the standard sense).

    (b) Show by means of an example that the routine on p. 189 may fail to declare a set S of statements CONSISTENT even though S has a model with a finite domain.

3.7   Axioms for Elementary Logic

The method of Sections 1.3 and 2.3—known, the reader will recall, as *natural deduction*—is only one of several methods that have been developed for deriving statements from sets of statements and for proving logical truths. Another one, which is older than natural deduction and different enough to deserve a brief treatment of its own, is the **axiomatic method.** It was originally designed for proving logical truths, and only subsequently extended to cover the derivation of statements from sets of statements.

The axiomatic method works thus. Certain logical truths, which are to be finite in number or—if infinite in number, as will be the case with us —of only finitely many different sorts, are first singled out as **axioms,** or what were once called *postulates*. A *finite* column of statements that closes with a statement A is next acknowledged as a *proof* of A if every statement in the column is an axiom or follows from previous statements in the column in accordance with one of a finite number of rules. A statement is then declared *provable* or a *theorem* if there is a proof of it.

The rules employed in a proof of the present sort are normally cast in the form

To infer B from A_1,

or the form

To infer B from A_1 and A_2,

or the form

To infer B from A_1, A_2, and A_3,

and so on. They do not involve subordinate derivations, as some of the rules of Sections 1.3 and 2.3 did: indeed, all they condone is adding a statement to a given column of statements if some other statement or statements already figure in the column. And they are usually fewer in number than the rules of Sections 1.3 and 2.3, the axioms (which automatically qualify as entries in a proof and, we shall presently see, in a derivation) making up the difference.

For some choices of axioms and rules (*ours will be one*), a column of statements that closes with a statement *A* is acknowledged as a *derivation* of *A* from a *finite or an infinite* set *S* of statements if every statement in the column belongs to *S*, or is an axiom, or follows from previous statements in the column in accordance with one of the rules. And a statement is said to be *derivable* from a set of statements if there is a derivation of the statement from the set.

To prevent confusion, we shall refer to derivations in the present sense as **a-derivations** ('a' for 'axiomatic'); we shall say that a statement *A* is **a-derivable** from a set *S* of statements if there is an a-derivation of *A* from *S*; and we shall use '*S* $\vdash_a A$' as shorthand for '*A* is a-derivable from *S*'. Proofs in the present sense may similarly be referred to as **a-proofs,** and a statement of which there is an a-proof may be said to be **a-provable** or to be an **a-theorem.** As expected, an a-proof of a statement *A* is an a-derivation of *A* from $\varnothing$, and hence an a-theorem is a statement that is a-derivable from $\varnothing$.

Axioms and Sample a-*derivations*

Borrowing from various sources, we adopt as our axioms:

(i)   all statements of any of the three sorts

    A1. $A \supset (B \supset A)$,
    A2. $[A \supset (B \supset C)] \supset [(A \supset B) \supset (A \supset C)]$,
    A3. $(\sim A \supset \sim B) \supset (B \supset A)$,

(ii) all statements of any of the three further sorts

    A4. $A \supset (\forall X)A$,
    A5. $(\forall X)(A \supset B) \supset [(\forall X)A \supset (\forall X)B]$,
    A6. $(\forall X)A \supset A(T/X)$, and

(iii) all statements of the seventh sort $(\forall X)A$, where—for some term *T* foreign to $(\forall X)A$—$A(T/X)$ counts as an axiom.

(A1–A6, incidentally, are known as **axiom schemata,** the first three as *truth-functional* axiom schemata, the last three as *quantificational* ones).[1]

---

[1] A1–A3 are a simplification by Jan Łukasiewicz of axiom schemata of Gottlob Frege in *Begriffsschrift* (1879); see Łukasiewicz and Tarski's "Untersuchungen über den Aussagenkalkül." *Comptes Rendus des Séances de la Société des Sciences et des Lettres de Varsovie,* Classe III, vol. 23, 1930, pp. 30–50. A4–A6 come from Fitch's "The consistency of the ramified *Principia*," *The Journal of Symbolic Logic,* vol. 3, 1938, pp. 140–49. And counting $(\forall X)A$ as an axiom if any conservative instance of $(\forall X)A$ is an axiom, is an adaptation of Fitch's practice in "Intuitionistic modal logic with quantifiers," *Portugaliae Mathematica,* vol. 7, 1948, pp. 177–85.

And we adopt *one* rule of inference, a close relative of $\supset$E known in the literature as **Modus Ponens:**

$$\text{R1. To infer } B \text{ from } A \text{ and } A \supset B.$$

To illustrate our choice of axioms, and the workings of clause (iii),

$$\text{Fa} \supset (\text{Gb} \supset \text{Fa})$$

counts as an axiom because it is of the sort A1;

$$(\forall x)[\text{F}x \supset (\text{Gb} \supset \text{F}x)]$$

counts as an axiom because, say, the result 'Fa $\supset$ (Gb $\supset$ Fa)' of replacing 'x' everywhere in 'Fx $\supset$ (Gb $\supset$ Fx)' by 'a' counts as an axiom, and 'a' is foreign to '$(\forall x)[\text{F}x \supset (\text{Gb} \supset \text{F}x)]$';

$$(\forall y)(\forall x)[\text{F}x \supset (\text{G}y \supset \text{F}x)]$$

counts as an axiom because, say, the result '$(\forall x)[\text{F}x \supset (\text{Gb} \supset \text{F}x)]$' of replacing '$y$' everywhere in '$(\forall x)[\text{F}x \supset (\text{G}y \supset \text{F}x)]$' by 'b' counts as an axiom, and 'b' is foreign to '$(\forall y)(\forall x)[\text{F}x \supset (\text{G}y \supset \text{F}x)]$';

$$(\forall z)(\forall y)(\forall x)[\text{F}x \supset (\text{G}y \supset \text{F}x)]$$

counts as an axiom because the result '$(\forall y)(\forall x)[\text{F}x \supset (\text{G}y \supset \text{F}x)]$' of replacing '$z$' everywhere in '$(\forall y)(\forall x)[\text{F}x \supset (\text{G}y \supset \text{F}x)]$' by any term you will, say 'a', counts as an axiom; and so on. Similarly,

$$(\forall x)\text{F}xa \supset \text{Fba}$$

counts as an axiom because it is of the sort A6; hence, so does

$$(\forall z)[(\forall x)\text{F}xa \supset \text{F}za];$$

hence so does

$$(\forall y)(\forall z)[(\forall x)\text{F}xy \supset \text{F}zy];$$

hence so does

$$(\forall x')(\forall y)(\forall z)[(\forall x)\text{F}xy \supset \text{F}zy];$$

and so on.

The restriction on T in (iii) is necessary. Without it, '$(\forall x)[\text{Fa} \supset (\text{Gb} \supset \text{F}x)]$', though *not* logically true, would count as an axiom since the result 'Fa $\supset$ (Gb $\supset$ Fa)' of replacing 'x' everywhere in 'Fa $\supset$ (Gb $\supset$ Fx)' by 'a' counts as an axiom; '$(\forall y)[(\forall x)\text{F}xa \supset \text{Fb}y]$', though *not* logically true, would count as an axiom since the result '$(\forall x)\text{F}xa \supset \text{Fba}$' of replacing '$y$' everywhere in '$(\forall x)\text{F}xa \supset \text{Fb}y$' by 'a' counts as an axiom; and so on.

The following are sample a-derivations (from $\varnothing$ in two cases). To compress things, we occasionally use '1' as shorthand for the first entry in an a-derivation, '2' as shorthand for the second entry, and so on.

EXAMPLE 1:   {P, P ⊃ Q, ~[(S ⊃ Q) ⊃ R] ⊃ ~P} ⊢ₐ R

(1)	P	
(2)	P ⊃ Q	
(3)	~[(S ⊃ Q) ⊃ R] ⊃ ~P	
(4)	3 ⊃ (P ⊃ [(S ⊃ Q) ⊃ R])	(A3)
(5)	P ⊃ [(S ⊃ Q) ⊃ R]	(R1, 3, 4)
(6)	(S ⊃ Q) ⊃ R	(R1, 1, 5)
(7)	Q	(R1, 1, 2)
(8)	Q ⊃ (S ⊃ Q)	(A1)
(9)	S ⊃ Q	(R1, 7, 8)
(10)	R	(R1, 6, 9)

EXAMPLE 2: ⊢ₐ (Q ⊃ R) ⊃ [(P ⊃ Q) ⊃ (P ⊃ R)].

(1)	[P ⊃ (Q ⊃ R)] ⊃ [(P ⊃ Q) ⊃ (P ⊃ R)]	(A2)
(2)	1 ⊃ [(Q ⊃ R) ⊃ 1]	(A1)
(3)	(Q ⊃ R) ⊃ 1	(R1, 1, 2)
(4)	(Q ⊃ R) ⊃ [P ⊃ (Q ⊃ R)]	(A1)
(5)	3 ⊃ [4 ⊃ ((Q ⊃ R) ⊃ [(P ⊃ Q) ⊃ (P ⊃ R)])]	(A2)
(6)	4 ⊃ ((Q ⊃ R) ⊃ [(P ⊃ Q) ⊃ (P ⊃ R)])	(R1, 3, 5)
(7)	(Q ⊃ R) ⊃ [(P ⊃ Q) ⊃ (P ⊃ R)]	(R1, 4, 6)

EXAMPLE 3: {(∀x)~Fx, ~(∀x)~Gx ⊃ ~(∀x)~Fx} ⊢ₐ Ga ⊃ Hb

(1)	(∀x)~Fx	
(2)	~(∀x)~Gx ⊃ ~(∀x)~Fx	
(3)	2 ⊃ (1 ⊃ (∀x)~Gx)	(A3)
(4)	1 ⊃ (∀x)~Gx	(R1, 2, 3)
(5)	(∀x)~Gx	(R1, 1, 4)
(6)	5 ⊃ ~Ga	(A6)
(7)	~Ga	(R1, 5, 6)
(8)	7 ⊃ (~Hb ⊃ ~Ga)	(A1)
(9)	~Hb ⊃ ~Ga	(R1, 7, 8)
(10)	9 ⊃ (Ga ⊃ Hb)	(A3)
(11)	Ga ⊃ Hb	(R1, 9, 10)

EXAMPLE 4:   ⊢ₐ (Fa ⊃ (∀x)Gx) ⊃ (∀y) (Fa ⊃ Gy).

(1)	(∀y) ([(∀x)Gx ⊃ Gy] ⊃ [Fa ⊃ ((∀x)Gx ⊃ Gy)])	(A1)²
(2)	(∀y) [(∀x)Gx ⊃ Gy]	(A6)³
(3)	1 ⊃ (2 ⊃ (∀y) [Fa ⊃ ((∀x)Gx ⊃ Gy)])	(A5)
(4)	2 ⊃ (∀y) [Fa ⊃ ((∀x)Gx ⊃ Gy)]	(R1, 1, 3)
(5)	(∀y) [Fa ⊃ ((∀x)Gx ⊃ Gy)]	(R1, 2, 4)
(6)	(∀y) ([Fa ⊃ ((∀x)Gx ⊃ Gy)] ⊃ [(Fa ⊃ (∀x)Gx) ⊃ (Fa ⊃ Gy)])	(A2)⁴
(7)	6 ⊃ (5 ⊃ (∀y) [(Fa ⊃ (∀x)Gx) ⊃ (Fa ⊃ Gy)])	(A5)
(8)	5 ⊃ (∀y) [(Fa ⊃ (∀x)Gx) ⊃ (Fa ⊃ Gy)]	(R1, 6, 7)
(9)	(∀y) [(Fa ⊃ (∀x)Gx) ⊃ (Fa ⊃ Gy)]	(R1, 5, 8)
(10)	9 ⊃ [(∀y) (Fa ⊃ (∀x)Gx) ⊃ (∀y) (Fa ⊃ Gy)]	(A5)
(11)	(∀y) (Fa ⊃ (∀x)Gx) ⊃ (∀y) (Fa ⊃ Gy)	(R1, 9, 10)
(12)	11 ⊃ [(Fa ⊃ (∀x)Gx) ⊃ 11]	(A1)
(13)	(Fa ⊃ (∀x)Gx) ⊃ 11	(R1, 11, 12)
(14)	(Fa ⊃ (∀x)Gx) ⊃ (∀y) (Fa ⊃ (∀x)Gx)	(A4)
(15)	13 ⊃ (14 ⊃ [(Fa ⊃ (∀x)Gx) ⊃ (∀y)(Fa ⊃ Gy)])	(A2)
(16)	14 ⊃ [(Fa ⊃ (∀x)Gx) ⊃ (∀y)(Fa ⊃ Gy)]	(R1, 13, 15)
(17)	(Fa ⊃ (∀x)Gx) ⊃ (∀y)(Fa ⊃ Gy)	(R1, 14, 16)

Note: Since by definition '(Q & R) ⊃ ~P' is short for '~(Q ⊃ ~R) ⊃ ~P', entries (1)–(9) in Example 1 also count as an a-derivation of '~R' from {P, P ⊃ Q, (Q & R) ⊃ ~P}; and, since by definition '(∃x)Gx ⊃ (∃x)Fx' is short for '~(∀x)~Gx ⊃ ~(∀x)~Fx', entries (1)–(11) in Example 3 also count as an a-derivation of 'Ga ⊃ Hb' from {(∀x)~Fx, (∃x)Gx ⊃ (∃x)Fx}.

We go on to show that, for any set *S* of statements and any statement *A*, *S* ⊢ₐ *A* if and only if *S* ⊢ *A*, and hence that the present method of derivation does exactly the same job as natural deduction.

Converting a-*Derivations into Derivations*

Any a-derivation of a statement *A* from a finite set *S* of statements can be provisionally recast in the form

---

² '[(∀x)Gx ⊃ Gb] ⊃ [Fa ⊃ ((∀x)Gx ⊃ Gb)]' is of the sort A1. Hence, (1) counts as an axiom.
³ '(∀x)Gx ⊃ Gb' is of the sort A6. Hence, (2) counts as an axiom.
⁴ '[Fa ⊃ ((∀x)Gx ⊃ Gb)] ⊃ [(Fa ⊃ (∀x)Gx) ⊃ (Fa ⊃ Gb)]' is of the sort A2. Hence, (6) counts as an axiom.

$$
\begin{array}{c|c}
1 & A_1 \\
2 & A_2 \\
\cdot & \cdot \\
n & A_n \\
\hline
n+1 & A_{n+1} \\
n+2 & A_{n+2} \\
\cdot & \cdot \\
n+p & A_{n+p},
\end{array}
$$

where A_1, A_2, ..., and A_n ($n \geq 0$) are the various members of S, A_{n+p} is A itself, and—for each i from 1 through p—A_{n+i} is an axiom or is obtained by one of the two rules R and $\supset$E. But, as the reader should verify on his own, any one of our axioms is provable in accordance with rules R, ~I, ~E, $\supset$I, $\supset$E, $\forall$I*, and $\forall$E. Hence any a-derivation of A from the set S can ultimately be turned into a derivation of A from S that uses just rules R, ~I, ~E, $\supset$I, $\supset$E, $\forall$I*, and $\forall$E. Hence, any statement that is a-derivable from a *finite* set of statements is sure to be derivable from the set in accordance with these seven rules.[5]

As an illustration, Example 1 can be provisionally recast in the form

1	P
2	P ⊃ Q
3	~[(S ⊃ Q) ⊃ R] ⊃ ~P

4	P	(R, 1)
5	P ⊃ Q	(R, 2)
6	~[(S ⊃ Q) ⊃ R] ⊃ ~P	(R, 3)
7	6 ⊃ (P ⊃ [(S ⊃ Q) ⊃ R])	(A3)
8	P ⊃ [(S ⊃ Q) ⊃ R]	(⊃E, 6, 7)
9	(S ⊃ Q) ⊃ R	(⊃E, 4, 8)
10	Q	(⊃E, 4, 5)
11	Q ⊃ (S ⊃ Q)	(A1)
12	S ⊃ Q	(⊃E, 10, 11)
13	R	(⊃E, 9, 12)

Since line 7 is provable in accordance with R, ~I, ~E, $\supset$I, and $\supset$E, and line 11 in accordance with R and $\supset$I, Example 1 can ultimately be turned into a derivation of 13 from $\{1, 2, 3\}$ using just rules R, ~I, ~E, $\supset$I, and $\supset$E.

Suppose next that A is a-derivable from an *infinite* set S of statements. Then A is sure to be a-derivable from a finite subset of S: the one

---

[5] It follows of course from the result that our axiomatization of elementary logic is sound.

consisting of the finitely many members of S which turn up in the a-derivation of A from S. Hence, by the result on p. 332, A is sure to be derivable from that subset of S in accordance with R, $\sim$I, $\sim$E, $\supset$I, $\supset$E, $\forall$I*, and $\forall$E. Hence, by the definition on p. 266, A is sure to be derivable from S itself. Hence, whether S is finite or infinite,

(3.7.1)   If $S \vdash_a A$, then $S \vdash A$.

Converting Derivations into a-*derivations*

Proof that any statement derivable in accordance with R, $\sim$I, $\sim$E, $\supset$I, $\supset$E, $\forall$I*, and $\forall$E from a set of statements is a-derivable from that set, calls for seven lemmas: (3.7.3), (3.7.5), (3.7.7)–(3.7.10), and (3.7.12). Proofs of some of these call in turn for (3.7.2), (3.7.4), (3.7.6), and (3.7.11).

(3.7.2)   If $S \vdash_a A$, then $S' \vdash_a A$ for any superset S' of S (i.e., for any set S' of statements of which S is a subset).

PROOF: Let S' be an arbitrary superset of S. In any a-derivation of A from S, any entry that belongs to S belongs to S' as well. Hence, any a-derivation of A from S qualifies as an a-derivation of A from S'. Hence (3.7.2).

(3.7.3)   If A belongs to S, then $S \vdash_a A$.

PROOF: The column made up of just A qualifies as an a-derivation of A from any set of statements with A as a member. Hence (3.7.3).

(3.7.4)   If A is an axiom, then $S \vdash_a A$.

PROOF: Suppose A is an axiom, and let S be an arbitrary set of statements. Then the column made up of just A qualifies as an a-derivation of A from S. Hence (3.7.4).

(3.7.5)   If $S \vdash_a A \supset B$ and $S \vdash_a A$, then $S \vdash_a B$.

PROOF: Let the column made up of the statements $C_1, C_2, \ldots$, and C_p constitute an a-derivation of $A \supset B$ from S, and the column made up of the statements $D_1, D_2, \ldots$, and D_q constitute an a-derivation of A from S. Since B follows from $D_q \, (= A)$ and $C_p \, (= A \supset B)$ by R1, the column made up of $C_1, C_2, \ldots, C_p, D_1, D_2, \ldots$, and D_q and B qualifies as an a-derivation of B from S. Hence (3.7.5).

(3.7.6) $\vdash_a A \supset A$.

PROOF: For any statement A the following column of statements constitutes an a-proof of $A \supset A$:

(1) $A \supset [(A \supset A) \supset A]$ (A1)
(2) $A \supset (A \supset A)$ (A1)

(3) $1 \supset [2 \supset (A \supset A)]$ (A2)

(4) $2 \supset (A \supset A)$ (R1, 1, 3)

(5) $A \supset A$ (R1, 2, 4).

Hence (3.7.6).

   (3.7.7) If $S \cup \{A\} \vdash_a B$, then $S \vdash_a A \supset B$.

PROOF: Let the column made up of the statements $C_1, C_2, \ldots$, and C_p constitute an a-derivation of B from $S \cup \{A\}$. We establish by mathematical induction on i that, for each i from 1 through p, $S \vdash_a A \supset C_i$, and hence that $S \vdash_a A \supset C_p (= S \vdash_a A \supset B)$.

BASIS: $i = 1$. Suppose first that C_i is a member of $S \cup \{A\}$ other than A or is an axiom. Then the following column of statements constitutes an a-derivation of $A \supset C_i$ from S:

(1') C_i

(2') $C_i \supset (A \supset C_i)$ (A1)

(3') $A \supset C_i$ (R1, 1', 2').

Suppose next that C_i is A. Then the column of statements in the proof of (3.7.6) constitutes an a-derivation of $A \supset C_i$ from S. In either case, therefore, $S \vdash_a A \supset C_i$.

INDUCTIVE STEP: $i > 1$.
Suppose first that C_i belongs to $S \cup \{A\}$ or is an axiom. Then $S \vdash_a A \supset C_i$ by the same argument as before. Suppose next that C_i follows by R1 from two previous entries C_g and $C_h (= C_g \supset C_i)$, and assume that each one of $A \supset C_1, A \supset C_2, \ldots$, and $A \supset C_{i-1}$ is a-derivable from S (this is the hypothesis of the induction). Then there is an a-derivation of $A \supset C_g$ from S, say the column made up of the statements $D_1, D_2, \ldots$, and D_p, and there is an a-derivation of $A \supset C_h$ from S, say the column made up of the statements $E_1, E_2, \ldots$, and E_q. But, if so, then the column made up of $D_1, D_2, \ldots, D_p (= A \supset C_g)$, $E_1, E_2, \ldots$, and $E_q (= A \supset (C_g \supset C_i))$, *plus* the following three statements:

(1'') $E_q \supset [D_p \supset (A \supset C_i)]$ (A2)

(2'') $D_p \supset (A \supset C_i)$ (R1, E_q, 1'')

(3'') $A \supset C_i$ (R1, D_p, 2''),

qualifies as an a-derivation of $A \supset C_i$ from S. Hence $S \vdash_a A \supset C_i$. In either case, therefore, $S \vdash_a A \supset C_i$.

To illustrate matters, we display side by side an a-derivation of '$R \supset Q$' from the set $\{P \supset Q, P\}$ (i.e., from the set $\{P \supset Q\} \cup \{P\}$), and the a-derivation of 'P ⊃ (R ⊃ Q)' from the set {P ⊃ Q} that we get by heeding the instructions in the proof of (3.7.7):

{P ⊃ Q, P} ⊢ₐ R ⊃ Q   {P ⊃ Q} ⊢ₐ P ⊃ (R ⊃ Q)

(1) P ⊃ Q
          (1.1) P ⊃ Q
          (1.2) 1.1 ⊃ [P ⊃ (P ⊃ Q)]   (A1)
          (1.3) P ⊃ (P ⊃ Q)   (R1, 1.1, 1.2)

(2) P
          (2.1) P ⊃ [(P ⊃ P) ⊃ P]   (A1)
          (2.2) P ⊃ (P ⊃ P)   (A1)
          (2.3) 2.1 ⊃ [2.2 ⊃ (P ⊃ P)]   (A2)
          (2.4) 2.2 ⊃ (P ⊃ P)   (R1, 2.1, 2.3)
          (2.5) P ⊃ P   (R1, 2.2, 2.4)

(3) Q   (R1, 1, 2)
          (3.1) 1.3 ⊃ [2.5 ⊃ (P ⊃ Q)]   (A2)
          (3.2) 2.5 ⊃ (P ⊃ Q)   (R1, 1.3, 3.1)
          (3.3) P ⊃ Q   (R1, 2.5, 3.2)

(4) Q ⊃ (R ⊃ Q)   (A1)
          (4.1) Q ⊃ (R ⊃ Q)   (A1)
          (4.2) 4.1 ⊃ (P ⊃ [Q ⊃ (R ⊃ Q)]) (A1)
          (4.3) P ⊃ [Q ⊃ (R ⊃ Q)]   (R1, 4.1, 4.2)

(5) R ⊃ Q   (R1, 3, 4)
          (5.1) 4.3 ⊃ (3.3 ⊃ [P ⊃ (R ⊃ Q)]) (A2)
          (5.2) 3.3 ⊃ [P ⊃ (R ⊃ Q)]   (R1, 4.3, 5.1)
          (5.3) P ⊃ (R ⊃ Q)   (R1, 3.3, 5.2).

(3.7.8) If $S \vdash_a \sim\sim A$, then $S \vdash_a A$.

PROOF: For any statement A, the column made up of any a-derivation of $\sim\sim A$ from S, plus the following seven statements:

(1) $\sim\sim A \supset (\sim\sim\sim\sim A \supset \sim\sim A)$ (A1)
(2) $\sim\sim\sim\sim A \supset \sim\sim A$ (R1, $\sim\sim A$, 1)
(3) $2 \supset (\sim A \supset \sim\sim\sim A)$ (A3)
(4) $\sim A \supset \sim\sim\sim A$ (R1, 2, 3)
(5) $4 \supset (\sim\sim A \supset A)$ (A3)
(6) $\sim\sim A \supset A$ (R1, 4, 5)
(7) A (R1, $\sim\sim A$, 6),

qualifies as an a-derivation of A from S. Hence (3.7.8).

(3.7.9) If $S \cup \{A\} \vdash_a B$ and $S \cup \{A\} \vdash_a \sim B$, then $S \vdash_a \sim A$.

PROOF: Suppose first that $S \cup \{A\} \vdash_a \sim B$. Since $\sim B \supset [\sim\sim(A \supset A) \supset \sim B]$ is an axiom (= A1), $S \cup \{A\} \vdash_a \sim B \supset [\sim\sim(A \supset A) \supset \sim B]$ by (3.7.4), and hence $S \cup \{A\} \vdash_a \sim\sim(A \supset A) \supset \sim B$ by (3.7.5). But, since

$[\sim\sim(A \supset A) \supset \sim B] \supset [B \supset \sim(A \supset A)]$ is an axiom ($=$ A3), $S \cup \{A\}$ $\vdash_a [\sim\sim(A \supset A) \supset \sim B] \supset [B \supset \sim(A \supset A)]$ by (3.7.4). Hence $S \cup \{A\}$ $\vdash_a B \supset \sim(A \supset A)$ by (3.7.5). Suppose next that $S \cup \{A\} \vdash_a B$. Then $S \cup \{A\} \vdash_a \sim(A \supset A)$ by (3.7.5), hence $S \cup \{\sim\sim A, A\} \vdash_a \sim(A \supset A)$ by (3.7.2), and hence $S \cup \{\sim\sim A\} \vdash_a A \supset \sim(A \supset A)$ by (3.7.7). But $S \cup \{\sim\sim A\} \vdash_a \sim\sim A$ by (3.7.3), and hence $S \cup \{\sim\sim A\} \vdash_a A$ by (3.7.8). Hence $S \cup \{\sim\sim A\} \vdash_a \sim(A \supset A)$ by (3.7.5), and hence $S \vdash_a \sim\sim A \supset \sim(A \supset A)$ by (3.7.7). But, since $[\sim\sim A \supset \sim(A \supset A)] \supset [(A \supset A) \supset \sim A]$ is an axiom ($=$ A3), $S \vdash_a [\sim\sim A \supset \sim(A \supset A)] \supset [(A \supset A) \supset \sim A]$ by (3.7.4). Hence $S \vdash_a (A \supset A) \supset \sim A$ by (3.7.5). But in view of (3.7.6) and (3.7.2) $S \vdash_a A \supset A$. Hence $S \vdash_a \sim A$ by (3.7.5). Hence (3.7.9).

(3.7.10) If $S \vdash_a (\forall X)A$, then $S \vdash_a A(T/X)$ for any term T.

PROOF: Let T be an arbitrary term. Since $(\forall X)A \supset A(T/X)$ is an axiom ($=$ A6), $S \vdash_a (\forall X)A \supset A(T/X)$ by (3.7.4). Hence (3.7.10) by (3.7.5).

(3.7.11) $\vdash_a (\forall X)A \supset (\forall Y)A(Y/X)$, where Y is foreign to $(\forall X)A$.[6]

PROOF: For any statement $(\forall X)A$, and any term variable Y that is distinct from X, the following column of statements constitutes an a-proof of $(\forall X)A \supset (\forall Y)A(Y/X)$:

(1)	$(\forall Y)[(\forall X)A \supset A(Y/X)]$	(A6)
(2)	$1 \supset [(\forall Y)(\forall X)A \supset (\forall Y)A(Y/X)]$	(A5)
(3)	$(\forall Y)(\forall X)A \supset (\forall Y)A(Y/X)$	(R1, 1, 2)
(4)	$3 \supset ((\forall X)A \supset 3)$	(A1)
(5)	$(\forall X)A \supset 3$	(R1, 3, 4)
(6)	$(\forall X)A \supset (\forall Y)(\forall X)A$	(A4)
(7)	$5 \supset (6 \supset [(\forall X)A \supset (\forall Y)A(Y/X)])$	(A2)
(8)	$6 \supset [(\forall X)A \supset (\forall Y)A(Y/X)]$	(R1, 5, 7)
(9)	$(\forall X)A \supset (\forall Y)A(Y/X)$	(R1, 6, 8).

Hence (3.7.11).

(3.7.12) If $S \vdash_a A(T/X)$, then $S \cup S' \vdash_a (\forall X)A$, so long as T is foreign to S and to $(\forall X)A$.

PROOF: *Part One.* Suppose the column made up of the statements $B_1, B_2, \ldots,$ and B_p constitutes an a-derivation of $A(T/X)$ from S, where T is foreign to S and to $(\forall X)A$, and let Y be X if X is foreign

---

[6] Here, of course, $A(Y/X)$ is the result of substituting the term variable Y for every occurrence of the term variable X in A. With Y required to be foreign to $(\forall X)A$, Y is sure to be distinct from X and foreign to A. Hence, for any term T, $((\forall X)A \supset A(Y/X))(T/Y)$ is the statement $(\forall X)A \supset A(T/X)$, and hence line (1) below is an axiom.

to each one of $B_1, B_2, \ldots,$ and B_{p-1},[7] otherwise let Y be an arbitrary term variable foreign to each one of $B_1, B_2, \ldots,$ and B_p. We establish by mathematical induction on i that, for each i from 1 through p, $S \vdash_a (\forall Y)B_i(Y/T)$, and hence that $S \vdash_a (\forall Y)B_p(Y/T)(= S \vdash_a (\forall Y)(A(T/X))(Y/T))$.

BASIS: $i = 1$. Suppose first that B_i belongs to S. Then $S \vdash_a B_i$ by (3.7.3). But, since $B_i \supset (\forall Y)B_i$ is an axiom $(= A4)$, $S \vdash_a B_i \supset (\forall Y)B_i$ by (3.7.4). Hence $S \vdash_a (\forall Y)B_i$ by (3.7.5). But, with T presumed to be foreign to S and hence to B_i, $(\forall Y)B_i(Y/T)$ is the same as $(\forall Y)B_i$. Hence $S \vdash_a (\forall Y)B_i(Y/T)$. Suppose next that B_i is an axiom. With Y presumed to be foreign to B_i, $(B_i(Y/T))(T/Y)$ is the same as B_i, and hence is an axiom. But T is sure to be foreign to $(\forall Y)B_i(Y/T)$. Hence $(\forall Y)B_i(Y/T)$ is an axiom. Hence $S \vdash_a (\forall Y)B_i(Y/T)$ by (3.7.4). In either case, therefore, $S \vdash_a (\forall Y)B_i(Y/T)$.

INDUCTIVE STEP: $i > 1$. Suppose first that B_i belongs to S or is an axiom. Then, by the same reasoning as before, $S \vdash_a (\forall Y)B_i(Y/T)$. Suppose next that B_i follows by R1 from two previous entries B_g and $B_h (= B_g \supset B_i)$, and assume that each one of $(\forall Y)B_1(Y/T)$, $(\forall Y)B_2(Y/T), \ldots,$ and $(\forall Y)B_{i-1}(Y/T)$ is a-derivable from S (this is the hypothesis of the induction). Then $S \vdash_a (\forall Y)B_g(Y/T)$ and $S \vdash_a (\forall Y)B_h(Y/T)$. But $(\forall Y)(B_g(Y/T) \supset B_i(Y/T))$ is the same as $(\forall Y)(B_g \supset B_i)(Y/T) (= (\forall Y)B_h(Y/T))$. Hence $S \vdash_a (\forall Y)(B_g(Y/T) \supset B_i(Y/T))$. But, since $(\forall Y)(B_g(Y/T) \supset B_i(Y/T)) \supset ((\forall Y)B_g(Y/T) \supset (\forall Y)B_i(Y/T))$ is an axiom $(= A5)$, $S \vdash_a (\forall Y)(B_g(Y/T) \supset B_i(Y/T)) \supset ((\forall Y)B_g(Y/T) \supset (\forall Y)B_i(Y/T))$ by (3.7.4). Hence $S \vdash_a (\forall Y)B_g(Y/T) \supset (\forall Y)B_i(Y/T)$, and hence $S \vdash_a (\forall Y)B_i(Y/T)$, by (3.7.5). In either case, therefore, $S \vdash_a (\forall Y)B_i(Y/T)$.

Part Two. With T foreign to $(\forall X)A$, $A(Y/X)$ is the same as $(A(T/X))(Y/T)$. Hence $S \vdash_a (\forall Y)A(Y/X)$ by Part One, and hence $S \vdash_a (\forall X)A$ if Y is the same as X. Suppose, however, that Y is distinct from X. Then X is sure to be foreign to $(\forall Y)A(Y/X)$. Hence, $S \vdash_a (\forall Y)A(Y/X) \supset (\forall X)(A(Y/X))(X/Y)$ by (3.7.11) and (3.7.2), and hence $S \vdash_a (\forall X)(A(Y/X))(X/Y)$ by (3.7.5). But, with Y presumed to be foreign to $A(T/X)$ and hence to A, $(\forall X)A$ is the same as $(\forall Y)(A(Y/X))(X/Y)$. Hence $S \vdash_a (\forall X)A$. Hence, whether or not Y is the same as X, $S \vdash_a (\forall X)A$. Hence $S \cup S' \vdash_a (\forall X)A$ by (3.7.2). Hence (3.7.12).

Now let there be a derivation (done in accordance with R, $\sim$I, $\sim$E, $\supset$I, $\supset$E, $\forall$I*, and $\forall$E) of a statement B from a set $\{A_1, A_2, \ldots, A_n\}$ of state-

---

[7] With $(\forall X)A$ presumed to be a statement, X is sure to be foreign to $A(T/X)(= B_p)$.

ments. It is easily shown by mathematical induction on d, the degree of complexity of the derivation, that B is a-derivable from $\{A_1, A_2, \ldots, A_n\}$. We just outline the argument, which parallels the one used on pp. 279–82 to prove the Soundness Theorem.

Suppose first that $d = 0$, and hence that the derivation uses none of $\sim$I, $\supset$I, and $\forall$I*. Then, by essentially the same reasoning as on pp. 279–80, but with 'B is a-derivable from $\{A_1, A_2, \ldots, A_n\}$' substituting for '$\{A_1, A_2, \ldots, A_n\}$ entails B', and with (3.7.3), (3.7.8), (3.7.10) and (3.7.5) respectively doing duty for (3.3.1), (3.3.3), (3.3.7), and (3.3.5), B can be shown to be a-derivable from $\{A_1, A_2, \ldots, A_n\}$.

Suppose next that $d > 0$, and assume that the result to be proved holds of any derivation (done in accordance with R, $\sim$I, $\sim$E, $\supset$I, $\supset$E, $\forall$I*, and $\forall$E) of a degree of complexity less than d. Then, by essentially the same reasoning as on pp. 280–82, but with (3.7.9), (3.7.7), and (3.7.12) respectively doing duty for (3.3.2), (3.3.4), and (3.3.6), B can be shown to be a-derivable from $\{A_1, A_2, \ldots, A_n\}$.

Since a statement, when derivable (in accordance with R, $\sim$I, $\sim$E, $\supset$I, $\supset$E, $\forall$I*, and $\forall$E) from an infinite set of statements, is derivable by definition from a finite subset of that set, we conclude that:

(3.7.13)   If $S \vdash A$, then $S \vdash_a A$,

this whether S is finite or infinite.[8]

Mechanical instructions for converting a-derivations into derivations, and vice versa, can be drawn from the proofs of (3.7.1) and (3.7.13). The task is left to the reader.

Incidentally, (3.7.7) was proved shortly before Jaśkowski and Gentzen devised the method of derivation of Sections 1.3 and 2.3. Known as the *Deduction Theorem*, it served at the time as an adjunct to the method of derivation of this section, and so did—under names of their own—(3.7.8), (3.7.9), (3.7.10), and (3.7.12). (3.7.7) guaranteed that any a-derivation of the consequent B of a conditional $A \supset B$ from a set S of statements *plus* the antecedent A of $A \supset B$ could be turned into an a-derivation of $A \supset B$ from just S, and hence could pass as an a-derivation of $A \supset B$ from just S. (3.7.8) guaranteed that any a-derivation of the double negation $\sim\sim A$ of a statement A from a set S of statements could be turned into an a-derivation of A itself from S, and hence could pass as an a-derivation of A from S. And so on. Natural deduction was born when Jaśkowski and Gentzen pooled these various adjuncts to the traditional method of derivation, and showed them to yield proofs of all the axioms then in use.

---

[8] It follows of course from the result that our axiomatization of elementary logic is complete.

Alternative Axiomatizations

The foregoing is only one of many axiomatizations of elementary logic that do the same work as natural deduction. We list a few others as samples.

(1)   The truth-functional axiom schemata A1–A3 can be turned in for a single one, to wit:

$$[([(A \supset B) \supset (\sim C \supset \sim D)] \supset C) \supset E] \supset [(E \supset A) \supset (D \supset A)].$$

(2)   When '$\sim$' and '&' (rather than '$\sim$' and '$\supset$') serve as primitive connectives, and $A \supset B$ serves as a definitional rewrite of $\sim(A \& \sim B)$, the following can do duty as truth-functional axiom schemata:

$$A \supset (A \& A),$$
$$(A \& B) \supset A, \text{ and}$$
$$(A \supset B) \supset [\sim(B \& C) \supset \sim(C \& A)].$$

(3)   When '$\sim$' and '∨' (rather than '$\sim$' and '$\supset$') serve as primitive connectives, and $A \supset B$ serves as a definitional rewrite of $\sim A \vee B$, the following can do duty as truth-functional axiom schemata:

$$(A \vee A) \supset A,$$
$$A \supset (A \vee B), \text{ and}$$
$$(A \supset B) \supset [(C \vee A) \supset (B \vee C)].$$

(4)   When ' | ' serves as sole primitive connective, the following can do duty as sole truth-functional axiom schema:

$$[A \mid (B \mid C)] \mid ([A \mid (C \mid A)] \mid [(D \mid B) \mid ([A \mid D] \mid [A \mid D])])$$

However, R1 must be turned in for the following rule of inference:

R1′: To infer C from A and $A \mid (B \mid C)$.

(5)   When all five of '$\sim$', '$\supset$', '&', '∨', and '$\equiv$' serve as primitive connectives, the following can do duty as extra truth-functional axiom schemata:

$$(A \& B) \supset A,$$
$$(A \& B) \supset B,$$
$$A \supset [B \supset (A \& B)],$$
$$A \supset (A \vee B),$$
$$B \supset (A \vee B),$$
$$(A \supset C) \supset ((B \supset C) \supset [(A \vee B) \supset C]),$$
$$A \supset [(A \equiv B) \supset B],$$
$$A \supset [(B \equiv A) \supset B], \text{ and}$$
$$(A \supset B) \supset [(B \supset A) \supset (A \equiv B)].$$

(6)   Under our original choice of truth-functional axiom schemata, and any one of the substitute choices listed in (1)–(5), clause (iii) on p. 328 can be dropped if a distant relative of $\forall$I—with $A(T_1,T_2,\ldots,T_n/X_1,X_2,\ldots,X_n)$ understood as the result of replacing X_1 everywhere in A by T_1, X_2 by $T_2, \ldots$, and X_n by T_n—is drafted as an *extra* rule of inference:

> R2. To infer $(\forall X_1)(\forall X_2)\ldots(\forall X_n)A$ from $A(T_1,T_2,\ldots,T_n/X_1,X_2,\ldots,X_n)$, so long as $A(T_1,T_2,\ldots,T_n/X_1,X_2,\ldots,X_n)$ is an axiom and—for each i from 1 through n—T_i is foreign to $(\forall X_i)(\forall X_{i+1})\ldots(\forall X_n)A(T_1,T_2,\ldots,T_{i-1}/X_1,X_2,\ldots,X_{i-1})$.[9]

(3.7.7) and (3.7.12) would call here for slightly more complicated proofs, which we leave to the reader.

Various axiomatizations of elementary logic are especially designed for proving statements (and call for slight adjustments in our account of an a-derivation when used to derive statements from sets of statements). We list three as samples.

(7)   With '$\sim$', '$\supset$', and '$\forall$' serving as primitive operators, axioms of *just* the five sorts A1–A3, A6, and

$$(\forall X)(A \supset B) \supset (A \supset (\forall X)B),$$

will do if the following relative of $\forall$I is drafted as an *extra* rule of inference:

> R2′. For any term T, to infer $(\forall X)A$ from $A(T/X)$, so long as T is foreign to $(\forall X)A$.

(8)   Again with '$\sim$', '$\supset$', and '$\forall$' serving as primitive operators, axioms of *just* the four sorts A1–A3 and A6 will do if the following relative of $\forall$I is drafted as an *extra* rule of inference:

> R2″. For any term T, to infer $A \supset (\forall X)B$ from $A \supset B(T/X)$, so long as T is foreign to $A \supset (\forall X)B$.

(9)   With '$\sim$', '$\supset$', and '$\exists$' (rather than '$\sim$', '$\supset$', and '$\forall$') serving as primitive operators, axioms of *just* the four sorts A1–A3 and

$$A(T/X) \supset (\exists X)A$$

will do if the following relative of $\exists$E is drafted as an *extra* rule of inference:

> R2‴. For any term T, to infer $(\exists X)A \supset B$ from $A(T/X) \supset B$, so long as T is foreign to $(\exists X)A \supset B$.

---

[9] With $A(T_1,T_2,\ldots,T_n/X_1,X_2,\ldots,X_n)$ presumed to be an axiom and hence a statement, and X_1, X_2, $\ldots$, and X_n presumed to be distinct, $(\forall X_1)(\forall X_2)\ldots(\forall X_n)A$ is sure to be a statement.

EXERCISES

E3.7.1.   Supply an a-proof of each one of the following statements:

a. $\sim P \supset (P \supset Q)$

e. $[P \supset (Q \supset R)] \supset [Q \supset (P \supset R)]$

b. $\sim\sim P \supset P$

f. $(P \supset Q) \supset [(Q \supset R) \supset (P \supset R)]$

c. $P \supset \sim\sim P$

g. $(P \supset \sim Q) \supset (Q \supset \sim P)$

d. $P \supset [(P \supset Q) \supset Q]$

h. $(\sim P \supset Q) \supset (\sim Q \supset P)$

i. $(P \supset Q) \supset (\sim Q \supset \sim P)$

E3.7.2.   With '&', 'V', and '$\equiv$' understood to be defined as on p. 254, supply for each argument in E1.3.3 an a-derivation of the conclusion from the premises.

E3.7.3.   With '$\exists$' understood to be defined as on p. 254, supply an a-proof of each one of the following statements:

a. $Fa \supset (\exists x)Fx$

d. $(\forall x)(Fa \supset Gx) \supset (Fa \supset (\forall x)Gx)$

b. $(\forall x)Fx \supset (\exists x)Fx$

e. $(\forall x)(\forall y)Fxy \supset (\forall y)(\forall x)Fxy$

c. $(Fa \supset (\forall x)Gx) \supset (\forall x)(Fa \supset Gx)$ f. $(\exists x)(\exists y)Fxy \supset (\exists y)(\exists x)Fxy$

g. $(\forall x)(Fx \supset Gx) \supset [(\exists x)(Fx \& Hx) \supset (\exists x)(Gx \& Hx)]$

h. $(\forall x)(Fx \supset Gx) \supset [(\exists x)Fx \supset (\exists x)Gx]$

i. $(\exists x)(Fx \supset Gx) \equiv [(\forall x)Fx \supset (\exists x)Gx]$

E3.7.4.   Using the definitions on p. 254, supply for each argument in E2.3.2 an a-derivation of the conclusion from the premises.

E3.7.5.   Show that every axiom is of the sort $(\forall X_1)(\forall X_2)\ldots(\forall X_n)A$, where—for some n terms $T_1, T_2,\ldots,$ and T_n such that T_i $(i = 1, 2,\ldots,n)$ is foreign to $(\forall X_i)(\forall X_{i+1})\ldots(\forall X_n)A(T_1,T_2,\ldots,T_{i-1}/X_1,X_2,\ldots,X_{i-1})$—the statement

$$A(T_1,T_2,\ldots,T_n/X_1,X_2,\ldots,X_n)$$

is of one of the sorts A1–A6.

E3.7.6.   Using the result in E3.7.5, show by mathematical induction on n that every axiom is provable in accordance with R, $\sim$I, $\sim$E, $\supset$I, $\supset$E, $\forall$I*, and $\forall$E.

E3.7.7.   Show that every line in an a-derivation of a statement from a set S of statements is entailed (either in the truth-value or in the standard sense) by S. (Do not use (3.7.1), from which the result follows, of course, by the Soundness Theorem.)

E3.7.8.   Show that:

(a) If $A \supset B(T/X)$ is a-provable, then so is $A \supset (\forall X)B$, so long as T is foreign to $A \supset (\forall X)B$;

(b) If $A(T/X) \supset B$ is a-provable, then so is $(\exists X)A \supset B$, so long as T is foreign to $(\exists X)A \supset B$.

E3.7.9.   With '$\sim$' and '$\supset$' still serving as sole primitive connectives, show that any statement of any one of the sorts displayed in (2), (3), and (5) on p. 339, is a-provable.

E3.7.10.   First under the circumstances described in (2) on p. 339, then under those described in (3), show that any statement of any one of the three sorts A1–A3 is forthcoming as an a-theorem.

E3.7.11.   Under the circumstances described in (6) on p. 340, supply substitute proofs of (3.7.7) and (3.7.12).

* *E3.7.12.*   Show that if $S \vdash_a A$, then $S(T'/T) \vdash_a A(T'/T)$, where $S(T'/T)$ consists of the results of putting T' for T in the members of S.

E3.7.13. With a set S of statements said to be *syntactically* a-*consistent* if there is no statement A such that both $S \vdash_a A$ and $S \vdash_a \sim A$, show that the double image of any syntactically a-consistent set of statements is syntactically a-consistent. (See (3.6.17) on this matter.)

E3.7.14. With A understood to contain no quantifiers, show that if there is an a-proof of A, then there is one using just A1–A3 and R1. (Hint: Show that upon deletion of any entry containing a quantifier, the original a-proof of A remains an a-proof of A.)

E3.7.15. With 0, 1, and 2 serving on this occasion as truth-values, and the two connectives '$\sim$' and '$\supset$' understood to obey the following truth-tables:

A	$\sim A$
0	0
1	2
2	1

A	B	$A \supset B$
0	0	0
1	0	2
2	0	0
0	1	0
1	1	0
2	1	0
0	2	2
1	2	2
2	2	0

show that:

(a) on any assignment of 0, 1, and 2 to its atomic components, any statement of either one of the two sorts A2 and A3 has value 0, and

(b) on any assignment of 0, 1, and 2 to the atomic components of $A \supset B$, B has value 0 or 1 if both A and $A \supset B$ do. (In view of (a) and (b), any statement a-provable by means of just A2, A3, and R1 is sure to have value 0 or 1 on any assignment of the three truth-values 0, 1, and 2 to its atomic subformulas.)

E3.7.16. Using the results in E3.7.14–15, show that '$P \supset (Q \supset P)$' is not a-provable without recourse to A1, and hence that this axiom schema is independent of the others.

E3.7.17. With 0, 1, and 2 serving again as truth-values, and '$\sim$' and '$\supset$' understood to obey the following truth-tables:

A	$\sim A$
0	2
1	1
2	0

A	B	$A \supset B$
0	0	0
1	0	0
2	0	0
0	1	1
1	1	0
2	1	0
0	2	1
1	2	1
2	2	0

show that:

(a) on any assignment of 0, 1, and 2 to its atomic components, any statement of either one of the two sorts A1 and A3 has value 0, and

(b) on any assignment of 0, 1, and 2 to the atomic components of $A \supset B$, B has value 0 if both A and $A \supset B$ do.

E3.7.18.   Using the results in E3.7.14 and E3.7.17, show that '$[P \supset (Q \supset R)] \supset [(P \supset Q) \supset (P \supset R)]$' is not a-provable without recourse to A2, and hence that this axiom schema is independent of the others.

E3.7.19.   Provisionally taking $\sim A$ to be true on a truth-value α to its atomic components if and only if A is true on α, and using the result in E3.7.14, show that '$(\sim P \supset \sim Q) \supset (Q \supset P)$' is not a-provable without recourse to A3, and hence that this axiom schema is independent of the others.

Appendix I

Set-Theoretic Matters

Throughout the book we deal as much with sets of statements as with individual statements; and in Chapter 3 we deal under the name of *domains* with all sorts of non-empty sets. So a few words about set theory may be in order.

Sets are collections of "things" in the broadest possible sense of the word, such as physical objects, statements, numbers, properties, even sets. Their members may have something in common, but need not. The members of the set {Taft,Eisenhower,Nixon}, for example, have much in common; those of the set {Nixon,7^2,redness} do not.

Some sets have only one member, like the set {Nixon} which consists of only one person, or the set {49} which consists of only one number. (They are often called **unit sets.**) Some sets have only two members, like the set {Julie,Tricia} which consists of only two persons, or the set {69,96} which consists of only two numbers. Some sets have only three members. And so on. Sets that have only finitely many members are called **finite sets.** Set theorists also acknowledge a set that has *no* members at all. They call it the **null** or **empty set,** and commonly refer to it by means of '∅'. ∅ also counts as a finite set.

By contrast, some sets—like the set consisting of all the positive integers (1, 2, 3, etc.), or the set consisting of all the irrational numbers—have infinitely many members. But we postpone specific discussion of these.

A set S is said to be **the same as** (or to be **identical with**) a set S' if S and S' have exactly the same members (not just the same number of members, but the very same members). The set consisting of all the primes between 2 and 20, and the set consisting of 3, 5, 7, 11, 13, 17, and 19, are the same. Note incidentally that when S and S' have no members, all the members of S are sure to belong to S' and *vice versa*. Hence, there is just one null set.

345

A set S is said to be a **subset** of a set S' if all the members of S belong to S'; and S is said to be a **superset** of S' if S' is a subset of S. Under these definitions, any set S is sure to be one of its subsets and one of its supersets, since all its members do belong to S. The subsets of a set S other than S itself are often known as the **proper subsets** of S. The set {Taft,Eisenhower} is a (proper) subset of the set of all the American Presidents, the latter set being, as a result, one of the supersets of {Taft, Eisenhower}.

A number of operations can be performed on sets to obtain new sets. We mention two simple ones, the first of which is often used in the text. Given two sets S and S', one can pool all their members together, thus obtaining the **union**

$$S \cup S'$$

of the two sets. And, given again two sets S and S', one can form the **intersection**

$$S \cap S'$$

of the two sets, consisting of all the members of S which also belong to S' (equivalently, all the members of S' which also belong to S). The union of the two sets {1,3,5} and {3,5,9,11}, namely:

$$\{1,3,5\} \cup \{3,5,9,11\},$$

is thus {1,3,5,9,11}, whereas their intersection

$$\{1,3,5\} \cap \{3,5,9,11\}$$

is {3,5}. (S may be a subset of S', in which case $S \cup S'$ is just S'.)

When S' is a unit set, i.e., a set with only one member, the union

$$S \cup S'$$

of S and S' consists of all the members of S *plus* the one member of S'. Supposing for example that S consists of all the primes between 2 and 20, the union

$$S \cup \{23\}$$

of S and {23} consists of all the members of S *plus* the one number 23, and hence is the set

$$\{3,5,7,11,13,17,19,23\}.$$

We frequently talk in Chapters 1 and 2 of the union of a set S of statements and the unit set $\{A\}$ of some statement A. That set will consist of all the statements in S *plus* the statement A (and of course will be just S when A already belongs to S).

As our practice so far may have suggested, one way of referring to a finite and non-empty set is to write down the *names* of its members (said names separated by commas when there is more than one), and enclose the resulting list within braces. The set whose only member is Humphrey can be referred to by means of

$$\{Humphrey\},$$

the set whose only two members are Humphrey and Nixon can be referred to by means of

$$\{Humphrey,Nixon\},$$

and the set whose only three members are Humphrey, Nixon, and Wallace can be referred to by means of

$$\{Humphrey,Nixon,Wallace\}.$$

Note incidentally the difference between the two sets

$$\{Humphrey,Nixon,Wallace\}$$

and

$$\{'Humphrey','Nixon','Wallace'\}.$$

The first set consists of three politicians, whose names we enclosed within a pair of braces. By contrast, the second set consists of the *names* of three politicians, and what we enclosed within our braces were therefore names of their names. We followed in this the customary convention whereby a name of a name (and, more generally, a name of a word or of a string of words) can be had by enclosing it within (single) quotation marks. Under this convention the set consisting of the three statements 'The Lord cometh', 'Old soldiers never die', and 'Mary had a little lamb' should be referred to by means of

$$\{'The\ Lord\ cometh',\ 'Old\ soldiers\ never\ die',\ 'Mary\ had\ a\ little\ lamb'\},$$

But no confusion can arise here. So we shall simply write

$$\{The\ Lord\ cometh,\quad Old\ soldiers\ never\ die,\quad Mary\ had\ a\ little\ lamb\},$$

often leaving blanks between the statements to function as quotation marks.

When a set has infinitely many members, there is of course no way of writing out the names of *all* its members. At times, a few sample names followed by dots will do the trick. For example, the set consisting of all the positive integers is often referred to by means of

$$\{1,2,3,4,5,6,...\}$$

or—preferably—by means of

$$\{1,2,3,\ldots,n,\ldots\};$$

the set consisting of all the positive integers that are even is often referred to by means of

$$\{2,4,6,8,10,12,\ldots\}$$

or—preferably—by means of

$$\{2,4,6,\ldots,2n,\ldots\};$$

and so on. But in most cases one must make do with descriptions like

the set of all the points on this line,
the set of all the irrational numbers between 0 and 1,

and so on.

Infinite sets, to embark on the discussion promised earlier, are familiar enough to students from mathematics, possibly less so to others. We mentioned four in the last paragraph, and there are of course countless others. The set consisting of all the positive integers from 2 on, the set of all the positive integers from 3 on, etc., are all infinite sets. And interestingly enough, they are all of the same size as the set of all the positive integers. The set consisting of all the irrational numbers between 0 and 1, on the other hand, is larger than any of them.

When the respective members of two sets can be paired *one to one*, so that to each member of the first set there corresponds a unique member of the second, and to each member of the second set there likewise corresponds a unique member of the first, the two sets are declared of **the same size** (or of **the same cardinality,** as mathematicians would put it). The two sets

$$\{1,2,3\}$$

and

$$\{2,3,4\},$$

for example, are of the same size because their respective members can be paired one to one:

$$
\begin{array}{ccc}
1 & 2 & 3 \\
\updownarrow & \updownarrow & \updownarrow \\
2 & 3 & 4
\end{array}
$$

By the same token, the set consisting of all the positive integers and that consisting of all the positive integers from 2 on are said to be of the same size, since their respective members can be paired one to one:

$$1 \quad 2 \quad 3 \quad 4 \quad 5 \ldots$$
$$\updownarrow \quad \updownarrow \quad \updownarrow \quad \updownarrow \quad \updownarrow$$
$$2 \quad 3 \quad 4 \quad 5 \quad 6 \ldots$$

Or take the two sets

$$\{1,2,3,\ldots,n,\ldots\}$$

and

$$\{2,4,6,\ldots2n,\ldots\}.$$

Their respective members can obviously be paired one to one:

$$1 \quad 2 \quad 3 \quad 4 \quad 5 \ldots$$
$$\updownarrow \quad \updownarrow \quad \updownarrow \quad \updownarrow \quad \updownarrow$$
$$2 \quad 4 \quad 6 \quad 8 \quad 10\ldots$$

The sets would therefore be declared of the same size.

To be sure, $\{2,4,6,\ldots,2n,\ldots\}$ is just a proper subset of $\{1,2,3,\ldots,n,\ldots\}$: infinitely many members of $\{1,2,3,\ldots,n,\ldots\}$ fail to turn up in $\{2,4,6,\ldots,2n,\ldots\}$! This paradoxical sort of situation does not arise in connection with finite sets, which are never of the same size as any of their proper subsets. But it arises in connection with *all* infinite ones. As a matter of fact, an infinite set is often characterized as one which is of the same size as at least one of its *proper* subsets.

Infinite sets whose members cannot be paired one to one are of course of different sizes. A criterion is readily had for determining which of two such sets is smaller than the other. Take again two finite sets, this time of different sizes, say:

$$\{1,2,3\}$$

and

$$\{1,5,7,9\}.$$

The first one could be declared smaller than the second because it is of the same size as some proper subset of the second. $\{1,2,3\}$ is indeed of the same size as four of the proper subsets of $\{1,5,7,9\}$: $\{1,5,7\}$, $\{1,5,9\}$, $\{1,7,9\}$, and $\{5,7,9\}$; whereas $\{1,5,7,9\}$ is not of the same size as any subset of $\{1,2,3\}$.

By the same token, an infinite set S is said to be **smaller in size** than an infinite set S' if S and S' are not of the same size *and* S is of the same size as some proper subset of S'; and of course S is said to be **larger in size** than S' if S' is smaller in size than S. The set consisting of all the positive integers is smaller in size than, say, the set consisting of all the irrational numbers between 0 and 1; and that set is smaller in size than many sets encountered in more advanced chapters of modern mathematics. But we cannot linger on these facts here.

Sets of the smallest infinite size are often said to be of size $\aleph_0$; and, as one set of size $\aleph_0$ is the set $\{0,1,2,\ldots,n,\ldots\}$ of all the so-called **counting numbers,** sets of size $\aleph_0$ are called **countable sets.** These sets are also called **denumerable sets,** and we so refer to them in Chapters 2 and 3. Incidentally, another label for the counting numbers is 'natural numbers'. We adopt it as our official label. So for us the **positive integers** are 1, 2, 3, etc., whereas the **natural numbers** are 0, 1, 2, 3, etc.[1]

Chapter 3 calls for a few extra notions. Pat and Dick Nixon, for example, can be made into a set, indifferently referred to by means of

$$\{Pat,Dick\}$$

and

$$\{Dick,Pat\}.$$

They can also be made into a so-called **ordered pair,** as a matter of fact into two different ordered pairs: the pair

$$<Pat,Dick>,$$

understood to have Pat at its first entry and Dick as the second, and the pair

$$<Dick,Pat>,$$

understood to have him as the first entry and her as the second. If along with contemporary set-theorists we construe **binary relations** as sets of ordered pairs, and for example think of the relation "wife of" as consisting of every pair $<x,y>$ such that x is the wife of y, and think of the relation "husband of" as consisting of every pair $<x,y>$ such that x is the husband of y, then $<Pat,Dick>$ will be one of the pairs that make up the first relation (but not the second), and $<Dick,Pat>$ will be one of the pairs that make up the second relation (but not the first).

Note incidentally that the two entries in an ordered pair need not differ. Whereas

$$\{Pat,Pat\}$$

is a unit set (with the name of its one member pointlessly repeated),

$$<Pat,Pat>$$

is a bona fide ordered pair, whose two entries just happen to be the same. It is one of the pairs which make up the binary relations "being a contemporary of," "being as well-dressed as," and so on.

Similarly, any three things can be made into an **ordered triple** as

---

[1] Readers of just Chapters 1 and 2 may omit the remainder of this Appendix.

well as into a set, and **ternary relations** (like that obtaining between three numbers x, y, and z when x is the sum of y and z, or x is the product of y and z) can be construed as sets of ordered triples.

More generally, any m things ($m \geq 1$) can be made into a so-called **ordered m-tuple** (as a matter of fact, into various ordered m-tuples),[2] and **m-ary relations** can be construed as sets of ordered m-tuples. Ordered pairs and ordered triples are thus only two sorts of ordered m-tuples, ordered pairs being ordered 2-tuples, and ordered triples being ordered 3-tuples. Note that m here may be 1. So we have 1-tuples as well, which for the occasion can be identified with their one entry, $<$Pat$>$ thus being just Pat, $<$96$>$ being just 96.

Given a set S, we can of course construct various ordered pairs of members of S, various ordered triples of members of S, and so on. Take S to be {Tom,Dick,Harry}, for example. We can turn out nine different ordered pairs of members of S:

$<$Tom,Tom$>$	$<$Dick,Tom$>$	$<$Harry,Tom$>$
$<$Tom,Dick$>$	$<$Dick,Dick$>$	$<$Harry,Dick$>$
$<$Tom,Harry$>$	$<$Dick,Harry$>$	$<$Harry,Harry$>$

We can turn out twenty-seven different ordered triples of members of S. And so on.

The set consisting of all the ordered pairs whose entries both come from a given set S is the so-called **Cartesian product** of S and S, often referred to as $S \times S$ or—for short—as S^2. The set consisting of all the ordered triples whose entries all come from a given set S is the so-called Cartesian product $S \times S \times S$, or S^3 for short. And so on. In such contexts it is often handy to refer to S itself as S^1.

With this terminology at hand, a set of ordered pairs of members of S is just a subset of S^2, a set of ordered triples of members of S is just a subset of S^3, and—more generally—a set of ordered m-tuples of members of S is just a subset of S^m. Conveniently enough, a set of 1-tuples of members of S, being a subset of S^1, proves to be—as expected—a subset of S.

Since all the pairs considered in Chapter 3 are ordered pairs, all the triples are ordered triples, and—more generally—all the m-tuples are ordered ones, we drop the qualifier 'ordered' throughout.

---

[2] Ordered m-tuples are usually treated as sets of a special kind, a matter we cannot pursue here.

Appendix II

Summary of Rules

Rules for making TREES

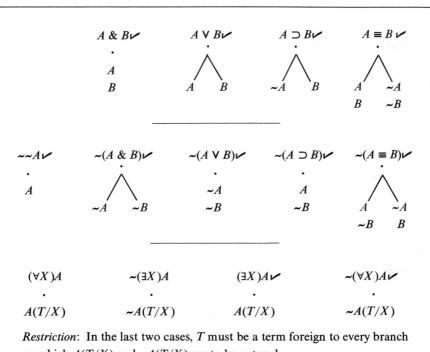

Restriction: In the last two cases, T must be a term foreign to every branch on which $A(T/X)$ and $\sim A(T/X)$ are to be entered.

Rules for Making DERIVATIONS

<table>
<tr>
<td rowspan="1">

R

</td>
<td colspan="2">

$$\begin{array}{l|l}
1 & A_1 \\
2 & A_2 \\
\cdot & \cdot \\
n & A_n \\
\cline{2-2}
\cdot & \cdot \\
p & A_i \qquad (\text{R}, i)
\end{array}$$

</td>
</tr>
<tr>
<td></td>
<td style="text-align:center">INTRODUCTION</td>
<td style="text-align:center">ELIMINATION</td>
</tr>
<tr>
<td>

~

</td>
<td>

$$\begin{array}{l|l}
1 & A_1 \\
2 & A_2 \\
\cdot & \cdot \\
n & A_n \\
\cline{2-2}
\cdot & \cdot \\
p & \quad\big|\; B \\
\cdot & \quad\big|\; \cdot \\
q & \quad\big|\; C \ (\text{or} \sim C) \\
\cdot & \quad\big|\; \cdot \\
r & \quad\big|\; \sim C \ (\text{or } C) \\
r+1 & \sim B \qquad (\sim\text{I}, p\text{--}(q,r))
\end{array}$$

</td>
<td>

$$\begin{array}{l|l}
1 & A_1 \\
2 & A_2 \\
\cdot & \cdot \\
n & A_n \\
\cline{2-2}
\cdot & \cdot \\
p & \sim\sim B \\
\cdot & \cdot \\
q & B \qquad (\sim\text{E}, p)
\end{array}$$

</td>
</tr>
<tr>
<td>

⊃

</td>
<td>

$$\begin{array}{l|l}
1 & A_1 \\
2 & A_2 \\
\cdot & \cdot \\
n & A_n \\
\cline{2-2}
\cdot & \cdot \\
p & \quad\big|\; B \\
\cdot & \quad\big|\; \cdot \\
q & \quad\big|\; C \\
q+1 & B \supset C \qquad (\supset\text{I}, p\text{--}q)
\end{array}$$

</td>
<td>

$$\begin{array}{l|l}
1 & A_1 \\
2 & A_2 \\
\cdot & \cdot \\
n & A_n \\
\cline{2-2}
\cdot & \cdot \\
p & B \supset C \ (\text{or } B) \\
\cdot & \cdot \\
q & B \ (\text{or } B \supset C) \\
\cdot & \cdot \\
r & C \qquad (\supset\text{E}, p,q)
\end{array}$$

</td>
</tr>
</table>

Rules for Making DERIVATIONS (cont'd)

	INTRODUCTION	ELIMINATION
&	1 $\quad A_1$ 2 $\quad A_2$ $\cdot \quad \cdot$ $n \quad A_n$ ——— $\cdot \quad \cdot$ $p \quad B \text{ (or } C)$ $\cdot \quad \cdot$ $q \quad C \text{ (or } B)$ $\cdot \quad \cdot$ $r \quad B \& C \quad (\&I, p,q)$	1 $\quad A_1 \qquad A_1$ 2 $\quad A_2 \qquad A_2$ $\cdot \quad \cdot \qquad \cdot$ $n \quad A_n \qquad A_n$ ——— $\cdot \quad \cdot \qquad \cdot$ $p \quad B \& C \qquad B \& C$ $\cdot \quad \cdot \qquad \cdot$ $q \quad B \qquad\quad C \quad (\&E, p)$
V	1 $\quad A_1 \qquad A_1$ 2 $\quad A_2 \qquad A_2$ $\cdot \quad \cdot \qquad \cdot$ $n \quad A_n \qquad A_n$ ——— $\cdot \quad \cdot \qquad \cdot$ $p \quad B \qquad\quad C$ $\cdot \quad \cdot \qquad \cdot$ $q \quad B \vee C \qquad B \vee C \quad (VI, p)$	1 $\quad A_1$ 2 $\quad A_2$ $\cdot \quad \cdot$ $n \quad A_n$ ——— $\cdot \quad \cdot$ $p \quad B \vee C$ $\cdot \quad \cdot$ $q \quad\quad\mid B$ $\cdot \quad\quad\mid \cdot$ $r \quad \cdot \mid D$ $s \quad\quad\mid C$ $\cdot \quad\quad\mid \cdot$ $t \quad\quad\mid D$ $t+1 \quad D \quad (VE, p, q\text{-}r, s\text{-}t)$

Rules for Making DERIVATIONS (cont'd)

	INTRODUCTION	ELIMINATION

$$\equiv$$

INTRODUCTION

1	A_1
2	A_2
.	.
n	A_n
.	.
p	$\quad B$
.	$\quad .$
q	$\quad C$
r	$\quad C$
.	$\quad .$
s	$\quad B$
$s+1$	$B \equiv C \quad (\equiv\text{I}, p\text{–}q, r\text{–}s)$

ELIMINATION

1	A_1	A_1
2	A_2	A_2
.	.	.
n	A_n	A_n
.	.	.
p	$B \equiv C$ (or B)	$C \equiv B$ (or B)
.	.	.
q	B (or $B \equiv C$)	B (or $C \equiv B$)
.	.	.
r	C	$C \quad (\equiv\text{E}, p, q)$

Rules for Making DERIVATIONS (concl'd)

	INTRODUCTION	ELIMINATION
$\forall$	1 A_1 2 A_2 $\cdot$ n A_n $\cdot$ p $B(T/X)$ $\cdot$ q $(\forall X)B$ $(\forall I, p)$	1 A_1 2 A_2 $\cdot$ n A_n $\cdot$ p $(\forall X)B$ $\cdot$ q $B(T/X)$ $(\forall E, p)$
$\exists$	1 A_1 2 A_2 $\cdot$ n A_n $\cdot$ p $B(T/X)$ $\cdot$ q $(\exists X)B$ $(\exists I, p)$	1 A_1 2 A_2 $\cdot$ n A_n $\cdot$ p $(\exists X)B$ $\cdot$ q $B(T/X)$ $\cdot$ r C $r+1$ C $(\exists E, p, q-r)$

Restrictions: In $\forall I$, T must be a term foreign to each and every one of A_1, $A_2, \ldots,$ and A_n, and to $(\forall X)B$.

    In $\exists E$, T must be a term foreign to each and every one of $A_1, A_2, \ldots,$ and A_n, to $(\exists X)B$, and to C.

Answers to Selected Exercises

Chapter One

Section 1.1

E1.1.1.

  a. Yes (= ~Hitler invaded England)
  b. No (When either of *A* and *B* is false, a statement of the kind *A because B* is sure to be false. But when both *A* and *B* are true, further information is needed to determine the truth-value of *A because B*.)
  c. Yes (= Tom is 6 feet tall & Jack is 6 feet tall)
  d. No (The statement is tantamount to 'Tom is the same height as Jack', which is atomic.)

E1.1.2.

A	*B*	*A* or *B*, but not both
T	**T**	**F**
F	**T**	**T**
T	**F**	**T**
F	**F**	**F**

E1.1.3.

  b. S ⊃ ~T
  d. (S & P) ∨ (~S & ~P)
  f. T & P
  h. ~S ⊃ ~P
  k. ([(P & Q) & ~R] ∨ [(P & ~Q) & R]) ∨ [(~P & Q) & R]
  m. (R & Q) & [(~S ⊃ ~P) & (S ⊃ ~P)]

E1.1.4. b. **T**; d. **T**; f. **F**; h. **T**; k. **T**; m. **F**

E1.1.5.

  c. (1) ~[~P ≡ ~(P & ~R)] ⊃ (~~R ∨ P)
      (2) ~[~P ≡ ~(P & ~R)]
      (3) ~~R ∨ P
      (4) ~P ≡ ~(P & ~R)
      (5) ~P
      (6) P (atomic)

  (7)   ~(P & ~R)
  (8)   P & ~R
  (9)   ~R
  (10) R (atomic)
  (11) ~~R

E1.1.6.

  b. (P ⊃ Q) ⊃ (R ⊃ S)
      ────────────────────
      T T T T F T F

  e. (P & ~R) ⊃ ~~S
      ────────────────
      T T TF F FTF

  h. P & [R ⊃ (~Q ∨ S)]
      ────────────────────
      T T F T   F T F F

E1.1.7.

  a. (P ⊃ ~P) ∨ (~P ⊃ P)
      ────────────────────
      T F FT T FT T T
      F T TF T TF F F
      Truth-functionally true

  g. ~(P ⊃ Q) & (~Q ⊃ ~P)
      ────────────────────────
      F T T T F FT T T FT
      F F T T F FT T T TF
      T T F F F TF F F FT
      F F T F F TF T T TF
      Truth-functionally false

  i. (P & ~Q) ∨ [Q ⊃ (R ≡ ~P)]
      ──────────────────────────
      T F FT F T F T T F FT
      F F FT T T T T T T TF
      T T TF T F T T F FT
      F F TF T F T T T T TF
      T F FT T T T T F T FT
      F F FT F T F F F TF
      T T TF T F T F T FT
      F F TF T F T F F TF
      Truth-functionally indeterminate

E1.1.8. Each conditional is true on any truth-value assignment on which its antecedent is false. So let the antecedent be true on, say, α:

  a. If either 'Q' or 'P' is false on α, the consequent is true on α, and hence a also
      is. If both 'Q' and 'P' are true on α, then 'R' is true on α (this because the

antecedent is true on α), hence the consequent is true on α, and hence a also is.

e. 'P ≡ Q' and 'Q ≡ R' are both true on α (this because their conjunction is true on α). But (i) if 'P' is true on α, then so is 'Q', hence so is 'R', and hence so is 'P ≡ R'; whereas (ii) if 'P' is false on α, then so is 'Q', hence so is 'R', and hence 'P ≡ R' is true on α. In either case, therefore, 'P ≡ R' is true on α, and hence e also is.

f. If 'P' were false on α, then '~P' would be true on α. But '~P ⊃ Q' and '~P ⊃ ~Q' are true on α (this because their conjunction is true on α). Hence if 'P' were false on α, then both 'Q' and '~Q' would be true on α, which is impossible. Hence 'P' must be true on α, and hence so is f.

E1.1.9.

a. Suppose ~~*A* is true on a truth-value assignment α; then ~*A* is false on α, hence *A* is true on α, and hence so is ~~*A* ≡ *A*. Suppose ~~*A* is false on α; then ~*A* is true on α, hence *A* is false on α, and hence ~~*A* ≡ *A* is again true on α.

d. Suppose *A* ⊃ *B* is true on α; then either (i) *A* is false on α, hence ~*A* is true on α, and hence ~*A* ∨ *B* is true on α, or (ii) *B* is true on α, and hence so is ~*A* ∨ *B*. Suppose ~*A* ∨ *B* is true on α; then either (i) ~*A* is true on α, hence *A* is false on α, and hence *A* ⊃ *B* is true on α, or (ii) *B* is true on α, and hence so is *A* ⊃ *B*. Hence *A* ⊃ *B* is true on α if and only if ~*A* ∨ *B* is, and hence (*A* ⊃ *B*) ≡ (~*A* ∨ *B*) is true on α.

g. Suppose ~(*A* ≡ *B*) is true on α. Then either (i) *A* is true on α and *B* is false on α, in which case *A* & ~*B* is true on α, and hence so is (*A* & ~*B*) ∨ (~*A* & *B*), or (ii) *A* is false on α and *B* is true on α, in which case ~*A* & *B* is true on α, and hence so is (*A* & ~*B*) ∨ (~*A* & *B*). Suppose (*A* & ~*B*) ∨ (~*A* & *B*) is true on α, in which case either *A* & ~*B* or ~*A* & *B* is true on α. If *A* & ~*B* is true on α, then *A* is true on α but *B* is not, hence *A* ≡ *B* is false on α, and hence ~(*A* ≡ *B*) is true on α. If ~*A* & *B* is true on α, then *A* is not true on α but *B* is, hence *A* ≡ *B* is false on α, and hence ~(*A* ≡ *B*) is true on α.

E1.1.10. a and i, b and e, c and j, d and g, f and h. That a and i are truth-functionally equivalent is borne out by the following truth-table:

a. ~P ⊃ Q   i.   ~(~P & ~Q)

FT	T	T		T	FT	F	FT
TF	T	T		T	TF	F	FT
FT	T	F		T	FT	F	TF
TF	F	F		F	TF	T	TF

E1.1.11.

b. {~[~(P & Q) ≡ ~Q], ~(Q ⊃ P)}

F	F	T	T	T		T	FT		F	T	T	T
T	T	F	F	T		F	FT		T	T	F	F
F	T	T	F	F		T	TF		F	F	T	T
F	T	F	F	F		T	TF		F	F	T	F

Truth-functionally consistent because of row 2 (**F** to 'P' and **T** to 'Q')

e.   {R V (P & Q), P ⊃ (Q & R), ~R}

T T T T T	T T T T T	F T
T T F F T	F T T T T	F T
T T T F F	T F F F T	F T
T T F F F	F T F F T	F T
F T T T T	T F T F F	T F
F F F F T	F T T F F	T F
F F T F F	T F F F F	T F
F F F F F	F T F F F	T F

Truth-functionally inconsistent

E1.1.12.

a.   P ⊃ Q   ∴~P ⊃ ~Q

T T T	F T T F T
F T T	T F F F T
T F F	F T T T F
F T F	T F T T F

Truth-functionally invalid because of row 2

d.   P V Q   P   ∴~Q

T T T	T	F T
F T T	F	F T
T T F	T	T F
F F F	F	T F

Truth-functionally invalid because of row 1

f.   P ⊃ (Q ⊃ R)   R ⊃ ~P   ∴~P V ~Q

T T T T T	T F F T	F T F F T
F T T T T	T T T F	T F T F T
T T F T T	T F F T	F T T T F
F T F T T	T T T F	T F T T F
T F T F F	F T F T	F T F F T
F T T F F	F T T F	T F T F T
T T F T F	F T F T	F T T T F
F T F T F	F T T F	T F T T F

Truth-functionally valid

i.

P ⊃ (Q ∨ R)	P ⊃ ~Q	∴.R ∨ ~P
T T T T T	T F F T	T T F T
F T T T T	F T F T	T T T F
T T F T T	T T T F	T T F T
F T F T T	F T T F	T T T F
T T T T F	T F F T	F F F T
F T T T F	F T F T	F T T F
T F F F F	T T T F	F F F T
F T F F F	F T T F	F T T F

Truth-functionally valid

E1.1.13.

b. On any truth-value assignment on which 'P ⊃ Q' is true, either (i) 'P' is false, hence '~P' is true, and hence '~Q ⊃ ~P' is true, or (ii) 'Q' is true, hence '~Q' is false, and hence '~Q ⊃ ~P' is true. So b is truth-functionally valid.

f. Consider any truth-value assignment α on which both 'P ⊃ (Q ⊃ R)' and 'R ⊃ ~P' are true. If 'R' is true on α, then '~P' must be true on α, and so must be '~P ∨ ~Q'. Suppose then that 'R' is false on α. If 'P' is true on α, then 'Q ⊃ R' must be true on α, hence 'Q' must be false on α, hence '~Q' must be true on α, and so must be '~P ∨ ~Q'. If on the other hand 'P' is false on α, then '~P' must be true on α, and hence again so must be '~P ∨ ~Q'. So f is truth-functionally valid.

g. Suppose there were a truth-value assignment α on which all of 'P ⊃ Q', 'Q ⊃ ~P', and 'P' were true. Then 'Q' would be true on α, hence so would '~P' be, and hence both 'P' and '~P' would be true on α, which is impossible. As there is no truth-value assignment on which all of 'P ⊃ Q', 'Q ⊃ ~P', and 'P' are true, there is none on which all of 'P ⊃ Q', 'Q ⊃ ~P', and 'P' are true and 'R' is false. So g is truth-functionally valid.

E1.1.14.

(a) Any atomic statement is false on the truth-value assignment that assigns it F. Hence no atomic statement can be truth-functionally true. Hence only truth-functional compounds can be truth-functionally true.

(b) Let A and B be truth-functional truths, and let α be an arbitrary truth-value assignment to the atomic components of A and to those of B. Since A is true on any truth-value assignment to its atomic components, A is sure to be true on any truth-value assignment to the atomic components of A and to those of B (why?), and hence to be true on α. The same result holds of B. Hence both A and B are true on α, and hence so is A ≡ B.

(c) First question: No by definition. Second question: Yes (the argument from '2 + 2 = 4' and '2 + 2 = 5' to '2 + 2 = 4' is truth-functionally valid). Third question: Yes (the argument from '2 + 2 = 4' to '2 + 3 = 5' is truth-functionally invalid).

(d) Both arguments are truth-functionally valid, since on any truth-value assignment on which either one of the two statements A and B is true, the other statement is then sure to be true.

E1.1.15.

(a) Let S be $\{A_1, A_2, \ldots, A_n\}$, where $n \geq 2$. Then S is truth-functionally inconsistent if and only if there is no truth-value assignment whatever on which $(\ldots (A_1 \& A_2) \& \ldots) \& A_n$ is true, i.e. if and only if $(\ldots (A_1 \& A_2) \& \ldots) \& A_n$ is truth-functionally false.

(b) Suppose S is truth-functionally inconsistent. Then so are $S \cup \{{\sim}A\}$ and $S \cup \{{\sim}{\sim}A\}$ for any statement A, and hence S truth-functionally entails both A and ${\sim}A$. Suppose on the other hand that S truth-functionally entails both A and ${\sim}A$ for some statement A. Then on any truth-value assignment on which all members of S were true both A and ${\sim}A$ would be true, which is impossible. Hence S must be truth-functionally inconsistent.

(c) Suppose S is truth-functionally inconsistent, and let A be an arbitrary statement. There being no truth-value assignment on which all members of S are true, there is none on which all members of S are true and A is false, and hence S truth-functionally entails A. Suppose on the other hand that S truth-functionally entails any statement you wish. Then S truth-functionally entails both A and ${\sim}A$, and hence by (b) S is truth-functionally inconsistent.

(d) Let S' be S *minus* some member A of S. Then S is $S' \cup \{A\}$, which is truth-functionally inconsistent if and only if $S' \cup \{{\sim}{\sim}A\}$ is. But $S' \cup \{{\sim}{\sim}A\}$ is truth-functionally inconsistent if and only if S' truth-functionally entails ${\sim}A$. Hence (d).

(e) Suppose S is truth-functionally inconsistent, and let S' be an arbitrary finite superset of S. There being no truth-value assignment on which all members of S are true, there cannot be any on which all members of S' are true, and hence S' is truth-functionally inconsistent. Suppose on the other hand that every finite superset of S is truth-functionally inconsistent. Since S is a finite superset of itself, S is truth-functionally inconsistent.

(f) Suppose S is truth-functionally inconsistent; then at least one non-empty subset of S is truth-functionally inconsistent, namely S itself. Suppose on the other hand that at least one non-empty subset of S is truth-functionally inconsistent. Since S is a finite superset of that subset, S is truth-functionally inconsistent by (e).

E1.1.16.

(a) By E1.1.15(e), $\{{\sim}A\}$ is truth-functionally inconsistent (i.e., A is truth-functionally true) if and only if for every set S of statements $S \cup \{{\sim}A\}$ is truth-functionally inconsistent—i.e. if and only if S truth-functionally entails A.

(b) By E1.1.15(e) also.

(c) By E1.1.15(f).

E1.1.17.   (a) $\sim A$: $A|A$

$A \,\&\, B$: $\sim(A|B)$, i.e. $(A|B)|(A|B)$

$A \lor B$: $\sim A|\sim B$, i.e. $(A|A)|(B|B)$

$A \supset B$: $A|\sim B$, i.e. $A|(B|B)$

E1.1.18.

(a)   See E1.1.7c

(b) $(A \supset B) =_{df} ((A \,\&\, B) \equiv A)$

E1.1.19.   (a) The truth-functional compounds of A by means of just '$\supset$' are A itself, $A \supset A$, $(A \supset A) \supset A$, $A \supset (A \supset A)$, $(A \supset A) \supset (A \supset A)$, etc. (i.e. A *plus* all compounds of the sort $B \supset C$, where B and C are themselves compounds of A by means of just '$\supset$'). Now on any truth-value assignment α on which A is assigned **T**, A is true, hence $A \supset A$ and $(A \supset A) \supset A$ are true since A is, hence $A \supset (A \supset A)$ and $(A \supset A) \supset (A \supset A)$ are true since $A \supset A$ is, etc. (i.e. A is true, and so is any compound of the sort $B \supset C$, where B and C are as above). But $\sim A$ is false on α. So $\sim A$ is not truth-functionally equivalent to any truth-functional compound of A by means of just '$\supset$'. As for the truth-functional compounds of A and B by means of just '$\sim$', they run A, B, $\sim A$, $\sim B$, $\sim\sim A$, $\sim\sim B$, etc., none of which is truth-functionally equivalent to $A \supset B$.

E1.1.20.   The truth-table wanted is that for $(B \supset A) \,\&\, (\sim B \supset C)$.

E1.1.21.   As regards the table for $\sim A$: if A is true (false) on every truth-value assignment, $\sim A$ is false (true) on every one, and hence $\sim A$ is truth-functionally false (true). If there is a truth-value assignment on which A is true, then there is one on which $\sim A$ is false; and if there is also one on which A is false, then there is one on which $\sim A$ is true. So if there is a truth-value assignment on which A is true and one on which A is false, $\sim A$ is truth-functionally indeterminate.

The table for $A \,\&\, B$ runs:

A	B	$A \,\&\, B$
2	2	2
1	2	1
0	2	0
2	1	1
1	1	1 or 0
0	1	0
2	0	0
1	0	0
0	0	0

Note that 'P & Q' is truth-functionally indeterminate (as 'P' and 'Q' are), but 'P & $\sim$P' is truth-functionally false (though each one of 'P' and '$\sim$P' is truth-functionally indeterminate).

Section 1.2

E1.2.1.   a.

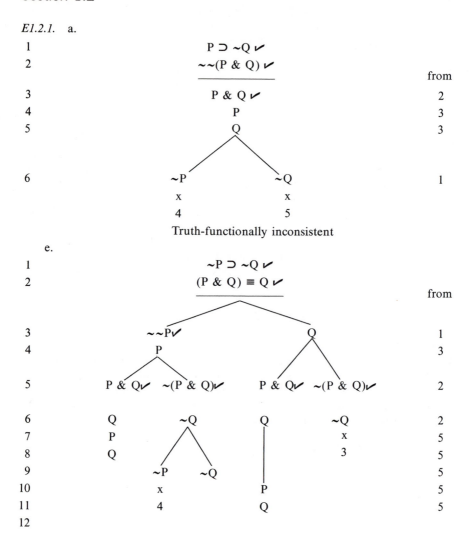

Truth-functionally inconsistent

Truth-functionally consistent: P—**T**

Q—**T**

(Whether or not there is a choice, we always recover *our* truth-value assignment from the left-most open branch of the tree; and, if an atomic component fails to occur either unnegated or negated on the branch, we automatically assign it **T**.)

h.

1	R V (P & Q) ✔	
2	P ⊃ (Q & R) ✔	
3	~R	from

```
                    R        P & Q✔              1
                    x          P                 4
                    3          Q                 4

                         ~P       Q & R✔         2
                          x         Q            7
                          5         R            7
                                    x
                                    3
```

Truth-functionally inconsistent

i.

1	P ⊃ (Q V R) ✔	
2	~P & (~Q & R) ✔	
3	~R ⊃ ~P ✔	from
4	~P	2
5	~Q & R ✔	2
6	~Q	5
7	R	5

```
           ~~R✔                      ~P              3
            R                                        8
      ~P     Q V R✔         ~P        Q V R✔         1
              Q    R                   Q    R
              x                        x
              6                        6
```

8		3
9		8
10		1
11		10
12		10

Truth-functionally consistent: P—F
Q—F
R—T

E1.2.2.   b.

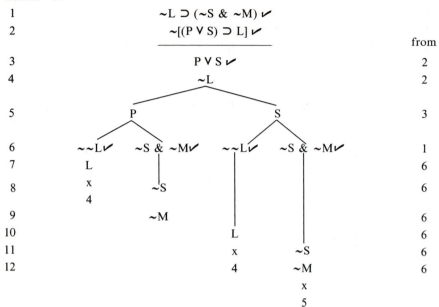

		from
1	~L ⊃ (~S & ~M) ✔	
2	~[(P ∨ S) ⊃ L] ✔	
3	P ∨ S ✔	2
4	~L	2
5	P S	3
6	~~L✔ ~S & ~M✔ ~~L✔ ~S & ~M✔	1
7	L	6
8	x ~S	6
9	4 ~M	6
10	L	6
11	x ~S	6
12	4 ~M	6

Truth-functionally invalid: L—**F**
                               M—**F**
                               P—**T**
                               S—**F**

g.

		from
1	N ⊃ [(B & ~P) ∨ R] ✓	
2	B & ~R ✓	
3	~T ⊃ P ✓	
4	~(~T ⊃ ~N) ✓	

from

5	B	2
6	~R	2
7	~T	4
8	~~N ✓	4
9	N	8

10	~~T✓ P	3
11	T	10
	x	
12	7 ~N (B & ~P) ∨ R✓	1
	x	
	9	
13	B & ~P✓ R	12
14	B x	13
15	~P 6	13
	x	
	10	

Truth-functionally valid

h.

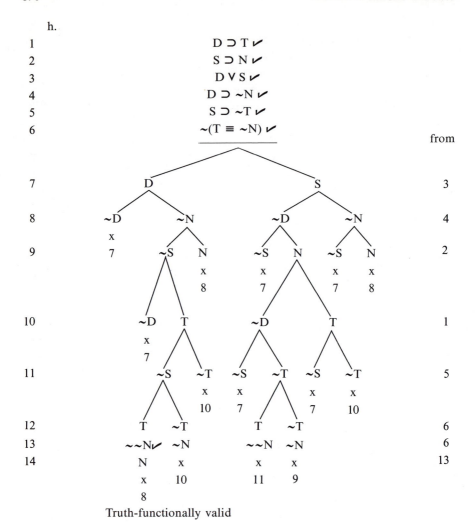

		from
1	D ⊃ T ✔	
2	S ⊃ N ✔	
3	D ∨ S ✔	
4	D ⊃ ~N ✔	
5	S ⊃ ~T ✔	
6	~(T ≡ ~N) ✔	
7	D / S	3
8	~D / ~N / ~D / ~N	4
9	~S / N / ~S / N / ~S / N	2
10	~D / T / ~D / T	1
11	~S / ~T / ~S / ~T / ~S / ~T	5
12	T / ~T / T / ~T	6
13	~~N✔ / ~N / ~~N / ~N	6
14	N / N	13

Truth-functionally valid

p.

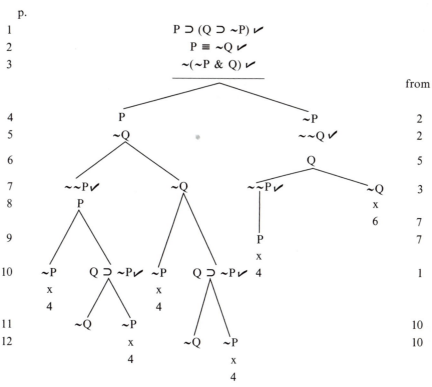

1   P ⊃ (Q ⊃ ~P) ✔

2   P ≡ ~Q ✔

3   ~(~P & Q) ✔

from

4   P   ~P   2

5   ~Q   ~~Q ✔   2

6   Q   5

7   ~~P ✔   ~Q   ~~P ✔   ~Q   3

8   P   x

                                          6   7

9   P   7

                          x

10   ~P   Q ⊃ ~P ✔   ~P   Q ⊃ ~P ✔   4   1

     x   x

     4   4

11   ~Q   ~P   10

12   x   ~Q   ~P   10

            4   x

                         4

Truth-functionally invalid: P—**T**

                              Q—**F**

t.

1   ~(~P ∨ Q) ≡ (R & S) ✔
2   ~R ⊃ (T & U) ✔
3   ~T ⊃ S ✔
4   ~(~P ⊃ T) ✔
                                                                          from
5   ~P   4
6   ~T   4
7   ~~T✔   S   3
8   T   7
              x
              6
9   ~~R✔   T & U✔   2
10   R   9
11   T   9
12   U   9
                                          x
                                          6
13   ~(~P ∨ Q)✔   ~~(~P ∨ Q)✔   1
14   R & S✔   ~(R & S)✔   1
15   ~~P✔   13
16   ~Q   13
17   P   15
          x
          5
18   ~R   ~S   14
                            x   x
                            10   7

          Truth-functionally valid

E1.2.3. d.

1   ~([P ⊃ (Q ⊃ R)] ⊃ [(P ⊃ Q) ⊃ R]) ✔

                                                          from

2   P ⊃ (Q ⊃ R) ✔   1

3   ~[(P ⊃ Q) ⊃ R] ✔   1

4   P ⊃ Q ✔   3

5   ~R   3

6   ~P   Q   4

7   ~P   Q ⊃ R ✔   ~P   Q ⊃ R ✔   2

8   ~Q   R   7

9   x   ~Q   R   7

                                5   x   x

                                                    6   5

Not truth-functionally true: P—F

                                    Q—T

                                      R—F

g.

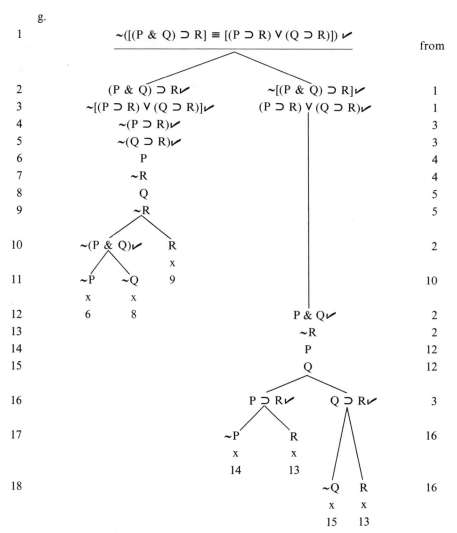

1   ~([(P & Q) ⊃ R] ≡ [(P ⊃ R) V (Q ⊃ R)]) ✔

                                                      from

2   (P & Q) ⊃ R✔   ~[(P & Q) ⊃ R]✔   1
3   ~[(P ⊃ R) V (Q ⊃ R)]✔   (P ⊃ R) V (Q ⊃ R)✔   1
4   ~(P ⊃ R)✔   3
5   ~(Q ⊃ R)✔   3
6   P   4
7   ~R   4
8   Q   5
9   ~R   5

10   ~(P & Q)✔   R   2
                       X
11   ~P   ~Q   9   10
      X   X
12   6   8   P & Q✔   2
13   ~R   2
14   P   12
15   Q   12

16   P ⊃ R✔   Q ⊃ R✔   3

17   ~P   R   16
                          X   X
                         14   13
18   ~Q   R   16
                                   X   X
                                  15   13

       Truth-functionally true

E1.2.4.   a.

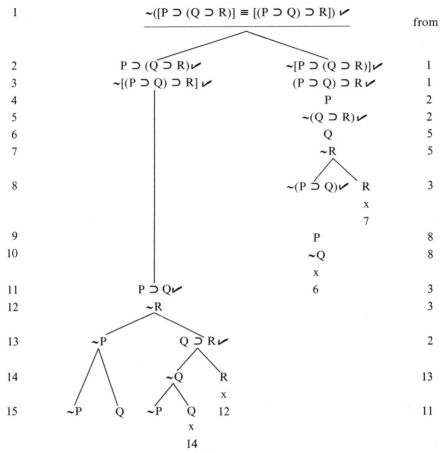

1   ~([P ⊃ (Q ⊃ R)] ≡ [(P ⊃ Q) ⊃ R]) ✔   from

2   P ⊃ (Q ⊃ R)✔   ~[P ⊃ (Q ⊃ R)]✔   1
3   ~[(P ⊃ Q) ⊃ R] ✔   (P ⊃ Q) ⊃ R✔   1
4   P   2
5   ~(Q ⊃ R)✔   2
6   Q   5
7   ~R   5

8   ~(P ⊃ Q)✔   R   3
                                               X
                                               7

9   P   8
10   ~Q   8
                                       X
11   P ⊃ Q✔   6   3
12   ~R   3

13   ~P   Q ⊃ R✔   2

14   ~Q   R   13
                             X
15 ~P   Q   ~P   Q   12   11
                X
               14

Not truth-functionally equivalent: P—**F**
                                    Q—**T**
                                    R—**F**

b.

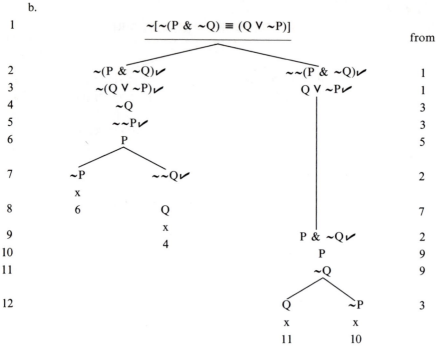

Truth-functionally equivalent

E1.2.5.   b.

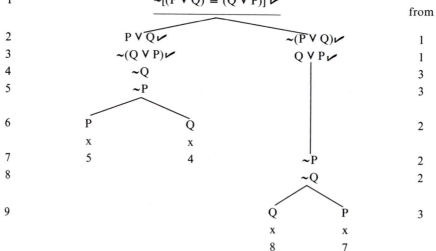

j.

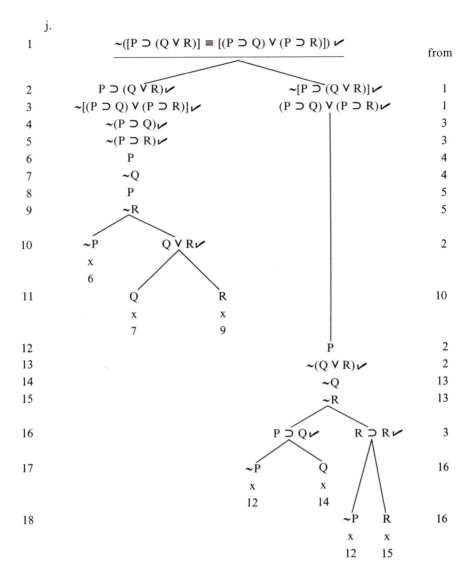

1

$\sim([P \supset (Q \lor R)] \equiv [(P \supset Q) \lor (P \supset R)])$ ✔

from

2     $P \supset (Q \lor R)$ ✔ $\sim[P \supset (Q \lor R)]$ ✔   1

3     $\sim[(P \supset Q) \lor (P \supset R)]$ ✔ $(P \supset Q) \lor (P \supset R)$ ✔   1

4     $\sim(P \supset Q)$ ✔   3

5     $\sim(P \supset R)$ ✔   3

6   P   4

7     $\sim$Q   4

8   P   5

9     $\sim$R   5

10     $\sim$P   Q $\lor$ R ✔   2

      x

      6

11   Q   R   10

      x   x

      7   9

12   P   2

13     $\sim$(Q $\lor$ R) ✔   2

14     $\sim$Q   13

15     $\sim$R   13

16   P $\supset$ Q ✔   R $\supset$ R ✔   3

17     $\sim$P   Q   16

      x   x

      12   14

18     $\sim$P   R   16

      x   x

      12   15

(b)   The reason why an atomic component—of a member of a set *S*—might not occur (unnegated or negated) on some one branch, or some two branches, etc. of a tree for *S* is clear from Example 3 on p. 62: 'Q' occurs only in the right-hand component of the conjunction 'P & [($\sim$P $\equiv$ Q) & ($\sim$P $\supset \sim$Q)]', and so never gets to be entered on the left-most branch of the tree. Turning now to the question asked in (b), note that (i) line 1 has got to be true on the result of assigning a truth-value to 'P' *and one to* 'Q' if line 2 (which comes from line 1) is true on that assignment, and (ii) line 2 ($= $ '$\sim$P') is true on the result of assigning **F** to 'P' and any truth-value you please to

'Q'. So line 1 has got to be true on *either* of the truth-value assignments retrievable from the left-most branch of the tree. These considerations are easily extended to cover the general case.

(c)   Graft to the branch a tree for the set $\{A, \sim A\}$. As claimed on p. 57, that tree is sure to be closed ($\{A, \sim A\}$ being truth-functionally inconsistent). So some atomic statement and its negation *will* turn up on every branch through A and $\sim A$.

E1.2.7.

(a)   Suppose you test a set $\{A_1, A_2, . . ., A_n\}$ for consistency, and some statement B occurs on every open branch of the tree. If you slip $\sim B$ between A_n and the horizontal bar separating $A_1, A_2, . . .,$ and A_n from the rest of the tree, B and $\sim B$ will occur on all the previously open branches of the tree; in view of E1.2.6(c), some atomic statement and its negation will eventually turn up on all those branches, and the tree will close. But, if a tree for $\{A_1, A_2, . . ., A_n, \sim B\}$ closes, then $\{A_1, A_2, . . ., A_n\}$ truth-functionally entails B. Hence $\{A_1, A_2, . . ., A_n\}$ is sure to truth-functionally entail B.

(b) A will be truth-functionally true if and only if from the open branches of a tree for $\{A\}$ you can retrieve *all* truth-value assignments to the atomic components of A.

E1.2.8.   a.

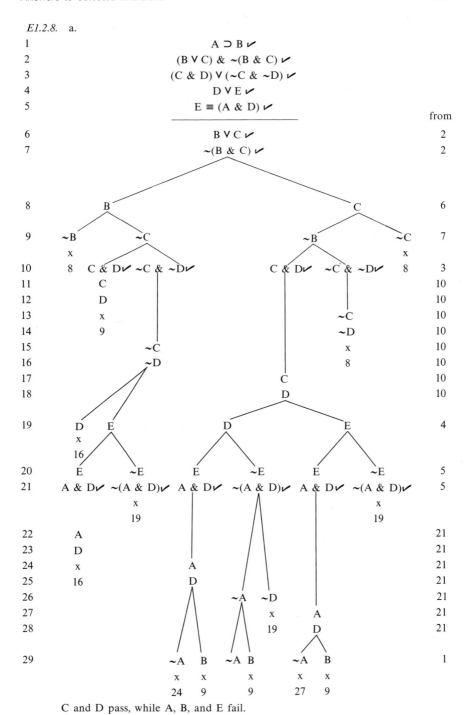

		from
1	A ⊃ B ✔	
2	(B ∨ C) & ~(B & C) ✔	
3	(C & D) ∨ (~C & ~D) ✔	
4	D ∨ E ✔	
5	E ≡ (A & D) ✔	
6	B ∨ C ✔	2
7	~(B & C) ✔	2

C and D pass, while A, B, and E fail.

E1.2.9. Given an open tree (Tree 1) for $\{A\}$ (there is sure to be one such tree if $\{A\}$ is truth-functionally consistent), make a tree (Tree 2) for the disjunction associate $(\ldots(B_1 \lor B_2) \lor \ldots) \lor B_n$ of Tree 1, and list all of the truth-value assignments corresponding to the open branches of Tree 2. These truth-value assignments and the ones corresponding to the open branches of Tree 1 will prove to be exactly the same. So A and $(\ldots(B_1 \lor B_2) \lor \ldots) \lor B_n$ are sure to be truth-functionally equivalent.

Section 1.3

E1.3.1. d.

1	$(P \supset Q) \supset (Q \supset R)$		
2		Q	
3			P
4			Q	(R, 2)
5		$P \supset Q$		($\supset$I, 3–4)
6		$(P \supset Q) \supset (Q \supset R)$		(R, 1)
7		$Q \supset R$		($\supset$E, 5, 6)
8		Q		(R, 2)
9		R		($\supset$E, 7, 8)
10	$Q \supset R$			($\supset$I, 2–9)

One might be tempted to try to reach 'Q ⊃ R' from line 1 (reiterated) and 'P ⊃ Q' by ⊃E. But this strategy will not work, since 'P ⊃ Q' is not entailed by—and hence is not derivable from—'(P ⊃ Q) ⊃ (Q ⊃ R)'.

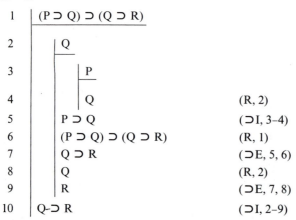

h.	1	$\sim\sim P$	
	2	$Q \supset \sim P$	
	3		$P \supset Q$
	4		$\sim\sim P$	(R, 1)
	5		P	($\sim$E, 4)
	6		$P \supset Q$	(R, 3)
	7		Q	($\supset$E, 5, 6)
	8		$Q \supset \sim P$	(R, 2)
	9		$\sim P$	($\supset$E, 7, 8)
	10	$\sim(P \supset Q)$		($\sim$I, 3–(4, 9))

1.

1	(P ⊃ ~Q) & (Q ⊃ ~R)		
2	S ⊃ Q		
3	S		
4	P		
5	S ⊃ Q	(R, 2)	
6	S	(R, 3)	
7	Q	(⊃E, 5, 6)	
8	(P ⊃ ~Q) & (Q ⊃ ~R)	(R, 1)	
9	P ⊃ ~Q	(&E, 8)	
10	P	(R, 4)	
11	~Q	(⊃E, 9, 10)	
12	~P	(~I, 4–(7, 11))	
13	S ⊃ Q	(R, 2)	
14	S	(R, 3)	
15	Q	(⊃E, 13, 14)	
16	(P ⊃ ~Q) & (Q ⊃ ~R)	(R, 1)	
17	Q ⊃ ~R	(&E, 16)	
18	~R	(⊃E, 15, 17)	
19	~P & ~R	(&I, 12, 18)	
20	S ⊃ (~P & ~R)	(⊃I, 3–19)	

p.   1 │ P ∨ Q
     2 │ (P ⊃ R) & (~R ⊃ ~Q)

     3 │ P ∨ Q   (R, 1)
     4 │   │ P
     5 │   │ (P ⊃ R) & (~R ⊃ ~Q)   (R, 2)
     6 │   │ P ⊃ R   (&E, 5)
     7 │   │ P   (R, 4)
     8 │   │ R   (⊃E, 6, 7)
     9 │   │ Q
    10 │   │   │ ~R
    11 │   │   │ (P ⊃ R) & (~R ⊃ ~Q)   (R, 2)
    12 │   │   │ ~R ⊃ ~Q   (&E, 11)
    13 │   │   │ ~R   (R, 10)
    14 │   │   │ ~Q   (⊃E, 12, 13)
    15 │   │   │ Q   (R, 9)
    16 │   │ ~~R   (~I, 10–(14, 15))
    17 │   │ R   (~E, 16)
    18 │ R   (∨E, 3, 4–8, 9–17)

E1.3.2. g.

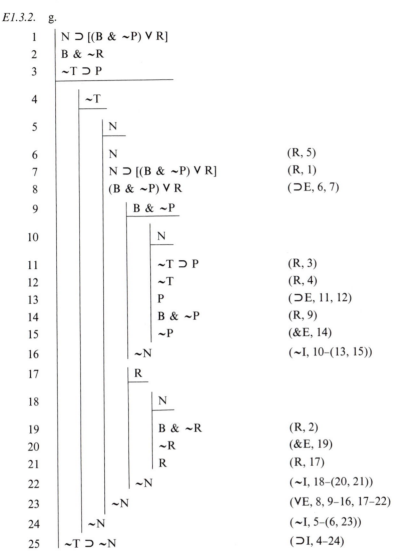

1	N ⊃ [(B & ~P) ∨ R]	
2	B & ~R	
3	~T ⊃ P	
4	~T	
5	N	
6	N	(R, 5)
7	N ⊃ [(B & ~P) ∨ R]	(R, 1)
8	(B & ~P) ∨ R	(⊃E, 6, 7)
9	B & ~P	
10	N	
11	~T ⊃ P	(R, 3)
12	~T	(R, 4)
13	P	(⊃E, 11, 12)
14	B & ~P	(R, 9)
15	~P	(&E, 14)
16	~N	(~I, 10–(13, 15))
17	R	
18	N	
19	B & ~R	(R, 2)
20	~R	(&E, 19)
21	R	(R, 17)
22	~N	(~I, 18–(20, 21))
23	~N	(∨E, 8, 9–16, 17–22)
24	~N	(~I, 5–(6, 23))
25	~T ⊃ ~N	(⊃I, 4–24)

Within the subordinate derivation headed by 'N' at line 5, we can easily derive the disjunction at line 8, and a different contradiction from each of its disjuncts. Review lines 9–22 to see how, availing ourselves of these two contradictions, we derive a single one from line 5.

h.   1 | D ⊃ T
     2 | S ⊃ N
     3 | D ∨ S
     4 | D ⊃ ~N
     5 | S ⊃ ~T

     6 | D ∨ S   (R, 3)
     7 | | D
     8 | | | T
     9 | | | D   (R, 7)
    10 | | | D ⊃ ~N   (R, 4)
    11 | | | ~N   (⊃E, 9, 10)
    12 | | | ~N
    13 | | | D   (R, 7)
    14 | | | D ⊃ T   (R, 1)
    15 | | | T   (⊃E, 13, 14)
    16 | | T ≡ ~N   (≡I, 8–11, 12–15)
    17 | | S
    18 | | | T
    19 | | | | N
    20 | | | | S   (R, 17)
    21 | | | | S ⊃ ~T   (R, 5)
    22 | | | | ~T   (⊃E, 20, 21)
    23 | | | | T   (R, 18)
    24 | | | ~N   (~I, 19–(22, 23))
    25 | | | ~N
    26 | | | | ~T
    27 | | | | S   (R, 17)
    28 | | | | S ⊃ N   (R, 2)
    29 | | | | N   (⊃E, 27, 28)
    30 | | | | ~N   (R, 25)
    31 | | | ~~T   (~I, 26–(29, 30))
    32 | | | T   (~E, 31)
    33 | | T ≡ ~N   (≡I, 18–24, 25–32)
    34 | T ≡ ~N   (∨E, 6, 7–16, 17–33)

You could derive 'T ≡ ~N' by ≡I, first deriving '~N' from 'T' by VE, and then deriving 'T' from '~N' by VE; but the resulting derivation would be longer than this one.

t. 1 | ~(~P ∨ Q) ≡ (R & S)
    2 | ~R ⊃ (T & U)
    3 | ~T ⊃ S

    4 | | ~P

    5 | | | ~T

    6 | | | | ~R

    7 | | | | ~R   (R, 6)
    8 | | | | ~R ⊃ (T & U)   (R, 2)
    9 | | | | T & U   (⊃E, 7, 8)
    10 | | | | T   (&E, 9)
    11 | | | | ~T   (R, 5)
    12 | | | ~~R   (~I, 6–(10, 11))
    13 | | | R   (~E, 12)
    14 | | | ~T   (R, 5)
    15 | | | ~T ⊃ S   (R, 3)
    16 | | | S   (⊃E, 14, 15)
    17 | | | R & S   (&I, 13, 16)
    18 | | | ~(~P ∨ Q) ≡ (R & S)   (R, 1)
    19 | | | ~(~P ∨ Q)   (≡E, 17, 18)
    20 | | | ~P   (R, 4)
    21 | | | ~P ∨ Q   (VI, 20)
    22 | | ~~T   (~I, 5–(19, 21))
    23 | | T   (~E, 22)
    24 | ~P ⊃ T   (⊃I, 4–23)

E1.3.3.   b.

1	T ⊃ V	
2	(U ⊃ ~L) & (O ⊃ D)	
3	~T ⊃ (U ∨ O)	
4	~V	
5	T	
6	T	(R, 5)
7	T ⊃ V	(R, 1)
8	V	(⊃E, 6, 7)
9	~V	(R, 4)
10	~T	(~I, 5–(8, 9))
11	~T ⊃ (U ∨ O)	(R, 3)
12	U ∨ O	(⊃E, 10, 11)
13	U	
14	(U ⊃ ~L) & (O ⊃ D)	(R, 2)
15	U ⊃ ~L	(&E, 14)
16	U	(R, 13)
17	~L	(⊃E, 15, 16)
18	~L ∨ D	(VI, 17)
19	O	
20	(U ⊃ ~L) & (O ⊃ D)	(R, 2)
21	O ⊃ D	(&E, 20)
22	O	(R, 19)
23	D	(⊃E, 21, 22)
24	~L ∨ D	(VI, 23)
25	~L ∨ D	(VE, 12, 13–18, 19–24)
26	~V ⊃ (~L ∨ D)	(⊃I, 4–25)

Line 3 is "obvious" not in the sense that it's obviously the premiss that's needed, but in the sense that it's obviously true.

f.

1	$G \equiv {\sim}I$	
2	$G \supset (W \mathbin{\&} S)$	
3	$D \supset ({\sim}S \lor {\sim}W)$	
4	${\sim}D \supset {\sim}C$	
5	C	
6	${\sim}I$	
7	D	
8	D	(R, 7)
9	$D \supset ({\sim}S \lor {\sim}W)$	(R, 3)
10	${\sim}S \lor {\sim}W$	($\supset$E, 8, 9)
11	${\sim}S$	
12	${\sim}S$	(R, 11)
13	${\sim}W$	
14	S	
15	${\sim}I$	(R, 6)
16	$G \equiv {\sim}I$	(R, 1)
17	G	($\equiv$E, 15, 16)
18	$G \supset (W \mathbin{\&} S)$	(R, 2)
19	$W \mathbin{\&} S$	($\supset$E, 17, 18)
20	W	(&E, 19)
21	${\sim}W$	(R, 13)
22	${\sim}S$	(${\sim}$I, 14–(20, 21))
23	${\sim}S$	($\lor$E, 10, 11–12, 13–22)
24	${\sim}I$	(R, 6)
25	$G \equiv {\sim}I$	(R, 1)
26	G	($\equiv$E, 24, 25)
27	$G \supset (W \mathbin{\&} S)$	(R, 2)
28	$W \mathbin{\&} S$	($\supset$E, 26, 27)
29	S	(&E, 28)
30	${\sim}D$	(${\sim}$I, 7–(23, 29))
31	${\sim}D \supset {\sim}C$	(R, 4)
32	${\sim}C$	($\supset$E, 30, 31)
33	C	(R, 5)
34	${\sim}{\sim}I$	(${\sim}$I, 6–(32, 33))
35	I	(${\sim}$E, 34)
36	$C \supset I$	($\supset$I, 5–35)

h. 1 | $[(O \lor Y) \supset A] \& [S \supset (\sim A \& P)]$
    2 | $S \lor (M \& I)$
    3 | $\sim(M \& F)$

    4 | $S \lor (M \& I)$ (R, 2)
    5 | S
    6 | Y
    7 | Y (R, 6)
    8 | $O \lor Y$ (∨I, 7)
    9 | $[(O \lor Y) \supset A] \& [S \supset (\sim A \& P)]$ (R, 1)
    10 | $(O \lor Y) \supset A$ (&E, 9)
    11 | A (⊃E, 8, 10)
    12 | $S \supset (\sim A \& P)$ (&E, 9)
    13 | S (R, 5)
    14 | $\sim A \& P$ (⊃E, 12, 13)
    15 | $\sim A$ (&E, 14)
    16 | $\sim Y$ (∼I, 6–(11, 15))
    17 | $\sim Y \lor \sim F$ (∨I, 16)
    18 | $M \& I$
    19 | F
    20 | $M \& I$ (R, 18)
    21 | M (&E, 20)
    22 | F (R, 19)
    23 | $M \& F$ (&I, 21, 22)
    24 | $\sim(M \& F)$ (R, 3)
    25 | $\sim F$ (∼I, 19–(23, 24))
    26 | $\sim Y \lor \sim F$ (∨I, 25)
    27 | $\sim Y \lor \sim F$ (∨E, 4, 5–17, 18–26)

j	1	M ⊃ S	
	2	F ⊃ J	
	3	(S ≡ J) ⊃ (G ∨ C)	
	4	~C & ~G	
	5	S ⊃ F	
	6	~M ⊃ ~J	
	7	B	
	8	S	
	9	S	(R, 8)
	10	S ⊃ F	(R, 5)
	11	F	(⊃E, 9, 10)
	12	F ⊃ J	(R, 2)
	13	J	(⊃E, 11, 12)
	14	J	
	15	~M	
	16	~M	(R, 15)
	17	~M ⊃ ~J	(R, 6)
	18	~J	(⊃E, 16, 17)
	19	J	(R, 14)
	20	~~M	(~I, 15–(18, 19))
	21	M	(~E, 20)
	22	M ⊃ S	(R, 1)
	23	S	(⊃E, 21, 22)
	24	S ≡ J	(≡I, 8–13, 14–23)
	25	(S ≡ J) ⊃ (G ∨ C)	(R, 3)
	26	G ∨ C	(⊃E, 24, 25)
	27	G	
	28	G	(R, 27)
	29	C	
	30	~G	
	31	~C & ~G	(R, 4)
	32	~C	(&E, 31)
	33	C	(R, 29)
	34	~~G	(~I, 30–(32, 33))
	35	G	(~E, 34)
	36	G	(∨E, 26, 27–28, 29–35)
	37	B ⊃ G	(⊃I, 7–36)

1.   1   │ (P ⊃ ~Q) & (Q ⊃ R)
     2   │ (R ∨ P) ≡ P
     3   │ ~S ⊃ Q
         ├─────────────────────────
     4   │   │ ~S
         │   ├────────────
     5   │   │ ~S   (R, 4)
     6   │   │ ~S ⊃ Q   (R, 3)
     7   │   │ Q   (⊃E, 5, 6)
     8   │   │ (P ⊃ ~Q) & (Q ⊃ R)   (R, 1)
     9   │   │ Q ⊃ R   (&E, 8)
    10   │   │ R   (⊃E, 7, 9)
    11   │   │ R ∨ P   (∨I, 10)
    12   │   │ (R ∨ P) ≡ P   (R, 2)
    13   │   │ P   (≡E, 11, 12)
    14   │   │ P ⊃ ~Q   (&E, 8)
    15   │   │ ~Q   (⊃E, 13, 14)
    16   │ ~~S   (~I, 4–(7, 15))
    17   │ S   (~E, 16)

n.   1 | (P ∨ Q) ∨ (R & S)
     2 | (~P & S) & ~(~P & Q)

     3 | (~P & S) & ~(~P & Q)   (R, 2)
     4 | ~P & S   (&E, 3)
     5 | ~P   (&E, 4)
     6 | (P ∨ Q) ∨ (R & S)   (R, 1)

     7 | | P ∨ Q

     8 | | P ∨ Q   (R, 7)

     9 | | | P

     10 | | | | ~R

     11 | | | | (~P & S) & ~(~P & Q)   (R, 2)
     12 | | | | ~P & S   (&E, 11)
     13 | | | | ~P   (&E, 12)
     14 | | | | P   (R, 9)
     15 | | | ~~R   (~I, 10–(13, 14))
     16 | | | R   (~E, 15)

     17 | | | Q

     18 | | | | ~R

     19 | | | | (~P & S) & ~(~P & Q)   (R, 2)
     20 | | | | ~P & S   (&E, 19)
     21 | | | | ~P   (&E, 20)
     22 | | | | Q   (R, 17)
     23 | | | | ~P & Q   (&I, 21, 22)
     24 | | | | ~(~P & Q)   (&E, 19)
     25 | | | ~~R   (~I, 18–(23, 24))
     26 | | | R   (~E, 25)
     27 | | R   (∨E, 8, 9–16, 17–26)

     28 | | R & S

     29 | | R & S   (R, 28)
     30 | | R   (&E, 29)
     31 | R   (∨E, 6, 7–27, 28–30)
     32 | ~P & R   (&I, 5, 31)

E1.3.4.   b.

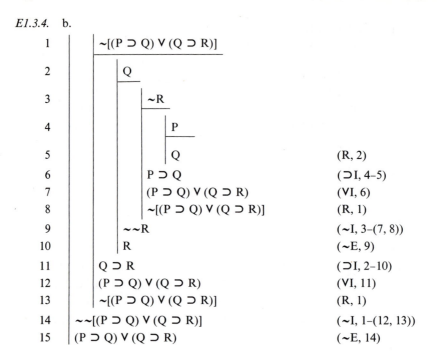

1	~[(P ⊃ Q) ∨ (Q ⊃ R)]	
2	Q	
3	~R	
4	P	
5	Q	(R, 2)
6	P ⊃ Q	(⊃I, 4–5)
7	(P ⊃ Q) ∨ (Q ⊃ R)	(VI, 6)
8	~[(P ⊃ Q) ∨ (Q ⊃ R)]	(R, 1)
9	~~R	(~I, 3–(7, 8))
10	R	(~E, 9)
11	Q ⊃ R	(⊃I, 2–10)
12	(P ⊃ Q) ∨ (Q ⊃ R)	(VI, 11)
13	~[(P ⊃ Q) ∨ (Q ⊃ R)]	(R, 1)
14	~~[(P ⊃ Q) ∨ (Q ⊃ R)]	(~I, 1–(12, 13))
15	(P ⊃ Q) ∨ (Q ⊃ R)	(~E, 14)

g. 1   (P & Q) ⊃ R

    2   ~[(P ⊃ R) ∨ (Q ⊃ R)]

    3   P

    4   ~R

    5   Q

    6   P   (R, 3)
    7   Q   (R, 5)
    8   P & Q   (&I, 6, 7)
    9   (P & Q) ⊃ R   (R, 1)
    10   R   (⊃E, 8, 9)
    11   Q ⊃ R   (⊃I, 5–10)
    12   (P ⊃ R) ∨ (Q ⊃ R)   (∨I, 11)
    13   ~[(P ⊃ R) ∨ (Q ⊃ R)] (R, 2)

    14   ~~R   (~I, 4–(12, 13))
    15   R   (~E, 14)
    16   P ⊃ R   (⊃I, 3–15)
    17   (P ⊃ R) ∨ (Q ⊃ R)   (∨I, 16)
    18   ~[(P ⊃ R) ∨ (Q ⊃ R)]   (R, 2)
    19   ~~[(P ⊃ R) ∨ (Q ⊃ R)]   (~I, 2–(17, 18))
    20   (P ⊃ R) ∨ (Q ⊃ R)   (~E, 19)

    21   (P ⊃ R) ∨ (Q ⊃ R)

    22   P & Q

    23   (P ⊃ R) ∨ (Q ⊃ R)   (R, 21)

    24   P ⊃ R

    25   P & Q   (R, 22)
    26   P   (&E, 25)
    27   P ⊃ R   (R, 24)
    28   R   (⊃E, 26, 27)

    29   Q ⊃ R

    30   P & Q   (R, 22)
    31   Q   (&E, 30)
    32   Q ⊃ R   (R, 29)
    33   R   (⊃E, 31, 32)

    34   R   (∨E, 23, 24–28, 29–33)

    35   (P & Q) ⊃ R   (⊃I, 22–34)

    36   [(P & Q) ⊃ R] ≡ [(P ⊃ R) ∨ (Q ⊃ R)]   (≡I, 1–20, 21–35)

E1.3.5.   a.

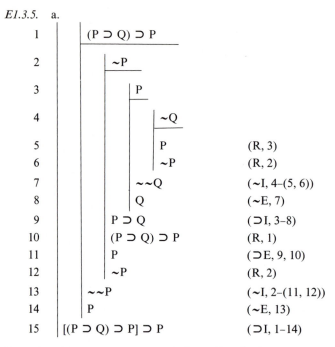

1	(P ⊃ Q) ⊃ P	
2	~P	
3	P	
4	~Q	
5	P	(R, 3)
6	~P	(R, 2)
7	~~Q	(~I, 4–(5, 6))
8	Q	(~E, 7)
9	P ⊃ Q	(⊃I, 3–8)
10	(P ⊃ Q) ⊃ P	(R, 1)
11	P	(⊃E, 9, 10)
12	~P	(R, 2)
13	~~P	(~I, 2–(11, 12))
14	P	(~E, 13)
15	[(P ⊃ Q) ⊃ P] ⊃ P	(⊃I, 1–14)

Note that 'P' (=14) cannot be derived directly from '(P ⊃ Q) ⊃ P' (=1) by ⊃E, since the antecedent 'P ⊃ Q' of '(P ⊃ Q) ⊃ P' is not entailed by—and hence is not derivable from—'(P ⊃ Q) ⊃ P' alone.

e.   1   P V (Q ⊃ R)

     2   P V Q

     3   P V Q   (R, 2)
     4   P

     5   P   (R, 4)
     6   P V R   (VI, 5)
     7   Q

     8   P V (Q ⊃ R)   (R, 1)
     9   P

    10   P   (R, 9)
    11   P V R   (VI, 10)
    12   Q ⊃ R

    13   Q ⊃ R   (R, 12)
    14   Q   (R, 7)
    15   R   (⊃E, 13, 14)
    16   P V R   (VI, 15)
    17   P V R   (VE, 8, 9–11, 12–16)
    18   P V R   (VE, 3, 4–6, 7–17)
    19   (P V Q) ⊃ (P V R)   (⊃I, 2–18)

    20   (P V Q) ⊃ (P V R)

    21   ~[P V (Q ⊃ R)]

    22   Q

    23   Q   (R, 22)
    24   P V Q   (VI, 23)
    25   (P V Q) ⊃ (P V R)   (R, 20)
    26   P V R   (⊃E, 24, 25)
    27   P

    28   ~R

    29   P   (R, 27)
    30   P V (Q ⊃ R)   (VI, 29)
    31   ~[P V (Q ⊃ R)]   (R, 21)
    32   ~~R   (~I, 28–(30,31))
    33   R   (~E, 32)
    34   R

    35   R   (R, 34)
    36   R   (VE, 26, 27–33, 34–35)
    37   Q ⊃ R   (⊃I, 22–36)
    38   P V (Q ⊃ R)   (VI, 37)
    39   ~[P V (Q ⊃ R)]   (R, 21)
    40   ~~[P V (Q ⊃ R)]   (~I, 21–(38, 39))
    41   P V (Q ⊃ R)   (~E, 40)
    42   [P V (Q ⊃ R)] ≡ [(P V Q) ⊃ (P V R)]   (≡I, 1–19, 20–41)

E1.3.6.   h.

1	R ∨ (P & Q)	
2	P ⊃ (Q & R)	
3	~R	
4	R ∨ (P & Q)	(R, 1)
5	R	
6	R	(R, 5)
7	P & Q	
8	P & Q	(R, 7)
9	P	(&E, 8)
10	P ⊃ (Q & R)	(R, 2)
11	Q & R	(⊃E, 9, 10)
12	R	(&E, 11)
13	R	(∨E, 4, 5–6, 7–12)
14	~R	(R, 3)

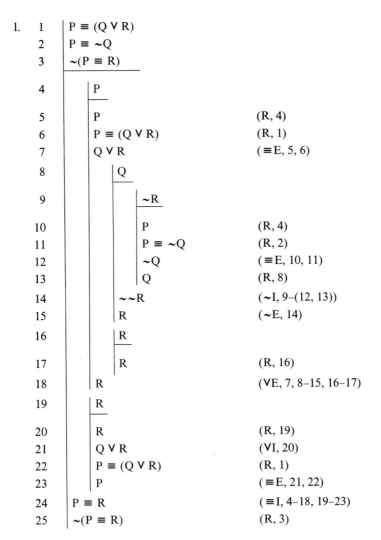

I.

1	$P \equiv (Q \lor R)$	
2	$P \equiv {\sim}Q$	
3	${\sim}(P \equiv R)$	
4	P	
5	P	(R, 4)
6	$P \equiv (Q \lor R)$	(R, 1)
7	$Q \lor R$	($\equiv$E, 5, 6)
8	Q	
9	${\sim}R$	
10	P	(R, 4)
11	$P \equiv {\sim}Q$	(R, 2)
12	${\sim}Q$	($\equiv$E, 10, 11)
13	Q	(R, 8)
14	${\sim}{\sim}R$	(${\sim}$I, 9–(12, 13))
15	R	(${\sim}$E, 14)
16	R	
17	R	(R, 16)
18	R	($\lor$E, 7, 8–15, 16–17)
19	R	
20	R	(R, 19)
21	$Q \lor R$	($\lor$I, 20)
22	$P \equiv (Q \lor R)$	(R, 1)
23	P	($\equiv$E, 21, 22)
24	$P \equiv R$	($\equiv$I, 4–18, 19–23)
25	${\sim}(P \equiv R)$	(R, 3)

E1.3.7.

(a) On any truth-value assignment on which all of $A_1, A_2, \ldots,$ and A_n are true, A_i is true.

(b) Let α be an arbitrary truth-value assignment on which all of $A_1, A_2, \ldots,$ and A_n are true. If $\{A_1, A_2, \ldots, A_n\}$ truth-functionally entails $B \supset C$ and B, then $B \supset C$ and B are sure to be true on α, and hence so is C.

(c) Let α be as in (b). If B is not true on α, then $B \supset C$ is. If on the other hand B is true on α, and $\{A_1, A_2, \ldots, A_n, B\}$ truth-functionally entails C, then C is sure to be true on α, and hence so is $B \supset C$ again.

E1.3.8.

    (a) No

    (b) S' being an arbitrary finite superset of S, enter all the statements in S' that do not belong to S at the top of your derivation of A from S. The result is a derivation of A from S'.

E1.3.9.

(a)

1	A_1		
2	A_2		
$\cdot$	$\cdot$		
n	A_n		
$\cdot$	$\cdot$		
p		$\sim B$	
$\cdot$		$\cdot$	Presumed derivation of $\sim\sim B$ from $\{A_1, A_2, \ldots, A_n\}$
q		$\sim\sim B$	
$q + 1$		$\sim B$	(R, p)
$q + 2$	B		$(\sim E^*, p\text{–}(q, q + 1))$

(b)

1	A_1			
2	A_2			
$\cdot$	$\cdot$			
n	A_n			
$\cdot$	$\cdot$			
p		$\sim\sim B$		
$p + 1$			$\sim B$	
$p + 2$		$\sim B$		$(R, p + 1)$
$p + 3$			$\sim\sim B$	(R, p)
$p + 4$	B			$(\sim E^*, (p + 1)\text{–}(p + 2, p + 3))$
$\cdot$	$\cdot$			Presumed derivation of C and $\sim C$ from $\{A_1, A_2, \ldots, A_n, B\}$
q	C			
$\cdot$	$\cdot$			
r	$\sim C$			
$r + 1$	$\sim B$			$(\sim E^*, p\text{–}(q, r))$

In place of $p + 1$ through $p + 4$, one could reiterate $\sim\sim B$ and infer B by $\sim E$, use of which was justified in (a).

E1.3.10–11. See pp. 254–55.

Chapter Two

Section 2.1

E2.1.2.

2. $(\exists x)(Dx \,\&\, Ax)$

4. $(\forall x)(Dx \supset Rx)$

9. $\sim(\exists x)(Dx \,\&\, Px)$

12. $(\exists x)[(Px \,\&\, Cx) \,\&\, (\sim Wx \,\&\, \sim Ax)]$

15. $(\forall x)([Px \,\&\, (Rx \lor Kx)] \supset [\sim Bx \supset Cx])$

17. $(\forall x)[(Px \,\&\, Sx) \supset \sim Dg]$

22. $(\exists x)(Tx \,\&\, Cx) \supset Cj$

23. $(\forall x)([(Px \,\&\, Jx) \,\&\, (\forall y)(Py \supset \sim Ly)] \supset Sx)$

27. $(\exists x)[(Dx \,\&\, Cx) \,\&\, Fx] \supset (\forall x)[(Dx \,\&\, Cx) \supset Fx]$

28. $(\forall x)(Sx \supset [(Mx \,\&\, Cx) \equiv Hx])$

33. $(\forall x)(Tx \supset \sim Lxp)$

36. $(\forall x)[Px \supset (\exists y)\sim Lxy] \,\&\, (\forall x)(Px \supset \sim\sim Lxs)$

38. $(\forall x)(Px \supset (\forall y)[(\exists z)(Czx \,\&\, Gzyx) \supset \sim(\exists z)(Pz \,\&\, Gxyz)])$

41. $(\forall x)[Lx \supset (\forall y)([Ty \,\&\, (\exists z)(Gz \,\&\, Sxzy)] \supset Exy)]$

45. $(\forall x)([Ax \,\&\, (\exists y)(Cy \,\&\, Bxy)] \supset (\forall y)[Dy \supset Bxy])$

46. $(\exists x)[Tx \,\&\, (\exists y)(Wy \,\&\, Hpyx)] \,\&\, (\forall x)[Tx \supset (\forall y)(Wy \supset \sim Hmyx)]$

49. $(\forall x)(\forall y)[Oxy \equiv (\exists z)(Pzx \,\&\, Pzy)]$

E2.1.3.

a. Barbara has something that Alan gave her.

d. Whoever gives something to Alan gives something to Barbara.

f. Everybody has something (or other).

j. There is someone who does not give anything to, or receive anything from, anyone.

n. No one has (any longer) anything that he gave away.

p. No one gives away anything he does not have.

t. There is no one who receives from a single person everything that is given to him.

E2.1.4.

a. Fa_3a_1—conservative
   Fa_3a_2—conservative
   Fa_3a_3—not conservative
   etc.

c. $Fa_2a_1 \,\&\, Ga_1$—conservative (why?)

f. $(\forall y)(Fya_1 \supset \sim Fa_2a_1)$—not conservative
   $(\forall y)(Fya_1 \supset \sim Fa_2a_2)$—not conservative
   $(\forall y)(Fya_1 \supset \sim Fa_2a_3)$—conservative
   etc.

E2.1.5.

   k. $(\exists x)Gx \supset \sim(\forall x)(Px \supset Wx)$

        $(\exists x)Gx$

        $\sim(\forall x)(Px \supset Wx)$

        $(\forall x)(Px \supset Wx)$

        Ga_1

        Ga_2

        Ga_3

        ⋮

        $Pa_1 \supset Wa_1$

        $Pa_2 \supset Wa_2$

        $Pa_3 \supset Wa_3$

        ⋮

        Pa_1

        Pa_2

        Pa_3

        ⋮

        Wa_1

        Wa_2

        Wa_3

        ⋮

E2.1.6.

(a) If $A(T/X)$ is an atomic statement for one term T, it would still be one (by Table VI, clause **C**) whatever other term were put for T. If $A(T/X)$ were the negation $\sim B(T/X)$ of the atomic statement $B(T/X)$, then $A(T/X)$ would be a statement whatever other term were put for T, because $B(T/X)$ would be one. If $A(T/X)$ were the conditional statement $(B \supset C)(T/X)$—i.e., $B(T/X) \supset C(T/X)$—of the atomic statements $B(T/X)$ and $C(T/X)$, then it would be a statement whatever other term were put for T, because $B(T/X)$ and $C(T/X)$ would be. And so on for the other compounds of atomic statements, and also for compounds of compound statements. As long as an atomic statement remains a statement with its terms changed, *any* statement will.

(b) If $A \supset B(T/X)$ is a statement, so are A and $B(T/X)$. But if $B(T/X)$ is a statement, then so is $(\forall X)B$. Thus if $A \supset B(T/X)$ is a statement, so is $A \supset (\forall X)B$ (but not necessarily $(\forall X)(A \supset B)$).

(c) Require that X occur in A.

(d) Suppose A is a statement and X is foreign to A; then—for any term T—$(A(X/T))(T/X)$ is the same as A, and hence by clause (4) $(\forall X)A(X/T)$ and $(\exists X)A(X/T)$ are statements. Suppose, on the other hand, that $A(T/X)$ is a statement; then X is sure to be foreign to $A(T/X)$, hence by clause (4') $(\forall X)(A(T/X))(X/T)$ and $(\exists X)(A(T/X))(X/T)$ are statements, and hence so are $(\forall X)A \ (= (\forall X)(A(T/X))(X/T))$ and $(\exists X)A \ (= (\exists X)(A(T/X))(X/T))$. $(\forall X)A(X/T)$ and $(\exists X)A(X/T)$ will prove vacuous when T is so chosen as to be foreign to A.

E2.1.7.

(a) When A is atomic, A is of the sort $P(T_1, T_2, \ldots, T_m)$, and by the definition on p. 138 its length is sure to be 1. When A is of the sort $\sim B$, the same predicates occur in $\sim\!B$ as in B, and they occur in $\sim\!B$ the same number of times as they do in B. Other than '$\sim$', the same logical operators occur in $\sim\!B$ as in B, and they occur in $\sim\!B$ the same number of times as they do in B. As for '$\sim$', it occurs in $\sim\!B$ one more time than in B. So the length of $\sim\!B$ is sure to be that of B plus 1. And so on.

E2.1.8.

(a) 'Fa$_1$a$_1$', which is a generating instance of '$(\exists x)Fxx$' only.

(b) If $A(T/X)$ is a generating instance of $(\forall X)A$, then T is foreign to A and hence $(A(T/X))(X/T)$ is the same as A.

(c) If T is foreign to $(\forall X)A$ and hence to A, then $(A(T/X))(T'/T)$ is the same as $A(T'/X)$, which is an instance of $(\forall X)A$. If, on the other hand, T occurs in $(\forall X)A$, then $(A(T/X))(T'/T)$ will contain T' both where A contains X *and where A contains T*, and hence $(A(T/X))(T'/T)$ will not count as an instance of $(\forall X)A$. Note that when T and T' are the same, $(A(T/X))(T'/T)$ is the same as $A(T/X)$, which counts as an instance of $(\forall X)A$ whether or not T is foreign to $(\forall X)A$.

(d) If $A(T/X)$ is a conservative instance of $(\forall X)A$, then T is foreign to $(\forall X)A$, and hence $(A(T/X))(T'/T)$ is the same as $A(T'/X)$.

E2.1.9.

(a) When all the quantifications in the statement, if any, are vacuous.

(b) S^* will be finite when every member of S is as in (a). S^{**} is sure to be infinite. For suppose 'Fa' belongs to S^*; then all of 'Fa', '$\sim$Fa', '$\sim\sim$Fa', '$\sim\sim\sim$Fa', etc. belong to S^{**}.

(c) Let $A_1, A_2, A_3, \ldots$ be the atomic statements in question. A_1 can be assigned a truth-value in 2 different ways; for each one of these 2 ways A_2 can be assigned a truth-value in 2 different ways; for each one of these 2×2 ways A_3 can be assigned a truth-value in 2 different ways; etc. Hence $A_1, A_2, A_3,$ etc. can be assigned truth-values in $\underbrace{2 \times 2 \times 2 \times \ldots}_{\aleph_0 \text{ times}}$ different ways. But 2 multiplied by itself $\aleph_0$ times is $2^{\aleph_0}$. Hence (c).

E2.1.10.

(a) i is false on α but true on α'; j is false on both α and α'.

(b)

i.	Fa	Fb		Fa $\supset$ ($\forall$x)Fx	
	T	F		F	F

iv.	Fa	Ga	Fb	Gb	(($\forall$x)Fx $\equiv$ ($\forall$x)Gx) $\supset$ ($\forall$x)(Fx $\equiv$ Gx)

| | F | F | T | F | F | | T | F | | F | F |

v.	Fa	Fb	Ga	(($\forall$x)Fx $\supset$ Ga) $\supset$ ($\forall$x)(Fx $\supset$ Ga)
	F	T	F	F	T	F	F

E2.1.11.

a. To determine whether a is logically true, we hunt for a truth-value assignment on which it would be false. Since a is true on any truth-value assignment on which '$\sim(\exists x)Fx$' is false, let '$\sim(\exists x)Fx$' be true on α; then '$(\exists x)Fx$' is false on α, hence all of 'Fa$_1$', 'Fa$_2$', 'Fa$_3$', etc. are false on α, hence all of 'Fa$_1 \supset$ Ga$_1$', 'Fa$_2 \supset$ Ga$_2$', 'Fa$_3 \supset$ Ga$_3$', etc. are true on α, hence '$(\forall x)(Fx \supset Gx)$' is true on α, and hence so is a. Hence also $\{\sim(\exists x)Fx\}$ entails '$(\forall x)(Fx \supset Gx)$'.

e. Let α assign **T** to all the instances of '$(\forall x)Fx$' but 'Fa$_1$', and **T** to all those of '$(\forall x)Gx$' but 'Ga$_2$'. Then all of 'Fa$_1 \lor$ Ga$_1$', 'Fa$_2 \lor$ Ga$_2$', 'Fa$_3 \lor$ Ga$_3$', etc. are true on α, and hence so is '$(\forall x)(Fx \lor Gx)$'. But neither of '$(\forall x)Fx$' and '$(\forall x)Gx$' is true on α. Hence '$(\forall x)Fx \lor (\forall x)Gx$' is false on α, and hence so is e. So e is not logically true. To show that it is not logically false—and hence that it is logically indeterminate—find a (different) truth-value assignment on which e is true.

f. Suppose that '$(\forall x)(Fx \lor Gx)$' is true on a truth-value assignment α, but '$(\forall x)Fx$' is not. Then all of 'Fa$_1 \lor$ Ga$_1$', 'Fa$_2 \lor$ Ga$_2$', 'Fa$_3 \lor$ Ga$_3$', etc. are true on α, but at least one of 'Fa$_1$', 'Fa$_2$', 'Fa$_3$', etc. is not. Hence one of 'Ga$_1$', 'Ga$_2$', 'Ga$_3$', etc. is sure to be true on α, hence so is '$(\exists x)Gx$', and hence so is f. Hence also $\{(\forall x)(Fx \lor Gx)\}$ entails '$(\forall x)Fx \lor (\exists x)Gx$'.

l. On any truth-value assignment, all of 'Fa$_1 \supset (\exists y)Fy$', 'Fa$_2 \supset (\exists y)Fy$', 'Fa$_3 \supset (\exists y)Fy$', etc. are sure to be true. Hence so is l.

m. Let α be the result of assigning **F** to all the atomic subformulas of '$(\exists x)(\exists y)Fxy$' but 'Fa$_1a_2$'. Then '$(\exists x)(\exists y)Fxy$' is true on α, but '$(\exists x)Fxx$' is not (this because all of 'Fa$_1$a$_1$', 'Fa$_2$a$_2$', 'Fa$_3$a$_3$', etc. are assigned **F** in α). Hence m is not logically true. Hence also '$(\exists x)Fxx$' and '$(\exists x)(\exists y)Fxy$' are not equivalent. (To show that m is logically indeterminate, find a truth-value assignment to its atomic subformulas on which it is true.)

E2.1.12.

(a) When $(\forall X)A$ is vacuous, $A(T/X)$ is the same as A for every term T, hence $(\forall X)A$ is true on a truth-value assignment α if and only if A is true on α for every term T, i.e. if and only if A is true on α. Hence $(\forall X)A$ and A are equivalent. For the same reason so are $(\exists X)A$ and A, and hence so are all of $(\forall X)A$, $(\exists X)A$, and A.

(b) Suppose we had only n ($n > 0$) terms, say 'a$_1$', 'a$_2$', ..., and 'a$_n$'. Then $(\forall X)A$ would be true on a truth-value assignment α if and only if all of $A(a_1/X)$, $A(a_2/X)$, ..., and $A(a_n/X)$ are true on α—i.e. if and only if $(\ldots (A(a_1/X) \,\&\, A(a_2/X)) \,\&\, \ldots) \,\&\, A(a_n/X)$ is true on α. For a like reason, $(\exists X)A$ would be true on α if and only if the disjunction of its instances were true on α. Note that a conjunction (disjunction) here has only finitely many conjuncts (disjuncts); so the point just made does not hold when the supply of terms is infinite.

E2.1.13.

(i) A is logically false (logically true) if and only if $\sim A$ is logically true (logically false).

A and B are equivalent if and only if $A \equiv B$ is logically true.

$\{A_1, A_2, \ldots, A_n\}$ entails B if and only if $((\ldots (A_1 \,\&\, A_2) \,\&\, \ldots) \,\&\, A_n) \supset B$ is logically true.

$\{A_1, A_2, \ldots, A_n\}$ is inconsistent if and only if $(\ldots (A_1 \mathbin{\&} A_2) \mathbin{\&} \ldots) \mathbin{\&} A_n$ is logically false.

(ii) A is logically true if and only if A and $A \supset A$ are equivalent.
A is logically false if and only if A and $\sim(A \supset A)$ are equivalent.
Then proceed as in (i).

(iii) A is logically true if and only if $\varnothing$ entails A. Then proceed as in (i).

E2.1.14.

(a) Let A be an arbitrary statement containing some term T_1, and let T_2 be any term distinct from T_1. It follows from (3.2.2) on p. 265 that there is a truth-value assignment on which A is not true if and only if there is one on which $A(T_2/T_1)$ is not true. Hence A is true on every truth-value assignment if and only if its term variant $A(T_2/T_1)$ is. (The result is trivially true when A contains no terms. In this case A is its only term variant.)

(b) The logical truth 'Fa $\supset$ Fa' is a term variant of 'Fa $\supset$ Fb' (which is logically indeterminate), and the logical falsehood 'Fa $\mathbin{\&}$ $\sim$Fa' is a term variant of 'Fa $\mathbin{\&}$ $\sim$Fb' (which is logically indeterminate).

E2.1.15.

(a) Suppose $(\forall X)A$ is logically true, and let α be an arbitrary truth-value assignment; then every instance of $(\forall X)A$ is true on α, hence at least one instance of $(\exists X)A$ is true on α, and hence $(\exists X)A$ is true on α. Suppose $(\exists X)A$ is logically false, and let α be as before; then every instance of $(\exists X)A$ is false on α, hence at least one instance of $(\forall X)A$ is false on α, and hence $(\forall X)A$ is false on α.

(b)   (i) See (a) above.

  (ii) If every instance of $(\forall X)A$ is logically true, then every instance of $(\forall X)A$ is true on any truth-value assignment, and hence so is $(\forall X)A$.

  (iii) Use Case 1 of the proof of (3.3.6) on p. 277, with S empty.

  (iv)–(vi) Adapt answers to (i)–(iii).

(c) The non-conservative instance 'Fa $\supset$ Fa' of '$(\forall x)(Fx \supset Fa)$' is logically true; the non-conservative instance '$\sim$(Fa $\supset$ Fa)' of '$(\exists x)\sim(Fx \supset Fa)$' is logically false.

E2.1.16.

$A(T/X)$	$(\forall X)A$	$(\exists X)A$
2	2	2
1	0 or 1	2 or 1
0	0	0

As regards row 2, note that (i) '$(\forall y)(Fy \mathbin{\&} \sim(\forall x)Fx)$' is logically false, though none of its instances 'Fa$_1$ $\mathbin{\&}$ $\sim(\forall x)Fx$', 'Fa$_2$ $\mathbin{\&}$ $\sim(\forall x)Fx$', 'Fa$_3$ $\mathbin{\&}$ $\sim(\forall x)Fx$', etc. is logically false; and (ii) '$(\exists y)(Fy \supset (\forall x)Fx)$' is logically true, though none of its instances 'Fa$_1$ $\supset$ $(\forall x)Fx$', 'Fa$_2$ $\supset$ $(\forall x)Fx$', 'Fa$_3$ $\supset$ $(\forall x)Fx$', etc. is.

E2.1.17.

a. On any truth-value assignment on which all of '$\sim$Fa$_1$', '$\sim$Fa$_2$', '$\sim$Fa$_3$', etc. are true, '$(\exists x)Fx$' is not; and on any one on which '$(\exists x)Fx$' is true, at least one of '~Fa$_1$', '~Fa$_2$', '~Fa$_3$', etc. is not. So there can be no truth-value assignment on which all members of the set in a are true.

b. On any truth-value assignment on which all of 'Fa$_1$', 'Fa$_2$', 'Fa$_3$', etc. are true, '($\forall x$)Fx' is true, and hence so is '~($\forall x$)Gx'. But on any truth-value assignment on which '~($\forall x$)Gx' is true at least one of 'Ga$_1$', 'Ga$_2$', 'Ga$_3$', etc. must be false.

c. On any truth-value assignment on which all of 'Fa$_2$', 'Fa$_3$', 'Fa$_4$', etc. are true, 'Fa$_1$' must be false if '~($\forall x$)Fx' is to be true. On any truth-value assignment on which 'Fa$_1$' is false and hence '~Fa$_1$' true, 'Ga$_1$' and '($\exists x$)~Gx' are true. But on any truth-value assignment on which all of 'Ga$_1$', 'Ga$_2$', 'Ga$_3$', etc. are true, '($\exists x$)~Gx' is false.

Section 2.2

We construct the trees here in accordance with the routine of p. 189, except in a very few cases where the tree so constructed would have been pointlessly long. When the tree is an open one (establishing consistency, invalidity, etc.), we note which of CASES 2 and 3 on p. 187 obtains, and pick our truth-value assignment from the left-most open branch in accordance with the instructions on p. 191.

E2.2.1.

b.

		from
1	($\forall x$)(Fx $\supset$ Gx)	
2	~($\exists x$)(Fx & Gx)	
3	($\exists x$)Fx ✔	
4	Fa	3
5	Fa $\supset$ Ga ✔	1
6	~Fa Ga	5
7	x ~(Fa & Ga) ✔	2
	4	
8	~Fa ~Ga	7
	x x	
	4 6	

Inconsistent

e.

		from
1	~(∀x)[Fx ⊃ (∀y)(Gy ⊃ Hx)] ✔	
2	(∃x)Fx & (∃x)~(Fx ∨ Gx) ✔	
3	~(∀x)(Fc ⊃ Hx) ✔	

		from
4	(∃x)Fx ✔	2
5	(∃x)~(Fx ∨ Gx) ✔	2
6	Fa	4
7	~(Fb ∨ Gb) ✔	5
8	~Fb	7
9	~Gb	7
10	~(Fc ⊃ Hd) ✔	3
11	Fc	10
12	~Hd	10
13	~[Fe ⊃ (∀y)(Gy ⊃ He)] ✔	1
14	Fe	13
15	~(∀y)(Gy ⊃ He) ✔	13
16	~(Gf ⊃ He) ✔	15
17	Gf	16
18	~He	16

Consistent (CASE 2): **T** to 'Fa', 'Fc', 'Fe', and 'Gf', and
F to all other atomic components

k.

		from
1	$(\forall x)[Fx \supset (\forall y)(Gy \supset Hxy)]$	
2	$\sim(\forall x)[Fx \supset (\forall y)(\sim Fy \supset Hxy)]$ ✔	
3	$(\forall x)(Fx \lor Gx)$	

---

4      $\sim[Fa \supset (\forall y)(\sim Fy \supset Hay)]$ ✔   2

5   Fa   4

6      $\sim(\forall y)(\sim Fy \supset Hay)$ ✔   4

7      $\sim(\sim Fb \supset Hab)$ ✔   6

8      $\sim Fb$ 7

9      $\sim Hab$ 7

10      $Fb \lor Gb$ ✔   3

11   Fb   Gb   10
            x
            8

12      $Fa \supset (\forall y)(Gy \supset Hay)$ ✔   1

13      $\sim Fa$ $(\forall y)(Gy \supset Hay)$ 12

14   x $Gb \supset Hab$ ✔   13
         5

15      $\sim Gb$ Hab   14
         x   x
         11   9

Inconsistent

n.

		from
1	$(\forall x)[\sim Fx \supset (Gx \lor Hx)] \supset (\forall x)(\exists y)\sim Ixy$ ✔	

2    $\sim(\forall x)[\sim Fx \supset (Gx \lor Hx)]$ ✔ $(\forall x)(\exists y)\sim Ixy$ 1

3    $\sim[\sim Fa \supset (Ga \lor Ha)]$ ✔   2

4    $\sim Fa$ 3

5    $\sim(Ga \lor Ha)$ ✔   3

6    $\sim Ga$ 5

7    $\sim Ha$ 5

Consistent (CASE 2): **F** to all atomic components

o.

1   ~(∀x)Fx ⊃ ~(∃x)(Gx ∨ (∀y)Hyx) ✔

2   ~(∀x)Gx✔

                                                                      from

3   ~Ga   2

4   ~~(∀x)Fx✔   ~(∃x)(Gx ∨ (∀y)Hyx)   1

5   (∀x)Fx   4

6   Fa   5

7   ~(Ga ∨ (∀y)Hya)✔   4

8   ~Ga   7

9   ~(∀y)Hya✔   7

10   ~Hba   9

11   ~(Gb ∨ (∀y)Hyb)✔   4

12   ~Gb   11

13   ~(∀y)Hyb   11

Consistent (CASE 3): **T** to 'Fa', 'Fb', 'Fc', etc., and **F** to all
other atomic components

E2.2.2.

   b.

1   (∀x)Fx ⊃ (∀x)Gx ✔

2   ~(∃x)(Fx ⊃ Gx)

                                                                      from

3   ~(∀x)Fx✔   (∀x)Gx   1

4   ~Fa   3

5   ~(Fa ⊃ Ga)✔   ~(Fa ⊃ Ga)✔   2

6   Fa   5

7   ~Ga   5

8   x   Fa   5

9   4   ~Ga   5

10   Ga   3

                                               x

                                               9

      Valid

c.

1                      $(\forall x)Fx \supset (\forall x)Gx$ ✔

2                      $\sim(\forall x)(Fx \supset Gx)$ ✔

                                                      from

3       $\sim(\forall x)Fx$ ✔ $(\forall x)Gx$ 1

4          $\sim$Fa   3

5      $\sim$(Fb $\supset$ Gb) ✔ $\sim$(Fb $\supset$ Gb)   2

6   Fb   5

7         $\sim$Gb   5

Invalid (CASE 2): **T** to 'Fb', and **F** to all other atomic
components

j.

1                 $(\forall x)(\forall y)(\sim Fxy \lor Gxy)$

2                 $\sim(\exists x)(\exists y)Gxy$

3                 $\sim(\exists x)(\exists y)Fxy$

                                                  from

4                $(\forall y)(\sim Fay \lor Gay)$ 1

5                 $\sim(\exists y)Gay$ 2

6                 $\sim(\exists y)Fay$ 3

7              $\sim$Faa $\lor$ Gaa ✔   4

8                  $\sim$Gaa   5

9                  $\sim$Faa   6

10        $\sim$Faa   Gaa   7

                            x

                            8

Invalid (CASE 3): **F** to all atomic components

k.

		from
1	$(\forall x)(Cx \supset Px) \lor (\forall x)(Rx \supset \sim Hx)$ ✔	
2	$\sim[(\exists x)(Rx \& Cx) \supset (\exists x)(Cx \& [Px \lor \sim Hx])]$ ✔	

3	$(\exists x)(Rx \& Cx)$ ✔	2
4	$\sim(\exists x)(Cx \& [Px \lor \sim Hx])$	2
5	$Ra \& Ca$	3
6	Ra	5
7	Ca	5
8	$\sim(Ca \& [Pa \lor \sim Ha])$ ✔	4

9. $\sim Ca$ $\sim[Pa \lor \sim Ha]$ ✔   8

10.   x $\sim Pa$ 9

11.   7 $\sim\sim Ha$ ✔   9

12. Ha 11

13. $(\forall x)(Cx \supset Px)$ $(\forall x)(Rx \supset \sim Hx)$ 1

14. $\sim Ca \supset Pa$ ✔   13

15. Ca Pa 14
     x   x
     7   10

16. $Ra \supset \sim Ha$ ✔   13

17. $\sim Ra$ $\sim Ha$ 16
     x   x
     6   12

Valid

r.

1	$(\forall x)(\forall y)(Fxy \supset Pxy)$	
2	$(\forall x)(Ax \supset Dx)$	
3	$\sim(\forall x)((\exists y)(Ay \& Fxy) \supset [(\exists y)(Ay \& Pxy) \& (\exists y)(Dy \& Fxy)]) ✔$	

from

4	$\sim((\exists y)(Ay \& Fay) \supset [(\exists y)(Ay \& Pay) \& (\exists y)(Dy \& Fay)]) ✔$	3
5	$(\exists y)(Ay \& Fay) ✔$	4
6	$\sim[(\exists y)(Ay \& Pay) \& (\exists y)(Dy \& Fay)] ✔$	4
7	$Ab \& Fab ✔$	5
8	Ab	7
9	Fab	7
10	$(\forall y)(Fay \supset Pay)$	1
11	$Fab \supset Pab ✔$	10

12	$\sim Fab \qquad\qquad Pab$	11
	x	
	9	
13	$Ab \supset Db ✔$	2

14	$\sim Ab \quad Db$	13
	x	
	8	

| 15 | $\sim(\exists y)(Ay \& Pay) \qquad \sim(\exists y)(Dy \& Fay)$ | 6 |
| 16 | $\sim(Ab \& Pab) ✔$ | 15 |

17	$\sim Ab \qquad \sim Pab$	16
	x \qquad x	
	8 \qquad 12	

| 18 | $\sim(Db \& Fab) ✔$ | 15 |

19	$\sim Db \quad \sim Fab$	18
	x \qquad x	
	14 \qquad 9	

Valid

t.

1             $(\forall x)(Px \supset {\sim}Hx)$

2             ${\sim}(Rd \supset [(\forall x)(Rx \supset Hx) \supset Pd])$ ✔

                                                 from

3   Rd   2

4         ${\sim}[(\forall x)(Rx \supset Hx) \supset Pd]$ ✔   2

5            $(\forall x)(Rx \supset Hx)$ 4

6                 ${\sim}Pd$ 4

7             $Pd \supset {\sim}Hd$ ✔   1

8              $Rd \supset Hd$ ✔   5

9         ${\sim}Rd$ Hd   8

                x

                3

10                       ${\sim}Pd$ ${\sim}Hd$ 7

                                x

                                9

Invalid (CASE 3): **T** to 'Ha', 'Hb', 'Hc', ...
                         F to 'Pa', 'Pb', 'Pc', ...
                         T to 'Ra', 'Rb', 'Rc', ...

E2.2.3.

b.

1       ${\sim}[((\exists x)Fx \supset (\exists x)Gx) \supset (\exists x)(Fx \supset Gx)]$ ✔

                                                 from

2               $(\exists x)Fx \supset (\exists x)Gx$ ✔   1

3                ${\sim}(\exists x)(Fx \supset Gx)$ 1

4      ${\sim}(\exists x)Fx$ $(\exists x)Gx$ ✔   2

5   Ga   4

6    ${\sim}(Fa \supset Ga)$ ✔ ${\sim}(Fa \supset Ga)$ ✔   3

7           ${\sim}Fa$ 4

8   Fa   6

9          ${\sim}Ga$ 6

10   x   Fa   6

11   7 ${\sim}Ga$ 6

                                       x

                                       5

Logically true

c.

		from
1	$\sim[(\exists x)(Fx \supset Gx) \supset ((\exists x)Fx \supset (\exists x)Gx)]$ ✔	
2	$(\exists x)(Fx \supset Gx)$✔	1
3	$\sim((\exists x)Fx \supset (\exists x)Gx)$✔	1
4	$(\exists x)Fx$✔	3
5	$\sim(\exists x)Gx$✔	3
6	Fa	4
7	Fb $\supset$ Gb✔	2

				from
8	~Fb		Gb	7
9	~Ga		~Ga	5
10	~Gb		~Gb	5
			x	
			8	

Not logically true (CASE 3): **T** to 'Fa', 'Fc', 'Fd', . . .
$\qquad\qquad\qquad\qquad\qquad$ **F** to all other atomic components

h.

		from
1	$\sim(\exists x)[(\exists y)Fy \supset Fx]$ ✔	
2	$\sim[(\exists y)Fy \supset Fa]$ ✔	1
3	$(\exists y)Fy$ ✔	2
4	~Fa	2
5	Fb	3
6	$\sim[(\exists y)Fy \supset Fb]$ ✔	1
7	$(\exists y)Fy$ ✔	6
8	~Fb	6
	x	
	5	

Logically true

j.

		from
1	$\sim[(\forall x)Fxx \supset \sim(\exists x)(\exists y)Fxy]$ ✔	
2	$(\forall x)Fxx$	1
3	$\sim\sim(\exists x)(\exists y)Fxy$ ✔	1
4	$(\exists x)(\exists y)Fxy$ ✔	3
5	$(\exists y)Fay$ ✔	4
6	Fab	5
7	Faa	2
8	Fbb	2

Not logically true (CASE 3): **T** to 'Faa', 'Fbb', 'Fcc', . . .
$\qquad\qquad\qquad\qquad\qquad$ **T** to 'Fab', 'Fcb', 'Fdb', . . .
$\qquad\qquad\qquad\qquad\qquad$ **F** to all other atomic components

E2.2.4.

a.

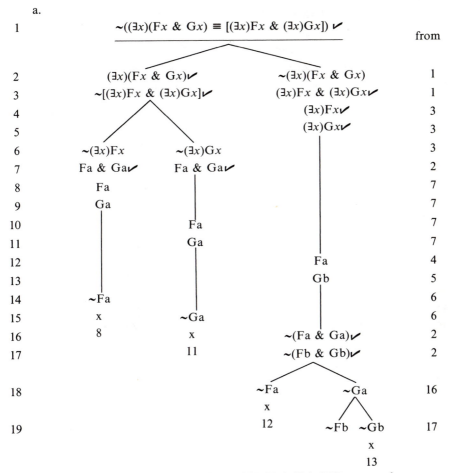

			from
1	~((∃x)(Fx & Gx) ≡ [(∃x)Fx & (∃x)Gx]) ✔		
2	(∃x)(Fx & Gx)✔	~(∃x)(Fx & Gx)	1
3	~[(∃x)Fx & (∃x)Gx]✔	(∃x)Fx & (∃x)Gx✔	1
4		(∃x)Fx✔	3
5		(∃x)Gx✔	3
6	~(∃x)Fx ~(∃x)Gx		3
7	Fa & Ga✔ Fa & Ga✔		2
8	Fa		7
9	Ga		7
10	Fa		7
11	Ga		7
12		Fa	4
13		Gb	5
14	~Fa		6
15	x ~Ga		6
16	8 x	~(Fa & Ga)✔	2
17	11	~(Fb & Gb)✔	2
18		~Fa ~Ga	16
		x	
19		12 ~Fb ~Gb	17
		x	
		13	

Not equivalent (CASE 3): **T** to 'Gb', 'Fa', 'Fc', 'Fd', etc., and
F to 'Fb', 'Ga', 'Gc', 'Gd', etc.

b.

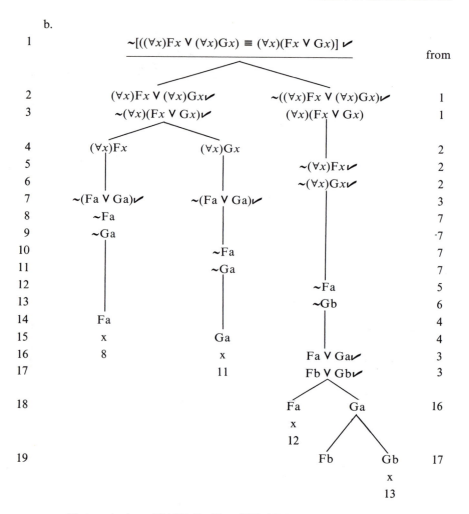

Not equivalent (CASE 3): **T** to 'Fb', 'Ga', 'Gc', 'Gd', etc. and
F to 'Gb', 'Fa', 'Fc', 'Fd', etc.

E2.2.5.

c.

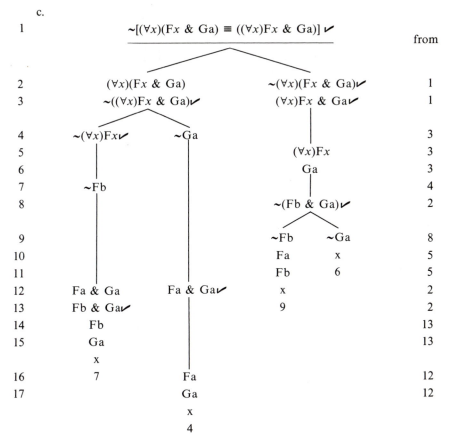

		from
1	~[(∀x)(Fx & Ga) ≡ ((∀x)Fx & Ga)] ✔	
2	(∀x)(Fx & Ga) ~(∀x)(Fx & Ga)✔	1
3	~((∀x)Fx & Ga)✔ (∀x)Fx & Ga✔	1
4	~(∀x)Fx✔ ~Ga	3
5	(∀x)Fx	3
6	Ga	3
7	~Fb	4
8	~(Fb & Ga)✔	2
9	~Fb ~Ga	8
10	Fa x	5
11	Fb 6	5
12	Fa & Ga Fa & Ga✔ x	2
13	Fb & Ga✔ 9	2
14	Fb	13
15	Ga	13
	x	
16	7 Fa	12
17	Ga	12
	x	
	4	

j.

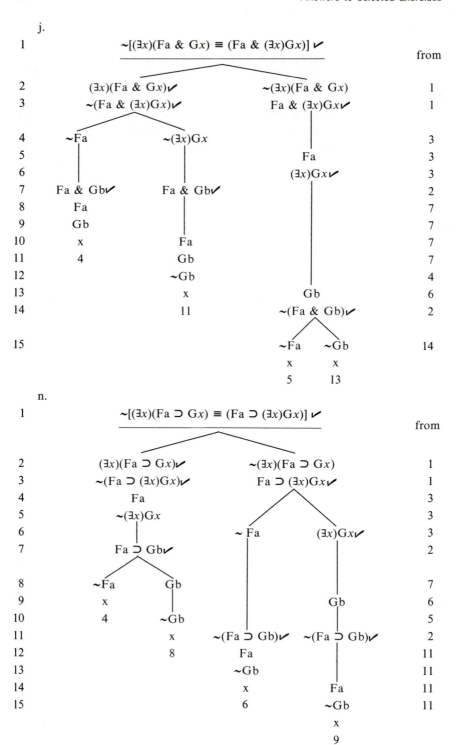

1   ~[(∃x)(Fa & Gx) ≡ (Fa & (∃x)Gx)] ✔   from

2   (∃x)(Fa & Gx)✔   ~(∃x)(Fa & Gx)   1
3   ~(Fa & (∃x)Gx)✔   Fa & (∃x)Gx✔   1

4   ~Fa   ~(∃x)Gx   3
5   Fa   3
6   (∃x)Gx✔   3
7 Fa & Gb✔   Fa & Gb✔   2
8   Fa   7
9   Gb   7
10   x   Fa   7
11   4   Gb   7
12   ~Gb   4
13   x   Gb   6
14   11   ~(Fa & Gb)✔   2

15   ~Fa   ~Gb   14
                                           x   x
                                           5   13

n.

1   ~[(∃x)(Fa ⊃ Gx) ≡ (Fa ⊃ (∃x)Gx)] ✔   from

2   (∃x)(Fa ⊃ Gx)✔   ~(∃x)(Fa ⊃ Gx)   1
3   ~(Fa ⊃ (∃x)Gx)✔   Fa ⊃ (∃x)Gx✔   1
4   Fa   3
5   ~(∃x)Gx   3
6   ~Fa   (∃x)Gx✔   3
7   Fa ⊃ Gb✔   2

8   ~Fa   Gb   7
9   x   6
10   4   ~Gb   Gb   5
11   x   ~(Fa ⊃ Gb)✔   ~(Fa ⊃ Gb)✔   2
12   8   Fa   11
13   ~Gb   11
14   x   Fa   11
15   6   ~Gb   11
                                                     x
                                                     9

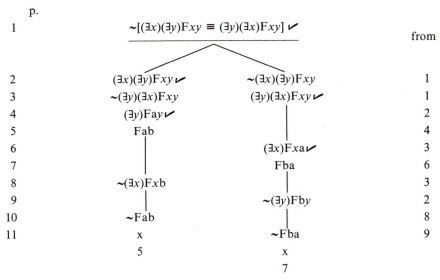

p.
1                         $\sim[(\exists x)(\exists y)Fxy \equiv (\exists y)(\exists x)Fxy]$ ✔   from

2	$(\exists x)(\exists y)Fxy$ ✔	$\sim(\exists x)(\exists y)Fxy$	1
3	$\sim(\exists y)(\exists x)Fxy$	$(\exists y)(\exists x)Fxy$ ✔	1
4	$(\exists y)Fay$ ✔		2
5	Fab		4
6		$(\exists x)Fxa$ ✔	3
7		Fba	6
8	$\sim(\exists x)Fxb$		3
9		$\sim(\exists y)Fby$	2
10	$\sim Fab$		8
11	x	$\sim Fba$	9
	5	x	
		7	

E2.2.6.

(b) The trees for $\{(\exists x)Fx\}$ are

    $\dfrac{(\exists x)Fx \text{ ✔}}{Fa_1}$ $\dfrac{(\exists x)Fx \text{ ✔}}{Fa_2}$ $\dfrac{(\exists x)Fx \text{ ✔}}{Fa_3}$ etc.,

all of which are finite.

    A typical tree for $\{(\forall y)(\exists x)[(Fy \supset Fy) \supset Fx]\}$ would begin as follows:

1                        $(\forall y)(\exists x)[(Fy \supset Fy) \supset Fx]$ from

2                           $(\exists x)[(Fa_1 \supset Fa_1) \supset Fx]$ ✔   1

3                             $(Fa_1 \supset Fa_1) \supset Fa_2$ ✔   2

4	$\sim(Fa_1 \supset Fa_1)$ ✔	Fa_2	3
5	Fa_1		4
6	$\sim Fa_1$		4
7	x	$(\exists x)[(Fa_2 \supset Fa_2) \supset Fx]$ ✔	1
8	5	$(Fa_2 \supset Fa_2) \supset Fa_3$ ✔	7
9		$\sim(Fa_2 \supset Fa_2)$ ✔ Fa_3	8
10		Fa_2	9
11		$\sim Fa_2$	9
		x	
		10	

As this portion of the tree shows, there will always be work to be done on the right-most branch (line 1 never being checked off), and no negation sign will ever appear on that branch. So the tree is sure to be infinite.

E2.2.7.

Let the set tested be $\{A_1, A_2, \ldots, A_n\}$, where all the quantifiers (if any) in A_1, $A_2, \ldots,$ and A_n are universal and initially placed. Suppose some statement B occurs on every open branch of the tree, and suppose the tree in question was made in keeping with the routine on p. 189. If every open branch is completed, then none of $A_1, A_2, \ldots,$ and A_n is a quantification, and the argument for E1.2.7 will suffice. If at least one branch is not completed, slipping $\sim B$ between A_n and the horizontal bar separating $A_1, A_2, \ldots,$ and A_n from the rest of the original tree will yield a second tree which abides by the ground rules on p. 188. (Note indeed that the only rule from Section 2.2 which can have been used is the one for decomposing universal quantifications, and that rule puts no restriction on the choice of the instantiating term T.) Grafting to each open branch of the second tree a tree for $\{B, \sim B\}$ will close the branch, and guarantee that $\{A_1, A_2, \ldots, A_n, \sim B\}$ is inconsistent.

The following two trees show why the above trick might fail when one of the quantifiers is existential or is universal but not initially placed:

$$
\begin{array}{lll}
1 & \underline{(\exists x)Fx\;\checkmark} & \underline{\sim(\forall x)Fx\;\checkmark} \quad \text{from} \\
2 & Fa_1 & \sim Fa_1 \qquad\qquad 1
\end{array}
$$

Note that if '$\sim Fa_1$' ('$\sim\sim Fa_1$') were slipped between lines 1 and 2 of the first (second) tree, then line 2 would violate ground rule **C**.

E2.2.8.

(a)–(b) Note that if you got to Stage 5, you must have just answered No to the questions posed at Stages 2, 3, and 4. But if you answered No to the question at Stage 2, then your tree is closed, or else there are lines still to be decomposed on all your open branches; and, if you answered No to the questions at Stages 3 and 4, then the only lines still to be decomposed on your open branches are unnegated universal quantifications or negated existential ones. So, if you got to Stage 5, either your tree is closed or else there are unnegated universal quantifications or negated existential ones on *all* your open branches. Should the latter possibility be ruled out (i.e., should you answer No to the first question at Stage 5), then your tree is sure to be closed.

E2.2.9.

(a) Inspection of the rules for making trees will reveal that if none of '$\sim$', '$\supset$', and '$\equiv$' occurs in any member of S, then no negation will be entered on the tree as the members of S are decomposed. So the tree is sure to be open.

(b) Modify the rule for decomposing $A \equiv B$ to read as follows:

$$
\begin{array}{c}
A \equiv B\;\checkmark \\
\diagup\!\diagdown \\
\sim A \qquad A \\
\sim B \qquad B
\end{array}
$$

Inspection of the rules for making trees will reveal that if '$\sim$' does not occur in any member of S, then no negation will be entered on the right-most branch of the tree (though negations may be entered on other branches) as the members of S are decomposed. So the tree is again sure to be open.

Section 2.3

E2.3.1.

a.
	1	$(\forall x)(Fx \supset Gx)$	
	2	Fa	
	3	Ha	
	4	$(\forall x)(Fx \supset Gx)$	(R, 1)
	5	Fa $\supset$ Ga	($\forall$E, 4)
	6	Fa	(R, 2)
	7	Ga	($\supset$E, 5, 6)
	8	Ha $\supset$ Ga	($\supset$I, 3–7)

d.
	1	$(\forall x)[(\exists y)Fxy \supset Gbx]$	
	2	$(\forall x)(\forall y)Fyx$	
	3	$(\forall x)[(\exists y)Fxy \supset Gbx]$	(R, 1)
	4	$(\exists y)Fby \supset Gbb$	($\forall$E, 3)
	5	$(\forall x)(\forall y)Fyx$	(R, 2)
	6	$(\forall y)Fya$	($\forall$E, 5)
	7	Fba	($\forall$E, 6)
	8	$(\exists y)Fby$	($\exists$I, 7)
	9	Gbb	($\supset$E, 4, 8)
	10	$(\exists x)Gxx$	($\exists$I, 9)

In lines 6 and 7, any other term (even 'b') could appear where 'a' is used.

e.
	1	$(\exists x)Fx \supset (\forall x)Gx$	
	2	~Ga	
	3	Fa	
	4	Fa	(R, 3)
	5	$(\exists x)Fx$	($\exists$I, 4)
	6	$(\exists x)Fx \supset (\forall x)Gx$	(R, 1)
	7	$(\forall x)Gx$	($\supset$E, 5, 6)
	8	Ga	($\forall$E, 7)
	9	~Ga	(R, 2)
	10	~Fa	(~I, 3–(8, 9))
	11	~Ga $\supset$ ~Fa	($\supset$I, 2–10)
	12	$(\forall x)(\sim Gx \supset \sim Fx)$	($\forall$I, 11)

h.   1 | $(\forall x)(\forall y)[(\exists z)Fyz \supset Fxy]$
     2 | Fab
     ───
     3 | $(\forall x)(\forall y)[(\exists z)Fyz \supset Fxy]$ (R, 1)
     4 | $(\forall y)[(\exists z)Fyz \supset Fdy]$ (∀E, 3)
     5 | $(\exists z)Faz \supset Fda$ (∀E, 4)
     6 | Fab   (R, 2)
     7 | $(\exists z)Faz$ (∃I, 6)
     8 | Fda   (⊃E, 5, 7)
     9 | $(\exists z)Fdz$ (∃I, 8)
     10 | $(\forall y)[(\exists z)Fyz \supset Fcy]$ (∀E, 3)
     11 | $(\exists z)Fdz \supset Fcd$ (∀E, 10)
     12 | Fcd   (⊃E, 9, 11)
     13 | $(\forall y)Fyd$ (∀I, 12)
     14 | $(\forall x)(\forall y)Fyx$ (∀I, 13)

j.   1 | $(\exists x)Fx$
     2 | $(\exists x)Gx$
     ───
     3 | $(\exists x)Fx$ (R, 1)
     4 | | Fa
     5 | | $(\exists x)Gx$ (R, 2)
     6 | | | Gb
     7 | | | Fa   (R, 4)
     8 | | | $(\exists y)Fy$ (∃I, 7)
     9 | | | Gb   (R, 6)
     10 | | | $(\exists y)Fy \ \& \ Gb$ (&I, 8, 9)
     11 | | | $(\exists x)[(\exists y)Fy \ \& \ Gx]$ (∃I, 10)
     12 | | $(\exists x)[(\exists y)Fy \ \& \ Gx]$ (∃E, 5, 6–11)
     13 | $(\exists x)[(\exists y)Fy \ \& \ Gx]$ (∃E, 3, 4–12)

k.　1 | $(\exists x)(Fx \ \& \ Gx)$

　　2 | $(\exists x)(Fx \ \& \ Gx)$　　　　　　　　　(R, 1)

　　3 | ┃ Fa & Ga

　　4 | ┃ ┃ $(\forall x)(Fx \supset \sim Gx)$

　　5 | ┃ ┃ $(\forall x)(Fx \supset \sim Gx)$　　　(R, 4)
　　6 | ┃ ┃ Fa $\supset \sim$Ga　　　　　　(∀E, 5)
　　7 | ┃ ┃ Fa & Ga　　　　　　　(R, 3)
　　8 | ┃ ┃ Fa　　　　　　　　　(&E, 7)
　　9 | ┃ ┃ $\sim$Ga　　　　　　　　($\supset$E, 6, 8)
　10 | ┃ ┃ Ga　　　　　　　　　(&E, 7)
　11 | ┃ $\sim(\forall x)(Fx \supset \sim Gx)$　　　($\sim$I, 4–(9, 10))
　12 | $\sim(\forall x)(Fx \supset \sim Gx)$　　　($\exists$E, 2, 3–11)

In this case it pays to ignore our strategy hint, which would have us reach the last line by $\sim$I. That approach proves rather more complicated than the above.

E2.3.2.

b.　1 | $(\forall x)(Qx \supset \sim\sim Ax)$
　　2 | $(\forall x)(Gx \supset \sim Ax)$

　　3 | ┃ Qa

　　4 | ┃ ┃ Ga

　　5 | ┃ ┃ $(\forall x)(Qx \supset \sim\sim Ax)$　　(R, 1)
　　6 | ┃ ┃ Qa $\supset \sim\sim$Aa　　　　　(∀E, 5)
　　7 | ┃ ┃ Qa　　　　　　　　　(R, 3)
　　8 | ┃ ┃ $\sim\sim$Aa　　　　　　　　($\supset$E, 6, 7)
　　9 | ┃ ┃ $(\forall x)(Gx \supset \sim Ax)$　　　(R, 2)
　10 | ┃ ┃ Ga $\supset \sim$Aa　　　　　　(∀E, 9)
　11 | ┃ ┃ Ga　　　　　　　　　(R, 4)
　12 | ┃ ┃ $\sim$Aa　　　　　　　　($\supset$E, 10, 11)
　13 | ┃ $\sim$Ga　　　　　　　　　($\sim$I, 4–(8, 12))
　14 | Qa $\supset \sim$Ga　　　　　　　($\supset$I, 3–13)
　15 | $(\forall x)(Qx \supset \sim Gx)$　　　　(∀I, 14)

e. 1 | $(\forall x)(Sx \supset [Gx \lor (Cx \ \& \ Ax)])$
    2 | $(\forall x)[(Gx \ \& \ Rx) \supset Lx]$
    3 | Sp & ~Lp

    4 | $(\forall x)(Sx \supset [Gx \lor (Cx \ \& \ Ax)])$ (R, 1)
    5 | Sp ⊃ [Gp ∨ (Cp & Ap)]   (∀E, 4)
    6 | Sp & ~Lp   (R, 3)
    7 | Sp   (&E, 6)
    8 | Gp ∨ (Cp & Ap)   (⊃E, 5, 7)

    9 | | Gp

   10 | | | Rp

   11 | | | $(\forall x)[(Gx \ \& \ Rx) \supset Lx]$ (R, 2)
   12 | | | (Gp & Rp) ⊃ Lp   (∀E, 11)
   13 | | | Gp   (R, 9)
   14 | | | Rp   (R, 10)
   15 | | | Gp & Rp   (&I, 13, 14)
   16 | | | Lp   (⊃E, 12, 15)
   17 | | | Sp & ~Lp   (R, 3)
   18 | | | ~Lp   (&E, 17)
   19 | | ~Rp   (~I, 10–(16, 18))
   20 | | Gp   (R, 9)
   21 | | Gp & ~Rp   (&I, 19, 20)
   22 | | $(\exists x)(Gx \ \& \ \sim Rx)$ (∃I, 21)
   23 | | $(\exists x)(Gx \ \& \ \sim Rx) \lor Ap$ (∨I, 22)

   24 | | Cp & Ap

   25 | | Cp & Ap   (R, 24)
   26 | | Ap   (&E, 25)
   27 | | $(\exists x)(Gx \ \& \ \sim Rx) \lor Ap$ (∨I, 26)
   28 | $(\exists x)(Gx \ \& \ \sim Rx) \lor Ap$ (∨E, 8, 9–23, 24–27)

k.   1 | $(\forall x)([Px \,\&\, (\exists y)(Dy \,\&\, Hxy)] \supset Sx)$
     2 | $(\forall x)(Px \supset Dx)$

     3 | Pa & Haa

     4 | $(\forall x)(Px \supset Dx)$ (R, 2)
     5 | $Pa \supset Da$ ($\forall$E, 4)
     6 | Pa & Haa   (R, 3)
     7 | Pa   (&E, 6)
     8 | Da   ($\supset$E, 5, 7)
     9 | Haa   (&E, 6)
    10 | Da & Haa   (&I, 8, 9)
    11 | $(\exists y)(Dy \,\&\, Hay)$ ($\exists$I, 10)
    12 | $Pa \,\&\, (\exists y)(Dy \,\&\, Hay)$ (&I, 7, 11)
    13 | $(\forall x)([Px \,\&\, (\exists y)(Dy \,\&\, Hxy)] \supset Sx)$ (R, 1)
    14 | $[Pa \,\&\, (\exists y)(Dy \,\&\, Hay)] \supset Sa$ ($\forall$E, 13)
    15 | Sa   ($\supset$E, 12, 14)
    16 | $(Pa \,\&\, Haa) \supset Sa$ ($\supset$I, 3–15)
    17 | $(\forall x)[(Px \,\&\, Hxx) \supset Sx]$ ($\forall$I, 16)

n.   1 | $(\exists x)(\exists y)Fxy \lor (\forall x)(\forall y)Gyx$
     2 | $(\exists x)(\exists y)Fxy \lor (\forall x)(\forall y)Gyx$ (R, 1)
     3 | | $(\exists x)(\exists y)Fxy$
     4 | | $(\exists x)(\exists y)Fxy$ (R, 3)
     5 | | $(\exists y)Fay$
     6 | | $(\exists y)Fay$ (R, 5)
     7 | | Fab
     8 | | Fab   (R, 7)
     9 | | $Fab \lor Gab$ (VI, 8)
    10 | | $(\exists y)(Fay \lor Gay)$ ($\exists$I, 9)
    11 | | $(\exists x)(\exists y)(Fxy \lor Gxy)$ ($\exists$I, 10)
    12 | | $(\exists x)(\exists y)(Fxy \lor Gxy)$ ($\exists$E, 6, 7–11)
    13 | | $(\exists x)(\exists y)(Fxy \lor Gxy)$ ($\exists$E, 4, 5–12)
    14 | | $(\forall x)(\forall y)Gyx$
    15 | | $(\forall x)(\forall y)Gyx$ (R, 14)
    16 | | $(\forall y)Gyb$ ($\forall$E, 15)
    17 | | Gab   ($\forall$E, 16)
    18 | | $Fab \lor Gab$ (VI, 17)
    19 | | $(\exists y)(Fay \lor Gay)$ ($\exists$I, 18)
    20 | | $(\exists x)(\exists y)(Fxy \lor Gxy)$ ($\exists$I, 19)
    21 | $(\exists x)(\exists y)(Fxy \lor Gxy)$ (VE, 2, 3–13, 14–20)

r. 1 $(\forall x)(\forall y)[(Fx \And Gy) \supset Hxy]$
    2    $(\exists x)(\exists y)[(Fx \And {\sim}Fy) \And {\sim}Hxy]$

    3    $(\exists x)(\exists y)[(Fx \And {\sim}Fy) \And {\sim}Hxy]$ (R, 2)
    4      $(\exists y)[(Fa \And {\sim}Fy) \And {\sim}Hay]$

    5      $(\exists y)[(Fa \And {\sim}Fy) \And {\sim}Hay]$ (R, 4)
    6        $(Fa \And {\sim}Fb) \And {\sim}Hab$

    7        $(Fa \And {\sim}Fb) \And {\sim}Hab$ (R, 6)
    8        $Fa \And {\sim}Fb$ (&E, 7)
    9        ${\sim}Fb$ (&E, 8)

   10   Gb

   11          $(Fa \And {\sim}Fb) \And {\sim}Hab$ (R, 6)
   12          $Fa \And {\sim}Fb$ (&E, 11)
   13   Fa (&E, 12)
   14   Gb (R, 10)
   15          $Fa \And Gb$ (&I, 13, 14)
   16          $(\forall x)(\forall y)[(Fx \And Gy) \supset Hxy]$ (R, 1)
   17          $(\forall y)[(Fa \And Gy) \supset Hay]$ ($\forall$E, 16)
   18          $(Fa \And Gb) \supset Hab$ ($\forall$E, 17)
   19   Hab ($\supset$E, 15, 18)
   20          ${\sim}Hab$ (&E, 11)
   21        ${\sim}Gb$ (${\sim}$I, 10–(19, 20))
   22        ${\sim}Fb \And {\sim}Gb$ (&I, 9, 21)
   23        $(\exists x)({\sim}Fx \And {\sim}Gx)$ ($\exists$I, 22)
   24      $(\exists x)({\sim}Fx \And {\sim}Gx)$ ($\exists$E, 5, 6–23)
   25    $(\exists x)({\sim}Fx \And {\sim}Gx)$ ($\exists$E, 3, 4–24)

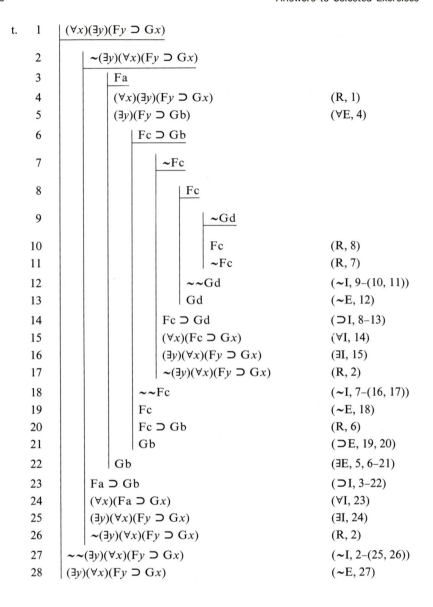

t. 1 $(\forall x)(\exists y)(Fy \supset Gx)$

2 $\sim(\exists y)(\forall x)(Fy \supset Gx)$

3 Fa

4 $(\forall x)(\exists y)(Fy \supset Gx)$ (R, 1)

5 $(\exists y)(Fy \supset Gb)$ ($\forall$E, 4)

6 Fc $\supset$ Gb

7 $\sim$Fc

8 Fc

9 $\sim$Gd

10 Fc   (R, 8)

11 $\sim$Fc   (R, 7)

12 $\sim\sim$Gd   ($\sim$I, 9–(10, 11))

13 Gd   ($\sim$E, 12)

14 Fc $\supset$ Gd   ($\supset$I, 8–13)

15 $(\forall x)(Fc \supset Gx)$ ($\forall$I, 14)

16 $(\exists y)(\forall x)(Fy \supset Gx)$ ($\exists$I, 15)

17 $\sim(\exists y)(\forall x)(Fy \supset Gx)$ (R, 2)

18 $\sim\sim$Fc   ($\sim$I, 7–(16, 17))

19 Fc   ($\sim$E, 18)

20 Fc $\supset$ Gb   (R, 6)

21 Gb   ($\supset$E, 19, 20)

22 Gb   ($\exists$E, 5, 6–21)

23 Fa $\supset$ Gb   ($\supset$I, 3–22)

24 $(\forall x)(Fa \supset Gx)$ ($\forall$I, 23)

25 $(\exists y)(\forall x)(Fy \supset Gx)$ ($\exists$I, 24)

26 $\sim(\exists y)(\forall x)(Fy \supset Gx)$ (R, 2)

27 $\sim\sim(\exists y)(\forall x)(Fy \supset Gx)$ ($\sim$I, 2–(25, 26))

28 $(\exists y)(\forall x)(Fy \supset Gx)$ ($\sim$E, 27)

E2.3.3. b.

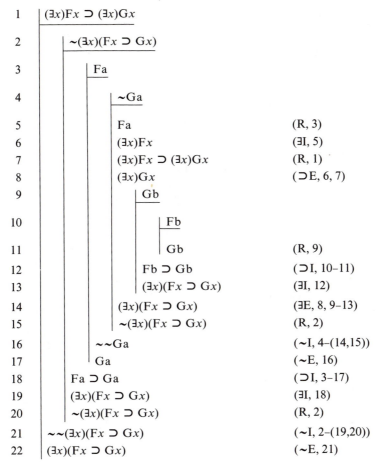

1	(∃x)Fx ⊃ (∃x)Gx	
2	~(∃x)(Fx ⊃ Gx)	
3	Fa	
4	~Ga	
5	Fa	(R, 3)
6	(∃x)Fx	(∃I, 5)
7	(∃x)Fx ⊃ (∃x)Gx	(R, 1)
8	(∃x)Gx	(⊃E, 6, 7)
9	Gb	
10	Fb	
11	Gb	(R, 9)
12	Fb ⊃ Gb	(⊃I, 10–11)
13	(∃x)(Fx ⊃ Gx)	(∃I, 12)
14	(∃x)(Fx ⊃ Gx)	(∃E, 8, 9–13)
15	~(∃x)(Fx ⊃ Gx)	(R, 2)
16	~~Ga	(~I, 4–(14,15))
17	Ga	(~E, 16)
18	Fa ⊃ Ga	(⊃I, 3–17)
19	(∃x)(Fx ⊃ Gx)	(∃I, 18)
20	~(∃x)(Fx ⊃ Gx)	(R, 2)
21	~~(∃x)(Fx ⊃ Gx)	(~I, 2–(19,20))
22	(∃x)(Fx ⊃ Gx)	(~E, 21)

h.

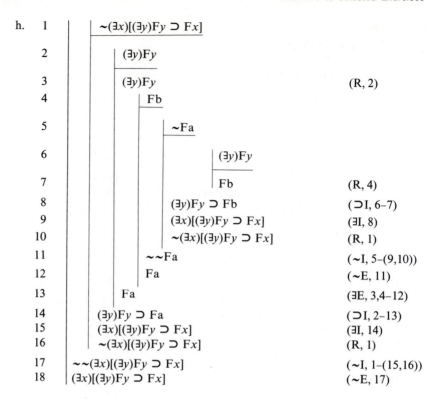

1	~(∃x)[(∃y)Fy ⊃ Fx]	
2	(∃y)Fy	
3	(∃y)Fy	(R, 2)
4	Fb	
5	~Fa	
6	(∃y)Fy	
7	Fb	(R, 4)
8	(∃y)Fy ⊃ Fb	(⊃I, 6–7)
9	(∃x)[(∃y)Fy ⊃ Fx]	(∃I, 8)
10	~(∃x)[(∃y)Fy ⊃ Fx]	(R, 1)
11	~~Fa	(~I, 5–(9,10))
12	Fa	(~E, 11)
13	Fa	(∃E, 3,4–12)
14	(∃y)Fy ⊃ Fa	(⊃I, 2–13)
15	(∃x)[(∃y)Fy ⊃ Fx]	(∃I, 14)
16	~(∃x)[(∃y)Fy ⊃ Fx]	(R, 1)
17	~~(∃x)[(∃y)Fy ⊃ Fx]	(~I, 1–(15,16))
18	(∃x)[(∃y)Fy ⊃ Fx]	(~E, 17)

k.   1 $(\forall x)(Fax \equiv Gx)$

2         $(\exists y)Fay$

3         $(\exists y)Fay$ (R, 2)

4   Fab

5   Fab   (R, 4)
6              $(\forall x)(Fax \equiv Gx)$ (R, 1)
7              $Fab \equiv Gb$ ($\forall$E, 6)
8   Gb   ($\equiv$E, 5, 7)
9              $(\exists y)Gy$ ($\exists$I, 8)
10        $(\exists y)Gy$ ($\exists$E, 3, 4–9)

11        $(\exists y)Gy$

12        $(\exists y)Gy$ (R, 11)

13   Gb

14   Gb   (R, 13)
15             $(\forall x)(Fax \equiv Gx)$ (R, 1)
16             $Fab \equiv Gb$ ($\forall$E, 15)
17   Fab   ($\equiv$E, 14, 16)
18             $(\exists y)Fay$ ($\exists$I, 17)
19        $(\exists y)Fay$ ($\exists$E, 12, 13–18)
20   $(\exists y)Fay \equiv (\exists y)Gy$ ($\equiv$I, 2–10, 11–19)
21   $(\exists x)[(\exists y)Fxy \equiv (\exists y)Gy]$ ($\exists$I, 20)

E2.3.4.   b.

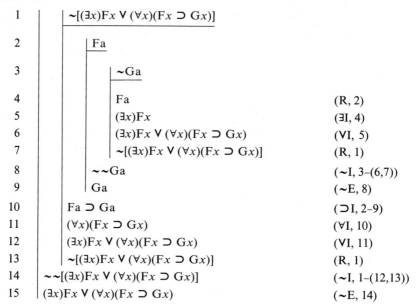

1	~[(∃x)Fx ∨ (∀x)(Fx ⊃ Gx)]	
2	Fa	
3	~Ga	
4	Fa	(R, 2)
5	(∃x)Fx	(∃I, 4)
6	(∃x)Fx ∨ (∀x)(Fx ⊃ Gx)	(∨I, 5)
7	~[(∃x)Fx ∨ (∀x)(Fx ⊃ Gx)]	(R, 1)
8	~~Ga	(~I, 3–(6,7))
9	Ga	(~E, 8)
10	Fa ⊃ Ga	(⊃I, 2–9)
11	(∀x)(Fx ⊃ Gx)	(∀I, 10)
12	(∃x)Fx ∨ (∀x)(Fx ⊃ Gx)	(∨I, 11)
13	~[(∃x)Fx ∨ (∀x)(Fx ⊃ Gx)]	(R, 1)
14	~~[(∃x)Fx ∨ (∀x)(Fx ⊃ Gx)]	(~I, 1–(12,13))
15	(∃x)Fx ∨ (∀x)(Fx ⊃ Gx)	(~E, 14)

e.

1	$(\exists x)(Fx \supset Ga)$	
2	$(\forall x)Fx$	
3	$(\exists x)(Fx \supset Ga)$	(R, 1)
4	$Fb \supset Ga$	
5	$(\forall x)Fx$	(R, 2)
6	Fb	($\forall$E, 5)
7	$Fb \supset Ga$	(R, 4)
8	Ga	($\supset$E, 6, 7)
9	Ga	($\exists$E, 3, 4–8)
10	$(\forall x)Fx \supset Ga$	($\supset$I, 2–9)
11	$(\forall x)Fx \supset Ga$	
12	$\sim(\exists x)(Fx \supset Ga)$	
13	Fb	
14	$\sim Fc$	
15	Fc	
16	$\sim Ga$	
17	Fc	(R, 15)
18	$\sim Fc$	(R, 14)
19	$\sim\sim Ga$	($\sim$I, 16–(17,18))
20	Ga	($\sim$E, 19)
21	$Fc \supset Ga$	($\supset$I, 15–20)
22	$(\exists x)(Fx \supset Ga)$	($\exists$I, 21)
23	$\sim(\exists x)(Fx \supset Ga)$	(R, 12)
24	$\sim\sim Fc$	($\sim$I, 14–(22,23))
25	Fc	($\sim$E, 24)
26	$(\forall x)Fx$	($\forall$I, 25)
27	$(\forall x)Fx \supset Ga$	(R, 11)
28	Ga	($\supset$E, 26, 27)
29	$Fb \supset Ga$	($\supset$I, 13–28)
30	$(\exists x)(Fx \supset Ga)$	($\exists$I, 29)
31	$\sim(\exists x)(Fx \supset Ga)$	(R, 12)
32	$\sim\sim(\exists x)(Fx \supset Ga)$	($\sim$I, 12–(30,31))
33	$(\exists x)(Fx \supset Ga)$	($\sim$E, 32)
34	$(\exists x)(Fx \supset Ga) \equiv [(\forall x)Fx \supset Ga]$	($\equiv$I, 1–10, 11–33)

E2.3.5.

b.　1　$(\forall x)(Fx \supset Gx)$

　　2　$\sim(\exists x)(Fx \& Gx)$

　　3　$(\exists x)Fx$

　　4　$(\exists x)Fx$　　　　　　　　　　　　　　　　　　(R, 3)

　　5　　Fa

　　6　　$(\forall x)(Fx \supset Gx)$　　　　　　　　　　　(R, 1)

　　7　　$Fa \supset Ga$　　　　　　　　　　　　　　　($\forall$E, 6)

　　8　　Fa　　　　　　　　　　　　　　　　　　　(R, 5)

　　9　　Ga　　　　　　　　　　　　　　　　　　　($\supset$E, 7, 8)

　10　　Fa & Ga　　　　　　　　　　　　　　　(&I, 8, 9)

　11　　$(\exists x)(Fx \& Gx)$　　　　　　　　　　　　($\exists$I, 10)

　12　$(\exists x)(Fx \& Gx)$　　　　　　　　　　　　　($\exists$E, 4, 5–11)

　13　$\sim(\exists x)(Fx \& Gx)$　　　　　　　　　　　(R, 2)

1.　1　$(\forall x)(\forall y)(\forall z)[(Fxy \& Fyz) \supset Fxz]$

　　2　$\sim(\exists x)Fxx$

　　3　$\sim(\forall x)(\forall y)(Fxy \supset \sim Fyx)$

　　4　　Fab

　　5　　　Fba

　　6　　　$(\forall x)(\forall y)(\forall z)[(Fxy \& Fyz) \supset Fxz]$　　(R, 1)

　　7　　　$(\forall y)(\forall z)[(Fay \& Fyz) \supset Faz]$　　($\forall$E, 6)

　　8　　　$(\forall z)[(Fab \& Fbz) \supset Faz]$　　　　($\forall$E, 7)

　　9　　　$(Fab \& Fba) \supset Faa$　　　　　　　($\forall$E, 8)

　10　　　Fab　　　　　　　　　　　　　　　　(R, 4)

　11　　　Fba　　　　　　　　　　　　　　　　(R, 5)

　12　　　Fab & Fba　　　　　　　　　　　　(&I, 10, 11)

　13　　　Faa　　　　　　　　　　　　　　　　($\supset$E, 9, 12)

　14　　　$(\exists x)Fxx$　　　　　　　　　　　　　($\exists$I, 13)

　15　　　$\sim(\exists x)Fxx$　　　　　　　　　　　　(R, 2)

　16　　$\sim Fba$　　　　　　　　　　　　　　　　($\sim$I, 5–(14,15))

　17　$Fab \supset \sim Fba$　　　　　　　　　　　　　($\supset$I, 4–16)

　18　$(\forall y)(Fay \supset \sim Fya)$　　　　　　　　　($\forall$I, 17)

　19　$(\forall x)(\forall y)(Fxy \supset \sim Fyx)$　　　　　　　($\forall$I, 18)

　20　$\sim(\forall x)(\forall y)(Fxy \supset \sim Fyx)$　　　　　　(R, 3)

E2.3.6.

See pp. 255–56.

E2.3.7.

(a) Toward answering (a), note that if $S \vdash \sim(\forall X)A$, then in view of Example 11 on p. 220 $S \vdash (\exists X)\sim A$. So if $S \cup \{\sim A(T/X)\} \vdash B$, where T is foreign to S, $\sim(\forall X)A$, and B (hence to S, $(\exists X)\sim A$, and B), then $S \vdash B$ by $\exists$E.

(b) See Example 10 on p. 219.

E2.3.8. (E2.3.1.d)

1	$(\exists x)(\exists y)(Fxy \vee Fyx)$	
2	$(\exists x)(\exists y)(Fxy \vee Fyx)$	(R, 1)
3	$(\exists y)(Fay \vee Fya)$	($\exists$E**, 2)
4	$Fab \vee Fba$	($\exists$E**, 3)
5	$\quad Fab$	
6	$\quad Fab$	(R, 5)
7	$\quad (\exists y)Fay$	($\exists$I, 6)
8	$\quad (\exists x)(\exists y)Fxy$	($\exists$I, 7)
9	$\quad Fba$	
10	$\quad Fba$	(R, 9)
11	$\quad (\exists y)Fby$	($\exists$I, 10)
12	$\quad (\exists x)(\exists y)Fxy$	($\exists$I, 11)
13	$(\exists x)(\exists y)Fxy$	($\vee$E, 4, 5–8, 9–12)

(E2.3.3.h)

1	$\quad (\exists y)Fy$	
2	$\quad (\exists y)Fy$	(R, 1)
3	$\quad Fa$	($\exists$E**, 2)
4	$(\exists y)Fy \supset Fa$	($\supset$I, 1–3)
5	$(\exists x)[(\exists y)Fy \supset Fx]$	($\exists$I, 4)

(E2.3.4.d—first half)

1	$(\forall x)(Fx \supset Ga)$	
2	$\quad (\exists x)Fx$	
3	$\quad (\exists x)Fx$	(R, 2)
4	$\quad Fb$	($\exists$E**, 3)
5	$\quad (\forall x)(Fx \supset Ga)$	(R, 1)
6	$\quad Fb \supset Ga$	($\forall$E, 5)
7	$\quad Ga$	($\supset$E, 4, 6)
8	$(\exists x)Fx \supset Ga$	($\supset$I, 2–7)

Index of Symbols, Abbreviations, and Tables

Index of Names

Index of Subjects

439